The American Department Store Transformed, 1920–1960

The American Department Store Transformed, 1920–1960

RICHARD LONGSTRETH

YALE UNIVERSITY PRESS   NEW HAVEN AND LONDON   *in association with*
THE CENTER FOR AMERICAN PLACES AT COLUMBIA COLLEGE CHICAGO

Published with assistance from Furthermore: a program of the J. M. Kaplan Fund.

Copyright © 2010 by Richard Longstreth.

All rights reserved.

This book may not be reproduced, in whole or in part, including illustrations, in any form (beyond that copying permitted by Sections 107 and 108 of the U.S. Copyright Law and except by reviewers for the public press), without written permission from the publishers.

Designed by Barbara E. Williams
Set in Minion and News Gothic type by BW&A Books, Inc.

Printed in China by Regent Publishing Services Limited

Library of Congress Cataloging-in-Publication Data

Longstreth, Richard W.
  The American department store transformed, 1920–1960 / Richard Longstreth.
     p. cm.
  Includes bibliographical references and index.
  ISBN 978-0-300-14938-8 (cloth : alk. paper)
  1. Department stores—United States—History—20th century. I. Title.
  HF5465.U5L66 2010
  381'.141097309041—dc22   2009029893

A catalogue record for this book is available from the British Library.

This paper meets the requirements of ANSI/NISO Z39.48–1992 (Permanence of Paper).

10 9 8 7 6 5 4 3 2 1

Jacket illustration: Marshall Field & Company department store, Old Orchard Shopping Center, Skokie, Illinois, 1956 (detail, fig. 215).

For Elizabeth, who loves to shop

CONTENTS

Acknowledgments, ix

Introduction, 1

1 Bigger and Bigger Stores, 5

2 Modernizing Stores, 33

3 Service Beyond the Stores, 61

4 Parking for Stores, 83

5 Branch Stores, 109

6 Station Wagon Stores, 137

7 Stores in Shopping Centers, 169

8 Stores Make the Mall, 183

9 Stores in the City, 219

Epilogue, 247

Appendix: Department Stores Studied, 251

List of Abbreviations, 257

Notes, 259

A Note on the Sources, 307

Index, 313

Illustration Credits, 324

ACKNOWLEDGMENTS

FOR MATERIAL, INSIGHTS, and valuable support in other ways I am grateful to many colleagues and other friends, including William Becker, Kenneth Breisch, Robert Bruegmann, Meredith Clausen, Bell Clement, Richard Cleary, Michael Corbett, Robert Damora, Paul Davidson, George Ehrlich, Stephen Fox, Jean France, Howard Gillette, Isabelle Gournay, Michael Hauser, the late Jay Henry, W. Dwayne Jones, Richard Karberg, Dennis McFadden, C. Ford Peatross, Eric Sandweiss, William Stern, Richard Striner, Alfred Tannler, Janet Wagner, Alex Wall, and Jan Whitaker.

The incomparable holdings of the Library of Congress were of immense value to this study, affording me the luxury of doing a major portion of my research close to home. Besides the vast general collection housed in the stacks, those of the Geography and Maps and Prints and Photographs divisions proved essential in ways too numerous to mention. Important collections from department store companies exist at several archives, including those of Marshall Field & Company at the Chicago History Museum; E. A. Filene's Sons at the Boston Public Library; Gimbel Brothers at the Milwaukee Historical Society; F. & R. Lazarus Company at the Ohio Historical Society, Columbus; Strawbridge & Clothier at the Hagley Museum and Library, Wilmington, Delaware; John Wanamaker at the Historical Society of Pennsylvania, Philadelphia; and Woodward & Lothrop at the Historical Society of Washington, D.C. The archives of the Dayton Company are well cared for in the offices of the Target Corporation, Minneapolis. Public relations staff at the former Famous-Barr (St. Louis), the former Foley's (Houston), and the former Kaufmann's (Pittsburgh), as well as archivists at Pei Cobb Freed & Partners, New York, and Perry Dean Rogers, Architects, Boston, supplied much additional material.

A number of real estate brokers, retail executives, and architects, mostly retired, allowed me to interview them, affording insights available no other way. They include the late Eaton Ballard (Carter Hawley Hale), the late Angelo J. Chiraella (Victor Gruen Associates, Midtown Plaza), Kenneth N. Dayton (Dayton Company, by correspondence), Robert Getz and R. Dean Wolfe (May Company), Joseph L. Hudson, Jr. (J. L. Hudson Company), Charles Lamb and Francis Taliferro (RTKL), Maurice Lazarus (Foley's, Filene's), the late Robert A. and the late Ruth Halle Little, the late William McAdam (Coldwell Banker), the late Albert C. Martin, Jr. (A. C. Martin Associates), the late Stanley Marcus (Neiman-Marcus), George D. Rinder (Marshall Field & Company), and Lacey Womack (Hecht Company). Regrettably, time precluded tracking down others who could have enriched the subject even further.

Many libraries at institutions of higher learning contained valuable material as well, including those at Columbia University's Avery Architectural and Fine Arts Library Archives; George Washington University; Mount Holyoke College; Rutgers University, Camden; Urban Archives, Temple University; University of Akron; University of Florida, Gainesville; University of Louisville; University of Maryland, College Park; University of Missouri, St. Louis; University of Pennsylvania, Architectural Archives; University of Southern California; Washington University; and Wichita State University.

Other libraries and archives used include the American Institute of Architects Archives, Washington, D.C.; California State Library, Sacramento; Chicago History Museum; Columbia Association, Columbia, Maryland; Historical Society of South Florida, Miami; Getty Research Institute, Los Angeles; Indiana Historical Society, Indianapolis; Lehigh County Historical Society, Allentown, Pennsylvania; Maryland Historical Society, Baltimore; Mercantile Library and Missouri Historical Society, St. Louis; Milwaukee County Historical Society, Milwaukee; Museum of the City of New York; New Haven Museum and Historical Society; New Jersey State Library, Trenton; New-York Historical Society,

New York; Oregon Historical Society, Portland; San Antonio Conservation Society; San Diego Historical Society; Western Reserve Historical Society, Cleveland; and Wichita-Sedgwick County Historical Museum, Wichita.

Public libraries offered a particularly important source for many newspapers not held at the Library of Congress. In some cases, newspaper clipping files or locally generated indexes facilitated the search. Libraries visited include those at Bessemer and Birmingham, Alabama; Berkeley, Beverly Hills, Contra Costa County, Glendale, Long Beach, Los Angeles, Oakland, Palm Springs, Palo Alto, Pasadena, Pomona, Richmond, San Diego, Sacramento, San Francisco, San Jose, San Mateo, San Rafael, Santa Monica, Vallejo, Ventura, West Covina, and Whittier, California; Bridgeport, Greenwich, Hartford, New Haven, Stamford, and West Hartford, Connecticut; Clearwater, Fort Lauderdale, Miami, Palm Beach County, St. Petersburg, Sarasota, and Tampa, Florida; Athens, Augusta, Brunswick, Columbus, and Macon, Georgia; Aurora, Chicago, Des Plaines, East Dundee, Elgin, Elmhurst, Evanston, Joliet, Kankakee, Lake Forest, Mount Prospect, Oak Park, Park Forest, Rock Island, Skokie, and Wilmette, Illinois; Bloomington, Hammond, Jeffersonville, and Lafayette, Indiana; Davenport, Des Moines, Iowa City, Newton, Oskaloosa, and Ottumwa, Iowa; Topeka and Wichita, Kansas; Lexington and Louisville, Kentucky; Baton Rouge and New Orleans, Louisiana; Portland and York, Maine; Baltimore, Rockville, and Towson, Maryland; Belmont, Beverly, Boston, Braintree, Brockton, Burlington, Cambridge, Falmouth, Framingham, Gloucester, Hyannis, Lexington, Magnolia, Malden, Medford, Northampton, Peabody, Quincy, Saugus, South Hadley, Springfield, Stoneham, Taunton, Wellesley, Winchester, Woburn, and Worcester, Massachusetts; Detroit, Flint, Grand Rapids, Harper Woods, Kalamazoo, Muskegon, and Pontiac, Michigan; Hennepin County, Rochester, and Southdale, Minnesota; Independence, Joplin, Kansas City, Kirkwood, St. Louis, and St. Louis County, Missouri; Omaha, Nebraska; Laconia, New Hampshire; Asbury Park, Atlantic City, Bloomfield, Camden, East Orange, Elizabeth, Hackensack, Long Branch, Metuchen, Millburn, Monmouth County, Montclair, Morristown, Paterson, Plainfield, Princeton, Summit, Trenton, and Westfield, New Jersey; Babylon, Batavia, Bay Shore, Garden City, Geneva, Great Neck, Hempstead, Hewlett-Woodmere, Hicksville, Huntington, Levittown, Manhasset, New Rochelle, New York/Queens, Niagara Falls, Rochester, Southampton, Syracuse, White Plains, and Yonkers, New York; Greensboro and Winston-Salem, North Carolina; Alliance, Barberton, Bowling Green, Canton, Cincinnati, Cleveland, Coshocton, Cuyahoga Falls, Dayton, Euclid, Findlay, Fremont, Lakewood, Lorain, Mansfield, Masillon, Maumee, Middletown, Parma, Sandusky, Tiffin, and Warren, Ohio; Norman and Oklahoma City, Oklahoma; Eugene, Portland, and Salem, Oregon; Allentown, Erie, Mount Lebanon, New Castle, Philadelphia, Pittsburgh, Scranton, and Tarentum, Pennsylvania; Memphis and Nashville, Tennessee; Dallas, Fort Worth, and Houston, Texas; Alexandria, Arlington, Charlottesville, Danville, Lynchburg, Richmond, and Roanoke, Virginia; Bellevue, Bellingham, Everett, Spokane, Tacoma, Walla Walla, and Yakima, Washington; and Manitowoc, Milwaukee, Oshkosh, and West Allis, Wisconsin.

Those who assisted me in the institutions cited above are far too numerous to list here, but particular thanks are due Beth Andersen, James Balga, Christopher Becker, Anne Blecksmith, James W. Campbell, Sean Casey, Christine Cordazzo, Kathleen Correia, Steve Daily, Scott Daniels, Joel Draut, Sandra Gates, Inna Guzenfeld, Karolee Harris, Twyla Thompson Hensen, John Hyslop, Anthony K. Jahn, Barbara Kellner, Ashley Koebel, Dana Lamparello, Gail Rogers McCormick, Bryan McDaniel, Carole Mazzotta, Chris Murtha, Janet Parks, John Pettit, Elizabeth Rose, James Scott, Jim Sluzewski, Beth Standifird, Judy Stevenson, Erica Stoller, Susan Sutton, Dacy Taube, Jeff Thomas, Amy Trout, Elmer Turner, Debbie Vaughan, Bettie Webb, Helen Weiss, Bill Whitaker, Jon Williams, Lisa Wood, and Helena Zinkham.

Pursuing a subject that warrants study in so many places is not easily undertaken. The best way to manage this endeavor, I discovered, was not by a nationwide journey encompassing many months but by comparatively short visits to one or a few places at a point when sufficient information was gathered to justify the trip. In a number of cases, expeditions to a given area were made two or more times when new material was found elsewhere. Combining such forays with annual meetings of the Society of Architectural Historians, Vernacular Architecture Forum, Society for American City and Regional Planning History, and Frank Lloyd Wright Building Conservancy, as well as with six years of SAH executive committee meetings—many of which benefited from subventions from George Washington University—greatly facilitated the enterprise. Similarly, lectures given at Columbia University; Detroit Museum of History; Foundation for San Francisco's Architectural Heritage; Getty Conservation Institute; Graham Foundation for Advanced Studies in the Fine Arts; Kansas State University; Los Angeles Conservancy and Petersen Automotive Museum; Mary Washington College; Savannah College of Art and Design; University of California, Berkeley; University of Kentucky; University of North Carolina, Greensboro; University of Texas, Arlington; and University of Virginia, as well as at the annual meetings of the Connecticut Trust for Historic Preservation, Kansas Preservation Alliance, National Trust for Historic Preservation, Preservation Maine, and Preservation Texas made many additional trips feasible.

Throughout the years taken to conduct this study I also had the great fortune to benefit from the hospitality of friends coast to coast. Special thanks in this regard go to Robert and Ethel Churchill, Fred and Mary Schmidt, Michael and Rosemary Sulzbach, and Robert Winter, with whom I have had the pleasure of staying on frequent occasions. Many others opened their doors to me as well, including Doreen Ashworth, Dorsey and Susan Brown, the late Polly Brown, Robert Bruegmann, Paul and Martha Capra, David De Long, John and Nadine Dillon, Dennis Domer, James A. Figg III, Dennis Gale, Bruce and Barbara Haldeman, Thomas and Carol Hanchett, Morrison and Fenella Heckscher, Jane Hope, Arthur and Wendy Hopper, W. Dwayne Jones, the late Steven Levin, Patrick McGrew and Robert Julian, David and Mary Alice Lowenthal, Eugene and Catherine Pasymowski, Robertson and Sandy Paton, Beth and the late John Reiter, Kim Spurgeon, Vicki Stansted, Radclyffe and Maria Thompson, the late Noel Train, and Richard Guy and Eleanor Wilson.

A grant from George Washington's University Facilitating Fund, as well as a very generous stipend from the Graham Foundation for Advancement in the Arts, covered the substantial cost of procuring illustrations and the permission to use them. I am also grateful to Furthermore, a program of the J. M. Kaplan Fund, for its support in the publication of this book.

I owe a substantial debt to George Thompson and his staff at the Center for American Places, who helped guide the development of the manuscript for a number of years and were always patient in response to my requests for additional time as the project grew in scope and complexity. My thanks go to the anonymous reviewers, who, at Thompson's request, offered enthusiastic and extremely useful comments.

I am deeply indebted to Michelle Komie at Yale University Press for her enthusiasm toward this project. It has been a privilege to work with her and with Heidi Downey, who has been the ideal manuscript editor. They and their colleagues, including Daniella Berman, John Long, and Mary Mayer, have made the production of this book a pleasurable, no less than a rewarding, experience.

INTRODUCTION

DURING THE DECADES BETWEEN 1920 and 1960, the department store in the United States became a wholly different phenomenon from what it had been in the early twentieth century. The changes that contributed to this transformation at once reflected and had a decisive impact on business practices, shopping patterns, design approaches, and, ultimately, urban structure. Operationally, the department store became much more a bastion of systemization. Assiduous methods of planning and control were instituted, whereby analysis of the market, purchase of goods, inventory of stock, and accounting of the myriad costs of doing business became core functions. Merchandising, too, experienced pronounced shifts, all focused on fostering the tendency to buy on impulse. Display of goods inside the store became a major thrust in presentation. The goods themselves were organized to enhance accessibility, both in perceptual and in logistical terms. The role of the sales clerk as an intermediary between customer and wares became diminished in a number of departments, fostering the sense of informality and personal choice among patrons. Increased consumption—due to metropolitan growth, stronger ties to outlying regions, and, after World War II, the emergence of a large, new mass market—led to unprecedented expansion. Companies frequently remodeled and enlarged their plants. In many cases wholly new stores were constructed downtown. Offsite support facilities were leased or erected to meet mounting storage and service needs and also in response to soaring land values in the retail core. Costly places for customer parking were developed to retain a key contingent of store clientele. Eventually, these building programs were matched and often surpassed by the development of large, full-line branch stores, which by the mid-1950s generally served as anchors for immense regional shopping malls.

The pursuit of greater markets in addition to greater efficiency in operation and greater effectiveness in sales all had a decisive impact on design. The layout of department stores changed markedly, moving away from regimentation to more varied arrangements devised to be customer friendly. Configurations that were organized to secure maximum perimeter glazing, supplemented by large skylit atria—both used to gain optimal natural light and air circulation—were supplanted by internally focused layouts designed to enhance the presentation of merchandise and human circulation that were made possible by improved lighting systems and the introduction of air conditioning. Escalators became the primary means of facilitating movement between floors. Goods were presented in an ever more artful, sometimes theatrical, manner. All these changes were crafted to attract trade, but the process was by no means a reactive one. Early on, department stores and other retail enterprises discovered the power of modernism in stimulating sales. From the store interior to the regional mall, the department store became a principal agent in bringing a modernist environment into the mainstream of middle-class life. Many physical changes were conceived to elicit the favor of females, who, retailers discovered by the 1920s, made up an astounding 85 percent of their customer base. Yet as department store companies embraced the regional mall, the agenda was modified to attract family attendance on a large scale.

Long before 1920, the rise of a highly centralized pattern of urban growth enabled the department store to emerge as a great, all-inclusive emporium that helped define the character and the purpose of the city. That process continued through the 1920s; thereafter, extensive remodeling and the more occasional expansion of department stores became a symbol of efforts at regeneration and retrieval of the retail core's dominant role. Concurrently, the development of department store branches became a key indicator of the rise in the importance of outlying areas as alternatives to downtown. Once the regional mall emerged as the mainstay of department store expansion, the metropolitan periphery began to assume functions once unique to the city center. In terms of its design, its consumer appeal, and its urbanistic role the department store was a catalyst for, as well as an indicator of, change.

If the department store's transformation had widespread and long-lasting effects on design, consumption, and metropolitan structure, it was wrought by external changes that were unwelcome and often seemed daunting to company executives. The meteoric rise of chain stores was a particularly unsettling occurrence in this regard. While chain companies were not directly competitive at first, the fact that they were growing at an unprecedented pace and could reap high profit margins became a source of widespread anxiety among department store leaders by the mid-1920s. During the years that followed, chains started to encroach on portions of the trade over which the great emporia had enjoyed hegemony. All the while, independently owned specialty stores were experiencing a comeback in many of the department store's prized realms, including both soft goods, such as apparel, and hard goods, such as furniture and appliances. Strengthening operational and merchandising practices as well as modernization and expansion of the plant were pursued as means of staving off this competition. The strategies that should be devised under such circumstances were the subject of ongoing debate among industry leaders. The department store had redefined retailing in the late nineteenth and early twentieth centuries; executives were unsure if they should redefine it again. Innovations such as self-selection of goods that had been pioneered by chain store and supermarket companies were frequently considered inappropriate, yet frequently proved unavoidable. At the heart of matter lay the unresolved question as to the nature of the department store: To what degree should it still be predicated on individuality and service versus efficiency and economy?

The vast influx of motorized vehicles into the city center during the 1920s and the fact that a sizable portion of the department store's most prized clientele now wished to use their cars for shopping expeditions posed another array of challenges as department store executives began to contemplate elaborate measures for off-street accommodation of automobiles. Soaring downtown land values coupled with the need to enlarge selling space led many department store companies to build remote-site support facilities. All these measures were costly in their own right, and department store profit margins remained small for much of the four-decade period. Branch development eventually became accepted as a means of improving sales by expanding a store's market. Large-scale branch building as part of multiple regional malls was propelled by this objective and held particular appeal since it initially enabled department store executives to exercise control over the nature and extent of competition by chain and independent specialty outlets alike. But the operation of a regional mall brought its own set of problems, and institutions financing the behemoths soon began to influence the selection of participating stores.

Examining the department store as a building type thus cannot be undertaken simply as a study of physical attributes. Nor can changes to that type be cast as a neat, linear sequence of developments. At any given point, multiple paths were taken to maintain and augment the department store's position in retailing. Far from abandoning downtown, for example, department store companies were conspicuous advocates in stimulating its revival through the mid-twentieth century. Ever more ambitious branch building campaigns thus went hand-in-hand with improvements to the parent store. The complexity of change was furthered by the fact that multiple, often conflicting views existed within the trade as to the optimal means of achieving objectives in realms as diverse as merchandising, warehousing facilities, branch size and contents, and even the basic character of the regional mall. Some challenges were seldom satisfactorily met, off-street customer parking downtown being among the most persistent examples. Throughout the period, transformation induced struggle as well as progress; change was seemingly constant; resolution all too frequently elusive.

By exploring how the department store was shaped by the intricacies of change—myriad obstacles; conflicting objectives; unanticipated results; slow, incremental shifts, often following circuitous paths, the ultimate outcome of which was seldom predictable; and abrupt alteration of circumstances, sometimes external, sometimes internal, that could play havoc with the best-laid plans—I seek to offer a fresh perspective on the development of architecture and the metropolitan landscape. The movement toward decentralization, for example, was neither an easy nor an obvious series of events; it frequently entailed prolonged struggles to resolve new problems that seemed perplexing at best to the people charged with addressing them. The department store affords especially rich insight into such processes, for no other commercial enterprise enjoyed a more pivotal position in affecting metropolitan growth, was so widely recognized and admired by the population, and, at the same time, so besieged by competing businesses.

Correlating the physical and business realms, while also considering their implications for the metropolitan landscape, presents only part of the story, of course. While cultural factors also play a prominent role in the history of the department store, developing this realm fully would entail exploring a great range of sources beyond the extensive number consulted in the course of my research. Moreover, the landmark historical works on the department store in the United States address the cultural and social spheres and also an earlier, formative period, when the department store emerged as the dominant force in retailing.[1] Even so, relatively little attention has been paid to a number of issues pertaining to race, ethnicity, and class in this sphere. Despite the major role long played by Jews in the operation of department stores and in retailing generally, for example, analysis devoted to the subject is limited.[2] The hierarchy of department stores in each city based on stylishness, with all the class connotations it carried, is another realm that begs detailed exploration. But irrespective of topic or period, scholarly examination of physical attributes has generally been of secondary concern at best.[3] *The American Department Store Transformed* aims to complement existing studies in its focus as well as in the time frame covered, addressing new material in the history of the type.

To keep the parameters manageable, I limit the scope to "major" department stores—loosely defined as those that ranked among the most sizable and prominent downtown-based emporia purveying a wide selection of merchandise that usually encompassed both soft and hard goods. To examine the department store phenomenon as a whole, I include examples that were oriented to the low, middle, and high ranges of the vast consumer market that frequented downtown, a market encompassing many people of moderate means, middle-class households with more disposable income, and affluent ones capable of regularly indulging in luxury goods. I have also included a few large, high-end departmentalized specialty stores trading primarily in apparel, accessories, and some home furnishings because of their important role in establishing patterns of interior design and branch development.[4] The geographic scope is limited to the nation's sixty largest cities in 1930, a date by which most of the key metropolitan centers in the U.S. during the mid-twentieth century had been established.[5] Communities of 138,000 and greater (in 1930) were identified so as to include important regional population centers in the southern and central parts of the country—Richmond, Nashville, Des Moines, Oklahoma City, Fort Worth, and Salt Lake City, for example—to attain a reasonably balanced national coverage. The pages of major trade organs, including *Women's Wear Daily* and *Dry Goods Economist,* make clear that many similar patterns could be found with downtown facilities of department stores in smaller communities as well.

To examine the range of issues addressed in this study, I have developed a topical structure that also adheres to an underlying chronological order. The first four chapters are devoted to downtown emporia and their support facilities. In Chapter 1, I focus on the boom period of the 1920s, when downtown department stores expanded at a rate that matched, and perhaps exceeded, that of previous decades as they made marked improvements to both design and operations. At the same time, department store executives had reason for alarm due to soaring costs, new and revived forms of competition, and limited space for expansion, among other factors. In Chapter 2, I explore changes wrought first by the Depression, then by tenuous recovery, and finally by the flush postwar years. All three phases contributed to the department store becoming one of the nation's foremost manifestations of modernity—inside and out. The striking changes that occurred as a result were primarily through alterations to existing plants; new construction on a large scale was limited. But even if such changes were often cosmetic, they led to a substantially new environment that was more internalized, flexible, and informal. Modernization and other agendas were facilitated by the rise of department store corporations, which, especially after World War II, became powerful instruments of operation nationally.

Soaring downtown land values in the 1920s spurred the process whereby numerous support functions were removed from the department store and placed in what became carefully designed, multipurpose service facilities by the decade's end. Situated at the periphery of downtown or even further afield, these outposts not only functioned as warehouses and places for such services as upholstering, they were nerve centers for the movement of goods—from manufacturers and wholesalers to customers. Remote site plants of this kind were practical only with motor trucks, the early development of which was propelled by department store companies to a major degree. In Chapter 3, I address the emergence of these plants and their subsequent transformation at mid-century owing to new tendencies in the design of industrial buildings and to the demands of serving a network of branches as well as the main store. Customer motor vehicles are the focus of Chapter 4, which analyzes the unforeseen and seemingly insurmountable problems caused by widespread automobile use as soaring volumes of vehicular traffic clogged the central arteries on which they depended for their trade. Department stores developed a number of strategies to address this problem, often becoming reluctant leaders in downtown initiatives to provide off-street parking. Yet no matter how concerted the effort, few of these endeavors appear to have met their objectives fully.

In the next four chapters I address the equally complex issues entailed in branch department store development.[6] During the interwar decades, branch building was experimental and tentative. In Chapter 5, I analyze the great variety found in such endeavors, as well as the underlying debates on whether branches served a valid purpose and, if so, what form they should take. The boom in new residential enclaves for the affluent and middle class, built on the metropolitan periphery, contributed to the call for branch store development in some quarters, but other retailers remained convinced that the downtown store was the sole facility needed. Only in Los Angeles did major department store companies establish large, full-line branches prior to 1940. The rate of participation grew decisively during the postwar years, while experimentation remained the norm. At first, many of these branches were developed as singular entities, located in existing or new outlying business centers. Others were constructed in town and city centers distant from the parent store in order to strengthen a large regional market. These emporia, the subject of Chapter 6, also varied considerably in size and scope. Collectively, however, they represented a clear trend that made branch building a major component of the industry.

A branch store could enjoy additional advantages if it was constructed as part of a shopping center. The early stages of this coupling are the subject of Chapter 7. A department store added prestige and appeal to the complex as a whole, while the department store enjoyed the benefits of a controlled mercantile environment and abundant off-street parking. All too often, however, the planning of these branches was fraught with shortcomings, rendering the department store more an independent appendage of, than a fully integrated contributor to, the ensemble. A viable means of remedying this situation became apparent by the early 1950s in the form of the regional shopping mall. The subject of Chapter 8, these sprawling complexes were quickly embraced by leading department store companies as the preferred means of achieving dominance in outlying areas. Those companies could exercise great power in determining all aspects of the mall, including its location, size, form, character, and tenancy. Competition was encouraged but also tightly controlled. Yet despite the numerous advantages the mall had to offer, it also carried substantial challenges and risks. Furthermore, the complex itself was rapidly evolving in the 1950s, the subject of vigorous discussions over its optimal form and complexion.

If, by the early 1960s, department store companies had reinvented themselves to meet the challenges that had begun to arise several decades earlier, they were far from home free. Despite continual efforts to update, even expand, the parent store through the postwar period, the issue of whether to embark on large-scale urban revitalization plans in order to rescue declining downtown retail districts intensified during the 1950s. That debate and some of its material results are analyzed in the final chapter. Throughout that decade, many department store chieftains participated in private-sector campaigns to draw more trade to the city center. These endeavors could include sweeping projects to improve highway access and to build nearby housing for the middle class, even the well-to-do. At the same time, the prevailing approach among retailers remained conservative as far as the shopping district itself was concerned. Dramatic changes under the aegis of urban renewal were for the most part resisted until a decade or two later.

Thus even though the department store had been effectively recast by 1960, challenges and changes persisted. Events that have occurred since then, including the collapse or near collapse of many forms of downtown retailing, the saturation of metropolitan and many rural areas with regional malls, the pursuit of new kinds of retail centers and indeed of new kinds of retail distribution, and the demise or conflation of all but four of the 185 companies examined in this study underscore the fact that change is as unpredictable as it relentless. As the department store emerged in embryo during the mid-nineteenth century, transformed itself at the turn of the twentieth century, did so again between 1920 and 1960, and has yet again since 1960, it is likely to so do in other ways over the next generation. The process is impossible to foretell and is difficult enough to understand in retrospect. Far from comprising a homogenous, straightforward, even dull environment, as it is sometimes still accused of being, the physical landscape of retailing embodies complex, multifaceted, sometimes conflicting, and frequently shifting concerns that can yield a wealth of insight on design, urbanism, business practices, and the things we value as a society. It is perhaps no coincidence that as subjects related to consumption have attracted a growing number of scholars in recent decades, the creation of retail facilities has acquired a new cachet among designers.[7] The richness of the past may be matched by the opportunities of the future.

1 Bigger and Bigger Stores

LIKE OTHER EVENTS of its kind, the opening of the enlarged Great White Store, in October 1922, elicited national attention in the retail trade and no small degree of excitement locally. At a cost of $1.5 million, a steel-frame pile extending eight floors above street level and two below, clad in ivory-colored terra cotta and containing nearly 120,000 square feet of floor space, had been erected in fourteen months. The emporium now housed 146 departments and an array of features that made it a publicist's dream. On the sixth floor lay a Temple of Music, with piano and Victrola salons, each boasting soundproof demonstration chambers. Nearby, the Men's Club Room was laden with sporting goods. The same floor also housed Toy Town, a children's barbershop, an attended playroom, and a noise-suppressing room for youngsters unwilling to observe adult boundaries of decorum. Three floors below were spaces for women's apparel, including a Louis XVI Room, a Black and White Room (mourning wear), a Japanese Room (negligees), four French rooms (millinery), a blouse shop, and a Costume Room, complete with stage and theater lighting, for the presentation of evening gowns. In between, on the fourth and fifth floors, lay home furnishing departments, including ten model rooms for "Homes that Reflect the Beauty of a Hundred Different Lands."

The service components of the Great White Store were no less impressive. A fur vault on the eighth floor had its own elevator and capacity for twenty-five thousand large pieces. For patrons seeking refreshment, there was the Ivy Tea Room, fitted with black and gold marble trim. Employees were treated to a glazed penthouse cafeteria, with blue and cream tile walls, as well as a reading room, solarium, and "silence room"—all open to a roof deck promenade. Fourteen passenger elevators were matched by as many escalators. Fourteen telephone operators could handle at least thirteen thousand calls daily. Direct lines ran to neighboring communities so that customers might order goods over the phone free of charge. The store generated its own power, with three immense boilers and four steam engines supporting the air filtration system, two forty-ton refrigeration machines, seventy-two thousand feet of steam pipes, and eighty miles of electrical wiring, among other equipment.[1]

The Great White Store was the popular name for L. Bamberger & Company, the Newark-based emporium that was preeminent in northern New Jersey and was seeking to compete with major New York establishments. In its short life, Bamberger's had been an unbridled success. When it opened in 1892, the store contained twenty thousand square feet on two floors of an existing building. Within six years the entire edifice was occupied and an addition completed, increasing floor space sixfold. Then in 1911–12, a new, purpose-built facility of five hundred thousand square feet—the Great White Store—was erected from plans by the prominent Chicago architect Jarvis Hunt.[2] Hunt's matching addition a decade later was followed by yet another of 1927–29, rising sixteen stories and bringing the total square footage to over 1 million (fig. 1).[3]

Bamberger's growth was more or less standard for department stores in large American cities, and not just in terms of the stores' rapid ascent at the turn of the twentieth century, but also in their continued expansion after World War I. Between 1919 and 1931 at least ninety large-scale construction campaigns were initiated at major department stores, taking form either as substantial additions or as wholly new facilities.[4] The pace had grown sufficiently intense that the editors of *Women's Wear Daily*, one of the most influential organs of the trade, speculated in 1924 that the predictions of the great London merchant H. G. Selfridge would soon be realized. Emporia would extend over many blocks, rendering current facilities as modest as they had made the shops of the previous century. The prospects seemed limitless.[5]

The 1920s was an important period in the development of the downtown department store on several fronts. The

1. L. Bamberger & Company department store, Market, Washington, and Halsey streets, Newark, New Jersey (1911–12, 1921–22, 1926–28). Jarvis Hunt, architect. Photo author, 1993.

intense building campaign culminated the fifty-year process that had propelled the type to retail dominance, which had become especially pronounced by the 1890s. The diffusion of new paradigms for ambience, merchandising, and service that had been consummated after 1900 by stores such as those for John Wanamaker and Marshall Field was, in this respect, merely interrupted by World War I. Many stores, like Bamberger's, did not fully emerge as grand mercantile palaces until the return of peace and the prosperous economic conditions of the 1920s. Only with such expansion did a number of these establishments begin to support the range of goods and services set by the industry's leaders.

The new decade brought a mounting array of uncertainties as well. In 1918 department store executives saw no serious challenges to their leadership in the retail field. Within a few years, however, anxieties began to rise over the revival of specialty stores, the expansion of mail-order companies into retailing, and the meteoric ascent of chain stores generally. No less ominous was a rise in operating costs that typically outpaced profits. The efficiencies wrought by ever more meticulous accounting and management practices failed to reverse the trend. By the late 1920s, merger and acquisition among department stores was becoming frequent, and some participants were calling for an extensive restructuring into huge national chains. Differences over the degree and course of change necessary were pronounced. A root problem was that growth in the consumer market, which underlay almost every basic merchandising policy, was substantially overestimated. Well before the stock market crash, department store executives feared crisis, not from an economic downturn, but from new competitors, lackluster profit margins, and other shifts in the field whose implications were not yet wholly grasped. By the decade's close, the complexion of retailing, and the department store's place in it, were substantially different from what they had been half a generation earlier. Moreover, those changes would have a profound effect on department stores for years to come. Throughout the 1920s there was nevertheless general agreement that no matter what the nature of the challenges facing the industry, an essential part of the solution was to expand operations by building bigger and bigger stores.

Business

Department store executives saw ample justification for continuing to do what they had done so well in years previous. From the mid-nineteenth century on, the growth of their establishments was, of course, directly related to increases in the number and size of urban centers, for both the large-scale manufacturing and the consumption of goods. Volume purchases and sales lay at the core of how the department store was able to gain dominance over other forms of retailing in cities. During the 1920s, the urban population continued to swell. Among the sixty largest cities, nearly half experienced growth rates of over 20 percent and nine others rose by more than 15 percent. Twelve cities had growth rates higher than the peak period of 1860 to 1890, when the urban population increased, on average, by 44 percent each decade. Many cities also now benefited from the burgeoning expansion of surrounding areas, where in twenty-seven of the same sixty metropolitan districts the population grew more than 44 percent. Newark's population, for example, rose only 6 percent in the 1920s, but the increase in outlying areas was over 45 percent, nearly 600,000 people.[6] Such increases were crucial to the department store because many newly populated districts contained a high number of households in medium-to-high-income levels, precisely those courted by the big emporia.

Equally important was the proliferation of technological advances that enabled department stores to reach their markets more effectively. Major strides were made in rapid transit systems for the largest metropolitan areas, including New York, Boston, Philadelphia, and Chicago, during the 1910s and 1920s. The latter decade also saw wholesale improvements to streets, facilitating auto access from outlying areas poorly served by public transportation. Motorized vehicles proved important in another respect as well, by substantially increasing the trade radius of major department stores. A trade radius of several hundred miles or more was common for many of these emporia in the years preceding the Depression. Among the hallmarks of service on which department stores built their reputations was efficient delivery of purchased goods. By the early 1920s, horse-drawn vehicles used for this purpose had largely been supplanted by fleets of trucks that contributed enormously to the speed and geographic scope of transfer, and metropolitan areas, if not larger regions, received the benefits of delivery within a day or two of the sale. The rapid rise in the use of home telephones boosted sales by enabling customers to order goods without going to the store. Expectations were rising, too, with a markedly higher rate of style consciousness, particularly among women, who, surveys of the 1920s indicated, constituted around 85 percent of the retail market.[7]

Expansion increased through the widespread adoption of more efficient management and accounting techniques. Analyzing changes in the field over the previous decade, William Nelson Taft, editor of the *Retail Ledger,* declared in 1928 that the "most important . . . [development] has undoubtedly been the great growth of statistical information available . . . , a growth which has been accompanied by a corresponding increase in interest in the facts which these statistics have brought to light." Before World War I, relatively few merchants expressed much concern for detailed study of the effect of costs—including salaries, rents, utilities, physical improvements, and advertising— or of sales and inventory on their operations. Statistical information was meager and sometimes inconsistent. One spur to upgrade accounting procedures came from the U.S. Department of the Treasury, which saw department stores' advanced inventory methods as a basis for income tax computation. But much of the impetus came from the growing realization that a detailed knowledge of costs was essential to running a large-scale store efficiently. Both encouragement and information in this sphere came from the National Retail Dry Goods Association (NRDGA), which was formed in 1911 and became a force in the industry after Lew Hahn assumed the presidency in 1918. Harvard University's Bureau of Business Research began to issue statistics on the operating expenses of department stores soon thereafter. A new emphasis on "scientific" management fostered by such organizations not only eliminated many wasteful practices but enabled store owners to better plan expansion. Looking back, Taft proclaimed that "work commenced between 1918 and 1928 will have more bearing upon the future of retailing and upon the ultimate cost of distributing to the buying public than that of any other ten years in the entire history of commerce." Many retailers agreed. A poll of NRDGA members in the mid-1930s yielded a majority response that improved control methods represented the industry's most important trend over the past quarter-century.[8]

An underlying impetus for the continued enlargement of department stores came from a substantial increase in consumption, reflecting the level of prosperity, at least among affluent households, during the years after World War I.⁹ Department stores generally enjoyed growth in patronage. Sales volume increased decisively through the first half of the 1920s and continued to rise through the decade, at a slower rate, to nearly twice the level it had been ten years earlier—an ascent that proved more tied to the growth of population in metropolitan areas than to widespread increases in personal income. Many accounts of stores' physical enlargement emphasized the rate of market growth, noting that existing facilities were stretched to capacity. Expansion was imperative, industry leaders agreed, if demand was to be met.

The prosperity of the era also caused more stores to upgrade their image as they jockeyed to improve their position in the local hierarchy. An informal ranking of stores, based on the elegance and quality of merchandise carried, services provided, and stature of the clientele, existed in each major city. These relationships between stores were never delineated in print, but merchants and the public alike recognized them. One emporium—Filene's in Boston, Wanamaker's in Philadelphia, Halle's in Cleveland, Marshall Field's in Chicago, Robinson's in Los Angeles—was the acknowledged leader in courting the most stylish local trade. Another store—Strawbridge & Clothier in Philadelphia, Bullock's in Los Angeles—might identify with this clientele as well. Several were directed toward the middle market, while still others focused on those of more moderate means, who nonetheless traveled downtown to fulfill many shopping needs, and those who simply were looking for bargains. Because of this ranking system, a number of companies sought to improve their status as consumption levels rose, primarily among the well-to-do. Although retailers had no way of quantifying the change, they sensed and in turn furthered the shift in expectations. The redesign of stores, the array of amenities offered, the increased emphasis on display, and the changes in merchandise all targeted prosperous households. Advertisements emphasized elegance and fashion, especially when a new building opened and during other events (fig. 2). Stylishness set the tone for most of the new work undertaken in the decade.¹⁰

At the same time, department store executives realized that they needed to attract a clientele well beyond the carriage trade. Many shoppers whose lot was not conspicuously improving could be attracted on occasion to an establishment that exuded exclusivity, but lower-cost merchandise of good value had to remain a staple of the big stores' offerings. Bargain-oriented departments also expanded significantly. To bolster sales among well-heeled and less prosperous consumers alike, stores began to establish credit plans in the early 1920s. Through the decade the aggressive marketing pursuit of installment buying, charge accounts, and even small loan programs captured a sizable share of business.¹¹

2. M. Rich & Brothers Company department store, Broad, Alabama, and Forsyth streets, Atlanta (1922–24). Hentz, Reid & Adler, architects; altered. Advertisement (*Atlanta Constitution,* 23 March 1924, 6-A).

Like the movie palace, the new department store exuded an aura of snob appeal at a time of widespread aspirations, yet it did not require extravagance to enjoy. Both were places where large numbers of Americans could feel important irrespective of their circumstances. The supply of elegant emporia, however, may well have exceeded demand.

In contrast to expectations and perceptions alike, the pronounced rise in per capita income during the 1920s was actually quite limited, encompassing only the top 7 percent of the nonfarm population. The other 93 percent remained stagnant or declined in their purchasing power. Furthermore, a mounting share of consumer income went to the purchase and maintenance of automobiles and to procuring appliances and electronic equipment (most of which were sold at specialty outlets), as well as to the pursuit of leisure activities that such goods fostered.¹² Department stores began to lose their share of the retail trade. Throughout the decade those with annual sales of $1 million or greater averaged a more or less steady percentage increase in expenses and a steady percentage decrease in net profits. The gains that department stores achieved in sales were to a significant degree offset by the rise in operating costs, despite new management and accounting techniques. Moreover, falling wholesale prices in clothing and home furnishings necessitated selling more goods at greater cost to maintain sales volume. Expensive advertising practices that did not always prove cost effective; spiraling downtown real estate values; customer demands for an ever greater array of goods, many of them with low turnover rates; and increasing competition further contributed to a situation markedly different from the decades of seemingly unchecked growth.[13]

Competitors

Probably the most compelling factor to spur expansion was the rapid ascendancy of competing distribution systems. Within a few years of the armistice, department store executives began to identify significant potential threats to their consumer base from both the independent specialty shop and the chain store.[14] Among the traditional strengths of the department store was the capacity to make purchases on a large scale, thus reducing costs. The company's substantial accumulation of capital further enabled it to take advantage of cash discounts, carry more complete stock, and diversify its risks. The scale of operation attracted talented executives. But size also tended to foster indifference and lack of specialized knowledge among the sales force, a weakness that had become a major problem by the 1920s.[15] While the specialty shop was the kind of outlet over which the department store had gained dominance in the late nineteenth century, it was now making a comeback because of its ability to offer a higher degree of personal attention, sales force expertise, and a more intimate, even exclusive, atmosphere. Many specialty shops capitalized on rising social aspirations, targeting a key component of the department store's clientele, and intimating that the emphasis that the big emporia placed on value resulting from large-scale purchases was tantamount to an admission that their goods were not of the highest caliber.

Most specialty outlets were quite modest in size and in the volume of goods sold. Yet during the 1920s numerous existing and new specialty businesses undertook construction of multistory buildings (with floor space ranging from 40,000 to 80,000 square feet or more) that were clearly oriented to a sizable market. Establishments of this kind were especially popular for purveying women's and men's clothing, as well as furniture and musical instruments.[16] Located on prime downtown blocks close to major department stores, they were direct competitors that were viewed by department store executives as a source of business erosion. At the decade's end, net sales in specialty stores represented only slightly more than 10 percent of those of department stores; however, the profit margins reaped by the bigger specialty stores were substantially higher.[17]

The chain store generated even greater consternation among department store executives. Chain companies proliferated between 1914 and 1930, their number expanding some 400 percent, while the number of stores increased 800 percent and the volume of business 1500 percent—a much greater gain than in any other form of retailing.[18] Especially ominous was the fact that many of these establishments were offering lines considered important to the department store. By the decade's end, variety chains had made serious inroads in the market for notions and many other goods that were the stock-in-trade of the ground floor at lower-end department stores. Among the largest companies, F. W. Woolworth increased its stores by more than half in the ten years after 1918; S. S. Kresge nearly doubled its units. Margins of profit were no less eye-catching. Averages between 1922 and 1926 for Woolworth were 10.53 percent; Kresge 12.33 percent; S. H. Kress 9.37 percent—conspicuously higher than most major department store companies. Medium-sized chains, including J. J. Newberry, G. C. Murphy, and F. & W. Grand were likewise engaged in ambitious expansion programs. Paul Mazur, a highly respected analyst of retailing who wielded considerable influence in the department store arena, declared that the five-and-ten-cent stores "are among the strongest economic institutions in the country." While many new avenues for improvement were being explored, only with these stores "does such evolution [in merchandising] seem to have arrived at a fairly permanent answer to a particular phase of problems in retail distribution."[19]

Other specialized businesses were growing as well. Shoe chains were virtually nonexistent in 1918; between 1925 and 1928, such companies increased their outlets from 1642 to 7000. During the same period, some clothing and accessory chains embarked on similarly intense development campaigns.[20] A number of these organizations, such as Lerner Shops (women's apparel) and Bond Company (men's clothing), traded in relatively low-priced merchandise and were not always seen as direct threats to leading department stores. Yet the emergence of so many retail establishments in such short order was unsettling for department store executives. Like their independent counterparts, many clothing and related specialty chain outlets were housed in modest quarters of a few thousand square feet. On the other hand, some companies occupied sizable buildings that were comparable to a number of the large independent specialty stores. In 1922, for example, New York–based Russek's opened a stylish "Fifth Avenue" store of five stories in the heart of Detroit's Woodward Avenue shopping district. Perhaps the biggest of these concerns was the Bedell Company, also headquartered in New York, which catered to a less upmarket audience and boasted nineteen units in cities coast to coast by mid-decade.[21] Large and small, these chains purchased prime locations in downtown shopping districts. By 1930, department store executives found their establishments surrounded by a host of competitors, many of which had not existed a generation previous. While the big stores remained the dominant forces of trade, their operators sometimes worried that their businesses might become like Gulliver in the land of the Lilliputians.

The reasons chain companies grew so quickly and extensively were a subject of great interest to department store executives. One of the most detailed studies of chains published prior to 1930 was by the *Dry Goods Economist*, principal organ of department and large specialty store operators.[22] The great advantage of the chain system, many independent merchants believed, was the low prices that could be offered thanks to high-volume purchases. But analysts noted that price was only part of the equation. More important was the carefully developed, systematized method of goods selection, concentrated on a limited variety of items, mostly in the low-to-medium price range, that enjoyed widespread demand and thus maximized revenues from stock. Key, too, were the advantages of regional or national advertising and the ability, owing to the potential for growth, to attract top-flight executives for the central office and as store managers. The chain store was viewed both as a threat and a phenomenon from which independent retailers could learn more effective business practices.

The chain enterprise that especially interested department store executives in the late 1920s was the J. C. Penney Company, which, of all the major chains, seemed the most directly tied to their own stores. Penney's was what was known at that time as a junior department store, purveying a limited range of items, mainly apparel, accessories, and basic household goods. Having begun in 1902 as a single, modest store in Kemmerer, Wyoming, the firm boasted some fifteen hundred units nationwide by the close of 1929, having nearly trebled its stores and its net profits over the previous five years alone. After much coaxing, Penney's president, E. C. Sams, spoke at the 1928 convention of the NRDGA, which had become the principal conclave of department store titans. His address was greeted as something of a revelation: "Any merchant may take the profits of his single store," Sams emphasized, "and—with the men he is able to train in that store—open up a second store, then a third store and so on until he has a chain, if he chooses to develop his business in this direction. His limitations are almost entirely concerned with the development and training of men. This is an educational problem, not a financial one." Penney's had always used its own capital to expand. Here, he suggested, was a way in which the beleaguered retailer could lay the foundations for growth and prosperity.[23]

Penney's was not the sole success story. The W. T. Grant Company was fast rising to national prominence, as were the newly formed retail operations of the country's two largest mail-order houses, Sears, Roebuck and Montgomery Ward. Indeed, between the time it entered the retail sphere, in 1924, and 1930, Sears opened no fewer than sixty-five full-line department stores in an expansion campaign that outdistanced those of virtually all other retail businesses.[24] All four companies catered to a different clientele than did the leading downtown emporia, by purveying goods that met basic needs, not fashion or other luxury-driven impulses, of persons of moderate means. Penney's and Ward's stores were also modest buildings, located in towns removed from the metropolitan centers. While not primary competitors, these chains were nonetheless seen as curbing the potential for department stores to expand and even lessening existing trade. Some low-cost items they carried had been a longstanding component of the merchandise in department stores. Furthermore, with travel now greatly facilitated by automobile, the trading area of major department stores was extending well into the territory increasingly occupied by Penney or Ward outlets. By the late 1920s, many department store executives were convinced that significant changes were required if their field was to survive. Among the most effective strategies for change, some believed, was establishing chains of their own.

Consolidation

A "chain" of major downtown department stores, as it then existed, was quite unlike a Penney's, Sears, or Woolworth's. Central administrative offices existed in both cases, but in the former, the role was one of consultation rather than direction and control. Each department store ran more or less independently, with its own executive management, buyers, and operating policies. The individual identity that had contributed so much to the store's reputation over its years of growth was cultivated to the point that the buying public remained generally unaware that it was part of a larger organization. These "chains" were in reality ownership groups, and the processes by which they developed were ones of consolidation through either acquisition or affiliation. The drive to form such companies was propelled largely by the advantages seen in sharing information on store operations, in group purchases of at least some goods, in diversifying the financial risks of such projects as store expansion, and in the prospects for increasing joint enterprises. Fear of competition combined with optimism about growth potential led many department store executives to entertain such ventures. Probably no other aspect of the business generated more debate during the decade.[25]

Consolidation among department stores began around the turn of the twentieth century and was part of the trend toward corporate expansion to a national scale that characterized so much business activity of that era. Some of the earliest of these retail ventures were tightly controlled by a family but still did not have a strong central organization. Most notable among these was the company created by

David May and his partners. After moving from Leadville, Colorado, to Denver, where it purchased a bankrupt store in 1889, the firm made similar acquisitions in St. Louis (Famous Company, 1892) and Cleveland (Hull & Dutton, 1901). Following its reorganization in 1910 as May Department Stores, the company purchased another St. Louis concern (William Barr Dry Goods, 1911) and one in Akron, Ohio (M. O'Neil, 1912), making it an unusually large enterprise of the period. Expansion continued after World War I with the acquisition of Hamburger's in Los Angeles (1923) and Bernheimer-Leader in Baltimore (1927).[26] Most of the stores bought were in weak condition, and May executives substantially reorganized and expanded each operation, though not according to a standardized format common to chains, to make their network one of the strongest and most profitable in the field.

The other major family-run company of this kind was Gimbel Brothers, which originated in 1842 as a trading post in Vincennes, Indiana. Nearly half a century later, Gimbel's began to move into major urban centers, first opening a store in Milwaukee (1887), then erecting a much larger one in Philadelphia (1894), and finally building an immense pile in New York (1910). Expansion continued after World War I with the purchase of a sizable Pittsburgh store, Kaufmann, Baer, which was reopened under the Gimbel name. While each unit was operated by sons and grandsons of the company's founder, Adam Gimbel, considerable differences appear to have existed in their styles of management. Family divisions became more pronounced than family unity.[27]

The third pioneer, H. B. Claflin Company, was established in 1890 on entirely different premises. Created by John Claflin in the course of reorganizing his enormous wholesale business, the organization soon began acquiring well-known retail outlets, including a number of department stores, in order to ensure steady demand for its goods. The consolidation was nevertheless the loosest of them all. Stores remained independent to the degree that they purchased from Claflin's competitors. Claflin collapsed in 1914 from overextension, but the eight major department stores (J. N. Adam, William Hengerer [Buffalo], Hahne [Newark], Lord & Taylor, James McCreery [New York], Powers [Minneapolis], Stewart [Baltimore], and Stewart Dry Goods [Louisville]) regrouped two years later as the Associated Dry Goods Corporation. The company focused on consolidated buying and within a few years had developed a research department focusing on merchandising methods. For this latter function Associated drew from the practices of the Retail Research Association (RRA), founded in 1916, whose membership consisted of independent stores that shared data on sales, control of stock, and other operations. The systematized exchange of information formerly closely guarded by each company proved beneficial to all nineteen participants and came to be seen as a major advance in retail practices. Like the RRA, Associated stores pursued what its members saw as a viable balance between cooperation and independence, with each member continuing to operate as a discrete unit, differing to a considerable degree in policies and merchandise carried.[28]

Both the acquisition of other stores and the formation *de novo* of corporate entities gained appeal among department store executives in the early 1920s. Not only did this path seem the most effective for checking competition from chain companies, consolidation could also be a means to accumulate capital for expansion and other improvements. Furthermore, at a time when the ownership of many stores was passing to a younger generation and problems were arising with taxes, disinterested heirs, and related matters, the idea of being part of a corporate system was attractive. Capital for these ventures was to a significant degree raised by the formation of public companies and thence the issuance of stock, a major break from traditional financing practices, in which expansion was funded by profits. Issuing stock enabled store owners to raise the needed money in short order and also spread the risk if the venture failed to meet expectations. Toward the decade's end, consolidation seemed a pervasive tendency in the department store field, though in fact the stores so affected were still in a minority.

Much of the stature the movement gained came from initiatives by industry giants such as R. H. Macy & Company, which purchased large, prominent stores in Toledo (Lasalle & Koch, 1924), Atlanta (Davison-Paxon, 1925), and Newark (Bamberger's, 1929).[29] Unlike May's managers, Macy's executives introduced few changes to their acquired offspring. Other prominent companies made similar purchases toward the decade's end. In 1927, the Emporium of San Francisco bought H. C. Capwell, the leading store in Oakland. F. & R. Lazarus of Columbus, Ohio, bought John Shillito, its Cincinnati counterpart, the following year, and Marshall Field acquired Frederick & Nelson in Seattle in 1929. A year earlier, Filene's purchased R. H. White, another large, if less prestigious, Boston store, both to broaden its base and to enlarge the scope of its merchandise, which had been primarily apparel and accessories.[30] On the other hand, Gimbel's used this strategy to increase its stature in New York. In 1922 the firm bought the building occupied by Saks, which lay across Thirty-Third Street from its own, with the idea of expansion, but instead it merged the next year, keeping Saks's identity as a complement to its own and nurturing a decisively more upmarket orientation of the new Saks facility on Fifth Avenue.[31]

Sebastian S. Kresge, who had developed one of the country's largest variety store chains, entered the department store field in 1923 with ample capital but no businesses. Kresge purchased L. S. Plaut of Newark that August, followed by the Palais Royal (Washington, D.C.) six months later and the Fair (Chicago) in 1925 as the nucleus of what he claimed would become a one-hundred-store empire.[32] Management problems plagued the company from an early date, however. Kresge's expertise in low-end merchandising was not always applicable to the new concern. After a much heralded start, the company failed to grow.

A far more ambitious and successful plan for assembling a group of retail establishments was launched in May 1928 as Hahn Department Stores. Eugene Greenhut and Arthur Weisenberger, specialists in promotion and advertising, conceived a national chain and soon enticed Lew Hahn, director of the NRDGA and a staunch advocate of consolidation, to consider the presidency. Inquiries were made to hundreds of department stores outlining the proposal. The response was sufficiently strong to secure Hahn's participation. Over the next several months the group became firmly established with twenty-seven prominent stores. Among the biggest concerns were Jordan Marsh (Boston), Rollman & Son (Cincinnati), Golden Rule (St. Paul), L. S. Donaldson (Minneapolis), Titche-Goettinger (Dallas), and Bon Marche (Seattle). Hahn believed that the retail field lagged behind manufacturing in developing large business organizations. While retailing did a much larger dollar volume annually than most spheres of manufacturing, he emphasized, none of its companies approached the size of U.S. Steel or General Motors. Hahn hoped that his new organization would become such a giant, but he advocated a slow, cautious path. The department store chain of the future, he argued, would create its own model rather than replicate existing ones. For the moment, he focused on devising an effective strategy for central buying and a regional structure that allowed managers to exchange information on controlling costs and maximizing sales. Hahn Department Stores was not only the largest group of its kind, but in 1927 it enjoyed net profits second only to those of the May Company, making it, for some, an exemplar of its kind.[33]

Mergers initiated by store executives themselves proved the most popular means of consolidation during the decade. The first such undertaking was National Department Stores, launched in February 1923 by five members of a research association, Affiliated Retail Stores, formed four years earlier. The new company was composed of large, well-established stores aimed at the lower-middle market: the Bailey Company in Cleveland, Nugent's in St. Louis, Rosenbaum's in Pittsburgh, and Geo. Stiffel and Geo. Taylor in Wheeling. Seven months later, these were joined by the three outlets of Frank & Seder (Philadelphia, Pittsburgh, and Detroit), a sizable firm specializing in apparel and accessories whose Philadelphia unit was developing into a full-fledged department store. National was able to implement some central buying for staple goods, but most purchases were made by the individual stores. Despite hopes for expansion coast to coast, National remained characterized more by its members' disparate practices than by uniform or even well-coordinated ones.[34]

A more closely knit organization, City Stores Company, was established in November 1923 with the aim of coordinating operations of major emporia in the South. The core group consisted of the Maison Blanche of New Orleans, B. Lowenstein & Brothers in Memphis, which the former had acquired three years previous, and Loveman, Joseph & Loeb in Birmingham, to which Kaufman-Straus in Louisville was added in 1924. The following year, however, City Stores began to alter its profile when Rudolph J. Goerke, owner of less prestigious stores that bore his name in Newark and Elizabeth, New Jersey, purchased controlling interest. Working with Bankers Securities Corporation, Goerke subsequently assumed control of a lower-middle-market Philadelphia store, Lit Brothers. While the group was an unlikely mixture, Goerke was aggressive in developing methods of operation that were effective for the group as a whole.[35]

One of the least consequential mergers when it occurred, yet one of the most important in the long term, was consummated in November 1929. Three of the nation's most prestigious emporia, Filene's, Abraham & Straus, and Lazarus, joined forces to create Federated Stores. Bloomingdale's entered the group a month later. The initial intent of this association was simply to spread risk; aside from its stock, each store remained a wholly separate entity. Eventually, however, Federated developed a strong central operation and rivaled May and Hahn as industry leaders.[36]

At the close of the 1920s department store consolidation remained in a nascent state and was yielding mixed results. Some companies, such as City Stores and May, enjoyed a steady increase in profits; Gimbel's and Hahn were less successful; National suffered losses.[37] The uneven record fueled the debate among retailers about how to expand operations most effectively. Some in the field believed that the change had not gone far enough. Perhaps the most vocal exponent of transformation in merchandising practices was Edward A. Filene, president of the venerable Boston emporium William Filene's Sons. Filene argued that department stores needed to embrace chain methods of large-scale buying and standardized operations. The individuality that was still cherished by store executives had to be abandoned, and with it the hierarchy among stores. The great store of the future, he emphasized, would cater to a broad segment of society, just like General Motors; departments would be highly specialized, just like a chain store; buying would be centralized to enable a high volume. As a result, manufacturing and distribution costs would be substantially reduced, leading to consumer savings. Filene was so certain of his idea that he predicted chains of fifty to one hundred department stores in the near future.[38]

Paul Mazur of Lehman Brothers advocated a similar objective, but he was less adamant about the department store shedding many of its distinguishing characteristics. Like Hahn, he believed that consolidation was essential if the great emporia were to continue to grow. Expansion within a single community had its limitations, he maintained, owing to what many then assumed would be a long-term stabilized population. Only through the new economies possible with consolidation could substantial increases in business be realized. Like Filene, he predicted that the change would be decisive and swift. Concocting a fictional narrative to develop his point, Mazur spun a picture of a great New York skyscraper in 1950, which "houses the central offices of the United States Department Stores Corporation, a company doing a business of over five hundred million dollars [annually], and representing a consolidation of over one hundred department stores. It is an extraordinary institution—strong as the Rock of Gibraltar and rendering great service to the consumers with whom it comes in contact. Its growth was one of the outstanding industrial developments of the decade from 1930 to 1940."[39]

Not everyone subscribed to so sweeping a view of the future. John Guernsey, a former executive of the NRDGA, enumerated in an analysis of the consolidation movement a multitude of shortcomings. He advocated a balance between adopting chain methods of buying and control and maintaining the distinction and individuality that were the department store's hallmarks.[40] The *Dry Goods Economist* editorialized that human nature resisted the complete standardization of products that would be inevitable if chain merchandising methods became pervasive, pointing to the rise of high-end specialty stores as evidence. If department stores embraced chain practices fully, they would lose their basic advantages while gaining little.[41] Even without strident uniformity, a department store chain could in theory yield the advantages of groups such as the RRA, by adopting uniform accounting practices, enlarging chances for advancement, applying successful methods to other stores, and improving weak links in the system.

Yet by the decade's end no clear model had emerged to demonstrate that consolidation could substantially reduce operating costs and generate an effective system of large-scale buying. Indeed, some of the most successful operations, such as May, eschewed central buying.[42] Opinions varied on the best way to combine the strengths of centralized management and volume purchases and sales, on one hand, and service, high quality, and individuality on the other. Still, one matter on which there seemed to be little disagreement was that, whether or not a department store became part of a group, enlargement and reorganization of its physical plant was essential to keeping the establishment competitive. The drive for physical expansion was fueled by the big department stores' tendency to earn substantially larger profits than small ones, and the fear among retail executives that failure to expand would leave them trailing in the race for consumer patronage. Enlarging the scale and often the scope of their operations locally, they believed, was essential to meeting the ever more intense competition.[43]

Building

Propelled by the omnipresent concern over maintaining leadership in the distribution of goods and by mounting trepidation over the consequences of not taking aggressive steps to achieve that goal, the department store construction campaign of the 1920s was relentless. Nearly fifty new facilities and more than sixty major additions were erected among the leading emporia during the course of the decade.[44] The pace of construction was more or less even, from the immediate post–World War I period, when the national economy was temporarily destabilized, into the early 1930s, only after which it became clear that the prosperity of previous years would not soon return. From Akron to Seattle, Hartford to Detroit, Washington to San Francisco, Atlanta to Dallas, the landscape of downtown retail centers was affected by the expansion of department stores.

To finance the building programs, many department store executives took steps that had been rare or nonexistent in earlier decades, when improvements were made using surplus capital. During the early 1920s a number of store companies issued mortgage bonds, often of $1 million or more. By mid-decade, establishing a public corporation and issuing stock also gained favor, just as it did for store consolidation. Stocks reduced the monetary risk for store owners and, like bonds, were an expedient way to generate large sums since many people saw them as lucrative. Stores no longer had to grow according to business achievements alone; they could expand on business projections.[45]

The number of entirely new facilities was impressive by any standard, equaling and perhaps even surpassing the number built during the ten years prior to U.S. entry into the war.[46] A few of the companies involved, such as Brown-Dunkin in Tulsa, were newly established, but most had been in business at least since the 1890s. Furthermore, almost all the schemes known to have advanced into the development stage were at least partially realized.[47] The businesses encompassed the hierarchical range. Some, such as the Fifth Street Store in Los Angeles, catered to the lower-middle market; others, such as Julius Garfinckel in Washington, ranked among the most fashionable stores in their respective communities. The majority of establishments lay somewhere between. Stores such as the Hecht Company

3. L. S. Plaut & Company department store, Broad, Cedar, and Halsey streets, Newark (1924–26). Starrett & Van Vleck, architects. Advertisement (*Newark Evening News*, 7 November 1925, 3).

4. Strawbridge & Clothier department store, Market and Eighth streets, Philadelphia (1928–32). Simon & Simon, architects. Photo author, 1988.

in Washington sought to bolster their position in the local arena, becoming more competitive with leading merchants and, perhaps, improving their place in the hierarchy. Sebastian Kresge no doubt financed the huge and elegantly appointed L. S. Plaut store in Newark hoping that a rise in stature would enable it to rival Bamberger's in attracting the lucrative northern New Jersey trade (fig. 3). With initiatives such as these, the business was transformed no less than the facility. But equally arresting changes could occur to long-established retailers such as Philadelphia's Strawbridge & Clothier, second to John Wanamaker in the local hierarchy, whose executives replaced a maze of nineteenth-century buildings with a towering, stepped-back pile touted as one of the most modern in the country (fig. 4).

In building new quarters, Strawbridge's and some other department stores employed phased construction techniques that had been developed in the first decade of the century—John Wanamaker and Marshall Field being the largest and logistically most sophisticated examples.[48] Phasing was often done in close sequence so that store operations could continue on site. In cases such as Louis Pizitz (Birmingham), Ernst Kern (Detroit), Hens & Kelly (Buffalo), Strawbridge's, and the Fifth Street Store (Los Angeles), the process lasted three or four years (fig. 5).[49] Phased construction was also undertaken when the management wanted to initiate a long-term expansion plan that could be implemented as needed and as the supply of capital allowed. This strategy proved especially prudent when growth failed

5. Ernest Kern Company department store, Woodward and Gratiot avenues, Detroit (1925–29). Smith, Hinchman & Grylls, architects; demolished 1966. Construction photo, 1928.

6. L. S. Donaldson Company department store, Sixth and Seventh streets, Nicolet and Marquette avenues, Minneapolis (1923–24). Graham, Anderson, Probst & White, architects; demolished 1982–83. Advertisement showing store as planned; left bays and tower unexecuted (*Minneapolis Tribune*, 1 January 1924, 3).

to materialize, as with L. S. Donaldson of Minneapolis or A. I. Namm of Brooklyn, where elaborate schemes did not proceed beyond the first building campaign (fig. 6).[50] External circumstances also could change; the Depression arrested phased construction of both Bloomingdale's in New York and Abraham & Straus in Brooklyn.[51]

Disrupting store operations was not an issue for slightly over a third of the new buildings, which were erected away from existing facilities. Such moves were sometimes prompted by the need for more acreage. Sometimes, too, the move was precipitated by the desire for a location that could be more easily reached or was considered more prestigious. In making these decisions, department stores continued to figure prominently as shapers of prime downtown districts.[52] The Bon Marche, for example, became the keystone in the development of Times Square, an area to the north of Seattle's existing business core. Saks and Company's new store on New York's Fifth Avenue not only represented a decisive move to attract an affluent clientele but also was the first large emporium on that thoroughfare above Forty-Second Street, eventually drawing additional high-end stores to its environs.[53] Perhaps the most dramatic such change occurred when the two largest department stores in Akron—M. O'Neil and A. Polsky—decided to relocate at the southern edge of the commercial center, decisively shifting the locus of trade (fig. 7). On the other hand, the Higbee Company's decision to build a new store as part of the Terminal Tower complex in Cleveland helped reverse the course of business migration east along Euclid Avenue, which had been occurring for some years.[54] Such changes were the exception, however. Most department store construction increased the density of business concentrations, reinforcing patterns that had evolved over previous decades.

Major additions to existing plants made up the primary thrust of department store expansion, literally building on the sizable facilities erected before World War I. In contrast to conventional practices of the late nineteenth and even the early twentieth centuries, when many companies grew

7. *(left)* View of downtown Akron, showing department stores of M. O'Neil Company (center; 1926–28), Graham, Anderson, Probst & White, architects, and A. Polsky Company, Main and State streets (left; 1929–30), Good & Wagner, architects.

8. *(below left)* Woodward & Lothrop department store, F, G, Tenth, and Eleventh streets, Washington, D.C. (1902–3; far left). Henry Ives Cobb, architect. Additions: 1912 (far right bay), Frederick Pyle, architect; 1913 (adjacent four bays), Clarence Harding, architect; 1925 (three bays to right of original building) and 1926 (remaining seven bays in center), L. K. Ashford, architect. Presentation drawing, probably by Ashford.

9. *(below right)* Hunt Building/Brown-Dunkin Dry Goods Company department store, Main and Fourth streets, Tulsa, Oklahoma (ca. 1920–21, eleven stories added 1927–28); demolished. Advertisement (*Tulsa Daily World*, 6 September 1931, 3).

by acquiring adjacent buildings, enlarging their emporia in a piecemeal fashion, the objective was now to make the totality seamless in both its physical and operational dimensions. When the core building was itself relatively new, as with Bamberger's, the Broadway (Los Angeles), Joseph Horne (Pittsburgh), F. & R. Lazarus (Columbus), Neiman-Marcus (Dallas), or Woodward & Lothrop (Washington), additions often were made so as to appear merely a continuation, replicating or nearly replicating the original exterior design (fig. 8).[55] In a few cases, most notably Lasalle & Koch in Toledo, the addition comprised an inconspicuous attic story and penthouse, which, given the building's enormous footprint, provided substantial amounts of new space.[56]

Store expansion could also be coupled with other business development. In 1927–28, the Brown-Dunkin Dry Goods Company of Tulsa added eleven floors to its four-story block, using three of them for the store, the remaining eight as income-generating office space (fig. 9).[57] A key precedent for such combinations had been set in the previous decade with the May Company's Famous-Barr store in St. Louis. Constructed in 1913–15, the twenty-one-story, block-square pile, called the Railway Exchange Building, housed the store on its lower six floors and basement. Between 1920 and 1928, May leased an additional six floors, nearly doubling the size of its facility with minimal disruption.[58] The most complex and sumptuous development of this kind was the Carew Tower in Cincinnati, which included a multistory office block, the city's premier hotel, a leading specialty store (Mabley & Carew), and additional space for the contiguous H. & S. Pogue department store (fig. 10).[59] Examples of mixed-use development were nevertheless rare in the department store field. Brown-Dunkin, for example, found that due to leasing agreements it had to expand into an adjacent building rather than occupy additional floors of the edifice erected only four years earlier. Rather than engage in building speculation or be subject to the demands of real estate developers, most merchants focused on creating physical plants for their exclusive use.

In planning additions, concern for unity and order on the exterior prevailed even when circumstances necessitated substantial changes. In several instances this tendency toward replication predominated even when the constraints of lot size and the demands for space required additions markedly higher than the original store. Elsewhere, the new section was composed as if it was a separate building, expressive of both its verticality and newness, yet care was taken to make the parts compatible. Some examples were relatively modest in scale. Others, including the second addition to Bamberger's and two additions to Macy's (1928–31), ranked among the largest department store building programs of the decade (fig. 11).[60]

No expansion campaign was more ambitious than that of J. L. Hudson of Detroit. Already the biggest store in the city, Hudson's erected a fifteen-story addition comprising nearly 500,000 square feet in 1923–25. Two years later a considerably larger section of sixteen stories was begun, bringing the total square footage to slightly under 2 million, a floor area surpassed only by Macy's (fig. 12).[61] To create this ensemble, Hudson's purchased Newcomb-Endicott, Detroit's most fashionable department store, and demolished its new, twelve-story quarters as well as Hudson's own original building, which had been among the largest in the nation when it opened in 1890 (fig. 13). The exterior design of both additions embodied a conscious effort to rectify the piecemeal approach taken with the store's first major addition, built in phases during the 1910s, to which two stories were added in a rather ungainly fashion in 1922–23.[62] Later work, in contrast, not only was unified in itself, but it brought coherence to the whole while mitigating the effects of its enormous bulk by differentiating the parts. Although most department stores of the period bore classicizing references, Hudson's additions drew from Byzantine and Romanesque sources integrated into a conventional three-part composition for tall buildings. They also had some of the character of a great industrial plant. Topped by a multistory tower—the only one of consequence to be realized on a downtown department store—the dark red brick walls rose above their neighbors in a manner evocative of a medieval fortress in modern metropolitan garb. It is doubtful whether any emporium in the country, save Wanamaker's palazzo in Philadelphia, had a more commanding presence.

Almost all department store expansion of the period was accomplished through construction of new facilities tailored

10. Carew Tower, Fifth, Race, and Vine streets, Cincinnati (1929–31). Walter W. Ahlschlager and Delano & Aldrich, associated architects. Rendering showing complex with additions to H. & S. Pogue Company department store (original building to right) (*Cincinnati Enquirer*, 19 October 1930, Rotogravure Section).

11. *(above left)* R. H. Macy & Company department store, Broadway, Seventh Avenue, Thirty-Fourth, and Thirty-Fifth streets, New York (1901–2). De Lemos & Cordes, architects. Additions: 1922–24, 1928–31, Robert D. Kohn & Associates, architects. Photo Irving Underhill, 1931.

12. *(above right)* J. L. Hudson Company department store, Farmer Street and Gratiot, Grand River, and Woodward avenues, Detroit. Additions: 1923–25 (left) and 1927–28 (tower and right), Smith, Hinchman & Grylls, architects. Demolished 1998. Photo ca. 1946.

13. *(right)* Newcomb-Endicott Company department store, Woodward and Grand River avenues, Detroit (from left: 1902, 1920, 1881); demolished ca. 1926. J. L. Hudson Company (right), additions of 1911–19 and 1922–23; Smith, Hinchman & Grylls, architects. Photo ca. 1925.

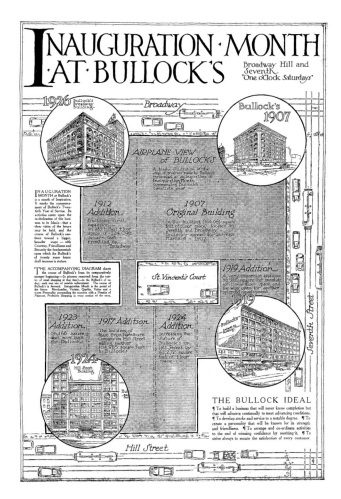

14. Bullock's department store, Broadway, Seventh, and Hill streets, Los Angeles. Site plan showing original store and additions (1926); all but purchased buildings by Parkinson & Bergstrom or John and Donald B. Parkinson, architects. Advertisement (*Los Angeles Times*, 11 March 1926, II-2).

to changing needs. A conspicuous exception was Bullock's, a leading Los Angeles emporium, which acquired recently erected contiguous buildings to accommodate its needs in 1917 and 1919. The first of these purchases then became the core of two narrow additions, constructed in 1923 and 1924 by an outside party and leased to the store. The final component, built in 1928, tied this agglomeration with the 1919 purchase and the original building (1907) to form one of the most complicated assemblages of its kind (fig. 14).[63]

Expansion to contiguous property was, of course, greatly preferred even as land costs reached unprecedented heights. In a few instances, however, stores had to leapfrog across streets to secure adequate space. Crowley-Milner of Detroit, whose ornate six-story building of 1908 had already been doubled in size to occupy the entire block, afforded a dramatic example. By March 1919, Crowley's had purchased the block to the north, including the recently constructed ten-story Emporium, which it now operated as part of its own business. Two years later a two-story addition to the original facility was complete, but it failed to meet expansion needs. As a result, the two complexes were joined in 1925 by an eleven-story extension to the Emporium, connected to Crowley's original building by a five-story bridge rendered in a monumental fashion befitting a civic edifice (fig. 15).[64] Although it connected most of the selling floors, so narrow a link was far from ideal. Nevertheless, it enabled the newer sections to function as part of a single plant rather than as separate entities.

Bridging public rights-of-way does not appear to have been a problem for Crowley's, or for L. S. Ayres of Indianapolis, which did so with its eleven-story addition (1928–29) over Pearl Street at all levels save the first, creating a near

15. Crowley, Milner & Company department store, Monroe and Gratiot avenues and Farmer Street, Detroit. From left: the Emporium (purchased 1918); addition to its rear and Library Street bridge (1925–26), and addition (1915–16) to original building (1905–7), with top two floors (1920–21). All portions save Emporium by Smith, Hinchman & Grylls, architects; demolished 1978. Photo Davis B. Hillmer, ca. late 1920s.

16. Halle Brothers Company department store, Euclid Avenue and Huron Street, Cleveland (1908–10, original building, at right). Henry Bacon, architect. Annex (1926–27, at left). Walker & Weeks, architects. Presentation drawing showing unrealized Huron Street Bridge, 1926.

17. J. L. Hudson Company music store, 68–70 Library Avenue, Detroit (1917–18). Smith, Hinchman & Grylls, architects; demolished. Photo ca. 1918 Thompson-Hudson Company.

tunnel in the process.[65] However, at least two stores encountered serious difficulties in this sphere. To utilize its 1919 building acquisition and the adjacent property purchased for later development, Bullock's had to construct a two-bay link over a dead-end alley, St. Vincent's Court, which was not owned by the city but by the holders of adjacent land. The primary link was in effect an extension of the two buildings, open only at street level and rising six stories above. In 1919, a special ordinance was passed granting Bullock's permission to construct the "bridge," but a year and a half later, when work was well under way, the City Council began to demur under pressure from William Randolph Hearst's *Examiner*. The newspaper's protests that Bullock's was abusing the public realm for its own selfish interest was prompted by Bullock's having refused to advertise owing to the *Examiner*'s pro-German stance in previous years. After several months Bullock's won its case in court, but the national attention that the dispute received in the trade press offered a warning to merchants about the hazards of expanding into the public realm.[66] A far more modest, single-tier bridge was proposed by Halle Brothers in Cleveland. Unable to acquire sufficient land contiguous to its immense facility, Halle's erected a sizable, six-story annex on Huron Road, directly opposite the main building's south front, in 1926–27. Care was given to design the bridge in a delicate, ornamental fashion, raising it to the fourth floor, with a wall area largely of glass, giving it minimal visual impact from the street (fig. 16). The scheme was denied by the city, and Halle's was forced to enlarge a tunnel connector that was originally intended for moving merchandise.[67]

Some space pressures could be more simply resolved. A few departments might operate efficiently, perhaps even optimally, apart from the main store, and a number of companies either leased or constructed separate facilities to house them. Hudson's six-story music store (1917–18), situated two blocks from its parent emporium, was an early and ambitious example (fig. 17). Both J. N. Adam (Buffalo) and the Hecht Company (Washington) opened separately run bargain departments, the former in its annex housing executive and merchandising offices, the latter in leased space across from the main store.[68] Perhaps the most popular outlet of this kind was the men's store. For some years department store owners had expressed frustration over the difficulties of expanding male patronage. Separate entrances and even special elevators were among the devices employed to lure males into a domain traditionally associated with

18. Liberty-Lincoln Building/John Wanamaker Men's Store, Broad and Chestnut streets, Philadelphia (1930–32). John T. Windrim, architect; altered.

19. Stix, Baer & Fuller Dry Goods Company department store, Washington and Lucas avenues, Sixth and Seventh streets, St. Louis (ca. 1907). Addition (1919–20, at left): Mauran, Russell & Crowell, architects. Advertisement (*St. Louis Post-Dispatch*, 6 November 1920, 5).

the opposite sex. So a completely separate facility carried appeal. As early as 1911, Marshall Field's had established the precedent for such an establishment when it constructed a twenty-story building on Wabash Avenue in Chicago, across from its main plant, the first six stories of which were used as the Store for Men. Sixteen years later rival Carson Pirie Scott opened a smaller facility, again in a new, multistory building two blocks to the south on Wabash—in the same block as the main store but on the diagonally opposite corner. Within three years Carson's had expanded this annex four times to include a bookstore, a rug store, and other departments.[69]

By far the most ambitious such venture was undertaken by John Wanamaker in 1928. Located a block from its Philadelphia emporium, the site lay in the heart of the financial district on one of the choicest sites in the city center. Replacing two thirteen-story piles constructed in the 1890s, the new edifice was one of the tallest buildings in the city at that time. The men's store occupied the first eight floors, with the remaining sixteen used for offices (fig. 18). Encompassing over 110,000 square feet, the outlet was reputed to be the largest of its kind operated by a department store in the United States, and it represented a major initiative by Wanamaker's to dominate the local trade in men's clothing.[70] Such ventures remained the exception, however. The department store's rise to hegemony in retailing had to a considerable degree been predicated on the convenience of having a wide array of goods and services under a single roof, and the great majority of owners strove to keep that feature. Separate facilities, or even ones that occupied more than a single block, remained peripheral developments in expansion programs of the 1920s, driven primarily by special circumstances.

Conservatism no less than unity in expression marked the character of the department store exterior. The image projected by the major street elevations was considered of paramount importance to a well-rounded merchandising plan.[71] The exterior functioned as a symbol of the establishment itself and was carefully depicted in advertisements

heralding the completion of a major construction campaign, anniversaries, and other special events. Thus portrayed, the store could assume the dimensions of a grand civic gesture, reflecting the aim that it be a defining component of a great city (fig. 19). Often, too, images depicted vignettes, emphasizing style consciousness (see fig. 2). A number of department stores constructed in the 1920s stood in the urban landscape as carefully designed commercial blocks, taking their place along with major office buildings, hotels, and institutions as elements that helped define the character of downtown but were not too conspicuous as individual gestures. Occasionally new construction assumed grander forms, as with the addition to Gimbel Brothers' Milwaukee store. Sited prominently on the Milwaukee River and heralding the eastern boundary of the downtown shopping district, the new section was dressed lavishly with a giant engaged ionic colonnade, suggestive more of a governmental building than a retail emporium (fig. 20).[72]

More pragmatic concerns predominated in most solutions, however. A building that seemed too extravagant could send the wrong message to consumers searching for reasonable prices. At the opening of the new Lowenstein's store in Memphis (1923–24) officials were quick to emphasize practicality. While some stores in other cities were more elaborate, they claimed, none combined "beauty of design with efficiency of service to such a degree," adding: "Many people will wonder how we can erect such a structure and still expect to give the people our stock at an economical price. They do not realize that we have eliminated

20. Gimbel Brothers department store, Grand Avenue, Sycamore Street, and Milwaukee River, Milwaukee (1901–2, original building, at right). D. H. Burnham & Company, architects. Addition (1922–24, center): Herman J. Esser, architect. Photo ca. 1951.

21. L. S. Ayres & Company department store, Washington and Meridian streets, Indianapolis (1905, original building, center right). Matching addition (1915, at right) and later addition (1928–29, left): Vonnegut, Bohn & Mueller, architects. Photo ca. 1929–30.

a thousand and one sources of waste."[73] Furthermore, since cost was a concern to store owners at a time of dwindling profit margins, many exteriors balanced notions of decorum and utility in a manner that frankly acknowledged the commercial nature of the enterprise yet also carried trappings of respectability.[74] Large, horizontally grouped windows, enunciating the bays of the steel frame in which they were set, restrained classical details, and an orderly overall composition remained signature components of many department stores through the mid-1920s (fig. 21). Thereafter, the exceptions to this treatment became more common. Some emporia, especially those catering to the upper end of the

22. Titche-Goettinger Company department store, Main, Elm, and St. Paul streets, Dallas (1928–29). Herbert M. Greene and La Roche & Dahl, associated architects. Presentation drawing.

24. Quackenbush Company department store, Paterson, New Jersey (ca. 1878). Storefront altered 1926. Photo late 1920s.

23. Abraham & Straus department store, Fulton, Hoyt, and Livingston streets, Brooklyn (1928–29). Starrett & Van Vleck, architects. (*Architecture & Building*, January 1930, 18.)

market, drew from more overtly palatial sources, giving the exterior an appearance suggestive of an elegant office or club building (fig. 22). Such treatment was made possible because natural light no longer played as important a role as it once had on the selling floors, and window area could be substantially reduced.[75] Hudson's was unique in its weaving of both pre-Renaissance and contemporary industrial sources. Whatever the inspiration, historicism prevailed until 1928, when Art Deco repertoires began to be introduced as a newly accepted emblem of sophistication and modernity. Among the first examples was for the prestigious Abraham & Straus store in Brooklyn, but the mode soon gained favor in the heartland as well, with such buildings as those for Halliburton-Abbott in Tulsa (fig. 23; see also fig. 35). The overall character of the outside nevertheless continued to be reserved and businesslike. One notable departure was Polsky's in Akron, whose exterior was lavishly coated in green terra-cotta ornamental panels; it ranked among the most flamboyant exterior decorative exercises for a large retail facility of the period (see fig. 7).[76]

The most marked programmatic change to the public face of department store exteriors in the 1920s was far less overt than the shift to stylish, French-inspired modernism. Whatever the expressive characteristics, the design of all new stores emphasized long, unbroken ranks of display windows and wide, centrally placed entrances to a degree that was more pronounced than in previous decades. Many existing fronts were remodeled at a time when exterior modifications were unusual. Corner entrances were now seen as detrimental to the flow of traffic inside the store, and many of them were eliminated. Broader and sometimes more entryways were introduced to facilitate movement into the premises. Window displays had long been considered crucial forms of advertising for department stores; now the tendency was to make the display area as open and unregimented by the exterior composition of upper floors as possible. Although such alterations could be substantially different from the fabric they replaced, they were generally designed to conform with the overall character of the exterior so that the change remained unobtrusive—a strategy diametrically opposed to that of later decades (fig. 24).

25. Halle Brothers Company department store, Cleveland, detail of ground-floor sales area. Photo late 1920s.

26. J. L. Hudson Company department store, Detroit, men's wear department. Photo late 1920s.

27. J. L. Hudson Company, children's wear department. Photo late 1920s.

Inside

The approach to change was less conservative on the interior, although here, too, the path was evolutionary. At no point was a radical departure introduced, and indeed many techniques appear to have been initiated earlier on a modest scale. Nevertheless, the cumulative effect was that by the late 1920s, interiors were conspicuously different from those of the pre–World War I years. Depicting the scene around 1910, an NRDGA account queried: "Can't you recall the hodge-podge of departments, the messy piles of merchandise, the goods crowded on high back fixtures and on every available ledge? Remember the crazy patchwork arrangement of departments, aisles which were laid out apparently with no thought of aiding the flow of traffic?"[77] While additions generally conformed to existing fabric on the exterior, interior work often entailed a complete restructuring of space and functions. The nature of change was multifaceted. Some modifications were aimed at enhancing display. Others addressed improving the efficiency of departmental layout. Substantial changes were introduced into the array of selling environments. Finally, considerable sums were spent improving circulation, horizontally and between floors. All of these changes, of course, were driven by the goal of making the department store a more effective vehicle for merchandising. The importance they were accorded in the trade was the underlying cause of both building anew and rebuilding extensively.

While display windows had long been the primary means of presenting merchandise in department stores; far less attention was given to interior presentation. Circumstances were clearly changing by the early 1920s, when a flood of trade literature accorded new importance to the subject.[78] It was essential to sales, industry experts incanted, to have the full range of stock in plain view of customers. An increasing array of items—from furniture to linens—was now placed so that customers could inspect them freely. The effect was the antithesis of techniques used a decade or so earlier, when many sales floors seemed more like storage rooms. Now large glass cases were being used to display smaller goods so that they could be artfully presented and easily seen—like a store window in miniature (fig. 25). Display cases and related fixtures were now readily available from manufacturers who claimed expertise in presentation. More sizable goods, from apparel to appliances, were selectively arranged on counters and floors to attract the eye. In some cases, store-owned furnishings—rugs, chairs, lamps, and the like—were introduced to enhance a setting conducive to the goods in a given section. Increasingly, too, the visual distinctiveness of each department was emphasized, creating memorable places with which customers could identify (figs. 26–28). This assemblage helped reduce the sense of

28. J. L. Hudson Company, luggage department. Photo late 1920s.

vastness in a large store while underscoring the richness and variety of the wares. Interior display—the creation of environments that stimulated sales—was now considered as important as any other component of merchandising.

Lighting that allowed goods to be seen to their best advantage was crucial. As in other aspects of display, significant breakthroughs in lighting technique had been developed in the previous decade, but the largest scale of application came after World War I. Lighting, accounts of the early 1920s made clear, was still a matter that many merchants took for granted. Systems that were inadequate or improperly maintained were legion. Lighting was a key to sales, not just because it could be flattering to merchandise but because it was a surrogate for daylight (fig. 29). Customers willing to take clothes and other goods to the nearest bank of windows to inspect their color were rapidly dwindling, and even under the best of circumstances the process consumed enormous amount of staff time. Items that were the "wrong" color once they were brought home ranked among the highest reasons for returns. Eyestrain caused by glare also was identified as a cause of customer and employee discomfort. Furthermore, the idea that lighting could be more or less uniform throughout the store was now discarded in favor of tailoring illumination to the requirements of many different kinds of spaces. The nature of lighting might vary to a substantial degree within a single department or from one department to the next or from sales to support areas. Maintenance was also given a new degree of attention. No matter how good the lighting system, accounts stressed, only an assiduous schedule of dusting and washing kept fixtures' performance acceptable. The costs were seen

29. L. Bamberger & Company department store, Newark, main floor as relamped in late 1920s. H. S. Whiting Company advertisement (*Dry Goods Economist*, 12 April 1930, 52).

30. Davison-Paxon Company, Peachtree, Ellis, and Spring streets, Atlanta (1925–27). Starrett & Van Vleck and Hentz, Adler & Schutze, associated architects. Main floor (*Dry Goods Economist,* 16 April 1927, 83).

as minor compared to other aspects of store operation. Proponents of good lighting stressed that in probably no other aspect of merchandising could so much benefit be gained for so little outlay.[79]

Expansion in the 1920s often entailed increasing store size by 30, 50, or 100 percent, and in some cases it resulted in a store several times larger than the one it replaced. Often, too, departments were not just enlarged, but new ones were added. For some companies such an expansion represented a transformation into a full-fledged department store.[80] Even when the scope of goods was not increased there was often a significant reordering of departments, so that those selling related or complementary items would be close to one another. Considerable thought was given to the kinds of merchandise a customer might be inclined to purchase on a single trip and to how those items might be most effectively grouped. Arrangements were considered for the convenience of the shopper and also to induce additional purchases. Relationships between department locations were increasingly conceived as part of an organic whole determined by purchasing habits. To address these merchandising factors, many department stores had existing portions extensively remodeled concurrent with the construction of additions to achieve a unified plant. Walls between an existing building and an addition were often removed in the construction process, sometimes requiring new structural reinforcement. The imperative for having a coherent interior was so great as to justify gutting facilities built even within the previous twenty years so they could become part of a modern selling facility.[81]

The layout of departments varied considerably from store to store. The number of selling floors, their size and configuration, as well as the specialties of the store, the nature of its clientele, and the strategy devised by its executives and designers all affected the plan. Nevertheless, the ground floor generally contained mostly small items, many of them aimed at impulse buyers. The next floors up usually were devoted to clothing and accessories for women, children, and sometimes men (a men's shop at ground level with its own entrances was also common). Upper floors tended to be reserved for items that a customer would likely plan a special trip to purchase—home furnishings, objets d'art, radios, appliances, glass, and china. Topmost levels were commonly used for offices and other support functions, as well as, perhaps, a restaurant. Basement levels were used for low-cost goods.[82]

Whether through additions or a wholly new plan, stores of the 1920s often were taller than their predecessors and occupied a larger ground area. Moreover, a greater portion of the floor space was devoted to selling, as support functions often were transferred to annexes or remote locations. Encouraging the movement of ever more people through this expanded area was pursued through psychological and physical means. Creating a sense of spaciousness was of paramount importance. While the multistory atria that distinguished a number of nineteenth- and early twentieth-century stores were now seen as counterproductive in their division and consumption of space, a lofty ground floor possessing monumental character was viewed as a valuable way of setting the tone of the establishment, even though upper floors were markedly less grand (fig. 30). In at least two cases, with L. S. Donaldson in Minneapolis and Gimbel Brothers in Philadelphia, stores were penetrated by arcades connecting one end of a block to another (fig. 31).[83] These passages served as ceremonial emblems of the stores, as draws for pedestrians who might not otherwise enter the premises, and as a means to improve ground-floor circulation. Part of the space was allocated to selling as well as to display, bolstering their integral place in the store as well as their role as eventful corridors.

Just as capacious entryways were now a priority, so was the layout of the display area. Many aisles were widened to facilitate traffic flow, and fixtures were positioned to encourage casual viewing but not impede customer circulation (fig. 32). The greatest hindrances to free circulation were the elevators, where consumers often had to wait, brave the crowds, and, once inside, stop at floors other than their destination.[84] By the 1920s, the best solution appeared to be the installation of escalators on a large scale. Escalators had been used in department stores since the turn of the twentieth century, but they were generally limited to one or two units connecting the lower floors. After World War I it became increasingly common to have an escalator system that extended to all selling floors and, in large buildings, to have several pairs in different sections of the store (fig. 33).

31. *(left)* Gimbel Brothers department store, Chestnut and Ninth streets, Philadelphia (1925–27). Graham, Anderson, Probst & White, architects. Presentation drawing of arcade (*Dry Goods Economist*, 22 January 1927, 58).

32. *(below left)* B. Lowenstein & Bros., Monroe and Main streets, Memphis (1923–24). Emile Weile and Hawker & Cairns, associated architects. Ground floor plan in advertisement ([Memphis] *Commercial Appeal*, 22 August 1924, 11).

33. *(below right)* Otis Elevator Company advertisement (*National Retail Dry Goods Association Bulletin*, January 1929, 53).

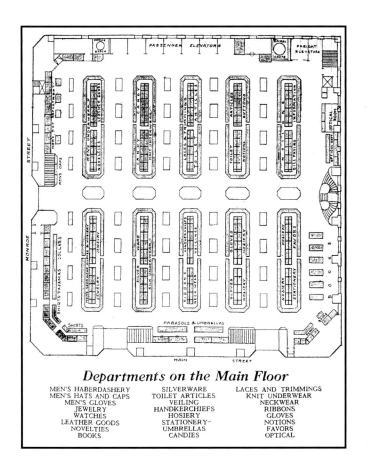

The great advantage of escalators, contemporary accounts emphasized, was that each could carry as many people per hour as about six elevators. Escalators consumed from one-third to one-half the floor space and were much cheaper to operate. They also could be installed without significantly disrupting store operation, and they did not have to be staffed, as elevators then were. Most advantageous of all, the public enjoyed them. No one had to wait, and the upper floors seemed more accessible; trips from one floor to the next were especially easy.[85] In terms of movement, escalators achieved what the great light courts of nineteenth-century department stores had gained in visual terms: a perceptual integration of multiple retail floors. By the decade's end escalators had become a major means of vertical circulation.

One change in layout for which there was little precedent prior to World War I was the advent of small departments organized and fitted as elegant specialty shops. A few intimate, well-appointed spaces for costly women's apparel, such as furs and evening gowns, had been present in big department stores for several decades, but most selling spaces were open and expansive. By the mid-1920s competition from specialty shops had led many department store executives to reassess conventional arrangements. Developing a group of small, fashionably decorated spaces was comparatively easy with the large, open, and adaptable floor plan of the department store. By having a number of such places stores could offer a variety found only at the largest of competitors, without compromising the sought-after aura of exclusivity. By remodeling one or two floors department store executives sought to counter the stigma of their establishments as vast, impersonal places (fig. 34). Costly merchandise sold by a pampering staff in elegant surroundings became viewed as a way that the more prestigious emporia could attract additional high-end customers and beat the specialty store at its own game. Within a few years many of the nation's leading department stores had embarked on such ventures.[86]

Well before the specialty shop was embraced, department store executives began to establish another beachhead with the opposite end of the market: the bargain basement. Filene's is credited with originating the idea in 1909, opening a space not for unsold merchandise but for basic goods aimed at a clientele for whom price was a major factor.[87] By purchasing goods at low cost; eliminating free delivery, charge accounts, phone orders, and alterations; avoiding expensive fixtures; and other readily achievable means, considerable savings could be passed on to consumers without the stigma of the basement as a repository of

34. Woodward & Lothrop department store, Washington, D.C., Walnut Room. Photo ca. 1930.

35. Halliburton-Abbott Company department store, Fifth Street and Boulder Avenue, Tulsa (1928–29). Frank C. Walter, architect; demolished. Advertisement for Thrift Store (*Tulsa Daily World*, 23 October 1929, 14).

unwanted goods. The basement store was operated as a discrete unit, with its own buyers, and it often contained a number of departments with a considerable range of goods. At the same time, efforts were made to imbue the basement with a sense of respectability that bargain hunters of all kinds would find appealing (fig. 35). The idea was slow to gain acceptance. Filene's basement failed to generate a profit until 1919, yet thereafter the concept gained widespread interest. Over the next half dozen years many store executives decided that it could induce a substantial and lucrative trade, and the basement moved from ancillary feature to significant attraction.[88]

Both the conceptualization and development of a department store plan had become intricate by the 1920s. Individuality in appearance was considered by many executives to be an important extension of the individuality of merchandise and service they had long cultivated. At the same time, the fiercely competitive market was among several factors that precluded conspicuous forays in nonconformance. Particularization was found more in decorative features than in the store's fundamental characteristics. To achieve a design that seemed distinct yet reflected the most current practices in department store planning required the collaboration of company executives, their architects, and manufacturers of store fixtures.

Numerous contemporary accounts of department store building campaigns indicate the prominent role taken by management in determining design.[89] Store executives frequently traveled, sometimes with their architects, to examine recent work firsthand and confer with their counterparts in the United States and sometimes abroad. The role of the merchant was crucial not just in determining the atmosphere of the new facility, but in delineating the myriad specifics of the operation. With input from buyers, the sales force, and other members of the staff, designers could form a sense of the functional dynamics of the establishment.

The great majority of architects who prepared plans for department stores in the 1920s, as in previous decades, were locally based. Many of these firms, such as Lewis Hobart (O'Connor Moffatt, San Francisco), John and Donald B. Parkinson (the Broadway and Bullock's, Los Angeles), Smith, Hinchman & Grylls (Crowley-Milner, Hudson's, and Kern's, Detroit), Walker & Weeks (Halle's, Cleveland), and Smith & May (Bernheimer-Leader, Baltimore), enjoyed prominent commercial practices in their respective regions. Their broad-based experience in the intricacies of conceiving and executing sizable urban buildings was clearly an important part of the equation, but their knowledge of the type was limited to a few large-scale retail schemes at the most. With the increasing emphasis now given to interior layout, especially, the appeal of architects who could bring specialized skills to the task markedly increased. D. H. Burnham & Company had pioneered this role with its work for Marshall Field and John Wanamaker, among other retailers.[90] Burnham's successor firm, Graham, Anderson, Probst & White, continued in this vein, realizing six major projects during the 1920s.[91] Another Chicago architect, Jarvis Hunt, secured two commissions in the East, but none in his own region.[92]

By far the most prolific contributor to the development of the new department store was the New York firm Starrett & Van Vleck. Goldwin Starrett had been a designer in the Burnham office before moving to New York in 1898. The following year he joined his brothers Theodore and Ralph to form the Thompson-Starrett Company, a major engineering and construction firm. Goldwin designed several buildings for Thompson-Starrett, including Hahne's department store in Newark, prior to establishing his own office with Ernest Alan Van Vleck in 1907. Before 1920 the firm enjoyed a prosperous commercial practice that included two major New York stores—Lord & Taylor (1913–14) and Abercrombie & Fitch (1916–17)—as well as the gigantic quarters for Lasalle & Koch in Toledo (1916–17). Over the next decade the firm became architects of preference, securing commissions for four of New York's leading emporia—Abraham & Straus (1928–29), Bloomingdale's (1929–30), Frederick Loeser (1929), and Saks Fifth Avenue (1922–24)—and for at least nine others throughout the country.[93] Starrett & Van Vleck's national prominence suggests that New York, perhaps even more than Chicago, had a decisive impact on department store design of the era. No other architecture firm would enjoy such prominence in the field during the 1920s and for over a decade thereafter.

If specialization in department store design was just emerging among architects, it had become established for the manufacturers of fixtures. Two organizations in particular, Grand Rapids Show Case Company and Welch-Wilmarth Corporation, advertised profusely in the *Dry Goods Economist,* promoting their expertise in layout. The sheer extent of such pieces over a prolonged period suggests that these firms often also served as interior designers (fig. 36).[94] Manufacturers boasted that they had not only studied display and other merchandising issues extensively but had acquired an enormous amount of experience developing installations in stores nationwide: no one could match the knowledge they brought to the job. Store owners were assured that they need not be experts in a constantly changing field when they secured the manufacturer's services. Fixtures and their layout were not the only realms in which such assertions were made. Manufacturers of lighting systems and escalators claimed much the same stature in their respective spheres. Whether manufacturers worked directly with the architect or with the store's staff is unclear. In at least several cases an interior design firm, Taussig & Flesch of Chicago, was hired to orchestrate the process, but

36. L. S. Donaldson Company department store, Minneapolis, layette department. Welch-Wilmarth Corporation advertisement (*Merchants Record and Show Window*, March 1926, 5).

it would be some time before operations of this kind became a major force in department store design.[95] Likewise, few stores appear to have had personnel focusing on such matters until later decades. Woodward & Lothrop in Washington hired its own architect, L. K. Ashford, to oversee interior modifications and additions to its plant, but his appointment appears to have been uncommon during the 1920s.[96]

Finale

On the evening of 31 October 1932, the official dedication of the new Strawbridge & Clothier store in Philadelphia was conducted with solemnity and fanfare. Store president Herbert J. Tily proudly announced that sales had been greater than ever before during the year in which the new building had been fully operational. With over 1 million square feet of space, the giant emporium had spurred business despite the worsening Depression. The building was a "reaffirmation . . . [of the] foresight, pioneering intelligence, integrity and zeal" of Justus Strawbridge and Isaac Clothier, who had created the company sixty-four years previous. "For as the founders' faith was never disturbed by temporary conditions," he continued, "we of today are in no wise disconcerted by the running of this largest building operation in our history into the period of world-wide depression. On the contrary, we regard it as the rarest of good fortune that we are ready for a period of general expansion such as has invariably followed every depression." He concluded: "It is firmly believed by us that this building . . . is an advance agent of that general prosperity, the return of which America is just beginning to glimpse."[97] When reporting to stockholders a year later Tily would be far less optimistic in explaining the worst decline in profits in the establishment's history.

Just as Tily could not have forecast the length and severity of the Depression, so he could not have realized when he gave his dedicatory address that the mammoth building was the last of its kind and that the ceremony was the finale of an era that, over a period of four decades, had encompassed a radical transformation in retailing. Throughout that period bigness had epitomized progress, and Tily was sure bigness would still enable business to triumph over the vicissitudes of the economy. But bigness had its limits. Several years earlier, at the height of the boom, Paul Mazur had observed that American production was in the unique position of supplying not needs, but wants. He warned that a "relatively small decrease in production . . . measures not the difference between excess profits and big profits, but the entire difference between profit and loss. It is a difficult problem we are facing—unique in history." Mazur was confident that the problem would be resolved through "scientific" means, such as more intense merchandising and business consolidation. At the same time, however, college president William Trufant Foster and industrialist-turned-banker Waddill Catchings, who were probably less well known to retailers, advised that pay was not keeping pace with production. The desire for consumer goods was widespread, but funds were inadequate to acquire the enormous volume of goods now being manufactured. Buying on credit had only postponed the inevitable depression.[98]

Department store executives had set their sights on what in fact continued to be a small portion of the public, building bigger and bigger stores to capture a market that proved narrower than they realized. The true mass consumerism that one might expect from this arsenal of great emporia was anticipated in retail circles, but it did not yet exist. Despite this weakness, the extensive construction programs of the 1920s cannot be dismissed as a blind error. The big, updated stores served their companies well for another generation, and had those piles not been realized, the department store might well have succumbed to chain competition. But the quest for bigness would never again be so concerted or be bolstered by such confidence. Five years after the stock market crash, the department store's traditional consumer base was narrower still. Merchants were scrambling to adjust their sights in ways they had yet to perceive fully, let alone comprehend. When recovery tenuously began in the mid-1930s, many department stores remodeled; some even undertook additions. After World War II, a few large downtown stores were constructed and many others substantially enlarged. The pace, however, did not match that of the previous era. New approaches to merchandising, new customer bases, and eventually new patterns in metropolitan growth wrought changes that altered the retail landscape in ways that Herbert Tily and his contemporaries could not have imagined.

37. Hutzler Brothers Company department store addition, 220–226 North Howard Street, Baltimore (1931–32). James R. Edmunds and H. C. Crisp, associated architects. Photo ca. 1932.

2 Modernizing Stores

THE EXPERIENCE OF WALKING AROUND the floors of Strawbridge & Clothier or many other major department stores in 1933 would likely give few indications of the severity of the Depression and the devastating impact it was having on retail sales and profits. The sequence of handsomely, sometimes elegantly, appointed spaces built or remade during the previous decade still looked new and well tended. The display of goods, including hundreds of items that carried hefty price tags, abounded in every direction. The staff might be reduced somewhat, but probably not conspicuously so. Customer service remained a keystone of merchandising; clerks were now especially eager to curry favor with the buying public since its disposable income had been so markedly reduced. The great emporium seemed, at least, like a bastion of stability, a haven from the outside world.

The department store also emerged as a symbol of defiance against the challenges of hard times. Strawbridge & Clothier's Herbert Tiley was not alone among prominent retail executives who urged colleagues to build for the future and, in the process, help reverse the effects of economic decline. Encouragement came from others as well. Building costs in 1930 were the lowest in a decade, proclaimed the president of New York's Turner Construction Company, one of the largest in the field; work could proceed more quickly with fewer projects at hand. In January 1932 the editor of *Retail Ledger* declared that this would be the "year of rebuilding." After two years of fiscal restraint, consumers would begin to replace "all lines from shoelaces to furniture." Stores had to keep up with the times, he asserted; new construction would probably not long remain so affordable.[1]

Locally, such initiatives drew effusive praise. In August 1931, for example, Hutzler Brothers, the premier Baltimore department store, announced plans to proceed with a multistory addition contemplated since 1924 but now recast in an elegant Art Deco vein that provided a centerpiece for its complex of buildings and seemed particularly bold in that tradition-bound city (fig. 37). At the opening fourteen months later, the mayor opined how "gratifying" it was "to find a firm which has the confidence in the future and is willing to back" it with a $1 million project, adding, "If 'big business' generally would follow the lead of Hutzler Brothers, I am firmly convinced we would see the end of this talk of depression and business would take an upward turn." Similarly, the Baltimore *Sun* editorialized: "In the midst of the depression, [Hutzler's] . . . has flung a challenge into the faces of the Jeremiahs [and] has affirmed its faith in the future."[2] Aside from public works projects, few building programs in the city matched its scale and sophisticated appearance.

But in sharp contrast to the previous decade, such undertakings were now rare. The heady expansion programs of downtown stores would never occur again with such intensity. Hutzler's was one of only six large-scale building programs initiated among major department stores nationally between 1931 and 1936.[3] Nevertheless, the unprecedented degree of adversity seemed to strengthen the sense of resolve. Department store executives were determined to hold a steady course until the worst years were past. Thereafter, many believed, the halcyon days of prosperity in the retail field would return. The great emporia would surely reemerge triumphant. That hope gradually faded during the years that followed, however. The Depression did not signal a death knell to the department store, as some observers had predicted. No major stores closed during the 1930s, and most were able to return to the sales volume they enjoyed before the stock market crash. But the industry became ever more challenged by competing forms of distribution, which in turn fueled insecurities and ignited debate concerning the function and character of the big stores.

What the department store should or should not become emerged as a preoccupation of many industry leaders between the mid-1930s and mid-1950s. Some believed the great emporium should uphold tradition and remain a bastion of elegance, individuality, and personal service. Others felt it should transform its merchandising methods, adapting ones used by chain stores with ever more success, streamlining operations and paring costs. Most sought a middle ground, for which there was likewise no consensus. By the time general agreement on the matter began to emerge, a decade or so following victory over Japan, the department store was a substantially different kind of business from what it had been in 1929 or even in 1940.

One aspect of department store operations that was enhanced by the Depression was the embrace of modernism in design and display. Modernism, soon adopted by all schools of merchandising, continued as a prominent feature throughout the ensuing decades. The ambient newness so fervently cultivated came to symbolize the capacity of great retail institutions to hold their ground and still look young. In some cases modernization could embody a conversion to an entirely different kind of establishment. Either way, the effects were conspicuous. Before and after the war alike, most of this new image was attained through remodeling; however, the appearance could be even more striking and memorable than that yielded by construction programs of earlier decades. Work performed on the inside, and sometimes on the outside as well, transformed buildings into places that seemed entirely unlike what they had been, as if earlier decades belonged to a distant past. Modernism became what bigness had been in the 1920s, the distinguishing feature that made the department store stand apart from other places, and a key defining component of the urban core. Thus recast, the great piles forcefully demonstrated a faith in economic regeneration and, by the late 1940s, a faith in downtown rejuvenation.

Challenges

The financial challenges identified by department store executives during the 1920s persisted over the next thirty years. Sales plummeted during the Depression, of course, but they were close to 1929 levels by 1936. They slumped in the recession that followed but returned again by 1941. Sales skyrocketed after the American entry into World War II, peaking in 1946–47. Subsequent increases were more gradual, interrupted by two minor declines, through the 1950s.[4] The percentage of revenues consumed by operating expenses, however, continued to plague profit margins. Having risen from 25.9 percent to 33.9 percent between 1920 and 1930, expenses peaked in 1932 at 39.5 percent and dipped to 28 percent in 1944, but generally hovered around the 1930 level, closing at 35.9 percent in 1960. Net profits were all but eliminated in the worst years of the Depression—many stores showed a loss—but they gained some ground by 1940, soared in the war years, then steadily shrank through the 1950s.[5]

Even more ominous was the fact that department store sales formed an increasingly smaller percentage of retail sales overall during the postwar years, declining from 7.4 percent in 1947 to about 5.8 percent in 1954. This trend went against most expectations. Two decades earlier, many department store executives had resigned themselves to the belief that their companies would no longer gain in their share of the market; growth would be predicated on population increase and the increase of its purchasing power. When the recession that some had predicted did not come after the war, many department store officials were optimistic. More people would have more disposable income. Department store growth, one analyst predicted, would dwarf that of the 1920s.[6] But even in the best of times it was all the industry could do to hold its own.

The failure to keep pace with the nation's economic growth was especially disconcerting, because many department store companies had worked hard to improve their operational efficiency. Lessons learned in the 1920s proved essential during the Depression, when every conceivable measure had to be taken to keep businesses afloat. Seasoned by hard times, executives continued to focus on ways to stimulate sales, increase the turnover of goods, streamline accounting procedures, maximize staff productivity, and provide related management objectives. Gains were continually offset, however, by rises in wages and in the cost of goods. Inflation became an undertow from which there seemed little escape.

Equally daunting was the challenge from competitors, primarily chain store companies. What was seen as a potential problem in the 1920s became a very real one in the 1930s as the low-cost items that chains purveyed appealed increasingly to a consumer public with shrinking disposable income. Even more threatening was the fact that chains were expanding the scope of goods they sold, treading ever closer to the department store's traditional base. Beginning in the Depression, leading variety chains dropped their twenty-five-cent limit on goods carried to encompass a spectrum of new lines, including inexpensive clothing and accessories. Store size increased substantially as well. In their dimensions, and to a certain degree in their appointments, new buildings erected during the late 1930s by Woolworth and Kress in New York emulated the grand department store more than the traditional five-and-dime outlet.[7] After the war and well into the 1950s, Woolworth's and other variety chains followed suit in cities nationwide with what was collectively the most ambitious downtown retail development program of that era. With sleek new facilities of 100,000 to 200,000 square feet, boasting a wide array of merchandise on several floors, the variety store in effect became a low-end department store, prominently situated cheek-by-jowl with its rivals.[8]

During the Depression, too, J. C. Penney began to move beyond the small towns where its units had proliferated, establishing stores of substantial size in major cities. Montgomery Ward continued the urban retail expansion program it had begun in the late 1920s, erecting large facilities in core and outlying areas alike. While it fell far short of the unprecedented building program of the late 1920s, Sears, Roebuck constructed at least eighteen large, full-line department stores between 1931 and 1942.[9] Equally important, by the mid-1930s these chains began to look to a broader audience, carrying more expensive and stylish lines that competed directly with those offered by downtown department stores. Sears and other chain companies also enjoyed substantially larger profit margins through the 1930s, especially during the Depression. Department stores gained equal footing in this sphere during the war, only to lose ground again for the remainder of the decade and into the next.[10] Proportionally, profit margins of the great emporia held steady during the 1950s but failed to recoup earlier losses. Well before that time, store executives understood that the struggle for survival did not end with the Depression.

The persistence of economic challenges to the big stores led to mounting debate over the future of the industry. Considerable discussion was percolating by the eve of the war over whether the basic way that business was conducted should change. At the core of the debate lay the department store's identity. Criticism of the status quo abounded. The return of high-volume sales with little or no rise in profit margins, which had plagued store owners for much of the previous decade, was the primary source of consternation. This "strange spectacle," as a writer for *Women's Wear Daily* described the phenomenon, was caused by antiquated sales methods—"horse and buggy techniques." Great effort was expended on getting consumers into the store, but then they were effectively "blocked" from the merchandise "until they have been properly introduced . . . by the salesperson." To make matters worse, most of this staff was "not well-informed, efficient, or resourceful." The problems would become acute at peak periods, when people had to wait to be served; many would leave, and the staff often hurried through a transaction, precluding the potential sale of additional items, in order to attend to the next customer. The process had to be "streamlined" so that the "merchandise is instantly accessible."[11] The latter remarks, made in 1941 by an executive of Sears, Roebuck, which had become an industry leader in self-selection merchandising, would never have attracted the notice of department store executives a decade earlier, but now industry leaders considered changing the relationship between customers and goods to be the issue of the hour. Increasingly, the great emporia were being admonished for employing sales methods that would surely bring about their demise.

Two major stores had already initiated experiments in streamlining sales. In 1937 the Columbus, Ohio, giant F. & R. Lazarus began a program of "size selling"—grouping merchandise by size rather than price—in its women's and children's ready-to-wear departments. It soon extended the practice to a number of other apparel lines. Four years later Macy's followed suit with an assemblage of Size Shops—expansive alcoves, each carrying a panoply of women's wear in just one or two sizes, all available on racks for customer perusal.[12] The point of these arrangements was to enable sampling and choosing of goods without the aid of a salesclerk unless requested. Proponents of self-selection, or simplified selling, as this method of merchandising was variously called, claimed that it not only provided convenience to patrons, it fostered better service because the staff could concentrate on those who needed assistance. Customers had become used to greater independence in shopping through the variety store and most recently the supermarket. As a result, self-selection was initially seen as applicable to departments selling lower-priced goods in high volume, not to department store merchandising more broadly.

What propelled self-selection from a few experiments to widespread application in department stores was the spiraling decrease in qualified sales personnel as the nation regrouped for war. By the end of 1942, store executives were desperate to staff their facilities, particularly since sales were rising, and they were willing to try new methods on an emergency basis if no other. Soon store after store began to adopt at least some aspects of self-selection to a few, sometimes many, of its departments.[13] But the shift was made with reluctance and anxiety. Many store executives were loath to be the pioneer in their respective communities for fear of wholesale customer rejection. More fundamentally, service was upheld as the hallmark of the department store's reputation. By abandoning this mode the great emporia would, in the words of one prominent retailer, surely lose much of their "character and prestige," becoming just another "low-cost distributor" like Penney's and Sears. "Dime store methods" surely would disengage the class of trade that had built the department store into so venerable an institution.[14]

The necessities of war nevertheless showed that customers approved of greater freedom on the floor. Sales increased; operating expenses were reduced. Shoplifting, which had been feared in many quarters, proved not to be a significant factor. At the same time, many retailers believed that with the return of peace, customers would be less sympathetic to the new measures and demand a return to full service. Through the war, industry leaders remained sharply divided on the issue. By 1946 the old ways were on the rebound.

Even for a middle-class clientele, an executive of A. I. Namm in Brooklyn emphasized, service is what differentiates the department store from the chains; without service, there is no reason these customers should come to the department store.[15]

While a few major stores adopted self-selection methods in facilities erected in the immediate postwar years, much of the industry appears to have ignored the issue at first. However, the success of those experiments, coupled with a pronounced decline in sales after 1946, caused many executives to alter their view. The soaring volume that characterized the period from 1941 through 1946 might not have represented a return to halcyon days of unabated prosperity, it was now feared, but instead be only an interlude in the longstanding problem of low profit margins and decline in overall retail sales. By mid-1949 the hand-wringing had begun again over the threat posed by chain competition. Perhaps for the first time, too, figures were marshaled to show industry leaders that they really did not cater to a mass market but rather to a relatively small component of the population, even with the swelling ranks of families with ever more disposable income. Paul Mazur, still a formidable voice in the trade, demanded that "many executives . . . revise their attitude" toward selling: "There must come a fundamental reshaping of the department store's basic emphasis."[16]

Throughout the lackluster performance years of the early 1950s the call for reform grew to a high pitch. In the decade's first year, on the occasion of his appointment as Lincoln Filene Professor of Retailing at Harvard's Graduate School of Business Administration, the most prestigious post of its kind in the nation, the normally reserved Malcolm McNair minced no words. A primary chronicler of the department store's business performance since the 1930s, he admonished the trade for failing to grasp changes in consumer habits brought about by supermarkets and other chain stores. The distinction between the kinds of merchandise these outlets sold, he intimated, was irrelevant. The lessons transcended such particulars and, when properly applied, generated greater sales at lower cost. He challenged department store executives in a tone that suggested he was running out of patience: "Suppose we visualize open display fixtures which will show our full range of stock to advantage, with attractive packaging and display . . . and suppose we visualize a few customer advisors or sales hostesses scattered about the floor; and suppose we visualize a service desk to which the customer can take her selection of merchandise and have the sale consummated rapidly by people who specialize solely in that kind of work, using the most up-to-date and speedy mechanical equipment. I don't think that this is by any means an impossible picture."[17]

A flurry of critiques ensued, all now strident in delineating the department store's intransigence. The great emporium was equated with the brontosaurus by one writer for *Women's Wear Daily:* "unable to cope with changing conditions." Department store executives should completely rethink their role and, in addition to adapting techniques pioneered by the chains, take such initiatives as sponsoring television programs to become prominent again in the public arena. "Many adults," the author noted in 1952, "grew up with the idea that their department store was the center of life of their community. Contrast that . . . with those who have grown up in the last 15 years or so. Today supermarkets, drug stores and many different retailers use hoopla to attract customers. . . . thousands of people [can be drawn to] the opening of a drive-in. . . . [But] the department store is not highlighting the excitement of visiting their establishment."[18] Furthermore, the consumer population had changed. Albert M. Greenfield, chairman of the City Stores, emphasized that many of those who shopped were comparatively young. Wartime routines and the self-service structure of the supermarket had conditioned them to independence. Merchants underestimated the intelligence of their public, he charged. Salesclerks were not only unnecessary but an intrusion: "If the woman is undecided, she wants time to browse. . . . A clerk hanging on her neck restricts her freedom of choice and is apt to make her feel self-conscious." The freedom to shop at one's own pace and in one's own way should be a foundation of merchandising for all except luxury items.[19]

A few analysts, most notably Columbia University marketing professor Harold Wess, strenuously opposed any changes that would make department stores more like the chains, but most others agreed that improved methods of selling based on greater customer independence were imperative. By 1953 the momentum was increasing among department stores to alter their practices, amid a near avalanche of drug and variety chains converting their stores to predominantly self-service operations.[20] The challenge was considerably greater for the big emporia, however, because of the enormous variety of goods sold. Not only did new fixtures have to be devised, they had to assume many forms to display different kinds of merchandise effectively and to avoid the homogenous character of display in most chain outlets.[21] The matter was hardly resolved toward the decade's end. Examining the prospects for 1957, McNair admitted no clear course had been charted. Questions lingered. Could the department store streamline selling practices and maintain its position as a distinctive and desirable place in relation to its competitors? Did department store management possess the flexibility to enable different kinds of sales methods to operate efficiently at the same time? There were no easy answers.[22]

Modernism

No such reluctance occurred in the department store's embrace of modernism, which had begun before the Depression. By the late 1920s, as nervousness mounted over dwindling profit margins and competition from specialty stores, purveying what was often simply called "modern art" emerged as a means for the great emporia to reaffirm their prestige and leadership. The stated aims were altruistic: to foster public understanding, to bolster American artists, and to encourage high quality among American manufacturers. At the same time, an increasingly aggressive merchandising strategy among participating stores indicated that modernism was being used to bolster their reputations as trendsetters in fashion, as bastions of exclusivity, and as quasi-civic institutions dedicated to elevating public taste. The initial focus on home furnishings also suggested that this was a method of gaining ground with the large furniture stores that had captured so much of that trade.

The primary means by which the department store initially pursued these objectives was by what was termed the "exposition." Making obvious reference to the 1925 decorative arts exposition in Paris, these events were temporary displays, usually arranged as a series of rooms containing a dazzling array of furniture, carpets, draperies, and objets d'art. In many cases each room was the work of an individual, well-known nationally and sometimes internationally, including Peter Behrens, Bruno Paul, Josef Hoffmann, Kem Weber, Paul Frankl, and William Lescaze. Macy's inaugurated the trend with its Exposition of Art in Trade, which ran for one week in May 1927 and occupied a substantial area of over 25,000 square feet. The public appeal of this venture prompted a second exhibition seven months later, this time focusing on items that were reasonably priced and well suited to the modest dimensions of a middle-class New York apartment. Other prominent New York stores—Lord & Taylor, John Wanamaker, and Abraham & Straus—soon followed with their own installations. Not to be outdone, Macy's staged an anniversary sequel to its pioneering venture, immodestly called the International Exposition of Art and Industry (fig. 38). Even before then, the attention given to these events was sufficiently great for the *Dry Goods Economist* to editorialize that public interest in the decorative arts had not been so high in the city since the opening of the Metropolitan Museum's American Wing four years earlier.[23] While all these undertakings were in New York, coverage in the retail trade literature suggested that the phenomenon would likely become national.[24] In March 1928, Macy affiliate Davison-Paxon in Atlanta staged the first such exhibition in the South. Within a few months similar offerings were being sponsored by major Midwest

38. "Modern art" interiors displayed at Lord & Taylor and R. H. Macy & Company, New York, 1928 (*Dry Goods Economist,* 31 March 1928, 57).

stores, including Marshall Field in Chicago and Rike-Kumler in Dayton. Field's executives became enthusiastic enough over the prospects for stimulating sales that they announced that a permanent gallery of twenty-three rooms would open soon after Christmas.[25]

Whatever the motivations, the department store became the place where large numbers of people were introduced to modernist design in the late 1920s. At a time when most museums ignored contemporary work, the grand emporium stood out as the foremost setting and, by inference, advocate of new trends in furniture and household decoration. In the eyes of some, the two types of institutions were complementary: as the museum was the sanctuary for the work of past eras, so the department store could become the staging ground for that of the present. Robert de Forest, director of the Metropolitan Museum of Art, was a leading advocate of and advisor for Macy's first show. Through such endeavors

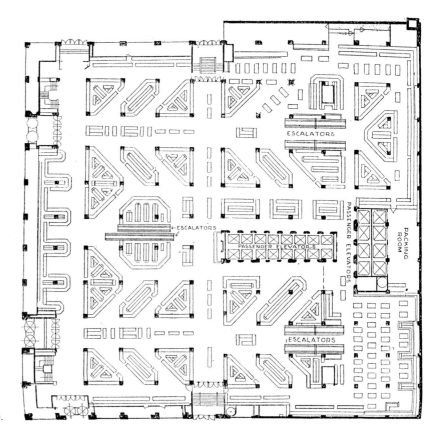

39. Kaufmann's department store, Fifth Avenue, Smithfield and Diamond streets, Pittsburgh (1898, 1913). Plan of first floor as remodeled 1929–30 by Jenssen & Cocken, architects; altered (*Retailing*, 14 June 1930, 8).

the department store could hold its ground as a distinguished and singular place that led others in the retail field.

Store executives were more conservative when it came to their own physical plants. Most major construction projects begun in 1928 and 1929 were of a vaguely historicizing nature. Those that did employ an Art Deco repertoire were relatively reserved in character and entailed few, if any, innovations in planning. This work was more a stylish updating of current practices than a departure from tradition. By the decade's end, however, some specialists were casting modernism as inevitable for retail establishments. Ernest Van Vleck, partner in the nation's leading architectural firm for department stores, spent the summer of 1928 studying new retail architecture in Europe; he pronounced it not a fad but a "very natural" movement.[26] Among the first major retailers to break with convention and use modernity as an instrument of change in merchandising was Edgar Kaufmann, owner of the Pittsburgh department store that bore his family's name. As early as 1925, Kaufmann envisioned an ambitious program to make the ground floor of his store a model of how modern art could be fully integrated with utility, commissioning the fashionable New York stage set and furniture designer Joseph Urban to prepare plans. The scheme apparently proved impractical, and Kaufmann embarked on an extended personal study, conferring with architects, painters, sculptors, and others about his vision that "beauty, design and other standards of fineness will become primary considerations of the housewife, instead of cost." In June 1929, after a five-month tour of European stores, he announced plans for an unusually expensive ($3 million) scheme "embodying some of the most far-reaching innovations yet attempted by an American store . . . [that] will be modernistic in the European sense, but not in the usual American interpretation." Eschewing the current infatuation with French work, he turned to Germany, "which is doing for display what she had done for her chemical industry, and is doing . . . so thoroughly that Paris will have a hard time to keep up."[27]

When it opened eleven months later, Kaufmann's first floor attracted attention nationally and was heralded by the *Dry Goods Economist* as the "most radical [design] . . . in the retail field." The layout, with counters set diagonally and with three sets of escalators, was organized to improve traffic flow and allow customers to see many parts of the floor at a glance (fig. 39). Display counters and the cabinets behind them were set on wheels to allow for changing arrangements. Equally unusual was the lighting system, designed to eliminate shadows as well as glare, with incandescent bulbs and reflectors encased in glass panels to form a ceiling grid that extended in two tiers down the forest of columns sheathed in black marble and Carrara glass (fig. 40). Framing the walls were murals by Boardman

Robinson depicting commerce and industry that Kaufmann saw as the "keystone" of the whole setting. The endeavor was a personal one. Kaufmann indicated that there was considerable resistance, presumably from his staff, to the scheme and to the murals in particular. One of the country's leading manufacturers of store fixtures refused the commission for the designs that were specified, fearing they might harm his company's reputation. Some customers were startled at first. But a favorable reception from the trade press and increased patronage during the first year made Kaufmann confident he had taken the right course. So costly a project in the most heavily traveled part of the store indicated his commitment to having modernist design play a truly public role. Kaufmann sought nothing less than having his store serve as a national model.[28]

For all the fanfare, the project had little, if any, direct influence, owing to its singularity and to the fact that many Americans did not associate German design with fashion.[29] Instead, the primary venue for change was the sumptuous and exclusive realm of New York's large departmentalized specialty stores, which carried high-end women's apparel and accessories. Inspired, at least in part, by a flurry of remodeling on the Rue de la Paix in Paris, Saks Fifth Avenue opened a new ready-to-wear floor in September 1929, a mere five years after the building's completion. Like many department and specialty stores before it, Saks's program called for remaking its fifth floor into a series of "shops," but while much of the remodeling of the 1920s was evolutionary, this design represented a complete break from the past. Much like the home furnishings exhibitions in other New York stores, the scheme possessed a sense of totality in its design, albeit without obvious domestic overtones. Arranged as a series of elegant salons with wares theatrically presented, a complex interplay of indirect and well as direct lighting, a panoply of colors selected to highlight the bold, abstract forms that defined each area, and stylish furniture, the ensemble seemed arrestingly new in every respect (fig. 41).[30] Saks's dramatic departure from convention was overshadowed, however, by the opening one month later of a twelve-story "citadel of modernism" housing Stewart & Company, a subsidiary of Arnold Constable. Here, the entire store was divided into intimate shops of intricately decorative design, with all furnishings custom made, the lighting all indirect, and almost no display of merchandise (fig. 42). Lauded as a significant development in store design, Stewart's was seen as a benchmark not just in the acceptance of modernism, but in adapting French precedent in an original, engaging, and sophisticated way.[31]

Yet such experiments could be risky. Stewart's lavish enterprise soon proved its undoing. In less than six months the citadel had closed its doors and was purchased by Bonwit Teller. Almost at once the new owners decided to gut the

40. Kaufmann's department store, general view of first floor. Frink Corporation advertisement (*Dry Goods Economist,* July 1930, 256).

interior, replacing it with an equally modern but far more reserved design. Bonwit's architect, Ely Jacques Kahn, was frank in stating the need to dispose of "trickiness"—effects that were "striking and dramatic"—in favor of an atmosphere that was "restrained, simple and efficient."[32] Spaces conceived as works of art defied their function, which was to provide the optimal setting to examine merchandise, whether it was displayed or shown by salesclerks. Kahn's penchant for openness on all floors was not shared by those colleagues and retailers who continued to embrace the shops concept for high-fashion goods. The fast-paced turn of events nevertheless occurred at a pivotal time, as the economy plummeted, demonstrating that department stores were not akin to art galleries; modernism must be used to foster basic functional needs rather than ignore them. Bonwit's success, coupled with complementary but varying approaches taken with the remodeling of Stern Brothers and with both new and remodeled sections of Macy's, all completed in the spring of 1931, made New York the primary

41. Saks Fifth Avenue store, Fifth Avenue, Forty-Ninth and Fiftieth streets, New York (1922–24). Starrett & Van Vleck, architects. Fifth floor remodeled 1929, Whitman & Goodman, interior designers; altered (*Dry Goods Economist*, 26 October 1929, 69).

42. Stewart & Company store, Fifth Avenue and Fifty-Sixth Street, New York (1928–29). Warren & Whetmore, architects; Whitman & Goodman, Carlu & Boyle, and Eugene Schoen, interior designers. All interiors demolished 1930. Perfume and French Lingerie shops, both Whitman & Goodman (*Architecture & Building*, December 1929, 377).

center for demonstrating modernism's efficacy for large-scale retail facilities.[33]

New York emporia indeed set the tone for department stores over the next decade in establishing modernism as the preferred course of design, both in the degree to which such work broke from conventions and in the extent that it was applied, often conveying the sense that the whole building was new. In other respects, however, their impact was limited. While the interiors of Kaufmann's, Saks, Macy's, and even Hutzler's were new in character and effect, they also represented the last spurt of expansive optimism from the 1920s. The cost of these projects made them indulgences that even the largest of stores could not afford to initiate as economic conditions continued to deteriorate. Many merchants came to view this pursuit of modernity with skepticism; it cost too much, and, in an industry marked by reserve, they feared it would soon appear dated.[34] The essential bridge and perhaps the greatest catalyst for the widespread acceptance of modernism as a basic part of department store development was instead the 1933 Century of Progress Exposition in Chicago.

While the 1925 Paris exposition had begun to affect store design in the United States several years after its closing, little attention was paid to it or other such enterprises, like the Philadelphia Sesquicentennial, in the literature of the trade.[35] The interest sparked by the new Chicago fair, by contrast, was immediate and widespread. This shift may have occurred in part because the event was conspicuously and self-consciously new in its ambience, the appeal of which was intensified by the search for new approaches to merchandising in the depths of the Depression. Yet even more interest was expressed in the trade toward the New York World's Fair six years later, which was less novel in appearance and was staged in more prosperous times. The underlying factor was not modernism in general but the kind of modernism developed, in particular the focus on display. Prior to the Century of Progress, exposition display had tended to be of the products themselves. Work in the decorative arts could be arranged in elegant ensembles, as at the 1925 exposition, but other goods were generally presented in a matter-of-fact or overtly commercial fashion. Inspired at least in part by recent designs for the stage, displays at Chicago assumed a more dramatic and interpretative mode, marshaling new effects with color and light as well as with graphics to tell a story in bold yet simple terms. Even before the fair opened, many of those involved in store display regarded it as an event of great importance for their work.[36] That impact was reinforced at the New York World's Fair. Headed by Grover Whalen, long the general manager of John Wanamaker's New York store and still closely identified with the city's retailers, the 1939 fair was frequently compared to a "vast department store, planned to give the 'shopper' the greatest efficiency in getting around." Most exhibits were on the ground floor of buildings that allowed "huge wall space to be utilized for interior display." With characteristic immodesty, Whalen trumpted this spectacle as the "greatest merchandising springboard in history."[37]

At Chicago and New York, display was in fact the basis of design. The results underscored what some display personnel had been championing since the 1920s, namely that their work lay not just with street-front windows but with presentations throughout the store. The fairs' exhibits dramatized the artistic attributes of display work on practical grounds, as a means by which to engage the public. The most literal demonstration of this point was made at General Motors' Futrama pavilion in New York, where a full-sized department store provided one of the anchors for the World of Tomorrow set and was conceived to give "dramatic emphasis merely by the use of surface treatment," which would fully express the character of merchandising within.[38] The importance of these expositions lay not in a single or small group of exhibits, but rather in the overall approach. For retailers, the modernity that prevailed was considered a triumph of pragmatism. Instead of a rarefied strain emanating from the studios of Europe, this modernism was billed as American, a fusion of art and utility, elevating the realm of commerce and rendering it more effective. During the 1930s, no events outside the immediate realm of retailing were so closely chronicled by the trade, and probably none had more lasting effect.[39]

Design

The greatest spurt in modernization came with economic recovery, beginning in the mid-1930s, propelled by the fact that, even with an improving market, profit margins remained low. After struggling for survival, stores now struggled to bolster profits amid relentless competition and rising costs. The widespread infatuation with newness had nothing to do with a love of art and little to do with making patrons forget hard times, but rather with conquering the renewed curse of what retailing guru Paul Nystrom termed "profitless prosperity."[40] The means to achieve that end, many retailers now believed, was to glamorize the atmosphere of selling just as the Century of Progress had done for display generally. The results, proponents stressed, significantly stimulated sales. A remodeled store not only attracted the public, it also fostered pride among the staff, improving its capacity to sell. New layouts could facilitate the movement of customers and further impulse buying. New materials could reduce the cost of maintenance. The money spent could be recouped through increased sales. Trade literature touting modernization was generally vague on the specifics of the cost-benefit relationship but never questioned that it was justified on economic terms alone.[41]

As the economic upturn slowly began in 1934, remodeling interiors became a ubiquitous practice among department store companies. Over the next eight years many stores undertook extensive projects, remaking most if not all of their selling space. Many more embarked on less ambitious programs that nonetheless had significant effects on the character of the establishment. The formal, reserved spaces decked with dark paneling and fixtures that were so assiduously cultivated in the 1920s were transformed by light colors and elegant yet low-key furnishings that exuded newness to a degree that made their immediate forebears seem to belong to another century (fig. 43).

Perhaps the most persuasive argument for modernization was linking it with fashion. Although store design had long been seen as a complement to merchandise, by the mid-1930s remodeling became equated with merchandising. How can a store "claim style-consciousness," one Chicago retailer queried, "while continuing to provide an environment that shrieks of yesterday's fashions." The public had become too aware of style to accept out-of-date stores, he continued. Any that fail to modernize "stick out like a sore thumb." The style-consciousness inculcated in customers, particularly women, was predicated on frequent change. The department store became a direct extension of this perspective. Stores were just like their clientele, observed Eleanor Le Maire, a New York interior designer who had become one of the leaders in the field by the mid-1930s. If Mrs. Jones "decided not to rejuvenate her wardrobe . . . [she] soon . . . would go down as being a very dowdy sort. . . . Well, just so with stores." The cycle had little to do with utility: "The modish life of apparel is hardly a fraction of its functional life." Similarly, "many a fixture is still functionally useful long after it should have been scrapped to make way for newer modes." Such replacements were practical from the standpoint of sales, advocates claimed. Modernization did not entail "merely a new layout, or merely new fixtures, or even a new front." Instead, like the Chicago fair, it was the "art of presentation, the power of stimulating showmanship; the opportunity for dramatization . . . motivating influences the power of which no merchant may overlook." Moreover, modernization should be self-perpetuating. It required a more-or-less continual process of "examining new ideas in arrangement, design, and planning, and of putting these new developments to work for the store as soon as possible."[42]

By the decade's end the department store was more akin to a stage than a museum. As sets were devised to enhance the motions and words of actors, so the store interior was tailored to the perambulation of customers and the dramatic display of goods. A growing number of retailers and designers alike believed that merchandising should constitute the basis for every aspect of a modernization plan. The results should not just improve efficiency, they emphasized, but generate pleasure. Remodeling, one chronicler intoned, should "make shopping more than ever the greatest indoor

43. Boston Store, Sycamore, Grand, and Fourth streets, Milwaukee (late nineteenth century, 1910, 1919–21). Second floor, probably latest addition, before and after ca. 1935 remodeling by Grand Rapids Store Equipment Company (*Dry Goods Economist*, 12 November 1935, 76–77).

sport, accepting the beauty and attraction of store service with all its modern facilities of entertainment and enjoyment, which really makes it more fun to shop than anything else one may do."[43]

To choreograph this activity, retailers turned increasingly to design specialists. While most interiors of the 1920s appear to have been the result of collaboration between the building's architect, the manufacturers of fixtures, and the store's staff, the Depression led to a greater reliance on display personnel. This corps was perhaps more responsible than any other in shifting the focus of physical alterations from fixtures to the merchandise itself. Displaymen (the overwhelming majority were male) retained a central role in the years that followed, contributing in conspicuous and significant ways to the character of the selling space.[44] Yet for major projects the tendency grew to hire a separate firm that focused on all aspects of the scheme. Layout, display, fixtures, lighting, furnishings, partitions, and color were among the aspects of what was conceived not only as new but total design. Some of those involved were architects, including Kenneth Welch from the Grand Rapids Store Equipment Company and E. Paul Behles. Eleanor Le Maire, who was arguably the most influential figure in the field prior to World War II, called herself an interior architect. Others, such as Robert Heller, Gilbert Rohde, and Raymond Loewy, were from the emerging arena of industrial design.[45] Taussig & Flesch, which had played so prominent a role in the 1920s, continued to do some work in this vein, even designing an entire addition for G. Fox & Company in Hartford, but it no longer appears to have been a major force in the field.[46] The interior designers professed themselves to be an elite corps, the only ones capable of grasping the needs of merchandising and translating them into three dimensions. Effective sales spaces could not be "achieved by ordering from a [manufacturer's] catalog," sniffed Rohde. "Store modernization in terms of 'fixtures' is over." Like those he debunked,

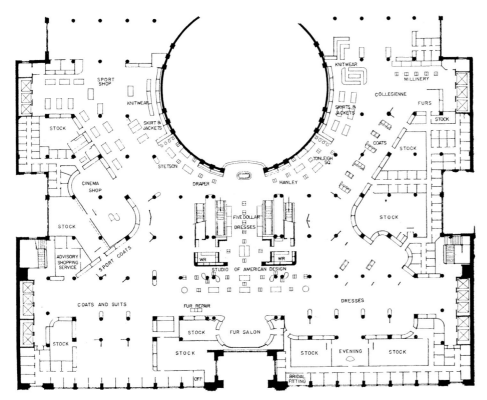

44. The Emporium department store, 835–65 Market Street, San Francisco (1896, 1908). Albert Pissis and Joseph Moore, architects. Plan of front section of second floor as remodeled ca. 1936; Eleanor Le Maire, interior architect (*Architectural Record*, January 1937, 47BT).

Rohde claimed success through thinking strictly in terms of sales in generating his scheme. Pragmatism also lay behind Behles's assertion that the architect should be a merchandiser.[47] But the approach they took was in fact different, manipulating form, space, light, and color in more dramatic and diverse ways than those involved with store design a decade previous would ever have considered.

At the core of this new view of store design lay the objective of facilitating customer traffic in portions of each floor where relatively few wandered of their own accord. The regimentation of fixtures, bespeaking the unity and order that had been a hallmark of department store interiors for some two decades, was now believed to discourage perambulation, creating many "dead" zones, frequented primarily when a patron came with the intention of buying something known to be there. Impulse purchases, so important to the merchandising plan, were close to nil in such areas. The shops concept introduced in the 1920s helped eliminate this problem as well as emphasize the department store as a center of fashion, but space so allocated constituted only a fraction of the total selling area. Designers argued that existing arrangements in many parts of the store had to be completely changed if sales were to increase.[48]

The planning that was central to the designers' approach was guided by maintaining a balance between freedom and order. As at the Century of Progress, spaces and spatial sequences should engage shoppers, attracting them to one area after another unconsciously. To achieve this end, of course, every aspect of the scheme, no matter how casual it appeared, had to be calculated. Spatial variety—in size, shape, alignment, fixtures, color, lighting, and ultimately character—was crucial to the equation. At the same time, the overall relationship of spaces had to possess sufficient order and unity to enable customers to circulate without losing their orientation (figs. 44–45). As sections or departments were differentiated, so vistas had to exist to enable easy viewing beyond the immediate area, often across considerable distances and in several directions. The freestanding fixtures that had formed the regimented aisles in years past were more freely arranged and reduced in number to facilitate circulation as well as improve sightlines. Sometimes, too, a conspicuous feature would be placed more or less centrally for the dual purpose of bringing customers to the middle of the floor and allowing them to see the surrounding spaces. Among the most dramatic examples of this kind was installed on the third floor as the Theatre of Fashion at Macy's Atlanta affiliate, Davison-Paxon, in 1938 (fig. 46). From an ovular space adjacent to the elevators, kept "dark, as in a theatre lobby," diagonal axes extended in several directions. Straight ahead lay the "dress circle," flanked by "brilliantly lighted stages," each with a mannequin. In the middle rose the Peacock Room, for fine dresses, with a domed ceiling of graduated colors from blue-black to pale green and walls of gold leaf blocks delineated by white

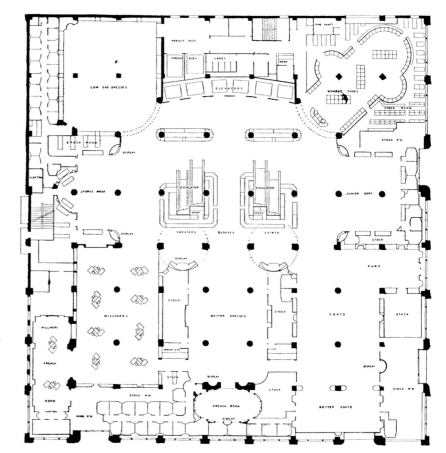

45. William H. Block Company department store, Illinois and Market streets, Indianapolis (1909–10). Arthur Bohn, architect. Plan of second floor as remodeled 1935–36, Vonnegut, Bohn & Mueller, architects; Kenneth C. Welch and Pereira & Luckman, associated architects of the interior (*Architectural Record,* January 1937, 6BT).

46. Davison-Paxon Company department store, Atlanta, third floor, remodeled as Theatre of Fashion, 1938. David Stetson, interior designer. Axonometric drawing (*Department Store Economist,* 25 October 1938, 22).

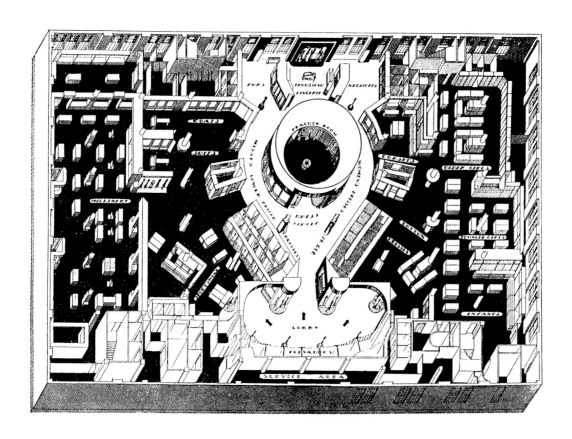

bands and framed in burgundy walnut. Wide openings led to other departments from both sides of this core, while to the rear lay intimate spaces for furs, lingerie, and negligees. At once intricate and direct, the ensemble was relentlessly seductive.[49]

The most fundamental design change, however, which greatly enhanced the possibilities of differentiating space and layout, was the allocation of the peripheral areas to stock and fitting rooms. Natural light, once so cherished, was now seen as wholly detrimental to selling goods (although exterior windows on upper floors were maintained for the sake of appearance). Once this break between indoors and out was made, the floor perimeter was considered the least attractive for selling, both in terms of circulation and display, but it made an ideal space for housing nonbulky goods that would otherwise clutter the sales area or have to be relegated to storage rooms elsewhere. Fitting rooms, too, could be close at hand without interfering with the central space. Together, these two functions helped the designer to justify on strictly practical grounds breaking a large floor area into relatively small, often intricately shaped "rooms" that were at the same time open to a central area. Much of that core space was devoted to circulation, so that the individualized areas around it remained part of an intelligible whole.

The new approach to layout was also predicated on the belief that the shops concept should be applied to more departments than was commonly done in full-fledged department stores during the 1920s. Toward the end of that decade new building programs for large, departmentalized stores specializing in high-end women's apparel and accessories did employ the concept pervasively, but these were the exception. A decade later, Raymond Loewy, by then a fast-rising star in the retail design sphere, emphasized that this pattern should be the norm, proclaiming: "The up-to-date department store is actually a series of specialty or internal shops. When one enters a modern department store, one is no longer confronted with a vast and seething sea of merchandise. Departments have become intimate, dramatic, individual and personalized."[50] Loewy's depiction represented this ideal far more than the reality at that time, yet it was shared by many retailers, increasing numbers of whom became his clients, in their pursuit of greater profits through a focus on individuality and fashion. Loewy's firm designed two of the most publicized schemes at the decade's close: a new third floor for Lord & Taylor as part of a plan for remodeling the entire store (1937–38) and the Dress Salon for Bamberger's (1940). Bold and varied color schemes, which the designers heralded as a key distinguishing aspect of department store interiors, were developed with particular intensity. The intricate play of spaces and theatrical lighting at Lord & Taylor was accentuated by greens, pinks, purples,

47. L. Bamberger & Company department store, Newark, Quality Dress Salon. Raymond Loewy Associates, designers, 1940.

and blues, offset by more neutral tones—all to mitigate the effect of "forbidding acreage" on the expansive floor. At Bamberger's an equally arresting palette was marshaled to help differentiate the three sections into which the salon was divided (fig. 47). The simplicity of the multiple vignettes no less than the unrelenting theatricality of presentation made both designs exemplify the objective articulated by one Loewy associate that the department store should "practice its own exclusive brand of specialization . . . supplying the complete needs of exactly the customer that is most productive"—that is, with the most disposable income.[51]

By the time Bamberger's new rooms opened, application of the shops concept was national. While much of this work remained on the floors displaying stylish clothing, Wanamaker's New York division embraced the concept as a guidepost for the entire remodeling, begun in 1935, of its venerable north building. Erected for A. T. Stewart in the mid-nineteenth century, the five-story pile was recast as a place devoted to women's and children's clothing and accessories. Designed by Kenneth Welch (in a more reserved manner than Loewy's), the shops concept was used throughout, even on the perimeter of the ground floor (fig. 48).[52]

Designers often described their new store interiors, however dramatized, in practical terms. Not only was the approach predicated on merchandising, they noted, excel-

48. John Wanamaker department store, Broadway, between Ninth and Tenth streets, New York (1859–62, 1866–68). John Kellum, architect; demolished 1954. Ground floor as remodeled 1935–36, Kenneth Welch, architect (*Architectural Record,* August 1936, 119).

lent results could be achieved without undue expenditure. This was not design based on frills, but on function. Welch elaborated that the "tools of modernization have so increased in efficiency, economy, and effectiveness, the new store of even 10 years ago suffers by comparison. . . . A modern interior . . . is like an improved diet applied to plants and human beings. They might live if not properly fed, but they will never really flourish."[53]

Besides its visual pyrotechnics, this "diet" encompassed a number of technical innovations. Without an array of dramatic effects made possible by advances in store lighting, the new approach to layout would have been impossible. By the 1930s most large-scale retailers were well aware of the important role that lighting played in sales, yet opinions varied on the optimal means in a given department. Critics of current illumination practices abounded; lighting problems seemed perpetual. As a result, the range of conditions and the time period from which lighting systems dated varied widely, even among leading emporia.[54] New techniques could be risky, as underscored by the brief embrace of indirect lighting as the primary means of illuminating large floor areas. Adopted by several of the nation's major stores in 1934, this method directed substantial amounts of incandescent candlepower at the ceiling from coves affixed to columns and beams. Spaces were twice or three times brighter as a result; however, shadows cast on customers and salesclerks, as well as the flat quality of light given to merchandise, pushed the costly installations from favor. Another innovation, recessed lighting, diffused through prismatic glass plates set flush with the ceiling, proved viable only in new construction or extensive remodeling; however, it failed to improve illumination sufficiently to warrant widespread application.[55]

A combination of spot and indirect lighting could be effectively applied to intimate, style-oriented departments, but not until near the decade's end did a new technology emerge that lent itself to a broad range of uses. Fluorescent lighting was reputedly introduced to retailing at the mammoth J. L. Hudson store in 1936 and began to attract widespread interest in the trade some two years later. Extensive use of these fixtures at the New York World's Fair intensified their aura as the ultimate solution to lighting dilemmas. Fluorescent lights could greatly increase candlepower while diffusing it, eliminating glare and shadows and thus bringing store interiors closer to daylight conditions. At the same time they generated much less heat than incandescent bulbs, thereby lowering operating costs and even reducing demands on cooling systems. The shape and relatively low temperature of fluorescent tubes also made them ideal for use in display cases and in other situations where lighting needed to be close to merchandise.[56] Fluorescents were generally not seen as a complete source of illumination in stores but rather to be supplemented by spot and other localized incandescent fixtures. In combination, these lights enabled a variety of effects tailored to the needs of each department or section. The theatrical presentations marshaled for haute couture could be tempered and hence more frequently employed in the overall lighting scheme. Both fluorescent lighting's inherent advantages and the technological improvements made during the war spurred wholesale application over the following decade.[57] The collective result helped to radically change the character of selling floors. Light was now omnipresent, generally at many times prewar levels, but also inconspicuous. Light also contributed to making parts of the department store interior more varied. In its new retail setting, the spectacle created by light elevated the routine and made the theatrical commonplace. The theater had permeated the store, transforming it and, in the process, transforming itself.

Air conditioning was arguably an even more significant technical advance, without which internally focused layouts would have been difficult to develop and orchestrate save on a very limited scale. Department stores had relied on mechanical ventilating systems that had become increasingly sophisticated. By the 1920s such equipment could not only warm and clean air but could cool and humidify it as well.[58] Still, interiors were often unduly dry in winter. During hot periods, open windows and fans supplemented the main system but could not fully overcome the effects of the season. Furthermore, little control was possible from space to space unless discrete systems were used—an ungainly solution at best. Arrangements that minimally impeded the circulation of air—internally and through open windows—were considered imperative, especially in warm periods. Even then, department store managers had long accepted the hottest months as those in which sales would be lowest.

With air conditioning, however, interiors could be made appreciably more comfortable in both winter and summer. Other advances, including the configuration of air ducts, made it possible to vary conditions in different parts of a space as well as in separate spaces. Under these conditions windows became detrimental: when opened they could significantly reduce the system's effectiveness, and when closed both the heat and cold that came through their glazing required the system to work harder. With air conditioning, the internal configuration was no longer a determining factor as long as it was shielded from the outside, quite the opposite of conditions affecting conventional forced air systems.

The first air conditioning equipment installed in a major department store was probably for Filene's basement in 1926, when such provisions were still a novelty for most of the public. Within a few years a number of new department store buildings had incorporated air conditioning on several floors, including Titche-Goettinger (Dallas), Strawbridge & Clothier (Philadelphia), and the Bon Marche (Seattle). Existing plants with major new additions, such as R. H. Macy, J. L. Hudson, and L. S. Ayres, also were fitted.[59] By the early 1930s this form of climate control had begun to attract substantial trade interest, and through the remainder of the decade the retail literature abounded in accounts advocating it use. Air conditioning, proponents maintained, drew customers into stores and kept them there longer; it improved the performance of the staff; and it reduced the soiling of merchandise. The high cost of installation, particularly in existing buildings, and the substantial expense of cooling soon began to be recovered through increased trade. Department store executives who had purchased systems were enthusiastic about the move on economic grounds alone.[60] On the eve of Pearl Harbor, many major department stores had at least partial air conditioning. After the war, air conditioning was generally considered by owners to be as important as heating. A survey of 435 department and specialty stores in 57 cities taken toward the close of 1952 indicated that 65 percent were fully air conditioned and 23 percent partially so. The effect on merchandising was profound. The following year, William Snaith, by then president of the Raymond Loewy Corporation, proclaimed that air conditioning "liberates design," freeing "department store buildings from every major physical disadvantage." Planning was uninhibited: space was saved with lower ceilings; restrictions no longer existed on interior materials, colors, or finishes; and all floors could be developed as prime selling space.[61] No other development had had as great an impact on the fundamentals of store design since skeletal construction.

While the majority of attention was given to the interior remodeling of department stores, considerable concern was expressed over the exterior as well. The rhetoric was much like that of the previous decade: the appearance of the outside was a key to attracting customers and to establishing the store's public identity. Most exterior remodeling of the 1930s, however, was confined to the street level, with new entrances and display windows—the zone with which pedestrians came in closest contact. Unlike many smaller shops of the period, most large department stores kept their exteriors more or less intact, one critic charged, because executives feared that a modern face would make the establishment seem undignified—or was simply unnecessary.[62] Even with the twenty or so major additions undertaken across the country between 1934 and 1942, seven replicated or emulated earlier portions of the complex, and five were of a low-key, visually subordinate nature.[63] A noteworthy exception to this pattern was J. W. Robinson, Los Angeles's most fashionable department store, which had the entire exterior of its 1914–15 building remade during the depths of the Depression. The change of character was an influential precedent, suggesting in the process that an exterior less than twenty years old was so detrimental to business as to justify sweeping alterations. Almost no other major department store followed this course prior to the war, but several did use the building of a large addition as an excuse to alter existing portions of the exterior, as well as the interior, in a radical way that made the entire premises seem new.[64]

The small cadre of these "new" stores was striking not just for how their exteriors exuded modernity on a large scale,

but also for how each made a strong, individualistic statement. Before the mid-1930s few major department stores really stood out in the urban landscape. Now they differed in composition, detail, and sometimes materials from many other buildings in the commercial center. But what made such work so arresting in the public eye was its size, which tended to give the exteriors visual dominance, even among larger buildings, in a way seldom pursued. The transformation no doubt seemed the more startling since the existing structures were antique by business standards—most of them dating from the nineteenth century. The "new" department store was often the largest and most openly modernist in its immediate area, and perhaps throughout the downtown. While sometimes clearly drawing from recent European examples, the architects avoided overt ties to any specific scheme by such noted continental practitioners as Erich Mendelsohn or W. M. Dudok. A significant programmatic difference existed: European retailers persisted in seeking as much natural light as possible, whereas their American counterparts were ever more partial to eliminating it.[65] The concern for expression, however, transcended such practical issues. Well before most American department store owners accepted the idea of eliminating exterior windows above street level, they allowed, and probably encouraged, their architects to give exteriors a distinctly new character—one that both parties likely wished to be identified with merchandising at home, not abroad.

The first such scheme was unveiled in 1935 by Starrett & Van Vleck, and it bore no visual ties to that firm's venerable legacy. Designed for J. N. Adam in Buffalo, the exterior was characterized as expressing a "modern American theme of horizontal lines," presumably to set it apart from earlier Art Deco patterns. But whatever the inspiration, the results ranked among the most stridently undecorated and suggestively functionalist schemes to be found in the commercial sphere on this side of the Atlantic (fig. 49). On the other hand, the new face of John Shillito in Cincinnati (1936–37) exuded a luxuriant, streamlined character (fig. 50). The project was the largest for a department store undertaken since the Depression. Besides covering the original facility, a great pile of over 250,000 square feet built in 1876, the scheme included an even larger addition. Existing spaces were

49. J. N. Adam & Company department store, Main and Eagle streets, Buffalo (late nineteenth and early twentieth centuries), additions and remodeling (1935). Starrett & Van Vleck, architects; altered. Photo ca. 1935 Underwood & Underwood (*Architectural Record,* August 1936, 116).

50. John Shillito Company department store, Race, Seventh, and Elm streets, Cincinnati (1877–78). James McLaughlin, architect. Additions and remodeling (1936–37): Potter, Tyler & Martin, architects. Photo author, 2008.

transformed as well, rendering the "New Shillito's" as total a manifestation of the modern department store as could be found until the late 1940s.[66]

At Joske Brothers in San Antonio (1938–39) the nineteenth-century store was likewise wrapped and extended, but the exterior treatment was markedly different. Breaking with a longstanding and nearly universal convention, Joske's president requested a regional image for his store, making it an emblem of "southwest" Texas. Situated one block from the Alamo, the building was intended to carry associations with the state's Spanish colonial heritage, but the stylish results drew at once from the modern classical strain of Art Deco and, in all likelihood, from the lively, Churrigueresque-inspired commercial buildings of the Los Angeles architects Morgan, Walls & Clements (fig. 51).[67] But the most decisive departure from precedent in department store design was the remaking of H. P. Wasson in Indianapolis (1936–37). Wasson's was the first downtown department store to use the new approach to floor layout as a basis for expression on the exterior. Its scheme completely remade the aged existing plant and added a large new corner section. Above street level, the elevations were treated primarily as solid walls, articulated only by slender strips of glass block to accentuate the sense of verticality and give scale to the mass (figs. 52–53). While the project failed to attract much attention, the concept of the "windowless" store would become standard after the war's end.[68]

Expansion

The immediate postwar years witnessed what seemed like a full-fledged comeback among major department stores. Defying the idea that the great emporium was a thing of the past, its size and intransigence self-defeating, downtown facilities expanded at an impressive rate, if not at the pace of the 1920s.[69] Between 1946 and 1955 over forty large-scale construction programs were consummated, including six new buildings. Remodeling was omnipresent. New lighting, dropped ceilings, air conditioning, new escalators, new layouts, and new fixtures appeared in department after department, floor after floor, in buildings nationwide. By the mid-1950s few major department store interiors bore much resemblance to what they were a quarter-century previous.[70] Capitalizing on wartime gains and the current national

51. Joske Brothers Company department store, Blum Street and Alamo Plaza, San Antonio (late nineteenth century; remade with additions, 1938–39). Bartlett Cocke, architect. Photo author, 1974.

52. H. P. Wasson & Company department store, Washington and Meridian streets, Indianapolis (1883, 1902). Photo early 1920s.

53. H. P. Wasson & Company, with additions and remodeling (1936–37). Rubush & Hunter, architects; later additions. Photo ca. 1937.

prosperity, companies sought to reaffirm their position as the premier force in retailing. Challenges had been mounting, to be sure, and not just from the chains downtown but from stores of all kinds in new outlying locations. The initial response was to do what had been done in the past: build bigger stores. Only in this way, many executives still believed, could the downtown and great emporia themselves remain dominant.

A key factor in postwar building was the ownership groups formed in earlier decades. While the value of such associations was still questioned at the close of the 1920s, and efforts toward further consolidation stymied by the economic decline of the following years, these organizations began to rebound toward the late 1930s, becoming corporations with strong, centralized management. Over the next quarter-century, department store corporations emerged as major forces in the industry, advancing ambitious new plans for purchasing, merchandising, systemization, and other facets of operation. Expanding markets was another element of their strategies, achieved in part by numerous acquisitions and mergers. Allied Stores (formerly Hahn Department Stores) was the most aggressive, adding nine companies to its portfolio before 1940, eleven more by 1950, and eight others during the subsequent decade. Most of these were stores in relatively small cities, but there were several major ones as well. Associated Dry Goods did not expand until the 1950s, when it added three large stores. Macy's purchased sizable operations in Kansas City and San Francisco in the mid-1940s. The May Company added four large stores and four smaller ones; City Stores a more or less equal number. Federated had the most ambitious program, acquiring seven large stores.[71] In 1960, many major independent companies remained, including such giants as John Wanamaker, J. L. Hudson, and Carson Pirie Scott. Yet by then the tendency to consolidate had long passed the experimental stage; many retailers now agreed with Paul Mazur's predictions of the 1920s that the national conglomerate was the only route to long-term success in the field.

One important cause of that shift was change in some of the organizations themselves. Being a corporation with dynamic, centralized leadership could attract business talent, providing expertise in a range of technical arenas that many independent stores could not provide. These corporations also had enormous sums of capital at their command to facilitate expansion of and improvements in the physical plant. Family-owned companies, on the other hand, could face difficulties when senior executives lost their drive and when heirs had little interest in or were incapable of running operations. Even with a smooth succession, heirs faced daunting taxes that could significantly reduce assets. Many independent businesses also suffered from inadequate financing and from increasingly stiff competition. The rise of the department store corporation into the heart of retailing was fueled by the needs of both sides.[72] The change was decisive. Store owners could no longer decide to "join" a corporation, as had occurred in the 1920s; they could only sell their businesses to such an enterprise.

The transformation of Allied Stores into a shaper of the industry was perhaps the most startling case of organization change. Despite the ambitious plans of the company when it was formed as Hahn Department Stores in 1929, the first several years brought only policies that, according to Fortune, "whipsawed the stores between central-office autarchy and local-management autonomy—losing money at both ends." Changes began in 1933 when B. Earl Puckett, an accountant who had recently entered retailing under the auspices of Mazur, became president and reorganized the company as Allied the following year. Puckett at once gave store managers greater authority while implementing a comprehensive reorganization in the main office. His retailing strategy, predicated on sales figures rather than on buying and promotion policies, became the basis of an elaborate merchandising plan that stores were given ample incentive to follow closely. The balance between, on one hand, a main office that offered innovative management tools, an abundance of comparative data, some central buying power, and even its own line of inexpensive women's apparel (to compete with Penney's and other stores of that ilk) and, on the other, full retention of local store character, yielded spectacular results. In slightly over a decade Allied had not only added well over a dozen stores to its portfolio, but its net profits had grown from $25,000 to about $20 million, making it one of the largest retailers in the nation.[73] The corporation had become a key force in the trade.

Two other multistore companies, May and Federated, jostled with Allied over the next decade for first place in sales. May Department Stores, probably the strongest such enterprise at the close of the 1920s, achieved much the same symbiosis as Allied through a gradual, evolutionary path. Federated, on the other hand, remained an ineffectual holding company until Fred Lazarus, owner of the two most profitable units (Lazarus and Shillito) took charge in 1945 and embarked on an aggressive restructuring and expansion program that appears to have been drawn in part from both May's and Allied's example. In each case the headquarters developed long-term strategy. Major building programs and the merchandising initiatives that lay behind them were ever less the product of the local retailer, ever more part of a multifaceted plan devised by the corporate management, while the individual character of each store was cultivated for the consumer. Each company possessed some singular characteristics. May, for example, had some of the strongest promotional strategies in the trade. Like Allied, the company focused on the lower-middle-to-middle range of the market.

54. Foley Brothers department store, Main and Travis streets, Lamar and Dallas avenues, Houston (1945–47). Kenneth Franzheim, architect; Raymond Loewy Associates, designers; later additions. Photo Bob Bailey, ca. 1947.

On the other hand, May provided a model for Federated in its pursuit of regional dominance, with each store outpacing its competitors in sales in its trading area.[74] Irrespective of management strategy, the big firms had access to far greater amounts of capital than did independent stores. Corporations were primary engines of expansion during the postwar years.[75] No better example exists than Federated's purchase and subsequent transformation of Foley Brothers department store in Houston.

Wartime profits enabled Fred Lazarus to embark on expansion that he considered essential to making Federated a serious competitor in the field. Yet both of his own stores had recently been enlarged to capacity, and two of the East Coast emporia (Bloomingdale's, Filene's) had little room to expand. Lazarus, who saw acquisitions as the most profitable route, eyed Foley's as the optimal first step in what he envisioned as an ongoing program. Although it was the city's largest store, Foley's had a much smaller sales volume than its trading area would suggest. The emporium's owner, George Cohen, had no interest in selling. But when Lazarus assembled a whole block in a prime downtown location, the threat of overwhelming competition led Cohen to sell for a substantial share of Federated stock. Lazarus had in part seized and in part created what he regarded as a golden opportunity: to build a mammoth store that embodied the latest ideas in merchandising and to dominate a bountiful market.[76] The old business continued in name only; Foley's was recast in Lazarus's image.

By all accounts, Foley's new store was a remarkable achievement. Not since Strawbridge & Clothier's emporium of 1928–32 had such an impressive pile been created *de novo* in the United States.[77] While not the first "windowless" downtown department store, as its owners claimed, the scheme seemed unique: its great bulk was sheathed in buff-colored Kasota stone broken by a lapping, "sawtooth" arrangement on the principal elevation (configured for hanging enormous seasonal displays), with vari-colored stone and brick striations on the sides—all without the glass block or streamline accessories characteristic to earlier examples (fig. 54). The design, at once grand and simple, arrestingly abstract and full of textural richness, was justified on the grounds of the savings it would yield in heating and air conditioning costs, but other treatments could have at-

55. *(left, top)* Foley Brothers, architect's rendering of Main Street display area and entrance, ca. 1945.

56. *(left, below)* Foley Brothers, negligee shop. Photo ca. 1947.

57. *(above)* Foley Brothers, "house dresses" section. Photo late 1940s or early 1950s.

Foley's also was a model application of another new feature, the show window canopy. Through the 1930s, awnings remained the primary means of shading window displays and sheltering pedestrians. Fixed metal canopies were installed around the entryways of a few new and remodeled stores prior to World War II, but Foley's was among the earliest to have so large a feature extend over its entire sidewalk perimeter. The canopy entailed a much costlier initial investment, but it obviated manual operation and offered better protection in inclement weather. As a year-round shield, the canopy could encourage passersby to linger over displays. Visually, it formed a barrier between the urban environment and the fantasy world portrayed behind glass. The effect could be enhanced at night when canopy lighting fostered the sense of a separate environment—safe, inviting, and conducive to consumption (fig. 55).

Inside were innovations as well. Foley's was probably the first major department store with escalators as the primary means of connecting its interior levels—here there were seven levels, six devoted to selling. During the 1930s this form of vertical transportation had become ever more widely used for upper floors. The main surge of installations, however, came during the postwar years, as emporia nationwide added and replaced units. Fitting these into buildings that had grown incrementally often led to less than ideal arrangements. But the benefits of what were now fast, almost noiseless moving stairs—they were sleek, modern, and a source of pleasure for the clientele—were considered overwhelming. Foley's demonstrated how crucial to department store layout and merchandising the escalator had become.[78]

tained comparable results. The solution was at least partially a matter of esthetic choice. When the large department store had emerged as a principal component of the urban core at the turn of the twentieth century, many examples ranked among the tallest buildings in their communities or, in the case of New York, their neighborhoods. Now office buildings and hotels in most cities were much taller. The huge, windowless mass not only created an imposing presence amid the forest of higher buildings, it also gave the store a distinct identity, emphasizing the great scale of retail distribution it manifested and dramatically setting it apart from all other building types.

Foley's selling floors further reflected the latest ideas in layout, the product of extensive studies undertaken by Federated's staff and the principal designer, Raymond Loewy Associates.[79] Sales areas were varied in character, their expanse mitigated by relatively small-scale "shops," with stock and fitting rooms on the periphery (fig. 56). Careful attention was given to display, and more than the usual emphasis was placed on self-selection, with divisions based on size and price (fig. 57). The results encompassed much of the variety that interior designers espoused, but in a more matter-of-fact way than at many of the prewar remodelings. Foley's helped set a new standard for interiors that appeared more practical than dramatic, inviting without overtones of elitism. Behind the scenes, the building was "mechanized," as William Snaith, Loewy's chief retail architect, described it, to a degree that set Foley's apart from predecessors. Goods traveled via conveyor belt from an underground garage across the street to the basement receiving and marking room, thence by lift to the appropriate floor. No department store on this scale had been planned so thoroughly from the standpoint of the movement of stock and effective merchandising, with all components "designed first and foremost as parts of an efficient *machine.*" "Don't get me wrong," Lazarus intoned, "we tried to add looks afterwards, and I think we did. But we didn't sacrifice one single bit of efficiency for the sake of looks."[80] The advocates of rational sales planning in retail design now had a monument.

Foley's was the opening salvo in a wave of downtown store expansion, led by the large corporations, during the immediate postwar era, defying observers who believed the big city store had become a creature of the past. In the two years after work on the new Houston emporium was begun announcements were made for another four new buildings of substantial size. The most adventurous was the second store purchased in Macy's new expansion program, John Taylor Dry Goods Company of Kansas City, Missouri, for which Lazarus had made an unsuccessful bid. The transformation that ensued was as sweeping as Lazarus's in Houston.[81] Following its acquisition in 1947, the business was closed, the existing building stripped to the frame and integrated into a plant three times the size. Reopening two years later under the Macy name, the facility was almost as large as Foley's and similarly conceived as a national model. The site conditions were a challenge. Unlike Foley's, which occupied an entire block, Macy's rose mid-block along a very narrow Main Street, but also on axis with Eleventh Street ("Petticoat Lane"), the premier retail corridor of the city. As a result, the facade was treated as a great unbroken wall of dark red aggregate—Gannux—and buff brick to form a striking visual terminus for the range of fine shops that lay to the east (fig. 58). Designed by Kivett & Myers, then a still young firm but considered the most avant-garde region-

58. R. H. Macy & Company department store, Main Street, Baltimore Avenue, Kansas City, Missouri (1947–49). Kivett & Myers, architects; Daniel Schwartzman and Gruen & Krummeck, architects of the interior; demolished ca. 1990. Main Street elevation.

ally, the scheme drew effusive praise from the *Architectural Forum,* whose editors, apparently disappointed with Foley's, sniffed that this was not only the "first big piece of 'modern' architecture [in] Kansas City . . . [but] also the first real chance 'modern' architects have had anywhere in the U.S. to show what they can do for the big downtown department store."[82]

The greatest demonstration value lay with the lively interior, created by two of the nation's leading retail architects, Daniel Schwartzman (New York) and Gruen & Krummeck (Los Angeles), along with several others advising. The results were a veritable showcase of how the department store could become a theater for selling, with circular and diagonal traffic patterns, dramatically illuminated displays, suspended acoustical ceiling and light panels that could be interchanged, and an equally flexible system of aluminum partitions, designed to be quickly moved to accommodate seasonal or other changes in merchandising needs (fig. 59). In contrast to Foley's somewhat matter-of-fact ambience, Macy's seemed glamorous and seductive, affirming that design tailored to self-selection was compatible with the theatrical approach to interior design developed some ten years previous.

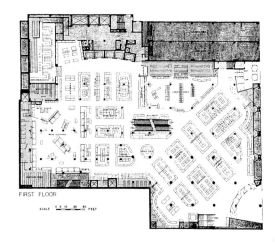

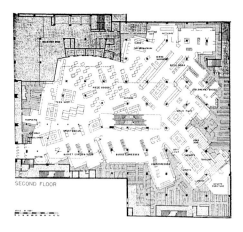
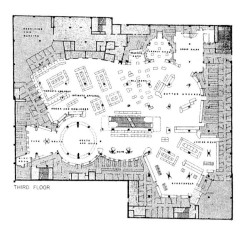

59. Macy's Kansas City, plans of second through fifth floors (*Architectural Forum,* February 1950, 92).

Allied Stores likewise emphasized how the latest developments in interior merchandising and layout were used in two large new stores in its group, Herpolsheimer's in Grand Rapids and Jordan Marsh in Boston. In both cases, Allied's own architect, George Ely, was primarily responsible for the inside, which he, like Snaith, described as a "merchandising machine." Ely's contribution to retail store design was a suspended grill ceiling devised both to obscure the mechanical area above and to diffuse the illumination so that it would, ostensibly, approximate daylight (fig. 60). In response to Herpolsheimer's constrained site, Ely also devised a "band system" of alternating storage and service floors with selling floors. The exteriors of the two buildings could not have been more dissimilar even though they, too, emanated from the same office: Perry, Shaw & Hepburn of Boston. Consistent with its inside, Herpolsheimer's was unabashedly abstract, although its three-story entrance window, framed on one side by a fin-like vertical sign punctured by circles, brought to mind the design conventions employed for chain specialty stores (fig. 61).[83]

The building for Jordan Marsh was much bigger, planned to occupy an entire block. It replaced the old store, that of a long-owned affiliate, C. H. Hovey, and a number of additional buildings as well. Designed eventually to rise fourteen stories, the vision was of a behemoth on the scale of the largest examples of the 1920s—one, its owners proclaimed, that would be the largest retail facility in the world. "No longer," effused Jordan's president, Edward Mitton, "will it be necessary to go to New York or Chicago for the latest there is, because it will be right here." To express these aspirations of distinctiveness, it was Mitton, in all likelihood, who requested a historicizing exterior, capitalizing on the city's venerable traditions. Drawing inspiration from the work of Charles Bulfinch and other turn-of-the-nineteenth-century sources they knew well, the architects developed an interplay of sculptural forms and large-scale classical elements to mitigate the effects of the enormous mass, just the opposite approach from that taken at Foley's and Macy's (fig. 62). At ground level, on the other hand, the effect was aggressively modern, accentuated by coved lighting, a curving canopy, and recessed display windows, made possible by a ten-foot cantilever of the floors above (fig. 63). Despite its novel effects and state-of-the-art interior, the scheme was snubbed by the architectural press and given far less trade press attention than its program would indicate. This cool reception suggests that the scheme sent too many signals of longing for *temps perdu,* or perhaps it reveals how executives and designers regarded digressions from modernism by the 1950s.[84]

The extent to which a modernist public face was cultivated among department store companies at the onset of the new decade is clearly indicated by the spate of additions and new facades constructed between 1950 and 1955. Through the 1940s and on occasion afterward, additions continued to be treated as most were in previous decades; that is, as visual extensions of the stores, compatible, even identical, in composition, details, and materials.[85] The Rike-Kumler store in Dayton was typical, with a new section of three bays and a two-story section atop the existing building (1911–12) added in 1936–38 and another three bays and a single-story addition above the extended part erected a decade later (fig. 64). But a third extension, begun in 1954, reflected a major shift in design. Rendered as little more than a planar slab supporting a six-story vertical sign, which was clearly intended as the visual focus of the ensemble, the scheme could not have been more defiant in its contrast. Here rose a veritable proclamation of how the store, which dominated its trading area, was advancing with the times, unencumbered by the traditions it had been instrumental in creating locally.[86]

A similar about-face occurred in a single project when Allied's Titche-Goettinger of Dallas planned an exact match of its elegant store of 1928–29 (see fig. 22) for an addition that would more than double the facility's size. It was unveiled in 1948 but construction of the scheme was delayed by the Korean War, and in 1952 the design was revised as a blank wall above street level, relieved only by the store's name in two-story-high letters.[87] By that time, little question seems to have existed that the building as a giant unadorned box was the favored symbol of the department store's continuance as a major force in retailing. The most ambitious such project was for Kaufmann's in Pittsburgh (1953–55), which the May Company had purchased in 1946. Planned

60. Herpolsheimer Company department store, Monroe and Division avenues and Fulton Street, Grand Rapids, Michigan (1947–49). Perry, Shaw & Hepburn, architects; George Ely (Allied Stores), architect of interior. View of sales floor. Photo ca. 1949.

61. Herpolsheimer Company, exterior view. Photo ca. 1949.

62. Jordan Marsh Company department store, Washington, Chauncey, Summer, and Avon streets, Boston (1947–57). Perry, Shaw & Hepburn, architects; George Ely, architect of the interior. Rendering of store in projected, fully developed state.

63. Jordan Marsh Company, detail of entrance.

64. Rike-Kumler Company department store, Main and Second streets, Dayton. Second Street elevation, showing (from right) original building 1911–12, Schenck & Williams, architects; first addition (two stories over original building and adjacent three bays to left), 1936–1938, Schenck & Williams, architects; and second addition (adjacent three bays and uppermost story), 1947–49, Lorenz & Williams, architects; and former Miami Hotel, purchased 1961, floors incorporated into store beginning 1962. Photo author, 1998.

as part of an extensive program that included a complete remodeling of the existing store interior, the addition encompassed over 200,000 square feet, making the complex among the largest in the country. Rising ten stories, the new section was sheathed simply in a grid of marble panels, affording stark contrast to earlier sections (fig. 65). Part of a sweeping downtown renewal effort spearheaded by citizens, including Edgar Kaufmann, a decade earlier, the rejuvenated store was touted as the essence of a new, vital spirit in the city, as well as in retailing.[88]

The focus on a conspicuous and complete remaking of the store's public face also spurred a rash of remodelings, which until the 1950s had been rare among major department stores. Fred Lazarus helped set the trend at the beginning of the decade when he commissioned the Loewy firm to redesign the front of his Columbus store. In 1948 the windows were covered to improve the control of heating and air conditioning. Concurrently, the ornate cornice was removed, probably out of concern for maintenance as well as for a more up-to-date appearance. With a minimalist treatment, Loewy's use of marble, granite, and brick nonetheless brought some panache to what had been a rather utilitarian treatment (fig. 66). Subsequent work, such as at Richard's Department Store in Miami (1950–51), which had been recently acquired by City Stores, and the May Company Denver store (1954) was more akin to the work at Kaufmann's, with vast expanses of terra cotta and stone aggregate panels, respectively.[89] However plain, such reworking entailed considerable cost. Protruding elements on the existing front had to be removed, and substantial anchoring was needed to secure the new veneer. In 1953, Thalheimer's of Richmond, Virginia, introduced a major innovation in exterior design. Prompted by one in a succession of additions of various heights and treatments and out of the desire to cover them all in a uniform, eye-catching way, store designers worked with engineers of the locally based Reynolds Metals Company to develop an aluminum curtain wall (fig. 67). The new face was not only much lighter than masonry counterparts, it required less removal of fabric, since its anchors could project from the existing wall plane. Aluminum was less expensive, required little maintenance, and was heralded as embodying the latest in architectural treatments.[90] With the facade no more than a continuous screen, the minimalist approach to exterior design that had been pursued since the war reached a new level of fulfillment.

The cache of the enormous box as a symbol for the modern department store was underscored with its adaptation by major specialty outlets carrying high-end women's apparel and accessories. But rather than the neutrality attained at Thalheimer's, these high-end emporia exuded elegance in their spare treatments. I. Magnin of San Francisco set the tone with one of the first new building projects of the

65. *(left)* Kaufmann's department store, Pittsburgh, addition 1953–55. Hoffmann & Crumpton, architects. Photo ca. 1955.

66. *(above)* F. & R. Lazarus & Company department store, High, Town, and Front streets, Columbus, Ohio (1909, 1921, 1925–26). Snyder & Babbitt and Starrett & Van Vleck, associated architects. High Street front remodeling (1950), Potter, Tyler & Martin, architects, Raymond Loewy Associates, designers. Photo ca. 1950.

67. *(below)* Thalheimer Brothers department store, Sixth and Broad streets, Richmond, Virginia (1922, 1928–29, 1935–36 [left]). Carneal & Johnson, architects. Additions and new veneer (1953–55; center right), Copeland, Novak & Associates, architects. Photo author, 2000.

postwar era, announced in October 1944 and begun two and a half years later. The new building, which replaced a facility that pioneered the shops concept, was prominently sited facing Union Square and was likewise conceived as a standard-bearer for stores of its kind.[91] Encasing an indulgent array of sumptuous, curvilinear salons, the exterior suggested a pristine jewel box sheathed in white Vermont marble. The regiment of mostly square, blue-tinted windows (some of them blind, others opening to fitting rooms) projected slightly from the wall plane to read more as surface decoration than as true voids (fig. 68). The year after Magnin's was completed, plans were unveiled for the new quarters of Sakowitz Brothers, Houston's counterpart and the southwestern rival to the Dallas-based Neiman-Marcus. Situated across the street from Foley's, the building was clearly intended to hold its own visually, with vast expanses of white marble veneer offset by tiered grillwork and two soaring portals, a leitmotif of fine stores since the 1920s, here magnified to monumental

proportions (fig. 69).⁹² Like I. Magnin's, Sakowitz's was a grand gesture, demonstrating how the "windowless" store could bespeak fashion and bigness at the same time.

A much-publicized alternative to what would soon become the norm was offered by Rich's, one of Atlanta's two main department stores, with additions that boasted extensive glazing. The program was no less unconventional. In February 1946, Rich's announced plans for trebling the size of its facility by adding to the existing store and erecting a six-story pile across a side street, connected by a four-level bridge as well as a wide underground passage (fig. 70). The new "bridge building" would have its own motor entrance and underground receiving area. While well connected, the new parts would be treated as a "downtown community of stores under one management" rather than a series of departments separated by floors. Glass curtain walls were marshaled to enunciate the distinctiveness of this arrangement while providing clear ties between the parts. Heat-resistant glass was used for the bridge and also for the adjoining wall of the Store for Homes, as the new building was christened, to emphasize connectedness and also provide an inviting exterior face to the narrow street between (fig. 71). Similarly, a glass curtain wall was used on the opposite face of the new store to herald the motor entrance, although that component went unrealized. Rich's management also hoped that strong visual ties to the outdoors would make the selling areas more cheerful and inviting; great lengths were taken to devise layouts and curtains to prevent fading of fabrics. Pleased with the results, Rich's management used the glass curtain wall as a signature element on the second addition,

68. I. Magnin & Company store, Geary and Stockton streets, San Francisco (1944, 1947–49). Timothy & Milton Pfleuger, architects, and Neal Parker, designer. Photo author, 1974.

69. Sakowitz Brothers store, Main and Fannin streets and Dallas Avenue, Houston (1949–51). Alfred C. Finn, architect; I. S. & S. J. Brochstein, designers; altered. Photo ca. 1951.

58 | MODERNIZING STORES

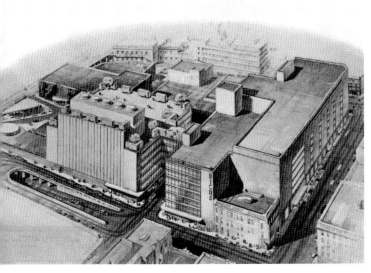

70. Rich's department store, Hunter, Forsyth, and Broad streets, Atlanta. Aerial perspective showing Store for Homes (left; 1946–48). Toombs & Creighton, architects; Eleanor Le Maire, interior architect. Store for Men (right, below existing store; 1950–51), Stevens & Wilkinson, architects, and Eleanor Le Maire, interior architect. Design modified in execution (*Progressive Architecture,* May 1947, 53). Store for Homes demolished 1994.

71. Rich's Store for Homes and bridge. Photo Jennifer Almand for Historic American Buildings Survey, 1994.

the Store for Men, begun two years later.[93] Rich's bold move to create a great retail magnet met with success. Within a few years the company claimed to be doing the largest volume of business of any store south of Philadelphia, and more than the total of the five next largest stores in the South. While the novel approach to expansion and design failed to attract a following, the big emporium stood as a sleek embodiment of the hopes of many department store executives, other retailers, and the business community alike that modernism could bring a revival of the prosperity known decades ago.

Rich's emporium was an embodiment of faith in the department store as a unique place, one that learned from distribution methods pioneered by chain companies and had dramatized them through modern design of a much more endearing sort. It manifested Richard Rich's belief that downtown could remain the heart of retailing if merchants were smart and aggressive enough in combating the forces of decentralization. By 1955, big "branch" department stores were beginning to dot the metropolitan landscape of not only Boston, New York, Philadelphia, Detroit, Chicago, San Francisco, and Los Angeles, but also of Baltimore and Washington, Cleveland and Indianapolis, St. Louis and Milwaukee, Denver and Seattle. They had not yet, however, come to Atlanta or Nashville, Dayton or Columbus, Richmond or Kansas City, Omaha or Des Moines, Portland, Spokane, or many other centers nationwide. Some cities, including Pittsburgh, had small branch department stores sprouting on the periphery, but Kaufmann's management was nonetheless certain that modernizing its great emporium would be a preferred alternative, attracting enough people downtown to bolster trade. Even in Houston, where department store branches and large chain units were proliferating by the mid-1950s, Fred Lazarus was certain that the best way to compete was to nearly double the size of Foley's so that it would continue to offer a selection of goods no other emporium could match.[94] Each of the forty-odd major additions and new buildings erected since 1945 was an expression of a commitment to keeping the urban core a vital component of the American experience. But the signs were abundant that fundamental change was at hand. No matter how impressive the legacy of postwar expansion downtown, it began to decrease after mid-decade. By the early 1960s, most of the energy and capital that department store executives could muster was channeled to building branch stores, increasingly large in size and miles away from their troubled parents.

3 Service Beyond the Stores

"'DRUG DEPARTMENT? I notice you have a sale of exquisite toilet soap today—twelve for 84 cents. Will you send me a dozen bars and charge it please?' . . . Now may I be connected with the grocery department?' . . . Mrs. Customer then places an order for some mayonnaise, dill pickles, canned goods, sugar, flour and oranges, and next she is transferred to the notion department where she orders a spool of thread. And even then she is not completed her shopping, for last of all she talks with the millinery department about a hat that she tried on the day before and was having held for her decision." This series of fictitious transactions was used to introduce the improved service facilities that had been constructed in 1927–28 for Meier & Frank in Portland, the dominant department store in Oregon. "Mrs. Customer" placed her call at 11 A.M., and it never occurred to her that her purchases would not be delivered that afternoon.[1] Meier & Frank received hundreds of such orders daily from its walk-in trade, as well as over the telephone. Thousands of items, most of them small and inexpensive, were delivered to customers' homes daily, often within twelve hours of the order. By the late 1920s this immense, complicated transfer of goods from store to consumer was hardly unusual. Some items were carried away by those who had just bought them, but many were delivered. Since the nineteenth century, efficient, free home delivery had been a hallmark of the great emporia, one that distinguished them from many other forms of retail distribution and one that the public had come to expect. In the minds of patrons, the service that a department store provided was as much associated with delivery as with the selling floor.

Although the sales areas were overt manifestations of the department store's special character, the spaces and fixtures needed to yield fast, cost-effective deliveries mostly lay behind the scenes. Mrs. Customer did not know about these spaces, nor did she give them any thought. She did know about the fleet of shiny delivery trucks, each bearing the store's name and manned by a uniformed driver, presenting a decorous image. She knew that the appearance of such a vehicle at her residence would probably be noticed by her neighbors, too. But the actual delivery was only the last step in a series of maneuvers that allowed her to receive her dozen bars of soap with such dispatch.

The logistics of delivery was a crucial component, and only one of several, that transformed the department store in ways largely unseen by the public. An expanding repertoire of in-house services, ranging from upholstery to fur storage, placed new demands on work spaces. Even more dramatic was the rise of large, bulky items carried in stock, which meant that the growth of department stores through the 1920s entailed more than just increased selling space. In some cases at least an equal amount of square footage was devoted to the ever more complex array of support functions associated with delivery, repair, and storage. These activities assumed their most dramatic three-dimensional manifestations during the 1920s and, at a lesser pace, in the half dozen years before American entry into World War II. At a time when downtown land values were escalating, downtown traffic reaching nightmare proportions, and the fever pitch of competition spurring ever more amenities for the customer, building bigger and bigger stores entailed not just aggrandizing the emporium but also constructing one or more large service facilities away from the city center, where access by motor vehicle was easier and the cost of property lower. This infrastructure, conceived to foster a centralized, delivery-oriented system of distribution, also proved invaluable to the shifts that occurred after the war, when large branch stores were being built and expectations of service were substantially changing.

Delivery

Delivery was long a defining feature of the department store, the natural outgrowth of the rise of large establishments that offered a seemingly limitless spectrum of goods. If middle-class customers were expected to buy liberally from this selection, they could not be expected to tote their bundles home on streetcars. Providing free delivery was also integral to the equation from the outset, since much of the department store's appeal lay with its reasonable prices. During the 1870s and 1880s such pioneering giants as R. H. Macy, Marshall Field, and John Wanamaker instituted this amenity, often first with couriers who walked or took public transportation and later with horse-drawn wagons. As similar emporia began to proliferate toward the century's end, competition ensured that the practice not only became universal but encompassed an ever larger territory. No establishment could call itself a great department store without providing free, fast delivery.[2] By that time, too, delivery came to be seen as a means of advertisement. A team of well-groomed horses pulling a handsomely painted wagon and driven by a courteous, liveried employee attracted attention along the city streets and made many customers feel important in a way seldom possible. The pampering atmosphere inside the store was thus given a public dimension cherished by status-conscious consumers.

Free delivery grew because it did not put significant strain on the store's physical plant. Space allocated within the building was limited to small areas for wrapping, generally on each of the sales floors, and a space in the basement where packages were held until the next morning, when they were brought to the street and sorted into the wagons. The introduction of motor vehicles, however, brought changes to the process, requiring ever more systematized methods and particularized spaces in which to perform them. This shift, in turn, led to the development of off-site facilities that became standard components of major department stores across the country during the 1920s and 1930s. A decade before the automobile started to influence the nature of these emporia, the truck was having a substantial impact of its own.

Department store executives did not embrace the motor truck at once. During the early 1900s the cost was deemed too high and the machines themselves too unreliable. A decade later, some store managers were reluctant to make the switch, and even into the 1920s horse-drawn conveyances continued to be seen in some quarters as the most efficient means of delivering goods to places within a mile or so of the emporium. Yet by then the basic shift had taken place. The key years of debate and change were from around 1910 to 1913, when a critical mass of large department stores purchased fleets of both electric and gasoline-powered trucks for many delivery functions. The truck was more reliable than the horse and wagon, proponents argued, especially in the hottest and coldest months. The initial cost was about a third greater for a truck; however, operating costs were significantly less. One truck could perform the job of two, three, or even four horse-drawn vehicles and as many as a dozen horses a day. Trucks could make two delivery trips each day, not just one. They occupied less space at the curb—one advocate believed that they would thus eliminate traffic congestion—and in storage. Furthermore, they were touted as the embodiment of progress and hence were of advertising value. But the greatest advantage from the retailer's perspective was that they could cover much more territory; without the truck, it would be increasingly difficult and expensive for the department store to keep up with the rapid dispersion of its clientele to outlying areas of the city and beyond. These middle- and upper-middle-class consumers expected rapid delivery. Moreover, most of them had acquired telephones during the 1910s and 1920s and, like Meier & Frank's Mrs. Customer, frequently called in small orders that did not warrant a trip downtown. The horse simply could not keep up with metropolitan expansion and the resulting consumer demand. By the early 1910s department stores had become the major purchasers of delivery trucks, and it was primarily for this field that such vehicles were built and refined until their widespread adoption in other commercial spheres during the 1920s.[3]

The truck brought a level of efficiency and order to the retail delivery system that was inconceivable only a few years previous, but to realize that efficiency, some major reorganization was required within the store. For trucks to be cost effective, they could not stand idle at the curb while sorting took place, as wagons generally had done. The pronounced increase of deliveries further intensified the cost of time-consuming procedures. Presorting packages for the expanding network of delivery routes; checking packages against the increasing range of payment options, especially credit; and protecting packages against damage from inclement weather, breakage in handling, and theft from sidewalk loiterers all emerged as objectives during the 1910s. The aim was to minimize the time the truck stood at the store. These functions were best performed inside the building and demanded considerable space. In many cases delivery trucks were brought inside to reduce the distance from the sorting room to the vehicles.

Beginning in the early 1910s and continuing through the next two decades, new and remodeled department stores alike had below-grade spaces devoted to the systematic sorting of packages. Gravity-fed spiral chutes connected wrapping stations on each floor with the delivery department. Upon arrival there, charged goods would be checked for their purchaser's credit rating, and C.O.D. packages would be marked. Everything would be passed to routers, then itemized and placed into locked bins, one for each driver. Packages would then be transferred to hampers and taken by the driver to his truck, generally by freight elevator (figs. 72–74). Details varied somewhat, but the basic procedure of meticulous accounting and fast sorting, using a substantial number of employees, each doing a simple, repetitive job, led to a more-or-less consistent pattern. For the first time, the movement of goods within the store was subject to careful programming for efficiency and cost-effectiveness, reflecting the doctrine of scientific management espoused by Frederick Winslow Taylor and his disciples.[4]

However well the subterranean system worked, store owners continued to be plagued by the practice of keeping delivery vehicles on the street. Some emporia, such as Marshall Field and Strawbridge & Clothier, abutted alleys or minor streets that had long been used for loading (fig. 75). Some others had interior courts arranged for the same purpose. But most department stores did not possess such arrangements, which in any event consumed substantial amounts of costly ground-floor space. Instead, delivery wagons and, later, trucks had to stand along the curb. At a time when urban vehicles were relatively few, this

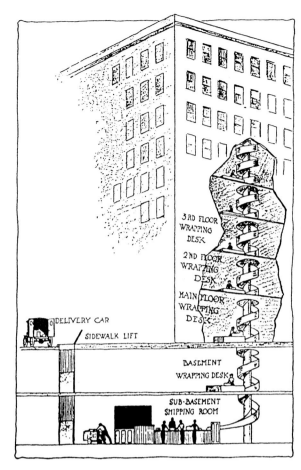

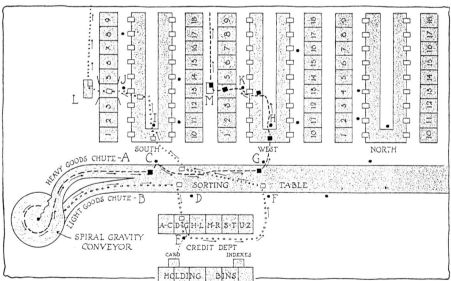

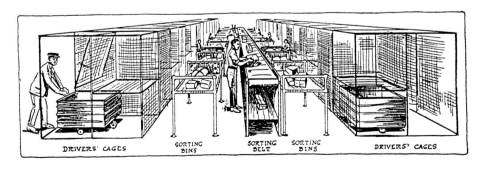

72. Halle Brothers Company department store, Cleveland. Sectional diagram of chute, sorting room, and elevator used to expedite deliveries (*Commercial Vehicle*, 1 May 1913, 10).

73. Rothchild & Company (later Goldblatt's) department store, 305–41 South State Street, Chicago (1909–12). Holabird & Roche, architects. Diagram of delivery department, showing sorting table, routing stations (H), delivery clerk stations (J, K), drivers' bins (numbered), and drivers' aisles leading to elevator (L, M) (*Commercial Vehicle*, 1 April 1913, 6).

74. Kaufmann, Baer (later Gimbel Brothers) department store, Southfield and Sixth streets, Pittsburgh (1913–14). Starrett & Van Vleck, architects. Perspective sketch of delivery room (*Commercial Vehicle*, 1 September 1914, 25).

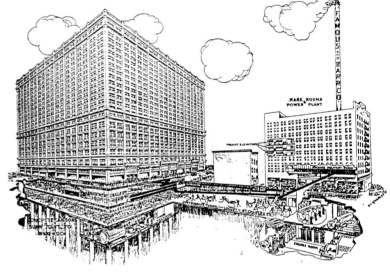

75. *(above)* Marshall Field & Company department store, State and Washington streets, Chicago (1878–79), Alley loading area. Photo late nineteenth century. Demolished 1900s.

76. *(above right)* Rosenbaum Company department store, Fifth Avenue and Market Street, Pittsburgh, various late nineteenth- and early twentieth-century buildings; demolished. View showing delivery vehicles (left) and movement of transfer hampers (lower left and right) (*Commercial Vehicle*, 1 September 1914, 21).

77. *(right)* Famous-Barr department store, Locust, Olive, Sixth, and Seventh streets, St. Louis (1911–13). Mauran, Russell & Crowell, architects. Cutaway diagram of store (in Railway Exchange Building) and warehouse at St. Clair Street; warehouse demolished. (*Dry Goods Economist*, 25 October 1913, 79).

arrangement posed little inconvenience; however, during the 1910s and 1920s curbside congestion became a serious issue. Even when relegated to side streets, trucks stymied traffic. The movement of goods from store to truck was slowed by pedestrian traffic, and often the elevator was some distance from the loading area. Equally important, the whole messy operation detracted from the atmosphere of stylishness and refinement that stores sought to impart. At the very least a section of show windows was obstructed while deliveries were being loaded (fig. 76).[5]

To improve matters, some stores built delivery departments that included space for the trucks themselves, which would be brought to the basement floor by elevator or ramp. This configuration demanded a large amount of additional square footage, however, so that all trucks could back up to the bins for loading and then exit freely. Examples of this arrangement could be found into the 1930s, but it never became standard, because such accommodations were costly to build, required extensive ventilation, and needed frequent maintenance for the elevators. But the biggest problem was lost time. Once loaded, drivers could wait as long as an hour for their turn to exit. Trucks with returned and nondelivered goods had to repeat the process in the evening. The larger the delivery fleet, the more cumbersome the process.[6]

The only feasible alternative was to remove the delivery department from the store and construct a facility tailored to its functions. This measure alleviated the pressure for space from the store at a time when ever more room was demanded for selling. During the 1910s at least five major department stores experimented with such arrangements, including the May Company's St. Louis store, Famous-Barr. The new building erected for the company in 1911–13 fronted four heavily traveled streets, which discouraged the use of any one of them for delivery vehicles. So a ten-story

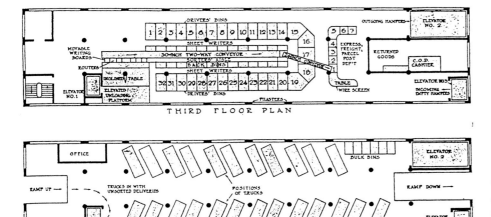

78. Rosenbaum Company, Pittsburgh, diagrammatic plans of garage and delivery department, 1914–15 (*Commercial Vehicle,* 1 September 1915, 25).

warehouse was constructed concurrently one block away, facing a less-used street (fig. 77). All save large delivery goods were sorted (according to whether they had been paid for, charged, or were being sent C.O.D.) at a central station in the store, then taken by conveyor belt via underground passage to the second floor of the warehouse. From this room, the routing was conducted, with each driver taking his stock to the ground-floor loading area.[7] The arrangement also facilitated the handling of incoming goods, which could either go directly to the storage floors or be conveyed through the tunnel to the store. The Famous-Barr scheme was revolutionary in its understanding of how both incoming and outgoing delivery functions were best conducted on a separate site and of how they were complemented by those of warehousing at the same location. Directly or otherwise, the solution had a decisive impact on practices over the next quarter-century.

Within a year, the Outlet Company of Providence was nearing completion of a similar facility, but this may have been the only case in which the Famous-Barr design was followed closely. The constraints of downtown locations, where land values were high and where a lightly traveled street was often not at hand, combined with many other variables—such as the layout, structure, and needs of the store—precluded adoption of a single plan. Gimbel Brothers' New York store, for example, opened a rear annex in 1919. Trucks had to take elevators two floors below for loading. This process was done in a space separate from the sorting and routing, which were conducted under the store proper. Filled hampers had to be individually rolled through a tunnel from one section to the other. A more efficient system was devised by the Rosenbaum Company of Pittsburgh, which had initially planned to follow the Famous-Barr scheme in building its new store. But when difficulty arose in securing permits for the connecting tunnel, store executives opted for redesigning the remote-site garage to accommodate deliveries instead. Goods were sorted by payment type in the store basement, then sent by transfer vans to the garage a quarter-mile away, where routing was done (fig. 78).[8] The advantages of this system were several. Much valuable space was saved at the store by removing the delivery department and by allocating room for only one large transfer vehicle. Delivery trucks could leave and return to the garage unimpeded by downtown traffic. Finally, the delivery department was located in a light, airy space rather than in a subterranean one, making for a more agreeable work environment. The costs incurred in transferring packages to this location were more than offset by the benefits. Still, the site limitations of the garage necessitated that hampers be wheeled from the transfer truck to an elevator, brought to the third floor for routing, and then returned by hamper to the first and wheeled again to the delivery vehicles. This flaw would be eliminated the following year (1916) in what was probably the first building conceived for delivery functions and situated away from the parent store—the ever-expanding plant of J. L. Hudson in Detroit.

Hudson's distributing station, as it was called, was part of a system developed, in the words of the delivery superintendent, for "doing things the easiest way and doing the thing at hand at once.... Instead of a concentration at one point of many operations," he explained, "the whole service is arranged so that recording and handling of the purchase shall progress as the package travels from its place of purchase to the very door of the buyer."[9] With this system, checking packages for credit, marking them for C.O.D. or special delivery, and other functions were conducted on each sales floor, where the packages were wrapped. "Bundle boys" placed wrapped goods in small quantities in a spiral chute to promote an even flow to the basement shipping room, which was quite small. In the shipping room a few employees were charged with assigning route numbers. All packages were placed in large crates, each with a capacity of

| 65

79. J. L. Hudson Company distributing station, Adams Street, Detroit (1916). Probably Smith, Hinchman & Grylls, architects; numerous later additions; demolished 2002. Exterior view, showing second-story addition of 1920.

80. Marshall Field & Company remote delivery station, 4355 Ravenswood Avenue, Chicago (1913). William E. Walker, architect. Photo ca. 1913.

seventy-five to one hundred bundles, then transported by escalator to transfer trucks, one of which was filled every ten minutes, forming a continuous flow of goods. At the distributing station the crates could be unloaded close to a central conveyor belt running nearly the length of the building. In this space, sorting and inventorying ("sheet writing") were conducted in a more or less conventional manner, but in this case the loading dock was directly on the other side of the drivers' bins, and that area, in turn, was adjacent to the street (fig. 79). Located a few blocks from the store, on the fringe of downtown, the station was ideally situated for trucks to reach the neighborhoods of Hudson's vast clientele without encountering traffic congestion. All the drawbacks of previous experiments were eliminated.

Though really the product of fast-paced evolution of delivery infrastructure over the previous five years, Hudson's scheme was billed as a "radical departure."[10] It apparently elicited great interest among managers of other stores and, during the 1920s, served as a springboard for numerous remote service facilities. Acceptance may also have been fostered by the fact that for a number of years another type of remote delivery building had been used by some of the nation's largest stores. These outposts were developed during the late nineteenth century as relay stations to bridge the ever-greater distances that delivery wagons had to travel in major cities. Located in or near target residential areas, the stations received goods in bulk from the store after hours; items were transferred to smaller wagons for delivery the next morning. As horse-drawn vehicles began to be replaced by trucks, some companies considered their stations outdated. Still, some of the industry's giants continued to rely on them. Marshall Field, for example, established a network of "barns" along railroad lines in 1902 so that goods could be transferred quickly to their outposts. As the company acquired a fleet of trucks it replaced at least several of these makeshift facilities with substantial relay stations, which remained in use until the mid-twentieth century (fig. 80).[11] In New York, both John Wanamaker and R. H. Macy built elaborate relay stations into the early 1930s, when they were developed into sorting facilities based on the Hudson's model. The size of the New York metropolitan area and its numerous topographical barriers, combined with the density and high land values in much of Manhattan, argued for a diffuse system, in which goods destined for suburban districts could be transferred in bulk to the outlying areas for sorting and distribution.[12] But New York was an exception. In most other cities, a single remote-site facility proved adequate. Hudson's plant, promoted to customers as a service amenity, proved so successful that by 1920 construction was under way for workrooms and for an adjacent warehouse that furthered the role of the building as a model.

Warehousing

If most aspects of the increasingly complex delivery system remained unknown to the public, warehousing was an even more obscure realm.[13] Through most of the nineteenth century few stores were large enough to require their own warehouses; wholesalers primarily performed the storage function. Even the emergence of major department stores does not appear to have warranted changes in building patterns. Many reserve stocks were stored conveniently in the building. If additional space was needed, one or more floors of a loft building could be rented, frequently next to the store or within a few blocks. Many department stores relied on this ad hoc method well into the twentieth century. The factors that eventually made such arrangements untenable were the unceasing demand for additional selling space, the escalation of land values, and the rapid rise in number and range of bulky goods carried. Soft goods and many other small items offered by the department store were for the most part easily kept on the premises. But the storage requirements of furniture, appliances, toys, and other such items led to the pursuit of offsite warehousing.

Storage facilities did not fully solve the problem when they were secured without a long-range strategy, for ongoing growth resulted in the use of multiple locations, often some distance from one another. The situation described by the chief executives of Lit Brothers department store in Philadelphia may have been extreme when it was written in 1937, but it cogently outlined the problems that had been shared by many firms. Delineating the need for a new, consolidated building, they wrote to Albert M. Greenfield, president of the parent City Stores, that Lit's was then using nine warehouses. One lay directly at the store's rear, but the others were on scattered, inconveniently located sites. They elaborated with an example: "We sell about 100 pieces of furniture from the floor a day. Merchandise is received at the train shed in building A, where it is checked and loaded on a truck and hauled to one of the other buildings to be stored. Later it is requisitioned to be sent to the store as a sample. It must then be loaded on a truck and hauled back to building A where it is finished and taken to the delivery platform where it is loaded on a truck and brought to the store." That was just the beginning: "When it is sold it must be sent from the store to a temporary location . . . because the delivery building is not large enough. . . . A day or two before the actual delivery date it must be picked up from the . . . location and carried back to the delivery building where it is assembled." They concluded: "The constant loading and unloading is bound to damage the furniture which adds to our labor cost and makes for numerous errors. . . . The customer suffers because the result is unsatisfactory service which in turn adds to the office cost in the furniture bureau of adjustment. The records necessary to keep track of all these movements are also a contributing factor in increased clerical expenses."[14]

Neighboring Strawbridge & Clothier may have seemed more in control of the logistical situation. In 1901, it opened a seven-story warehouse and stable on Race Street, just two blocks from the store and perhaps among the earliest of its kind to be purpose-built. In 1918, the company constructed a second, considerably larger warehouse about a mile north of the store. This, too, proved inadequate to meet all the expansion needs. Six years later, three buildings to the rear of the store that had been acquired at various times for its now defunct wholesaling operations were converted for administrative and storage purposes (fig. 81). But even if it did not achieve consolidation, Strawbridge's was a pioneer among department stores in constructing its own warehouses on carefully chosen sites. The 1918 facility, in particular, was noted as a model (fig. 82).[15] Not only was it a more modern

81. Commercial buildings, nineteenth century, adapted in 1924 for storage and administrative functions of Strawbridge & Clothier, Filbert and Eighth streets, Philadelphia; demolished for new warehouse ca. 1955. Photo ca. 1950.

82. Strawbridge & Clothier warehouse, Ninth and Poplar streets, Philadelphia (1918). Photo 1920s.

83. William Filene's Sons service building, Memorial Drive and Main Street, Cambridge, Massachusetts (1920–21), demolished.

plant than most used by department stores at the time, it was laid out to provide the most efficient flow of stock and operations. The building was designed to house furniture and other household furnishings, as well as related finishing and upholstering jobs. Goods came directly to the building on a spur of the Reading Railroad line, which entered the premises on the second level. Most stock remained in the warehouse until it was delivered to purchasers, who selected pieces from samples in the store. Thus the facility did not have to be close to the emporium; indeed, it was in an area with low land values and of marginal use for many industries, but close to arteries that would allow delivery trucks easy access to their destinations. Like Hudson's distributing station, Strawbridge's warehouse was among the first of a new generation of facilities to fully avail itself of the advantages that motor transportation allowed. It served as a basis for similar facilities constructed during the next decade.

Integration

In the spring of 1920, Edward Filene felt compelled to announce that, contrary to rumor, his company's plans for a sizable edifice in Cambridge, just over the Charles River from Boston, was going to be neither an employees' recreational facility nor a branch. Instead, as part of an expansion program that included opening two annexes near the store that year, Filene's would erect a six-story service building in which delivery operations, storage, marking and receiving, support functions such as printing, and even the manufacturing of garments would occur under one roof (fig. 83).[16] When the facility opened a year later, the store whose name had become synonymous with innovation in retailing made another breakthrough: the nation's first fully consolidated, remote-site service center built for a department store. More or less concurrently, Hudson's was transforming its distributing station into a comparable plant of roughly the same size, 100,000 square feet.[17]

Other companies were slow to follow at first, perhaps owing to both the newness of the idea and unsettled economic conditions. Once department store expansion picked up, however, the idea quickly became a trend. Before 1920, the number of warehouses (aside from those for companies with wholesale divisions) well adapted to the department store's needs appears to have been quite limited, and the number of remote delivery stations (aside from the relay type used in Chicago and New York) almost nil. But between 1922 and 1931 nearly forty large remote-site, purpose-built service facilities were realized, and at least fourteen more were built between 1936 and 1941.[18] The great majority were planned as multistory buildings encompassing 100,000 to nearly 600,000 square feet. No particular type of department store prevailed among those that undertook such projects. Some companies—including Bullock's in Los Angeles and Woodward & Lothrop in Washington—ranked among the leading department stores in their respective cities. Others—such as the May Company in Cleveland, the Boston Store in Milwaukee, and Famous-Barr in St. Louis—were less fashionable but commanded a major share of the local market. A third group—such as S. Kann Sons in Washington, and Powers Dry Goods Company in Minneapolis—were lower in the hierarchy. All sought to improve their physical plants, but few of these projects were undertaken as an integral part of a comprehensive expansion program.

No geographic area dominated, either. Washington was

84. Woodward & Lothrop service building, First, M, and Pierce streets, N.E., Washington, D.C. Built as a U.S. Army medical supply depot ca. 1917, converted 1927, demolished ca. 2002. Photo late 1920s.

unusual, with five of its six major stores so equipped by 1939. Most large cities had at least one example, although a number of smaller centers, including Atlanta, Omaha, and Dallas, apparently did not. When combined with many others that were adaptations of existing buildings, and yet a third group built or in remodeled facilities adjacent to the store, the total represented a substantial portion of major companies nationwide. The shifts in delivery and warehousing practices that occurred after 1920 had a decisive impact on the industry in terms of systemization of operations and of divorcing a number of important functions from the main facility.

The primary causes of this phenomenon had not changed since the 1910s; they had only intensified. Downtown land values continued to escalate as the perceived need for expansion among department store executives was reaching new highs. Under these circumstances alone it was desirable to allocate the maximum amount of floor area to selling space. The fact that department stores were carrying ever more bulky goods—especially furniture, appliances, and radios—substantially contributed to the need. But sales of these bulky goods could be made from samples, with the actual piece delivered from another location. This practice, adopted by increasing numbers of stores during the 1920s, was made possible by the development of offsite storage plants. Rapid advances in motor truck technology during the late 1910s and 1920s contributed as well. Fleets of electric vans, once favored for many short-distance runs, were replaced by ones powered by internal combustion engines. Motors that were ever more reliable and could carry increasingly heavy loads at ever greater speeds, as well as improved suspension systems and the introduction of pneumatic tires, which enabled smoother rides, all contributed to the process. On the other hand, the exponential rise in downtown motor vehicle traffic during the same years spurred many department store executives to remove their new delivery fleets from the traffic quagmire.

The cost of building a new service facility was substantial. Constructing a moderate-sized plant of about 200,000 square feet could run between $400,000 and $500,000; the largest projects ran between $1 million and $2 million. Perhaps for this reason, shared facilities were constructed in at least two instances.[19] However, many companies opted to purchase or take long-term leases for existing warehouses, modifying them to suit their needs. Woodward & Lothrop, for example, purchased a sprawling complex in 1927 that had been constructed only about a decade earlier as a U. S. Army medical supply depot (fig. 84). Located a dozen blocks east of the store, the facility encompassed over 100,000 square feet and could accommodate warehouse, delivery, and repair functions, as well as provide a garage. Other advantages included reinforced-concrete construction, large glazed areas to admit abundant natural light and air, and a number of loading bays. The horizontal configuration was less than ideal, however, at a time when moving goods to and from the stockrooms was still done largely by hand.[20] A similarly well-endowed plant of 1913 was acquired by Boston's Jordan Marsh Company the same year. Replacing makeshift accom-

85. Gimbel Brothers warehouse, Tenth and Clyborn streets, Milwaukee. Built as clothing factory, late nineteenth or early twentieth century, converted ca. 1922. Photo ca. 1921.

modations at a former U. S. Army warehouse on Commonwealth Pier, the 134,000-square-foot complex rose five stories on a prominent site in Cambridge not far from Filene's service building.[21] But here, too, the structure's configuration, with a 60-foot depth that was ideal for some factories, compromised its efficiency for storage and delivery operations.

In the rush to attain more space for selling, many department stores settled for buildings poorly suited to their service needs. As a group, these adapted quarters were characterized as dark, poorly ventilated, and susceptible to fire, as well as lacking adequate dock space and elevators. The turn-of-the-century clothing factory that Gimbel Brothers converted to a warehouse for its Milwaukee store in the early 1920s was probably typical of many such undertakings (fig. 85).[22] Finding a sufficiently large building also proved difficult, and acquired facilities could soon prove inadequate. The Hecht Company of Washington invested heavily in turning a loft across from the store into its new, consolidated service facility. But only a year after the 1933 opening Hecht's had to lease two small warehouses some distance away in order to meet storage demands, re-creating the conditions it had just sought to correct.[23] The scattered facilities that so frustrated Lit's executives were common during the interwar decades.

For companies that made the substantial investment in a new facility, planning was of utmost concern. Store executives and their architects visited new projects elsewhere to observe their attributes and to confer with colleagues. The lengthy descriptions of new service buildings that proliferated in trade literature during the second half of the 1920s suggest not only the importance of the subject, but a keen interest among the readership. Siting was seen as among the most crucial factors. Because of the continuous movement of goods to and from the store, it was ideal to locate the service building within a mile radius; two miles was usually considered the maximum distance. Ample space could be found in the industrial districts that skirted city centers, where land values were relatively low. Access to a railroad spur was deemed highly advantageous, so that incoming goods could be directly transferred. At the same time, the site had to be on or close to major roadways so that delivery trucks could reach residential neighborhoods with ease. Finally, the site had to be big—many were large enough to permit expansion—and unencumbered, so that the building would receive ample natural light and ventilation, preferably on all sides. The latter consideration was seen as particularly important for workrooms, where finishing and repairs were made, but also for storage spaces at a time when artificial cooling systems for most types of warehouses remained limited.

While the basic elements of the service building and warehouse had been developed decades earlier, their consolidation required a more complicated arrangement, as well as a significant increase in scale. Designed as the initial part of a complete service complex, Bamberger's delivery building (1924–25) had spaces for loading more than a hundred delivery trucks. The facility, among the most publicized schemes of its kind, appears to have played an important role in codifying what quickly became industry standards. Another influential project, particularly for integrating delivery with storage and service functions, was the plant built for Famous-Barr a year later, which could accommodate nearly seventy delivery vehicles.[24] The movement of goods to and from trucks had always occurred inside the building to protect merchandise from the elements and theft. Paired ranges of sorting tables, bins, and loading platforms, rather than the single range employed at Hudson's, became the rule. Rather than have trucks back into the bays from the street, they entered and exited the building through one or two portals, with all interim maneuvers conducted inside (figs. 86–88). A separate loading area was provided for furniture and other large items. Extensive maintenance and repair facilities were close at hand. These activities consumed almost the entire ground floor in cases where warehousing and related functions were included.

The increased scale of operation also required more office space, as well as a large area for the receiving, sorting, and marking of incoming goods—generally at the second level (fig. 89). Commodious locker rooms and lavatories for employees became common features, in some cases supplemented by cafeterias or recreation areas—all part of a concerted effort by department stores to make working conditions more agreeable. The scope and volume of stored goods rose, and as a result differentiation of storage areas became common.[25] Goods were segregated by size and type, often with steel shelving used for small pieces and, later,

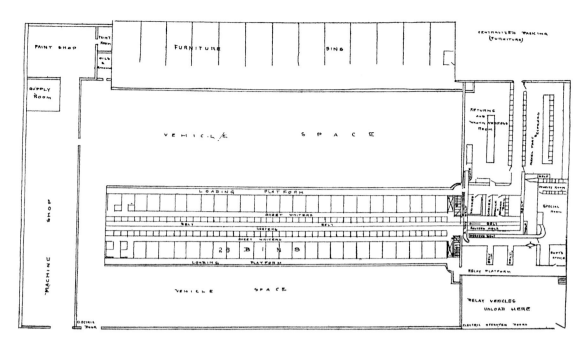

specially made bins to hold bulky items so that space could be maximized. In many examples, a large area was developed as a cold storage unit for customers' furs. At least one workroom existed for the finishing, repair, and sometimes even custom manufacture of furniture. Freight elevators transferred large goods from one floor to another; spiral chutes or, in some later instances, sloping conveyor belts moved smaller goods. By the late 1920s, *Women's Wear Daily* emphasized, the design of these facilities had developed into an "exact science." Far from being conventional loft structures, department store service buildings were home to a spectrum of particularized functions, all tailored to the needs of the individual client. The support building could seem to be almost as intricate and costly a venture as the store itself.[26]

The only drawback of these new facilities was, of course,

86. *(top)* Famous-Barr Company service building, Spring Avenue and Market Street, St. Louis (1925–26). Will Levy, architect; altered. Diagram of ground floor plan (*Dry Goods Economist,* 13 March 1926, 98).

87. *(above, left)* Famous-Barr service building, bins and loading platform. Photo ca. 1920s.

88. *(above, right)* Bloomingdale Brothers service building, Hunter's Point Avenue and Fourth Street, Brooklyn (1927–28). Abbott, Merkt & Company, architects-engineers. Truck loading and maneuvering area, similar to that at Famous-Barr's service building. Photo 1928.

89. Strawbridge & Clothier delivery station, 950 North Ninth Street, Philadelphia (1928). Abbott, Merkt & Company, architects-engineers. Second-floor sorting area. Photo ca. 1928.

90. F. & R. Lazarus Company service annex, Front and State streets, Columbus, Ohio (1939). Richards, McCarthy & Bulford, architects. Addition of 1958 (left) and store (right). Photo Bob Fite, 1969.

their remote location. In some instances, circumstances allowed department store executives to develop a large new service building close to the store, as Famous-Barr and the Outlet had done. In a rare example of a plan that was an integral component of an extensive remodeling and expansion campaign, G. Fox of Hartford, Connecticut, erected a large new plant in 1929–30 across a secondary street from its store, connected by a two-story bridge. Slightly earlier, the Dayton Company in Minneapolis incorporated its delivery department in the sub-basement of a new customer parking garage adjacent to the store.[27] Fred Lazarus combined these features, taking them one step further with his two Ohio emporia. Six months after unveiling plans for a complete transformation of the recently purchased John Shillito in Cincinnati, Lazarus announced that the plant would be bigger still, with a new rear section containing a service facility for small-sized goods and a garage for patrons.[28] Above the four parking decks, stock and workrooms were placed as close to their parent departments as possible, with connections at each level. As a result, time spent in moving goods was significantly reduced. Even before the project was completed Lazarus embarked on a similar addition at his home store in Columbus. The building was about the same size—300,000 square feet—but without the parking facilities that occupied over a third of Shillito's extension (fig. 90). All selling floors thus enjoyed direct connection to the service areas. Furthermore, since the latter spaces did not need to be as high as those it served, mezzanine levels were introduced for additional functions, such as training and personnel offices. The sloping site also enabled the west side to be used as a selling area at street level. Enough space existed to allow room for expansion, which was not possible at Shillito's. The importance of this provision was soon evident; in 1941, Lazarus had to purchase a seven-story, 98,000-square-foot warehouse some distance from the Cincinnati store to accommodate its growing needs.[29] Despite the praise and publicity that the Columbus project received, Lazarus's approach never became a general tendency.[30] Like G. Fox, the two Ohio emporia had the unusual advantage of being able to build contiguous service extensions on acreage that was not in high demand for other business purposes, and at a time when land values were low. After World War II, when the opportunity arose for other stores to make similar expansions, the role of the service building was fast changing.

Expression

If all the intricacies of the service building and the processes it housed lay outside the public's consciousness, the image did not. Most department stores that invested in new facilities tried to use them to enhance their reputations. At the time of its completion, the service building was often featured in newspapers as part of its store's advertising agenda, presented as a means of bringing tangible benefits to the customer. The Golden Rule in St. Paul was one of several emporia that emphasized how deliveries were enhanced by the new outpost so that even remote areas of the region could be well served (fig. 91). The Dayton Company in nearby Minneapolis offered a jazz-age impression of its delivery department to convey a sense of speed and efficiency, suggesting that purchases would arrive sooner and in better condition (fig. 92).[31] Often, the building was opened for public inspection. Lazarus staged a storewide

91. Golden Rule service building, Lafayette and Woodward streets, St. Paul, Minnesota (1927–28). Clarence H. Johnson, architect. Advertisement (*Saint Paul Pioneer Press*, 3 May 1928, 24).

92. Dayton Company service building, 24–38 Eighth Street, Minneapolis (1927–28). Advertisement (*Minneapolis Journal*, 8 September 1928, 3).

sale in conjunction with the ceremonies for his Columbus plant. But such fanfare was brief. A service facility had more enduring value in its exterior, which many companies strove to make memorable.

Part of the challenge in creating a service building as a visual advertisement lay in the locations that were best for practical reasons. Most of the public did not frequent the industrial areas where department store service facilities stood except, of course, along major commuting routes. Since those routes were also advantageous for delivery truck access to and from the building, many companies, including Filene's and Bamberger's, constructed service quarters on streets passed by thousands of motorists daily. Others, such as Famous-Barr's, commanded somewhat more removed sites that nonetheless allowed them to be seen from a distance. Straddling the shores of the Allegheny River, the eight-story Joseph Horne service building loomed large not only from several bridges, but also from downtown Pittsburgh, which lay directly across the water. Large signs identifying the business were commonly painted on the wall or were mounted as freestanding, illuminated letters.

The second challenge to creating a distinctive image was that service facilities were by nature utilitarian. Costly exterior treatment was something that most department store executives did not entertain even for the main building, let alone an adjunct one. Some facilities, especially those erected in the early 1920s, were without adornment of any kind. But most had at least some decorative qualities, bene-

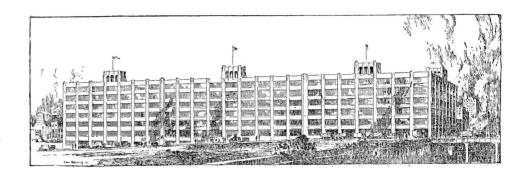

93. Bloomingdale Brothers service building, presentation drawing (*Women's Wear Daily*, 7 July 1928, 7).

94. May Company service building, Payne Avenue, East Forty-First and Forty-Third streets, Cleveland (1927–28). Lehman, Schmidt & Company, architects. Photo author, 1995.

fiting from a shift in attitude toward industrial architecture that had emerged in recent decades. Since the turn of the twentieth century, a growing contingent of architects had focused on the design of warehouses, manufacturing plants, power stations, and other structures that had long been ignored by most of the profession. Architects were able to establish themselves in this lucrative area not just by attending to programmatic needs but by convincing clients that they could address those needs better than could engineers or builders alone, creating plants that were more efficient and cost-effective. A well-planned building was important for the welfare and productivity of the workforce. Appearances, designers argued, boosted morale. Furthermore, appearances were important as advertising; the public face suggested the character of the operation inside in more than functional terms. A carefully studied exterior heralded a modern, progressive business, and high-caliber design need add little to the cost. The best results were achieved by expressing the building's purpose; attention to mass, proportion, materials, and detail were the essential factors, not the application of ornament. By the 1920s, many business owners were convinced that this approach was viable. Examples were numerous of warehouses and other buildings that were dignified, purposeful, and even refined, without being pretentious.[32]

The range of expression that could be achieved using this approach was considerable, which not only accommodated varying budgetary constraints but also gave latitude for varying tastes and concerns for individuality. The enormous service building constructed for Bloomingdale Brothers in 1927–28, for example, resembled numerous light-manufacturing plants of the period in its no-nonsense, exposed concrete frame, brick spandrels, and steel sash windows (fig. 93). The designer, Hunley Abbott, was proud that the exterior "reflects its purpose. . . . It is massive, strong and simple, without unnecessary decoration or ornamentation, but the proportions are dignified and pleasing."[33] A more overtly decorous character was chosen for the May Company's Cleveland service building, which employed both classicizing compositional patterns and some medievalizing motifs—the corners suggesting towers; the intermediate piers, buttresses—associated with more ornate commercial

and institutional work of the period (fig. 94). To enhance the image further, a range of display windows extended across the front at street level to capture the eyes of motorists along what was then a heavily traveled route into the city center.[34] On the other hand, applied ornament was kept to a minimum, and the expansive areas of steel sash gave a clear sense of the building's general function.

Two of the most ambitious examples of exterior treatment were designed for rival Washington stores, the Hecht Company and Woodward & Lothrop, both of which found their adapted facilities inadequate within a decade. Hecht's was probably the first major department store to embark on constructing a service facility after the worst years of the Depression, announcing plans for a great pile of more than 400,000 square feet in January 1936. The preliminary scheme was given much the same dignified sense of order and solemnity as the May Company building, but within six months the plans were completely revised. As built, the structure was sheathed in horizontal bands of glazed brick and glass block to form one of the most striking large-scale

95. Hecht Company service building, New York Avenue and Fenwick Street, N.E., Washington, D.C. (1936–37). Abbott, Merkt & Company, architects-engineers. Photo author, 1970.

streamlined exteriors in the commercial sphere of the period (fig. 95). At a time when glass block was still new, the building employed it liberally to enhance the diffusion of light in the workspaces lining the window walls.[35] The composition was given a dynamic focus with a rounded corner capped by a multifaceted glass crown illuminated at night from within by a colored beacon. In a city notorious for its architectural conservatism, the Hecht service building made a conspicuous departure, its minimalist treatment exuding sleekness and modernity. Prominently placed along what soon became one of the major routes into the city and one of the most heavily traveled rail corridors on the eastern seaboard, the building was an instant landmark. Two factors probably contributed to this unprecedented exuberance. Hecht's was the youngest of Washington's major department stores and for years had been among the least prestigious. Aggressive efforts to improve its status had begun with a new store building in the 1920s and were accelerated during the next decade. The service building, which executives trumpeted as the largest in the East south of New York, appears to have been conceived not so much to reflect the store's image as to enhance it. In addition, the revised design included a limited amount of ground-floor space for selling, and the entire scheme was developed so that much of it could be converted to retail functions. Should the northeastern sector of the metropolitan area have become a site for large-scale middle-class residential development, company officials were poised to convert part of their elegant building into a branch store.[36]

Woodward & Lothrop, long considered the city's most

96. Woodward & Lothrop service building, 131 M Street, N.E., Washington, D.C. (1938–39). Abbott, Merkt & Company, architects-engineers. Photo author, 1997.

prestigious full-line department store, could not be upstaged by erecting a less imposing facility than Hecht's. Nor could it emulate its upstart rival, which would be tantamount to conceding that Hecht's was the pacesetter. So the company opted for a more conservative treatment, true to its reputation, loosely in the spirit of the modern classical public buildings then in vogue for federal projects (fig. 96). Although Woodward & Lothrop shunned much of the ballyhoo in which Hecht's indulged, the company was clearly bent on making a statement of its own.[37] Similar in size, configuration, structure, and internal features, the two great piles stood as conspicuous symbols of the department stores' solidity and strength despite the ravages of the Depression. More than any remodeling done to either store, these service buildings suggested a new era of progress, affording a pronounced case of how a utilitarian outpost could project a compelling image for its owner. Even without an intracity rivalry, appearances became increasingly important in the 1930s. The Lazarus service buildings in both Cincin-

nati and Columbus were carefully designed to complement their adjacent stores, in contrast to many earlier instances where nearby leased, or even purpose-built, quarters were much more mundane in appearance. Hecht's, especially, seems to have made an impression on the executives of Lit's, who found the logistics of scattered-site facilities so frustrating. One of the last major projects of its kind before World War II, the building boasted the latest conveniences, designed to minimize the internal movement of goods and the number of hands required to perform those operations. Lit's officials took pride not only in the claim that their new 600,000-square-foot, $2 million facility was the largest industrial building undertaken locally by the private sector since the 1920s, but also in its appearance (fig. 97). Like Hecht's, the design bespoke modernity, here balancing a traditional, academic sense of order and containment with an avant-garde love of transparency and machinelike precision, rising like a beacon in Philadelphia's industrial landscape to herald hopes for a new era in retailing.[38] While not on a major thoroughfare, the building was sited so as to be prominent from the city center, with enormous neon letters on its parapet that would make a strong impression from some distance.

To plan such facilities, many department store executives relied on the architects they had used to build or expand their stores, who in turn often worked closely with employees in charge of the pertinent operations. The visits to recently developed facilities elsewhere that became standard practice in the early stages of a project would have given both designers and their clients a clear sense of the intricacies involved. One engineering firm pursued specialization in this arena from an early date. The New York–based Abbott, Merkt & Company, established in 1923, entered the limelight with its design for Bamberger's delivery station. Months before construction began on the project, Abbott and his client presented a detailed report on the merits of type before the retail delivery contingent at the National Retail Dry Goods Association's convention. Abbott, Merkt also frequently advertised in trade organs. Coupled with the extensive publicity the scheme itself received, these steps elicited considerable attention. Soon commissions were secured for service buildings in Washington and Cincinnati, as well as for a new Hecht Brothers store in Baltimore.[39] Bloomingdale's service facility, one of the largest of its kind, followed. By the eve of World War II, Abbott, Merkt had prepared plans for at least fourteen such projects, including the giant ones for Hecht's and Woodward & Lothrop. Most of this work lay between New York and Washington, D.C.; however, examples could be found in Hartford, Rochester, Detroit, and St. Louis, as well as in Los Angeles, which housed a much-praised depot for United Parcel Service. Abbott, Merkt had established a niche as a national leader in

97. Lit Brothers service building, Buttonwood Avenue, Seventeenth and Eighteenth streets, Philadelphia (1939–40). Simon & Simon, architects; demolished. Photo ca. 1940.

this specialized realm.[40] The firm had not invented the consolidated, remote-site service facility, but it was responsible for some of the most prominent examples from an early stage in the type's development. This distinction would serve Abbott, Merkt well in its efforts to redefine the modern service building after the war.

Transformation

Even before the return of peace in 1945, plans were announced for a huge addition to Famous-Barr's remote-site facility. Within a matter of months the projected size was increased. The seven-story, $1 million building was urgently needed, its owners-to-be claimed, if their company was to embark on a much costlier expansion program that entailed building three giant branch stores in the northern, southern, and western portions of the metropolitan area. In the early 1920s the service building was well sited in relation to the downtown store and its clientele, and the location was equally suitable for a much larger center that would serve a network of retail outlets. Within months of the announcement the affiliated May Company in California unveiled plans for a service plant of 800,000 square feet, perhaps the largest ever built, conceived to serve two large new branches in Los Angeles.[41]

Both projects helped inaugurate a new thrust in service building construction, which was guided by large-scale development in outlying areas of cities. Branch store buildings increased the need for storage, especially since early stores were typically designed with little on-site capacity for reserve stock. Coordinating merchandise and its movement at a central location became imperative if distribution to multiple outlets was to occur in an efficient, cost-effective manner. The distance between the stores and the service building mattered less than in earlier decades; spans of several miles became common. The construction of better arterial routes and, by the mid-1950s, high-speed thoroughfares, combined with improved design in trailer trucks, lessened the time spent transporting goods. Far more important was the positioning of reserve stock so that it could be received from the manufacturer in a single location and shipped to one outlet or another on short notice as demand warranted. In both St. Louis and Los Angeles the May Company realized that it could not launch its ambitious branch building plans without having the service building in place. On the East Coast, the Hecht Company, also among the first to embark on a large-scale branch building plan, adapted its service facility to this new function, increasing its size by nearly a third in the process.[42] From an operational standpoint, such facilities were becoming less an adjunct to the store and more a nerve center in their own right. Pioneered by chain stores during the 1920s, the central distribution facility was readily adaptable once department store executives decided to implement the change.[43] Within a few years most service buildings constructed, added to, or leased by the great emporia assumed this role.

Conditions were changing in other ways as well. Cus-

tomer delivery remained an important function and symbol of the department store's stature, but the range of goods delivered began to narrow. Greater reliance on cars for shopping trips downtown and a nearly complete dependence on them for shopping at branches meant that most goods were now personally transported; most customers preferred the convenience of immediate acquisition to waiting for the delivery van. Mrs. Customer was far less likely to instigate the ritual of delivery for a dozen bars of soap or a hat than she had been two decades earlier.

What still required delivery, of course, were bulky goods: furniture, bedding, rugs, appliances, large toys, and other items for which department stores sought to retain a substantial market share over the chain and independent specialty outlets. The department store's continued role in selling such wares and in providing services most chains did not offer, while also opening new branches, further necessitated larger service facilities. As a result, at least as many sizable, purpose-built service complexes were erected or had major additions made to them in the decade after World War II as had been constructed during the 1920s.

Prewar patterns clearly influenced some of the new work. Fred Lazarus more or less replicated his Columbus store's annex with a large addition to Federated's Abraham & Straus

98. H. & S. Pogue Company service building, Race Street, Cincinnati (1946–49). Harry Hanke and Harry Hanke, Jr., architects. Photo author, 2008.

99. J. L. Hudson Company service complex, Adams, Brush, and St. Antoine streets and Madison Avenue, Detroit. Warehouse 1 and other 1920s buildings (center midground), Smith, Hinchman & Grylls, architects; Warehouse 2 (just visible to immediate right of Warehouse 1), 1924, Smith, Hinchman & Grylls, architects; delivery building (right), 1937–38, Abbott, Merkt & Company, architects-engineers; addition to Warehouse 1 (center-left foreground), 1945–47, Smith, Hinchman & Grylls, architects (three stories added 1953–54); delivery building altered; other components demolished 2002. Photo ca. 1947.

100. F. & R. Lazarus Company bulk service building, West Whittier Street, Columbus, Ohio (1948–49). Austin Company, architects-engineers. Building in foreground; store to right of second bridge from top (*Architectural Forum,* December 1950, 109).

store in Brooklyn (1945–47). He hoped for a somewhat similar arrangement in his new showcase store, Foley's in Houston. A large section of each floor in the mammoth store was designed as a stockroom for apparel and other small items. The basement of the adjacent garage was devoted to receiving and delivery, with goods taken to and from the store by subterranean conveyor belts. The third component, converting a warehouse next to the garage for the storage of bulky goods, proved infeasible, so a new facility was constructed some miles distant.[44] Two Ohio stores followed Lazarus's inclination to erect service buildings downtown, if not in so integrated a fashion. In 1949, Halle Brothers opened a seven-story service center to supplement several warehouses as part of a major expansion program for its main building, and a small branch in Shaker Heights. The service center abutted the annex building of the 1920s, and the exterior emphasized a continuity in the store's design that had prevailed since the first section was erected in 1909–10. H. & S. Pogue of Cincinnati, which had built a remote-site facility in the mid-1920s, now opted for a much larger building half a block from the store. Rising eleven stories, the front was elegantly treated in a sleek, modernist vein more suggestive of a company headquarters than a structure devoted to storage, delivery, and repairs (fig. 98).[45] A few remote-site facilities retained the basic multistoried configuration of prewar examples as well. The May Company's Los Angeles building was a primary example even though it was substantially larger and bore none of the refinements common to work of previous decades. J. L. Hudson continued to make major additions to its plant. What had begun in 1916 as a one-story delivery depot had become, by the late 1920s, an immense complex covering the better part of a city block. In 1937–38, a four-story delivery building was added across the street. Less than a decade later, the ensemble received a sizable appendage to the warehouse, which, in turn, was doubled in size within a few years (fig. 99).[46]

The great majority of work, by contrast, differed in a number of basic ways. Sites were not only further afield but larger—often between ten and twenty acres. The buildings themselves were sprawling affairs of one or two stories, enclosing as many as 600,000 square feet. Finally, the movement of goods of all kinds within these walls was accomplished primarily with mechanical devices rather than human exertion. The service building was reinvented in the ongoing effort to improve efficiency and reduce the relentless problem of escalating operational costs. One of the two pioneering examples of this new breed came from Fred Lazarus, who sought to complement the innovations he had brought to service buildings for small-sized goods.

The F. & R. Lazarus Bulk Service Building, as it was called, opened in April 1949, replacing four separate facilities downtown. Manufacturers from across the country came to view what was touted as an important "step in the evolution of the department store." Visiting the premises would not necessarily have led anyone to believe the facility was associated with a great emporium downtown (fig. 100). It lay not far from the city center, but it was isolated on marginal land in a setting more rural than urban. The 250,000-square-foot building appeared nearly limitless in its expanse. A small section in the front was devoted to offices, but most of the vast, horizontal mass was sheathed in unadorned brick with unbroken bands of steel-frame windows just below the roofline. In every respect the design suggested a modern manufacturing plant, not part of a retail enterprise. Lazarus executives would agree. In the words of one observer, it was "looked upon as an operation rather than a building."[47]

Lazarus credited company employees, including those who worked daily in the many jobs associated with the movement of goods, with helping to provide the ideas that led to the plan. But the results were more than a patchwork of novelties. At some point during the planning period, a new concept arose that the traditional multistory warehouse configuration should be discarded in favor of a design that had been used for manufacturing plants since the 1920s and had enjoyed preeminence over the past decade. Goods were not made in the service facility, but their patterns of movement could and indeed should be analogous to those of articles produced on an assembly line. Through a choreographed series of linear progressions a breakthrough could be attained in reducing time and labor. It was no doubt for these reasons that Lazarus went neither to his firm's regular architects in Columbus nor to a retail specialist elsewhere, but to the Cleveland-based Austin Company, an architecture and engineering firm internationally known for its work in buildings devoted to manufacture.[48]

Given these parameters, the siting objectives included a property big enough for goods to be organized laterally, for future expansion, for staging of delivery and transfer trucks, and for visitor and worker parking. Shipments to and from the premises occurred on opposite sides of the building's considerable length to minimize lateral movement. Indoors, goods were to move ("flow" was the popular term of the period) from the receiving side to the delivery and transfer side over the shortest distance possible, preferably in a straight line and never more than the building's width of 242 feet (fig. 101). Traditional practices, which relied on human muscle to move goods in small quantities, came at a high cost in terms of time, damage to merchandise, and strain on employees. To make the process more efficient, handling was kept to a minimum and largely achieved through mechanized equipment: floats (trailers with ladderlike sides that enabled them to be shelved) and dollies (for some appliances) pulled by small tractors, as well as roller conveyers

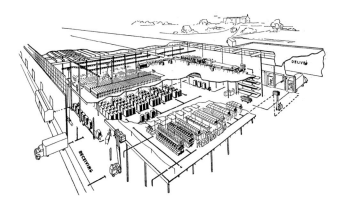

101. Lazarus bulk service building, perspectival section (*Women's Wear Daily*, 7 April 1949, 62).

102. Lazarus bulk service building, interior view of forklift tractor raising float to mezzanine. Photo ca. 1949.

(to speed unloading from freight cars and trailers). Without these devices the lateral configuration of the plant would have been impractical. Storage was on two levels, the upper a mezzanine, to which forklifts transferred goods, still on their floats (fig. 102). This arrangement was devised to preclude the extent of space on one level from being too great while avoiding reliance on freight elevators. Storage space was fluid, with no fixed shelving or other devices that would preclude ready use of an area for different kinds of goods.

Portable shelving was crucial, on the other hand, to maximize space, with just over a two-foot clearance between merchandise and the ceiling. Every item was assigned a location to facilitate accountability and quick retrieval.

To streamline the process further, a large area was set aside for "preprocessing" goods—uncrating and assembling them to ensure swift delivery when they were purchased and also to identify any damage or other flaws. Space was also allocated for customers who chose to pick up items that they could transport easily by vehicle. The concern for natural light and air that had been a driving force in prewar work was replaced by an effort, which now guided factory design generally, to create an artificially controlled environment. Neither this building nor most of those that followed it over the next half dozen years was air conditioned, but they were equipped with sophisticated circulation systems that kept the atmosphere clean and temperate. Natural lighting was replaced primarily by fluorescent tubes on movable tracks that could be arranged to suit merchandise storage, rendering the level of illumination fairly even throughout. The building housed only large items—about a quarter of the store's business—which greatly simplified the movement and storage of goods. Everything else continued to be handled at the 1939 service annex, where items were stored near their respective selling floors. Lazarus considered the new plant to be an experiment but also a model, much as he had conceived Foley's as a paradigm for the modern downtown store. His expectations appear to have been fully met. After a year's operation the facility had reduced handling costs between 10 and 46 percent, depending on the type of merchandise.

An equally important departure was made by Bamberger's new service building, which opened a month after Lazarus's. Located four miles from the store in the center of its most concentrated delivery area, the complex likewise replaced four older plants and was devoted primarily to bulky goods. One-third larger in square footage, the plant was organized on a single floor so that it occupied three times the ground area of the Columbus building. This configuration, combined with a more constrained site, resulted in a slightly more complicated flow pattern for merchandise (fig. 103). But in other key respects the scheme was similar. It was described as an "assembly line warehouse" that used the "Willow Run system," referring to the great Ford Motor Company bomber plant near Detroit of 1941–42. Designed by Abbott, Merkt, the scheme was the result of extensive study, which in all likelihood was done with little or no detailed knowledge of the approach taken for its Columbus counterpart; the parent companies, Macy's and Federated, had no reason to exchange their unorthodox plans before the fact.[49] Like the Lazarus building, too, the scheme received extensive favorable publicity. Their collective impact

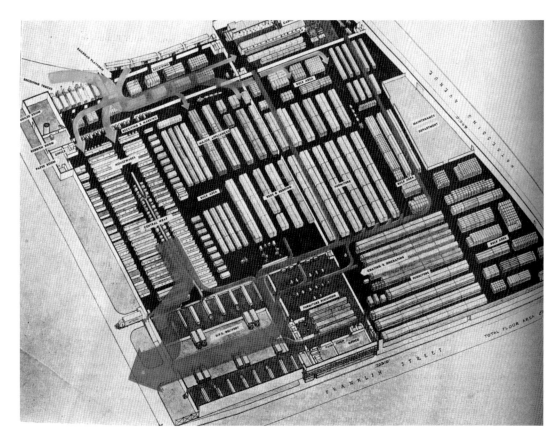

103. Bamberger's service building, Franklin Street and Watsessing Avenue, Bloomfield and Belleville, New Jersey (1947–49). Abbott, Merkt & Company, architects-engineers. Diagram of layout (*Stores,* February 1953, 59).

was substantial. Over the next decade, at least a dozen service complexes were executed along similar lines coast to coast.[50]

Bamberger's new plant was also a boost to its designer, Abbott, Merkt, for it assured the firm a continuing leadership role in the design of service buildings. Over half the new facilities constructed during the postwar era came from the firm, while no others are known to have been done by the Austin Company. Richard Tatlow III assumed presidency of Abbott, Merkt in July 1946, after his discharge from the Army. During the years immediately previous he had been a member of the Construction Advisory Committee of the War Department and then placed in charge of all new industrial plants of the Army's Production Division. Tatlow knew intimately the innovations that had occurred in the design of assembly and other manufacturing plants, as well as storage facilities, and within a year he provided one of the most detailed rationales for the changes that would be manifest in both the Bamberger and Lazarus plants. Most department stores wanted more service space, he argued, but the cost of providing that space was high—twice that of a decade earlier. So space had to be used more efficiently. Techniques and equipment developed or improved during the war years provided the means to realize this efficiency and to cut labor costs. What was needed was careful study of a department store's needs to adapt lessons learned from the war to maximum benefit.[51]

The symbolic role of many prewar service buildings had little place in this equation. The new generation of facilities was, with the exception of small office headhouses, unabashedly utilitarian. The shift to a one- or two-story arrangement was not a primary factor; examples abounded of decorous industrial plants in this configuration from the 1920s and 1930s. Just as with the department store itself, rising construction costs were a major cause of simplification. So were esthetics. A machine-inspired minimalism had been advocated by the modernist avant-garde for a generation. The exigencies of war had helped propel that esthetic into the mainstream, giving it a logic, perhaps even an inevitability, that it had never seemed to have before. In the process, the esthetic became less driven by abstract formalism and more by pragmatism. Industrial buildings of the 1940s and thereafter were heralded as embodiments of progress in this way. Their owners were proud of how they looked—not as buildings but as operations. Even if Mrs. Customer had seen them she probably would not have cared less. She was getting her television, patio furniture, and gas range quicker and in better condition than ever before.

4 Parking for Stores

THE AUTOMOBILE, no less than the delivery truck, at first seemed to be a boon to the department store's business. As retailers found that they could disperse more goods more quickly and over a greater distance with company vehicles during the 1910s, so they discovered that many of their well-heeled customers were beginning to use their cars on shopping expeditions. For the well-to-do, especially women, the car was seen as a liberating device. No longer were shoppers beholden to rail transit or to the slow pace of their carriages. With posh residential enclaves built ever further from the commercial core, the automobile seemed to conquer space—to make the drive of several miles rather easy and to accommodate the demands of a busy personal schedule. At an early date, the car made the department store even more attractive as a place for the affluent to shop.

The early euphoria induced by the automobile among high-end retailers was epitomized by modifications introduced in 1919 when the B. H. Dyas Company moved into its new quarters in downtown Los Angeles. One of the premier sporting goods stores in the region, the company boasted a vast array of camping equipment on its basement level. Dyas pampered male customers by installing a freight elevator that carried them, still in the driver's seat, to a subterranean fantasy, where they could alight from their vehicles in a mock auto campground, where tents and displays were offset by photomurals, and where a log "lodge" offered both a lounge and material on choice destinations (fig. 104).[1] Such an extravagance was conceived under the assumption that only a few patrons would avail themselves of it in a given day and that a sizable portion of them would indulge in costly purchases. But even as Dyas unveiled the theatrical showroom, automobile use was substantially exceeding the levels known prior to World War I. Car ownership was growing at an exponential rate, and cars were being used increasingly for routine transportation needs. "The chariots that rage in the streets," as one chronicler described them, were beginning to revolutionize the daily patterns of many thousands of urban dwellers and in the process transform the shape and function of the places they went.[2]

By the early 1920s, merchants were viewing the advent of widespread automobile use as a formidable challenge, even a curse, rather than the blessing they had believed it to be. Less than three years after the new Dyas store opened, a writer for the *Dry Goods Economist* lamented that in Los Angeles the days of customers parking in front of great emporia were over. The flood of downtown traffic had led to a conspicuous lack of curbside space and also to parking restrictions. Motorists now had to search for a place, generally some blocks from the store, and then had only forty-five minutes in which to walk to the premises, conduct their business, and return. Instead of a leisurely excursion that was seen as conducive to impulse buying, the time frame for shopping was now quite brief, often resulting in no more than a single purchase, which itself might not be made with adequate care due to anxieties over receiving a ticket.[3] The scenario was common in cities nationwide, and department store owners had no idea how to resolve it. The characteristics that had made their great piles ideal for capturing the large pedestrian trade, most of which entered downtown by rail, posed mammoth problems for large numbers of automobiles. The drivers of those cars—the cream of the consumer trade—were among those most irritated by congested streets, parking restrictions, and all the related inconveniences. The change was so swift and intense that no group knew how to address its ramifications. But merchants appear to have been particularly frustrated by traffic issues, which were far removed from those they traditionally handled. New competitors, new management and operational strategies, as well as new expansion programs posed a sizable corpus of challenges; nevertheless, experience gave

You Motor Right Into This Store

104. Ville de Paris and B. H. Dyas stores, Seventh and Olive streets, Los Angeles (1916–17). Diagram of auto access route to camp goods department (*Retail Ledger*, 15 October 1919, 10).

store executives some basis for tackling them. Catering to motorists, on the other hand, was wholly removed from the retailer's purview, making it a source of bewilderment as well as frustration.

Developing solutions for a clientele that immediately grew attached to its cars posed an unending series of problems for merchants. Expedient and extravagant solutions alike were devised, some of them effective in the short term, but the ground gained was inevitably eroded by the ever greater volume of cars. Many downtown store owners felt they were scarcely better off thirty years later. Increases in the scale, complexity, and ambitiousness of off-street parking facilities for shoppers peaked in the 1960s only because downtown store patronage was beginning to stagnate, even wane. Until that downward trend became irreversible, no matter how many spaces for cars were provided, parking remained among the most vexing issues facing department store owners. Contributing to their dilemma were the multiplicity of ways advanced to solve the parking problem, and the frequent shifts in viewpoint that could soon render the latest thinking obsolete or of marginal value. As an issue, parking was a sea of constantly shifting sand.

Traffic

The early 1920s were depicted as years of a traffic-induced crisis for many American cities. Nationally, automobile registration had soared to five times its 1914 level—from 1.6 to 8.2 million in six years. While the largest percentage of car owners lay among the rural population, a sizable portion of urban dwellers embraced driving as a basic mode of conveyance. In many cities, the rise in car registration paralleled or even exceeded the national average.[4] In addition, many inhabitants of towns and rural areas found that the car made urban centers much more accessible, and they more frequently used their vehicles for shopping and other trips. Use of motor trucks also expanded as more and more businesses discovered the efficiencies they afforded. Fewer than eighty-seven thousand trucks were registered in 1914; by 1920, there were more than a million.

The volume of motor vehicles circulating on downtown streets seemed overwhelming to observers. Cities were ill equipped to handle the onslaught. Many streets were narrow, and almost none had any regular means of controlling the flow of traffic—signals and lane divisions were virtually unknown. Negotiating major intersections became slow and arduous. Movement was rendered more difficult by the trolley tracks that occupied the center of many routes, and curb lanes became lined with stationary vehicles. The continued presence of horse-drawn conveyances further slowed traffic. Conditions worsened as the decade progressed: Automobile and truck registrations alike more than doubled between 1920 and 1925 and continued to rise substantially over the following five years. In large cities, increases of twenty thousand to thirty thousand cars were not uncommon between 1925 and 1930.

As traffic congestion grew, motorist frustrations mounted, but drivers continued to enter downtown—for work, for shopping, and for pleasure—expecting to find free parking on the street. The belief that parking was a right, not a privilege, which stemmed from traditions established long before the motor age, held fast despite the obvious impediments. In city after city public officials and civic groups began to develop strategies for overcoming the melee.[5] Toward the decade's end they took on a repertoire of ambitious programs for improving access to and bypasses around downtown; for widening thoroughfares within the core; for building speedier rail transit systems; and for using mechanized signals. Individually or in coalitions, merchants generally supported such measures in the hope that they would make downtown more attractive to their clientele. The issue, however, that elicited their greatest involvement and often their sharpest dissent was the easiest and least expensive to implement, yet also the one that appears to have had the greatest psychological impact on the public's attitude toward continuing to use downtown as the primary retail and entertainment center. That issue was restricting parked vehicles along the streets.

Because parking regulations on public rights-of-way could be issued with dispatch, and because both law enforcement officials and street railway companies often lobbied strenuously for their implementation, they were among the first steps taken to ease downtown traffic. In city after city, ordinances were passed that prohibited curbside parking along major streets during rush hour and eliminated parking near intersections. Provisions also limited parking to a set period of time—usually between thirty minutes and two hours—to facilitate turnover. At first, merchants were the most vocal element in opposing restrictions. Even if many shoppers did not park their cars for long, those who spent the most money were more inclined to take more time. Parking restrictions discouraged going to several stores for comparison shopping. Finally, critics claimed, these limits presented a psychological barrier to the popular concept of downtown as a place of consumer excursion. Yet by the second half of the decade, merchants tended to accept parking ordinances, realizing that conditions would only continue to deteriorate if such measures were not taken.

Furthermore, the clientele to which many lower-middle to middle-market retailers catered did not rely on automobiles for downtown trips; overall, the great majority of shoppers still relied on public transportation.[6]

Where conflict did erupt, however, was over programs calling for the elimination of curbside parking. Probably the first such measure to be implemented was in Los Angeles, but it was substantially modified soon after it took effect in April 1920, as downtown interests protested that it would ruin business and property values. Yet the issue was hardly moot. Within less than four years, the State Conference of Mayors proclaimed that soon all cities would establish such sweeping bans.[7] Syracuse had already taken a major step in that direction.

Launched in January 1924, Syracuse's parking ban illustrated that, however well-intentioned, city officials could be utterly incapable of comprehending the ramifications of widespread automobile use. The premise lacked logic: parking would be prohibited along downtown thoroughfares except on South Salina Street, the main axis of retail development, where congestion was most likely to occur. Merchants not on that street cried favoritism, prompting restrictions on it as well. The chorus of complaints swelled, which led the commissioner of public safety to allow police to enforce the ordinance at their discretion. Chaos ensued, with officers responding in myriad ways and motorists viewing their options akin to those of Russian roulette. The mayor stuck by the parking ban and, as leading merchants mounted pressure, made the extraordinary statement that "it is not a fair spirit . . . to say that trading should be done entirely downtown or to ask that the city concentrate business in the downtown section." Retailers, meanwhile, cited huge losses. Some of the dropoff was attributable to in-town customers who used automobiles by choice, but a substantial share came from clientele in the region, for whom the car facilitated access to the city. At a time when the automobile was extending the radius of trade, retailers claimed, municipal policy was destroying that progress. By mid-October a nonpartisan commission ruled in favor of the merchants' proposed thirty-minute parking limit.[8] Still, the episode, which received national coverage in the retail press, no doubt made many store owners aware of how vulnerable their businesses were to automobile-related issues. Suggestions in other cities that such bans might be tried were met with strenuous opposition from this contingent.[9]

It was thus with great interest and no small degree of trepidation that merchants nationwide followed the boldest experiment in parking restrictions of the interwar decades. Based on an exhaustive ten-month study by Miller McClintock, perhaps the period's most knowledgeable and sophisticated analyst of the automobile's impact on the metropolis, the city of Chicago instituted a parking ban within the

Loop, beginning on 1 January 1928. McClintock argued that for Chicago, at least, the ban would improve business. The great majority of parked cars that so impeded traffic flow belonged to salesmen, not shoppers. Indeed, he claimed that fewer than 2 percent of shoppers actually drove to the Loop. Executives from most of the major State Street stores were compliant, arguing that the plan needed to have a sustained trial run if the results were to be fully known.[10] Despite careful planning and cooperation, the initiative began to lose favor by summer's end. One store owner said that the ban created a "mental barrier" among many shoppers to coming downtown, even if they had not relied on curbside parking previously. Colleagues noted receiving a flood of complaints. The effectiveness of the plan was also questioned. A single stationary truck or taxi could impede traffic flow for an entire block. Statistics gathered toward the end of the year, on the other hand, suggested that the ban was achieving its goal of improving the movement of vehicles. Some proponents of traffic control advocated that it be adopted elsewhere, but such proposals failed to gain general acceptance. Chicago was billed as an exception, in part because several thousand cars could be lodged nearby in Grant Park. Furthermore, one critic noted, the city's premier retail section was no longer defined by the department stores on State Street, but rather by the specialty shops on North Michigan Avenue, where no such ban existed.[11] The Chicago plan represented the most extensive governmental program to control parking patterns in the 1920s. But elsewhere, the time limitations imposed on curbside parking that became commonplace by mid-decade, and ubiquitous a few years later, necessitated alternative solutions to reliance on public rights-of-way for the storage of cars. Numerous experiments were launched, virtually all of them at the instigation of the private sector in a frantic search to maintain business and property values or in an attempt to capitalize on that need.

Buses

Among the ideas that elicited widespread interest was busing. Establishing a system that kept cars away from downtown altogether was deemed highly desirable because its operating costs represented a small fraction of those required to accommodate motorists by any other means. The commercial motor bus was a new phenomenon in the early 1920s but was fast proving itself to be an effective conveyor of people on inner- and intra-city routes alike. Buses did not require the expensive infrastructure of rail lines, and their routes could be easily modified according to shifts in demand. Buses could also reach many residential areas not well served by streetcars or trains. By the end of 1923, merchants in a number of cities, mostly on the East Coast, were calling for the creation of special lines that would terminate downtown. With urban bus depots still few in number and primitive in accommodations, newly formed carriers, jostling for a share of the emerging business, welcomed the opportunity to have a destination that would foster patronage. Among the first bus lines implemented to serve a specific store began in 1925 with a daily express bus from Bridgeport, Connecticut, to Macy's in New York. Operated by a New Haven–based carrier, the trip cost $3.50 and included lunch at the store. Within a few months, Abraham & Straus consummated a similar arrangement, with buses taking sixteen daily trips from Queens and outer sections of Brooklyn. Arnold Constable followed suit, with trips from Stamford and Greenwich, Connecticut; the fare would be halved with a purchase of $10 or more. Other routes serving the big New York stores were established for northern New Jersey.[12]

No other metropolitan area appears to have experienced comparable developments, because in no other place were shoppers so reliant on public transportation to reach the city center. Many of the bus lines to New York proved alternatives to taking the train, not to driving. Yet the bus did offer advantages over cars in linking cities with rural communities at a time when roads were primitive and some small town and farm families harbored inhibitions about urban driving. The great role that the bus could play in making these people regular customers at a major department store is suggested by the ambitious scheme of the St. Louis giant Famous-Barr. In 1926 the store purchased a garage that was modified to accommodate seven bus lines whose routes penetrated the hinterland. Famous-Barr ran a free shuttle over the four-block distance between depot and store and even conducted an advertising campaign on behalf of the participating carriers.[13] The substantial purchase, conversion, and operation costs of the venture seem to have kept it an anomaly, however. In addition, the urban bus depot became an established feature by the decade's close. Led by the fast-rising Greyhound Bus Company, carriers no longer saw an advantage to teaming up with a single or even a few merchants to enhance business.[14]

Still, the bus's utility to the department store could be manifest in other ways. As early as 1920 a carrier persuaded Chicago's Carson, Pirie, Scott & Company to allow it to run a shuttle between the store and two of the city's railroad stations, a service that was said to bolster suburban trade substantially. Washington-based Woodward & Lothrop may have adapted this idea once parking limitations were put into effect there. In October 1923, the emporium began operating a free shuttle bus continuously from 9:15 A.M. to 6 P.M. on a circuit of some eighteen blocks to the north and west of the store, making eight stops where parking remained unrestricted (figs. 105–6). The appeal of the conveyance quickly mounted, with an average of nearly twenty-six thousand people using the bus each month by mid-1925. The

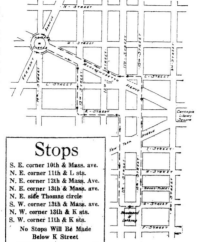

105. Woodward & Lothrop parking shuttle service advertisement, 1923 (*Washington Post*, 27 October 1923, 2).

106. Woodward & Lothrop parking shuttle bus. Photo ca. 1923.

O'Neill Company in Baltimore soon launched a similar program, although it appears to have been short-lived. Toward the decade's end, twenty-six Boston emporia, including all the major department stores, joined forces to subsidize a shuttle between two recently completed parking garages and their establishments.[15] So used, the bus could aid in overcoming consumer fears of entering the central shopping district, but many department store executives seem to have been reluctant to incur the expense, particularly at a time of increased operating costs, stagnant profit margins, and major expansion. As a result, the role of buses remained marginal in the drive to maintain and enhance the patronage of motorists.

Parking

During the 1920s most department stores turned to off-street parking as the primary means of accommodating customers' cars—retailers saw this solution as the most cost-effective, and their clientele saw it as the most convenient. The challenges presented by this course, however, were numerous. The last thing most store owners wanted was to enter the parking business; those that made the commitment did so only because they were convinced they had no viable alternative.

Creating off-street space for cars was difficult in itself. At the outset of the decade most cities had virtually no such accommodations oriented to shoppers.[16] Limited storage capacity existed at garages built for automobile repairs and sales, the majority of which lay some distance from the retail center. Much of the land in proximity to a major department store was too valuable to devote to parking, so the facilities that were developed tended to be several blocks away. Parking lots were the cheapest form of accommodation to create and run, but their holding capacity generated modest returns and thus they made economic sense only where land values were relatively low. With the rise in downtown property values during the 1920s, many parcels devoted to parking were soon acquired for new buildings. Multilevel parking garages also suffered from significant drawbacks: they were costly to construct and did not yield profits commensurate with those of other commercial buildings. These utilitarian structures were mostly erected where demand for more lucrative functions was not strong. Even then, doubts persisted as to their capacity to yield a reasonable return on the investment.

The great majority of off-street parking facilities developed during the 1920s were created by independent entrepreneurs. If one or more of these businesses was established near a department store, the easiest course was to contract

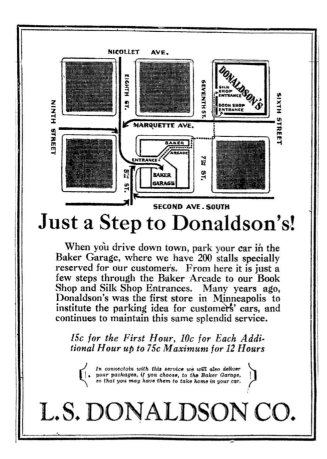

107. L. S. Donaldson Company, Minneapolis, advertisement for customer parking (*Minneapolis Journal*, 20 September 1928, 13).

108. Marshall Field & Company, Chicago, publicity photo of chauffeur service inaugurated in 1925. At left is Charles Pritzlaff, head doorman for several decades. Photo Chicago Architectural Photographing Company, ca. 1925.

with that owner to care for the emporium's clientele. The principal cost to the store was covering some or all of customers' fares. By the late 1920s many department stores had established such relationships with parking lot and garage owners alike, making their clientele well aware of the service through newspaper advertisements and even pamphlets (fig. 107). Some establishments sought to recapture part of their outlay by requiring motorists to pay a fee or make a minimum purchase of goods; others offered the service for free in the belief that the return in sales would justify the expense.[17] In a few cases where off-street parking was not readily at hand and the stores were catering to an affluent clientele, chauffeur service was introduced. Franklin Simon, a large women's apparel store on Fifth Avenue in New York, was among the first to implement this amenity, announcing it less than two weeks before Christmas in 1924. Without charge, a customer could leave her car in the hands of a driver in front of the store. The driver would proceed to Simon's West Side garage, used to house delivery trucks at night, where the car could be serviced, if requested. Vehicles were returned within ten minutes of notification. Response was enthusiastic; some 350 persons availed themselves of the service on the first day. The plan's success may have prompted Marshall Field's to follow suit the following year (fig. 108). To offset the substantial costs, however, Field's charged seventy-five cents for the first hour, and ten cents for each additional one—a hefty fee at that time—which apparently discouraged extensive use.[18]

Relying on the facilities of others may have lessened the demands on a store's management force, but it entailed distinct drawbacks. Parking lots were frequently replaced by new construction in the 1920s, so reliance on them could be chancy. Parking garages were more permanent, but their owners could raise rates or otherwise change the terms of an agreement as demand for the space they offered continued to swell.[19] This factor, coupled with the dearth of large downtown parking structures in most cities until near the decade's end, led many department stores to develop parking facilities of their own. This was the most complicated and costliest means of reconciling motorists' demands, and it was the one store executives were probably the least enthusiastic about adopting, but the fear of losing customers and of being upstaged by competitors led them to embark on such extravagant projects.

A few stores were fortunate enough to secure space for car lots close to the premises. Perhaps the first property dedicated exclusively to customer parking for a department store was unveiled in February 1920 by Wolff & Marx of San Antonio not long before it commenced an aggressive campaign to enlarge its customer base. Encompassing 20,000 square feet on land directly across from the emporium—the newest in the city—this Automobile Park no doubt seemed a remarkable luxury when it opened, and it was the setting for Santa Claus to receive children that December (fig. 109). Three years later, when the Boston Store in Milwaukee opened a lot likewise sited, it still received national coverage as an unusual amenity even though the space was nearly half the size and catered to a much larger emporium.[20] Whatever their cachet, most store-owned car lots were utilitarian in the extreme, without embellishment, framed by the exposed side walls of adjacent buildings, the ground surface graded and graveled but rarely paved (fig. 110). The space alone was an adequate attraction. A pronounced departure from this pattern was manifested in the Auto Parking Station built by Meyer Brothers of Paterson, New Jersey, in 1926. Probably conceived to upstage rival Quackenbush's more than 40,000-square-foot lot opened the previous year, and perhaps also to help keep local residents from patronizing larger stores in Newark and New York, the facility boasted iron gates punctuated by decorative masonry piers and an elaborate waiting room. The ensemble suggested more the entrance to a great country place than a utilitarian staging ground and no doubt played to the pretensions of some customers (fig. 111). Two buses provided a shuttle service over the four-block distance to the store, one leaving either place every ten minutes. While highly popular, the service no doubt represented an extreme in the minds of many store executives who were looking for ways to trim the cost of parking, not inflate it.[21]

Garages

The course that elicited the most attention and the greatest investment among department store executives was constructing a garage. By so doing, a retail firm could ensure permanent quarters for its clientele and could reap revenue from others who took advantage of the facility as well. By this method it was hoped that a garage would at least come close to paying for itself over time. Equally important, the garage would bolster the motorist trade while adding to the store's prestige. Almost no retail businesses other than major department stores could command the capital necessary for such an undertaking; having a garage in one's name was a mark of prominence in the field. The dozen or so companies that took this course during the 1920s were upheld as standard-bearers for the industry. Most projects were for large, multistory structures that held several hundred cars at a time.[22]

109. Wolff & Marx Company department store, 100 East Houston Street, San Antonio (1912–13). Marshall R. Sanguinet and Carl G. Statts, architects. Advertisement for parking (*San Antonio Evening Express*, 16 February 1920, 7).

110. H. Leh & Company parking lot, Allentown, Pennsylvania. Photo late 1920s or early 1930s.

The New Auto Parking Station Free to Patrons

Now Open for Your Convenience and Comfort

On Godwin Street, between Bridge and Washington Streets, with Free De Luxe Auto Bus Service every 10 minutes between Station and Store.

THIS new feature of Meyer Brothers service to customers will be welcome news to those who find it desirable and necessary to do their shopping by automobile—a convenience that will mean quick, safe, comfortable shopping, free from parking worries.

Now you can Park Your Car Free in Meyer Brothers new Auto Parking Station, centrally located on Godwin Street, between Bridge and Washington Streets—easy of access, and take Meyer Brothers Free De Luxe Bus to the store, do your shopping quickly and most satisfactorily, without traffic or parking problems to inconvenience you, and tire you out.

And besides the convenience of the station itself for parking, there are other conveniences which will mean much to your comfort and satisfaction.

Free Parcel Checking Room
Women's Lounging Room
Women's Lavatories
Men's Lavatories

All of which are fitted with the most modern and substantial equipment, and adequately arranged.

Absolutely No Tipping. You will not be annoyed to buy Gas or Oil or Accessories of any kind

And remember it is free to customers, with Free Bus at your service, and uniform attendants to serve you.

So, all customers who shop by automobile and who find it desirable and have not cared to do so on account of the traffic and parking problems, are invited to take advantage of this Free Service, for they will find it most convenient and satisfactory.

All Roads lead to the Free Parking Station and to Pateson's Foremost Store

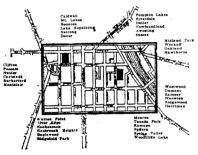

The Lounging Room

WELL appointed for comfort, attractively fitted so as to be a most pleasant meeting and resting place. Here you may await friends or members of your family. There are telephone booths for your convenience.

Parcel Checking Room

IF YOU have packages or bags or bundles, you may check them at the Parking Station Checking Room for safekeeping, without any cost. The convenience will save you much carrying of cumbersome parcels.

The De Luxe Auto Bus

A COMFORTABLE De Luxe Auto Bus will take you to and from the store every ten minutes free of charge. It runs on 10-minute schedule, which assures you no waiting at the Parking Station or at the Store. This Auto Bus is comparable to the finest Auto Buses in service today, with accommodations for a great many passengers. It is Free to customers.

MEYER BROTHERS
Patersons Foremost Store

111. Meyer Brothers "Auto Parking Station," Godwin Street, Paterson, New Jersey (1925–26). Advertisement (*Paterson Morning Call*, 5 April 1926, 7).

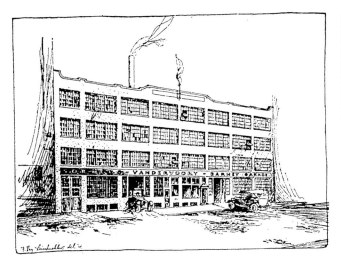

112. Scruggs, Vandervoort & Barney Dry Goods Company garage, St. Charles Street between Eleventh and Twelfth, St. Louis, 1922; demolished ca. 1999. (*St. Louis Globe-Democrat,* 1 January 1922, 14a).

113. Scruggs, Vandervoort & Barney advertisement diagramming garage in relation to the store (*St. Louis Globe-Democrat,* 15 August 1922, 2).

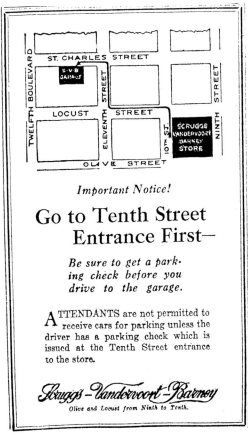

The pioneering venture was announced by Scruggs, Vandervoort & Barney, then the most fashionable St. Louis department store, on 1 January 1922. Opened eight months later, the building featured the latest innovation in garage design: staggered floors connected by ramps. Rising four stories and with a capacity of nearly four hundred cars at a time, the facility also contained two waiting rooms (one for women, the other for chauffeurs) and an automobile accessory shop (fig. 112). Parking was free for the first four hours, with a nominal charge thereafter. The program suffered from some weaknesses, however. Parking was self-service, and although the first two floors were reserved for women drivers, experience soon showed that most of them were loath to perform this task given the dark, confined quarters, as well as the maneuvering characteristics of cars of the period.[23] While the garage lay only two and a half blocks from the store, it fronted a narrow street—in effect an alley. Motorists had to drive to the store first, get a ticket from the "footman," then drive to park their cars and retrace their steps on foot—a routine that advertisements diplomatically had to remind frustrated customers to follow (fig. 113).

Not to be outdone, nearby Famous-Barr announced plans in February 1922 for a six-story pile with space for one thousand cars, which would have made it among the largest in the country. The most innovative feature of the scheme was that half of each floor formed a continuous ramp on which cars could park, minimizing space devoted to circulation. This configuration's experimental nature and the high cost of the project in general probably led to the extensive revisions that were soon introduced to the plan. As realized, the garage was only two stories high and held slightly over two hundred cars. It was farther from the store than was Vandervoort's garage, but chauffeur service relieved patrons of the task of parking. St. Louis's third major department store, Stix, Baer & Fuller, operated a parking lot one block from its premises, which probably opened the same year as the facilities of its two rivals. Five years later the store supplemented this space with the leased floor of a nearby garage.[24] Competition between these emporia reportedly spawned the projects. Vandervoort's assumed it enjoyed the majority of the carriage trade; the store's two leading rivals refused to let it make the claim unchallenged. The situation propelled St. Louis to the forefront of retail accommodations for motorists at mid-decade, but such jousting was not common among department stores in the 1920s. Most of the companies that built garages were alone in their respective cities.

The course taken by four retailers in Seattle was in fact precisely opposite of that of their St. Louis counterparts. In November 1924, two of the city's department stores, the Bon Marche and Rhodes, and two large apparel stores, Fraser-Paterson and MacDougall-Southwick, unveiled plans for the cooperatively run Four Stores Garage (fig. 114). Patrons drove to the structure, which lay within two blocks of all

114. Four Stores Garage, First Avenue and Union Street, Seattle (1924–25). Thomas & Grainger, architects. Opening advertisement (*Seattle Times*, 6 April 1925, 25).

the sponsoring establishments, but could hire a chauffeur to drive them to another destination. Unlike its St. Louis predecessors, this facility was operated as a public garage, with a five-hundred-car capacity. Structural provisions were made for a two-story addition if needed. Nearby property owners could store their automobiles on the premises; anyone else could partake of the service as well. When they made purchases at the sponsoring stores, customers got a substantial rebate, and they could have large packages delivered to the site. Gasoline and oil could be purchased, as was common in commercial garages of the period.[25] The venture set a new standard as a business investment as well as for the conveniences it provided. But most department store executives seem to have been either unwilling to join forces or unable to find a site that was equally beneficial to all participants. Cooperative ventures among the retail giants remained rare over the decades that followed.[26]

During the mid-1920s several department stores individually embarked on building mammoth structures as long-term solutions to the intensifying problem of automobile storage. In Boston, where narrow, winding streets and poor access routes to the main shopping district were more pronounced than in most large cities, Jordan Marsh executives decided by early 1924 that existing arrangements for customers to park free at three commercial garages were insufficient. That June they announced plans for an immense pile, with a five-hundred-car capacity, that would be reserved exclusively for the store's clientele

115. Jordan Marsh Company, Shoppers' Garage, 14–22 Beach Street, Boston (1924–26; altered) (*Boston Globe*, 14 June 1924, 10).

during the day. Site limitations led to the unusual height of eight stories, supplemented by a roof deck for use in good weather (fig. 115). The Shoppers' Garage, as it was called, lay close to the store, and customers who chose not to take the three-minute walk could avail themselves of a shuttle bus.[27] On the other hand, the building fronted a small side street that likely seemed difficult to reach, and the operation was self-service, requiring in many cases the negotiation of multiple levels. Bostonians seemed unfazed by such routines, however, for the equally tall and much larger (two thousand cars) Motor Mart Garage, which opened less than four months after Jordan Marsh's, had the same internal arrangement. Strategically located facing Park Square, with bus service to the fashionable shops nearby in the Back Bay and, later, to the downtown stores (including Jordan Marsh), the Motor Mart was a veritable palace. It looked like a stylishly updated Filene's on the exterior and boasted an array of services and amenities inside.[28] Neither operation appears to have suffered from the lack of assistance in parking.

The Motor Mart was part of a trend toward embellishment that became pronounced during the second half of the decade. Many garage owners came to believe that it was essential to have the facade complement nearby buildings when their establishment was conspicuously located; anything less would be viewed negatively no matter its convenience. The unadorned, utilitarian qualities that characterized many early examples were no longer considered appropriate as the garage business became more firmly established and was held as an important function of the modern urban core.[29] For some department stores, a decorous garage was also seen as good advertising—an emblem of standing among local businesses. The most ambitious schemes in this realm were undertaken by the May Company for its big stores in Cleveland (1925) and Los Angeles (1926–27). The Cleveland garage lay some distance from the store and was used primarily by attendants, who drove female customers' cars from the emporium. On the other hand, it stood directly opposite the ornate Cuyahoga County Court House (1912) on a prominent thoroughfare.[30] While not as imposing as the Motor Mart, the exterior was clearly designed to take advantage of its site and catch the eye of the thousands of motorists who passed it daily (fig. 116). The Los Angeles garage had no civic neighbors but was even more ornamental, setting a local standard for structures of its type.[31]

Finding a suitable location for a department store garage posed considerable challenges; any site more than a few blocks away was perceived as too far removed to attract customers, and use of attendants and shuttles proved an expensive part of the operation. The optimal place was adjacent to the emporium itself, but few companies were situated to build in this way. Many stores occupied most or all of their respective blocks. In other cases, adjacent land could not be purchased, at least not at a suitably low price. Like the service building, the garage was not economically viable on prime downtown lots. A rare exception was the Dayton Company in Minneapolis, which in 1928 built a four-story garage (with a delivery station in the basement) on highly valued land next to its immense store. In harsh Minnesota winters, especially, walking inside from garage to the main shopping floor was a welcome change. Two years later, Daniels & Fisher in Denver followed suit with a rear addition designed to appear as a part of its ornate emporium (fig. 117).[32] In planning new quarters (1926–28) for their Akron store, M. O'Neil, May executives chose a large site on the southern edge of the shopping district with enough space to build not just a much larger retail facility, but also a four-hundred-car garage at the rear (see fig. 7). A year after O'Neil's opened, rival A. Polsky unveiled plans for an elegant emporium across the street that likewise included a rear garage, albeit one of more limited dimensions. These integrated facilities were the exception during the 1920s, but they afforded a model for major downtown building programs over the next thirty years.[33]

By the decade's end, the viability of the department store garage was being questioned despite its appeal among shoppers. The construction costs could run between $250,000 and $500,000. Maintenance, utilities, staffing, insurance, shuttle buses, drivers, and other related expenses contributed to a substantial operating budget, estimated in some cases as being between $30,000 and $40,000 a year. Use at full-market rates by noncustomers of the parent store, auto service and accessory sales, and other means of securing additional income only partly offset the outlay in many cases.

116. May Company parking garage, Lakeside Avenue, Cleveland (1924–25). Lehman & Schmidt, architects; demolished. Opening advertisement (*Cleveland Plain-Dealer*, 21 June 1925, 10-A).

The president of the Rosenbaum Company in Pittsburgh, which transformed its pioneering remote delivery station into a garage in 1925, declared that the project would never pay for itself; it must be considered a luxury. Merchants associations in several large cities, including Columbus, Detroit, Indianapolis, and Pittsburgh, agreed not to provide free parking for their clientele. In 1929 the vice president of the nation's largest builder of garages told retailers that customers were willing to pay commercial rates and should be so charged. The loss otherwise, he calculated, was between fifty cents and a dollar per car, a substantial figure given the average capacity of several hundred cars. A decisive factor in rethinking the issue was the erection of numerous commercial garages beginning in the mid-1920s, which greatly increased options for shoppers. The president of the giant San Francisco–based Emporium dismissed the department

117. Daniels & Fisher Stores Company, Sixteenth and Arapahoe streets, Denver (1910–11). Varian & Sterner, architects. Parking garage added 1929–30; demolished late 1950s. Opening advertisement (*Rocky Mountain News,* 24 August 1930, 7).

118. Halle Brothers Company, Cleveland, parking advertisement (*Cleveland Plain Dealer,* 29 May 1927, 8-B).

store garage as a "passing fad," insisting that the garage business would fully address market needs. Others questioned the willingness of the consuming public, which still clung to the notion that free street parking was an inalienable right, to pay for commercial parking. Garages were underused, they charged, because motorists were unwilling to bear the expense. Whatever one's views, the disturbing reality was that even in cities where major stores offered a parking service of some kind, traffic congestion was no better than in places where stores did not.[34] Halle Brothers, the largest and most fashionable department store in Cleveland, was probably one of many emporia whose leadership steered clear of direct involvement in parking, occasionally advertising the facilities available but dispensing no passes or special rates (fig. 118). The Depression, of course, put an abrupt end to the debate. However, once the economy began to rebound, parking problems arose again, soon with greater intensity, spurring conditions that executives of the big stores could not rely on others to resolve.

Transition

Although the parking problem seemed to diminish significantly during the Depression, appearances were deceiving. Automobile registrations declined for only a brief period—between 1930 and 1933—then quickly surpassed the previous peak. By the close of 1940 the number of cars has risen 13 percent, or over 4 million, during the past ten years.[35] Even more telling was the rate of gasoline consumption; in two years it regained the high it had reached in 1931, and then it grew at the same pace it had during the 1920s. Average miles driven per year rose an estimated 28 percent between 1930 and 1940. As a result, the influx of cars downtown quickly reemerged as a major traffic problem. To make matters worse, curbside parking restrictions often had been minimally enforced in the immediately preceding years, and thousands of motorists were in the habit of ignoring them. Double parking and the omnipresent streetcars added to the quagmire. The public, some observers complained, seemed to assume that such conditions were inevitable. Many merchants still clung to the notion that curbside parking was essential to their businesses. Public officials recognized the problem but were not taking steps to address it.[36]

If downtown traffic seemed as messy as it had a decade previous, it also seemed much more threatening. Beginning in the early 1920s, some critics predicted that congestion would drive businesses from the core. Many small-scale retailers had in fact left the city center, but primarily over spiraling rents, not traffic. In some of the largest cities, a few major stores had established branches in outlying areas toward the decade's end. National chain store companies had targeted such locations as well, and some outlying stores had become sizable. Yet most city centers also continued to grow, many at a feverish pace, with land values sometimes spurred more by speculation than actual demand. Whatever downtown's problems, there seemed no overt signs that it would face a crisis. By the late 1930s, however, the picture was different. Downtown property had declined in value in many cities; new construction was meager, a tiny fraction of what it had been in earlier decades. Many buildings now deemed obsolete were demolished for car lots, which, their owners hoped, would yield some income. Yet improvements to these properties were minimal, and the land was often not well located. Parking lots, which had been seen as a means of alleviating traffic congestion, were now also symbols of the core's failure to rebound.[37] On the other hand, many outlying business districts were again flourishing and new ones were emerging, driven especially by the chains, which were entering ever more lines of the retail field. For the first time, the city center seemed truly threatened. Decentralization, as it was termed, became a preoccupation of downtown business interests nationwide, and traffic problems were considered its root cause.[38]

The outlook for retailers was ominous indeed. In 1939, sales at leading St. Louis department stores were nearly 24 percent below what they had been in 1929, and well below the national average. Over the same period, downtown building and land valuation had dropped one third more than the citywide average. Downtown Kansas City suffered from neglect and disinvestment. Twelve major theaters had closed their doors, and "night life [was] near to the vanishing point."[39] But Detroit was cast as experiencing some of the most acute problems. In 1939, three-quarters of the downtown blocks had at least some vacant land; ninety-six buildings had been demolished in the previous three years, and more were deemed too old to rehabilitate profitably. As in many other cities, much of this newly vacant land was now used for parking, but much of it, too, was on the periphery and not ideally suited for downtown businesses. A shuttle service had been implemented, but not all observers were convinced that such a measure would suffice. Furthermore, at least double the available off-street space was estimated as necessary to meet needs in the foreseeable future. As in St. Louis, downtown department store sales remained significantly below 1920s levels. But in Detroit, neither the stores nor other retail businesses did much to accommodate motorists. In contrast to Los Angeles, which had larger outlying business centers but also a reasonably strong (if not growing) downtown, Detroit epitomized merchants' worst fears of how the city center might actually cease to perform in its traditional role. Its loss caused others to worry that the nation's fifth-largest metropolis would cease to provide the foundation for its own tax base.[40]

Oakland, California, by contrast, was widely hailed as an example of how decentralization could be effectively countered. The Downtown Property Owners Association, formed in September 1931 to stem the impact of the declining economy, had implemented a series of measures to lure shoppers to the core. In nine years the group orchestrated the remodeling of thirty-four buildings (three times the number modernized in St. Louis's much larger core), worked with city officials to reduce property taxes, established six parking lots that shoppers could use without charge, and developed a spirited promotional program. The results were impressive. Ground-floor vacancy rates plunged from 25 percent to 5 percent, and forty-three chain store companies erected or leased new quarters in the district.[41] No other program so underscored the need for a planned, multifaceted approach and for cooperation between the private and public sectors.

By the late 1930s there appears to have been widespread agreement that decisive action was needed on numerous fronts, and that off-street parking was a key factor. Relying on curbside space was now seen as preposterous. Although Chicago was still the only city to impose a downtown ban on street parking, many analysts argued that the measure should be adopted elsewhere. Detailed surveys of traffic and parking conditions needed to be made in places where none had been recently conducted. The location, features, and operation of off-street parking facilities required regulation as part of a comprehensive program to improve conditions for the general welfare. Some parties went so far as to advocate municipal control of parking lots and garages. At the same time, proponents of reform stressed that major generators of traffic—hotels, theaters, office buildings, and department stores—should make their own, complementary parking provisions.[42] Whether or not store executives shared that view, a growing number of them saw that they could no longer remain on the sidelines. Between 1937 and 1941, almost as many new garages designed to serve the big emporia were developed as had been in the entire previous decade, and these were only a prelude to the proliferation that occurred after the war.

Need was not the only factor that propelled the depart-

119. Kaufmann's department store parking garage, Smithfield and Diamond streets, Pittsburgh (1936). Metzger-Richardson Company, designers; demolished 1956. (*Architectural Record,* June 1937, 76.)

ment store garage back into the limelight. A substantially new approach to the design of these buildings reduced their construction costs by around three-fifths, and greatly reduced operating costs as well. Born out of the exigencies of the Depression, the so-called "open-deck" or "wall-less" garage initially consisted of a conventional concrete frame without windows. The prototype was attributed to the Cage Garage in Boston of ca. 1932. Some four years later, a more sophisticated version was introduced for Kaufmann's in Pittsburgh. Announced in August 1936 and operating three and a half months later, the facility could not have offered a more striking contrast to its elaborate forbears. The building was no more than a grid of columns, spaced thirty feet on center, supporting decks that were terminated by low parapets (fig. 119). All parts were exposed to the elements save a stairwell and waiting room. The need for lighting, ventilating, heating, and sprinkler systems was eliminated.

The bare-bones approach taken at Kaufmann's garage was feasible because of changes in automotive technology. Open cars, which constituted slightly under half of those on the road in 1925, were now few and far between in urban areas. Improvements in engine starters, gasoline, batteries, and motor oils, as well as the now common use of antifreeze, permitted cars to be left in the open during cold weather. The open-deck arrangement was accepted by consumers because it was no less convenient than earlier facilities and because of budding interest in minimalist design esthetics.[43] Indeed, such a function-driven scheme was championed in many circles. Kaufmann's structure became the model for countless examples nationwide over the next fifteen years. In its appearance, as well as in its cost, the parking garage was revolutionized.

The impact of Kaufmann's garage on others built by department stores was soon evident. Abbott, Merkt & Company, in an initiative to develop a business in this sphere just as it had done with service buildings, drew closely from the design in plans for the Hecht Company garage in Washington, which were prepared the following year. Not long thereafter, Hecht's rival Woodward & Lothrop built a similar design. Stix, Baer & Fuller did likewise, giving it the most up-to-date facility among its St. Louis competitors.[44] Most of these garages were smaller than the behemoths of the 1920s, with an average capacity of about 275 cars. At the same time, experience was yielding plans in which space could be used to maximum effect. Even when demand warranted, department store owners could be reluctant to build on the scale of the previous decade. Gimbel Brothers commissioned Abbott, Merkt to design a four-hundred-car garage for its Philadelphia store, but it refused to be identified with the operation out of fear that customers who might not get a parking place would be irate.[45] Yet even with this anonymity, store executives wished the structure to be more decorous than Kaufmann's. Eschewing streamlined minimalism, the exterior was composed in a more traditional manner, in concert with the recently built post office nearby (fig. 120). Buffum's in Long Beach, California, likewise opted for an elaboration of the open-deck scheme, with the facade of its Autoport looking as much like a new commercial building as a storage facility for cars.[46]

Not every experiment enjoyed complete success. The three-hundred-car garage integrated into the remaking of the John Shillito store in Cincinnati (1937) provided welcome relief but did not begin to satisfy demand. As a result, the company had to build another structure, with over

120. Gimbel Brothers Thrift Park Garage, Eighth and Chestnut streets, Philadelphia (1940–41). Abbott, Merkt & Company, architects-engineers; Silverman & Levy, consulting architects. Photo author, 1996.

three times the capacity, less than ten years later.[47] On the other hand, the expansion plans of Snellenbergs department store in Philadelphia were programmed into an ingenious scheme. Store executives collaborating with the owners of the block to the south developed a "Building of Tomorrow," with nine stores at ground level surmounted by three parking decks, two enclosed and one on the roof, with a six-hundred-car capacity (fig. 121). Patrons could enter Snellenbergs directly through an inside connection or return to the street to reach the smaller establishments, some of which had complementary functions. At least one additional deck could be added to the ensemble. The tight arrangement necessitated the use of elevators to transport cars, a means that was both slower and more expensive than ramps. On the other hand, the scheme attracted considerable interest as a demonstration of how store parking could be accommodated when property values were high and land was scarce.[48]

Crisis

The war years brought reprieve for cities in the battle to stem traffic congestion, but the hiatus was brief. Car registrations increased by 5 million between 1945 and 1947, then jumped another 10 million during the next three years. The rate of increase slowed somewhat during the 1950s; still, by the decade's close an additional 20 million automobiles were on the road. Urban travel swelled from over 141 million miles to an estimated 195 million between 1941 and 1950 and continued to soar in the years that followed. The impact on cities, especially, was depicted as far more ominous than it had ever been. While a 1946 study by the Urban Land Institute declared that "automobile parking is the most serious problem facing the central business district of large cities today," an analogy offered by a spokesman for Seattle's Municipal League expressed the emotions of many involved: "Downtown property owners, retail stores, theaters and other establishments are now in the position of the Mississippi River bottom farmer standing knee deep in a flood and watching the waters carry away his land wealth. Thousands of automobiles cruising around downtown blocks, backing in and out . . . constitute a menace to the very prosperity of the city."[49] There was no dearth of ideas. Municipal governments, civic groups, and business associations coast to coast called for decisive action. Detailed studies of how and where to place stationary automobiles abounded within a few years' time. There was no dearth of experts. Increasing legions of planners, highway engineers, and even architects became authorities on traffic and parking problems. Yet by the early 1950s, the situation still seemed to be worsening. Kenneth Welch, long a prominent figure in store layout and now a leader in the planning of regional shopping centers, went so far as to declare the situation insoluble.[50] Motorists held hard to their habit of expecting to park close to a destination. Around one thousand feet was considered the limit of tolerance—and considerably shorter distances posited as optimal—for shoppers, even in large cities.[51] There were numerous accounts of consumers who traveled to the urban center infrequently or not at all because conditions were perceived as too inconvenient.

Effective countermeasures were inhibited in many cities as public officials and business disagreed over how to solve the parking problem. By the mid-1940s a growing contingent of planners and other municipal authorities had come to believe that a public-run parking program was the only sound means of addressing needs. Such programs had existed since the 1920s, but they were relatively few in number and primarily confined to small cities and towns. Now the approach was advanced as an essential one for major urban centers as well. Since the very life of downtown depended on adequate parking accommodations, those accommodations were no less a public responsibility than streets. Only municipal government was equipped to address the formidable challenges of comprehensive planning and site acquisition. Furthermore, cities could operate garages and lots as a public service at minimal cost to patrons—a cost

121. Stephen Girard Center, Chestnut Street between Eleventh and Twelfth, Philadelphia (1939–41). Ballinger Company, architects-engineers; altered. (*Women's Wear Daily,* 5 January 1940, 45.)

much lower than the private sector charged—or indeed at no cost at all.

If anyone doubted the imperative of municipal parking, proponents were quick to note, the private sector provided all the evidence that was needed. Many parking facilities, especially lots, were operated on a strictly temporary basis. They were often ill kept and poorly situated. Operators were bound to charge the highest prices they could and thus worked for scarcity rather than abundance of parking space. Despite having more than twenty years to address parking needs, the industry had failed miserably. Parking facilities were not optimal business investments, critics charged, and so they did not attract adequate capital. Often the implication, at least, was that those so engaged had less than sterling credentials. This viewpoint attracted a growing contingent of followers through the early 1950s. H. Stanley Marcus, then executive vice president of Neiman-Marcus in Dallas, was among the first prominent retailers to advocate such a course in the public forum.[52]

But many colleagues disagreed. Business interests generally tended to take a dim view of government usurping private enterprise. In 1956, the senior vice president of Woodward & Lothrop declared: "Let us not be lulled into the belief that parking is primarily a matter of public interest. . . . If we work with the parking industry, free enterprise will assure adequate parking space for everyone at a reasonable price." Some proponents of this view allowed that parking might be subject to a degree of public oversight and regulation, as was done with utilities, but it should not be government operated. The most vocal opponents, not surprisingly, were the owners of parking garages and lots. In a campaign to further their position and in the process improve industry standards, the National Parking Association was formed in 1952. NPA advocates stressed that members could rise to the occasion if given the chance. Owners were now focusing more on analyzing sites and on the potential market, as well as on lowering construction and operating costs. Privately run garages and lots were improving in the service they offered as well. Investment in new facilities and in upgrading old ones had been stymied, they claimed, by plans for government takeover. Municipalities charged less for parking because they paid no taxes. The loss to the tax base, as well as the monies encumbered by construction and operation, was an expense borne by everyone, even though only the motorists benefited directly. The business should be left in the hands of professionals, not bureaucrats, they maintained.[53] Even more neutral accounts stressed that by the early 1950s planning had made the garage industry a profitable one. The huge structures of the late 1920s were too expensive to build and certainly to operate. More than a few owners of these piles had been forced to declare bankruptcy during the Depression. The parking industry could not be judged on this record, but rather on what it was able to accomplish now.[54]

Ultimately, neither approach attained national dominance. Public programs were adopted in a number of large cities, including Pittsburgh (1946), Rochester (1947), and Chicago (1952), while in others the private sector became the driving force. Whatever strengths or weaknesses each sector possessed in the abstract, the crucial decisions seem to have been predicated on local circumstances. Some municipalities proved eager and able to assume this major new responsibility. Others were more reluctant, intimidated by the substantial costs, among other factors. The private sector proved capable of earning the public trust in many cases, but by no means all. By the mid-1950s the debate had subsided; a commitment to one or the other course had been made in most cities, and the task of building to meet the still growing need was well under way. Yet the complex task of determining who would meet the challenges of off-street parking and who would pay for such accommodations led to frequent delays in those building programs and exacerbated the problems that both contingents wanted to solve.

Under the circumstances, it is not surprising that many department store executives realized that they would have to take the initiative on their own. A few observers of the trade still questioned the need to cater to motorists. As late as 1950 the editors of the *Department Store Economist* insisted that the fraction of people coming to the big emporia by car was so small as to be negligible. Retailers should instead focus on ways to improve public transit, which continued to carry the great majority of patrons. But by far the more prevalent view was that off-street parking facilities were critical to a profitable merchandising plan. One department store owner noted: "I place a fixed value of $20,000 per year in sales on each parking stall I provide for my customers. . . . I figure that the 75 cents per car space per day it costs me is equivalent to only one per cent of the sales that car space generates." Another study cited by the NPA estimated that each stall generated a third again as much in sales.[55] Rapidly mounting delivery costs also entered the equation. Shoppers in outlying areas were used to taking purchases home in their cars. Adequate parking downtown would facilitate that process, reducing deliveries perhaps by two-thirds or more.[56] Such figures gave reason for an unprecedented construction campaign of store-owned facilities. Between 1946 and 1951 alone, well before most municipal programs in large cities had begun any actual projects, as many garages were built for the big emporia as had been constructed throughout the 1920s. Nor did the pace slow over the ensuing years as the public and private sectors alike launched more programs. Parking for department stores became a big business, but more as an extension of individual merchandising programs than as part of larger parking networks.

Proliferation

Well before the war's end the parking crisis that would follow was anticipated by some department store executives, who took what limited measures they could to prepare for it. In 1944, Richmond's Miller & Rhoads purchased an elaborate 375-car garage of the 1920s and soon began securing adjacent land for eventual expansion.[57] That fall, Bamberger's launched a two-year program to develop a chain of seven car lots that would ring its big Newark store. Called Bamparks, the parcels were improved with paved surfaces; boundary rail fences and landscaping; discrete ornamental signs; and embellished kiosks—all designed in a manner that "suggests the atmosphere of old Williamsburg." The lots held a total of a thousand cars, probably the most that any department store could hold on its own. The lots were available to all, but Bamberger patrons received reduced fees, and the locations clearly favored that clientele. Trumpeted as "New Jersey's finest parking service," Bamparks were aggressively marketed, with signs along main routes to the city and advertising prominently featured in the newspapers of outlying communities.[58] At a time when car lots were still generally considered expedient and utilitarian cuts in the urban fabric, Bamberger's celebrated them as civic assets, setting a new and probably influential standard for the parking industry.

The following year, A. Harris of Dallas created a no less innovative scheme. Rather than attempting to carve out parcels in the dense business core, whose narrow streets exacerbated congestion, Harris executives developed a large lot some seven blocks to the north and provided a free shuttle service every five minutes (fig. 122).[59] This fringe parking concept had already been inaugurated in Chicago on the initiative of the State Street Council, using existing lots outside the Loop and a private carrier, capitalizing on many residents' habit of taking public transit to the city's core.[60] Harris's project differed in two ways: it was entirely run by the store and was in a city where motorists took a dim view of buses. Acceptance took more than six months, but eventually the service won steady patronage. With a waiting room and service station, the five-hundred-car lot was touted as a model for the fringe-parking concept. The scheme never achieved widespread acceptance, however, owing to the belief among retailers that motorists would resist leaving their cars so long before arriving at the store.[61]

Between the mid-1940s and mid-1950s, most purpose-built parking facilities developed by department stores were variations on the open-deck design pioneered by Kaufmann's. The garages of the postwar generation were larger than those of earlier decades; space for four hundred to five hundred cars was not uncommon. Often, too, attempts were made to give exteriors a more distinctive presence. Federated Department Stores set the pace with two enormous garages for John Shillito in Cincinnati and F. & R. Lazarus in Columbus, both of which opened in 1947. The capacity of each was around 750 cars in marked spaces and another 250 in the aisles—equaling the behemoths of the pre-Depression years. Yet their large floor plates kept the number of levels to four, minimizing movement on ramps and facilitating quick retrieval. Lazarus's garage, especially, embodied this idea of efficient horizontality in its sleek profile, its curved ends offering a poetic response to the triangular lot, its great length displayed to striking advantage along the banks of the Scioto River (fig. 123). This facility soon proved insufficient, however, and a second garage with a 550-car capacity was erected in 1953. Over the next eight years Lazarus expanded its second unit and built two more—all located within two blocks of the store. The ensemble could house some three thousand cars, a capacity that rivaled those of regional shopping centers and probably exceeded that of any other downtown store.[62] The ambitious program was possible because, with the store's site near the edge of the city center and few new construction projects in the works, ample inexpensive land lay close by.

The conditions that favored Lazarus were by no means uncommon in the urban core, and they were crucial in the multiplying of garages during the postwar era. Before then, property owners and planners alike had hoped that the decline in downtown land values was a momentary affair, wrought by the Depression and perpetuated by traffic, and that soon a new rush for parcels on which to erect large buildings would occur. In fact, few such projects were realized during the late 1940s and 1950s in most city centers. But if downtown was not going to grow at the rapacious rate it had in the 1920s, some of the land could be profitably used to further sustain important operations already there. New municipal regulations encouraged the shift. Beginning with Los Angeles in 1946, a number of cities enacted zoning

122. A. Harris & Company Parking Center, Munger between North Akard and Field streets, Dallas (1947) (*Off-Street Parking*, 32).

123. F. & R. Lazarus Company, Town Street Garage, Riverside Drive, Town, and Ludlow streets, Columbus (1947). Potter, Tyler & Martin, architects; altered.

provisions that stipulated off-street parking accommodations on or close to the premises for all new buildings whose functions were considered significant generators of automobile traffic—including hotels, office blocks, and department stores.[63] The primary argument behind such moves was to curb the growth of traffic, but these widely accepted measures helped legitimize parking as a planned land use among the business community.

Federated also set an important example for integrated parking in the design of Foley's, the immense new Houston store that was enthusiastically presented as a national model. Like O'Neil's twenty years earlier, Foley's was erected on a site several blocks from the heart of the shopping district, where ample acreage could be procured at a reasonable price. Yet the Houston garage was much larger than its Ohio precursors, occupying half a city block directly

124. Foley's Garage, Travis, Lamar, and Milan streets, Houston (1945–47). Kenneth Franzheim, architect; demolished. Photo ca. 1949.

across the street from the rear of the store, rising five decks above ground level, with a capacity of around six hundred cars (fig. 124). Below ground lay parallel connections to the emporium, one for garage patrons who wished shelter, the other for merchandise entering and leaving from the service facility in the garage's basement.[64] In its size, siting, and uses the structure was treated as a key component of the retail operation, and in this respect it was no doubt more influential on postwar practices than were the few integrated schemes that preceded it. Indeed, between 1948 and 1960, at least eighteen department store companies erected garages adjacent to, sometimes directly connected with, their plants. J. Goldsmith & Sons in Memphis (1953) had an underground link and service facility; the Golden Rule in St. Paul (1955) and a new Kaufmann's garage in Pittsburgh (1955–56) had bridges. O'Neil's expanded its 1920s facility twice, in 1947 and in 1954. Five years later, Dayton's replaced its 1920s garage with a much larger one, which held nearly 750 cars.[65] A scheme that was especially poignant in reflecting the changes then under way in the retail core was a 600-car garage built in 1959 for Abraham & Straus. To make room for the structure, the Brooklyn company purchased and demolished the adjacent, recently defunct Namm-Loeser department store.[66] Along Fulton Street, one of the nation's best-known retail corridors, parking now enjoyed center stage.

As the size and prominence of new department store parking garages increased, new avenues were explored to bolster the return of the investment. By the time it opened, Abraham & Straus's facility was one of many that contained retail outlets (in this case, the store's furniture showroom) at street level. Even with the slow rate of business development that characterized most city centers of the period, a strategically placed site still offered opportunities for modest expansion. Automobile accessory stores had been placed at street level in some department store garages since the 1920s, Foley's being one of the latest examples. However, incorporating businesses that drew from the pedestrian trade generally was new. Miller & Rhoads in Richmond undertook what was perhaps the first such venture. To realize a program that more than doubled the capacity of the enclosed garage purchased in 1946, the store entered a partnership with its rival, Thalheimer Brothers, whose building lay directly across the street from the site. In this strategic location, street-level stores not only provided an additional source of revenue, they enhanced the specialized shopping atmosphere of the precinct. At the same time, the J. L. Hudson Company erected an immense (850-car) facility, occupying an entire block in garage-starved Detroit. The structure was a short distance from the emporium it served, along a secondary shopping street that enjoyed an active trade in convenience goods. As a result, the fourteen stores housed in the building catered to routine needs—a mix that was no doubt appreciated by many Hudson patrons as they returned to their cars but was also targeted to a large in-town clientele.[67]

Not all department stores were able to gain capacious quarters for parking. ZCMI's holdings in Salt Lake City were among the most constrained, as its building was hemmed in by other commercial enterprises. Meeting these challenges led to a striking, innovative design that was also an important testing ground for other ways to bring economy to parking operations without compromising customer service. Erected between July and October 1954, ZCMI's Parking Terrace stood in the block's interior, at the rear of the store, and was reached by a narrow two-way passage. An old service building on the site was partially demolished, but a new one had to be constructed at ground level—without interrupting operations—before the decks that would hold more than five hundred cars could be set above. Structurally, the solution was a tour de force, with two staggered, interlocking sections connected by ramps in the middle and at both ends (fig. 125).[68] Each section was supported by only twenty pre-stressed concrete columns, fifty feet in height and configured somewhat like lozenges (four feet wide, ten to eighteen inches deep) to minimize intrusion on parking space. Once in place, the columns were tied by steel beams that in turn provided the anchors for the formwork of the

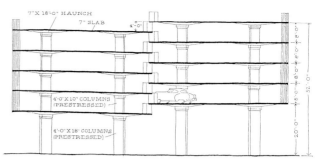

125. *(above)* ZCMI Parking Terrace, Regent Street, Salt Lake City (1954). Bowen, Rule & Bowen, engineers; demolished. Section (*Architectural Forum*, May 1955, 165).

126. *(left)* ZCMI Parking Terrace, exterior view (*Architectural Forum*, May 1955, 164).

five levels of concrete floor slab. Experimenting with models led to precision placement of reinforcing bars, a process that enabled the decks to be unusually thin, thereby reducing floor-to-floor dimensions. The height between the first and fifth decks in each section was only thirty-two feet—a key factor in minimizing the incline of and the space occupied by the ramps. On the perimeter, the thinness of the decks was accentuated by a sawtooth profile and the absence of parapets, the edges defined instead by thin, closely spaced steel rods (fig. 126). While most customers would never see this animated manipulation of structure from the outside, they would experience the effect of openness and light within. They would further benefit from the ease of angle parking and from a location that allowed direct entrances from the decks to the second, third, and fourth floors of the store. Unlike many predecessors, the Parking Terrace was designed for motorists to park their own cars.

Self- or self-service parking remained limited in the mid-1950s. For garages and lots alike, attendant parking allowed for substantially higher capacities. Most motorists, furthermore, disliked maneuvering cars in the enclosed structures of the pre-Depression years. Among department stores, which placed so much emphasis on customer service in all areas of merchandising, attendant parking was long the dominant form. Yet by the early 1950s, conditions were beginning to change. Escalating labor costs made staffing an ever-greater operational burden. A 550-car garage required between twenty and thirty attendants for full service. Furthermore, garages oriented to shoppers faced relatively short peak periods of incoming and outgoing cars. Adequate attendant staffing for these periods left many employees idle the rest of the time, while fewer attendants promised prolonged car retrievals, which annoyed patrons. With staff-ing costs as high as 40 percent of gross income by the early 1950s, parking facility operators were eager to find alternatives to maintaining or creating a large workforce. When customers were left on their own, the primary staffing need was cashiers at exit booths. Equally important, self-service greatly enhanced turnover, so that while attendants enabled more cars to park at a given time, self-service could raise overall capacity on a daily basis. Since short-term parking was the most lucrative kind, the impact on revenue could be significant, which in turn helped keep fares competitive. Operators also discovered that in parking lots, at least, many motorists preferred to be left on their own, alleviating worries about vehicle damage, lost keys, and slow retrieval.[69]

In the mid-1950s, the great majority of self-service operations lay removed from the city center and were on open lots. The proliferation of supermarkets before and after World War II was often cited as a factor that got many women customers acclimated to self-parking away from the curb, but it had also been a standard feature at most department store branches since the late 1920s. Through both types of outlets, self-parking came to be seen as a convenience rather than a chore. It was the department store, too, that appears to have been instrumental in introducing customers to self-parking in a garage, the pioneering examples of which were likewise in outlying areas, not downtown.[70]

A decisive step was taken in 1950 by the Hecht Company of Washington to overcome the limited acreage available at what was otherwise considered a prime site in Arlington County, Virginia, some four miles west of the city center. While the branch planned was 300,000 square feet, then one of the largest in the country, and would serve as anchor to a thirty-store complex, the tract was a mere fifteen acres, far too small to accommodate surface parking. To resolve

127. Parkington shopping center, Randolph Street between Glebe Road and Wilson Boulevard, Arlington, Virginia (1950–51). Abbott, Merkt & Company and Kahn & Jacobs, associated architects. Department store altered, other components demolished ca. 1985.

this impediment, Hecht's took the risk of departing radically from convention and relying on a multideck parking garage for most of the required spaces (fig. 127). Reputedly possessing the largest square footage of any such structure in the world, the four-deck behemoth held at least sixteen hundred cars. Attendant parking never seems to have been seriously considered, given the high cost and the customer expectation of self-parking in outlying locations. At the same time, every measure was taken to make the garage appealing to customers. Straight ramps ran to each deck outside so that motorists would not have to negotiate curving ones on the inside. Each deck had a direct connection to the department store. The distance most customers would have to walk, accounts emphasized, was no more than three hundred feet, and the path was sheltered from the elements. To underscore the garage as an amenity, Hecht's executives christened the complex "Parkington," trumpeting that the garage was "so far ahead of its time, it . . . let[s] you park on the floor you shop on."[71] Although the pathbreaking introduction of self-parking to a garage of this scale was downplayed, no doubt to avoid any consumer inhibition over a novel practice, the scheme set a key precedent for downtown projects and also for branches, whose spiraling client base demanded ever more space in which to store their vehicles.[72]

The innovations that department stores brought to the design and operation of parking facilities were, of course, generated by their own needs. Despite the widespread anxieties over the future of the urban core and the viability of its businesses, department store executives did not always view their concerns as synonymous with those of others. Many cooperative efforts failed to attract the participation, let alone the leadership, of the big emporia. Washington's Park & Shop plan was among the most ambitious venture of this kind, with some one hundred merchants covering the costs for shopper parking at over twenty-five thousand existing spaces downtown. Still, the city's major department stores, two of which had their own garages, ignored the campaign out of the belief that they would be subsidizing the smaller enterprises. Similar attitudes prevailed in nearby Baltimore.[73] Some major retailers were responsive elsewhere, but usually toward a specific new project rather than a comprehensive plan.[74] Thus, in their pursuit of solutions to parking, department store executives tended to act more as lone wolves than as collaborators in a broad initiative.

Two notable exceptions to this pattern occurred during the postwar years. In 1953 Downtown Parking was incorporated in Milwaukee, spearheaded by executives of the Boston Store, Gimbel Brothers, and three large banks. An offshoot of the Milwaukee Downtown Association, the group was formed to develop a comprehensive network of facilities. The initiative was triggered by four large shopping centers that were either in the planning or construction stages and threatened to become a substantial drain on trade by mid-decade. Parking facilities downtown, on the other hand, were considered poorly located, operated, and maintained. Capitalized with donations from the organizers and stock available to all downtown merchants, the corporation soon engaged the Los Angeles–based Systems Auto Parks

Garages to manage a chain of nine city-owned and around eleven privately owned lots. In addition, a large area on the lakefront was targeted for all-day parking. Within two years, fifteen hundred spaces were controlled by the organization, whose leaders eventually hoped to dominate the field. Inspired by the Oakland merchants' program, begun over two decades previous, the scheme was widely heralded as a model of its kind.[75]

An even more aggressive parking program was launched some years earlier in Pittsburgh. Conceived as an integral part of that city's much-heralded redevelopment campaign, the initiative created the Public Parking Authority of Pittsburgh in 1947. Using revenues from parking meters, the agency floated bonds to build a network of garages, the operation of which was conducted by experienced commercial firms. By mid-1953, two garages with a combined capacity of over fourteen hundred cars were in business, and the nearly nine-hundred-car underground garage at Mellon Square was under construction. Edgar Kaufmann, who was active in many facets of the city's renewal and served as a member of the Urban Redevelopment Authority, appears to have played a prominent role in fostering merchant cooperation. At the close of 1955, the Parking Authority announced that it would purchase the existing Kaufmann's garage and replace it with a much larger (seven-deck, 830-car) structure, which it would in turn lease to the store (fig. 128). Not long thereafter, plans were made for a second garage with a somewhat smaller (500-car) capacity, located two blocks away. Opened in 1956, the pair ranked among the most advanced of their kind, with layouts designed to facilitate self-parking, using space efficiently, but also more generously than was possible with their ZCMI precursor. Kaufmann's was not the only department store to collaborate with the Parking Authority. The same year as Kaufmann's garages opened, Joseph Horne Company embarked on a similar venture, with a 650-car structure located adjacent to its emporium.[76]

With this triad and other authority garages, Pittsburgh's motorist shoppers were as well accommodated as any in the United States at the decade's end. Indeed, probably no other city had taken so many steps in this arena to support its downtown's traditional role as the metropolitan retail core. Yet like so many other store parking programs, Pittsburgh's remained distinguished more by its singularity than by its influence.[77] During the late 1950s and the opening years of the next decade, most department stores that expanded in this sphere built their own facilities. The scale of Pittsburgh's garages, however, was no longer unusual. With the swift rise of the regional shopping center during this same period, retailers became convinced that their downtown emporia would remain competitive only if accommodations for the motorist reached epic proportions.

128. Kaufmann's Diamond Street Garage, Smithfield and Diamond streets, Pittsburgh (1955–56). Hoffman & Crumpton, architects.

Climax

The revived trend toward giantism in garages was propelled by an underlying belief among many merchants, property owners, and others heavily invested in the urban core that the parking dilemma could be resolved and, more importantly, that it was worth resolving. By the mid-1950s observers began to assert that the specter of decentralization posited in the 1930s and again with renewed vigor during the postwar years was not nearly as ominous as believed. Outlying areas were growing faster than the city center, but that did not mean that the core was headed for extinction. Downtown still performed vital functions for a metropolitan area and would continue to do so long into the future.[78] Adequate parking and other measures could not reverse decentralization; the boom in outlying commercial centers, including regional shopping malls, made that situation readily apparent. But decisive measures were essential if downtown was to remain competitive. To do that, the scale of accommodations found at new shopping centers must be created in the core.

An important model for parking facilities of this kind was the Downtown Center Garage in San Francisco, which opened in 1954, about a month's after ZCMI's garage. A speculative venture erected to serve a large number of

105

129. Bon Marche Third Avenue & Pine Street Garage, Third Avenue, Pine, and Stewart streets, Seattle (1958–60). George Applegarth, architect. Photo author, 2004.

130. J. L. Brandeis & Sons garage, Seventeenth and Douglas streets, Omaha (1959–61). Photo author, 1996.

stores, theaters, and other businesses, the structure rose eleven levels and could hold twelve hundred cars. Since all parking was self-service, the size of the facility had few precedents, save the Hecht Company's Parkington. The great volume of traffic served, combined with the minimal staffing required, enabled its operators to keep fares low. Vehicular movement was facilitated by a double circular ramp placed at one corner that separated in- and outbound cars and also kept vertical passage apart from the maneuvers of those entering and leaving stalls. The scheme proved appealing and profitable; it was also relentlessly promoted by its operators. The parking industry considered the garage a major breakthrough.[79] Department store executives took careful note.

Four years later Seattle's Bon Marche unveiled plans for a nearly identical structure by the same architect. When it opened in March 1960, the garage was trumpeted as the "finest . . . in the world," with a thirteen-hundred-car capacity (fig. 129). Advertisements spared no superlatives: "You'll find nothing like it in New York, Chicago or Los Angeles . . . in London, Paris, Brussels or Rome. . . . [It] DOUBLES the parking [capacity] in your central downtown shopping area. And it's fast. Two minutes after you drive in, you've parked and locked your car and have been whisked by elevators to the very heart of Seattle's shopping . . . district. . . . —just a step away from The Bon Marche." An enclosed bridge, dramatically poised at the seventh level, spanned the considerable width of Third Avenue to enable patrons to enter the store "without ever going out doors!" The parking behemoth transformed the emporium into a "drive-in department store," no less accessible, it was implied, than the company's big branch at Northgate, the nation's first regional shopping mall.[80] And, much like the immense car lot at Northgate, the downtown garage was scaled to support more than the Bon Marche. Patrons making a purchase at any of nearly one hundred stores were entitled to an hour's free parking.

No other department store matched the size of the Bon Marche's garage, but some seemed no less like leviathans in their respective settings. J. L. Brandeis's 653-car garage all but overwhelmed the venerable Omaha store to which it was added in 1960–61. Above a drive-in bank and other facilities at ground level, six decks rose and projected for a third of their length over the intervening street to connect to the store in much the same way as occurred at Parkington (fig. 130).[81] Even in the dense core of St. Louis and with a design intended to harmonize with the immense parent store, Famous-Barr's new garage of 1960–62 had a strong presence. Its proud owners boasted that the ten-level, eight-hundred-car structure was the largest building erected in the urban core since the 1920s. May Company officials stressed that the project was closely tied to other downtown renewal projects—upper-income high-rise housing complexes, the

Jefferson National Expansion Memorial, and Busch Stadium. As part of a multimillion-dollar renovation program begun three years earlier, the scheme was considered a symbol of faith and optimism. The store's general manager was confident that the garage would "provide women shoppers with the same easy access to their automobiles at our downtown store as they would have from the parking lot of a suburban branch store" (fig. 131).[82]

But for customers who resided on the urban periphery, a drive to the core of St. Louis was not the same as one to Clayton or to other outlying retail centers. Highway, and soon freeway, construction enabled many others who lived between the two to drive in an outbound direction no less swiftly than to make the traditional pilgrimage to the city center. Even when people came downtown they still faced crowded streets. And for all the praise its owners gave it, Famous-Barr's immense garage, like many others of its kind, required careful maneuvering and probably seemed ominous even to seasoned motorists. Once drivers found a space, walking to the elevator or stairs, descending to the third level, and then proceeding to the bridge that connected to the store was perhaps equally inhibiting from a psychological standpoint. True, Famous-Barr's big Clayton and bigger Southtown branches had vast car lots that had to be negotiated behind the wheel and on foot, and getting to those lots often entailed driving through high volumes of traffic, but the perception, at least, was one of greater ease, and often the reality was as that well. For these and other reasons the attempts to maintain a balance between downtown and branch stores was generally doomed to failure. Ironically, the downtown parking problem began to be solved not because garages and other infrastructural improvements were meeting demands, but because the increase in those demands was now directed primarily to outlying areas.[83] Downtown, by contrast, was in decline. The Famous-Barr garage was among the last of its kind because the need for such behemoths had, at best, stabilized, whereas the need for investment in branch development continued to intensify. The parking problem did not go away; it merely created mischief in different places.

131. Famous-Barr Company parking garage, Sixth, Seventh, Olive, and Pine streets, St. Louis (1960–62). Schwarz & Van Hoefen, architects. Opening advertisement (*St. Louis Globe-Democrat*, 8 October 1962, 18A).

5 Branch Stores

SPEAKING BEFORE the National Retail Dry Goods Association's annual meeting in the early months of 1926, John Ihlder, manager of the Civic Development Department of the U.S. Chamber of Commerce in Washington, was supremely confident about the department store's future. Like most of those in the audience, he predicted that the department store would continue to expand, but he differed from the majority in his vision of the form that process would take. Bigger and bigger stores was not the solution; they "can become top heavy . . . eating up . . . profits" as a result. "Merchants will find it increasingly harder to confine their expansion to one spot and still prevent their business from outgrowing itself." A much more effective way to grow, he said, was through the "establishment of smaller units in the neighborhood communities." The lateral growth of cities that was already a pronounced trend would continue, even accelerate. The department store, he argued, should likewise cast itself into multiple parts; it made no sense simply to enlarge what were already behemoths.[1] Ihlder was off the mark is forecasting that high-end stores would just remain in the city center, but in other respects his prediction was strikingly accurate.

Few merchants listening to Ihlder's remarks would have been so confident. For them, the future was anything but clear, and the matter of branch store development ranked among the most vexing challenges. Charles Mears, a Cleveland-based marketing consultant, no doubt expressed the frustrations of many retailers in an address he gave before the Executive Club in Chicago the following year. The current business situation, he suggested, was analogous to a tornado: "Nothing else could so adequately represent the present movement in its speed, its power, its wreckage and its enveloping cloud of dust." The growth of large shopping districts in outlying areas posed one of the most serious of many problems that department store executives were facing, he noted, but he offered no hint of what might be done to address the situation.[2] A survey conducted some months earlier by *Women's Wear Daily*, polling executives of major stores in seventeen large cities, revealed that little branch development had occurred aside from a few businesses headquartered in Boston, New York, and San Francisco. Most importantly, merchant responses gave scant indication that the situation would change soon, if at all. Representatives of Chicago department stores, for example, were "loath to believe that they will have to open up suburban branches. . . . [because] the cost of operating such an establishment would be excessive and out of all proportion to the results."[3]

The fast-paced growth of metropolitan areas, the emergence of business centers well removed from downtown, and the traffic and parking problems that plagued the urban core prompted such discussions, but the concept of branch store development seemed daunting because it was so expensive. A branch store of substantial size could easily represent a total investment (building, land, and fixtures) of $1 million, to which were added the costs of stock, personnel, and operation. Equally inhibiting was that no model existed for what a branch department store should be. Ihlder mentioned that chain companies provided a major precedent, but in the mid-1920s most chains were still made up of food, drug, and variety stores, which in outlying areas were quite modest in size and appearance and carried everyday goods. Were one to build a branch department store, should it likewise be small, or should it be a bigger operation that would dominate the area as the parent store did downtown? Should the store carry most or even all of the variety of goods of its parent, or should it specialize? Should it seek a new clientele or concentrate on retaining the existing customer base? Should it be situated in an established business center or should it follow the example just initiated by Sears, Roebuck and have a lone-wolf location, apart from all but a few scattered businesses?[4] Such questions made the prospects of branch development seem problematic indeed. Given the expenses of developing new merchandising and operating strategies, enlarging and remodeling downtown stores, building service facilities, and accommodating customers' parking needs, it is hardly surprising that most department store executives hoped that the pressures to move beyond the city center would abate or that others would undertake the risky task of establishing the ground rules for sound branch development.

But just as with the other spheres that were beginning to transform the department store during the 1920s, branch development could not be ignored. Within a year of the *Women's Wear Daily* survey the situation had changed dramatically. Branch stores had begun to emerge as a major trend in the field and to grow over the next several years. After some setbacks during the Depression, the tendency returned with renewed vigor until extenuating circumstances once more curtailed growth in the early 1940s. Throughout the interwar decades, branch development remained experimental. Had department store owners been polled in 1941, it is doubtful whether any consensus would have existed on the optimal kind of branch or even on the future role of branches. Nevertheless, branch stores had become an important component of the industry, and lessons learned from the myriad endeavors to build and operate them afforded an essential foundation for the postwar years, when large-scale branch development soon was regarded as key to the survival of the parent store.

Parameters

Just what constituted a branch department store was difficult to define in concise terms because so many different varieties were created. At one extreme, a branch could encompass a room or two in a resort hotel, operate two or three months a year, and carry a very limited array of goods; at the other, it could occupy its own lavish quarters of 100,000 square feet or more, operate year round, and carry much the same spectrum of articles found in the main store. Branches were located in posh suburbs but also in cities and towns beyond the store's primary trading area. Most branches were developed to increase profits; however, some were built more for prestige. Most department store companies that opened branches during these decades were oriented to a reasonably affluent, sometimes elite, trade. Others employed branches to expand their business within a market of more moderate means. The types of branches varied widely from company to company and from one region to another. Differences in operating policies were as numerous as the participating companies themselves. Besides full-fledged department stores, sizable, departmentalized specialty stores carrying clothing, accessories, and often other "soft" goods played an important role both in the early decades of branch development and during the postwar era when they served as major destinations of their own or as anchors in shopping centers.[5]

Given all the variables, a branch can be best understood as an extension of, and lying some distance from, an existing, or parent, store trading under the same name. The stores would be operated by the same top-level management and usually would share administrative staff for accounting, advertising, buying, and other operational functions.[6] Branches were not annexes that specialized in music, men's wear, or cheap goods not carried in the main plant. Instead, they were conceived to duplicate at least some of the lines of the parent store, even in the cases where they catered to a more prestigious trade. This relationship also made them fundamentally different from units in a chain organization, which were run in more or less the same way by management that was not tied to any one store and often operated from a separate administrative headquarters. A few stores referred to themselves as chains, from the elegant I. Magnin & Company in San Francisco to the popular-priced Hearn Department Stores in New York. Furthermore, the chain store in concept, as advocated by Edward Filene and Paul Mazur, appears to have helped guide the process of developing branches for a number of firms. Yet most of the basic conceptual and operational parameters differed. At the onset of branch development, the mass-market-oriented chains were probably the last things on the minds of department store executives. With the value of branch expansion on a substantial scale remaining very much in question, no firm made a commitment in this sphere until the late 1920s. During most of that difficult decade, the pioneering companies tested the waters in a much less ambitious way by opening small specialty shops in exclusive resort and college communities.

Specialty Shops

An intimately scaled shop selling sportswear, shoes, and perhaps accessories on a seasonal basis in an elegant resort hotel or store block might seem an unlikely progenitor to the big department store branches that became a ubiquitous fixture during the 1950s, but the former indeed laid an important foundation at a time when the idea of branch stores was being avidly debated. Not only were resort and college stores among the first erected beyond the urban core by major mercantile companies, several of those companies soon expanded their programs to include year-round branches within a metropolitan context. Furthermore, the resort store quickly became an important instrument for enhancing the parent store's position as a trendsetter when fashion assumed a major place in defining the great emporium's role in retailing. Stores in stylish watering places could attract a new clientele; equally important, these small outlets func-

132. Wm. Filene's Sons store, opened 1927 in corner units of the Queen's Buyway, North Main Street and Palmer Avenue, Falmouth, Massachusetts (1925–26). Whitten & Sons, architects. Photo author, 2001.

tioned as useful proving grounds for merchandise among a discriminating audience. Finally, while most such branches lay in communities frequented by the well-to-do from the cities in which their respective parent stores were located, they attracted many others as well, enabling the stores to expand their customer bases among an elite clientele from different parts of the country.

The pioneers in this rarefied realm were prestigious departmentalized stores devoted to clothing, accessories, and some household goods: Saks Fifth Avenue in New York, Filene's in Boston, and I. Magnin in San Francisco.[7] Magnin's took the lead, opening hotel shops in the West Coast's two premier winter resorts, Santa Barbara and Pasadena, in 1912 and 1913, respectively. The network expanded to include the equally fashionable Hotel Del Monte at Pebble Beach (1914) and Biltmore at Montecito (1927), as well as the Ambassador (1921) and Biltmore (1927) hotels in Los Angeles. Saks Fifth Avenue's program was similar, with its first store in Palm Beach (1926), followed by others in Atlantic City (1927), Long Branch (New Jersey), Miami Beach, and Southampton (all 1929). Filene's entered the field with stores in York Harbor, Maine, and Hyannis (both 1923), Magnolia (1926), and Falmouth (1927), Massachusetts.[8] Among these companies, Filene's had some of the largest shops, occupying buildings of their own or substantial sections of store blocks (fig. 132). Miami's leading department store, Burdine's, sought to enhance its stature, competing directly with the New York emporia by opening branches in Miami Beach (1929) and Palm Beach (1930). By the late 1920s, the aura of a resort shop was such that R. H. Macy also opened one in Palm Beach, with store executives frankly admitting the venture had more to do with image than revenues.[9]

Concurrently, Filene's began to cultivate another outside market: female college students. Shops were opened in the Massachusetts towns of Wellesley and Northampton (Smith) in 1924 and South Hadley (Mount Holyoke) two years later.[10] Like the resort store, the outlets held the potential for attracting a new client base, in these instances at an early age. However, the idea failed to gain widespread application, perhaps because most women's institutions of higher learning were relatively small and somewhat remote. In 1927 the Dayton Company adapted the concept to a larger, coeducational clientele at the University of Minnesota, as did Kerr Dry Goods Company for the University of Oklahoma (1936) and Younker Brothers for Iowa State University (1941), but such outlets, too, remained far more the exception than the rule.[11]

Early on, store executives recognized that the appeal of some of their seasonal outlets warranted expansion, not just of space and stock, but also of clientele. The best-known success with such a program was Filene's 1,000-square-foot shop at Wellesley, which was enlarged three times between 1925 and 1932 to accommodate the needs of area residents as well as students. When these campaigns proved insufficient, the facility was rebuilt in 1938 to encompass an area twenty times that of the original store (fig. 133). A less dramatic shift occurred in Northampton, where in 1930 the store moved to substantially larger quarters in the main shopping district. Three years later Magnin's relocated its Pasadena store from the once venerable Hotel Maryland to a sizable two-story building in the retail core.[12]

The experience of establishing resort and college branches may also have contributed to the decision by most of the companies involved to open sizable, year-round emporia in cities well outside their respective trading radiuses. While much smaller than their parent stores, these establishments represented substantial investments and carried a considerable array of goods; some were in fact department stores in

133. Wm. Filene's Sons department store, 50 Central Street, Wellesley, Massachusetts (1938). J. E. Holmes, architect; altered. (*Retailing,* 29 August 1938, 8.)

134. I. Magnin & Company store, 6340 Hollywood Boulevard, Los Angeles (1922–23). Myron Hunt, architect; altered. Main sales floor (*American Architect,* 5 February 1926, 231).

their own right, purveying most of the goods found at the parent. Little precedent existed for such enterprises when I. Magnin opened an elegant store on Hollywood Boulevard in Los Angeles in 1923. Smaller, high-end apparel stores had participated in the movement to develop resort branches since the 1910s, and some of them were beginning to create establishments in outlying metropolitan communities, but most of this latter group was very modest in size. A few major companies, most of them New York–based, had begun to establish outlets in other cities, but these were aimed at a much broader market and appear to have been more closely modeled on chain organizations.[13] And unlike virtually all branches at that time, Magnin's Hollywood store did not occupy an existing building but had its own specially designed quarters, making it a landmark in a shopping district then beginning to emerge as an upmarket competitor with downtown. The work of Myron Hunt, one of southern California's most prominent architects, the building lacked the characteristics of most retail spaces. The facade suggested a bank as much as a store, while the two-story selling area, with paneling, fireplace, and only a few goods displayed, elicited comparisons with the lobby of a fine hotel (fig. 134). To the rear lay a garden. Three scarcely less elegant store units lay to one side, one used by Magnin's for millinery, the other two available for future expansion. Much praised upon its completion, the design was still hailed, several years later, as the "high water mark to date in store architecture in this country," according to the editors of the *American Architect.*[14] At a pivotal point in branch store development, Magnin's set a standard not only for appearances in general but also for how this type of retail establishment could possess an identity of its own that was quite different in character from most downtown emporia and was appealing to affluent consumers who resided ever further from the core.

The Hollywood store also seems to have enjoyed sufficient trade to prompt its owners to announce plans for additional ones in Seattle, Portland, and Oakland some two years after its opening. While the plans for Portland never materialized, the other two constituted substantially larger enterprises than their predecessor. Occupying 35,000 square feet, the Seattle unit (1925–26) was the primary tenant of a seven-story building that was in its final planning stage when the agreement was reached. With a lavish suite of rooms fashioned after a variety of historical periods—from Italian Renaissance to English Georgian—the interior drew rhapsodic praise from observers. At the opening, a reporter for the *Seattle Times* cooed that "Like Alice in Wonderland, who walked through the looking glass into another world, Seattle femininity yesterday afternoon stepped through the artistic bronze doors of the new . . . store into a bit of the Rue de la Paix."[15] Less than two years later, small, temporary quarters were opened in Oakland, which was more easily accessible to well-to-do residents of the extensive East Bay communities than the parent store in San Francisco. The venture quickly proved its worth, and by August 1929 plans were under way for the largest branch yet, a four-story,

80,000-square-foot pile rendered in an elegant Art Deco vein.[16]

If I. Magnin was the nation's leader in branch building among large, departmentalized specialty stores, a New York counterpart was quick to follow suit. In 1929 Saks Fifth Avenue opened a 51,000-square-foot store, which was by far the largest of the fine shops along Chicago's North Michigan Avenue. Magnin's Oakland and Seattle stores were similarly located in new, "uptown" shopping districts that real estate interests were promoting for the high-end consumer market. At an early stage, the branch store not only became an important instrument for department store expansion, it also was demonstrating its capacity to have a catalytic effect on the growth of new business areas in larger cities.[17]

Momentum

As Saks was planning its Chicago outlet, and Magnin's contemplating its Oakland branch, a number of full-fledged department store companies began to address the branch issue in earnest, not to capture trade in resorts or in other cities, but to consolidate and expand trade on home ground. Between 1928 and 1932 sixteen large branches were opened in outlying sections and satellite communities of cities from New York to Los Angeles. Merchants and industry observers alike considered this trend the primary and probably the most risk-laden one in branch development of the period. Skeptics, including many store owners, believed that branches would only erode the business of the parent store while consuming large amounts of capital to operate. Furthermore, the argument ran, branches could not begin to offer the variety of goods that was one of the most important attractions of downtown emporia. If, then, department store executives resisted temptation and concentrated on expanding and otherwise improving their big stores, the public would continue to come downtown in droves.[18]

Yet to others in retailing, the forces of change seemed overwhelming. The population was dispersing at a rate inconceivable a generation previous. As a result, the big stores' principal customer base was located ever farther from the core. Chain and independent specialty stores alike were leading the drive to meet consumers on their new home territory. But these factors alone might not have tipped the scale toward building large-scale branches, at least not at so early a date. During the late 1920s one of the most discussed cities in terms of retail decentralization was Detroit, where small and medium-sized establishments proliferated in a galaxy of business nodes beyond downtown. Yet the city's dominant department store, J. L. Hudson, and its two, considerably weaker rivals, Crowley-Milner and Ernest Kern, ignored all pressures for branch building until well after the Second World War, continuing to expand their downtown plants instead.[19] Even in Los Angeles, which experienced probably the most intense decentralization of its populace, industry, and business in the nation during the 1920s, department store executives maintained a tacit agreement not to succumb to branch development until the newest and weakest among their cadre broke from the fold.

Period accounts minced no words in pointing the finger at downtown traffic congestion and parking as the foremost factors in justifying expansion through branches. The issue that was so vexing to merchants in maintaining the viability of their main facilities thus also triggered the move to provide alternatives. Most of the stores that so engaged themselves catered to the upper portions of the market. It was precisely these consumers who were relocating toward the urban periphery where the female head of the household was most inclined to use her automobile on shopping expeditions. If the store did not meet this clientele close to home, branch proponents believed, it would begin to lose them and also fail to gain the growing number of young, affluent women who were entering the consumer market. Children exacerbated the problem in the retailers' opinion. Many women might be willing to endure the challenges of driving to the congested central district, disposing of their car, and braving the pedestrian crowds, but toting along children significantly complicated the situation. If a mother was shopping for her children or simply did not want to have to arrange for a surrogate when she went downtown, the prospects could be daunting. Given these circumstances and the fact that department stores were ever more dependent on exuding an aura of fashion, on purveying ready-to-wear clothing (for children as well as adults), and on featuring a wide array of goods associated with leisure time, having stores that were easily reached by the prosperous middle class and the well-to-do were considered an essential investment by some prominent figures in the field. Department store branches could be efficiently run, proponents asserted, because much of the overhead costs for advertising, buying, accounting, and other core functions were already incurred by the parent store. Branches did not carry an abundant stock, either. As inventory ran low on certain items, they could be quickly replenished by truck from the main store or the warehouse. Finally, branch stores could boost business at the core, proponents were certain. Persons in the habit of going to a branch would then likely decide to go to the parent operation for items they could not purchase close to home.[20] The nation's leader in taking this approach near the close of the 1920s was the legendary Marshall Field's.

As one of the largest retail enterprises in the United States and the dominant department store in its region, Marshall Field's was in a good position to expand its business through building large branches. Field's strategy was to establish stores in several key locations, effectively trumping any competitor. The three communities chosen were

Lake Forest, lair for many of the city's richest and most socially prominent families, and Evanston and Oak Park, strategically situated among enclaves of the upper middle class, and with existing business centers of some size. To implement this program, however, the company began with a trial run, taking a cue from the stores that had found little shops in resort and college communities to be rewarding. In Field's case, the focus was on children, which the store's executives seem to have identified early on as a crucial part of the equation for a branch. In September 1928 juvenile shops were opened in Lake Forest and Evanston. Both were sufficiently well received that they were expanded within two months, the Evanston shop relocating in the process. By March the following year, the latter outlet had increased in size twice more.[21]

Field's executives did not wait long to commit to their main agenda. Plans for one of the largest branch stores yet proposed (about 70,000 square feet) were unveiled for Oak Park on the eve of Thanksgiving 1928 and for an even larger unit (about 100,000 square feet) for Evanston on the first of March 1929.

When they opened, in time for the 1929 Christmas season, Field's big branch stores stood quite apart from others of the type. On the exterior they possessed an elegance and a restraint associated with the finest buildings being erected in uptown business districts such as Chicago's North Michigan Avenue, and in this respect were comparable to Magnin's Seattle and Saks's Chicago branches (fig. 135). At the same time, they possessed a singular identity that speculative buildings did not, their corners accentuated with masonry walls, the upper-level window bays in between unified as insets sheathed in bronze, giving the composition a monumental quality. On the other hand, the fifth floor made reference to the residential communities the stores served, with a mansard roof that at once unified the mass and distinguished it from the great majority of commercial buildings. This urbane character was directly tied to Field's merchandising strategy of presenting the stores as a great State Street institution transplanted to the suburbs. Both the goods and services found downtown were available at the branches. Doormen were stationed at the entrances; even the restrooms were located on the same floor as in the parent store. The interior had a sophisticated air: "The very simplicity and quality of the decorations, fixtures and furnishings imparting a richness which is immediately impressive." Imported veneers distinguished fixtures and elevator cabs alike. Upper floors followed the latest fashion in being arranged like a series of fine specialty shops (fig. 136). Much

135. Marshall Field & Company department store, Sherman Avenue and Church Street, Evanston, Illinois (1929). Graham, Anderson, Probst & White, architects. Photo ca. 1929.

136. Marshall Field & Company department store, Lake Street and Harlem Avenue, Oak Park, Illinois (1928–29). Graham, Anderson, Probst & White, architects. Women's apparel departments, fourth floor. Photo ca. 1929.

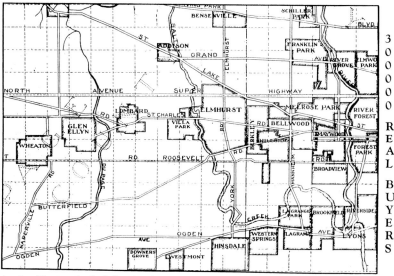

137. "West Suburban Marketable Area" for Oak Park commercial center (lying off the map just to the east of River Forest (*Hemingway Organizer*, October 1929, 4).

of the selling space was devoted to goods for women and children; two floors carried furniture, hardware, and other items tailored to the needs of prosperous suburban households. The finest in downtown retail luxury had arrived in places that a decade previous had little to offer beyond staple goods.[22]

Marshall Field executives appear to have carefully studied the optimal locations for the branch stores. The company had to continue to attract a huge number of patrons to its State Street store; branches sited within the city would likely weaken that draw. Evanston lay some ten miles to the north of the Loop; Oak Park about eight to the west. In both cases, the distance was sufficiently far not to erode city constituents. The primary audience instead came from the fast-growing communities that lay beyond these towns,

as a consumer market map for potential investors in Oak Park commercial real estate, prepared in conjunction with the Field store's opening, graphically illustrated (fig. 137).[23] The rapid rise in this new outlying population, much of which lay apart from major public transportation lines, was the key factor in transforming downtown Evanston and Oak Park, which had traditionally provided a limited spectrum of merchandise and services to a nearby population, to magnet business districts for major portions of the metropolitan area. Evanston began to assume this new role by the mid-1920s. A pronounced rise occurred in the number of small, fashion-oriented specialty shops that opened. Longstanding Loop merchants and national chain companies entered the arena as well. A ten-story building erected to house physicians and dentists joined a rising

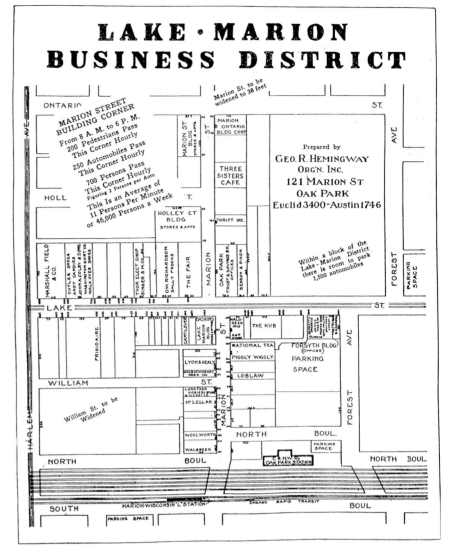

138. "Saving Time," Evanston Chamber of Commerce advertisement (*Lake Forester*, 28 May 1926, 4).

139. Map of main business district, Oak Park, showing location of major businesses (*Hemingway Organizer*, October 1929, 5).

number of facilities catering to professional services.[24] In 1926, the Evanston Chamber of Commerce sponsored a series of advertisements in suburban newspapers from Chicago's north side to Lake Forest, emphasizing the time saved, the convenience to motorists, the variety of stores, and the abundance of stylish merchandise that awaited consumers who came there (fig. 138).[25] By the time Field's committed to its large store, nearly fifty Chicago businesses already had outlets in the community.[26] Oak Park's commercial center was smaller, more compact, and slightly later in ascending to regional prominence. Yet by the late 1920s, the precinct had the same strong combination of local merchants, Chicago branches, chain units, and professional offices (figs. 139–40). Field's was hardly a pioneer in these communities, but it did capitalize on recent development, assuring both places the status of major commercial centers and stimulating additional growth, despite the Depression.[27] In its early stages, the economic downturn had little impact on Field's expansion plans. Less than a year after the two big stores opened, the company announced plans to operate an expanded branch in Lake Forest. Occupying 6,500 square feet, the outlet was much smaller than the other two, but it had ample room in which to grow. Formerly occupied by a bank and a utility company, the lavish new home provided the centerpiece for Market Square, which was erected in the 1910s as the nation's first comprehensively planned shopping complex. Plans for including additional space took form a few months after the store opened in May 1931; by the eve of World War II the entire building was occupied.[28] With these three units, Field's had the most extensive network of suburban branches among department stores in the United States until the late 1940s.[29]

Marshall Field's branch expansion strategy was widely covered and praised within the trade, but few department stores emulated it. The one company that appears to have drawn substantially from this precedent, Strawbridge &

140. Main business district, Oak Park, looking northeast. Marshall Field department store is at center left. Photo early 1930s.

Clothier, did so for somewhat different reasons. In Philadelphia, John Wanamaker enjoyed the dominance Field's had in Chicago. Both Wanamaker's and Field's had been industry pioneers; had played a major role in recasting the department store as a palatial emporium at the turn of the twentieth century; continued to be national leaders; were the largest stores in their respective cities; and purveyed the most stylish merchandise. While a venerable establishment with a solid reputation, Strawbridge's held a distant second, not unlike Carson, Pirie, Scott & Company in Chicago. When Strawbridge's announced its multimillion-dollar campaign to erect branches as well as a grand downtown store, it was in all likelihood to challenge Wanamaker's hegemony. The firm would not only have the newest facilities, it would have a front line near the leafy enclaves where many of Wanamaker's best customers resided. Locally, the precedent for big stores situated well beyond the city center had been set by George Allen, a fashion-oriented retailer specializing in women's accessories and dry goods. In the final weeks of 1927, Allen opened a 50,000-square-foot branch in Germantown, a "suburb" within the city limits that had been an area of choice among prominent Philadelphians since the mid-nineteenth century. Allen's store was not only three times the size of its downtown parent, it carried a wider range of goods, including apparel.[30] But Strawbridge's did not select Germantown or any comparable area. Instead, it followed Field's example, locating in enclaves beyond the sprawling neighborhoods of the city.

In September 1929, when plans for the first Strawbridge branch were made public, company president and chief architect of the plan, Herbert Tily, stressed how the downtown store and its suburban offspring would complement one another. The branch represented a "natural and logical extension of the present-day scheme of merchandise distribution." "Modern conditions of living," he asserted, "demand modern methods of merchandising if the public is to

141. Strawbridge & Clothier department store, Montgomery Avenue and St. James Place, Ardmore, Pennsylvania (1929–30). Dreher & Churchman, architects; altered. Architect's rendering.

142. Strawbridge & Clothier department store, Ardmore, main floor. Photo ca. 1930.

be provided with what it needs." Located in Ardmore, which for Philadelphia's Main Line functioned much like Evanston for Chicago's North Shore, the store was multistory and carried a substantial array of goods.[31] At 60,000 square feet it was not quite as large as Field's two purpose-built branches, but it resembled them in its urban character. Employing a restrained repertoire of Art Deco motifs, the building exuded a stylish sophistication inside and out (figs. 141–42). In contrast to Field's, however, Strawbridge's emphasized how it was catering to affluent Main Line customers rather than

how it was bringing the retail luxuries of downtown to the suburbs. The difference was more one of presentation than substance. Field's channeled a carefully selected range of the medium- to high-grade stock from its State Street store; Strawbridge's did likewise. No special buying occurred for the suburban clientele.[32] But Tily seems to have been more concerned than his Chicago colleagues in winning over new customers, creating a reputation as much as capitalizing on the existing one.

Customer access no doubt figured prominently in selecting a site for the store. Field's new buildings were located on the edge but were nonetheless integral parts of their respective commercial districts. In Ardmore, comparable siting would have entailed property on Lancaster Avenue, a comparatively narrow and by then somewhat congested thoroughfare along which the business center extended for a number of blocks. Instead, Tily opted for a site on the other side of the railroad tracks oriented to Montgomery Avenue, which was mostly lined with fine houses and was the preferred route of many area residents. The developer of this tract, a syndicate known as the Suburban Company, had already erected several one-story store blocks in hopes of luring shoppers to an area were vehicular movement and parking were easy. Strawbridge's commitment to the site radically altered the nature of the complex, making it a major destination. Over the next several years, the developers succeeded in creating a full-fledged shopping center, which was eventually called Suburban Square. Though the process occurred in increments, with little if any initial conception of the eventual outcome, Strawbridge's nonetheless took a pioneering step in establishing the branch department store as a key component of an integrated retail development.[33]

Tily and his associates seem to have been aware of the potential benefits a planned retail center could bring. Six months after the Ardmore store opened, they revealed plans for the second, larger branch of 87,000 square feet in Jenkintown, which would serve a fan of affluent enclaves north of the city. The site lay completely apart from the town's commercial center. Plans prepared by the Suburban Company called for the branch to lie at the heart of a sizable shopping center, which could have rivaled, even eclipsed, the existing retail core.[34] Worsening economic conditions precluded realization of most of this precocious scheme, which seems to have enjoyed almost no publicity and soon was forgotten. The big store, on the other hand, was constructed, opening to great fanfare in September 1931.[35] Far more than at Ardmore, the exterior was unabashedly theatrical, proclaiming its role as an eye-catching landmark on its somewhat isolated hilltop site (fig. 143). Besides curbside parking along streets intended to serve the shopping center, the building featured an underground garage where customers could have their cars serviced and from which they could enter the

143. Strawbridge & Clothier department store, Old York and Rydal roads, Jenkintown, Pennsylvania (1930–31). Dreher & Churchman, architects; altered.

store directly, another unusual feature that would be used a generation later.

Strawbridge's Jenkintown store was the last of the big branches to open until 1936, when economic recovery had become a distinct, if not entirely stable, trend. The Depression curtailed branch building in many quarters, just as the phenomenon was gaining momentum. But even if business had remained strong, it is doubtful whether many stores would have followed Marshall Field's lead in erecting several large branches. Besides the high cost of such ventures, many metropolitan areas were not sufficiently decentralized to support such a galaxy of emporia oriented to the high end of the market. Even Sears, catering to a much broader clientele, erected two or more of its department stores only in the largest cities.[36] The perspectives that leading retailers had toward the matter also entered into the equation, as was quite evident in New York.

Variation

The prestige of the big Fifth Avenue stores and the widespread view of New York as the center of the retail trades ranked among the factors that led leading department store executives to relegate branch development to a marginal position at best. The man who most forcefully challenged this outlook was Philip LeBoutillier, president of Best & Company, a prominent store specializing in women's and children's clothing. Between November 1929 and October 1930 he opened branches in Garden City, Long Island; Mamaroneck, in Westchester County, New York; and East Orange, New Jersey. An outspoken advocate of making stores accessible to motorists, LeBoutillier chose sites that were on the edge of existing business districts or, in the case of Mamaroneck, in a lone-wolf location—away from concentrated commercial development—to ensure minimal congestion

144. B. Altman & Company department store, Mamaroneck Avenue and Post Road, White Plains, New York. Opened 1930 in M. A. P. Building (1929); altered. Editorial cartoon (*Daily Press*, 5 May 1930, 1-B).

and ample space for cars.³⁷ The stores were not big, however. The Garden City store was less than 2,000 square feet; Mamaroneck and East Orange around 25,000 and 35,000, respectively. LeBoutillier appears to have believed, along with many others in the trade, that the region's topography was a key determinant of size. With affluent suburbs fanning thinly over broad areas separated from one another by Long Island Sound and the Hudson River, as well as many lesser topographical barriers, no one area was seen as possessing the critical mass to sustain a large branch.

LeBoutillier's example may well have influenced the decision-making of two major department stores, B. Altman, one of the largest of the Fifth Avenue establishments, and James A. Hearn & Son, the city's oldest, still at its long-standing location on Fourteenth Street. Altman's first step was cautious, with a shop of about 2,500 square feet containing a limited array of women's and children's apparel and accessories. The establishment was located in White Plains, the business and population center of Westchester County, in a new speculative building along Mamaroneck Avenue, which was emerging as an enclave of high-end specialty stores. Altman's, however, was the first major New York establishment to enter the scene. The White Plains business district, which was larger than those in Evanston and Oak Park, heralded the opening of Altman's tiny branch as an event tantamount to the transplantation of Fifth Avenue on local ground (fig. 144).³⁸ White Plains and its many surrounding communities could likely have sustained a store at least as large as Field's biggest branch; given the shop's reception, Westchester residents were starved for such an outlet.

The popularity of their initial venture appears to have caused Altman's leadership to think in more expansive terms for the second branch, the plans for which were announced four months after the White Plains shop opened. The site chosen was East Orange, a sizable community in its own right and, much like Evanston and Oak Park, in a pivotal position between dense population centers and well-to-do residential enclaves. LeBoutillier had already selected East Orange for his third branch, but Altman's chose a property some distance afield, removed also from the existing business district, even though a number of sites in the latter were considered. The property lay some blocks to the south, along Central Avenue, which had the best highway connections to many of the western suburbs. Since the mid-1920s, the Baldwin Construction Company had been erecting commercial buildings that by 1930 formed an alternative business center. Aside from a small Sears store and an A&P market, most tenants were local. As at White Plains, Altman's seems to have been one of the first New York stores of any consequence to commit to the emerging district. In this case, however, the company commissioned its own three-story building of nearly 55,000 square feet and containing a wide variety of goods (fig. 145).[39] With a facade and selling spaces designed to evoke those of the urban parent store, the building was as close as any in the region to its Chicago counterparts. And, much like Strawbridge's in Ardmore, the store proved a catalyst for making Central Avenue the prime retail area, along which a number of New York specialty stores opened branches in later years.[40]

Altman's was thanked by Hearn's executives, along with Best's and Strawbridge's, in a rare public disclosure of specific precedents studied for its branch program. The example of the latter company may well have induced Hearn's leadership to open a "complete" department store; that is, one with the full range of goods characteristic to the type. But Hearn's deviated from the others in having the store operate on as independent a basis as possible. Buying was done in New York, but especially for the branch. Hearn's also sought to stake out its own territory, moving beyond Mamaroneck and White Plains to Stamford, Connecticut, the major business center for Fairfield County, which was almost as big as White Plains. Still, Hearn's executives opted for a small store, completely remaking a late nineteenth-century building that contained only some 17,000 square feet. Opened in September 1930, the branch had all the appearances of an exclusive uptown specialty shop and could hardly have lived up to the promise of the endless array of goods that advertisements suggested.[41]

Los Angeles department store executives were as resistant

145. B. Altman & Company department store, 570 Central Avenue, East Orange, New Jersey (1930–31). Frederick G. Frost, architect. Photo Wurts Bros., ca. 1931 (*Architectural Record*, July 1932, 11).

to branch buildings as their New York colleagues, until one among them broke ranks. But even then development was of a limited and particularized nature until the late 1930s. The nature of activity, however, could not have been more different than that in greater New York. Although discussion of creating a new shopping district along Wilshire Boulevard, some three miles to the west of downtown, had occurred among several major retailers in the mid-1920s, the program never materialized. As long as all the big stores agreed to focus only on their downtown plants, the sentiment ran, customers would have few other choices.[42] The shift in strategy was triggered by Bernal Dyas, who announced plans in July 1927 to erect a multistory building of around 150,000 square feet in Hollywood. The approach was not unlike that of George Allen's in Philadelphia. The Hollywood store was larger and carried more lines than its parent (fig. 146). For some years Dyas had operated a high-end sporting goods business, expanding its repertoire with the purchase of the Ville de Paris dry goods store in 1920 (see fig. 104). Still, the company enjoyed only a fraction of the business transacted in the city's largest department stores, Bullock's, the May Company, the Broadway, and J. W. Robinson. The new Hollywood store would greatly facilitate expansion by attracting both the array of rich consumers tied to the now booming movie industry and the many other well-to-do Angelenos who were gravitating to the Hollywood hills. Dyas could, in effect, significantly enlarge his audience. As realized, nothing about the building suggested a branch store. Its unprecedented size, multilevel configuration, and corner site at one of Hollywood's major intersections all suggested a downtown store. Inside, departments were organized as suites of elegant shops. Nowhere else was branch building then part of so ambitious an expansion agenda.[43]

146. B. H. Dyas Company department store, Hollywood Boulevard and Vine Street, Los Angeles (1927–28). Fred R. Dorn, architect. Preopening advertisement depicting downtown store at the upper right and Hollywood store at left (*Hollywood Daily Citizen*, 6 February 1928, 5).

Three years after Dyas opened his dream store it was sold to the Broadway, a victim of overextension. The building's new owner used the facility for similar purposes. The Broadway ranked toward the lower end of the local department store hierarchy. The Hollywood store allowed it to purvey a higher grade of goods and target a more well-heeled clientele. At about the same time, the May Company was rumored to be contemplating a large Hollywood branch, but store officials vehemently denied such a plan.[44] The only department store company that responded to Dyas's move initially was Bullock's.

Bullock's position in the local hierarchy was somewhat like Strawbridge's in that it was second to Robinson's. At the same time, Bullock's was much larger, having undergone an aggressive expansion campaign over the previous decade. For volume of trade, it rivaled the May Company as the biggest store in the region. Shortly after the Dyas store's opening, John Bullock announced his company's plans to

147. Bullock's department store, 3050 Wilshire Boulevard, Los Angeles (1928–29). John and Donald B. Parkinson, architects; Jock D. Peters, associate of Feil & Paradise, interior designer. Photo Mott Studios, 1929.

construct a branch on Wilshire Boulevard. Within the next six months, however, the scheme was markedly altered. The revised plan, unveiled in November 1928, called for a building of almost 200,000 square feet. Rather than being an echo of the downtown plant, its design bespoke a very elegant suburban store—freestanding, with a landscaped perimeter and an enormous rear parking area to accommodate 375 cars. The scale and stepped massing of Bullock's Wilshire, on the other hand, suggested more a great civic building (fig. 147). The operational program was equally unorthodox. The store would be run more or less independently of the downtown emporium, with its own buyers and with merchandise of the highest grade. Like Dyas, Bullock sought to enlarge his clientele, catering to some of the richest households in the metropolitan area. Significantly, he did not try to compete with Dyas in Hollywood but instead chose a site near the residential areas favored by the Los Angeles oligarchy in the mid-Wilshire district and readily accessible from other bastions of wealth along the Adams Avenue corridor. Aside from Sears' new stores, it was the first sizable emporium to be erected in a lone-wolf location—in this case, poised as a beacon to well-heeled motorists.[45]

Bullock's Wilshire was indeed atypical in almost every respect. At a time when some of the major New York stores were beginning to associate themselves with European modernism through exhibitions and household furnishings, Bullock's embraced the phenomenon. An account of the opening in the *Los Angeles Evening Express* waxed that the design was "thoroughly modern, but it is not the popular aspect of modernism. It is, rather, a rarified classic spirit of modernism expressed in as orderly a manner as a Greek sculptor would have expressed beauty. . . . Above all, it is far, far from the popular conception of 'shop moderne.'" Not long thereafter, Pauline Schindler, wife of one of the country's most innovative avant-garde modernist architects, wrote that the visitor was "not merely in a luxurious establishment cleverly planned in an authentic mode, but in the presence of a work of art." Along with others, Schindler emphasized that the spaces were hardly derivative in character; they represented a "new utterance, breathing sharply and independently from the parent stem of European modernism. The interior shows an amazing fecundity of creative vitality. . . . The achievement is equal in magnitude to the designing of a great medieval cathedral." The results were seen as symbolizing the emergence of artistic maturity in the region. "The spirit that is Southern California," gushed one reporter, "has been caught and crystallized in Bullock's Wilshire."[46] The modernist esthetic was not only developed to an unusual extent, it was done with considerable innovation.

Central to the quality of expression on the ground floor was the layout. There as well as on the upper floors designers adapted the shops concept, with some departments occupying expansive, lofty spaces while being treated as separate rooms, each with a distinct character (fig. 148). The principal entry opened not into a vast selling floor but into a grand concourse sheathed in marble, with display cases arranged almost as if in a museum (fig. 149). Most spaces were given an intimate scale, with luxurious materials and furniture (figs. 150–51). The display of goods was minimal and carefully integrated with the overall design. The Men's Shop, connected to the main part of the store through a sequence of small rooms, was no less lavish (fig. 152). While differentiated, the spaces throughout formed a coherent whole. "Every room," enthused Schindler, "flows into the next by way of a design transition in form and color." "The old box architecture is over," she proclaimed, "Each unit . . . is designed not alone as an individual item, but in relation to the whole. There is a fine organic integration, a harmony of thousands of individual parts."[47] Another touted attribute of the ensemble was that it was a collaborative effort. The designer of the interiors, Jock Peters, worked with the building's architects, the venerable Los Angeles firm of John and Donald B. Parkinson, as well as with a number of artists. Coordinating the program was a new Bullock's employee, Eleanor Le Maire, who had recently arrived from the East Coast. The project was reputedly her first and would swiftly propel her to preeminence as a designer of store interiors.[48]

Le Maire's role was just one aspect of the endeavor that prompted *Los Angeles Times* reporter Amy Whitaker to dub Bullock's Wilshire a Temple to Women. Le Maire's involvement, she believed, made "all the splendor, dignity, and utter magnificence . . . so cleverly tempered with soft lighting and color psychology to dispel any awe that its sumptuousness might engender. No room for an inferiority complex in this temple. One immediately responds and expands to the superiority of the surroundings." At a time when the operation of a department store remained largely the province of men, Whitaker noted that many of the departments there were run by women instead. Besides its design and operation, the conveniences of the store, which included not only attendant parking but a large, supervised play area for children, made the experience an unusual one. "Never before anywhere," she exulted, "have we been invited to trade under such entrancing conditions."[49]

Highly praised in design, retail, and consumer circles alike, Bullock's Wilshire received probably the most coverage of any department store constructed during the interwar years. From a historical perspective, it ranks as a major landmark in the development of retail architecture. Bullock's Wilshire remained an anomaly among branches; however, it helped establish a spectrum of key precedents that eventually would be of central concern in the building of branch stores. For executives of downtown emporia, it demonstrated that a lone-wolf location and huge parking lot were highly desirable. It further revealed that a large store catering to the top of the market need not be limited to the city center, as those of I. Magnin and Saks had been. Its operating policies showed that a branch need not carry the same goods as the parent store; the nature of merchandise could be adjusted according to the location. It probably did as much as any other endeavor to equate stylishness with modernity in the public's mind. Finally, together with Dyas's short-lived venture, it established a scale for department store branches that other Los Angeles companies would follow a decade later and that would become an industry standard in the 1950s. For a store that remained unique, its impact was widespread and lasting.

While companies in Chicago, New York, and Los Angeles were developing branch plans suited to the biggest metropolitan areas, Halle Brothers Company pioneered one for cities then considered of insufficient size to sustain branches. The largest and most prestigious store in Cleveland, Halle's embarked on a program of opening small stores in towns and cities beyond its normal trading radius. The pattern echoed somewhat that established for resort and college shops by the large specialty stores, but had a stronger regional focus. The marketing strategy of having a big department store draw from an extensive hinterland, which was particularly strong in the Midwest, was thus reinforced. In rapid succession, Halle's opened five branches between January 1929 and February the following year in a string of small cities and large towns extending from the northeast to the southwest of Cleveland—Erie and New Castle, Pennsylvania, and Warren, Canton, and Mansfield, Ohio—with a

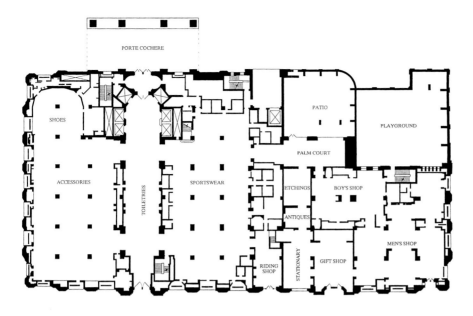

148. Bullock's Wilshire, first-floor plan. Drawn by Paul Davidson, after *Architectural Record,* January 1930, 52.

149. Bullock's Wilshire, central corridor. Photo Mott Studios, 1929.

150. Bullock's Wilshire, women's sportswear department. Photo Mott Studios, 1929.

151. Bullock's Wilshire, Collegienne Shoe Department. Photo Mott Studios, 1929.

radius of between fifty and eighty-five miles.[50] Most of these outlets occupied no more than 2,000 square feet in existing buildings; however, the Canton store was at least ten times that size in a specially constructed two-story edifice with a rear lot for parking. While Halle's had few immediate followers, its approach, too, would broaden in use by the late 1940s.[51]

Economy

The principal thrust of department store branch development into the early 1930s was to bolster sales among the many prosperous households that were, by all accounts, moving ever farther from the urban core. Shortly before the late 1920s, however, the movement began to include several stores targeted to a much larger portion of the market. Consumers with middle-to-moderate incomes were also moving to the outskirts in great numbers. They, too, were increasingly mobile through the use of cars, and they were perhaps even less inclined than their well-to-do contemporaries to travel downtown if comparable shopping choices existed closer to home. Department store companies undertook experiments in several cities, almost all of them launched just prior to the Depression. In Chicago, The Fair, one of the least prestigious stores in the State Street hierarchy, opened sizable branches along Milwaukee Avenue, serving a large blue-collar population, and also in Oak Park, a block from where Field's would soon build. The two districts were quite different demographically and likely presented a challenge to the retailer. On Milwaukee Avenue, the firm purchased the 180,000-square-foot building of a major neighborhood department store, E. Iverson, to capture a respectable share of the local market. In Oak Park, The Fair was likely targeting the large lower-middle-class population that lived primarily to the south and east, as well as others looking for bargains. Here the quarters purchased were less than half the size of the Milwaukee Avenue store. Both stores enjoyed a substantial patronage, with the Oak Park unit expanding to twice its original dimensions in 1936.[52]

Concurrently, a very ambitious branch building program was undertaken by the Cleveland-based ownership group National Department Stores. Formed in 1923, National was smaller than most other such conglomerates, and its stores catered largely to the low end of the downtown consumer market. But unlike many ownership groups at that time, National had a relatively strong central organization. Under the aegis of its president, Victor Sincere, the company embarked on an aggressive expansion campaign primarily through opening branch stores. Sincere was an advocate of branch building due to the low operational cost and appeal among customers. As did many of his colleagues, he pronounced the traffic problem sufficiently pressing to spur branch building. He proudly noted, "We have eliminated those

152. Bullock's Wilshire, Men's Shop. Photo Mott Studios, 1929.

things that exhaust a patron's patience. She is not required to force her way through crowds, to cross dangerous traffic-jammed streets, and she does not return home as tired as a basketball player after a court struggle. She is in a more receptive buying mood."[53]

Sincere's enthusiasm may well have been sparked by the experience of running a branch that was already in operation when his organization was formed. One of the participating stores, B. Nugent of St. Louis, had in fact opened a branch some three miles west of downtown in 1913, the first and only example of its kind until the late 1920s. Although the store was a modest 15,000 square feet and appears never to have been well known in the trade, it provided an essential proving ground for the branch concept with Sincere and his associates. Once they were convinced of its viability, they embarked on one of the most ambitious branch development programs of the interwar decades.[54] Between June 1929 and the following April, four new units were opened—two for the Bailey Company in Cleveland, another for Nugent's in St. Louis, and the fourth for Frank & Seder in Philadelphia. These stores were between 45,000 and 75,000 square feet. All carried a wide range of merchandise. The Bailey stores had their own rear parking lots; the other two had arrangements with independent lot operators so that

153. Bailey Company department store, Detroit Avenue and Warren Road, Lakewood, Ohio (1929–30). Morris & Weinberg, architects; altered. (*Chain Store Age,* February 1930, General Merchandise Sect., 6.)

patrons could park for free. Although most were in existing buildings that were constructed speculatively, the second Bailey store was specially built for the company. None of these stores had the stylishness characteristic of the upper-end branches. Instead, they were representative of mainstream commercial architecture of the period—orderly and respectable and without much flourish (fig. 153).[55] National was consistent in locating these stores in outlying business districts serving a large number of moderate- to middle-income households—places that by then were favored by the growing array of large chain store companies. In this respect National succeeded in targeting a major consumer base.[56] Although the company's program proved especially vulnerable to the economic downturn, it established a key precedent that was adapted by some of the country's leading large-volume department stores after World War II.

Regrouping

The Depression dealt a severe blow to branch expansion, arresting development at a point before numerous initiatives had had time to demonstrate their merits. Doubts in fact arose well before the full impact of the downturn was felt. In October 1930, when branch building remained active, the National Retail Dry Goods Association issued a report that predicted a limited role for such stores in the future. The authors asserted that the very nature of the large department store lay at odds with the branch concept: "It is not to be expected that a department store that owes its prestige to completeness of stock can so well maintain its clientele in small branch stores. . . . Branch store development is for that type of organization that gains a large part of its prestige from smartness and style, rather than from completeness of stock. It is for the specialty shop . . . rather than for the department store."[57]

As conditions worsened, the sentiment became widespread among department store executives that branches were not a profitable form of expansion. Like many ventures of the 1920s, branches came to be seen as overly ambitious projects that were costly mistakes for those who had undertaken them. National's plunge into bankruptcy in 1933 and the closing of the two Nugent branches only reinforced the view that such projects were misguided.[58] Attitudes did not change much with the return of more prosperous conditions. In 1936 a writer for the *New York Times* noted that branches were likely to grow for the big specialty stores such as Saks Fifth Avenue but summarily dismissed the whole endeavor among full-fledged department stores. The latter "had tried out the branch store plan in the 1929 era [the period of greatest excess], but the results were not satisfactory." Most State Street store executives agreed, despite the earlier successes of Marshall Field's and The Fair. Branches, they argued, could not begin to carry the assortment of stock that customers expected; further expansion outside the Loop was best conducted by chain companies and neighborhood establishments.[59]

Except for Nugent's, however, no branch department stores, aside from a few very small ones, closed during the 1930s. The problem, some observers began to realize, lay not with the basic concept but in the way it was realized. By the decade's end, the shortcomings of early branch expansion were being more accurately identified as ones of merchandising and management. Too often, retail analysts charged, the branch was not developed as a "complete" store focusing on its trade area, but as a "feeder" for the parent store. The array of goods was wide, perhaps, but the stock was thin. Moreover, customers would seek the branch for the elegant wares they associated with the parent, only to find more mundane merchandise. Finally, branches were frequently seen as aloof institutions whose staff did not participate in the community or even advertise in local papers. The whole initial phase of branch development, one consultant then involved with the planning of several such stores indicated, was reactive. Store executives "were in a hurry, had no time for scientific planning. In some cases, they plumped a branch right down beside the first branch store in the area. In others, they decided hastily just which was the 'second-best' location. . . . In every case, however, one thing was obvious. All of these retailers were negative in their approach to the problem. They were forced into branch operation. . . . Their aim was not necessarily to build up a satisfactory branch profit, but to protect the parent store's profit percentage."[60] Not all ventures suffered in this way, of course. Some of the most ambitious programs, including those by Bullock's, Field's, and Strawbridge's, appear to have enjoyed considerable success after the worst years of the Depression. Yet the problems were sufficiently extensive to capture the industry's attention. Just how problematic branch development remained on the eve of World War II was underscored by the widely publicized debacle experienced by R. H. Macy.

Other than its resort outlet in Palm Beach, Macy's had remained apart from the first stage of branch building, so when store executives announced the creation of new emporia that might redefine the nature of such development, it was received with great interest by retailers nationwide. Unveiled in August 1940, plans called for an experimental store in Syracuse, New York, which, if successful, would serve as a prototype for many others. The strategy behind the initiative seemed simple enough, but it departed markedly from the conventions of department store merchandising. Macy's appears to have based its program on the supermarket, which had achieved a meteoric rise to prominence in food distribution during the years immediately previous. Like the supermarket, Macy's Syracuse would be structured for high-volume merchandising, with a rapid turnover of items. Goods would be limited to the best-selling wares, mainly clothing and accessories, in the New York store. The operation would be one with no frills. For the most part customers would help themselves. Sales would be strictly cash. These provisions would keep costs down and prices low. To foster the agenda, Macy's commissioned Raymond Loewy Associates to create sales floors that optimized contact between merchandise and customers, where dramatic display techniques were matched by a prevailing sense of openness and easy access. Modernity, economy, efficiency, and highly popular goods would all contribute to a lucrative trade, Macy's executives believed. The emporium, they intoned, was of a new kind: it was not a chain store, not a specialty shop, and certainly not an ordinary department store, but rather a "best-seller" store. With this concept, they hoped, lay the future of retail expansion.[61]

Despite enthusiastic projections, performance was lackluster when Macy's Syracuse opened shortly before the start of the Christmas season in 1940. Sales proved so poor over the months that followed that company executives decided to close the operation two days after Christmas 1941. What was arguably the most pronounced failure of the era among department stores was precipitated, Macy officials discovered, by unmet expectations. Area residents anticipated a grand emporium. They were unimpressed with the goods presented and with the prices; what may have been a bargain in New York was hardly so in Syracuse. The stigma attached to the building, which had been a low-end store prior to Macy's lease, was reinforced by the self-service orientation. Customers routinely commented that it looked like a variety store. By embracing chain store methods, the enterprise did not seem innovative but rather mundane—manifesting fears that many department store executives had harbored about change since the 1920s. Embarrassed, Macy executives chose to terminate rather than to modify their notorious experiment.[62]

Reentry

Whatever the risks associated with branch development and however much some industry leaders downplayed its viability, the phenomenon could not be ignored for long. During the second half of the 1930s the population of metropolitan areas continued to disperse ever farther from the business core. The expansion of established outlying commercial districts and the creation of new ones increased steadily. Chain companies, ever more of them purveying apparel and accessories that competed directly with the department store's merchandise, targeted these satellite shopping districts as optimal for the new units. A resurgence of small specialty shop development in outlying centers also occurred. By the late 1930s the issue of decentralization was the source of widespread anxiety among downtown-based retailers, who saw their future seriously threatened. Surveys such as that published by *Sales Management* magazine in March 1940, which found that housewives in the Philadelphia metropolitan area preferred downtown stores to those beyond the core by only a narrow and probably diminishing margin, were cause for discomfort.[63]

Given the prevailing viewpoint, the large, departmentalized specialty stores not surprisingly assumed the leading role in branch development between 1935 and 1942. Now, however, almost all the locations selected were in outlying areas. Saks Fifth Avenue was the most aggressive. After opening a small outlet in Greenwich, Connecticut (1937), the company built a 30,000-square-foot building in Beverly Hills (1937–38)—the first large store to be established in that fashionable community. The California enterprise proved so popular that an addition encompassing one-third again as much area was announced seven months after the initial opening. An even larger facility was launched in 1940, occupying two floors of a major office building in Detroit's New Center—a business district rising some two miles northwest of downtown that had been developed in large part by General Motors in the 1920s.[64] In a metropolis where the major department store companies staunchly resisted

branch building, the Saks emporium was certainly the most elegant outlying store and, with the exception of two Sears units, among the largest until the mid-1950s.

Yet nothing Saks developed could rival the grand Wilshire Boulevard store of I. Magnin, which opened in February 1939, replacing the Hollywood store. Located a few blocks west of Bullock's, the establishment was clearly conceived as a rival as well as a means of upstaging Saks. Like Bullock's, its principal entrance lay at the rear, enunciated by an elegant porte-cochere where attendants took cars to an expansive parking lot. Magnin's interior spaces were not as artistically adventurous as Bullock's had been a decade earlier, but they were similarly rendered as a series of sumptuous salons. Clad in marble, rising five stories, the building encompassed over 120,000 square feet and at once became a landmark along the burgeoning Wilshire corridor (fig. 154).[65] Just as Bullock's had done a decade earlier, the big Saks and Magnin stores became significant forces of change for their respective environs, transforming their sites into shopping destinations. Julius Garfinckel accomplished much the same effect, albeit on a more modest scale, in 1942 with the first large branch of a downtown store in Washington, D.C.[66] Filene's, on the other hand, opted for intimate shops in the Boston suburbs of Winchester (1940) and Belmont (1940–41). Developed as part of store blocks, both branches capitalized on a domestic aura that many well-to-do consumers considered a hallmark of their leafy enclaves (fig. 155).[67]

Full-fledged department store companies were much more reluctant about reentering the branch field. Most were New York–based, including Frederick Loeser of Brooklyn, which opened a sizable store in the Long Island suburb of Garden City, and Hahne & Company of Newark, which established a much more modest outlet in the northern New Jersey community of Montclair (both 1937). Arnold Constable built near-twin stores of between 50,000 and 60,000 square feet at New Rochelle in Westchester County (1937) and Hempstead on Long Island (1939–40), which attracted notice in the field for their strong community orientation.[68] After James A. Hearn & Son was purchased and recast to appeal to a broad, moderate-income market, the firm purchased sizable emporia in the Bronx and Newark (both 1937) as the initial units of a planned area-wide network. Trading under the name of Hearn Department Stores and depicting itself as a chain, the business may well have been inspired by the success of neighborhood-based chain department stores in Chicago.[69] The enterprise experienced some difficulties, however, in finding a suitable niche, particularly in Newark, and hopes for rapid expansion had to be shelved.[70] The popular-priced market nevertheless gained renewed appeal for branches. Shortly before its experimental store opened in Syracuse, Macy's announced plans for a more

154. I. Magnin & Company store, Wilshire Boulevard and New Hampshire Avenue, Los Angeles (1938–39). Hunt & Chambers, architects; Timothy Pflueger, interior architect. Photo author, 1987.

155. Wm. Filene's Sons store, Main and Thompson streets, Winchester, Massachusetts (1940–41), in Locatelli Block (1935–1936, 1938). Photo author, 1990.

conventional branch of 100,000 square feet to serve the enormous planned residential community of Parkchester in the Bronx.[71] In contrast to its upstate sibling, the Parkchester store proved highly successful and provided the company with a foundation for an aggressive postwar development program. Other New York–area stores pioneered the concept of a branch devoted exclusively to appliances. By the 1930s, these fixtures had become a major component of the household inventory. A branch devoted to them freed considerable space in the parent store, and locating the branches closer to consumers' homes, proponents believed, helped stimulate sales. Abraham & Straus introduced the idea with an outlet in the Jamaica section of Queens in 1934. The Newark-based Kresge Department Stores followed suit with units in Elizabeth (1936) and Plainfield (1937), New Jersey.[72]

By the late 1930s, too, some indication existed that branch department stores might become a phenomenon that affected more than a few of the largest metropolitan areas. In 1941, Burdine's purchased a sizable department store at West Palm Beach five years after it was built. Kerr Dry Goods Company opened a small branch close to the most fashionable residential districts of Oklahoma City (1936–37). John Gerber Company in Memphis did likewise in 1941. Just before the store's opening, Gerber's president proudly indicated that branch building carried prestige for the community as well as for the business: "Memphis is now in the major leagues and demands the more efficient service which a suburban store can give."[73] While all newly constructed buildings or extensively renovated ones were touted as exemplars of the latest features in department store design, few boasted significant innovations. Two prominent exceptions were the new resort stores in Miami Beach for Burdine's (1935–36) and Saks Fifth Avenue (1939), which were not only much larger than most of their ilk but also testaments to the department store's role as a pacesetter of modernity. Designed by Eleanor Le Maire, Burdine's interior, especially, elicited considerable interest among retailers. The openness of its layout, an exuberant color palette—including "maize, lettuce green, blue, white, and lemon"—along with its extensive use of indirect lighting rendered it one of the most unusual selling environments in the country (fig. 156).[74]

Generally, however, the most discussed new work in department store interiors occurred with remodeling downtown buildings, not constructing new branches. Branch development on the eve of the Second World War was marked by how little rather than by how much was accomplished—in conspicuous contrast to a decade earlier. Nevertheless, amid the prevailing mood of caution and uncertainty, two projects were undertaken on opposite ends of the continent that not only manifested unbound optimism in the future of branch expansion but established important precedents

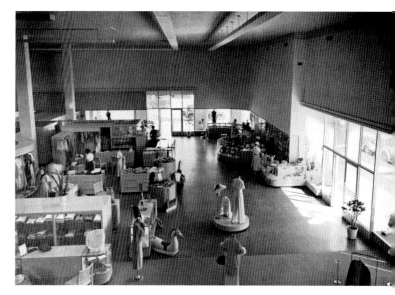

156. Burdine's department store, 800 Lincoln Road, Miami Beach (1935–36). Robert Law Weed, architect; Eleanor Le Maire, interior architect. View of main selling area. Photo Gottscho, 1936 (*Architectural Record,* May 1936, 387).

when such work became the dominant thrust in the industry's growth after World War II. One lay in the western part of Los Angeles, not far from Beverly Hills. The other was built outside the town center of Manhasset to serve an array of prosperous suburban tracts along Long Island's North Shore. Both were part of a new kind of linear commercial development conceived as a competitor with downtown, a precursor to the regional shopping mall that became known as the Miracle Mile.

Miracle Mile

Los Angeles department store executives appear to have harbored none of the doubts about branch development that most of their colleagues did in the post-Depression years. Between 1935 and 1940, three of the five major companies embarked on ambitious construction campaigns. Bullock's, which had opened a relatively modest college store in the planned shopping district of Westwood Village in 1932, enlarged it three times in rapid succession so that eight years later it had become a "complete" department store offering a wide variety of goods to consumers of all ages. Building on its success with the purchased Hollywood store, the Broadway sought further to upgrade its standing with a new 95,000-square-foot branch, which opened in 1940 in the heart of Pasadena's shopping core. Boasting an exuberant corner tower and a rear "carriage entrance" with an adjacent parking lot, the store exuded a stylish modernity previously associated primarily with Wilshire Boulevard.[75] But by far the most lavish investment was made by the May Company in a store designed to dominate the trade in western Los Angeles County. Having resisted erecting a branch in Hollywood some years earlier, Tom May, head of the company's West Coast division, devoted considerable time to determining the location and nature of the one he believed would inevitably be built. The importance of planning was heightened by the fact that this would be not only the company's entry into a highly competitive bid for trade beyond downtown Los Angeles, but the first branch within the extensive May Company system. Apparently several years were devoted to searching for a site easily accessible to a large share of the region's affluent and prosperous middle-class population. Like Bullock's Wilshire and the Broadway Hollywood, this store was to enhance the prestige of its parent company, but it was also intended to have broad-based appeal. Operating on a property removed from his direct competitors also seems to have been a determining factor. In the early 1930s no place afforded this combination of assets, but near the decade's close a part of the Wilshire corridor emerged as an ideal location. Lying more or less equidistant from the posh mid-Wilshire district to the east, the Hollywood Hills to the north, and Beverly Hills and Westwood to the northwest, the precinct was also surrounded by vast tracts of new middle-income housing. Several prominent downtown clothing stores had established branches there in the late 1920s, and the area was becoming a major commercial center. In 1937 the Coulter Dry Goods Company announced it would close its downtown store and build a four-story emporium containing over 120,000 square feet in the heart of this precinct, greatly intensifying the level of its retail activity. Christened the Miracle Mile by its developer, A. W. Ross, this seventeen-block stretch of Wilshire Boulevard was not a fully integrated shopping center, but it did enjoy the benefits of more attention to the nature and quality of building than did the vast majority of outlying retail districts then in existence.[76]

Even as it became one of southern California's premier business centers the Miracle Mile still offered space for new buildings. May chose a site removed from Coulter's and other stores, apparently for several reasons. Lying at the northeast corner of Wilshire and Fairfax Avenue, an artery, the property was easily reached from the exclusive hillside enclaves. Visually the site was oriented to Beverly Hills more than to sections of Los Angeles to the east. Finally, two contiguous blocks could be secured in their entirety, allowing ample room for an immense store and car lot, as well as for expansion. In size, the May Company Wilshire store was indeed unprecedented among branches. Rising five stories, it encompassed more than 270,000 square feet. Its vast rear parking area could accommodate 450 cars, more than any other retail facility in the country at the time.[77] Unlike Bullock's Wilshire, the store was planned as a complete extension of the downtown plant, although emphasis was given to higher grades of merchandise. May adapted the approach pioneered by Marshall Field's and Strawbridge's, developing a branch that was a sizable, full-fledged department store in its own right. At the same time, he greatly increased the scale of the operation, anticipating a huge volume of trade. Even though May went to great pains to emphasize that erecting a sumptuous new store in no way signaled a decline in the importance of the downtown plant, he moved the company offices to the new building, in effect making it the flagship.

Both the size of the store and the approach that May took in developing it as a retail facility probably contributed to some of the conventional aspects of its design. On the outside, the massing, composition, and character gave no hint of the open site and low-density development all around, but rather suggested a downtown store (fig. 157). While proclaiming its modernity with a bold corner element counterpointing unadorned elevations, the design was also quite conservative, its basic arrangement a traditional one, creating somewhat the impression of an older store that had been resurfaced. Inside, the main selling floor and the array of departments treated as shops bespoke the atmosphere of a grand emporium in the center of a metropolis—glamorous, but not unorthodox (fig. 158). It was not the building, then, that embodied significant innovations, but rather the idea of setting a big-city store in an outlying location. None of these qualities were likely accidental. The principal designer for the project, including the interiors, was May's brother-in-law, Samuel Marx, with whom he worked closely on transforming his ideas into three dimensions.[78] The results accomplished much more than consummating the Miracle Mile's place as a leading commercial center for southern California. When the store opened in September 1939 it was hailed as the showcase facility for the whole May Company network. Its great size, mainstream merchandising approach, and subdued modernism all provided a basis for the May Company's branch expansion after World War II, a campaign that ranked among the most ambitious and influential in the nation. Tom May was confident that large-scale branch development was the way of the future, and that he knew how to give it mass-market appeal, tempering newness with familiarity.

The other Miracle Mile—actually one of many nationwide inspired by its Wilshire Boulevard namesake—would not coalesce until around 1950. The creation of a Long Island builder, Sol Atlas, this Miracle Mile gained fame as a concentration of Fifth Avenue store branches.[79] Set along Northern Boulevard, an east-west arterial route, Atlas's Miracle Mile was much less densely developed than its Los Angeles counterpart. Small store blocks, individual buildings, and a four-story medical center stood free amid landscaped yards and capacious parking lots. The urban ambience that Ross

157. May Company department store, Wilshire Boulevard and Fairfax Avenue, Los Angeles (1938–39). Albert C. Martin, architect; Samuel A. Marx, associate architect and interior designer. Photo author, 1990.

158. May Company Wilshire store. Main selling floor (Emrich Nicholson, *Contemporary Shops in the United States,* 142).

159. Lord & Taylor store, Northern Boulevard and Shelter Rock Road, Manhasset, New York (1940–41). Starrett & Van Vleck, architects; Raymond Loewy Associates, designers; later additions. Interior view. Photo Robert M. Damora, 1941 (Emrich Nicholson, *Contemporary Shops in the United States,* 108).

160. Lord & Taylor Manhasset, exterior view. Photo author, 1988.

cultivated along Wilshire Boulevard and that was stalwartly maintained by the big May Company store was wholly absent. Instead, the development celebrated its "country" setting in a way virtually unknown for large outlying commercial districts before the war. The precedent for this approach to shaping a retail center came in large part from its first building, which was erected as a lone-wolf store some years prior to the coalescing of the Miracle Mile. That building was the initial branch of the venerable Fifth Avenue emporium Lord & Taylor.

In spring 1940, Lord & Taylor president Walter Hoving decided to situate his store on a two-acre parcel along Northern Boulevard just beyond the edge of concentrated settlement in Manhasset. It was an unusual decision for the time, as the most obvious location on Long Island then was Garden City, where Loeser's had recently built its branch department store and a number of Fifth Avenue specialty shops were operating. These enterprises were situated along a corridor set aside for the purpose. It had ample space not only for buildings but for car lots, which were part of one of the most comprehensive municipal parking programs in the country. Hempstead, lying eight miles to the north, had Nassau County's largest established commercial district, in which Arnold Constable was just completing its second branch store. Manhasset and other communities near the Lord & Taylor site were much smaller, but they also lay closer to many of the most prosperous suburban enclaves that had been developed since the First World War, for which Northern Boulevard was the principal spine. Easy access for many of the area's most prosperous households and an absence of nearby competition, then, appear to have been primary factors. But in contrast to most lone-wolf locations—including those of Bullock's Wilshire or, closer to home, Best & Company in Mamaroneck—the property was not surrounded by extensive, low-density development. Rather, it lay on the suburban fringe in an area that could be termed country. That association appears to have been a decisive factor in the site's appeal, and it became a major determinant of the store's design.

Much like Bullock's Wilshire, Lord & Taylor's Manhasset store broke new ground not only in its siting, but also in its design. In this case, however, the scheme enjoyed a much greater direct impact on later work, becoming a paradigm for postwar expansion. Hoving wanted a store that would fit in with the popular notion (if fast-disappearing reality) of Long Island as an elegant rural retreat. The design that emerged carried no urban overtones. To execute this concept, he secured the services not only of Starrett & Van Vleck, which had prepared plans for the Fifth Avenue store in 1913, but also of Raymond Loewy Associates, which was primarily responsible for the scheme, inside and out. Much like others in the field by 1940, Loewy's approach was to develop an open, informal interior arrangement, but without the constraints of an urban site. Perhaps for the first time the main selling floor of a department store fully embodied the spirited informality that designers had pursued over the previous decade (fig. 159). Here, too, the exterior set a precedent in embodying comparably free, casual qualities, set back from the street, embellished by landscaping on all sides. The building also was strikingly modern among retail establishments of the period, with none of the classicizing arrangements of form and composition associated with Art Deco (fig. 160). Lord & Taylor was of a more avant-garde cut, with a dynamic play of abstract forms. Glazing was used extensively, not for traditional display windows but to make the interior itself function as a display, especially when illuminated at night. The large window areas further allowed the selling spaces to seem more a part of their open setting and gave customers ample opportunity to examine goods in natural light—something that was considered a luxury. The arresting composition was calculated to attract the eye of the passing motorist at a time when architecture of this kind barely existed in the public sphere.[80]

Yet if the scheme was one of the most unorthodox among department stores of the prewar period, it also possessed attributes calculated to appeal to an affluent and largely conservative clientele. The exterior veneers, brick and fieldstone, were selected to suggest the area's "colonial" past, and the interior spaces, while far from historicizing, were intimately scaled. In a very different way from the May Company Wilshire store, Lord & Taylor Manhasset struck an effective balance between modernity and tradition that was likewise conceived to hold popular appeal. Here, Loewy and his patron pushed the boundaries of architectural expression in the retail sphere, but they did so in a way that would seem comforting, not alien, to their well-heeled customers. The Manhasset store was not just "modern"; it was billed as "country modern"—a term that captured many of the allusions, but also the illusions, of life in American suburbs at mid-century. Here was a place that concretized the atmosphere everyone wanted to have on the fringes of the metropolis in a way that seemed not only enticing but inevitable.

6 Station Wagon Stores

TOWARD THE MIDDLE of October 1951, well-heeled inhabitants of greater Dallas were introduced to the first branch of Neiman-Marcus, which lay seven miles from the city center in University Park, amid the metropolitan area's best residential districts. Dubbed a Town and Country store, the elegantly understated emporium offered, according to *Women's Wear Daily,* "facilities never before available in a suburban store in the Southwest." Besides a beauty salon and a restaurant, the building boasted private rooms for dining and "afternoon entertaining." The building did not sit on the generous site in the way Lord & Taylor Manhasset did, but its design was clearly an offspring. Here, to mitigate the effects of a constrained lot, two-story glazed walls opened onto a patio garden (fig. 161). Designed by Eleanor Le Maire, the interior was calculated to evoke "wide open spaces," with Indian motifs and southwestern colors integral to the design. But the effect was neither provincial nor historicizing (fig. 162). It is unlikely that a more suave modernist building could have been found in the immediate region, or perhaps anywhere in Texas. A sizable mobile by Alexander Calder was only one of many features that gave the store

161. *(right)* Neiman-Marcus Company store, Preston Road near Westwood Drive, University Park, Texas (1949–51). De Witt & Swank, architects; Eleanor Le Maire, interior architect; demolished.

162. *(top)* Neiman-Marcus University Park, interior view. Photo c. 1951.

an aura of cool sophistication.[1] What impressed the editors of *Architectural Forum* and no doubt many others was that the scheme achieved an elusive balance. The *Forum*'s coverage began: "How do you make a suburban store so informal that women will run in and out to shop there so casually as in the neighborhood supermarket? How at the same time do you make it so suggestive of luxury that it will put every shopper in the mood to spend more money than she planned to spend?" The emporium was cast as a new breed that reflected not only the massive movement of affluent and middle-income households alike ever farther from the urban core, but also the generational shift in taste and habits that entailed a new level of convenience, casualness, and, at the same time, material betterment. *Forum*'s name for this establishment could not have been more appropriate: "station wagon store."[2]

Nearly a half-century later, Stanley Marcus offered a very different perspective on the project, the planning for which he spearheaded. His father, Herbert Marcus, then president of the company, was adamantly opposed to building branch stores. He believed that they undermined the meticulous merchandising organization and personal service that had made his business so renowned. The elder Marcus went against his better judgment, however, because he and especially his son feared that a New York store such as Saks Fifth Avenue, which had an aggressive branch building program in many parts of the country, would come to Dallas. Were that move made, the store would not be downtown, Stanley Marcus suspected, but rather in an outlying area. Neiman-Marcus's genteel station wagon store was conceived and executed foremost as a "defensive outpost."[3]

No matter how prominent the company and how determined its leadership might be to erect a branch that would keep the competition in its place, the process was often difficult. Stanley Marcus worked on creating a branch for half a decade, first unveiling plans in March 1946 for an equally fine store slightly closer in than the site eventually used. The initial location lay across from Highland Park Village, one of the country's pioneer shopping centers and a mecca for well-to-do Dallasites who lived nearby. While the shopping center's management did not oppose the plans, the Highland Park town council resisted expanding commercial development beyond the shopping center's limited boundaries for fear of adverse impact on adjacent residential property—one of many such governmental actions taken during the postwar period. Marcus had to wait three years until plans coalesced for another, more expansive, shopping complex to the north. Even then, the one lot available was a long, narrow one not ideally suited for a freestanding store. Once construction was under way, the Marcuses made what turned out to be the wrong merchandising decision by predicting that demand would be for moderate-priced goods.

Customers instead clamored for expensive wares, and a complicated restocking program was undertaken. The store proved exceedingly popular, but site limitations precluded its enlargement. What was initially considered to be a generous off-street parking area also proved inadequate. Elaborate plans were prepared for an unobtrusive parking garage, but local authorities refused to grant a variance for its construction. A little more than a decade after the store's opening, plans were made for relocating the operation so that present and future needs could be fully addressed—now as part of a vast, enclosed regional shopping mall that seemed worlds apart from the intimate station wagon store.[4]

Like all aspects of department store operation, branch building was complex and risky. What distinguished it from the others was the scale to which it grew and the central importance it acquired in retailing during the fifteen years after World War II. Whereas most members of the industry regarded this phenomenon as a tentative and peripheral activity before Pearl Harbor, it became identified as the most significant tendency in the field by the time Neiman-Marcus opened its first branch. Stanley Marcus and colleagues coast to coast realized that without creating such outposts their businesses would be unable to expand or perhaps even to survive. Amid all the efforts to upgrade downtown stores, improve merchandising and other operational techniques, and combat the intensifying problems of vehicular congestion and parking, no agenda was held more urgent than creating new outposts, defensive or otherwise.

Despite the wide range of experiments in branch development during the 1920s and 1930s, major retailers appear to have had little sense of the best way to fulfill their objectives in the immediate postwar years. For all his business savvy, Marcus admitted that he and everyone else so engaged had no real sense of what they were or were not accomplishing. Precedents probably played a greater role than most department store executives admitted or perhaps realized, but they felt as though they were simply going "by the seat of their pants."[5] The new Neiman-Marcus branch and other station wagon stores embodied the optimism of the postwar era. They were landmarks of a purportedly new and better metropolitan order, one abundant in green open space, conducive to relaxation, predicated on convenience—an environment touted as clean, healthy, and safe, ideal for families and for progress of all kinds, a world absent all the difficulties that many Americans believed were endemic to more traditional forms of urban life. But the ideal was often far from the reality. Even in a prosperous and expanding market most consumers could not afford to purchase goods at such an emporium on a regular basis. Department store executives who sought to fashion their new branches in a similar vein were making a costly error, according to E. B. Weiss, one of the most perceptive and outspoken analysts of the industry. By creating "aristocratic stores" retailers were alienating their real market, he charged. Most department store executives should never try to emulate Neiman-Marcus; they should learn from Sears and other chain operations instead.[6]

Branch development did in fact emerge as a multifaceted phenomenon at the very beginning of the postwar era and continued as such for well over a decade. Just as metropolitan residential growth was hardly limited to the stereotype of gardenlike suburban enclaves, so department store branches were cast in a variety of ways to serve an increasingly diverse and large audience. The extent of this spectrum was generated as much by differing views among retailers about what a department store branch should be as it was grounded in careful study of the market, and it affected every aspect of the enterprise. Widely differing viewpoints persisted as to the optimal location for, as well as size and character of, the branch department store. The range and depth of stock carried, the logistics of acquiring merchandise, and indeed almost every facet of operation were sources of debate. As a company opened additional branches, which collectively rivaled or exceeded the downtown store in sales volume, some executives questioned the basic concept of a parent and a branch, arguing that their businesses were in effect chains. Others saw this shift as a threat to the very nature of the establishments in their charge. Irrespective of such divergences, change was omnipresent and ongoing. By the 1950s branch development dominated the field, transforming it in the process. The downtown stores, whose owners sometimes still planned to enlarge them, remained significant bases of operation, but their hegemony was a thing of the past. In many cases they were simply the largest units in a galaxy that encompassed the metropolitan area and sometimes greater regions. Appearance, merchandising, and support systems had all changed in the process. In less than a generation, the department store became a very different entity than it had been in the prewar years.

Inauguration

The "retail rush" to outlying areas, as one account depicted the situation in the mid-1940s, was a conspicuous and remarkable phenomenon by any standard.[7] Even before the war's end, major department store companies announced plans to open branches, and a number of others disclosed their intentions to do so. The pace accelerated with the return of peace. By the close of 1945, plans to open no fewer than thirty-two new branches had been made public by more than twenty companies, half as many as had been realized between 1931 and 1942. Over one hundred announcements were added to the roster during the next four years. These figures soon seemed unimpressive compared to those of the next decade. More than 150 projects were announced between 1950 and the end of 1954; 52 more in 1955 alone; and nearly 200 from 1956 through 1960. The great majority saw realization—more than 530 in seventeen years.[8] The space encompassed by these branches was even more impressive, roughly 38 million square feet, compared with some 4 million in branches opened between 1920 and 1941. The size increase was progressive. Square footage added between 1950 and 1954 was nearly double that of the previous six years but was only about a third of that added from 1955 through 1960. Perhaps the most telling indication of the shift in priorities was that the total square footage of branches established between 1944 and 1960 was nearly five times the figure added to downtown emporia over the same period and was probably over 10 million square feet more than all additions and new buildings constructed for the major department stores in the urban core between 1920 and 1960, even though branches were almost always much smaller than parent stores.[9] In quantifiable terms, the magnitude of the collective endeavor was unrivaled in the industry.

The principal reason that virtually all the major department store companies committed to branch development by 1950 and continued to expand in this realm thereafter was the epochal shift of their primary market from established urban districts to outlying, sparsely settled areas. The process of lateral growth had, of course, long characterized urban expansion in the United States. The 1920s ranked among the most intense periods of such development. Toward that decade's end the population shift began to be seen by some department store executives not as a premise for enlarging the downtown store but as a potential threat to their business. The concern over decentralization mounted anew among retailers after the worst years of the Depression.

If in some respects, post–World War II trends were merely a continuation of patterns that were by then firmly established on the American landscape, important differences existed. First were the vast numbers of middle- and upper-middle-class people involved. Nationally, savings tripled between 1940 and 1965. From 1946 to 1965 residential mortgage debt swelled from $17.7 billion to $208.7 billion. The construction rate of new residences in the 1950s was more or less double that of the previous decade and six times that of the 1930s. The overwhelming majority of new residential development occurred, of course, on the urban periphery. During the 1950s the population in "central cities" increased 8.2 percent, while that in "suburban sections" rose 47.2 percent. Contributing to this suburban growth was the rising prosperity of many households. The new mass consumer market that observers, including retailers, had thought was emerging in the 1920s in fact arose a generation later. Moreover, in contrast to the previous generation, the "new" consumers tended to view purchasing goods as a virtue, an act necessary to improving the standard of living and the quality of life.[10] Not only was the consumer market larger and moving farther afield, its settlement patterns were often more diffuse and sprawling. Pervasive automobility rendered vast areas of open space opportune territory for middle-class and prosperous blue-collar residential tracts alike, and also fostered a more generous use of land for those dwellings. Traditional urban models, with lots of comparatively narrow frontage organized on a grid, were eschewed in favor of ones previously associated with enclaves of the affluent, with houses set on capacious yards in tracts that increasingly boasted irregular, curving streets.

The cumulative result of this shift was a substantial decrease in population density in newly developed areas, accelerating the distances from the city center in which new development occurred. That center had continued to function as the dominant retail magnet as long as shoppers remained within a three- to five-mile radius and could rely on public transportation that converged on downtown. During the postwar years, however, the distances involved grew to be more in the five- to ten- or even fifteen-mile radius, which made the core seem ever more remote and difficult to reach. In reality, too, the exponential increase in automobile usage for everyday functions that occurred during the mid-twentieth century rendered the city center a markedly less convenient place.

The need to drive greater distances over increasingly crowded streets culminated in downtown congestion and parking challenges. A major portion of the department stores' key audience was fast moving beyond the range of the downtown emporia. Moreover, automobility also dealt a devastating blow to public transportation, diminishing the systems that had been the lifeblood of downtown's great growth. Whereas department store executives had long striven to erect bigger stores to enlarge and retain their market, they now labored hard to sustain a clientele sufficient to justify the huge physical plants they had created. The era of the downtown department store was hardly over in the 1950s, but its key role in the distribution of goods had peaked. Henceforth, more attention would be devoted to recapturing, retaining, and enlarging the department store's consumer base close to its new home ground.[11]

Even with sweeping population shifts and changes in routine transportation modes, department store executives might have resisted the expense and difficulty of branch building. But the chain store remained an omnipresent threat. Downtown retailers had witnessed the accelerating expansion of chain companies in outlying areas since the mid-1920s and were all too cognizant of their vigorous growth during the postwar years. To make matters worse, chains had not only usurped the department store's dominance in the sale of many low-cost goods, these businesses were expanding their lines, making greater inroads into the department store's traditional territory. Competition also now existed from comparable downtown establishments, just as Herbert and Stanley Marcus feared. Being the first major store to open a branch in a lucrative new trading area was a coup. Furthermore, once one department store made such a move in a given metropolitan area, others felt compelled to do the same or lose a conspicuous share of the booming suburban market. Conventional wisdom held that an aggressive expansion policy was a necessity. And the more that branch development occurred, the more the process intensified.

Despite the circumstances, many department store executives undertook branch development reluctantly. The investments they had made in downtown plants were huge, and they feared that branch building might in fact erode existing trade, not enhance it. The urban core had been neglected since the onset of the Depression, but it could be renewed, they insisted, and no outlying business district could begin to match the array of goods and services downtown continued to offer. The very idea of a great department store, in the minds of most of their owners, was based on its comprehensiveness, not on the limitations inherent in a branch. Yet the first round of branches that opened after World War II proved enormously popular. They were profitable and, as it turned out, did not significantly undercut sales at the parent store. Branches could even improve downtown patronage.[12] These factors, combined with retail competition and the steady outward movement of the population, spurred the pronounced rise in branch building during the postwar years. But the process was sufficiently daunting that it was compared to crossing a minefield.[13]

Scope

The planning was complicated by the multitude of divergent views among department store executives as to a sound strategy for branch development. Between 1945 and the early 1950s the focus was on building or acquiring individual stores; only thereafter did the tendency shift to planning branches as integral parts of regional shopping centers. During the earlier period, especially, opinions differed widely as to the optimal size and location of a building, as well as the scope and nature of its operation. A few retailers considered the branch as a purely supplemental venture, at least in the initial years of planning. The most common outlet of this sort was the appliance and/or furniture store where samples of bulky hard goods could be displayed close to customers' homes. But even within this realm, noticeable differences in location occurred. Newark-based Kresge Department Stores and Bamberger's opened several such outlets during the mid-1940s in the suburban business centers of sizable, affluent communities: Summit, East Orange, and Millburn. Herpolsheimer's in Grand Rapids, Michigan, selected four sites in that city's blue-collar neighborhoods. Maas Brothers in Tampa opened a home furnishings store specifically tailored to the Cuban-American community. Hartford's G. Fox, on the other hand, erected a building of substantial dimensions for outdoor furniture in a quasi-rural site that was readily accessible by highway. Not all such programs were focused on hard goods, however. New York–based Hearn Department Stores contemplated building a network of linen stores in 1947, but only one was realized.[14] In most cases, store executives emphasized that the branch was not a dumping ground for items that failed to sell at the parent. Washington's Woodward & Lothrop, on the other hand, successfully ran a small branch in nearby Bethesda, Maryland, as a "budget store." Customer demand warranted the construction of an additional floor on the small building in 1953–54. When it burned a few months later a new edifice of more decorous design was hastily erected (fig. 163). On the other hand, Wm. H. Block of Indianapolis opened a small branch devoted to women's and children's apparel of high grade in that city's most stylish residential district. Few full-fledged department store companies pursued expansion through college shops, as some had before the war. Saks Fifth Avenue, on the other hand, strengthened its appeal to male customers by establishing several outlets in college communities. "Navy and Army Shops" were opened in Ithaca, New Haven, and Princeton, among other locations, while the nation was engaged in combat. Subsequently, larger facilities were built in New Haven (1948) and Cambridge (1957).[15]

The resort store never regained the major role it had enjoyed in branch development during the prewar years, but several companies sought to expand the purview of such outlets in significant ways. Precedent for such programs was set as early as 1934, when Kresge purchased the Steinbach Company—the "world's largest resort store"—whose five-story, block-long pile stood in the heart of Asbury Park, the northern New Jersey shore's main business center. Open year round, the emporium catered both to vacationers and a sizable resident population. By substantially enlarging the spectrum of merchandise available, the new owners sought to enhance the glamorous associations of a beach outlet with the metropolitan character of a great department store. The venture lasted only about a decade, however, and in 1946 Kresge's opened a much more modest resort shop in the community's major hotel.[16] A dozen years later the Philadelphia-based Snellenbergs followed Kresge's first move, acquiring the even larger M. E. Blatt in Atlantic City to capitalize on the sizable resident and tourist populations alike (fig. 164). Well before then, Burdine's vacated its Miami

163. Woodward & Lothrop Budget Store, 7201 Wisconsin Avenue, Bethesda, Maryland (1955). Arthur P. Starr, architect; demolished. Photo ca. 1955.

164. Snellenbergs department store, Atlantic and South Carolina avenues, Atlantic City, New Jersey. Built for Braunstein-Blatt Company (1919–21), Price & McLanahan, architects; acquired by Snellenbergs (1958); altered. (*Atlantic City Daily News,* 16 January 1921, Braunstein-Blatt sect., 1.)

165. Bullock's department store, Palm Canyon Drive, Palm Springs, California (1945–47). Wurdeman & Becket, architects; demolished ca. early 1990s. Photo author, 1987.

Beach quarters to a much larger new building that was likewise a full-fledged department store.[17] Even without a large all-year population to serve, some resort stores were now conceived as substantial outlets in their own right. The tone was set by the very elegant Bullock's Palm Springs emporium, which opened in 1947 (fig. 165). Three times the size of the previous store, the building contained a wide selection of hard goods, as well as apparel and accessories, in a setting trumpeted as the "expression of desert living." Not to be outdone, both J. W. Robinson and Saks Fifth Avenue erected posh establishments nearby in the next decade.[18] Through such projects the resort store was transformed from a modest shop into a destination in its own right.

Much the same change characterized the evolution of mainstream branches during the postwar years. Chronicles of the process repeatedly criticized stores of the 1940s and even early 1950s as being too small, but just what this deficiency entailed in terms of actual size was seldom specified.[19] The majority of branches constructed before the mid-1950s were of less than 100,000 square feet, which was indeed small by the standards of even a few years later. Among those not built as part of shopping centers or of the specialized nature of an appliance or linen store, over a third were under 40,000 square feet. A few of these were built in outlying sections of metropolitan areas. The first branch of Joseph Horne, Pittsburgh's premier department store, affords a good example. Opened in May 1945, the unit lay in the heart of the business center of Mount Lebanon, a prosperous, middle-class suburb of thirty thousand lying some five miles south of the city center. Occupying two store units totaling probably less than 10,000 square feet, the outlet was limited to merchandise that many department store executives believed would be most desired in such locations: apparel and accessories for women and children. Four years later an adjacent store unit was added, as were two more in 1953, bringing the total area to 28,000 square feet (fig. 166). With each expansion came additional departments or enlargement of existing ones, yet the space fell far short of that needed to provide a good representation of all the goods offered at the parent store. Such ventures were not limited to middle- and upper-middle-income enclaves. Buffalo's Hens & Kelly, which targeted a broader market, opened its first branch (18,000 square feet) in 1950 in a store it had purchased to serve prosperous blue-collar neighborhoods on the city's south side.[20] Still, most of the smallest branches were located not in or near large cities, but in communities of lesser size that lay outside the parent store's primary trading radius, places where their limited size generally proved adequate.

Far more branch stores serving major cities lay in the 40,000- to 99,000-square-foot range, and it was probably within this category that most problems occurred. If it was unusually elegant in its design, Neiman-Marcus's University Park store seems to have shared the drawbacks of limited space with many other branches. The difficulties stemmed from the fact that most department store executives strove to have their new outlets function as "complete" stores. Announcements that a new branch carried the full range of goods found at the parent abounded, but the enormous difference in size between the two facilities meant that the

166. Joseph Horne Company department store, 711–21 Washington Road, Mount Lebanon, Pennsylvania. Remodeling of existing store blocks (1945, 1949, 1953); altered. Photo author, 2008.

branch had to be severely limited in its selections. If the store operated with numerous departments, the choices (breadth of stock) among goods in at least some of those departments had to be quite meager, and the quantity (depth) of any given item small. Even when the departments were fewer, inadequate stocks was an endemic problem. Initially, senior management believed that stocking would not be an issue; anything not available in the branch could be delivered from the main store or the warehouse within a matter of hours. Customers held a very different perspective, however. The great appeal of branches was their convenience. Shopping at a branch often was not so much a recreational expedition as it was a task performed along with others during the course of the day. In most cases, patrons wished to take purchases home with them, a habit retailers encouraged since it greatly reduced delivery costs.[21] Under the circumstances, if the right model, size, or color of a given item was unavailable at the moment, customers often declined to purchase and, even worse, might go to a competing store. As with virtually all other matters pertaining to branch stores, opinions varied widely as to how to rectify the situation. By the early 1950s, this basic issue was identified as the most difficult one in branch store merchandising and became a central factor in defining the very nature of what a branch should be.[22]

Adequate stocking, under the circumstances, was closely tied to the particularities of consumer demands in a given location and with a specific store. A number of medium-sized branches proved too limited soon after their operation was established. Half a dozen years after it opened in 1947, B. Altman's Miracle Mile branch of about 45,000 square feet, which served a well-heeled clientele on Long Island's North Shore, began an expansion that increased its floor area two and a half times. An even bigger increase occurred less than a decade after the completion in 1949 of Bamberger's initial major branch (66,000 square feet) in Morristown, New Jersey, which served a considerably broader market. The management of Lit Brothers, who took over an 85,000-square-foot building formerly occupied by Frank & Seder in Upper Darby, Pennsylvania, planned to add a third story but did not anticipate the need to do so immediately. Yet the demands of the moderate-income shoppers who were the company's core customers were sufficiently great that the decision was made to embark on the expansion only six months after completing an ambitious yearlong renovation.[23] Announcements of such projects emphasized the stores' great successes, but in fact changes were often made to compensate for inadequate market assessment. In other instances, stores of about the same size functioned perfectly well when the range of stock was more focused. Abraham & Straus purchased Frederick Loeser's 80,000-square-foot store in affluent Garden City, Long Island, to address a limited range of needs while planning a branch nearly three times larger only a few miles away in Hempstead that would purvey a much greater assortment of wares to a commensurately broad clientele. Defying observer skepticism, the two stores operated well in this complementary relationship. In a somewhat parallel situation, Scruggs Vandervoort Barney, the most fashionable of St. Louis's department stores, erected a 74,000-square-foot branch in Clayton (1950–51), just west of the city. Instead of competing with Famous-Barr, which had previously announced plans for a much larger store a few blocks away, Vandervoort's opted for an elegant emporium carrying a limited array of high-end merchandise (fig. 167).[24] Similarly, major fashion-oriented departmentalized specialty stores such as Lord & Taylor, Saks Fifth Avenue, and I. Magnin often found that branches of 60,000 to 90,000 square feet were adequate, given the scope of merchandise and clientele.

For companies that intended their branches to meet

167. Scruggs Vandervoort Barney department store, Forsythe Boulevard and Hanley Road, Clayton, Missouri (1945–51). Harris Armstrong, architect; Amos Parrish & Company, interior designers. Photo Julius Shulman, ca. 1951.

a broad spectrum of needs among the immense middle market, buildings over 100,000 square feet proved optimal.[25] Some of these retailers ranked among the leaders in their respective cities, including Hahne's in Newark, Hengerer's in Buffalo, Wanamaker's in Philadelphia, Hutzler's in Baltimore, and Woodward & Lothrop in Washington. Others were targeted to more budget-conscious households, including Macy's (New York), Lit's (Philadelphia), Hecht's (Washington), Famous-Barr (St. Louis), and Bon Marche (Seattle). Like the big Los Angeles branches, these afforded sufficient space to provide both breadth and depth of stock. But the new plants sometimes proved insufficient. One of the first companies to build a "complete" branch for the middle market was Hecht's, which unveiled plans for a 160,000-square-foot branch in Silver Spring, Maryland, in November 1945. Four years later work began on an addition of 64,000 square feet, and a 45,000-square-foot enlargement was announced five years after that. Famous-Barr executives apparently considered their enormous (256,000-square-foot) Clayton branch too small soon after it opened in 1948, but they never made a major addition. Abraham & Straus, on the other hand, began work on the third story of its Hempstead store seven years after its opening in 1952, adding 140,000 square feet to an existing plant of 236,000.[26] As much as any facet of operation, the scope of merchandise underscored the variables that permeated the branch field and the futility of seeking to establish guidelines that applied across the board.

Operation

The debates over the optimal breadth and depth of stock to carry were indicative of more fundamental issues that affected not just branches, but the entire business structure of which they were a part. During the prewar and immediate postwar years, most department store executives considered branch operation comparatively straightforward. All the key operational components—buying, accounting, marking, advertising, promotion, display, and the like—were already in place at the parent store. Branch personnel followed the directives of central management. This relationship seemed both efficient and cost-effective in principle. However, having a large branch with a multitude of departments and subsequently having several branches severely challenged existing methods. Staff members found themselves overworked. Often, too, parent-store personnel gave little attention to the needs of the branch; time was inadequate even if the interest existed. The condition was particularly acute among buyers. To address the tastes of its clientele successfully, a branch required its own profile of stock, one consistent in overall terms with that of the parent store, yet also distinctive in terms of types of goods, price ranges, styles, and even colors. The purchasing patterns of branch patrons often proved quite different from those of shoppers in the parent store. Simply ordering additional quantities of a given item for the branch, based on assumptions or abstract projections of demand, proved woefully inadequate, as many retailers discovered. The demands of space allocation in a branch could markedly differ as well. Furthermore, the profile of one branch in a given company seldom matched that of another, so that the demands for the buyer's attention grew more complex with expansion.[27]

Logistics were another concern. During the early postwar years conventional wisdom held that all goods destined for a branch would be processed—inventoried, priced, and stored, if necessary—at the parent store, then delivered for display and sale. This kept support spaces at the branch to a minimum. Theoretically, replacement stock could be quickly transported from the parent store or warehouse. In practice, however, the most popular goods, which were critical to profits, often could not be replenished quickly enough. Branch managers clamored for more space for reserve stock and also for the most sought-after goods to be shipped directly from the manufacturer.[28] So doing not only necessitated yet additional space but also more personnel for processing. Yet the drawback of frequently running out of items became the overriding factor. By the early 1950s an increasing number of department store companies were allocating substantial amounts of space and people to these support functions.

At the heart of the matter was the degree to which the branch operated autonomously. Bullock's set the precedent for more-or-less independent stores with its Wilshire Boulevard branch in the late 1920s and continued that pattern as it established new outlets after World War II.[29] With this arrangement branch personnel performed all functions; integration with the parent organization occurred only at the highest levels of management. But as with every other aspect of branch development, opinions varied widely as to the best operational structure. Most department stores did not follow Bullock's lead even as branches became bigger and more numerous. Some companies opted for continuing a parent-based structure while enlarging or reorganizing their staffs to handle branch needs. A few, mostly notably Saks Fifth Avenue, adapted chain store methods.[30] But most department store personnel had a longstanding prejudice against chains. Once a big emporium operated several branches, as many did by the mid-1950s, the network was essentially a chain. Much could be gained, some analysts insisted, by adopting chain methods. The best chain companies, such as Sears, had through considerable trial and error developed sound mechanisms for accommodating the particularities of individual units without losing the efficiencies of a large-scale, centralized business. The stigma attached to chains was so great, however, that department store personnel frequently resisted any change remotely associated with those businesses. Only when trial ventures allowed the staff to see the benefits on home turf would they endorse such methods, one industry observer noted.[31]

The impetus for change was pressing, nevertheless. By the mid-1950s branches were reaping an ever-larger share of department store profits. One survey of fifty major cities showed that while downtown stores commanded over 78 percent of department store sales in 1948, that figure had shrunk to less than 54 percent six years later. Figures varied greatly between places and companies. Filene's reported that around 40 percent of sales came from branches by mid-1956; Macy's reported the same a year later. In Los Angeles, the network of enormous branches operated by major department stores attained or even exceeded 50 percent of sales by 1956. Stores in some other regions were reporting similar figures a few years later.[32] In the minds of nearly everyone involved, branches had ceased to be a mere extension of the main store and a defense against competition. They were engines of the industry and had to be run accordingly. At the decade's end, most department store companies with branches had embarked on significant changes in this sphere. No department store executive predicted that they would eventually replace the parent store, at least not publicly. Most retailers could not conceive of such a shift, and they had every reason to want their enormous investments downtown to remain economic mainstays. But branches were approaching equal partnership, which necessitated a more complex operational structure and hence more intricate planning than most parties had anticipated a decade previous.[33]

Planning

At the outset of postwar expansion, many department store executives were uncertain about virtually all aspects of establishing a branch. Contemporary accounts convey not only a sense of frustration, but they also suggest that much strategizing was conducted by empirical methods. The longstanding opinions, gut feelings, and casual impressions that had been the basis for branch development were identified as sources of innumerable difficulties. Such depictions, made by those in the business of "scientific" planning for retailers, were perhaps exaggerated in order to strengthen the client base. But criticism came from other quarters as well. In 1949, E. B. Weiss admonished department store executives that the "early post war models of these branch units may prove to be as sour lemons as some of Detroit's postwar [automobile] models." Enough retailers admitted that the problems were significant as to suggest that the critics were not wholly unfounded. Precedents existed, of course, from the prewar years, but many of these proved inadequate.

Early postwar branches, retailers conceded in retrospect, were indeed too small, lacked sufficient off-street parking, and were hampered by stock limitations.[34] Equally important, as many involved were quick to recognize, precedents often did not apply because each case had its own determining factors. What may have worked well in one instance could yield quite different results in another. Each project had to be thought anew. The particularized nature of branch development was one of its greatest challenges.

By 1950 the planning process had achieved greater clarity. Department store executives realized that many issues lay outside their realm of expertise; the services of economic and real estate analysts were essential. These consultants undertook copious surveys, gathering a spectrum of data to determine the optimal course for their clients. Among the overriding matters to address in this procedure was determining the geographic radius for branch operation; that is, whether the stores were best confined to a metropolitan area or could profitably extend to a greater region. In examining specific communities in which to locate, store executives had to weigh the nature and extent of the employment base, the particulars of household income, and the past and projected rate of population growth. These and other considerations—ranging from automobile accessibility to land costs—helped determine the store's size and location. Matching a branch to a community required not only a clear profile of the local inhabitants, but also of the parent store's existing customers. The latter information was out-of-date or otherwise incomplete in many cases, necessitating additional research. Without a good sense of customer wants, a branch operation could prove shaky. Surveying the competition—present and anticipated—in the community was no less essential. Finally, an attempt to estimate the sales potential and profit margin of the branch was advised even though such projections were rough at best.[35]

The intricacies of the relationship between gathered information and the design of the store itself led to a pronounced change in the latter process, which increasingly became dominated by a corps of specialists. The interior design field, which had risen to prominence in retailing during the 1930s, provided a major springboard for such work, but now most leading practitioners in this realm had training and experience as architects. The traditional process of an architect producing the basic form of a building and the interior designer working within that matrix was abandoned in favor of a more integrated approach. An important and widely publicized precedent for this was pioneered by Sears, Roebuck at its Pico Boulevard store in Los Angeles (1938–39), which placed merchandising needs at the heart of the design process.[36] The plan was the result of analyzing arrangements for selling in all departments, both individually and in relation to one another. From this perspective the building's structure and enclosing elements were no more than efficient responses to internal programmatic needs. The people who really determined a store's plan, therefore, had to possess detailed knowledge of retailing issues, as well as expertise in design.

The new prominence accorded to interior design was fostered, and in all likelihood shaped extensively, by what by the 1950s was called the Raymond Loewy Corporation. The celebrated industrial designer had established a department of architecture and interior design in 1937 when he was commissioned to remodel a number of spaces at Lord & Taylor's Fifth Avenue store. Loewy chose William Snaith to run the operation. After training as an architect Snaith had worked as a set designer and with decorator Elsie de Wolfe before joining the office in 1936. Under Snaith's direction the department quickly became a major component of the firm. While responsible for the disastrous experiment of Macy's at Syracuse, it also produced the stunning scheme for Lord & Taylor at Manhasset. Seven years after it was established, Snaith's department became the Raymond Loewy Corporation, retaining the name but functioning as a nearly independent business.[37] Between 1945 and 1960 the firm played a key role in the design of at least forty branch department stores. Sometimes the firm had complete charge of the project, providing all design services. In many other instances, when Snaith and his associates worked in collaboration with another architectural office, they nonetheless appear to have played the dominant role. Retailers found that Snaith had a fertile imagination and was completely sympathetic to their needs—in conspicuous contrast with many architects.[38] Snaith's own writings indicate that his office was prepared to take an active role in advising department store companies on some of the fundamental aspects of size, location, and merchandising well before the design stage.[39] The Loewy Corporation secured an impressive portfolio of clients by any standard. While many projects were in the Northeast, the practice was national in scope. Besides all the postwar branches of Lord & Taylor, others were done for companies coast to coast, including Bloomingdale's (New York), Filene's (Boston), Woodward & Lothrop (Washington), J. W. Robinson (Los Angeles), Burdine's (Miami), Halle's (Cleveland), Gimbel's and the Boston Store (Milwaukee), Hengerer's (Buffalo), and Wm. H. Block (Indianapolis). The prestige of these commissions, combined with their sheer volume, made the Loewy Corporation one of the standard-bearers in the field throughout the postwar years.

While Snaith's firm arguably dominated the design of department store branches, it was by no means the only one. Five other New York–based offices figured prominently in the field as well: Copeland, Novak & Associates (later Copeland, Novak & Israel); Meyer Katzman; Amos Parrish; Ketchum, Gina & Sharp; and Abbott, Merkt. Peter Copeland, who described himself as an "industrial architect," had worked with several New York–area firms specializing in commercial buildings and also in the design offices of Macy's before establishing his own office in 1934. He was joined eighteen years later by Adolph Novak, who had worked for theater architect John Eberson and then for John Wanamaker for five years. The firm specialized in department store interiors, mostly for New York and Philadelphia companies, but also for others farther afield by 1960. Meyer Katzman was employed by architects in Detroit and New York before joining Macy's staff in 1930, remaining there for six years. After a stint at freelance store design he entered Copeland's office in 1946 and began his own practice three years later. At first, he, too, focused on department store interiors, but he broadened the scope to include entire buildings by the mid-1950s. Parrish, on the other hand, was a leading retail consultant who expanded his services to include interior design after World War II. While that arm of the practice does not appear to have been extensive, it was national in scope. In a vein probably inspired by Loewy, a principal of the firm proudly coined the phrase "engineered designing" to describe the ostensibly scientific process his staff followed.[40] With all these offices, the idea of interior as theater that was so emphasized in the 1930s was replaced by touting efficiency and convenience. Interior design firms now sold themselves to retail clients on the basis of their technical prowess in addressing the challenges of layout and character in a branch store. Eleanor Le Maire, who had enjoyed such a prominent role before the war, played a marginal one thereafter, even though she proved her adaptability with the first Neiman-Marcus branch.

Staying in favor with retailers was by no means easy. The architecture firm Ketchum, Gina & Sharp began the postwar years as a leading innovator. Morris Ketchum, who had extensive experience in the design of small specialty shops, became an exponent of innovative new approaches to store design more broadly. The firm worked on several interiors for Macy's and its affiliate Davison-Paxon and enjoyed much favorable publicity for the Hutzler's branch in Towson, Maryland (1950–52). Ketchum also wrote a leading text on store design. Yet his scheme for one of the nation's first regional shopping malls, Shopper's World in Framingham, Massachusetts (1948–51), experienced considerable financial difficulties. Coupled with the experimental nature of other proposals, the complex seems to have undermined his reputation, and the firm did little work for department stores after the early 1950s.[41] Abbott, Merkt, on the other hand, took a consistently pragmatic approach. Having become well known to retailers nationally for its work with service buildings, the firm expanded into the retail sphere before the war's end, with designs for branches of Burdine's and Hecht's. Thereafter, Abbott, Merkt became one of the most prolific firms in the field, working primarily with companies in New York, Rochester, and Washington, D.C. Given the engineering origins of the firm, however, no pretense was made in the realm of interior design, which was always done by a collaborating office.

No other metropolitan area began to equal New York as a center for department store design, but Los Angeles emerged as a strong second by the early 1950s through the work of two architectural firms—Welton Becket & Associates and Victor Gruen Associates—both of which were responsible for the interior and exterior design of most of their department stores. Becket applied his experience as an architect of houses for Hollywood stars to the design of Bullock's store in Pasadena (1944–47), which thrust him into the national limelight. Aside from Loewy's, his became the largest practice in this sphere, designing over thirty major department stores throughout the country between 1945 and 1960. Like Ketchum, Gruen attained considerable note for his specialty shop design before World War II. His first department store was a branch for Milliron's in Los Angeles (1946–49), which generated an avalanche of publicity. Experimental aspects of the scheme, however, hurt his reputation locally. Only with the subsequent design of regional shopping malls for J. L. Hudson and Dayton in the Midwest did he reemerge in the forefront of retail design, expanding his practice into a national one. The third leading figure outside New York was John Graham of Seattle, who likewise became well known across the country for his designs of regional shopping malls, beginning with Bon Marche's Northgate (1948–50). By the mid-1950s the demands of developing a department store branch as an integral component of a shopping center became crucial to reinforcing the architect's key place in shaping the retail landscape. Any architectural firm prominent in the realm of branch stores also had to be a specialist in the planning of shopping centers.

Design

With a relatively small number of specialists setting the pace, opinions showed almost no variation, let alone substantial difference, as to the proper approach to designing a new branch department store once its basic program was prepared. However much retailers disagreed as to aspects of size, scope, and operation of their ventures, they seem to have been entirely willing to entrust the physical solution to the designers they hired. As a result, many basic characteristics of branch design during the postwar years were relatively uniform in tone, especially on the interior. The merchandise more than the setting in which it was presented provided the principal indicator of the clientele targeted by the store in many cases. Except for top fashion stores like I. Magnin, hierarchical distinctions tended to be less pronounced than in department stores of the prewar

168. Burdine's department store, Meridian Avenue and Seventeenth Street, Miami Beach (1952–53). Raymond Loewy Corporation, architects. General view of interior. Photo Gottsch-Schleisner, 1953.

decades. At the same time, designers spent considerable energy on tailoring the particulars of a given scheme to its individual requirements. In describing his firm's approach to the design of the big Rich's branch in Knoxville, Snaith emphasized: "We have made no concession in the plan or design to false ideas of what is practical and what is typical. Rich's, like all well-designed stores, is completely atypical."[42] Guided by general principles, over which there appears to have been no debate by the mid-1950s, department store branches seemed more or less similar, but their design had become particularized.

The design of branches was also now at the forefront of department store design generally. For years, the mainstay in this arena had been adding to and remodeling existing plants, where those involved had to cope with tight configurations, longstanding structural grids, and often a disjointed sequence of component buildings assembled over time. The new branch offered a welcome sense of freedom in which the scheme could be resolved without encumbrances. Two factors were unwaveringly identified as underlying goals of the process. First, the store should be arranged for maximum efficiency in every respect. The movement of goods, shoppers, and staff into and through the premises; the organization of selling and support spaces, individually and in relation to one another; the distribution of light—artificial and natural—as well as the installation of such building systems as air conditioning were all crucial aspects of that objective. Second, and equally important, the store should have strong customer appeal. Those coming to the facility should find it convenient, relaxed, and inviting, but also stimulating. That appeal, designer and retailer alike believed, was rooted in what was often termed "ultra modern." "Ultra modern" did not, however, entail radical departures from precedent in configuration and layout. Proposals for huge, one-story stores, stores set above parking lots, and a variety of other schemes that were presented as bold, innovative conceptions never gained much credibility.[43] Instead, "ultra modern" suggested an approach to design rooted in pragmatism from which an ambient newness was a direct, logical result.

Efficiency and modernity were thus closely interrelated pursuits, both of which were seen as contributing to the fundamental objective of fostering sales. Almost without exception were new branches cast in a modernist vein—not out of esthetic preference per se, but because department store executives had been convinced by designers that a modernist approach was essential for maximum efficiency. Predetermined ideas that merchants might have concerning image, layout, or features should be cast aside, according to this canon, and the process begun as a tabula rasa, with the core programmatic needs driving the solution. A description of Bamberger's branch in Plainfield, New Jersey (1951–54), for example, read almost as if it were adapted from a functionalist manifesto for avant-garde modernism in the prewar years. The store "is a mammoth showcase, with every square foot planned to pay its own way. Lighting, fixtures, and spaciousness are balanced components that supplement each other toward the single end objective of a continuous selling function. Beauty has not been added. It emerges as a natural result of the self-sufficient whole." Any esthetic attributes were thus deemed merely the outcome of addressing pragmatic concerns. Recessed lighting, for example "is strictly functional, not . . . a self-conscious attraction, but . . . an unconscious selling attraction, because it does a thorough job of showing off the merchandise while creating a pleasing, subdued lighting effect."[44] The customer appeal of ultra modern design in stores was rooted in the conveniences and relaxed atmosphere it offered as much in its novelty.

Most of the basic innovations that began to be introduced to downtown stores during the 1930s were now stock components of the new branches: air conditioning, a near complete reliance on artificial lighting, extensive use of interior display, informal layouts, wide aisles, and some use of self-selection. If the theatricality that characterized a number of fashion-oriented departments in the prewar years was now generally downplayed, the underlying concept of selling space as flexible space grew even stronger (figs. 168–69). Accounts repeatedly stressed the desirability of fixtures, layouts, and even whole departments that could

be easily changed, a facet made all the more desirable since many branch managers found they had to rethink the stock they carried during the early years of operation.[45] Although designed from the inside out, the building that resulted was analogous to a vessel, containing neutral space with minimal definition that could be finished and modified in a seemingly infinite variety of ways. The structural configuration, therefore, was tailored less to a particular set of initial functions than to enabling numerous internal changes in the future. The spatial openness that permeated the selling floors of new branches reflected this malleability, but it was championed by retailers primarily because it gave customers a clear sense of the floor as a whole and facilitated their perambulation. At the same time, some intimacy in scale and departmental identity was deemed just as important. To achieve this balance, the overall character of new branch interiors was low key, with fixtures, finishes, and lighting subordinated to displays. Departments were distinguished by subtle differentiations in layout, detail, illumination, and color (figs. 170–71). The sequence was developed to offer a smooth, even unconscious, transition from one area to another. Irrespective of the particulars of each area, the display of merchandise dominated the environment. The role of design as background had never been more thoroughly developed in a building type.[46]

However much flexibility was afforded by these spaces, their layout remained carefully orchestrated, following the general pattern established in the 1930s. A floor devoted to fashion items was typically organized with a more-or-less circular array of departments, often treated as discrete "shops," around a core area reserved for vertical circulation (escalators and sometimes elevators). Catering to an unusually affluent clientele, Robinson's Beverly Hills branch (1950–52) had both of its main floors organized in this manner (fig. 172). The lowest level, carrying household goods,

169. *(top, right)* Rich's department store, Henley and Locust streets, Church and Clinch avenues, Knoxville, Tennessee (1954–55). Stevens & Wilkinson and Barber & McMurry, associated architects; Raymond Loewy Corporation, interior architects; Garret Eckbo, landscape architect. General view of interior. Photo Gottscho-Schleisner, 1955.

170. *(bottom, right)* Thalheimer Brothers department store, 500 West Fourth Street, Winston-Salem, North Carolina. Built in late 1920s as Sosnik's department store; interior remodeled 1949, Raymond Loewy Corporation, interior architects. Salon. Photo Gottscho-Schleisner, 1950.

171. *(top, left)* Bloomingdale Brothers department store, Route 4 and Hackensack Avenue, Hackensack, New Jersey (1958–59). Parsons, Brinkerhoff, Hall & Macdonald, architects-engineers; Raymond Loewy Corporation, interior architects. Green Room, Sutton Place. Photo Gottscho-Schleisner, 1959.

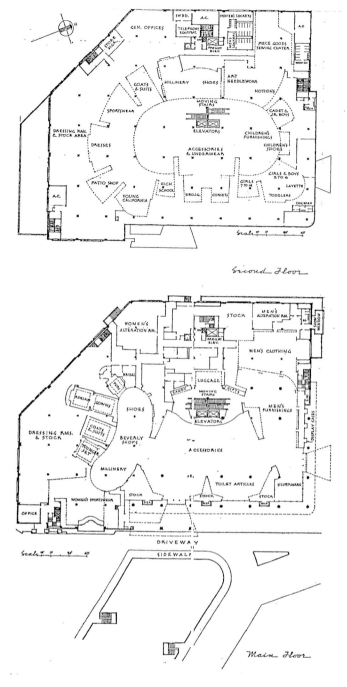

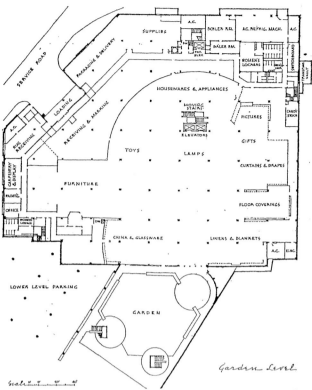

172. J. W. Robinson Company department store, 9900 Wilshire Boulevard, Beverly Hills (1950–52). Pereira & Luckman and Charles O. Marham, associated architects; Raymond Loewy Corporation, interior architects. Floor plans (*Progressive Architecture,* August 1952, 82–83).

was less manipulated but nonetheless adhered to the basic pattern of encouraging circuitous movement. In larger selling areas carrying less expensive goods the same design concept was adapted by employing curvilinear walls around the periphery and rounded fixtures so that movement was meandering if not always along a circular path. The Hecht Company's Silver Spring branch, which catered to a broad middle market, was an early and influential example (fig. 173). Some larger stores adhered to a more rectilinear layout but employed skewed circulation paths to foster diag-

onal movement, as occurred on the main floor of Abraham & Straus's Hempstead branch (1950–52). Customer circulation was also stimulated by a more or less linear sequence of thematically related merchandise, as with the Aisle of Fashion at Rich's Knoxville or the Avenue of Shops at Burdine's Miami Beach.[47] Multiple entrances were commonly used to facilitate access from parking lots and streets, as well as to encourage internal circulation. Changes in grade on the site became a welcome means of placing entrances on two levels, again to encourage maximum pedestrian traffic to all portions of the store. On occasion, topography was manipulated to achieve this end.[48] Two levels of selling space were considered optimal for a sizable new branch. Sometimes a third was constructed below grade, but it was always referred to as the ground floor, lower floor, or even garden floor rather than as the basement to ensure no association with that component of urban emporia.

While ostensibly the byproduct of the interior design, the outside treatment of postwar branches was crucial to the success of the operation. The results clearly showed that architects devoted considerable time to the exterior, even if they downplayed its role. From the retailers' perspective, a

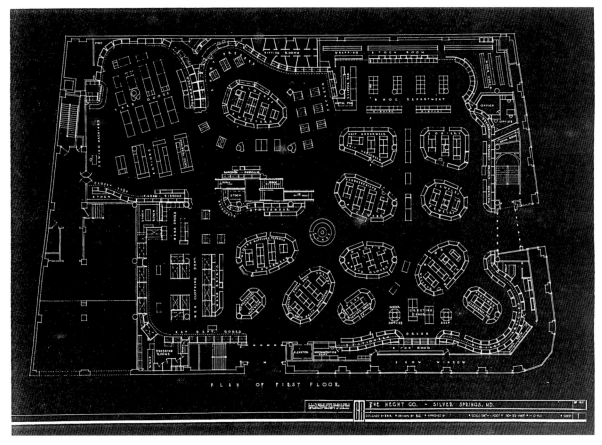

173. Hecht Company department store, Fenton Street and Ellsworth Drive, Silver Spring, Maryland (1945–47). Abbott, Merkt & Company, architects-engineers; Sue Williams, interior designer; altered. Plan of first floor (Louis Parnes, *Planning Stores That Pay*, 41).

strong first impression was key to attracting trade as their businesses ventured into new territory. Within the field, a consensus appears to have emerged at an early date that a new branch should be conspicuous irrespective of its location and even its size. Equally prevalent was the view that the most effective means of achieving that end was through appearances no less ultra modern than those inside. Historicizing motifs that continued to proliferate in the outlying residential areas where these stores were built were nearly absent in the new branches.[49] So were traces of stylish Art Deco designs that had persisted in a number of commercial buildings for at least several years after World War II.[50] Instead, branch exteriors typically exuded a bold, abstract quality that was rare for many other buildings prior to the mid-1950s. This singularity was not discussed in the trade press, but it was a trait that retailers wanted or at least were willing to accept in their efforts to retain leadership in an ever more complex and competitive field.

Like other facets of the department store's modernity, exterior boldness was spurred by practical considerations. Since most new stores were oriented primarily to the motorist, the visual prominence of the facility had to be pronounced—both striking and appealing at a glance. Large rooftop signs of the kind that had proliferated on commercial buildings during the interwar decades and large freestanding signs of the kind that advertised many roadside businesses never appear to have been viewed as appropriate for an establishment of the department store's stature. Instead, the building itself stood as the foremost signifier of its function. This role was achieved through abstract means, principally the manipulation of form, materials, and in some instances a few large elements. The fact that windows above ground level were generally undesirable left broad expanses of wall surface, which, when treated as abstract sculpture, could be developed to attract the eye of motorists. Mural wall surfaces also afforded an effective backdrop for large letters, often molded in script, that proclaimed the store's identity in a manner deemed suitable for a fine emporium. As unprecedented as these branches must have seemed rising on the metropolitan periphery, they tended to convey a sense of decorum rather than the exaggerated and flashy qualities that characterized many commercial establishments of the period. In all these respects, the Lord & Taylor Manhasset store appears to have been a significant model.

174. Lord & Taylor store, White Plains Post and Wilmot roads, Eastchester, New York (1946–48). Starrett & Van Vleck, architects; Raymond Loewy Corporation, interior architects; William Lee Moore, landscape architect. Photo Gottscho-Schleisner, 1968.

Although E. B. Weiss admonished retailers for building "aristocratic stores," the pursuit of elegance was widespread through the postwar period among department store companies that cultivated associations with the well-to-do. Lord & Taylor's flock of postwar branches cast in the same genre reinforced the attraction of its Manhasset store in this realm. The store at Eastchester, near White Plains (1946–48), in particular received widespread coverage and high praise for its suave, understated character—"designed to blend [into] and enhance the surrounding community rather than to be glaringly commercial" (fig. 174).[51] No less influential was the enormous store erected for Bullock's in Pasadena, which opened in September 1947, before any of Lord & Taylor's postwar branches. Encompassing nearly 300,000 square feet, the store was also one of the largest of its generation. "Retailers throughout the nation await a new concept of store design," a *Women's Wear Daily* reporter purred shortly before the opening, to which the local press added: "Probably nowhere in America is there a store building anything like it." For the exterior of this "Taj Mahal of the merchandising world," architect Welton Becket expanded on what Snaith did at Manhasset, developing the concept in his own, exuberant vocabulary, giving it a commanding presence on the street, while at the same time creating a separate experience of approach, oriented entirely to the parking lots, from which the main entrances emanated (fig. 175). Seldom had this three-dimensionality, without the dual "front" and "back" entrances, been so pronounced in a department store. The parking lots were no longer rear appendages but key spaces in the entire site plan and central determinants of the location and arrangement of the store. Capitalizing on the salubrious climate, Becket also made terraces a conspicuous component of the scheme. Inside, the design was most novel. Treating each major group of merchandise as a separate business operation led to far more departmental differentiation than was found at most stores. Each sphere was rendered with unusual lavishness as well as intimacy, the whole comprising one of the most intense panoplies of settings found in the retail realm. Inside and out, the effect was likened to a club more than to a retail establishment (fig. 176).[52]

Just how many clubs—in town or country—looked like Bullock's at that time is problematic, and how many customers could partake of such establishments even more so.

Without apparent prototypes in the rarefied world of exclusive social institutions, Becket and Snaith each created stores that looked to the consumer as if they *should* be clubs—or perhaps posh resorts.[53] The palatial allusions of many downtown emporia in the early twentieth century thus were replaced by associations scarcely less elite but markedly different in character. The uptown ambience cultivated in branches such as those of Marshall Field and Strawbridge & Clothier less than two decades earlier was likewise discarded. Instead was a suggestion of a quasi-rural retreat, a store that appeared to stand in splendid isolation even when, as in the case of Bullock's, the site lay within an established urban district. With this atmosphere, patrons could forget the crowds and congestion, the rush and the fears of the city, and forget, too, their own worries, immersed in an elegant and efficient environment that seemed to leave the vagaries of depression and war in a far distant past. The new world of shopping was indeed entirely new. Escapism in this sphere had never been more pronounced.

The stores built by Lord & Taylor and Bullock's set the tone for others erected by a number of high-end retailers, including B. Altman and John Wanamaker. But many others pursued a less extravagant course, creating branches of "modest opulence," as one account described them.[54] The companies involved—for example, Hutzler's in Balti-

175. Bullock's department store, 401 South Lake Avenue, Pasadena, California (1945–47). Wurdeman & Becket, architects; altered. Photo Julius Shulman, 1947.

176. Bullock's Pasadena, women's apparel department. Photo Julius Shulman, 1947.

177. Hahne & Company department store, South Park and Church streets, Montclair, New Jersey (1949–51). Fellheimer & Wagner, architects; altered. Photo Gottscho-Schleisner, 1951.

more, Woodward & Lothrop in Washington, Burdine's in Miami, or Maas Brothers in Tampa—were generally the most prestigious ones in their respective cities. At the same time, all these retailers sought a relatively broad mix in their patronage. Like many downtown stores of earlier decades, the branch had to possess some snob appeal yet not seem intimidating to shoppers of less than substantial means. The stores were conceived as major magnets, better than most emporia in the immediate environs and catering to a sizable segment of the population. Site constraints in many cases also precluded too elaborate an external design. Hahne's branch in Montclair, New Jersey (1949–51), was typical of this widespread approach.[55] Materials of high quality were employed throughout, and some flourish was accorded the corner section, which trumpeted displays instead of the traditional entrance, while most of the exterior was given scant detail above street level (fig. 177). Nevertheless, the scale of the building and the pervasiveness of its modernity guaranteed it a striking presence when viewed from any direction. Probably the most ingenious solution of this genre was for Hutzler's branch at Towson, Maryland, where site constraints were turned into an advantage. A street that bifurcated the property was rebuilt at a higher level as an integral component of the design, enabling direct access to the store from the parking lot below. This configuration, coupled with a three-dimensional but otherwise extremely simple play of masses, gave the store an arresting appearance that made it an iconic design of the period (fig. 178).[56] Department store executives tended to place great value in the image projected, irrespective of its particulars. Even though the Hempstead store was to complement the tonier Garden City branch, Abraham & Straus officials commissioned the renowned modernist architect Marcel Breuer to design the exterior to enhance its prestige at a time when such practice was just beginning to become popular among corporations for their headquarter offices and research parks.[57]

A more utilitarian approach was taken for exteriors of branches targeted to the mass market. In this realm, the Hecht Company was among the pioneers. Lying just north of the District of Columbia, Hecht's big Silver Spring emporium opened in November 1947, as one of the first large branches to be completed after the war, one of the first to carry an array of stock comparable to that of the parent store, and one of the first to target the swelling middle market. Without any pretense at exclusivity, the building's street faces exuded a matter-of-fact plainness then highly unusual for retail establishments of any import (fig. 179). The great bulk of the building emphasized its unadorned qualities; looming above neighboring one- and two-story commercial establishments and houses, the pile seemed more like a latter-day version of the household goods warehouses that had been erected in many urban residential districts since the 1920s than a beacon for shoppers.[58] This no-frills approach to exterior design was cast as a virtue—an esthetic that embodied the efficiency and practicality of the modern consumer. Accounts of the period give no sense that the effect was seen as merely expedient or utilitarian. With a state-of-the-art interior that carried glamorous overtones, no embellishment was deemed necessary outside. A similar approach was taken with Macy's Jamaica branch, which opened slightly earlier and received widespread publicity. Here, however, with only one and a half stories above ground, the configura-

178. Hutzler Brothers Company department store, Joppa and Dulaney Valley roads, Towson, Maryland (1950–52). Ketchum, Gina & Sharp and James R. Edmunds, associated architects; altered. Photo Ezra Stoller, 1952.

179. Hecht Company department store, Silver Spring, Maryland. Photo ca. 1947.

tion was a more horizontal one, which was used for many subsequent branches in the 100,000-square-foot category (fig. 180).[59] Both designs demonstrated the degree to which the exterior could be pared down when appealing to the broad middle class. As Weiss had cautioned, the new mass market could be ill at ease amid pretentious surroundings. Straightforward, no-nonsense simplicity was not only economically practical, it was esthetically desirable. The two buildings were instrumental in laying the groundwork for a new image of the modern department store as a large boxlike container, enunciated by only a few low-key openings and signs, which became the hallmark of the type as anchors to the shopping centers of the 1950s.

Such external plainness was possible, of course, only because the windowless store pioneered by Sears in the 1930s was now widely accepted. High-end departmentalized specialty stores such as Lord & Taylor and Neiman-Marcus and comparable department stores such as Bullock's still featured extensive glazing so that customers could view in

180. R. H. Macy & Company department store, 89th Avenue and 165th Street, Jamaica, New York (1944–47). Robert D. Kohn and John J. Knight, architects; Richard G. Belcher, consulting architect; Daniel Schwartzman, interior architect; Kenneth C. Welch, consulting interior architect; altered. Photo ca. 1947.

181. Saks Fifth Avenue store, Millburn Avenue, Springfield, New Jersey (1956–57). Kahn & Jacobs and Abbott, Merkt & Company, associated architects. Photo Felix Gilbert, 1957.

natural light the costly goods they were considering, and architects used this factor to enhance the varied treatment of the exterior to achieve a signature design. A few companies experimented with multistory display windows at the main entrance, as Sears had done at several of its stores in the mid-1930s.[60] After opening its Jamaica store, Macy's took an entirely different approach with its next branch (1946–48) in the commercial center of Flatbush, where the trade was almost entirely pedestrian. Here, with a comparatively narrow frontage, the entire facade was glazed, with three levels

of displays, and the building was serviced by an elevator that was an integral component of the presentation. The next branch (1948–49), in the Westchester County business hub of White Plains, had a more conventional layout, but still a huge, semicircular window around the entry, extending the height of the building's curvilinear front. Not long after that store opened, however, a Macy's executive minced no words in explaining that such features were a mistake.[61] While the glazed corner was used in several other instances, such as Hochschild-Kohn's branch in the Belvedere neighborhood of Baltimore (1947–48) and John Wanamaker's branch in Wilmington (1947–50), the practice was limited. By the mid-1950s the idea of a glazed entry zone was revived for a number of high-end departmentalized specialty store branches, especially those of Lord & Taylor and Saks Fifth Avenue. The use of multiple window locations in these stores no longer held currency, in all likelihood because ever more emphasis was given to controlled illumination, with interior lighting techniques improving accordingly. Instead, a great window bay at principal entry points helped offset the extensive wall surfaces all around and added the requisite sense of elegance to the composition (fig. 181).

Display windows at street level remained a standard feature for most branch stores that retained a street-front orientation, even though the locations, on the periphery of business districts or in lone-wolf settings, did not always attract much pedestrian traffic. This practice was to a certain degree generated by what one architect long involved in department store design later admitted was the persistence of "urban thinking" among retailers and designers alike. The display window lay at the heart of how the department store had presented itself to the public since the nineteenth century. Besides a reluctance to discard this venerated feature, many of those involved simply never considered the fact that it would have a less central role when most shoppers were in automobiles rather than on their feet.[62] In some instances, however, experiments were made to orient displays to the motorist. These breaks with convention appear to have been instigated by the architects involved rather than by their clients. In designing the branch for Milliron's store in the Westchester business district of Los Angeles, Victor Gruen ignored the prevailing trend of simplicity.[63] Even though the store was oriented toward shoppers of moderate means, the exterior was vigorously composed with patterned brickwork, clerestory windows, vertical fins, a wide projecting parapet slab, and an imposing vertical signboard. Amid this lively, polychromatic arrangement, four angled display kiosks extended far onto the sidewalk to catch the attention of those driving by on one of the most heavily traveled routes of the area (fig. 182). Hutzler's Towson store did not have display windows as such; instead, most of the street frontage was composed of continuous glazing, so that

182. Milliron's department store, 8739 Sepulveda Boulevard, Westchester, Los Angeles (1947–49). Gruen & Krummeck, architects; altered. Photo Julius Shulman, 1949.

the sales floor would serve as a surrogate display, especially when illuminated at night. Some years later, architects Pereira & Luckman took this idea further in their design of Robinson's branch at Palm Springs (1957–58). Here, most of the exterior was glazed and set under a wide projecting roof to create the effect of a "jewel case" (fig. 183).[64] Well before that time, however, the majority of new department store branches were being planned as part of shopping centers, where the opportunity for display windows was generally limited to the areas around the store entrances.

Whatever doubts may have lingered among department store executives in the prewar years about providing off-street parking, they had dissipated by the mid-1940s. All but the smallest of newly built branches included one or more lots that were controlled by the store.[65] The absence of discussion in period trade publications over how much parking to provide suggests that ample precedent existed, most likely from the large branches of the late 1920s and 1930s erected by the May Company, Bullock's, and Strawbridge & Clothier.[66] Whatever the source, dedicating an area at least two and preferably two and a half times the store's square footage appears to have become the industry standard save in a few dense, urban settings, where heavy pedestrian traffic was anticipated. In most cases, the parking area was treated as utilitarian, and hence essentially residue, space at the side and/or the rear of the store. However vital this acreage was

183. J. W. Robinson Company, Palm Canyon Drive and Bariste Road, Palm Springs, California (1957–58). Pereira & Luckman, architects; Raymond Loewy Corporation, interior architects. Photo Julius Shulman, 1958.

for the life of the operation, it was ancillary in terms of the store design.[67] A few high-end retailers, notably B. Altman, Bullock's, Lord & Taylor, and Wanamaker's, commissioned branches where the movement and storage of cars became a springboard for innovative site and store planning alike. In such cases, both designer and retailer seemed to have realized that parking need not be just a convenience; arrival at a store by car could be a pleasurable esthetic experience, enhancing the shopper's mood and, perhaps, the tendency to make purchases.

Location

Ideally, the station wagon store was situated close to its core constituents; getting there by car was convenient and parking was easy. These attributes, incanted continuously in accounts of the period, were much the same as those that distinguished a big Sears store of the interwar decades and were to a lesser extent characteristic of some prewar branches as well. But the station wagon store often appeared very different in its setting, where the grounds were landscaped and the atmosphere informal. The desired effect was markedly less urban in every way, with low-slung, abstractly composed buildings rising amid gardenlike settings. The new department store was not to evoke its downtown forebears but rather to manifest the relaxed, spacious, leafy world of the postwar suburb. Such emporia were vanguard emblems of a modern metropolitan order that was intended to break decisively from its predecessors. In reality, of course, the location of postwar branches varied as much as any other aspect, and some were used to bolster established business centers. Nevertheless, the ideal of locating the station wagon store in a wholly different kind of place enjoyed widespread appeal throughout the industry and had significant impact on siting practices.

As in design, the ideal in site selection was nurtured by practical economic concerns. Chastened by their intensifying troubles downtown and by the stunning success of Sears, department store executives were nearly unanimous in seeking land with lots of space that was well connected to arterial routes. As Sears and some pioneering department stores such as Bullock's had discovered in the late 1920s, property situated away from existing development carried the dual advantage of low cost and convenient access.[68] But now this retail frontier often lay not in established residential districts of the city that were crossed by sparsely developed boulevard frontage. Instead, the prime sites were identified beyond the city, sometimes many miles beyond, in newly evolving, spacious, tranquil bedroom communities where large-scale commerce seemed anathema.

The model for such siting was Lord & Taylor's Manhasset branch, which possessed what many retailers considered optimal characteristics: land large enough for landscaping, parking, and expansion situated at the intersection of two key routes connecting a loose and fast-growing network of middle- and upper-middle-class enclaves. Not surprisingly, Lord & Taylor adhered to this pattern in planning its program for continued branch development around New York and farther afield. In March 1945, company president Walter Hoving announced plans to build about ten new stores within a five-hundred-mile radius of the city following the Manhasset concept—one of the most ambitious branch development programs of the period. Initial efforts were focused on suburban New York. An ill-fated attempt to locate a branch near New Rochelle, New York, was quickly followed by successful ventures nearby in Eastchester and in Millburn, New Jersey (1947–48). Later the focus shifted to well beyond the metropolitan area, to West Hartford, Connecticut (1951–53).[69] At Millburn the store was located near to yet distinctly apart from the existing town center, much the way it was at Manhasset. The Eastchester and West Hartford stores, on the other hand, were well removed from outlying business districts, surrounded almost entirely by residential tracts. Millburn had the smallest property, eight and a half acres, which nonetheless was vast compared to a downtown site for a building of comparable size. The other two had some fourteen acres each, providing space for the later development of complementary specialty stores.

Equally important as a model was Bullock's Pasadena, which drew inspiration from its Wilshire Boulevard predecessor in the use of a lone-wolf site surrounded by the urban grid and residential blocks of earlier vintage. Here the property lay four blocks south of Colorado Boulevard, Pasadena's main commercial thoroughfare, and more blocks east of the primary business district. Yet the scheme was as evocative of an open setting on the metropolitan periphery as those of the Lord & Taylor stores, with its principal entrances away from the street, oriented instead toward landscaped parking lots. As a full-fledged department store carrying a broad spectrum of goods, Bullock's Pasadena quickly became another standard-setter for the era. One of the most striking examples of its impact was Wanamaker's first branch, near Wilmington, Delaware. While less than two miles from that city's core, the site was a wooded hillside property of over sixteen acres, completely removed from commercial development and just beyond the municipal boundary. Initial plans for a 62,000-square-foot store, slightly smaller than the Lord & Taylor branches, were scrapped as a result of a detailed market survey. A new scheme of nearly three times the size was unveiled in 1949.[70] With a sprawling building sheathed in fieldstone and sandstone, flanked by terraced parking areas rendered as if they were in a park, few branches made comparably declarative statements of how unlike the established urban order such a place could be (fig. 184).

Lone-wolf locations generally remained the province of high-end department stores and thus possessed an aura of exclusivity. Early examples include Filene's branch in Newton and Brookline, Massachusetts (1949–50); Woodward & Lothrop's near Chevy Chase, Maryland (1949–50), and in Alexandria, Virginia (1951–52); and J. W. Robinson's in Beverly Hills (1947–52). The practice continued throughout the decade, with Sakowitz's in the Post Oak district of Houston (1958–59) and Hahne's in Westfield, New Jersey (1960–63), for example. The prestige of the store, combined with easy access, proved sufficient to ensure success; indeed, their clientele preferred not having to battle dense traffic to reach these destinations, as was demonstrated at Bullock's Wilshire two decades earlier. Curiously, most department store companies oriented to a broader market avoided such locations, despite the example of Sears. A major exception was the immense (285,000 square feet) Southtown branch of Famous-Barr (1950–51) erected at the intersection of two major arteries in a sea of moderate-income St. Louis neighborhoods (fig. 185).[71]

Locations in outlying business centers proved the most popular for branches of all sizes and types operating within the metropolitan area of the parent store, just as they had in the prewar years. By so situating their new establishments department store executives could capitalize on the attraction such places already possessed. Through the early 1950s, at least, conventional wisdom held that the optimal place for a new branch was a commercial core, even though that core now lay well beyond the city center. In a few cases, the precincts selected were major neighborhood centers of long standing. Macy's branches in Jamaica, the principal business district of Queens, and in Flatbush, an important outlying center for Brooklyn—both magnets for persons of modest means—were the two primary examples. But most cities did not sustain such concentrated outlying development within their boundaries. More importantly, the population shifts that were driving branch development were focused farther afield, near the metropolitan periphery, where settlement was new and much less dense. The neighborhoods of the late nineteenth and early twentieth centuries thus generally were skirted in favor of newer ones boasting higher per capita incomes. Yet even on the metropolitan periphery, the relationship between the branch and other stores in the community was rooted in the tradition of the downtown store and establishments around it.

The persistence of traditional patterns in new places was most clearly evident with a number of branches that opened in buildings previously occupied by local department stores in the cores of longstanding town business centers. Bloomingdale's, for example, purchased and remodeled the former Ware department store in New Rochelle (1947–48), as did Jordan Marsh with the Joslin Company in Malden, Massachusetts (1953–54), and Macy's with the two Albert's department stores in Richmond and San Rafael, California (1953).[72] Likewise, Lit's eagerly took the lease on the former Frank & Seder branch in Upper Darby, the largest outlying business center of metropolitan Philadelphia, where it had been considering a branch since the late 1930s. If the proper kind of building was unavailable, however, adequate space in the middle of such precincts was hard to assemble. In 1946, Bamberger's benefited from a fire that destroyed a large building on the central square of Morristown, New Jersey, while Macy's was able to purchase the grounds of the recently vacated high school in the center of White

184. John Wanamaker department store, Augustine Cut Off and Eighteenth Street, New Castle County, Delaware (1947–50). Massena & du Pont, architects; C. E. Swanson Associates and Joseph B. Platt Associates, associated interior designers; William Lee Moore, landscape architect. Photo ca. 1950.

185. Famous-Barr Company department store, Kingshighway and Chippewa Road, St. Louis (1949–51). P. John Hoener, architect; Taussig & Flesch, interior designers; demolished 1990s. Photo early 1950s.

Plains for its branch the previous year. Yet such opportunities were the exception, and downtown property values in these communities were often so high that department store executives generally focused their attention elsewhere when searching for a branch site.

The locations that held the greatest appeal for developing a sizable branch lay on the edge of the outlying business district, where the land was not only cheaper and more readily assembled, it was also more easily reached by motorists who were finding that suburban centers were generating traffic problems of their own. Abraham & Straus's huge branch in Hempstead, for example, lay several blocks removed from the core, as did Hahne's branch in Montclair. Gilchrist's in Framingham, Massachusetts (1948); B. Altman (1949–51) and Saks Fifth Avenue in White Plains; and Bamberger's in Plainfield were similarly situated. The big Famous-Barr store in Clayton was sited some distance from that community's business core, but on a strategic entrance route to the business district from established neighborhoods to the east. Hutzler's branch in Towson similarly formed a gateway, but in this case it lay immediately adjacent to that community's small and theretofore unimportant business district. Silver Spring, the site of Hecht's first branch, likewise had previously functioned as a modest retail district for nearby residents. Both Hutzler's and Hecht's positioned their stores optimally for projected growth rather than for existing settlement.

Up to the mid-1950s, the sizable, freestanding branch that served a metropolitan population was primarily a phenomenon of major cities in the northeastern states, St. Louis, and the Los Angeles and San Francisco Bay areas. In many other places, especially in the South, Midwest, and Northwest, the prevailing pattern was to establish branches well beyond the parent store's primary trading area in small cities and towns that lay dozens, sometimes hundreds, of miles afield. While seldom discussed in accounts addressing trends, this practice represented a significant share of postwar branch development through the 1950s. In most cases, the retailers that advanced this extraterritorial strategy were based in cities considered too small to justify suburban branches and also well removed from competing urban centers. For decades, big emporia in predominantly rural states had attracted customers from considerable distances who came by train and, later, automobile. Creating a network of branches bolstered this trade, adding a substantial new customer base in the process. Pioneered by Halle's in the late 1920s, this strategy was adopted by seventeen companies in almost as many states during the 1940s and by six other firms during the following decade.[73] In 1960, about sixty such outlets were operating throughout the country.

Among the most ambitious programs for regional branch development was for companies in the Macy's corpora-

186. Davison-Paxon Company department store, Broadway and Twelfth Street, Columbus, Georgia (1946–49). Ketchum, Gina & Sharp and Harold M. Heatley, associated architects. Photo author, 1999.

tion. For Atlanta-based Davison-Paxon Macy's purchased existing department stores in Augusta (1944), Macon (1945), and Athens (1953), Georgia, as well as in Columbia, South Carolina (1946). The first of these was soon replaced by a considerably larger and strikingly modern building (1947–49), while a similar store was erected in Columbus, Georgia (1946–49) (fig. 186).[74] With the exception of Savannah, Davison's had outlets in all of its home state's leading population centers. Containing between 56,000 and 106,000 square feet, the Georgia stores also ranked among the largest in their respective communities. Davison's own reputation, and that of several of the companies purchased, further contributed to the prominence that these branches enjoyed in their respective locales. The firm now promoted itself as Davison's of Dixie, suggesting regional dominance. Community boosters, for their part, trumpeted the arrival of these stores as bringing the prestige of the metropolis to Main Street. Another Macy company, Lasalle & Koch of Toledo, embarked on a somewhat less sweeping program, remodeling a building in Bowling Green (1944–45) and constructing new ones in Tiffin (1947), Sandusky (1947–49), and Findlay (1954–55), Ohio.[75] While smaller (29,000 to 46,000 square feet) and nearer the parent store, these branches enjoyed a local prominence equivalent to that of Davison's. The Kansas City–based Macy's, on the other hand, pursued territorial expansion on a grand scale, purchasing major stores in Joplin, Missouri (1954), and Wichita, Kansas (1955).[76] Constructed during the interwar decades for the George Innes Company, the Wichita store had long enjoyed the reputation as that region's leading department store. Encompassing 275,000 square feet, it was over half the size of the Kansas

187. Bon Marche department store, Main, Howard, and Wall streets, Spokane. General view showing the remodeled Welch Building (constructed as Culbertson's Department Store, 1914, 1921 [right]), partially masked by new Main Street front, with addition (left), 1954–57, John Graham & Company, architects. Skywalks added as part of Parkade parking garage (1965–67). Photo author, 2004.

City emporium and among the largest branch acquisitions in the country.[77] Spurred by the success of these operations, Macy's unveiled plans in 1960 for what would be the biggest retail facility in Topeka, although a series of difficulties postponed its realization for over half a decade.[78]

In the Northwest, Allied stores matched Macy's aggressiveness in territorial expansion. The Seattle-based Allied subsidiary Bon Marche opened seven branches between 1947 and 1957. The first purchase, made by Allied, was a ten-story emporium in Spokane, nearly three hundred miles to the east. Subsequent branches lay closer to home—in Everett (1949) and Tacoma (1952)—but stores in Walla Walla (1951), Yakima (1953), and Bellingham (1957) extended the company's presence as the major store in most of the state's population centers.[79] Allied and Bon Marche were determined to attain hegemony. A competing Spokane department store was purchased and its quarters sold in 1952. Two years later, a new construction campaign was launched, with a ten-story addition that expanded Bon Marche and also gave it a more lateral configuration, while developing the upper six floors as leased office space.[80] The existing plant was completely remade inside to conform to the addition; however, the stark modernist front extended only to the corner of the side elevation (fig. 187). The store's market significantly expanded again with the development of a new building in Eugene, Oregon (1953–54), one hundred miles south of Portland. The move effectively challenged Meier & Frank, that state's dominant store, whose leadership a few months before Allied's announcement unveiled plans for a large branch in Salem, midway between Portland and Eugene. Subsequently, Allied's proposal to invade Portland itself was shelved, but Meier & Frank experienced some competition on its home turf from Lipman Wolfe & Company, which built its own Salem branch more or less concurrently (1953–54). Thereafter Lipman's opened a branch in Corvallis, thirty miles north of Eugene, probably in part to limit Bon Marche's draw.[81]

Competition between department stores for the conquest

of new territories also occurred elsewhere. Executives of Allied's Minneapolis-based affiliate Donaldson's, for example, did not hesitate to proceed with plans in October 1952 for a branch in Rochester, Minnesota, less than two months after a larger scheme for that city had been unveiled by Dayton's, the dominant emporium in Minneapolis and much of the state.[82] In some cases, however, store executives may have reached a mutual understanding that their new territories would not overlap. Thalheimer's in Richmond, Virginia, for example, opened branches to the southwest in Danville (1955), as well as in Winston-Salem (1949) and Greensboro (1957), North Carolina, while rival Miller & Rhoads pursued territory to the west, with stores in Charlottesville (1955–56), Roanoke (1955–57), and Lynchburg (1957).[83] The May Company's M. O'Neil of Akron demonstrated that being surrounded by larger cities—including Cleveland, where May had another large subsidiary—was not necessarily a disadvantage in such expansion programs. Between 1945 and 1956, the firm opened small branches in two neighboring communities and five additional towns beyond, forming an arc sixty miles to the west and south and twenty-five miles to the southeast, effectively saturating the northeastern portion of the state aside from the Cleveland and Youngstown metropolitan areas.[84]

Unchallenged by any rival stores at home or in other regions, Younker Brothers of Des Moines developed one of the most extensive networks of extraterritorial branches. Between 1942 and 1956 the company opened eight units throughout Iowa, as well as in Rock Island, Illinois, and Omaha, Nebraska. Most branches were in purchased or leased buildings of modest dimensions (20,000 and 40,000 square feet) that nonetheless became key destinations in their respective towns. Concurrently, a sizable (160,000 square feet) store was purchased in Sioux City (1947) and one nearly as large was built in the outskirts of Omaha (1955), a city dominated by J. L. Brandeis.[85] But such expansion had its limits. Younker's purchased the Innes store in Wichita three years before Macy's, but the company proved ill equipped to manage so big an operation that far afield. Younker's joint acquisition in 1954 of Daniels & Fisher in Denver proved short-lived for the same reason.[86] Otherwise, regional saturation proved very effective, netting its firm no small amount of publicity in the process.

A number of firms viewed acquiring department stores well beyond their home base as a complement to building large suburban stores. Amid its statewide expansion program, Bon Marche planned Northgate (1948–50), the nation's first realized regional shopping mall, in Seattle. Complementing its Rochester store (1952–54) and one purchased in Sioux Falls, South Dakota (1954), Dayton's planned Southdale (1952–56), just outside Minneapolis, which was the first regional shopping mall to be both fully enclosed and with dual anchor department stores.[87] Expansion through extraterritorial branches did not end as suburban branch development intensified in the mid-1950s with the building of such shopping centers. Besides Macy's huge Wichita store, Carson Pirie Scott of Chicago purchased department stores in Aurora and Kankakee, Illinois, as well as closer by, in Chicago Heights, toward the decade's end.[88] Even as the department store was on the front line of large-scale commercial development on the metropolitan edge, it was making a major commitment to fostering trade in the core of small cities and towns farther afield.

The dualities of such initiatives were evident in the conception of Rich's branch at Knoxville, Tennessee. Not wishing to challenge Davison-Paxon branches in other cities, the Atlanta-based retailer instead looked to an area deemed markedly underserved. Much as Federated had done with Foley's in Houston, Rich's acquired a local department store whose building was far too small to address the purchaser's objective of drawing customers from forty-one counties throughout eastern Tennessee and beyond. Encompassing over 200,000 square feet, the facility that Rich's commissioned far surpassed local department stores in size and selection; company president Richard Rich called it the largest in the state. No location was seriously considered aside from downtown, even though the density of the retail core necessitated building on a site several blocks away. Rich firmly believed that a great, centrally located store would always be more attractive than outlying branches, and he had expanded his Atlanta emporium accordingly in the postwar years. The Knoxville store followed that strategy. At the same time, its ambience was intended to provide a marked contrast with the traditional downtown store. Announcements of the plan emphasized the "suburban character" of the design, and once it opened, the store was heralded as a "regional shopping center." Faced in glazed tile and glazed brick, the multicolored exterior was set back on two sides by exuberantly composed terraces designed by the celebrated San Francisco landscape architect Garret Eckbo (fig. 188). "Rich's," cooed a reporter upon the store's completion, "is a suburban shopping center in the heart of Knoxville."[89] Here, in other words, was the best of both worlds—the most ambitious emporium ever built in the region, with virtues antithetical to the traditional urban scene in which it stood.

Catalyst

The executives of Rich's, Younker's, Bon Marche, and other department store companies opened extraterritorial branches in large part because such places were the only ones believed to be viable for expanding a large retail operation beyond the nation's major metropolitan areas. For New York and San Francisco, Chicago and St. Louis, or even Washington and Cleveland, on the other hand, outlying

188. Rich's department store, Knoxville. Photo Gottscho-Schleisner, 1955.

areas were almost always considered the only ones where branch development could flourish. Yet one prominent figure in field, Albert M. Greenfield, was convinced that as the department store had been a determining factor in the emergence of great downtowns in the late nineteenth and early twentieth centuries, so it should now be a catalyst for expansion and renewal of business centers near the company's home base. As chairman of the board of City Stores, Greenfield headed one of the largest department store corporations in the country, but unlike his colleagues he was intimately familiar with the dynamics of urban development. The real estate firm that bore his name had long dominated the commercial sphere in the Philadelphia area and was among the largest in the nation during the postwar era.[90] Greenfield was able to translate his views into reality through the expansion of one of his largest stores, Lit Brothers, which was based in his home city.

Lit's first branch lay in Upper Darby, just to the west of the Philadelphia city line and about five miles from the downtown retail district. This satellite center became established in the 1920s and emerged as second only to the city's core in retail sales throughout the metropolitan area by the eve of World War II. The branch lay right in the heart of that district, occupying a building that was extensively remodeled for the purpose. Greenfield's strategy was to strengthen the core of a business center whose potential remained underestimated, not extend its boundaries or set up a competing node.[91] His decision, in turn, quickly prompted a number of other downtown-based and chain companies to plan major units close by.[92] In January 1949, not long before the Upper Darby store opened, Greenfield's purchased Swern's, a large, low-end department store in Trenton, New Jersey, some thirty miles northeast of downtown Philadelphia. The emporium enjoyed a substantial customer base not only in that predominantly industrial city and neighboring New Jersey jurisdictions, but also in burgeoning lower Bucks County, Pennsylvania.[93] The most important and unusual venture in this direction was the construction of a large new store in the center of Camden, New Jersey (1951–55), right across the Delaware River from its parent store in Philadelphia.

The impetus to build a store in Camden came from the fast-paced growth of the surrounding area. Greenfield correctly recognized that Camden, Burlington, and Gloucester counties, which had been primarily devoted to agriculture, were rapidly becoming a part of metropolitan Philadelphia. He avoided locating the store along one of the area's well-developed network of highways, however, choosing instead a block in the core of the city. Up to that point, Camden's business district remained relatively small, serving basic needs of the blue-collar population that dominated the community but remaining subservient to downtown Philadelphia, which was a short subway ride away. The new Lit's was sizable, encompassing 180,000 square feet, more than twice the size of the Upper Darby branch and reputedly larger than any other in the state save Bamberger's Newark emporium (fig. 189).

The project entailed more than the usual challenges in branch building. Whereas decision makers in most outlying jurisdictions welcomed the prospect of a big new store and often took pains to facilitate the process, Greenfield and his lieutenants engaged in lengthy and difficult negotiations with Camden's municipal government to secure the acreage—the site of the former courthouse—and ensure that the city would erect a multideck parking garage a block away to attract the critical mass of motorists needed to support the operation.[94] Four and a half years elapsed between the time the plan was unveiled and the store was opened. The objective of this complicated, sometimes contentious process was no less than to transform Camden "into South Jersey's greatest shopping and business center." When the store opened, Greenfield stated that it "carries . . . a significance which reflects itself in the entire economic development of South Jersey. . . . It [the store] is not a goal unto itself. It is one phase of a greater program."[95] Just as with expansion campaigns of parent stores in major cities, Greenfield believed that major satellite business centers—close in, as with Camden; some distance away, as with Trenton; and in between, as with Upper Darby—could be strengthened as, or even transformed into, retail magnets serving a broad geographic radius. Greenfield proved correct in predicting the fast-growing demand for retail goods in southern New Jersey, but his gamble with Camden proved far less effective than the previous expansion in Upper Darby. When other major retailers initiated plans, they eyed outlying locations. Lit's big store had almost no impact on development in the downtown commercial district.[96]

If Greenfield's views lay at one end of the spectrum concerning the role of branch building in the dynamics of metropolitan development, Walter Hoving's outlook lay at the opposite end. As president of Lord & Taylor, his ambitious postwar expansion program entailed several sites that were completely surrounded by residential areas. Like churches or schools, these new stores would remain isolated amid the sylvan atmosphere of the enclaves they served without adverse impact. No plan more fully epitomized the suburban ideal that the growth of metropolitan amenities could occur without disrupting the bucolic order of elite areas on the periphery. Nearby homeowners tended to disagree, however, and often they joined forces to stave off what they saw as an encroachment that would forever change the nature of their tranquil communities. Grassroots opposition appears to have taken Hoving and other store executives by surprise, for they regarded their emporia as great community assets; it never seems to have occurred to them that the public would consider a new branch as anything but a beneficial neighbor. Yet the idea of a large business, or perhaps any business, entering the neighborhood seemed to well-heeled residents antithetical to the world they had cultivated. Such a practice ran against the covenants that were implemented to protect long-term property values in many high-end residential tracts, and also against the zoning ordinances that many citizens had labored to enact in their communities. Now zoning proved to be the activist's primary weapon, for variances often were needed in order to erect the elegant new lone-wolf stores.

In June 1945, residents of New Rochelle, New York, were

189. Lit Brothers department store, Broadway, Sixth, Market, and Federal streets, Camden, New Jersey (1951–55). Thalheimer & Weitz, architects; Copeland Novak & Associates, interior architects; altered.

girding for battle against Lord & Taylor's first planned postwar branch. The protest came primarily from business interests, who feared that the proposed store, near the Hutchison River Parkway several miles from downtown, would undercut commerce in the core. Allowing the project, by granting a zoning variance, would create a dangerous precedent, critics charged, and encourage other businesses to decentralize as well. Indeed, after about a month of debate, it was reported that the executives of several leading downtown stores were contemplating relocation to the periphery if the Lord & Taylor project went ahead. Because the site lay in a relatively undeveloped area, homeowners were slow to make their sentiments known, but eventually a number of them joined the opposition, expressing outrage over the prospects of spot zoning. Opponents were sufficiently vocal to delay what Hoving had hoped would be a swift process, and at the summer's end the city council voted against the variance.[97]

Subsequently, Lord & Taylor secured a site in Eastchester, close to White Plains, with little opposition. No doubt taking these experiences into account, the site of the next branch lay adjacent to the commercial center of Millburn, New Jersey, and thus was welcomed by the town's business leaders. Furthermore, the site was buffered from nearby residential blocks so that its physical impact on them was minimal. Here, however, homeowner resistance was swift and vehement. It was not so much the store itself, citizens argued, as the effect it would have on future development. Early on in the debate, an ad hoc citizens group concluded that the proposal represented no less than a "turning point in the life of the community, with the township deciding if it will remain a quiet residential town or become the business center for the surrounding territory." Not all residents believed that the impact would be ominous, yet opinions were sufficiently divided to generate a delay of several months before local authorities amended the zoning ordinance to allow the project to proceed.[98]

Citizen opposition proved a resurgent issue for a number of department stores seeking lone-wolf sites in affluent residential enclaves—and sometimes even in less prosperous ones. The most protracted battle, which lasted five years, was over plans announced in November 1946 by Washington's Woodward & Lothrop, which sought to build a branch in neighboring Arlington, Virginia. Although county officials approved a zoning amendment to erect a 150,000-square-foot store amid tracts of modest, middle-class houses and apartments, the move was challenged by William Day, a nearby resident and a lawyer who worked as assistant to the U.S. attorney general. Day's suit complained that the store itself would be a nuisance; it would generate traffic congestion that would, among other things, endanger children; it would intrude on the privacy of residents; and it would "greatly reduce" property values. When the county decision was upheld, Day appealed to the state supreme court, adding that the store "will be merely the opening wedge for other commercial interests." When defeated again, he tried other legal tactics, even though widespread community opposition to the project never materialized. Ultimately Woodward & Lothrop won its case, but by that time company executives were reconsidering the viability of the location given the rapid pace of growth into adjacent Fairfax County. Although the company refused to abandon the site, it eventually chose one several miles farther afield as part of the area's first fully developed regional shopping center.[99] In some other cases, department store executives simply withdrew, not wishing to incur ill feeling among existing and potential customers. Fierce resident opposition to Wanamaker's proposed site in Wilmington caused the company to relocate outside the city limits, where no zoning ordinance was in effect. On the other hand, as a result of citizen protest, Hecht's abandoned plans altogether for a large branch in the small residential community of Somerset, Maryland, just north of an emerging commercial center on the District of Columbia line.[100] Such disputes got detailed coverage in *Women's Wear Daily* and must have given retailers a new sense of caution before they committed to an otherwise well-situated property.

For department store companies that pursued locations in existing business districts, the challenge could be significant as well. Such locations often were not of the right kind, not in the right location, had inadequate or overpriced land, or already had a department store. The challenge was to secure a more isolated site around which complementary retail activities could develop. The rewards could be great if this strategy was successful. Department store executives could work with the owners of surrounding property in setting the tone for the district and the value of the land, to which the anchor store could add dramatically. The model for such initiatives was Bullock's Pasadena. Capitalizing on how the Wilshire Boulevard store had spawned an array of high-end specialty shops nearby, Bullock's purchased a site on Lake Avenue with the hope that its plans would stimulate comparable development in Pasadena. Store executives worked closely with the Coldwell-Banker real estate firm, and land across from the store was sold to a select group of developers for the erection of fine stores. Within a few years South Lake Avenue emerged as a major fashion center for the region.[101]

But when multiple parties were involved the process could be lengthy and laden with risks, as Woodward & Lothrop's leaders discovered in their attempts to develop the store's first large branch. Located at the intersection of two major thoroughfares, Wisconsin and Western avenues, just over the District of Columbia line, the site lay amid a sizable, largely undeveloped area tangent to the affluent, unincorporated residential enclave of Chevy Chase, Maryland. The rationale for selecting this location was not disclosed when the project was announced in August 1945 or in the months that followed, but it is likely that the appeal lay in drawing well-heeled customers from several directions. Significantly, Woodward's chose not to expand in Bethesda, less than two miles farther north on Wisconsin Avenue, where its budget store operated but which had never attracted a critical mass of fashionable stores. Chevy Chase and comparable enclaves in Washington were not well served by existing facilities, aside from those purveying convenience goods. The metropolitan area's most stylish shopping precinct lay several miles to the southeast along Connecticut Avenue, close to downtown. Aside from Sears and a small branch of Julius Garfinckel, a high-end departmentalized specialty store, no major retail establishments existed within a radius of over three miles.[102]

The executives of Woodward's clearly sought to make their establishment the locus of a new center. The initial design called for a four-story, 100,000-square-foot building rendered in a reserved urban mode analogous to that used for Marshall Field and Strawbridge & Clothier some fifteen years earlier. Disputes soon arose over the zoning, with nearby homeowners objecting to the proposed change of residentially zoned acreage for the store's parking lot. The dispute was resolved when the county council amended the ordinance.[103] For reasons unknown, however, Woodward's held off construction for four and a half years. By the time ground was finally broken, in October 1949, the store plans had been completely revised. Opening in November the following year, the branch quickly became a regional magnet, attracting trade from Virginia, where the company's branch plans remained in limbo, as well as from Washington and Maryland.[104]

190. Silver Spring business district, aerial view looking west, showing Hecht Company store at left and subsequent retail development along Colesville Road at center and right. Photo 1953.

Yet Woodward's branch stood more or less in isolation for several years, and when related development did occur, it unfolded very gradually. In October 1953, the Chevy Chase Land Company announced plans for a shopping center directly across Wisconsin Avenue that would encompass both convenience and high-end specialty stores, as well as professional offices, but it was not until near the decade's end that the office space was realized. The momentum increased in June 1958 when Lord & Taylor revealed plans to erect a large store on the other side of Woodward's. Subsequently, Saks Fifth Avenue announced its intention to build a three-story emporium adjacent to the shopping center.[105] More specialty shops followed, and the area became the region's most stylish shopping district by the mid-1960s, some two decades after Woodward's had sparked the transformation.

The outcome could be less unpredictable when a large branch was erected in a small but established outlying commercial district, of which the Famous-Barr store in Clayton was a premier example. Among St. Louis department stores, Famous-Barr, the home-based emporium of the huge May Company, ranked third in prestige behind Scruggs Vandervoort Barney and Stix, Baer & Fuller. For the first branch, president Morton J. May wanted to expand the clientele to encompass an affluent trade, much as his brother, Tom May, had done on Wilshire Boulevard before the war. Surrounded by virtually all the metropolitan area's fashionable residential enclaves, Clayton was an ideal community under the circumstances. By the late 1930s, the town center had begun to harbor small, elegant shops. Postwar growth patterns only reinforced Clayton's strategic position as a center for the well-to-do. May announced the project in October 1944. Opened four years later, the 256,000-square-foot branch was one of the largest in the country at that time.[106] Following the strategy used for the Wilshire store, May chose land on the edge of the community so that the emporium would be the first reached by the majority of its motorist clientele. Between the property and the center of Clayton lay several blocks along a major east-west thoroughfare, Forsythe Boulevard, that were now ripe for retail development. The impact of the new store was immediate and decisive. Even before construction began, other downtown St. Louis retailers began making plans for opening branches nearby. Scruggs Vandervoort Barney was the first, followed by Boyd's, a major apparel store. By the early 1950s Clayton was not only the metropolitan area's most prestigious shopping district, it was the dominant one outside central St. Louis itself.[107]

Success could be a mixed blessing, however. Even before Clayton's transformation into a retail hub was consummated, Silver Spring, Maryland, attracted national attention as a commercial boomtown that, seemingly overnight, had become the second largest business center in the state and a second "downtown" for metropolitan Washington (fig. 190).[108] Recent rezoning aimed at spurring such development, coupled with a much-touted public parking program, contributed to the phenomenon, but the most important trigger for growth was the Hecht Company's large branch, which opened in November 1947. Silver Spring was as strategically poised to draw middle-income households as Clayton and Chevy Chase were for more affluent ones. Hecht's store changed Silver Spring's localized trade orientation, attracting large numbers of patrons from Washington neighborhoods to the south and fast-growing Montgomery County communities all around. Within five years an array of branches of downtown Washington and chain stores had opened or were under construction nearby.[109]

On the surface, Hecht's flourished; however, company officials expressed growing displeasure with local conditions. For reasons that remain unclear, they had not sought or were unable to secure a site on either of the thoroughfares that defined the new district, instead building on a side street a block away. This unusual location did not seem to hinder business at first, but as patronage swelled, Hecht's executives found it increasingly difficult to obtain adequate parking space and room for expansion.[110] Circumstances suggest that Hecht's initially may have sought to add to its store so that it would have a front on Colesville Road in the heart of the new retail center. Soon thereafter, the owner of that property, real estate entrepreneur Sam Eig, built his own four-story store and office building on the site. Subsequently, Hecht's agents secured the adjacent parcel for its second addition. Colesville frontage was achieved, but at the price of a narrow extension, necessitating awkward interior layouts. The tortuous configuration was reminiscent of some downtown stores whose expansion in the early twentieth century was often thwarted by the inability to purchase adjacent parcels. In a rare public display of irritation, Hecht's officials let their dissatisfaction be known. Silver Spring had enjoyed unprecedented prosperity because of their store, yet, they complained, they were constantly hampered in their efforts to nurture their own business. Not only could they not expand in an optimal manner, they had no control over who their neighbors were.[111]

The latter situation was, of course, normal in central and outlying business districts of all sizes, but the fact that Hecht officials singled it out as a liability indicates that, in their promise never to repeat the mistakes of Silver Spring, they were convinced that the only viable way to continue building branches was to invest in planning stores as integral parts of shopping centers. Zoning disputes, ever intensifying competition, and the vagaries of minimally planned development all contributed to a shift in thinking within the industry that was gathering momentum by the early 1950s. Branch building, irrespective of how ambitious the scale, was not enough; if the department store was to retain—or regain—its dominance in the retail field, it would have to do so in an environment over which it exercised majority control. The shopping center was the one instrument with which that control could be acquired and maintained.

7 Stores in Shopping Centers

WRITING IN MARCH 1960, near the conclusion of his 110-part series on the shopping center phenomenon, *Women's Wear Daily* columnist Samuel Feinberg related a story told to him by New York real estate broker Benjamin Strouse about a professor of economics. Called on the carpet by the college president for giving the same examination ten years running, the faculty member replied that other departments had to change their exams annually because the answers are always the same. However, "in economics, we use the same questions every year because the answers are always different." That dynamic, to Feinberg, neatly summarized the "gargantuan growth" of shopping centers over the past decade—"growth accomplished by men playing largely by ear and progressing by trial and error." The best predictions of even a few years previous had to be revised. To drive home the continually shifting situation, Feinberg drew from B. Earl Puckett, president of Allied Stores, one of the most aggressive department store corporations in developing shopping centers. In 1955 Puckett maintained that only twenty-five metropolitan areas in the United States could sustain a large shopping center; now his estimate ran upwards of seventy-five such places, many of which could support two great retail complexes. In 1956, Puckett predicted that 75 to 80 percent of Allied's business would always be downtown. Now that figure was lower by 5 percent. Since the beginning of the decade, Feinberg added, the size of what was considered a large, full-line department store branch had doubled. In closing his series, the columnist incanted the quote from Lincoln Steffens, with which he had begun his observations six months before: "I have seen the future and it works." The shopping center was retailing's great promise.[1]

But the "future" came at a price. In 1953, Homer Hoyt, one of the nation's foremost market analysts in the planning of shopping centers, emphasized the chaotic aspect of the initial development phase: "The first scramble away from the old commercial patterns based on mass transit routes was like the Klondike gold rush. Claims were staked on vacant tracts on the periphery of cities.... Time was always of the essence, because when there were several vacant tracts of suitable size and equal accessibility, the first one to secure commercial zoning and a commitment from a major store was often the winner." The "winner" was not always an exemplar of good fortune. The following year, a cover story in the advertisers' journal *Tide* observed that "right now, few [shopping] center owners or merchants know much about either their methods or their markets. Most of them still feel their way along by tedious trial and dreadful error." David Bohannon, a nationally recognized builder of tract houses and pioneer developer of shopping centers remarked about the same time that "the number of mistakes that the ... entrepreneur can make when developing [such a complex] seems limitless."[2]

The shopping center experienced a difficult birth and an even more difficult adolescence. During the mid-1940s, few department store executives probably gave the shopping center very much thought, but that attitude had changed by the decade's end. Over the next several years, most major firms entered the difficult realm of the shopping center, some of them tentatively, others with a serious commitment. Joining with other stores was perhaps as effective in attracting the outward-moving clientele as was building in peripheral business districts. But the complications in realizing such a facility could be substantially greater and more time consuming. Experimentation was widespread; resolution elusive. The confidence that Feinberg could exude in 1960 was hardly a foregone conclusion a decade earlier.

Conception

In the minds of most observers, then and later, postwar shopping centers seemed to spring from nowhere—a pronounced departure in conception and appearance from earlier retail environments. These new complexes were often far from established districts. They had low-slung, sprawling masses that were generally set well back from the arteries that served them, visually engulfed by acres of parking lots. The character of their design, too, was different, with storefronts defined mostly by glass and signage. Chroniclers of the phenomenon intimated, at least, that these complexes were virtually without precedent. Architect Victor Gruen, who by 1953 had emerged as a leading designer and exponent of shopping centers, contributed to the myth of their origins: "Although the . . . idea is a relatively new one (the theory of the planned shopping center was developed and discussed during the war years, the first shopping center plans were drawn about five or six years ago [i.e., 1947–48], and construction on shopping centers started only about four years ago), some very definite characteristics have crystallized." The revolutionary nature of this development was not to be underestimated. The widespread publicity that the shopping center received in all forms of media, he explained, was "because we are confronted with a truly new building type, with a new architectural concept, such as is born only every few hundred years."[3] Gruen's hyperbole advanced his cause; however, the basic ideas that lay behind the shopping center were created not by his generation, but by the previous one. Those ideas afford the best sense of what both pre- and postwar advocates meant by the term "shopping center."

As a concept, the shopping center was, and is, an entity characterized by comprehensiveness and completeness. It is designed, built, and operated as a single unit. All tenants are selected on the basis of not only the kind and quality of goods and services they provide, but also on how they contribute to a larger whole so that each tenant benefits by the presence of the others, without unnecessary duplication or unmet market needs. This integration of businesses is predicated on a specific set of consumer requirements. Detailed study is necessary to determine the extent and nature of that market, the most suitable location for serving it, and whether the site is large enough. Customer convenience is a paramount objective. Reaching the site should be easy; so should be vehicular circulation, parking on the premises, and walking to the stores once parked. Stores should be grouped so as to foster movement throughout the complex in order that all portions are well patronized. The plant should also be physically attractive to patrons—unified in design, appealing to the eye, and provisioned with amenities. Once in operation, large shopping centers should be aggressively promoted, with management and tenants working together to keep the operation in the public eye. "Shopping mall" has become used interchangeably with "shopping center," but strictly speaking a shopping mall is a shopping center whose stores are primarily oriented to one or more pedestrian walkways instead of the parking lot or street; that is, a complex with an internalized more than an externalized configuration.

While the origins of the shopping center extend to the nineteenth century, the coalescing of these ideas into a coherent program realized on a substantial scale occurred during the 1920s under the aegis of the Kansas City–based real estate developer J. C. Nichols. By the opening of that decade, Nichols was considered the dean of comprehensively planned residential districts for middle- to upper-income households. For him, the shopping center was merely an extension of his endeavors—to provide the commercial functions that prosperous homeowners desired close at hand in a way that added to the long-term value of their real estate. Nichols's concerns were partly esthetic; he loathed the visual cacophony of unplanned conventional development along streetcar lines. But economic considerations underlay his argument. The strip detracted from the value of the adjacent residences, and strip businesses were often poor investments. A fully planned retail development, on the other hand, was a sound, long-term commercial venture in itself, as well as one that well-heeled householders would consider an asset to their neighborhood, protecting them from the alleged blight caused by uncontrolled arterial development. Nichols's Country Club Plaza, begun in 1922, was the principal manifestation of his ideas. Planned to be implemented in increments as capital and demand allowed, the multibuilding complex gave the appearance of an idealized village, its blocks carefully orchestrated not just for visual effect but so as to render all parts desirable, without a pronounced hierarchy of business locations. Most stores were specialty shops catering to an affluent trade, but everyday goods and services were supplied as well. The Plaza was also tailored to the motorist, with wide streets, parking lots, and service facilities. As it evolved during that decade and the next, defying the vagaries of the Depression, the Plaza afforded stunning validation of its developer's approach. Through the early 1950s, at least, the complex also functioned as a mecca for developers and retailers who were interested in adopting Nichols's methods. The developer's ideas were further disseminated through the Washington-based Urban Land Institute, which he helped form in 1940 and which became a highly influential champion of the shopping center concept during the postwar years.[4]

As a reality, however, the shopping center remained far more the exception than the rule in retail development through the mid-1940s. Not until the late 1920s did the Country Club Plaza develop sufficiently for its effectiveness to be demonstrated. Most projects patterned after it were arrested or at least retarded by the onset of the Depression. Since these complexes were generally constructed as part of residential developments for the well-to-do, insufficient demand for new centers on a comparable scale existed once economic recovery began in earnest. Smaller examples that adopted the drive-in concept—where off-street customer parking became a primary determinant of site and design—were introduced as early as 1930 and enjoyed some popularity toward the decade's end. The Federal Housing Administration embraced these neighborhood-oriented facilities for the tracts of garden apartments and modest single-family residences whose mortgages it insured. Others were built independent of housing developments in outlying districts where demand existed. Nevertheless, the extent of all these retail ventures remained quite limited, hampered by uncertain economic and global conditions. Even more inhibiting was the amount of time and money required for proper planning and execution of such a scheme. Constructing a single store or small block of them—either for a predetermined client or on speculation—along public transit lines was far more expedient and remained the prevailing pattern.[5] Through the mid-1940s the shopping center thus was still in an experimental stage. In all but a few cities where the small drive-in centers enjoyed some acceptance, most people had probably never even heard of the type. For them "shopping center" denoted any concentration of retail activity, not the meaning Nichols advanced to identify a specific kind of project that was largely of his own creation.

What transformed the shopping center from a somewhat marginal reformist ideal in retail development to the mainstream phenomenon that it became within only a few years of the war was the inadequacy of existing methods of retail development to meet the great influx of middle-class and prosperous working-class households moving to outlying parts of metropolitan areas. New work in the commercial sphere initially tended to rely on prewar practices. Well-established business centers such as Hempstead, Long Island; Stamford, Connecticut; Evanston, Illinois; or San Mateo, California, continued to grow. Other nodes that had been quite small, such as Silver Spring, Maryland, or Clayton, Missouri, rapidly expanded into major destinations. However, the bulk of the rising consumer population's reliance on automobiles for shopping and almost every other routine exceeded the capacity of conventional commercial districts irrespective of how new they were. Supplying the enormous amount of space needed for moving and parked automobiles was the biggest stumbling block. A rapidly growing business center was still hailed as an embodiment of progress, just as it had been in the 1920s and earlier, but now the greater the development the worse parking options and congestion became. Merchants were not always aware of how acute the need for parking could be. Even if the problem was fully understood, resolving it posed an array of challenges. Private-sector initiatives were generally inadequate, and local officials were frequently reluctant to enter the parking business.[6] Multiple property ownership made assembling land difficult for car lots of any size; often, available land was not well positioned relative to existing or proposed stores. Often, too, nearby residents protested commercial expansion, especially for parking. Congestion along streets that were created long before heavy automobile traffic was anticipated added to the cauldron of dilemmas facing commercial and civic interests alike as outlying commercial centers increasingly experienced problems that had plagued downtown.

To avoid the costs and headaches of operating in suburban business districts, a number of retailers erected single stores along sparsely developed portions of major traffic routes. The proliferation of residential construction near these corridors rendered formerly rural acreage, suitable for only the occasional service station, motel, or roadside stand, into prime territory to serve households. But unlike the lone-wolf locations of the interwar decades, such as that chosen for Bullock's Wilshire, these lay not amid a tightly woven fabric of residential developments but in far more open terrain, with housing tracts often widely scattered within a radius of several miles or more. Situating a business far removed from others might work well for certain enterprises, such as furniture stores, which could operate as destinations unto themselves, or discount stores, which depended on unusually low prices to attract customers, but it was less than satisfactory for many other retail functions that had traditionally congregated in business districts. In isolation, an apparel store, a shoe store, a drug store, or even a department store branch would not likely attract sufficient trade and would also be vulnerable to larger, more diverse retail developments that might be erected nearby.

The highly competitive scene on the metropolitan periphery generated a boom atmosphere in which success seemed within easy reach, but also in which fear of usurpation was omnipresent. The principal stops and transfer stations along public transit lines that had been the basis for so much prewar strip development had proved tenuous enough. Now the automobile gave access to abundant, cheap land along the open road, often only loosely tied to residential tracts, rendering this frontage a locational free-for-all. So removed from established concentrations of commerce, many stores could be highly vulnerable if left on their own. The only alternative in such places was to regroup in a way attractive to motorists—to have an assemblage of related stores served by generous off-street parking facilities.[7]

The shopping center thus emerged as the most viable means of survival for many retailers in a new, dispersed landscape premised on everyday automobile use. Given the vagaries of the situation, retailers and developers alike became willing to undertake the extra costs and time in creating a shopping center. By the late 1940s, such com-

191. Halle Brothers Company department store, Shaker Square, Shaker Boulevard, Cleveland (1947–49). Conrad, Hays, Simpson & Ruth and Robert A. Little, associated architects; altered. Photo 1949.

plexes had become widespread; soon it was the prevalent form for many of the commercial functions associated with a traditional town or city center. The shift to shopping center development received a decisive boost as executives of retail companies that were key to attracting other businesses decided that these complexes afforded the most advantages for their new stores. Regional supermarket chains played a leading role. While food stores had always been a staple of shopping centers of all sizes, most supermarket operators saw their establishments as sufficiently large to attract customers without a supporting cast of emporia. Once this viewpoint began to change in the late 1940s, more or less as the supermarket was consolidating its dominance in food distribution, a major new impetus for shopping center construction emerged.

Fuel was added to the process when the national variety and "junior" department store chains—those carrying a spectrum of merchandise, but in more limited lines than found in a full-fledged department store—likewise made the conversion a few years later.[8] That shift, in turn, prompted the growing number of apparel and shoe chain store companies to follow suit, just as they had to unplanned business districts in previous years. The shopping centers that were developed as a result constituted more than just a neighborhood-oriented facility catering to routine needs, or a collection of fine specialty shops targeted to a well-heeled trade. They were a major source of goods and services used by the burgeoning middle- and moderate-income population on the metropolitan periphery.

The mounting interest that variety and junior department store chains had in the shopping center was likely a major factor in attracting the attention of department store executives, and one reason they did not plan more freestanding stores. The chains, after all, were considered a significant competitive threat that had spurred branch department store development before the war and greatly accelerated it once peacetime returned. Again, the depart-

ment store had to meet its rivals on the same field. But this imperative was not clear for some years, as the chains themselves were deciding whether to embrace the shopping center. In the meantime, the relationship between the department store and the shopping center was tentative at best. Most department store executives proved reluctant to build a branch outside established outlying business districts during the immediate postwar years. To many of them, shopping centers—generally still quite modest in size and appearance—did not possess anything near the prestige they sought. Up through the early 1950s, moreover, industry leaders continued to debate the basic strategies for branch development. Conventional wisdom held that building branches of modest size—under 50,000 square feet—and carrying a limited array of lines supplied directly from the parent store and warehouse was the best course. Many shopping center developers wanted to have a department store as part of their project, but store executives often remained ambivalent. This position among retailers ensured that developers generally had the advantage in shaping the shopping center during the first half dozen or so years after the war.

As a result, relatively few department store branches were introduced as part of shopping centers by 1950. Some were small outlets carrying a limited array of goods in complexes that catered to an affluent clientele. In 1949, Emery, Bird, Thayer Company, Kansas City's most prominent department store, leased a 28,000-square-foot building in Nichols's Country Club Plaza. Concurrently, Sanger Brothers, second only in prestige among Dallas stores to Neiman-Marcus, took over a 16,000-square-foot space in Highland Park Village (begun 1930), a complex inspired by the Plaza and located in the most fashionable part of its metropolitan area. No suitable space existed in Cleveland's Shaker Square (1928–29), another pioneering complex of the Plaza genre, so Halle Brothers built a new facility at one edge of the development in 1947–48. The arrestingly abstract, sculptural design of the store stood in marked contrast to its Georgian-inspired neighbors and received much favorable publicity when it opened (fig. 191). Encompassing 32,000 square feet, the branch was quite modest in scope. For their next branch (1950) Halle executives had to settle for even less space in order to have a store in the recently completed Cedar-Warrensville Center, the premier business development in affluent University Heights.[9]

In several other instances branches were built as centerpieces to new shopping centers of comparatively modest dimensions. Frederick & Nelson's 16,000-square-foot store in Bellevue Square (1945–46) was in fact the first department store branch to open in a shopping center since Strawbridge's at Suburban Square over fifteen years previous. Built to serve the growing population east of Seattle, the

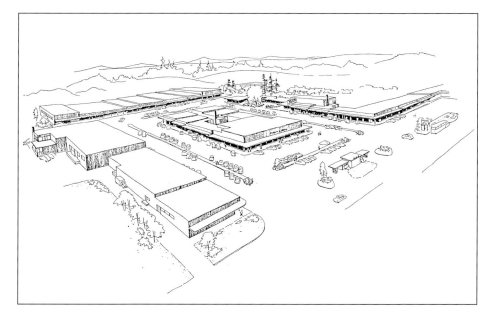

192. Bellevue Square, 104th Avenue, N.E., Bellevue, Washington (1945–46). Moore & Massar, architects; no longer standing. Aerial perspective drawing with Frederick & Nelson store in center (*Architectural Forum,* April 1947, 77).

193. Edmondson Village, Edmondson Avenue between Old Frederick Road and Hilton Street, Baltimore (1946–47). Kenneth Cameron Miller, architect. Hochschild, Kohn store (vacant) in center. Photo author, 1985.

complex contained thirty-five businesses organized around a square, a variation on the village configurations characteristic of the most fashionable prewar shopping centers. Here, however, the department store lay in the heart of the square, a small but conspicuous focal point of the ensemble (fig. 192). Another pioneering venture was Hochschild, Kohn's 30,000-square-foot branch at Edmondson Village in Baltimore (1946–47). Located amid middle-class row house districts developed some two decades earlier, the twenty-eight-store complex was organized in a linear pattern as a large drive-in shopping center, with the Hochschild unit as the centerpiece. The ensemble was clothed in historicizing imagery inspired by the Williamsburg restoration (fig. 193). Most shopping centers, however, were cast in a modernist vein, generally without much pretense. Some catered to a middle market, such as the John Wanamaker store at North Shore Mart in Great Neck, Long Island (1950–51). Others were more oriented to prosperous blue-collar households, such as L. B. Smith Plaza (1950–51), south of Buffalo. This complex was an anomaly, however, in having small branches (20,000 square feet each) of two department stores, E. W. Edwards and Hens & Kelly, in embryonic form heralding the dual-anchor tenancy that would become a hallmark of much larger shopping centers a decade later.[10]

Such early ventures by department store companies strengthened the draw but did not dominate the nature and volume of retail activity of the shopping centers in which they were located. For the most part such a department store branch functioned much like the food, drug, and variety outlets that were the primary tenants in all but the largest of these complexes. Yet by 1951, the tentative nature of department store participation had begun to change, with a rapid rise in the number and size of units planned. About

sixteen department store branches were introduced to shopping centers between 1946 and 1950; over the next five years, more than sixty more were opened. Thirteen of the first group contained fewer than 100,000 square feet; three contained more. Between 1951 and 1955 around thirty were opened with fewer than 100,000 square feet; however, about the same number were larger.[11]

The rapidly increasing participation of major department and chain store companies in shopping center development during the early 1950s led to the conceptualization of distinct categories for these developments based on size, complexion, and target audience—categories that remained industry standards for at least three decades. The "neighborhood" shopping center generally had fewer than twenty businesses, anchored by a market (increasingly a supermarket) and a drug store, providing basic goods and services to a clientele in the environs. The "community" shopping center averaged twenty to forty businesses, was anchored by a variety and/or junior department store as well as one or two supermarkets, included more specialty goods in addition to those routinely purchased, and was oriented to a clientele of up to one hundred thousand. Finally, the "regional" shopping center had at least forty businesses, was anchored by a sizable branch of a major department store, included a wide spectrum of goods and services, and was intended to serve a population above one hundred thousand (usually several times that number) with most of the goods and services that population needed. Even though regional shopping centers never carried as great a variety of consumables as a sizable city center, these complexes were intended to function as surrogates for downtown among the rising population on the metropolitan periphery. By the mid-1950s virtually all regional shopping centers were designed as malls.

Not everyone agreed on the particulars of each definition. Increasingly, analysts also maintained that a true regional center had to have at least sixty businesses; those with fewer were "sub-regional."[12] Furthermore, many shopping centers did not conform to these categories. In some cases, the total number of stores was relatively small, but the department store branch and sometimes several other units were sufficiently sizable for the complex to function as a regional shopping center. In other cases, a complex could boast a much larger number of stores, but most of them, including the department store branch, were small, and the ensemble could hardly be seen as a counterpart to the city center. What constituted a regional or sub-regional center, especially, could not always be determined on a fixed statistical measure. Still, the emergence of a clear hierarchy helped clarify the nature of these undertakings for the parties involved—developers, retailers, and lending institutions all got a better sense of what a given scheme could and could not realistically accomplish in the marketplace. This differentiation also provided the framework in which the department store consolidated its position of preeminence in locations well beyond existing commercial districts.

That consolidation process was hardly achieved overnight. Through the first half of the 1950s, the great majority of department store branches were erected in shopping centers of community or sub-regional size. Out of sixty shopping centers opened or substantially enlarged with branches of major department stores between 1951 and 1955, thirty-nine had fewer than forty businesses; twelve had between forty and fifty-nine businesses; nine had sixty or more. Not until 1956 did the number of new branches in indisputably regional centers begin to rise to a significant degree. From that year to 1960, fifty-one new or expanded shopping centers with department store branches had fewer than forty businesses; thirty-eight had between forty and fifty-nine; twenty-four had sixty or more.[13] During the first half of the decade, strategies for the size, layout, character, and business complexion of shopping centers planned with department store branches remained experimental in nature, and not until the decade's end did the patterns of such development emerge clearly in the minds of many involved in these projects.

Experiments

A major precedent for demonstrating the efficacy of a large department store as the anchor unit of a shopping center occurred with development of the enormous Broadway-Crenshaw Center in Los Angeles (1946–47). The Broadway's store alone encompassed some 220,000 square feet—it was bigger than most shopping centers built before the mid-1950s—and the entire complex totaled 385,000 square feet. While the store was announced well before the war's end, the decision to build it as an anchor to a shopping center was not made public until February 1946, in all likelihood to outmaneuver the archrival May Company, which had announced plans to build an equally big branch just across the street. While the Broadway's tract, thirty-five acres, was ample for such a complex, the May Company's was not. May executives hastily revised their plans to include seven additional stores, but not as an integrated shopping center, losing land earmarked for parking in the process. This was probably the first demonstration of the advantages that a planned shopping center possessed over a single store, although the lesson was obscured by the fact that, rather than undermining one another, the two combative giants attracted a much greater trade than either expected.[14] For the first time, retailers could see the value in having two behemoths in a single outlying node. The design of the Broadway-Crenshaw Center was also arresting. In layout and appearance it bore no relation to comparably sized prewar shopping centers. Components were cast in an exuberant modernist vein, with the sculpted forms of the immense department store poised at the intersection, dual storefronts developed on a billboard scale facing both street and car lot, and, with a capacity of 2,500 automobiles, by far the biggest parking facility created for a retail complex (fig. 194). Overwhelmingly larger than any other shopping center opened prior to 1950, the Broadway-Crenshaw Center attracted widespread attention as an emblem of the postwar retail landscape.

Despite the conspicuous success of the Broadway-Crenshaw Center, it did not serve as a direct model for subsequent endeavors. Huge branches had thrived in Los Angeles since the late 1920s because of the extent of metropolitan decentralization. At the close of 1948 or even a few years later, merchants in many other parts of the country believed that their communities could not sustain so big a store beyond the urban core. Furthermore, as the shopping

194. Broadway-Crenshaw Center, Crenshaw Boulevard and Martin Luther King Avenue, Los Angeles (1946–47). Albert B. Gardner, architect; all but department stores demolished. Broadway store in center, with May Company store above.

center concept gained greater acceptance, several aspects of the complex drew criticism. Its street-front orientation, with the parking lot at the rear, soon came to be seen as antiquated. Little reason existed to have storefronts near the street when the great majority of customers drove to the premises. The parking lot could accommodate those shoppers; however, its one-sided relationship with the buildings necessitated lengthy walks from the farthest parking stalls. Moreover, the linear configuration of the main block, with the Broadway at one end, rendered establishments at the opposite end beyond the main paths of customer circulation. Finally, the supporting cast of fifteen businesses was viewed as too few for so big a department store.[15] An object lesson as much about what to avoid as what to emulate, the complex remained an anomaly.

Subsequent endeavors involving a large department store branch were no less one-of-a-kind. Around the time the Los Angeles giant opened, plans were finalized for the first branch of Bloomingdale's in the Fresh Meadows Shopping Center, which was part of a huge housing complex (population eleven thousand) developed by the New York Life Insurance Company in the New York borough of Queens. With thirty-seven stores and the Bloomingdale's branch encompassing over 100,000 square feet, the complex drew from a burgeoning population in that part of the city and also in nearby Nassau County, Long Island. Unlike most such ventures, a large portion of Fresh Meadows's trade comprised pedestrians; parking, therefore, was limited. The design was also quite conservative, with a series of individual store blocks, most of them fronting internal roadways in a manner reminiscent of some of the large prewar centers (fig. 195). The great mass of the department store rose amid what was conceived as a town center updated with off-street parking.[16]

In several instances, the department store completely overwhelmed the shopping center to which it was supposedly related. After the frustrations experienced in Silver Spring, Hecht Company executives determined to embrace the shopping center as a means of controlling the retail environment of additional branches. Announced in April 1950, the firm's initial venture in this realm included the largest department store branch yet realized (300,000 square feet), from which two modest wings, each encompassing slightly over 50,000 square feet, extended to the rear. The site seemed strategically positioned at the confluence of two arteries and surrounded by well-developed residential districts of Arlington, Virginia, just across the Potomac River from Washington, D.C. The available twelve-and-a-half-acre site was too small, however, to enable adequate on-grade parking for the department store, let alone the entire center, so that a multilevel parking deck holding twenty-two hundred cars—purportedly the biggest of its kind at the time of completion—was constructed at great expense in the wedge formed by the buildings (see fig. 127). The garage

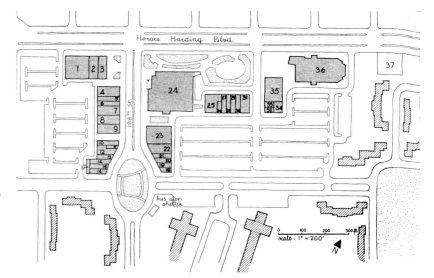

195. Fresh Meadows Shopping Center, Horace Harding Boulevard and 188th Street, New York (1947–49). Voorhees, Walker, Foley & Smith, architects; Kahn & Jacobs, consulting architects; altered. Site plan (Geoffrey Baker and Bruno Funaro, *Shopping Centers: Design and Construction*, 250).

196. Langley Park Shopping Center, New Hampshire and University avenues, Langley Park, Maryland (1953–55). Abbott, Merkt & Company, architects-engineers; altered. Rendering.

was directly tied to several levels of the Hecht branch, but customers had to take a circuitous route to the stores, which had dual fronts—on the abutting streets and on the small surface car lots wedged between the buildings and parking structure. Besides the awkward configuration, the size of many stores and their limited number (under thirty) proved an insufficient complement to the department store. Parkington, as the complex was named, in many respects functioned as two independent developments rather than an integrated whole. The Urban Land Institute's staff considered the arrangement sufficiently unfortunate to publish a case study "to direct the thinking of architects, developers and merchandisers toward a more careful consideration of the amenities of the site."[17]

Eight months after Parkington was announced, S. Kann Sons, a smaller Washington-based rival, unveiled plans for its first branch, which was to rise less than ten blocks away. It, too, had a small group of adjacent stores, in this case undertaken by a separate developer in coordination with the department store.[18] Opening within two weeks of one another in November 1951, the Hecht and Kann stores drew from the same market base but were not close enough to reinforce one another to the degree that occurred at the Broadway-Crenshaw Center and the adjacent May Company store. Further fragmentation stemmed from the fact that both complexes lay a short distance from Clarendon, then the major business district for Arlington County, where a number of chain companies had located during the late 1940s. If shoppers wished to take advantage of the full array of stores these places had to offer, it necessitated driving or taking public transportation to three destinations, not one.[19]

Examples of such disjuncture continued to appear throughout the decade. A third Washington store, Lansburgh & Brother, erected a 127,000-square-foot branch as part of the Langley Park Shopping Center (1953–55), which had nine other stores—the largest, a supermarket—and lay across intersecting arterial routes from two other shopping centers of slightly greater size (fig. 196).[20] The Washington area by no means had a premium on examples. The Castor-Cottman Shopping Center (1952–54) in Philadelphia's burgeoning northeast section contained a sizable branch of Lit Brothers (145,000 square feet), a supermarket, and a few other stores. Albert M. Greenfield, the president of Lit's parent company, City Stores, had little interest in integrated retail complexes. He correctly gauged that the immediate environs would develop into a major business center (his real estate firm negotiated many of the transactions) but appears to have been unconcerned that neither he nor anyone else could exercise more control over the evolving district. Lit's remained the dominant store until it was challenged by rival Gimbel Brothers, which unveiled plans in 1960 for a considerably larger store two blocks away, adjacent to but independent of the neighborhood-sized Cottman-Bustleton Shopping Center.[21] Concurrently, John Wanamaker erected the largest branch yet in Philadelphia (250,000 square feet) in a prestigious location in Wynnewood, Pennsylvania. The big emporium was nominally part of a complex named the Main Line Shopping Center that otherwise was composed of a supermarket and a few other convenience-goods stores. Five months before the new branch opened, Bonwit Teller committed to build a 26,000-square-foot facility in an adjacent building that would also house four small shops oriented to high-end fashion. These offered a fitting complement to Wanamaker's, but the ensemble remained fragmentary.[22]

Adaptation

The sequence of construction at the Main Line Shopping Center was symptomatic of a practice that contributed to the varied nature of these complexes. Adding department store branches to existing shopping centers was a common practice throughout the postwar period. Out of roughly 220 complexes in which such branches were operating by 1960, over one third of those branches were added without being part of the initial plan.[23] This pattern was spurred by the fact that department store executives were frequently stymied in finding locations where an entirely new complex could be erected. Part of the problem stemmed from an attitude toward site selection that still had ties to the conventional patterns of outlying retail development. It was far preferable, the reasoning went, to erect a branch in a residential area that was well developed and to capitalize on the proximity of other businesses than to develop a site farther afield, apart from established commercial centers and residential districts. From this perspective, an established shopping center was an asset on which the department store could build. Shopping center owners, in turn, were delighted by the prospects of transforming their plants into more important consumer magnets.

In some instances, adding the department store was part of an extensive remaking of the complex, as occurred when a Lansburgh's branch was erected at Shirlington in Arlington County, Virginia (1957–59). Sometimes, too, accommodating a number of additional businesses was part of the construction campaign, as when Jordan Marsh was built at the Sunrise Shopping Center in Fort Lauderdale (1959–60); the Emporium at the Signal Hills Shopping Center in St. Paul (1960–61); or the May Company at both the Parmatown Shopping Center near Cleveland (1959–60) and the

197. Irondequoit Shopping Plaza, Hudson and Titus avenues, Irondequoit, New York (1950–51), and Sibley, Lindsay & Curr Company department store (1955–57). Abbott, Merkt & Company and Sumner Schein, associated architects; altered. Department store at left.

University Hills Shopping Center in Denver (1953–55).[24] In a similar move, the Broadway coordinated construction of a 226,000-square-foot branch with the concurrent development of a large store block, greatly increasing the size of an unintegrated business district, called the Panorama City Shopping Center, in Los Angeles's San Fernando Valley.[25] But by far the highest incidence was of simply adding the department store branch as a single building. Such projects could be realized expeditiously, with little or no disruption to operating stores. This mode of branch development appears to have been preferred among some firms. Sibley, Lindsay & Curr, the dominant department store in Rochester, New York, used it for all three of its branches in that metropolitan area during the 1950s (fig. 197).[26] The principal drawback of such projects was that the department store was placed where the land was available, at one end of the complex, so that the new emporium often operated somewhat independently of other tenants, whose owners might benefit little from the relationship. So widespread was the practice of adding to shopping centers in this way that industry analysts soon pronounced it a serious problem.[27]

Such difficulties were exacerbated when sufficient land could not be assembled for a large additional building and the department store company opted for acquiring its own property close by and constructing a discrete facility. After appending a 150,000-square-foot branch (1953–54) to the

Northwood Shopping Center (1949–50) in Baltimore, more than doubling the size of the complex in the process, Hecht's acquired land across from Edmondson Village, erecting a store similar to Northwood's in 1955–56. While separated by a heavily traveled artery, the store dominated the ensemble; even with several additions, the Hochschild Kohn store was slightly over one third the square footage of Hecht's branch. The transformation in retail dynamics was even more pronounced when the May Company in Cleveland constructed a branch of over 350,000 square feet across from the Cedar-Warrensville Shopping Center in 1955–57. Rising in splendid isolation amid a parking lot for two thousand cars, the immense pile dwarfed all the neighboring establishments, including Halle's 25,000-square-foot store. Kaufmann's 230,000-square-foot branch in Monroeville, Pennsylvania (1959–61), was more a complement to the adjacent Miracle Mile Shopping Center (1953–54), which was of approximately equal size and could be reached by a covered walkway.[28] In all these cases, department store executives could capitalize on the existing trade and recognition that the shopping center possessed, but it did not need to negotiate with the owners of those complexes or participate in the ongoing demands of operating them. Shopping center owners benefited from the increased trade that the department store drew, yet the latter facility was also a competitor. Less inclined to patronize establishments on both sides of a busy roadway than in a unified complex, customers could be siphoned off from some of the older stores. Moreover, any coordination, let alone cooperation in merchandising and promotion, between the department store company and the shopping center management was voluntary and often not fully utilized to mutual benefit.[29]

Regularization

Amid the panoply of patterns produced in attempts to make the department store a major component of the shopping center, a growing number of examples were planned with sizable branches—most of them between 100,000 and 200,000 square feet—utilizing arrangements that were enlarged variations on ones that had proven viable for neighborhood and community shopping centers. With a linear sequence of stores facing a front parking lot, the complex could form a more-or-less straight range, be slightly bent at one or two points to form a shallow V, or be divided into two parts to form an L. Irrespective of these differences, the department store was generally placed at one end, but sometimes at or near the center—positions occupied by the supermarket and variety store, respectively, in most smaller shopping centers. This emerging pattern appears foremost to have been the work of the real estate developers who initiated the projects and, perhaps, their architects, drawing from their own experience or from study of other examples.

Either way, the shift to building at a larger scale would not have been difficult from a design perspective. For developers and department store executives alike, this approach brought a predictable order to the project, enhancing its efficiency as a unified merchandising center. The challenges of securing an optimal location, financing, and any needed zoning changes could increase with the size of the project, but the basic physical organization did not.

An important precedent for this pragmatic approach was set by Evergreen Park Shopping Plaza (1951–52). The well-known Chicago real estate broker Arthur Rubloff developed Evergreen Plaza as the city's first regional shopping center—with nearly 500,000 square feet of enclosed space and some five dozen businesses—in an established residential area on the far South Side. The tenant mix was better rounded than in many early examples. The Fair had a 169,000-square-foot branch and Carson Pirie Scott one about a quarter that size. These were supplemented by a 32,000-square-foot branch of Lytton's, a major downtown clothing store, three women's stores and one men's store, a variety store, four shoe stores, a drug store, an appliance store, and two supermarkets, among other outlets covering most goods and services its target audience would purchase most of the time. Like a number of developers in the immediate postwar years, Rubloff decided not to venture too close to the metropolitan periphery but to choose a key intersection amid a large network of lower-middle-class and prosperous blue-collar residential districts.[30]

The price Rubloff paid for his choice of location was a site that was relatively narrow for much of its length and that was assembled with great difficulty. As a result, the buildings had to be configured to the tract rather than for maximum merchandising advantage. The arrangement was ingenious under the circumstances, with the primary, and most constrained, area defined by an L-shaped range of businesses framing a large parking area. Beyond lay a second, much deeper car lot set at a lower level to conform to topography (fig. 198). The Fair lay at the apex, which, together with Lytton's and Carson Pirie Scott, was easily accessible from both parking areas and served to tie the sprawling complex together perceptually. Still, the upper lot seemed by far the more accessible and precluded customers from having to take a flight of steps to the main level. The most innovative aspect of the scheme was placing several small, freestanding specialty shop groupings as a buffer between the larger stores and the parking lot at the upper level so that the long (over one thousand feet) sidewalk was accorded a sense of variety as well as shelter from the acres of automobiles beyond. The pedestrian environment was not all-inclusive, as it was with the regional mall, yet it was a canny response to the large scale of the enterprise. Frequently noted in retail publications of the period, the complex appears to have enjoyed considerable influence. Parking accommodations, on the other hand, almost immediately proved inadequate even though many customers came on foot or by public transportation. The acreage devoted to automobiles, along with its bifurcated plan, were conspicuous shortcomings.[31]

A less well known, concurrent project, the Metropolitan Merchandise Mart in Wilmington, Delaware (1950–52), demonstrated other challenges encountered when expanding a shopping center's scale. Initiated by veteran commercial real estate developer Don Loftus and backed by a group of well-heeled local investors, the scheme was the first major shopping center to be realized in the Delaware Valley since Suburban Square two decades earlier. Sited along a major highway, the Merchandise Mart was planned to draw from a wide radius, including the industrial communities between Wilmington and Philadelphia, affluent Chester County to the north, and southern New Jersey counties to the east. Philadelphia's Strawbridge & Clothier agreed to build the anchor store, probably in part to ensure that the newly opened Wanamaker branch a few miles away did not enjoy the area market alone. Constructed in phases over several years, by the spring of 1955 the complex boasted over forty stores and parking for three thousand cars. Nothing in the greater Philadelphia area rivaled it until the Cheltenham Shopping Center in Montgomery County opened in 1960 and Strawbridge's Cherry Hill Mall opened in New Jersey the following year. The range of tenants at the Merchandise Mart was much the same as that at Evergreen Plaza.[32] Here ample space existed, but maintaining strong visual ties between all the storefronts and the highway appears to have been an underlying concern. As a result, the more-or-less centrally placed department store stood close to the road, apart from the other establishments, which were grouped in two, very long, L-shaped ranges. This configuration facilitated patronizing the department store without going elsewhere and made it difficult to traverse more than a segment of the complex on foot, especially when toting purchases. Ample space existed for cars, but customers no doubt moved their vehicles one or more times within the complex if they chose to visit a number of its businesses.

Whatever the drawbacks of a long, linear layout, they did not prevent it from being used, with some modifications, in even larger projects of subsequent years. North Hills Village near Pittsburgh (1955–57), developed by Edward J. De Bartolo, who had already made a specialty of building community shopping centers, streamlined the arrangement a bit, placing the 130,000-square-foot Gimbel's store at the apex of the two long wings, each set at a slight inward angle to lessen the perceived length. The most ambitious example was the Northland Shopping Center near St. Louis (1952–55), which the May Company itself developed. The Famous-Barr branch, with 325,000 square feet on four

198. Evergreen Park Shopping Plaza, Western Avenue and Ninety-Fifth Street, Chicago (1951–52). Holabird, Root & Burgee and Howard T. Fisher, associated architects; altered. Model. Photo Hedrich-Blessing ca. 1951.

199. Northland Shopping Center, Lucas Hunt Road and West Florissant Avenue, Jennings, Missouri (1952–55). Russell, Mullgardt, Schwarz & Van Holfen, architects; Marx, Flint & Schonne, consulting architects; demolished 2005.

levels, was framed by sprawling store blocks that extended to each side and contained fifty other businesses in another 400,000 square feet (fig. 199). The ensemble was one of the largest shopping centers in the nation when it opened. But while walking distances could be formidable, the situation was somewhat mitigated by having the five-thousand-car parking lot surround the complex, much as at a regional mall, rather than lying on one side.[33]

Fully capitalizing on a large department store branch in a shopping center was rendered even more difficult when the

200. Fair Oaks Shopping Center, River Oaks Boulevard and Quail Trail, Fort Worth, Texas (1951–52). Gruen & Krummeck, architects. Photo author, 2004.

big emporium rested at one end of the complex, as occurred with Abraham & Straus's branch at South Bay Shopping Center in West Babylon, Long Island (1956–57), Hutzler's branch at Westview Shopping Center near Baltimore (1955–58), and the Crowley-Milner branch at Westborn Shopping Center in Dearborn, Michigan (1957–59).[34] The latter two complexes had supermarkets and other stores catering to routine needs at the opposite end, which tended to polarize the functions of the complex as a whole rather than foster circulation throughout. Indeed, the basic role of such complexes remained that of a community shopping center; the big department store was an additional amenity, but not a fully integrated part of the whole.

Throughout the decade, the community-sized shopping center also became the host to numerous full-line department stores of between 50,000 and 80,000 square feet. The primary reason for this relationship was a retailer's belief that the metropolitan area served was not large enough to sustain a bigger branch. One of the pioneers in this realm was Adam, Meldrum & Anderson in Buffalo, which opened a 4,500-square-foot store in 1947 as part of the five-year-old University Plaza. Over the next twelve years, the outlet was expanded four times to encompass some 40,000 square feet. Three more small branches opened in rapid succession between 1949 and 1952, two of them likewise growing considerably larger through additions. After gaining a clear sense of its market on the urban periphery, AM&A opened a 60,000-square-foot store in 1957 at Thruway Plaza, then the largest shopping center in western New York. This strategy was deliberately formulated to "feel our way and enlarge only when proved profitable." According to president Robert B. Adam: "We decided to crawl before we should walk."[35] In an urban area where most established neighborhood business centers were too close to downtown for a branch, the shopping center provided a safe haven for a small outlet closer to the fringe of settlement. Following AM&A's example, E. W. Edwards & Sons and McCurdy & Company in Rochester each opened modest branches in two shopping centers between 1953 and 1961.[36]

The pattern of multiple small units in shopping centers remained the exception, but was by no means exclusive to upstate New York. In Forth Worth, the Fair of Texas embarked an ambitious expansion program in 1951, commissioning Victor Gruen to develop its master plan. The Fair initiated the scheme by developing its own shopping center, Fair Oaks (1951–52), the first Gruen design anywhere to see realization, with a 40,000-square-foot branch at its apex (fig. 200). Two more branch stores were opened by the Fair over the next two years. Subsequently, the firm extended its presence nearby to Arlington, thence to Dallas, opening 90,000-square-foot branches in established shopping centers there in 1960.[37] One or two ventures were more common in cities where the outlying population remained insufficient to support a regional shopping center, especially in the South. J. Bacon and Kaufman-Straus of Louisville took this course, as did Castor-Knott in Nashville, B. Lowenstein in Memphis, Maison Blanche in New Orleans, Miller & Rhoads in Richmond, and Macy's in Kansas City.[38] In at least two larger cities, Pittsburgh and Cincinnati, Joseph Horne and the McAlpin Company, respectively, at first built small branches in shopping centers because topographical divisions were thought to preclude serving a larger market.[39] In most of these metropolitan areas, regional shopping centers were planned or well under way by the decade's end, however, fueled by highway improvements and a burgeoning outward-bound populace. Prior to then, modest branches in community shopping centers constituted an important transitional phase.

Predicament

The piecemeal nature of developing department store branches in many shopping centers underscored the challenges faced by those involved and also the experimental nature of their work. Even some of the nation's foremost department store companies accepted practices that would soon be avoided because so little basis existed to determine the optimal solution or even whether a single such solution could be found. With the continued boom in population growth around the metropolitan periphery, fueled by a strong economy through the mid-1950s, most endeavors yielded handsome profits irrespective of shortcomings. But once the economy began to weaken in 1956, attitudes changed. For several years some observers had charged that the market had been saturated, perhaps even oversaturated in certain places. Too many shopping centers meant that sales would be stunted in each and that once lucrative operations might fail. The matter became a source of considerable discussion as early as 1953, and the debate intensified over the next several years. Between 1955 and 1957, no topic

180 | STORES IN SHOPPING CENTERS

seemed more to preoccupy retailers, real estate interests, and others involved with shopping centers.[40] A barrage of criticism was leveled over design flaws: many shopping centers were poorly located, too small, had inadequate parking, or required customers to walk inordinately long distances, among other shortcomings. Rubloff was one of the first to voice alarm. His Evergreen Plaza was enjoying success; however, he feared that "many of the larger centers are even losing their appeal.... Weary of the novelty and carnival-like attractions," customers often find "the traffic on congested arteries and parking just as difficult as downtown where there is generally a greater assortment and greater values." Architect William Snaith, who had become a national leader in the design of branch department stores, was no less unsettling: "As with chain letters, the first names on the list with the biggest untapped circle of friends reap the biggest rewards. Five years ago it didn't seem as if any store could build too big a branch. Maybe the next five will find the stores that can."[41]

Part of the problem lay with the numerous shopping center developers whose background in house building and speculative commercial development was of a much simpler sort. Their mindset, critics charged, was to construct and sell. The careful selection of site and of tenants needed to plan a shopping center frequently eluded them. The responsibilities of long-term management were even less appealing to many involved. This situation was especially a source of distress to the growing number of companies formed to specialize in shopping center development. These firms sought to capitalize on a field that could be spectacularly lucrative but also undermined by a poor reputation. As a growing sense of order was influencing the planning, design, and operation of shopping centers, their developers sought to have their businesses acquire the respectability of a profession, not be cast as fly-by-night enterprises. The International Council of Shopping Centers was founded in 1956 by a group of these developers who wished to guide a growing enterprise into maturity and take steps to curb amateurish and excessive practices.[42]

The proliferation of shopping centers was significantly boosted by changes in the federal tax code implemented in 1954 that allowed for accelerated depreciation of commercial property. Under the new law, profits earned from building a shopping center could be tax free since they were effectively negated by the paper loss from depreciation. At the end of the five-year depreciation period, the property could be sold at a handsome profit.[43] Many developers took advantage of this provision in order to keep capital fluid for new projects. Edward J. De Bartolo had produced sixty-five shopping centers in Ohio and neighboring states by the close of 1961, yet still owned only about twenty-six. Even so, DeBartolo and a number of his colleagues who sought to bolster the reputation of their field deplored development driven foremost by the lure of profitable resale. Quick resale, critics complained, undermined the efficacy of the shopping center concept. Often the design was cheap, necessitating sizable expenditures for maintenance. Even more disturbing, the developer, according to the vice president of Food Fair Properties, a prolific shopping center development subsidiary of the supermarket chain, "is tempted to rent space to any financially qualified tenant so as to be able to show a prospective buyer that the center is fully occupied."[44] Achieving a good tenant mix was sacrificed for expediency.

The lure of accelerated depreciation and quick resale added fuel to the belief that too many shopping centers were not the root cause of the problem, but rather too many poorly planned ones. Opportunity for growth still existed, but success demanded a more careful approach than many entrepreneurs had taken. The shopping center should not be a disposable commodity but a long-term investment, irrespective of whether the property changed hands. To achieve that goal, meticulous planning was necessary to assess the nature of the market, location, and tenant mix. Equally detailed physical planning was needed to create a tightly unified complex tailored to the specific circumstances of the case. In both spheres, the scope and complexity of planning were markedly greater than that undertaken in all but a few of the largest shopping centers since World War II. Any doubts about making such a commitment were quickly dissipated by the insistence among the insurance companies and other institutions, which lent the huge sums necessary to construct shopping centers, that a comprehensive approach to planning be conducted and premised on sound models. Those models existed primarily when the regional shopping center was developed as a mall, examples of which had been operating since 1950 but which some retailers had seen as overly extravagant. It was the department store executives and corporations, sometimes working in concert with top-of-the-line developers, who eventually rendered the regional mall a mainstream phenomenon. Through their efforts this form of shopping center became the premier form of retail development—the one that made Feinberg so optimistic about the future.[45]

8 Stores Make the Mall

JUST BEFORE THE 1951 OPENING of Shoppers' World, the second regional mall to see realization, the project's landscape architect, Sidney Shurcliff, had a nightmare. In it, he and others from the project team were aboard a "rather rickety airplane" piloted by Huston Rawls, the project's maverick developer. "We were all rather tense," Shurcliff recalled, because "we were accelerating, but far too slowly, down a steeply inclined runway. On each side, just beyond the wing tips, great tree trunks sped past, for this runway was located in a remote forest somewhere in Canada. Its surface was full of potholes. At the far end the sun shone on a remarkably steep up-slope that had been graded like a ski hill, and beyond this to the right, there was a clearing extending at a sharp angle. . . . Rawls held the throttle wide open as we slowly gathered speed. . . . 'We are going to try a "bounce take-off,"' [he] yelled. . . . 'Since the runway isn't long enough for a straight take-off, we gather all the speed we can going down hill and then we wham into the up-ramp. This will bounce us into the air and to the right, where we can finish our take-off run through the clearing, which is out of sight.'" Shurcliff was not convinced by his pilot's ingenuity. Indeed, "all the passengers . . . were terrified. Rawls, too, looked terrified but determined. His eyes had a maniacal glare. 'I'm going to get this damn thing off the ground if it is the last thing I ever do!' he shrieked. The up-ramp rushed at us like a wall of dirt. My heartbeat was out of control. I couldn't breathe. . . . With a terrific crunch the under-carriage hit the up-grade. Were we crashing or had we bounced . . . ? I woke up gasping. . . . Nevertheless the Grand Opening was still rushing at me; it would begin in a very few hours."

Scion to the redoubtable Boston landscape architecture firm established by his father in 1904, Shurcliff had little enthusiasm for either Rawls or shopping centers.[1] Yet, however caustic, his analogy captured a sense of the highly unorthodox nature of the regional mall—a regional shopping center with its stores oriented inward to pedestrianways—at its nascent stage. The economic perils were multifold. Few members of the business community were confident that undertakings of this kind constituted a sound investment. Someone with sufficient entrepreneurial audacity to bring a regional mall to fruition could reap sizable profits and acquire fame. Failure, of course, could bring financial ruin and destroy a reputation.

Shurcliff knew the enormity of the challenge. He had been involved with Rawls's vision for half a dozen years. Having worked in newspaper production, manufacturing, banking, and real estate, Rawls was in his early fifties when he decided to retire to stylish Beverly Farms on the Massachusetts North Shore in 1945. An avid sportsman, he joined some of the area's most fashionable clubs, and he soon took up a business venture with several Boston friends. His idea was to create a small, elegant retail complex catering to the elite clientele of which he and his associates were a part. In consulting with Harold Hodgkinson, vice president for merchandising at Filene's, he was criticized for the modest nature of the scheme: it was too small, too limited in scope, and the parking plan was entirely inadequate.[2] Responding to Hodgkinson's admonishment, Rawls took a dramatically different course. Near the close of October 1946 he unveiled plans on a new site for an enormous shopping complex—the "largest in the United States"—that must have appeared to some observers as a harbinger of the space age (fig. 201).

Situated eighteen miles from the heart of Boston, on the outskirts of the large industrial town of Beverly, Rawls's North Shore Center lay adjacent to an interchange of the projected ring freeway, State Route 128. Two long ranges of one-story buildings straddled a pedestrian green, culminating at one corner in a round department store capped by an immense saucer dome. Parking for three thousand cars encircled the complex, and landscaped buffer zones extended beyond. Not every aspect of the scheme was stridently

201. North Shore Center, State Route 128, Conant, Dodge, and Ellsworth streets, North Beverly, Massachusetts (1946–48). Ketchum, Gina & Sharp and Anderson & Beckwith, associated architects; Arthur and Sidney Shurcliff, landscape architects; project. Model of initial scheme (*Women's Wear Daily*, 20 November 1946, 71).

futuristic, for this was to be part of a new "community." Between the retail complex and a side street lay a collection of eighteenth-century houses, moved to form an idealized enclave, which Shurcliff and his father were asked to develop along the lines of their landscape plan for the reconstruction of Williamsburg over a decade earlier. The name associated with the oldest dwelling in the group became the namesake for Rawls's company, Conant Real Estate Trust. Land was to be purchased for residential development beyond this superblock to ensure that the environs grew in a compatible manner. Commerce would not grow unchecked, as it commonly did along arterial routes. The North Shore Center was a contained entity. It did not represent decentralization, its promoters hastened to note, but rather "recentralization" of the commercial functions that routine automobile use had tended to disperse.[3]

Rawls took no credit for conceiving this vision; that went to Kenneth Welch, an architect and planner who for many years had worked for the Grand Rapids Store Equipment Company and was now its vice president. Welch was well known within the retail field for his expertise in store layout and other retail planning issues. He had advised Strawbridge & Clothier to erect its first branch in what became Suburban Square on Philadelphia's Main Line in 1930 and may well have done similar consultations with Filene's for its branch expansion program during the prewar years. Welch had never undertaken a scheme so ambitious in scale or concept as the North Shore Center. Still, Hodgkinson introduced him to Rawls as the expert who could guide him through an uncharted course.[4] Welch probably seized the opportunity to develop ideas he had been nurturing, for he quickly arrived at what was a bold strategy.

At the heart of Welch's concept lay the premise that city centers could not possibly accommodate the rising consumer market given current and projected levels of automobile use. Instead, downtown had to be matched by outlying shopping centers with comparable drawing power. The location, layout, and size of these huge complexes, as well as their mix of tenants, would be such that sales volume would far surpass that of branch stores and would eventually help lower the price of goods. To achieve this volume, the potential market area not only had to be thoroughly analyzed, the extent of that area had to be determined by the length of time it took consumers to drive to the site, not by distance alone. A limited-access highway such as the proposed Route 128 could greatly enlarge the actual trading area and permit operation on a much larger scale than most analysts were projecting. By making the center isolated and self-contained, motorists could ostensibly reach this destination unimpeded by the traffic that increasingly clogged many thoroughfares. Welch thus adapted the idea of the lone-wolf location to the now greatly expanded and more diffuse postwar metropolitan landscape. Organizing stores around a pedestrian mall ensured compactness and thus helped intensify retail activity. It was among the most revolutionary plans in the history of retail facilities.[5]

Welch, in turn, introduced Rawls to Morris Ketchum, a New York–based architect who had elicited much favorable publicity for his designs of several specialty shops just prior to the war, but who likewise had no experience at large-scale projects.[6] Ketchum proved up to the task, giving Welch's conceptual dictates a fresh and vigorous presence in three dimensions—a presence that eloquently captured the radical nature of the proposition and also exuded a relaxed, informal, and inviting atmosphere considered synonymous with the suburban ideal. Soon the project team was expanded to include as advisors the noted Boston architectural firm Anderson & Beckwith; Frederick Adams, head of Massachusetts Institute of Technology's school of architecture; and Thomas Church, a pioneer modernist landscape architect. Over the next year the scheme underwent numerous refinements. Commitments from the retailers who could transform the plans from vision to reality were slow in coming, however. In all likelihood, some retailers were reluctant because the proposal was so different from anything they had previously encountered. Furthermore, Rawls assumed that Hodgkinson would bring in Filene's as the anchor tenant, prompting others to follow. When Hodgkinson demurred, Rawls approached B. Earl Puckett, president of Allied Stores, whose affiliate, Jordan Marsh, was the largest department store in New England. Within a few years Puckett would become an outspoken advocate of regional malls, but at this stage he was still studying the viability of so major a commitment. In March 1948, soon after launching plans

202. Shoppers' World, Worcester Turnpike, near Greenview Street, Framingham, Massachusetts (1949–51). Ketchum, Gina & Sharp, architects; Arthur and Sidney Shurcliff, landscape architects; demolished 1994. Photo 1951 (*Landscape Architecture,* July 1952, 144).

for a regional mall to accommodate Allied's Seattle affiliate, Bon Marche, Jordan Marsh's president announced that his company would be the linchpin at Beverly. An official groundbreaking occurred that December, but Rawls failed to acquire all the land needed for the expanded scheme; the project was scrapped some five years later.[7]

Rawls was nonetheless determined to "bounce" out of the remote forest in which he had landed. As the Beverly center's momentum was faltering, he pressed ahead for a second complex in what he hoped would become a national network.[8] This new scheme, soon called Shoppers' World, lay along the Worcester Turnpike, the major east-west route in the state, and near the projected path of the Massachusetts Turnpike—not far from the town center of Framingham and eighteen miles west of downtown Boston. Shoppers' World was larger (500,000 square feet), with two levels of stores and parking for six thousand cars on a two-hundred-acre tract (fig. 202).[9] From an early stage Rawls anticipated attracting two department stores. Shoppers' World benefited from all the exploration undertaken in the planning of the Beverly complex, with the same team of specialists devoted to the new undertaking. Two months after Shoppers' World was announced in January 1948, Jordan Marsh committed to tenancy there as well as at the North Shore Center. Design refinements were made quickly, but construction was delayed, perhaps due to Rawls's continuing efforts to secure Filene's. Those hopes were dashed in January 1949, when that company unveiled plans for its flagship branch much closer to Boston.[10] Rawls pressed ahead nevertheless. Within two weeks, contracts began to be let; ground was broken that April; the complex opened in June 1951. A wave of favorable publicity followed in professional and popular journals alike.[11] Shoppers' World, it seemed, had emerged as a national model in the brave new world of shopping center development.

But Rawls was never able to lure a second department store to the complex. The only other major Boston stores were the markedly less prestigious Gilchrist's, which had recently committed to building a branch on the edge of downtown Framingham, and R. H. White, which soon undertook a branch to the west on the outskirts of Worcester.[12] He may have approached firms more equivalent to Filene's, such as Lord & Taylor and Saks Fifth Avenue, but Framingham and its environs did not harbor a large affluent population, which was their mainstay. Indeed, the site lay farther on the fringe of the metropolitan area than many observers considered prudent for so large a retail complex. Rawls had to wait for the population to catch up to his enterprise. At the same time, he had less operating capital and higher operational costs than anticipated, which, combined with inadequate lease agreements, lack of a strong promotional strategy, and problems with the layout, contributed to his company's filing for bankruptcy in July 1955. After two years of study and negotiations, Shoppers' World was purchased by Allied Stores, which, with immense resources at its disposal, successfully operated it for some years.[13] Still, the publicity generated by the episode branded Shoppers' World a failed experiment in the eyes of some retailers. Perhaps because the design was seen as contributing to these misfortunes, Ketchum's reputation as an architect of shopping centers eroded and he never again enjoyed a strong position in a fast-growing field.

Rawls, on the other hand, bounced once again. Even before the bankruptcy he had formed yet another organization, National Planning and Research. Despite his difficulties, Rawls apparently impressed Puckett and Jordan Marsh executives enough to let him plan an entirely new scheme for the North Shore Center. Rawls's firm selected the site, farther east on Route 128, near the town of Peabody, and conducted elaborate market studies, secured zoning changes, and negotiated the land purchases. On his third attempt Rawls was now able to secure Filene's as a second anchor tenant, persuading the company to relinquish plans to build in a stalled shopping center project nearby.[14] This coup elicited considerable interest nationally: although it was not the first time that two major downtown department stores had agreed to erect large branches in a shopping center prior to its construction, such schemes were still rare. The scale of the undertaking also ranked among the largest in the country. At over one million square feet, the North Shore Center was more than twice as large as Shoppers' World. Jordan Marsh's branch alone contained 243,000 square feet, more than the entire complex that Rawls had envisioned for Beverly. The combined drawing power of the two department stores and sixty other establishments, as well as the center's immense size, made it the dominant one in the region for some years after it opened in August 1958.[15] In just over a decade, Rawls helped propel the regional mall from a radical conception into an effective reality that was widely regarded as the foremost new instrument in retail distribution. Despite its slow start, the regional mall approached maturity in a rather short period of time.

The swiftness of this ascent, the epic nature of the formative projects, and the bravura of the retailers, developers, and architects who were key figures in the process all make for a compelling story of how the department store came to enjoy preeminence in the new postwar landscape, transforming the character and function of outlying areas in the process. But the actual events whereby the regional mall came to enjoy such a pivotal place are far more complicated than the Rawls progression might suggest. Once a number of department store companies became interested in the shopping center as a means of expansion, and after they were convinced that the scale of that expansion had to be large, the regional malls such as Shoppers' World that stole the limelight—then and in recent accounts as well—were only a part of the equation. For much of the 1950s, many department store executives considered the regional mall only one possibility—an expensive one that was neither possible for, nor suited to, all occasions. Experimentation was widespread in terms of the size, location, layout, and tenant composition (or mix), as seen in the previous chapter. Among those partial to the regional mall, disagreement also was widespread over matters of size, configuration, character, and even defining a viable market area. Consensus began to build by the close of the decade, but only after numerous experiments, and even then some basic issues remained unresolved. The runway was not quite as tortuous as that in Shurcliff's nightmare, but taking off could still give cause for no small degree of anxiety.

Dominance

The rise of the regional shopping mall was heralded as a phenomenon of unusual importance well before such complexes became the dominant mode of large-scale retail development. To participants and observers alike, the creation of these enormous complexes, occupying sixty acres or more, with buildings that encompassed from 700,000 to over a million square feet, encircled by parking lots capable of holding three thousand to nearly eight thousand cars—more cars than could be parked in the downtowns of many modest-sized cities—seemed remarkable.[16] Their immense size was matched by their unorthodox configurations, with stores opening inward, to tranquil, landscaped pedestrianways. In character as well as scale they seemed antithetical to the piecemeal complexion of most outlying shopping districts, and their customer-friendly inner sanctums offered a sharp contrast to the sidewalks, parking lots, and signs and other accouterments of retail centers generally. The regional mall seemed the ultimate rational response, not just for new outlying areas but for retail development as a whole. "No construction is more dynamic," cooed the editors of the *Department Store Economist* in 1954, "or as likely to influence a reform of the usual urban and suburban hodgepodge of big and little buildings, vacant lots, dumps and slums." Welton Becket, who became one of the nation's leading architects of regional malls, expressed a view held by many of those involved when he claimed its inevitability. Writing to chain store executives in 1951, when only a single such complex had been completed, he declared: "The regional shopping center became a foregone conclusion when the automobile became a reality."[17]

What Becket and other champions of the regional mall framed as a direct, logical step in retail development hardly looked that way a few years earlier. After much experimentation in layout during the immediate postwar period, orienting the shopping center to face a large front parking lot became the preferred arrangement for most projects, irrespective of size by 1950. Placing stores along an inner, pedestrian space, on the other hand, was so marginal an idea among retail and real estate interests that it was scarcely recognized, let alone considered an option. Initially the mall was championed by architects and planners who called for basic reforms in community design and believed that a pedestrian orientation would foster human interaction and a sense of community in new residential areas—qualities, they maintained, sorely lacking in contemporary, automobile-driven development. But very few such projects had been built, and those that had were created under federal auspices, mostly due to the exigencies of World War II.[18] Welch was the catalyst in altering that perspective of oblivious real estate and retail interests. The great respect he commanded from department store and other retail executives gave his proposals for Rawls a rare legitimacy for the time. Welch transformed a concept generated by social concerns into one driven by retail needs; he also increased the scale and the scope of goods and services purveyed so that his complexes would serve as "complete" centers, ostensibly equivalent in retail fuction to the core of a large town or small city. This latter concept was new. J. C. Nichols and other developers of large-scale shopping centers before the war envisioned them as complementary to downtown; they assumed that their generally well-heeled clientele would always rely on the urban core for certain shopping needs. Welch, on the other hand, suggested that his regional malls were a new kind of downtown, surrogates for city centers that had reached capacity.

An equally new idea was that the department store branch was the key component to achieving equivalency. Previously, shopping centers and department store branches had developed independently of one another, with Strawbridge & Clothier's first branch introduced to Suburban Square the primary exception. Having advised Strawbridge's on this project, Welch took the lesson to heart as a cornerstone in his conceptualization of the regional mall.[19] But Welch's own record may not have been enough to propel his concept into the heart of the retail field, as he was then focusing on the mostly stillborn projects of Rawls.

The key factors in giving Welch's ideas proposed efficacy were their adoption and refinement by department store executives themselves. The underlying reason these chieftains undertook projects of such enormous cost—many complexes ran between $10 million and $30 million—that necessitated years of planning and construction and that were laden with innumerable unforeseen difficulties was that they came to believe the regional mall could ensure dominance in the fast-evolving, highly competitive, decentralized market. In contrast to conditions with freestanding branches and branches added to existing shopping centers, department store companies could exercise nearly complete control over the retail and physical environments. The great size of these complexes not only ensured hegemony in customer draw, it ostensibly discouraged competitors from locating nearby, as the May Company had done on Crenshaw Boulevard and Hecht's and Kann's were doing in Arlington, Virginia. Instead, the competition would be internalized, between the department store and the smaller establishments in the complex, so that customers could indulge in comparison shopping as they did downtown without leaving the premises. At the same time, department store executives could choose that competition, because their company was either functioning as the developer or working in close alliance with one. The fears that industry leaders had harbored for some three decades over chain store encroachment were at least mitigated by this unprecedented controlling relationship.

The physical configuration of the regional mall also possessed advantages from a merchandising perspective. Having so large a complex was proving unwieldy when arranged along the conventional linear and L-shaped plans that were common to neighborhood and community shopping centers. Placing stores along a pedestrianway cut the walking distance from end to end by at least half and psychologically made the complex seem more compact and easily navigable. This condensed format also facilitated making the department store the major focus of the ensemble. At the same time, divorcing customers from their cars fostered perambulation throughout the premises and induced them to spend longer periods of time there. Encircling the buildings with a parking lot rather than confining that space to one or two sides minimized the walking distance from automobile to store. The mall configuration was more expensive to construct and maintain, but once its strengths became clear they were difficult to ignore.[20] Few businesses could command the funds needed to construct a regional mall. The financial strength of major emporia and, especially, of those that were part of corporations were central to the mall's realization. In this realm of development, the department store was in a league of its own.

The pivotal work in demonstrating the efficacy of the regional mall concept was Northgate Shopping City in Seattle (1948–50) (fig. 203). Conceived by Rex Allison, president of the Bon Marche department store, working closely with architect John Graham, the complex was designed with merchandising the foremost concern. Allison took pains to ensure a "complete" shopping environment, with other stores selling every kind of product offered by his establishment and also encompassing a greater price range of goods. In its size and location the Bon Marche dominated the ensemble, yet the retail dynamics were intentionally on a highly competitive scale. To facilitate comparison shopping Allison broke another convention of shopping center

203. Northgate Shopping City, 5th Avenue, N.E., and 100th Street, Seattle (1958–60). John Graham & Company, architects; altered. Photo Pacific Aerial Surveys, 1950 (*Architectural Forum*, August 1950, 117).

planning. Normally, stores with the most customer draw were placed throughout the complex to foster circulation. At Northgate, stores selling related merchandise were grouped together to shorten walking distances. To maximize locations throughout, key functions were situated at each end of the spine that traversed the complex as well as in the center. Welch's work was never acknowledged in contemporary accounts as a source of inspiration. Allison and Graham later implied that they arrived at their plan independently; both the approaches to tenant mix and mall configuration, they later recalled, were inspired by Seattle's main shopping corridor. Not long after the opening Graham described the scheme as a "merchandising city without the usual inequities of downtown retailing"; that is, without the great disparities in the merits of location in the shopping district. Northgate's plan was intended to manifest to a degree seldom achieved the parity of all locations that Nichols had espoused since the 1920s. Both the nature of the merchandising plan and use of it as the basis for layout were new. At the same time, it is difficult to believe that either man could have been unaware of Welch's revolutionary conception given the coverage it received in business and design journals alike.[21]

B. Earl Puckett, chairman of Allied Stores, of which the Bon Marche was an affiliate, was also a likely agent of transfer since he was intimately familiar with Welch's and Rawls's plans for the North Shore Center. An account prepared several years later stated that around 1947, Puckett and his associates had embraced the objective of "recentralization" and decided that the regional shopping center was the most effective means of achieving that objective.[22] Allison's preliminary planning of Northgate that year may have convinced Puckett to approve his scheme and have Jordan Marsh commit to Rawls's projects early the year following. Or perhaps it was the years of experience that Welch brought to bear on the subject that was a deciding factor as much as the plans advanced by Allison, who was only in his mid-thirties. Indeed, the confluence of the two initiatives could have fostered a major change in policy. Whatever the circumstances, Puckett became an outspoken proponent of the regional mall. Opening in April 1950, Northgate was hailed as a resounding success in the ensuing months, and it became the industry's model. Had the complex not been realized, it is debatable whether the regional mall would have had much of a future, given the stigma attached to Rawls's work. Instead, Allied was heralded as the pioneer in the development of regional malls. "For dominance in the suburban market," Puckett declared in his typically brusque manner, "build a center to end all centers in the region." Merchandising needs, he maintained, must shape the scheme in all its aspects. "Shopping centers must be planned and executed by retailers, not real estate prospectors thinking in terms of leases." Between 1952 and 1955 he unveiled a massive expansion program that, in addition to the recast North Shore Center, included Bergen Mall in Paramus, New Jersey (1952–57); Gulfgate Shopping City in Houston (1954–56); Mid-Island Shopping Plaza in Hicksville, Long Island (1955–56); and Swifton Center in Cincinnati (1953–56).[23]

While Allied was the acknowledged industry leader in spurring the development of regional malls, it was soon joined by competitors. Among the corporations, only the May Company approached the same scale of development before the mid-1950s, with its immense Lakewood Center in Los Angeles County (1950–52) and the much smaller O'Neil-Sheffield Shopping Center near Lorain, Ohio (1952–54). Independently owned department stores undertook some of the most ambitious projects during the same period. Three months before Northgate's opening, the San Francisco–based Emporium announced plans for a larger store in a 1-million-square-foot regional mall called Stonestown. By mid-fall, Marshall Field had done likewise with a complex later named Old Orchard. John Wanamaker executives were exploring plans for what became the immense Cross County Center in Yonkers. The most daring initiative, however, was taken by the J. L. Hudson Company in Detroit, which unveiled long-range plans to build four regional malls ringing the city, the first two of which, Eastland and Northland, would be considerably larger than any others realized over the next decade.[24] Even though the regional mall still had no clear track record, some of the foremost department store companies in the nation were willing to take the substantial risk and translate the concept into bricks and mortar.

For the first time since the great emporia had reigned unchecked downtown did the problems that arose in the 1920s—expansion, customer access, parking, and chain competition—seem to be headed toward conclusive resolution. The analogy between what the department stores had once achieved in the urban core and what they were now starting to do on the periphery was not lost on those involved. In an immodest reflection, the *Department Store Economist*'s editors were triumphant: "A new generation of department store men and women are reaching out to create new centers today. These descendants are showing the same high responsibility to their communities that their grandfathers showed when they helped create the great down towns which we know today in hundreds of cities."[25] The department store was both the defining element of and the driving force behind the regional mall.

To realize their objectives, many department store executives, like Allison and Puckett at Northgate, were willing to enter the field of real estate development, about which they knew very little. In the Chicago region, Marshall Field's competitor, Carson Pirie Scott, took this course at Eden's Plaza (1953–56) and joined with Wieboldt's and Montgomery Ward to build the immense Randhurst Center (1959–62). Allied's initiative to build the North Shore Center induced Filene's to undertake South Shore Plaza (1955–61). Hudson's example inspired Dayton's to do the same at Southdale (1952–56) outside Minneapolis. Macy's committed to projects for its affiliate, Bamberger's, at Garden State Plaza (1951–57) in northern New Jersey and for its California division at Bay Fair near Oakland (1953–58) and Valley Fair near San Jose (ca. 1955–57). After its success with the Crenshaw Center, the Broadway developed three large malls, the Broadway-Anaheim Shopping Center in Orange County, California (1954–57), Del Amo Center in southeastern Los Angeles County (1957–59), and Chula Vista Shopping Center near San Diego (1959–62). Bullock's did similarly at Santa Ana (1956–58) and in the San Fernando Valley (1959–64). After building the O'Neil-Sheffield Shopping Center (1952–54) in northern Ohio and the enormous Northland outside St. Louis (1952–55), the May Company created a subsidiary, May Shopping Centers, which was based in Los Angeles but responsible for work across the country, including Westland Shopping Center near Denver (1957–60) and Mission Valley Shopping Center in San Diego (1957–61). Such ventures were not limited to the industry giants, however. A. Harris built Oak Cliff Shopping Center in Dallas (1953–55), as J. L. Brandeis did Crossroads Shopping Center in Omaha (1959–61).[26]

Initially, the commitment to serve as developer often was made because, as Puckett explained at Northgate, no one else was prepared to undertake a project of this kind. Within a few years, however, some companies found that the process also could yield handsome profits beyond those generated by the store. May vice president Frank Clark, Jr., enthused before a group of New York security analysts: "A department store operator is in the real estate business whether he likes it or not. We happen to like it . . . [because] we are adding very substantially to our stock for our stockholders. . . . our half interest in the residual land value in this project [Mission Valley Shopping Center] will show a maximum appreciation of several million dollars over our cost." He continued: "Major population shifts . . . during the last 10 years have created a constantly increasing real estate opportunity for the department store operator. . . . A regional shopping center with a May store as its nucleus creates economic value far in excess of the actual land and construction costs."[27]

Not all department store executives were inclined to assume the developer's role. A year and a half after announcing Old Orchard, Marshall Field's formed a subsidiary company to implement the project. But by the close of 1953 Field's chairman, Hughston McBain, turned over the project to developer Philip Klutznick, with whom he had established a good working relationship in planning a branch in Park Forest (1953–55). McBain admitted that his firm simply did not have the expertise to undertake the venture.[28] Even when a department store company did muster the talent, the preference often was to work cooperatively with a developer. Puckett stated that Northgate Allied had orchestrated the creation of the North Shore Center and Bergen Mall only because satisfactory developers could not be found; an independent party had charge of construction and management of most other Allied regional malls. For some retailers, too, the real estate business was best avoided.[29] Securing an experienced staff was expensive, and the whole operation diverted time and energy from the pressing business of branch development itself. The demands could be particularly great on an independently owned company, which could not draw from the centralized staff of a corporation. Yet finding a developer up to the task could be challenging as well. Many of those developers who rushed to enter the field had previously focused on residential property and had little or no experience in the commercial sphere. Many also proved to be impatient with the extensive planning needed to secure a shopping center that was sound for the long term. Department store executives apparently received innumerable proposals from real estate developers to build regional centers, the great majority of which were turned down.[30]

Nevertheless, some entrepreneurs succeeded in convincing a department store to participate in a plan for a regional mall that they had already initiated. Temple Buell, head of one of Denver's leading architectural and construction firms, secured a commitment from the Denver Dry Goods Company to join his venture for Cherry Creek Shopping Center (1950–54). Subsequently, the retailer was courted by veteran real estate developer Gerri von Frellick and agreed to be the focus of his Lakeside Center (1954–56). Macy's was wooed by William Zeckendorf, president of Manhattan giant Webb & Knapp, to be the centerpiece of Roosevelt Field in Hempstead, Long Island (1953–56). Garfield Kass, who had the most experience in commercial properties throughout the Washington area, convinced the venerable Woodward & Lothrop to anchor his 7 Corners Shopping Center in northern Virginia (1953–56). In some cases, firms seasoned primarily in residential development were able to attract a major store. Macy executives on the West Coast and veteran house builder David Bohannon reportedly found each other while both were contemplating a regional center on the San Francisco peninsula, leading to the development of Hillsdale in San Mateo (1952–54).[31] Allied signed up with three such firms: Stackler & Frank for the B. Gertz branch at Mid-Island Plaza; the Jonathan Woodner Company for the Rollman's branch at the Swifton Center; and Roy Pletz for the Joske's branch at Plaza de Las Palmas in San Antonio (1956–57).[32]

In many other cases, the department store took the lead, gravitating toward real estate developers with a good record on large-scale commercial projects. Halle's executives chose Anthony Visconsi, with whom they had established a solid working relationship, to develop Westgate (1951–54), the Cleveland area's first regional mall. For the Cross County Center, Wanamaker's teamed with Sol Atlas, who had acquired considerable stature for the Miracle Mile on Long Island. Allied joined forces with Boston real estate entrepreneur Theodore W. Berenson and his associates for Gulfgate and Northline (1960–63) in Houston. L. S. Ayres, the leading department store in Indiana, chose the Chicago firm Landau & Pearlman for the Glendale Center in Indianapolis (1954–58). Marshall Field's continued to collaborate with Klutznick at Oak Brook 1959–62) on Chicago's far west side, while choosing Froedtert Enterprises, which had pioneered shopping center development in Milwaukee, for its giant Mayfair Shopping Center (1953–59) in that city's western suburbs. In December 1955, Shillito's, Cincinnati's largest department store, announced its intention to build the Tri-County Shopping Center on that metropolitan area's northern fringe. When plans coalesced more than three years later, Shillito's leadership had enlisted Joseph Meyerhoff, who had pioneered shopping center development in Baltimore.[33]

On occasion, department stores found unusual partners. San Francisco's Emporium-Capwell worked with the real estate arm of Stanford University to create the large Stanford Shopping Center (1954–56) as a means of generating income for the university. Similarly, Rich's in Atlanta joined forces with the Noble Foundation of Ardmore, Oklahoma, which had selected the Georgia city as an ideal location for a regional shopping center, to build Lenox Square (1957–59), the largest in the South at the time it opened. Sometimes, too, an alliance was founded on unforeseen circumstances. Strawbridge & Clothier's project in Camden County, New Jersey, with residential developer Eugene Mori collapsed when he could not secure financing. Strawbridge's assumed control of the enterprise and in 1960 brought in the Baltimore-based Community Research & Development, headed by James Rouse, a rising star in the shopping center field. The resulting Cherry Hill Shopping Center opened the following year as the largest in the Philadelphia area and in Rouse's portfolio to date. Woodward & Lothrop's experience at Wheaton Plaza in Montgomery County, Maryland, was somewhat the reverse. When plans were unveiled in 1958, the developer was the Yonkers-based Eastern Shopping Centers, which had also undertaken another regional mall, Prince Georges' Plaza (1957–59), in the neighboring county. Before the year ended, however, Eastern had abandoned the project, which then fell to the local representatives, a real estate agent and developer, both of whom lacked experience in this sphere. Nevertheless, work proceeded; Wheaton Plaza was touted as the area's premier retail facility when it opened in March 1960.[34]

Irrespective of who was charged with the tasks of development, the department store enjoyed enormous influence over the shape and complexion of the regional mall. Knowing that the stores' presence was essential to the creation of such a facility, executives demanded optimal positions for their buildings, lease agreements that were far more favorable than those with the other businesses involved, and sometimes veto power over potential tenants. Having felt besieged by competition, especially from chain stores, department store executives took pains to ensure that the assemblage of tenants in a shopping center would work to their advantage. But achieving a strong, balanced tenant mix was only a part of the equation. Developing a regional mall was far more complex and demanding than any previously experienced in the retail field.

Planning

The challenge of development was foremost one of comprehensive, long-term planning. Nichols had stressed the need for this since the 1920s, and it was likewise championed by the Urban Land Institute, which he helped found. Nevertheless, the value of this endeavor was lost on many developers, who were eager to capitalize on the postwar boom. The requirements of thorough planning were far more extensive than those for an independent branch store, or even a shopping center of smaller size. The market survey had to assess the demand for a wide range of goods over a large geographic area, examining current and projected competition from both outlying areas and the city center. Welch's work for Rawls in this sphere helped set the stage for what became an important new commercial realm in planning during the 1950s. Welch advised on a number of projects, most notably several undertaken by Rouse. Homer Hoyt in Chicago and Larry Smith in Seattle were the most prominent planners, commissioned by developers and department store companies coast to coast. Since the 1930s Hoyt had been well known for his studies of location and its impact on commercial values. Smith likewise focused on the commercial sphere, counting Allied Stores, Sears, J. C. Penney, and J. J. Newberry among his clients when he began to work as a real estate consultant on some of the pioneering regional malls, including Northgate, Stonestown, Hillsdale, and Eastland.[35] Their planning, which could take a year or more to conduct, formed the basis for every other decision made as to the size, scope, and location of a regional mall. The department store was the linchpin and often the initiator in creating these behemoths; however, the real estate analyst arguably had the most decisive role in realizing them.[36]

Smith and his colleagues targeted peripheral areas in transition—ones that had experienced significant population growth in recent years and were likely to continue to grow. Sites closer to the core were too small, too expensive, and not positioned well to serve the population settling farther afield in the years to come. The households earmarked were the department store's prime, traditional clientele, and thus the areas served were overwhelmingly made up of new freestanding, single-family houses occupied by the middle class. Sometimes more well-to-do enclaves were nearby, but to a greater degree regional malls were accessible to prosperous blue-collar households that, arguably, were approaching middle-class status, with a rising amount of disposable income. Irrespective of such differences, the target population was overwhelmingly white, reflecting both the demographics of outlying areas and longstanding racial prejudices. The regional mall was conceived to draw from a substantial geographic radius, but the critical mass of clientele had to live nearby. Most patrons, consumer studies found, lived within five to ten miles of the complex.[37]

Once the general location had been determined, selecting the site was also a challenging task. The property had to include room for stores, motor vehicles, and expansion. The fifty acres set aside for Northgate became more or less the minimum size for a truly regional mall; most subsequent examples occupied between fifty and eighty acres. Sometimes additional acreage would be purchased for the development of office space and other revenue-generating facilities, as occurred at Lakewood and Roosevelt Field.[38] Concerns arose, too, about creating buffer zones so that the complex would not be surrounded by unwanted competition. Department store executives, especially, were concerned that the environs be developed in a way that would enhance the regional mall, as Welch understood in his initial conception for the North Shore Center. Some of these retailers also saw the potential to benefit from the enhanced property values created by the mall. Hudson's had one of the most ambitious projects of this nature, securing 409 acres for Northland, 161 of which were allocated to the mall complex and its service facilities, with the remainder set aside for office buildings, a hospital, a theater, apartment houses, and single-family dwellings. Following Hudson's lead, Dayton's took similar steps at Southdale, purchasing a total of 462 acres so as to surround the mall's site with office buildings, a medical center, and a residential enclave (fig. 204).[39]

Adequate parking was a central consideration as well. Experience with smaller shopping centers during the late 1940s and early 1950s revealed the tendency for developers to underestimate the number of spaces required. Welton Becket cautioned retailers in 1951 that parking was a core issue. The Urban Land Institute, which took the lead in setting standards for shopping center parking, continually revised its figures, determining by 1953 that three square feet of parking space for every one square foot of retail space was optimal. Some experts argued for more, however, and many admitted that no ratio worked across the board, because some stores generated more automobile traffic or higher automobile turnover than others.[40] But without any real precedent for determining the capacity of early regional malls, decision makers had to rely largely on judgment. Surveying the initial plans for Old Orchard, the editors of *Architectural Forum* concluded, "Nobody really knows how much parking is necessary to take care comfortably of the combined pulling power of a center like this." Welch, they noted, "has always hammered the importance of having enough for 'the last Saturday before Christmas.'" Others claimed the growth rate of automobile ownership would not be as great as it had in the recent past.[41]

As it turned out, Northgate's planners proved to be on target, providing space for five thousand cars when the complex opened in 1950. Through the decade, most regional malls averaged between four thousand and six thousand

204. Southdale Shopping Center, France Avenue between Sixty-Sixth and Sixty-Ninth streets, Edina, Minnesota (1953–56). Victor Gruen, Associates and Larson & McLaren, associated architects; altered. Site plan as developed prior to L. S. Donaldson Company's agreement to enter complex with the second anchor store.

spaces, but the biggest were larger. Mid-Island, Garden State Plaza, North Shore, and Mayfair all had eight thousand spaces. Land had to be set aside for increases in accommodation as well. Northland's seventy-five hundred spaces were augmented by twenty-five hundred more within three years of opening—a pattern that proved common by the decade's end.[42] Increasing car size during the 1950s also led some developers to enlarge the space allocated to each vehicle, the cumulative results of which were significant. The property had to be configured so that parking could be evenly distributed around all portions of the complex. And so extensive a parking area had to have its own circulation systems in order to move a large volume of cars through the premises. Those involved in planning soon realized that connections to streets on at least three sides were essential when dealing with so much traffic.[43]

Many early regional malls were tied to boulevards or to highways with unlimited access. By mid-decade, however, adjacency to a high-speed, limited-access route, as well as to other thoroughfares—a locational strategy pioneered in the siting of the unrealized North Shore Center, Northgate, Cross County Center, and Old Orchard—became increasingly common (fig. 205). Plans for Roosevelt Field were scrapped when those for an adjacent extension of the New York Thruway were terminated, then revived with announcement plans to build the Meadowbrook State Parkway along one side of the property. Gulfgate's creation was tied to the newly completed Gulf Freeway (I-45), Houston's first. The selected site lay at the intersection of the partly completed South Loop Freeway (I-610). The value of this location apparently was judged sufficient to warrant a bifurcated parking lot on the South Loop side, with a pedestrian bridge connecting the two parcels. Similarly, the Tri-County Center was predicated on the development of the Mill Creek Expressway (I-75) to Dayton and a major loop (I-275), although by that point planning had begun well enough in advance to secure a larger, undivided site near the intersection.[44] Not all properties selected for regional malls through the 1950s were so served. In some cases the value of such access appears to have been underestimated. Bottlenecks generated by traffic traversing an inadequate street system to reach Mid-Island Plaza underscored the importance of transportation planning.[45] The regional mall became ever more a creature of the fast-changing landscape of efficient motor transportation.

The sites chosen had to be largely open, of course; otherwise, acquisition and demolition costs were prohibitive. Previous uses encompassed a variety of functions associated with the metropolitan periphery, including charitable institutions, airports, amusement parks, country estates, even a town dump. In many other cases, the land had been used for agricultural purposes or was untended. Irrespective of its past, the land was generally subject to some form of zoning by the 1950s. Often outlying acreage was given the blanket designation of low-density residential use, but sometimes land fronting thoroughfares was zoned for commercial use, following a pattern that became pervasive in cities after World War I. Neither community planners nor

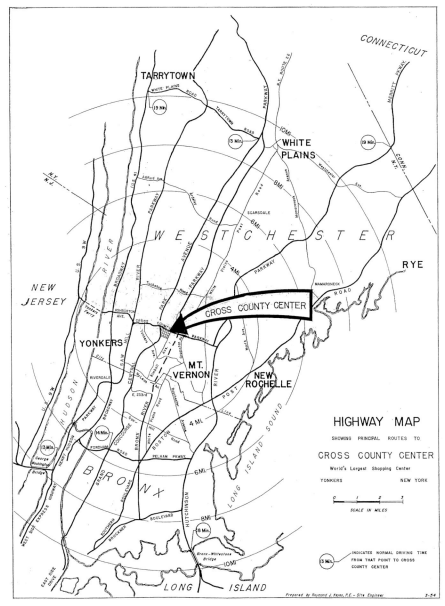

205. Cross County Center, Central Park Avenue and Cross County Parkway, Yonkers, New York (1947–55). Lathrop Douglas, architect; altered. Map of highways, showing driving times and distances from the complex, prepared by Raymond J. Keyes, site engineer, March 1954.

zoning officials anticipated the proliferation of immense retail complexes consuming fifty to eighty acres or more. In most jurisdictions, officials were delighted by the prospects of a shopping center, especially a regional mall, and variances were dutifully bestowed to developers. But just as with some lone-wolf branches, shopping center proposals could encounter citizen or even business opposition. When Filene's executives agreed in July 1948 to provide the anchor store for the Townlyne Shopping Center in Peabody, Massachusetts, they probably expected their decision would remove the plan from the local political imbroglio it had experienced during the previous months. Rezoning failed to occur over the next year, however, and the store eventually located in the North Shore Center instead. Nearly a decade later, Filene's encountered strong citizen opposition to a proposal regional mall it planned in Lexington. After months of bitter debate, the plan was scrapped. Soon thereafter, the company announced plans to undertake a regional mall nearby in Burlington.[46] Yet complications prevented the store from opening until 1968. In both cases, the failure to secure rezoning cost the store a delay of about a decade.

Instances where a regional mall went unrealized due to rezoning disputes appear to have been few, perhaps in part because the acreage needed was large enough to demand sites that were removed from well-established residential and business areas. Still, protests could cost a project's sponsors valuable time. Homeowners in Garden City, Long Island, the jurisdiction in which a small part of Roosevelt Field was located, held up rezoning for nearly a year.[47] The May Company's decision to enter San Diego with the enormous Mission Valley Shopping Center generated a storm of protest among downtown business interests. Once the city council approved the rezoning petition, a small group of opponents pressed for a referendum. The fracas was not resolved until seven months after the request for rezoning was initiated.[48] A far more pervasive problem was the steadily rising cost of land. After World War II, acreage removed from established metropolitan development generally could be secured at bargain prices, but as the move to such areas swelled during the 1950s, land values escalated.[49] Ideally, a regional mall's site was procured years ahead of need so as to obtain a strategic location at reasonable cost. Yet purchases made too far in advance carried risks, since residential growth and other development might deviate substantially from projections.

Well before any petition for rezoning, preliminary design studies were undertaken and the search begun for tenants. Both the latter processes had to be well advanced before financing could be pursued. The tens of millions of dollars required to realize a regional mall posed a significant challenge. Prior to the war, Nichols's Country Club Plaza and the few shopping centers that emulated it were built incrementally, capitalizing on the considerable funds and high credit rating of the companies that sponsored them. In the years that followed, developers who did not have comparable resources at their disposal generally found it easy to get financing from banks and other traditional lending institutions for neighborhood or community shopping centers given the booming market. Building a regional mall, on the other hand, encumbered more money than most single businesses wished to commit. Department stores, especially those that were a part of leading corporations, could draw from their own substantial resources, as well as issue additional stock, just as they had financed construction before the war. Yet as the size and cost of branches rose, the period required for them to show an initial profit grew as well. Furthermore, at a time of unprecedented expansion, which was occurring on multiple fronts and could include enlargement or remodeling of the downtown store, building a new service facility or parking structure, and developing several large branches, even the biggest firms sought major funding from outside sources.[50]

From the start, the principal source of financing was insurance companies. Intensive lobbying by the insurance industry had yielded changes in state laws right after the war, enabling investment in real estate. With vast sums available from maturing war bonds, insurance companies initially concentrated on new residential development. By 1950, however, a confluence of circumstances rendered a sizable component of that activity—apartment houses—no longer attractive. The new crop of regional malls being planned at that time proved an appealing alternative. At least one financial analyst pronounced well-planned shopping centers to be the most profitable investment available in outlying portions of metropolitan areas with over a half million people.[51] The New York Life Insurance Company had developed Fresh Meadows in conjunction with the large housing project of the same name and directly experienced the profits a well-run center could generate. Early on, too, Northwestern Mutual Life Insurance Company purchased the Broadway-Crenshaw Center, an arrangement that allowed the department store to keep its assets liquid as it continued to plan branches.[52] Prudential Life Insurance Company was perhaps the most committed in this sphere, with a portfolio that included Roosevelt Field, Southdale, North Shore Center, Prince Georges Plaza, and Mayfair, among others.[53] As the supply of money grew tight in the mid-1950s, these firms demanded more to safeguard their investments. Beyond the basic attributes of planning, their foremost concern was the tenant mix. The best way to ensure a profitable future for the complex, they believed, was to enlarge the galaxy of chain operations complementing the department store, a policy that department store executives did not welcome but had to accept. The parties most hurt by this shift, however, were the independent merchants, who had made up a large segment of the early regional malls.

Tenants

Developers and department store executives alike preferred to have the majority of tenants comprise independent merchants. Such outlets were frequently offshoots of existing businesses that were well known and respected in the community. Their owners, moreover, tended to be willing to invest the most time and labor to ensure that the enterprise succeeded. The president of the International Council of Shopping Centers (ICSC)—founded in 1956 by developers involved in the process—reminded colleagues in 1961 that the "small independent is the tenant who gives our shopping centers their image and charm, pays the most rent, and usually earns us the most money." For their part, independent merchants found locating in a regional mall a boon to business as long as they were scattered along primary pedestrian traffic routes. Segregation in their own court or quarter, on the other hand, could be disastrous, since it was the roster of major stores that attracted most shoppers.[54] The shift to including a higher ratio of chain stores—at the expense of the independent ones—began in 1956 as insurance companies demanded the highest credit ratings among tenants occupying at least 70 percent of the selling space. By the decade's end the situation had become sufficiently acute to prompt Senate hearings on charges of favoritism, at which architect Victor Gruen testified that only federal intervention was a solution. Concurrent efforts within the industry were beginning to rectify matters, especially with refinements in the layout of the enclosed mall, in which Gruen himself was taking a leading role. Still, the problem was challenging enough to engage the assistance of the Small Business Administration, which began to explore ways to assist independent merchants in 1960.[55]

After some hesitation during the immediate postwar years, chain store companies quickly embraced the shopping center as the prime location for new units. Finding sales volume declining in both downtown and established outlying business districts where they had invested heavily during the 1930s and 1940s, chains now made the shopping center their principal focus of expansion. Beginning in 1953, the May issue of that industry's principal organ, *Chain Store Age,* was devoted to shopping center planning and operation. By the decade's end some major chain companies found that the shift to shopping centers had led to operational improvements as well as bolstered sales.[56] From an early date, however, a number of chains ran their stores primarily as company units at the expense of the integrated business development. In 1960, the president of the ICSC lamented: "I know of no other industry which is more in need of a clearer spirit of understanding and cooperation." Chains could cause innumerable problems in the development stage, as well as after the complex was operating.[57]

As all those involved soon discovered, planning did not end with the construction of a regional mall. "The developer," a prominent advertising executive noted, "should realize that he is not a retail operator. . . . On a long term basis, he has the greater concern in his center's developing a desirable personality . . . and quickly becoming part of the shopping habit of the trading area." To achieve those ends it was necessary to have an aggressive program of merchandising and promotion orchestrated by a professional manager. As in many other ways, Northgate afforded a model. James Douglas, president of the subsidiary company that developed the complex, emphasized to retailers that "with no promotion . . . the customers would eventually be won over by the convenience [of shopping here, but with] . . . the proper type of promotion, this period has been shortened and the tempo has been accelerated." He added: "Northgate is like a fine Swiss watch. The design is perfect, the workmanship great—but you have to wind it to make it tick."[58] But the manager alone could not ensure success. By the mid-1950s, many of those connected to the shopping center field realized that a strong, effective association of merchants was an essential component of running a regional mall. Participation could not be voluntary, critics charged, as was the case in a number of early shopping centers; all tenants must contribute a reasonable share of time and money.[59] In this realm, too, chain companies could prove reluctant partners, refusing to allocate funds for or otherwise participate in efforts to promote the shopping center as a whole. Even when chain companies were willing to sponsor promotions their approach could differ substantially from that of other stores. By 1960, chain companies began to counter that most merchants' associations were not effective; if the organization was a strong one, they would be happy to participate.[60]

Given their role in the creation of the regional mall, department store companies might be expected to take a leadership role in promotion, but such was often not the case. In numerous instances a central office downtown generated advertising for all the company's stores, with little or no attention paid to advancing the cause of the shopping centers in which branches were situated.[61] Knowing that their establishment was the cornerstone to the regional mall, department store executives negotiated extremely favorable leases from developers. The big emporia were for all intents and purposes subsidized by other merchants, who carried a larger burden of the operational costs. Chain store companies soon followed the department store's lead in this respect, especially once insurance companies demanded their presence in force. As a result, the independently owned stores often bore the biggest brunt of expense, causing no small degree of friction in the process. The shopping center—and especially the regional mall—was conceived as a fully integrated operation in which all components benefited from a well-balanced, equitable relationship. Yet the rivalries of the city center persisted. In fact, no bigger rivalry or more formidable planning problem existed with the regional mall during the 1950s than getting the department stores to cooperate among themselves.

The idea that two major department stores in a single shopping center would enhance trade for each other and for the ensemble as a whole was demonstrated in the late 1940s by the unorchestrated presence of both the Broadway and the May Company at the Crenshaw Center. Besides increasing their draw simply by virtue of their combined size and the possibilities of comparison shopping, two department stores could broaden the clientele of a shopping center by each targeting a somewhat different income group. Finally, this arrangement could greatly benefit the other tenants. By 1956, Homer Hoyt had experienced enough experimentation in the field to declare: "The ideal type . . . is the regional center with two major department stores, each at opposite ends of the mall, with an unbroken line of apparel and fashion goods between them, on one level, with no intervening street separating them. The department stores should not constitute more than 50 percent of the total store area . . . so that they will not overshadow and dwarf the other stores. If [this arrangement is followed] there is no weak end . . . [and all the stores] will do the most business."[62] But not until the mid-1950s did such a regional mall actually open. The Crenshaw precedent may have prompted or reinforced Rawls seeking what soon became known in the trade as dual anchor stores at Shoppers' World, a pairing he had pursued earlier. Both Wanamaker's and developer Sol Atlas planned to have a second major store at the Cross County Center as early as 1950, but only in 1953 did Gimbel's agree to build there. Similarly, Marshall Field's anticipated having a second and perhaps a third major department store at Old Orchard without securing a commitment until 1955. Chicago's Evergreen Plaza, one of the few regional shopping centers without a mall plan, opened in 1952 with two department stores, the Fair and Carson Pirie Scott. But the latter was a much smaller unit, operating essentially as a specialty store.[63]

The resistance to dual anchors among department store executives was based to a significant degree on hubris. Each company wanted to be the dominant force in a shopping center, not to cooperate with a downtown rival. From the department store's perspective, the regional mall derived much of its identity—both in physical and psychological terms—from that emporium's presence. Dual anchors would dilute this prestigious position, it was feared, and some of the largest retailers simply did not want to share the limelight. After being trumped by the Broadway on Crenshaw Boulevard, Tom May apparently grew adamant about pursuing solo performances, building branches, generally as part of regional malls, that were so immense that no rival would attempt to compete nearby.[64] The hubris could intensify when large corporations were involved. Negotiations between Allied and Macy's in 1954 failed to produce a union for a mammoth regional mall in Paramus, New Jersey, the two companies opting to construct their own, equally ambitious, centers—Bergen Mall and Garden State Plaza—less than two miles apart. The traditional hierarchy of department stores downtown could also enter the equation. Some companies saw suburban expansion as a means of raising their stature.[65] Carson Pirie Scott was courted by Marshall Field's for Old Orchard but turned down the offer because company executives did not want to be the "second" store there, as they were on State Street. Instead, they chose to build their own shopping center, Edens Plaza, close by. Perhaps because of that proximity Carson's could not secure the funds to develop a comparable center; Edens Plaza was one-sixth Old Orchard's size and thus doomed to a subsidiary role.[66]

But obtaining dual anchors encompassed problems beyond identity and pride. If a department store spearheaded the creation of a regional mall—itself or through a developer—securing the second emporium could require rents sufficiently low as to amount to a subsidy, resulting in a less than equal partnership. The primary means of avoiding this dilemma was for the second store to construct and own its facility independent of the rest of the complex. But this arrangement could undermine the integrated nature of the ensemble, with a major component operating more or less apart from all the rest.[67] Not until department store companies decided to collaborate at the outset could a regional mall with dual anchors be optimally planned, a collaboration that appears to have been rare until the 1960s.

Department store duels, of course, went against the very idea of a regional mall, which was to contain and control retail competition in a single complex serving a sizable geographic area. The booming northern New Jersey market was so underserved that the two Paramus complexes fared well. But the pitfalls of creating single-anchor regional malls that competed with one another in the same vicinity attracted national attention with the opening of three giant complexes in Nassau County, Long Island. Macy's fired the initial salvo with its 343,000-square-foot branch in the 1.2 million-square-foot Roosevelt Field in August 1956. Two months later, Gimbel's followed suit with a 218,000-square-foot store at Green Acres Shopping Center (1954–56), which was as large as Roosevelt Field, eight miles away. The same day, Allied's B. Gertz opened a 325,000-square-foot behemoth at the slightly smaller Mid-Island Shopping Plaza five miles from Roosevelt Field. These complexes, combined with other, smaller shopping centers and new freestanding stores, such as the giant Abraham & Straus branch at Hempstead, seriously oversaturated the market, analysts believed.[68] Some observers saw the phenomenon as a clear sign of too many shopping centers being constructed; others believed that it was not the shopping center itself that was the problem but the single-anchor department store. The hope was that dual anchors would forestall unnecessary competitive forays.

The first regional mall specifically designed for and constructed with dual anchors was Southdale, outside Minneapolis. Significantly, the scheme was developed to preclude the duplication of facilities, which would soon occur near Chicago and New York. Southdale was planned by the Dayton Company, then the dominant department store in Minnesota. Not long after plans were unveiled, Allied subsidiary L. S. Donaldson announced its intention to build a rival center less than two miles away. Dayton's took the initiative and eventually coaxed Donaldson's into joining forces. Toward the close of October 1953, plans for a revised, dual-anchor scheme were completed.[69] A year and a half later, similar arrangements were made by W. H. Block to join L. A. Ayres at Glendale in Indianapolis. At an even earlier stage, developers secured dual anchors for Eastpoint Shopping Center in Baltimore (1955–56)—Hutzler's and Hochschild Kohn—and for 7 Corners outside Washington—Woodward & Lothrop and Julius Garfinckel.[70] Yet such initiatives remained the exception for the rest of the decade.

Augmenting the dual anchor trend were department store branches added to existing regional malls, beginning with Gimbel's branches, which opened at both Garden State Plaza and Roosevelt Field in 1960.[71] Even then, many major downtown store companies seem to have preferred teaming up with Sears or Montgomery Ward, which were more differentiated, complementary establishments, rather than with one of their own kind.[72] As late as 1960, plans for regional malls of substantial size in major metropolitan areas were being unveiled with a single department store.[73] Only during the next decade, with the revenues generated by dual-anchor malls, combined with the ever more competitive retail market and the demands for optimal planning by those who financed those complexes, did the dual-anchor arrangement become ubiquitous. The regional mall was heralded as a spectacular solution to the changing postwar scene, but it also introduced a welter of problems that were not being resolved until the 1960s.

Appeal

If department store executives took their time accepting the efficacy of dual anchors, they were quick to assess the value of the mall itself as a magnet for customers. The sequestered pedestrianways not only reduced walking distance between stores, they enhanced the relaxed, informal atmosphere that many middle-class consumers appreciated. Embellished with landscaping, benches, pools and fountains, even artwork, the mall proper was a place where people could walk in comfort at a leisurely pace. The setting was not only the antithesis of downtown shopping streets, but also presented a marked contrast to the sidewalks of shopping centers fronted by car lots. The pace of the mall was that of the pedestrian. Likewise the sounds of the mall were those of human interaction, augmented in many cases by piped-in music, without the noise of motor vehicles, streetcars, traffic police, or sidewalk hucksters. The mall's atmosphere was especially important for department stores, as they were now frequently charged with being archaic and stuffy institutions. As part of a mall, they seemed more approachable to a new generation of consumers disinclined to dress up to go shopping. "The suburban housewife," noted a reporter in 1956, is "certainly a lot different from the suburbanite of 20 years ago who used to leave her household and family in the hands of 'day help,' get all dressed up to travel into the city and make a day of her shopping sprees. Today's housewife . . . doesn't have to save . . . all [her errands] for a weekly or even a monthly excursion. Almost as quickly as she can write down a shopping list she can drive to her nearby shopping center. With shopping speeded up, most women do not want to spend a lot of time dressing up for it, so shopping costumes are getting more informal. The absence of hats and gloves . . . is noteworthy, and stockings are rarely seen, except in winter."[74]

The novelty of the mall also had its appeal. In metropolitan settings where newness prevailed, the latest development held great attraction, particularly to a consumer audience that was young and born to modest means. A real estate writer for the *New York Times* observed that a "housewife may drive miles past an old-style store to reach one of the new retail centers." Similarly, the *Chicago Tribune*'s research manager emphasized the importance of "building a shopping center which presents a coherent picture . . . of modernity, up-to-dateness and progress."[75] As they began to open, regional malls suddenly made other shopping centers seem antiquated. The fact that many consumers were under forty was a crucial factor. The publisher of *Seventeen* magazine advised that the shopping center "be designed especially for young housewives," who were "today's 'major consumers.' They want shopping centers modern but not stark, sane but not meager, gay but not garish, functional but not austere."[76]

But the appeal was also more fundamental. As a setting, the regional mall was especially conducive to the outlook that marketers ascribed to the young females who made up their greatest clientele: women who were value conscious but not bargain hunters; who knew what they wished to buy but wanted a relaxed atmosphere in which to make decisions, in places that were convivial but not crowded. Perry Myers, research director for Allied Stores, emphasized that young housewives wanted "middle styling"—neither too expensive for her budget-conscious outlook nor "too cheap for her taste." "Suburbia," he intoned, "demands good styling, high utility and a moderate price and it isn't getting them now." On another occasion, he emphasized that the clientele in most new outlying areas was different from that in older ones, who traditionally patronized downtown stores. A "typical" customer was not only younger, but "[m]any of her needs are different. She wears different sizes and often may pay different prices. The timing of her buying is different. The problem of reaching her and attracting her business is different." Members of the younger generation were "setting up their own living pattern. . . . [They] have made a sharper break with . . . [the patterns of their] parents than almost any generation before." Moreover, according to the *Tribune*'s research manager: "We find that [the young female consumer] believes that spending is good. She sacrifices savings and future security to the acquiring and using of goods now. She is emotionally more secure in the shopping situation, she is less hounded by feelings of guilt. She feels that she can indulge herself; she feels that shopping is not a grim household task but a pleasantly challenging game. . . . And she has an eye on value." The regional mall seemed tailor-made for this typecasting of women who were at once confident and relaxed, careful and fancy-free—the clientele who were essential to get if the department store was to continue to expand.[77]

Perhaps the most important facet of the mall's appeal was to families. Family shopping was a relative rarity downtown, but it became common in new outlying areas. Most middle-class households still owned only one car. When the breadwinner drove to work he could preclude his spouse from ambitious shopping trips in a setting where public transportation was poor or nonexistent. The preponderance of small children in many households further discouraged women from taking them unaccompanied. Furthermore, the female workforce grew during the 1950s. All these factors contributed to a rapid rise in after-hours shopping trips taken by the family as a whole. Most retailers did not anticipate this phenomenon at first, but as it began to accelerate during the mid-1950s, many of them were eager to respond by expanding night openings to several times a week. By the decade's close, the ICSC reported that up to 60 percent of shopping took place between 6 and 9 P.M. "Shopping is an event," declared the manager of Prince Georges Plaza. "The family has dinner together [here] . . . and does the shopping afterwards." Another manager added: "You could shoot a cannon down the mall of any shopping center at midday and not hit a soul." While based largely on pragmatic concerns, family expeditions had the potential to boost sales. Traditionally, of course, women had been by far the dominant patrons of retail precincts of all kinds. The shopping center afforded a rare opportunity for merchants to cater to the male population as well. "After a hard day at the office," an industry analyst in Florida observed, "a man likes to get into a sport shirt, walking shorts and sandals and relax. But if he can go as is, he doesn't mind piling the wife and kids into the car and riding over to the shopping center after dinner." Even when men failed to purchase much themselves, they enabled the family to make prompt decisions about major purchases, such as appliances and furniture.[78]

The regional mall was an especially important stimulus to family outings. As an environment it was safe from traffic and from the unsavory characters long associated with downtown. The configuration was conducive to all but the youngest members of a family branching out and regrouping without serious incident. Independence and togetherness could coexist in the desired measure. Commenting on Garden State Plaza and Bergen Mall, a writer for the *New York Times* marveled that within six miles of Manhattan lay places that "suggest, in miniature, the 1939–1940 New York World's Fair. Pennants whip in the wind, and music carols along the promenades." Each center "lives a night, as well as a day, existence, glittering like a city when the sun goes down." But unlike the city: "It is a world of informality—of women shoppers in slacks and men in flannel shirts, of hot dogs and loudspeakers that blare alarms of missing children." At the large Hillside Shopping Center southwest of Chicago (1954–56), the manager reported that Sundays attracted thousands of window shoppers even though all but the drug store was closed, adding, "It's a real family pastime here."[79]

The regional mall was also particularly suited to staging special events by virtue of its inward-looking plan and great size. Held in copious pedestrianways, surrounded by stores, these promotional endeavors could markedly enhance customer draw. An art show, claimed the promotion director of the Park Forest Plaza outside Chicago, "is just [the] type of 'semi-sophisticated' approach that enables the typical shopper to assume an 'identity' with the center."[80] The Cross County Center held an athletic event of unspecified nature under the auspices of *Sports Illustrated*. Concerts, boat shows, children's contests, civil defense demonstrations, circuses, flower shows, ballet classes, dog obedience training programs, lessons in gun handling, cooking schools, and science fairs were among the panoply of events devised to attract more customers and keep them coming on a regular basis. At a time when specialized community facilities were few or nonexistent in many outlying areas, the regional mall also served a variety of temporary functions, housing branch libraries, high-school dances, and even worship services. A *New York Times* reporter marveled that regional malls represented a "new aspect of suburban living . . . They have become new centers of community activity. . . . They serve as the automobile age counterpart of the old village hall."[81] Nichols had developed a rich program of public entertainment at the Country Club Plaza beginning in the 1920s, and many other subsequent shopping centers had some form of special events. Downtown merchants associations likewise had entered the world of entertainment to compete with outlying centers. Yet no place seemed to harbor so many and so wide a range of such attractions as the regional mall.

The cost of staging events, which were free to the audience, could be substantial, and owners of stores specializing in fashion goods sometimes maintained that these events were not helpful to them. Nevertheless, entertainment became a staple of regional mall operations. Complementing these short-term events were those facilitated by the complex itself. One or more meeting rooms for civic groups and performances existed in most of these complexes—either in the department store or elsewhere. Among the most elaborate was Bergen Mall's Playhouse Hall, with a stage and seating capacity of nearly six hundred. Here and at a number of other centers small amusement grounds were developed for children. At the Cross County Center, a World's Fair–like "Crossmobile" offered inexpensive rides for weary adults and excitement-seeking youngsters alike. Roosevelt Field had an ice-skating rink that likewise catered to nearly all ages.[82] Amid all the ballyhoo, strong differences arose concerning the fundamental purpose of the regional mall and the character of its design. To what degree should the regional mall be a magnet for social interchange and amusement, as well as for shopping? Did such activities in fact enhance business? Or should these complexes just be lean, efficient machines for selling?

Design

The advocates of a no-frills approach to regional mall design held the upper hand at the outset, based on the success of Northgate. Indeed, well before it opened, the Seattle complex became an industry paradigm. The fact that it was the first of its kind to be realized gave the scheme an unusually large amount of publicity, but the clarity and logic of its design were crucial to the conception of subsequent regional malls. Department store executives no doubt approved of the emphasis given the Bon Marche, its great mass placed in the middle of, and projecting from, the ensemble to dominate the view from the highway (see fig. 203). The careful arrangement of stores with complementary functions elicited praise. At a time when numerous proposals for shopping centers entailed complicated, multidirectional spaces, the linear spine at Northgate made the vast center easily comprehensible to patrons and helped ensure viable locations for all establishments. Moreover, this space was narrow—forty-eight feet wide—carefully calculated so that pedestrians could easily see stores on both sides and enter them without much deviation from their path (fig. 206). The mall itself had few adorning features in order to facilitate pedestrian flow. Building exteriors were likewise straightforward modernist envelopes, with neither flair nor embellishment. Some observers criticized the appearance, charging that the building resembled a nearby aircraft plant. Northgate's president retorted: "The $22,000,000 we spent [on construction] could have been boosted another $10,000,000. Some centers spend a lot more on frills, but they'll never get their money back. The main thing is that Northgate makes money."[83]

Scarcely less influential was the design of Stonestown on the west side of San Francisco (1950–52), the plans for which were announced a few months before Northgate opened. The architect chosen was Los Angeles–based Welton Becket, perhaps because of his celebrated Bullock's Pasadena store. Here, however, the program could not have been more dissimilar in its emphasis on economy. The architect rose to the occasion. Stonestown's anchor, the Emporium, was touted as a marvel of efficiency. Becket, it seemed, now looked to the pragmatism that had guided the design of Sears stores since the late 1930s for his methods. The store's manager explained: "Long before actual plans were drawn up . . . Becket . . . and his 100-man staff of specialists, working closely with the Emporium management, spent months of research determining the flow patterns for merchandise, store personnel and customer traffic. . . . The result is an absolute minimum of time and effort to complete the merchandising cycle from the delivery of goods . . . to the moment a shopper leaves the store with his purchases."

206. Northgate Shopping City, view of central pedestrianway. Photo 1950.

207. Stonestown, Nineteenth Avenue and Winston Drive, San Francisco (1950–52). Welton Becket & Associates, architects; altered. Photo Alan J. Canterbury, 1964.

While this approach was widely condoned in principle among retailers and store designers alike, Becket apparently developed the consummate example and, equally important, applied this approach to the entire complex. In April 1954, after a meeting held in Santa Barbara, executives from Abraham & Straus, Joseph Horne, L. S. Ayres, and other leading department stores across the country made a detour to examine the scheme and effusively praised its clarity and efficiency. Becket appears to have drawn extensively from Northgate, although an existing roadway precluded placing the department store in the center. Here, the exterior treatment was even more Spartan, with unadorned volumes allowed to stand virtually on their own (fig. 207).[84]

Slightly earlier, the same basic approach was taken in the design of Lakewood Center (1950–52), near Long Beach,

208. Shoppers' World, view of inner court. Photo author, 1988.

California, for the May Company and developer Joseph Eichenbaum. Architect Albert C. Martin, Jr., recalled that the conceptual bases for the shopping mall's layout was the department store aisle and his extensive work with May's interior design staff.[85] Together with Northgate, the two California centers constituted the critical mass of regional malls opened by the end of 1952. All of them had been created under the auspices of a department store company, and the design of the department store interior appears to have been a springboard for the overall schemes.[86] The only other regional mall operating at this point was Shoppers' World, which, prior to bearing the stigma of bankruptcy, was suspect for its design. The layout on two levels around a large open court ran counter to the underlying objective of the mall, which was to shorten walking distances while maximizing exposure to stores (fig. 208). Architect Morris Ketchum's point of departure for the arrangement had nothing to do with retailing but looked instead to the New England green as an archetype. Similarly, his conception for the Jordan Marsh department store was developed during the initial stages of planning the North Shore Center, well before Jordan Marsh agreed to anchor the complex. The configuration, essentially a great circular space under a prestressed reinforced concrete dome, made a dramatic sales floor but proved difficult to modify and even more difficult to expand as departmental needs changed.[87] The degree to which retailers, developers, and architects rejected Ketchum's approach was emphatically reflected by the fact that the design had almost no influence on subsequent regional malls. Instead, the work that ensued continued to be shaped by the example of the department store and the concerns of its leadership.[88]

The challenge to the no-frills approach instead came from Victor Gruen, who, like Ketchum, had been one of the first architects to embrace the concept of the regional mall.[89] He was especially attracted to the potential to bring a sense of focus and vitality to community life in outlying areas. At the same time, Gruen followed the example of William Snaith and others who had made a specialty of designing store interiors. He immersed himself in the intricacies of retailing so that he could address business interests on their own terms. Teaming up with Larry Smith, Gruen also honed his faculties in site selection, following Welch's example. Gruen was a superb salesman as well and proved able to convince store executives that his visions were sound. That rapport was not consummated overnight, however.

Matching Gruen's persuasiveness was his seemingly insatiable appetite for experimentation. In a field where risk-taking designs were shunned, the architect seems to have wanted to live dangerously—to push the limits of his conservative clientele, continually challenging them to think in new ways. His adventurous agenda did not always yield rewards. In 1947 Gruen had a falling out with the Grayson-Robinson apparel chain after designing many of its stores. Even worse, others in the Los Angeles area perceived the theatrical exteriors of those stores as needlessly flamboyant and counterproductive to profitable sales. Gruen's design for Milliron's branch department store in the Westchester district of Los Angeles (1947–49)—his first major retail commission—had immense iconic value (see fig. 182). But Milliron's circuitous layout proved inconvenient for the same reasons as Ketchum's for Jordan Marsh and, with a central core, also disoriented shoppers. This variation on the planning taken for the high-fashion floor at downtown department stores in the 1930s ran against the tendency toward simplicity and openness of the main sales floors in postwar emporia. Two schemes he designed thereafter for an immense regional shopping center in Los Angeles never advanced beyond the preliminary stage. Gruen became stigmatized among retailers in his adopted region for some time.[90] To build his reputation as a leader in regional mall design, the architect had to turn elsewhere.

Gruen's opportunity came in 1949 with Detroit's J. L. Hudson. Later he claimed that he persuaded Hudson's president, Oscar Webber, to build branches, but Webber had already taken the initiative thanks to competition from a chain, Federal Department Stores, which had a number of its units in the area. The striking inadequacy of downtown parking facilities to handle the metropolitan population was also an important factor. Webber interviewed a number of architects, but he chose Gruen, perhaps because the two had similar inclinations in many respects. Webber had a keen sense of planning and design; he loved landscaping and outdoor sculpture. He was also intent on building enormous branches. Hudson's had no strong competition among downtown department stores in Detroit, but the city's sizable outlying retail districts, where the small Federal stores flourished, did pose a threat. The stores and shopping centers that Hudson's developed would have to be so big they would completely eclipse these arterial precincts, just as the Hudson's store downtown dwarfed the remainder of the retail core.[91] Gruen had met someone who shared his passion for creating on a grand scale. The designs that resulted were in all likelihood the result of the close relationship the two men came to enjoy. Like Northgate and Stonestown, these were collaborative works. Still, Gruen's penchant for pursuing unorthodox solutions guided his efforts at first.

The initial scheme for Eastland, the first of what would eventually be four Hudson shopping centers, broke from all convention (fig. 209). Organized as a polygonal lozenge, the complex looked as if the North Shore Center had been pulled open, enlarged several times, and its expanse of lawn converted to an enormous car lot. Gruen allocated parking to the inner space as well as on the periphery to minimize walking distance from automobile to store, but the traffic patterns created by this arrangement would have been complicated. Gruen apparently did not give much consideration either to the enormous perimeter distance to be traveled if a shopper wanted to go by all the hundred-plus stores in the 1,250,000-square-foot complex. Furthermore, he was still wedded to a circuitous department store plan. After generating much publicity, the scheme was put on hold as a result of materials restrictions during the Korean War. Over the next two years, someone involved saw the plan's fundamental flaws, and it was scrapped at great expense. Webber kept Gruen on nonetheless, in all probability because the architect was able to rethink the program completely and develop a scheme that was eminently more sensible.[92]

Due to complications in land assembly for Eastland, Hudson's brought its second projected regional mall, Northland, to the fore.[93] For the latter complex, Gruen produced the antithesis of its stillborn predecessor. Northland was even bigger, its buildings encompassing 1,317,000 square feet; the department store alone 475,000—both the biggest in their respective categories anywhere in the nation.[94] Yet the layout was remarkably compact, with five pavilions arranged around Hudson's building in a loose pinwheel pattern, which Gruen called the "cluster" plan (fig. 210). Instead of forming a linear path, pedestrian space comprised a series

209. Eastland Center, Eight Mile and Kelly roads, Harper Woods, Michigan, original scheme (1950). Gruen & Krummeck, architects; project. Model (*Architectural Forum*, August 1950, 111).

210. Northland Center, Northwestern Highway and Greenfield Road, Southfield, Michigan (1952–54). Victor Gruen Associates, architects; altered. Photo 1954.

211. Northland Center, inner court and J. L. Hudson store (*Architectural Forum*, June 1954, 102).

of six courts, varied somewhat in size and shape, expansive yet intimate. The clarity of this sequence facilitated perambulation while keeping pedestrians oriented. All the pyrotechnics of Gruen's earlier work were avoided, yet the atmosphere was a vibrant one, boasting an array of plants and sculpture (fig. 211). From almost any vantage point, the enormous department store remained the landmark, its mass articulated by a concrete frame, rendered more like a museum or other civic building of the period and quite distinct from its boxy counterparts at Stonestown and Northgate.

Northland was both dignified and relaxed, grand and modest in its ambience. The restraint exercised by Gruen in developing the building exteriors allowed them to be at once effective definers of space, of paths of movement, and of interior function, while also serving as a background to art, landscaping, and human activity. Gruen drew on preindustrial European town centers, especially memories of his native Vienna, but the effect was entirely new in scale, form, and character, without any overt urban associations. The importance of this traditional orientation was not lost on observers. In the mind of a writer for *Architectural Forum,* the connection validated its efficacy. Here a complex with storefronts equaling those along both sides of Fifth Avenue between Thirty-Fourth and Fifty-First streets was humanized in a way analogous to a centuries-old market town: "Shopping traffic has come full circle. It is right back where it started—with the pedestrian." But the impact that this atmosphere had on merchandising was a key feature to its success. The editors of *Stores,* organ of the National Retail Dry Goods Association, enthused that "for the first time, construction has caught up with the rapidly evolving theories of what the regional shopping center should be. . . . It is bound to lift the middle-class consumer's buying job to a brand new level of importance in her own mind. To surround the shopping expedition with such lavish evidence of planned convenience and comfort, plus much incidental pleasure, is basic and effective sales promotion." A writer for the *Ladies' Home Journal* was no less captivated. Northland "is a model of enlightened planning and of social co-operation between merchants, architects, sculptors, artists and civic minded citizens and it is entirely the creation of private enterprise."[95] Over the next two years sales at the complex exceeded the expectations of its owners. The spectacular design was a spectacular success.[96] By the mid-1950s, Gruen was enjoying the national limelight as the foremost architect of regional malls.

Gruen repeated his triumph in the revised scheme for Eastland (1955–57), which was only slightly smaller.[97] Yet his much-touted cluster plan had few significant offspring. Part of the reason this arrangement proved short-lived was the growing concern for at least allocating sufficient space for a second department store. Even when a suitable mate could not be secured prior to construction, the option was left open for one at a later date by placing the department

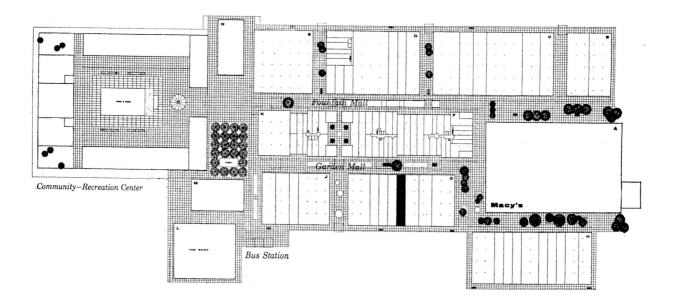

store at one end of a complex. In other cases, the latter arrangement was used strictly out of preference so that the department store could get maximum visual exposure. The opposite end was balanced by stores used for everyday items, such as a supermarket, following an organizational structure employed at Stonestown.[98] A straight pedestrianway was simpler to design and also to service than the cluster plan. Beginning with Northgate, a linear tunnel beneath the pedestrianway was used for deliveries and other service functions—a provision adapted from the Broadway-Crenshaw Shopping Center. The great size of Northland and Eastland justified a more extensive underground arrangement, but for projects that were half their size a single path was all that was needed. Even for very large complexes, other store configurations were tried. At Roosevelt Field (1.2 million square feet), the immense Macy's store rose at the end with two parallel pedestrianways (fig. 212). This layout was somewhat disorienting and not altogether conducive to perambulation throughout the premises, relegating some locations to second-class status. For Gulfgate at Houston (800,000 square feet), Graham introduced a modified "T" plan, with a different major function at each end. Joske's and Sakowitz lay at one end, chain variety and junior department stores at another, and an enormous supermarket at the third (fig. 213). Shortly thereafter, Graham employed a similar arrangement for the North Shore Center. The T plan proved especially compatible to a later stage of regional mall development in the 1960s and 1970s, when three anchor stores became increasingly common.

A far more influential aspect of Northland's design was the pedestrianway as a lively center for social activity and the underlying belief that the regional mall should be a community center. Gruen had not been alone in this viewpoint,

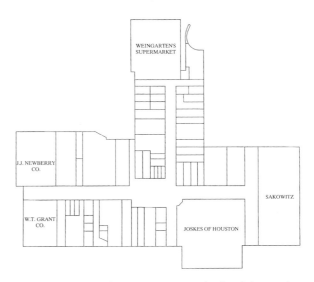

212. Roosevelt Field Shopping Center, Meadowbrook State Parkway, Hempstead, New York (1953–56). I. M. Pei & Associates and Boehler & Brugman, associated architects; Robert L. Zion, landscape architect; all but department stores demolished. Plan.

213. Gulfgate Shopping City, Holmes Road, Woodbridge Drive, and Gulfgate Freeway, Houston (1954–56). John Graham & Co. and Irving R. Klein, associated architects; altered. Diagrammatic plan drawn by Paul Davidson after *Houston Post,* 20 September 1956, VII-21.

of course. Besides Ketchum's plans for Rawls were those that four architectural firms had prepared at the request of Marshall Field's for Old Orchard in 1950. Though different in character and configuration, each scheme afforded a lush variety of embellished pedestrian spaces. With the regional mall still in its infancy, these well-publicized designs for one of the industry's leading firms were valuable expositions of the possibilities afforded by developing such a complex as a great new business and community center.[99] Without

214. Old Orchard Shopping Center, Skokie Highway between Gulf Road & Harrison Street, Skokie, Illinois (1954–56). Loebl, Schlossman & Bennett, architects; Lawrence Halprin & Associates, landscape architect; altered. Rendering.

215. Marshall Field & Company department store, Old Orchard. Photo Hedrich-Blessing, 1956.

Northland's success, however, this approach to regional mall design might well have faded into the background or have dissipated altogether in light of Northgate's renown. Instead, making the mall proper a distinctive place conducive to various forms of social interaction, including special events, became an important thrust in design through the rest of the decade.

In its realized form, Old Orchard made a significant contribution to this phenomenon as well. Informality was emphasized by a seemingly casual grouping of store blocks to either side of the immense (370,000 square feet) Field's store—an arrangement that was very different from the cluster plan's tight spatial organization (fig. 214). Despite its dimensions, Field's building exuded the chic "country" associations cultivated so well at Lord & Taylor branches (fig. 215). The pedestrian spaces to each side, designed by San Francisco landscape architect Lawrence Halprin, who would soon become one of the luminaries in his field, were rich and varied. The second anchor (the Fair) and other stores oriented to mid-level merchandise enveloped a broad, T-shaped court, treated as a plaza, punctuated by circular planters and pools. On the other side, surrounded by high-end specialty shops and a professional office building, the space was smaller, with a vivacious, curvilinear pool running down the middle (fig. 216). To one side, next to Field's, the space became at once more intimate and rustic (fig. 217). Save for Field's and the office building, store exteriors were rendered as abstract, neutral backdrops. The lively landscape and the people who occupied it were clearly what made the experience memorable. Few regional malls celebrated the outdoors to the same degree. Some years later, Old Orchard's architect, Richard Bennett, discussed the design, emphasizing that a linear plan was more suggestive of a bowling alley and an enclosed mall more like a department store. Instead, "shopping should be an adventure. . . . you don't 'find anything on a straight path, you find it around a corner. So we gave [customers] . . . a sense of 'finding' things." Field's vice president for architecture

216. Old Orchard Shopping Center, north court. Photo Hedrich-Blessing, 1956.

217. Old Orchard Shopping Center, south court. Photo Hedrich-Blessing, 1956.

and design, John Moss, incanted: "Don't tell everything in one view." At the same time, Bennett cautioned that "people know quality instinctively. And if a thing looks like a carnival, a midway, they think it's cheap."[100] Giving people an environment that they could not find elsewhere in the area, one that was both lush and understated, quickly made Old Orchard a primary focus for its surrounding communities.

Old Orchard was unusual in the extent of design attention lavished on the pedestrianway, but hardly an isolated case. In the East, Roosevelt Field set a high standard, with its architecture—Macy's was designed by Skidmore, Owings & Merrill, the remainder by I. M. Pei— employing an elegantly rendered Miesian vocabulary. Most of the store blocks had the enclosed areas deeply recessed so that much of the surrounding pedestrianways were framed (and sheltered) by the structure. Between these lofty extensions, which were much taller than the usual canopies, the open area was enlivened by fountains, trees, and benches—all crafted with the same elegant restraint. The work of Robert Zion, another young landscape architect who would achieve national distinction, these spaces encompassed a subtle variety of materials, textures, and colors that rendered the overall minimalist vocabulary a lively background for the crowds that traversed them (fig. 218).[101]

Few examples attained the level of design sophistication manifested at Old Orchard or Roosevelt Field, but a number of regional malls used esthetic appeal as a means of enhancing trade. "Tourists will find a new attraction in northern Dade County," a reporter for the *Miami Herald* predicted enthusiastically about the 163rd Street Shopping Center (1954–56). The "free display of gardens and institutional art . . . is expected to lure visitors in much the same manner as the grounds around Rockefeller Center in New York." Those responsible for the Tri-County Shopping Center near

218. Roosevelt Field Shopping Center, Fountain Mall. Photo Ezra Stoller, ca. 1956.

219. Swifton Center, Seymour and Reading roads, Cincinnati (1954–56). David B. Liberman, architect; National Landscaping Organization, landscape designers. View of mall. Photo author, 2001.

Cincinnati were under no illusions that their complex would be a tourist mecca, but they nonetheless gave considerable embellishment to the pedestrianway. The work of Baltimore landscape architect Martin Funnell, the space was planned to be "casual and informal, yet . . . give the impression of quiet dignity—the feeling of walking into a delightful garden." Similarly, at the Mayfair Shopping Center, situated in one of greater Milwaukee's best outlying areas, the "most pleasant first impression . . . is its landscaping, and that impression is lasting. . . . It's an informal effect, quiet to the shoppers who stop to rest in the green surroundings."[102] Just as with most other retail buildings, regional malls tended to employ vocabularies that were national rather than local in character. But sometimes the pedestrianway was an exception. At the May Company's Westland outside Denver, Beverly Hills landscape architect John Ratekin used large red rocks and a palette of plant materials to evoke a setting in the mountains nearby. A tropical lushness, complete with waterfall, characterized the central spaces of the College Grove Shopping Center in San Diego (1958–60), developed under the auspices of the Walker Scott department store. Likewise, Jonathan Seymour, formerly the landscape architect for Coral Gables, Florida, was commissioned to create a "tropical foliage garden" for the pedestrianways at Dadeland Shopping Center south of Miami (1960–62).[103]

Even when less attention was lavished on it, the mall proper tended to be an inviting showpiece, conducive to social interaction on a small scale as much as to movement from one store to another (fig. 219). Visually, these spaces became the more important with the generally plain treatment of the buildings around them. The substantial cost of developing and maintaining a regional mall as well as rising construction and labor costs throughout the period increased the pressure to economize on the design. As a result, the exterior of the department store and other blocks in the complex tended to be stark, in the manner that Graham and Becket had established early on. Retailers wanted consumer attention focused on store interiors, but the mall spaces ranked a close second in terms of appeal and identity.

Enclosure

Even before Northland opened, Gruen's fame as a designer of regional malls that were places of enjoyment and gathering as well as of consumption gained further ground from his design of Southdale, which not only had dual anchors but was completely enclosed (fig. 220). Based on Hudson's example, president Donald Dayton decided to inaugurate the move to the metropolitan periphery with a regional mall, hiring Larry Smith as marketing consultant and Gruen as architect on Webber's recommendation. After a yearlong study Smith identified a site six miles southwest of downtown Minneapolis in the fledgling community of Edina, which he believed lay along the principal axis of growth for upper- to middle-income households.[104] The climatic extremes of the region led Gruen, in turn, to resuscitate an idea he had developed for an unrealized project in Houston several years earlier: treating the complex as a single structure so that patrons could have the benefits of a completely sheltered, air-conditioned climate year round.[105] The cost of controlling both temperature and humidity in so large a space was mitigated by an efficient heat pump system, purportedly the largest in the world at that time, which was combined with the air-conditioning units. The losses accrued from the thousands of times shop doors opened daily was significantly reduced when outdoor connections were limited to a few mall portals, which were equipped with double banks of doors to provide airlocks. Costs were further reduced by minimal enclosure of stores at their fronts, which carried the added advantage of encouraging customer entry. The enclosed mall was still an expensive undertaking, but it was economically practical, according to Gruen.[106]

The greatest benefit of the enclosed mall from both the architect's and the client's perspective was the great appeal it would have among consumers. The customarily low returns that characterized shopping days when the weather was very hot, very cold, and/or inclement would receive a substantial boost, so the argument ran. Trade would also increase across the board because of the appeal of an interior environment as a community center. The visual impact of that space was greatly enhanced by expanding it to two levels. Since Shoppers' World, a two-floor configuration had been studiously avoided, but Gruen believed that it could work by adapting a device frequently used in department store branches: taking advantage of topographical changes to have major entrances on both levels.[107] This circulation system, coupled with the compact interior, he maintained, would generate ample pedestrian movement throughout. That prospect was substantially enhanced when Dayton's leadership persuaded that of Donaldson's to become the second anchor. Gruen altered his plan, placing the two department stores at opposite corners of a central gathering area (fig. 221). Dubbed the Garden Court, that space fulfilled Gruen's ideas of what a shopping center should be far more than the open pedestrianway because it combined the best of indoors and out. Natural light, landscaping, and pavement all suggested an open setting, with the freedom and variety it implied.[108]

At the same time, the sheltered, climate-controlled environment was more conducive to informal gatherings and social exchange than were outside places. Interviewed at the time of Southdale's opening Gruen said the court was at once like the Piazza San Marco in Venice and the Galleria Vittorio Emanuele II in Milan: "It's a square . . . a place where people will learn how to stroll again and look around

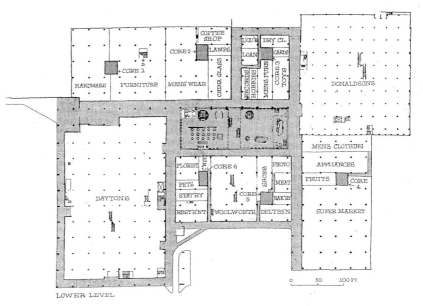

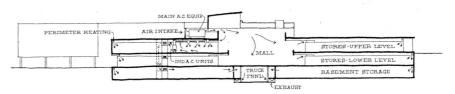

220. Southdale Shopping Center, Edina, Minnesota, aerial view.

221. Southdale Shopping Center, plan of ground level and section (*Architectural Forum*, December 1956, 121, 122).

222. Southdale Shopping Center, Garden Court, ca. 1956.

them at other people and things and stop and talk if they want to. . . . I hope it becomes a crystallizing force for the sprawling suburban area . . . [with] places for meetings and concerts and galleries of paintings . . . and rooms where classes can be held and places to eat. This is the town square that has been lost since the coming of the automobile." While nurtured by experiences of his youth and early manhood, Gruen's love of European public spaces was shared by many architects and planners of the period. Similarly, too, he viewed the residential areas upon which Southdale depended as bleak: "Families move to the sprawling suburbs where the women are bored to death and there is no social life. . . . They lose the values of an urban civilization. So cities must have more than one center." A passionate lover of traditional cities, Gruen sought to re-create that world at the regional mall. "It was designed in my dreams," he noted.[109]

What set Gruen apart from his colleagues was his successful adaptation of European precedent to this wholly American building type, redefining that type in the process. Only American technology made such a place as the enclosed mall plausible; only American prosperity made it possible. But in expression, too, the space was distinct from contemporary work abroad—a melding of practical and theatrical, of homey and futuristic, of expansive and intimate attributes—evocative of nothing from the past and without the insistent, often somber, abstractness of new European town centers.[110] With paving designed to evoke the streets of Copenhagen and ancient Rome; trees, vines, bushes, flowers, and pools; a "sidewalk" café; an array of murals and sculpture, including the fifty-foot-tall "Golden Trees" by Henry Bertoia, the court seemed an exceptional place when it was new (fig. 222). Equally important were the wide, open thresholds that linked stores to the pedestrianways that radiated from the court (fig. 223). The differences between indoors and out that alike characterized stores in an open-air shopping center and along the street were all but eliminated, minimizing the inhibitions about entering retail spaces that many shoppers were thought to possess.

In this "Cecil B. DeMille conception of a shopping center," as a reporter for *Women's Wear Daily* remarked, the court and surrounding stores proved to have immense draw. Some five months after the complex opened, a spokesman noted that an average of twenty-five thousand people came on Sunday just to windowshop and take in the scene. A quarter of those visiting on a given Saturday were tourists— "the biggest tourist business of any [shopping] center in the country"—or others from beyond Southdale's trading area. Like Northland, Southdale was a stunning retail success.[111] Gruen deserved credit for the center's design innovations. At the same time, his client was committed to civic as well as to mercantile leadership. Like Hudson's, Dayton's downtown store was considered an institutional bulwark of

Minneapolis. The decision by Dayton and his brothers to make Southdale an exceptional place, a landmark for the community, was simply extending a policy long cultivated in the city center. Southdale was, in this respect, an updated interpretation of Dayton's great downtown store.[112]

Contrary to most assertions, then and now, Southdale was not the first fully enclosed shopping mall to open. At least two others preceded it. In Omaha, a five-level structure called simply The Center (1953–55) combined parking decks with stores. The building component of this complex was bisected on four levels by enclosed central passages that connected to the Younker's department store branch, other retail facilities, and professional offices. Most stores also opened directly onto adjacent portions of the parking deck. This unusual arrangement probably stemmed from the compact, steep-sloping site, which was chosen for its access to a large number of well-established residential neighborhoods. Far from presenting a model, The Center was among the last shopping complexes attempting regional status to sacrifice acreage for an in-town location. The other example, Lakeside Center in Denver (1954–56), opened just over a month before Southdale. Here, skylit interior passages extended through the middle of the two large store blocks that lay to each side of the centrally placed Denver Dry Goods Company branch. As at the Minneapolis complex, these sheltering spaces were touted for the protection they afforded from the region's climatic extremes. But in neither case were the pedestrianways developed beyond practical considerations to become important places in their own right.[113]

Nor was Southdale the principal model for a number of enclosed malls built in the years immediately following. Some real estate developers apparently viewed Southdale as an expression of Dayton's largess, created without great concern for cost. However attention-getting, the scheme was not, in their minds, a suitable one for emulation.[114] As a result, a number of the first generation of enclosed malls were in fact quite modest affairs of less than 150,000 square feet, constructed to serve a small trading area, with a supermarket or variety store as the anchor. A number of others likewise fell well short of the regional category, encompassing less than 400,000 square feet, with a variety store, junior department store, branch of a small city department store, or chain department store as its anchor.[115] At the same time, most such examples were located in towns or minor cities well removed from the metropolitan sphere. In Billings, Montana; Waco, Texas; or Poplar Bluff, Missouri, these complexes could have at least as much impact on the surrounding area as a regional mall in a metropolitan setting. This kind of shopping center possessed little of the élan of Southdale. Two concurrent projects in Newton and Spencer, Iowa, undertaken by the same Nebraska developer

223. Southdale Shopping Center, pedestrianway and open storefronts, ca. 1956.

224. Newton Shopping Center, First Avenue E. and Seventeenth Street, Newton, Iowa (1958–60). J. & G. Daverman Company, architects. Photo author, 2003.

responsible for The Center and likewise working in conjunction with Younker's, exemplified the type. Encompassing 160,000 square feet, with twenty-five stores each, these one-level complexes were designed in a straightforward manner, with a generous central space but scant embellishment (fig. 224).[116]

Even among regional malls, few of the twenty that opened during the half dozen years after Southland matched its size, its range of merchandise, or its panache. Almost half were under 600,000 square feet; only five had dual anchors comprising major department stores.[117] Southdale's modified cluster plan was soon considered disadvantageous because its multiple entry corridors proved poor locations for the stores facing them, since they received only a fraction of the overall pedestrian traffic. The linear plan prevailed. When enclosed, this long, corridorlike space was a challenge to make inviting. Many early examples were relatively dark and plain, without much sense of the meeting ground. With broad expanses of uninterrupted wall surface, exteriors were often criticized as appearing more like fortresses or warehouses than commercial centers.[118] Big Town in Dallas (1956–59), built by the same developer as Lakeside and the second enclosed regional mall to see realization after Southdale, affords apt illustration. With Sanger Brothers and Montgomery Ward stores as anchors, the 750,000-square-foot shopping center was second in size only to Gulfgate statewide. With ranges of stores open to the car lot on each side of Sanger's and at right angles to the mall, some effort was made to mitigate the effects of enclosure. Still, the behemoth's no-frills design and its vast dimensions remained the dominant visual qualities.[119] The enclosed shopping mall could be big but also lackluster.

The principal reason enclosed malls were not livelier was tied to debates concerning their merits and costs. No one argued that shopping in an enclosed mall was less pleasant than one without this amenity during periods of precipitation and temperature extremes. The disagreement arose over how much that difference would bolster trade relative to construction and maintenance costs. Most architects, developers, and retailers involved were skeptical of Gruen's claim that enclosing the mall would pay for itself through savings in other arenas as well as through sales increases. After Southdale opened, both Gruen and some of his associates expanded their economic argument, emphasizing such factors as increased revenues from vendors in the mall proper and improved spaces for promotions and special events. Most important, the considerable expenses of constructing a service tunnel could be eliminated. Minimizing portals enabled screened delivery areas on grade at scattered locations around the building's perimeter.[120] Despite such advantages, the common belief among those involved in developing shopping centers was that both construction and temperature control costs were greater for an enclosed mall and that these increases could be borne by tenants if it could be clearly demonstrated that the configuration would augment sales enough to offset higher rents. Even the economies of a single air-conditioning system at Southdale were debated. As a result, all those concerned tended to seek economies in other aspects of the design. Until better data was available, at least, prudence was the order of the day. Moreover, the number of places where the climate was unpleasant enough to warrant enclosure was believed to be limited; most early examples were in regions where either long periods of heat or cold prevailed. Even Gruen maintained that only some parts of the country had climatic variations sufficient to justify enclosure. Much like the embrace of jet aircraft for passenger travel at about the same time, when industry planners believed that the advantages lay primarily with transcontinental or transoceanic flights, the acceptance of enclosed malls was substantial yet still tentative. In 1960 a writer for *Chain Store Age* observed that the phenomenon "is not expected to sweep the country, but the chances are that enough enclosed mall centers will be built to take them out of the 'strange and wonderful' category."[121]

The economics of enclosed mall development and operation also brought to the fore the debate over design. Those who considered Gruen's work excessive offered few public challenges in the wake of the successes of Northland, Eastland, and Southdale. Toward the decade's end, however, criticism mounted. James Douglas, the president of Northgate since its opening, warned members of the National Retail Dry Goods Association in 1958 that the "shopping center developer of the future must curb his champagne appetite. We must learn that less expensive construction and better utilization of floor space will produce the same volume of sales." Welton Becket did not admonish spendthrifts directly but emphasized that the enclosed mall improved the opportunities of creating the same degree of efficiency that he had achieved at Stonestown. A writer for *Chain Store Age* explained the architect's views: "The enclosed mall . . . is similar to a huge department store . . . and should be designed and laid out in exactly the same way. . . . It becomes an integrated shopping area that is literally an extension of the department store concept, except that each department is an individually owned shop."[122]

John Graham was even more blunt. Addressing the ICSC convention in 1962, he shared Gruen's and Becket's enthusiasm for the enclosed mall—"the most important single advancement in shopping center planning since the early establishment of the regional center." At the same time, he said, a "regional center is a business, [and] just as in manufacturing plants, the planning must be based upon the efficiency of operation. It may be timely to remind developers and planners that their principal assignment is to create a facility for retail distribution, not a recreation area." In a direct swipe at Southdale, whose layout he, as Donaldson's architect, had argued against, Graham asserted that "garden-court type planning dilutes the traffic, creates dead corners, poor locations, hot or cold sides of the street, makes for difficult situations in handling merchandise service, and above all, increases costs on a rentable square foot basis. While in the case of the open mall, this type of planning may produce harmful effects on some stores . . . , in the case of enclosed malls, the increased cost plus the reduced efficiency may become disastrous for the center." Graham was not opposed to some embellishment of the mall, only against those features that "interfere with the efficiency of the retail operation, . . . with the traffic flow [and with] . . . visual sight lines." Just as in Northgate, the mall's width should be between forty and sixty feet. Planting might best be "contained within small movable units." Echoing Becket, he intoned that "as we gain more experience in planning . . . new centers, I expect we will come closer to the planning philosophy accepted by the primary department stores of the country. . . . simple, straightforward, easy to operate with a minimum [building] area . . . , otherwise the cost will get out of hand."[123]

Graham also sparred with Gruen on exterior treatment, over which their differences seemed to be reversed. While the latter argued for few if any store signs on the exterior, developing building mass and landscaping in ways to elicit visual interest, the Seattle architect voiced vehement opposition: "No matter how thoughtfully the facades of the 'introverted' center are done, or what materials are used, it still resembles a warehouse, without the grace to let the approaching customer know that it is a collection of merchants the developer is proud of." The liveliness, Gruen maintained, should be concentrated inside, but Graham advised that an enclosed regional mall would be hurt by "hiding good names on the mall side," adding that a "variety of properly designed storefronts and signs on the center's exterior lend a lot of gaiety and excitement to the architectural complex."[124]

But Gruen was the most experienced in the field. At the close of 1962, not only had he designed more operating regional malls of all kinds (fifteen) than either Becket or Graham (twelve each), but by far the largest number of enclosed malls (six, versus one and two, respectively). Gruen also had arguably the most prestigious roster of department stores coast to coast as his clients, including Macy's in San Francisco, L. S. Ayres, Strawbridge & Clothier, Joseph Horne, Filene's, and Carson Pirie Scott, as well as Hudson's and Dayton's.[125] On two of these projects, he also worked with a developer who became equally outspoken in championing the enclosed mall and the regional shopping center as an exciting place that afforded focus for the community. That developer was James Rouse.

Aside from J. C. Nichols, probably no one has achieved the legendary status that Rouse has with the building of shopping centers, and few have with real estate development more broadly. A mortgage banker who had financed a number of shopping centers in his adopted home of Baltimore, Rouse decided to enter the real estate field when the opportunity arose to build on a large tract of farmland only some three miles from the city center. Working with architects Pietro Belluschi and Kenneth Welch, he created a scheme for a regional mall, Mondawmin (1952–56). The project was unusual not only in its in-town location but in its design, combining the two-tier arrangement of Shoppers' World with a plan that drew from both the linear and cluster types. Around the time the complex opened Rouse formed a public corporation, Community Research and Development (CRD), to spearhead shopping center and other projects.

No less than at Mondawmin, his approach continued to be one of a maverick.[126] Developers specializing in regional malls were almost unknown in the mid-1950s. Sol Atlas had achieved renown for the Cross County Center and was embarking on other, less ambitious complexes. Philip Klutznick had created the sub-regional mall and the surrounding community of Park Forest, Illinois, and was now engaged with Marshall Field's in building Old Orchard. Locally, Joseph Meyerhoff had made a specialty of developing shopping centers, including Baltimore's first, Edmondson Village (1946–47), and largest, dual-anchor Eastpoint.[127] But these individuals were the exception. Furthermore, the idea of developing through a corporation other than a department store subsidiary was still quite new. The advantage of this method was that higher cash equities could be obtained through the issuance of stock (or in the case of CRD debenture bonds), reducing the debt burden and hence rents.[128] Corporate status thus allowed the developer more latitude in determining the scope, complexion, and physical character of the center, a position very important to Rouse.

Among the things that most distinguished Rouse in the early years of his career as a developer was his outspoken advocacy of the enclosed mall as an optimal place for fostering human activity and interaction—a "wonderfully peaceful, easy, gracious environment in which people feel at home." Rouse's brother and chief lieutenant, Willard, was no less blunt. Addressing colleagues in 1961, he opened his remarks on the ostensibly dry subject of "Construction and Operation" of enclosed malls with: "Let's not forget we're in a fun business, because this is a business of fun." The "fun" of a regional mall was not a self-indulgent extra but stemmed from a basic human need, he intoned. A year later James Rouse emphasized that a shopper "should feel warmed by [the shopping center's] beauty and comfortable in its scale. He should enjoy the sense of being served by it rather than being 'promoted' into it. He should have a true sense of possession of the center and a sense of pride in that possession. In its design, the center should relax and refresh the families who use it and promote friendly contact among people of the community. And in its management, the center should fulfill its enormous opportunity to enrich the community life." The need was endemic to the modern era: "The central city has deteriorated further and further. Its excitement, interest and liveliness, its activity and the diversity of its cultural offering to the community has gone steadily downhill. The suburbs on the other hand have provided none of this through their natural growth. The little towns around have not been places that have had this kind of active, lively central core."[129] The regional mall was the only logical place for such activity to occur. Like Gruen,

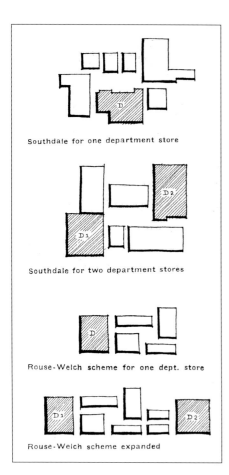

225. *(left)* Diagrammatic drawings of original and revised layouts for Southdale and of layout devised by James Rouse and Kenneth Welch whereby a second department store could be added without changes to original portion of the regional mall (*Architectural Forum*, December 1956, 178).

226. *(below)* Garden State Plaza, New Jersey routes 4 and 17, Paramus, New Jersey (1951–55). Abbott, Merkt & Company, architects-engineers; altered. Site plan drawn by Paul Davidson after "Traffic Report, Garden State Plaza," n.p.

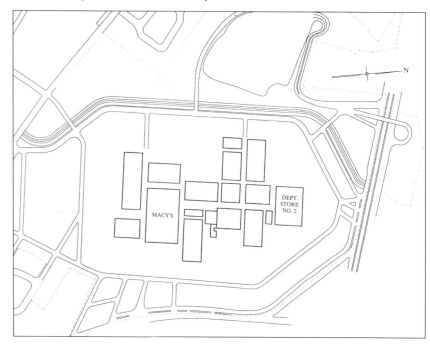

Rouse believed that it should play an essentially urban role without traditional urban physical characteristics.

Like Gruen, too, Rouse considered design to be a central issue in the equation. To date, the record was not an especially admirable one in this realm. In 1960 he admonished colleagues: "Until now . . . we can't be proud of what we've done. . . . In our company . . . there is no other area that concerns us so much as how we can humanize these centers that we're building. The buildings are too massive, they're out of scale with human beings, they're cold and impersonal whether closed mall or open mall. The steady procession of stores all look alike. . . . We need to deliberately break things into [a] scale in which people feel at home."[130] Rouse was strongly influenced by Gruen, but also by Nichols, whose Country Club Plaza he believed was a more important source of inspiration than contemporary work. Rouse also seems to have understood Nichols's example in how a high level of design and of human appeal was advantageous to business. But in realizing that integration, he came up with a rather novel scheme. Working with Welch on Mondawmin, Rouse sought to avoid the problem of potential expansion should a second department store be secured at a later date. The redesign of Southdale after Donaldson's agreed to participate incurred substantial costs, but Gruen claimed this course was far better than initially designing an open-ended linear plan for a second, yet-to-materialize anchor, as at Shoppers' World. For Mondawmin, Rouse wanted a layout that would be whole with only a single department store but could also be enlarged to accommodate a second in a seamless way. An ingenious mixing of linear and cluster plans was the result (fig. 225).[131] This configuration formed the basis for several subsequent projects and also appears to have been quickly adopted in the design of Garden State Plaza, which came to rival Northland in size by the decade's end (fig. 226). Here, Abbott, Merkt used the cluster arrangement for the initial phase, then, for the second and third stages, extended one of the pedestrianways to culminate in the second department store (Gimbel's) and, off that path, extended a cross axis as Graham had done at Gulfgate.[132]

But design was not the only component of Rouse's conception. At the heart of his argument lay the matter of tenant mix: "The space yielding highest rents in a shopping center is that rented by optical, millinery, jewelry, hearing aid, candy, and beauty and barber establishments, plus all sorts of little impulse and kiosk businesses." The features billed as essential to making the mall "fun" and a place of vital activity were also some of the most profitable, he maintained. Indeed, they could make the difference not just in receiving a handsome return on the investment, but in being able to invest enough in the center to make it an

227. Harundale Mall, Ritchie Highway, Glen Burnie, Maryland (1956–58). Rogers, Taliaferro & Lamb, architects; demolished 1998.

attractive place: "Here is the bonanza, glittering beyond the bread and butter. This is the very business most sensitive to the shopper's attitude about the center; this is the extra that flourishes spectacularly in a center which shoppers find fun to go to, appealing to traverse, seductive to hang around in." Aesthetics and business went hand in hand. Rouse believed that he had found the end of the rainbow and pursued it vigorously.[133]

The initial venture of CRD, Harundale in Glen Burnie, Maryland (1956–58), manifested Rouse's approach more fully than Mondawmin. The venture was in part spearheaded by Hochschild Kohn, the pioneer and also the most aggressive in branch department store development in Baltimore. At the same time, Hochschild's was not the city's leading emporium, and the location, some eight miles south of downtown, was in an area developing primarily with moderate-income housing tracts. Plans were announced in 1954; however, little was apparently done on the scheme until after CRD's founding. Reinforced, if not determined, by Southdale's precedent, Harundale was the first enclosed mall of any size completed after the Minnesota complex and the only one of its kind until CRD's second project opened in Charlotte, North Carolina, a year later.[134] Rouse worked closely with the young modernist firm of Rogers, Taliaferro & Lamb (later RTKL) to refine the ideas introduced at Mondawmin. Continually challenging the architects to tackle and resolve difficult issues, he thrived in what Francis Taliaferro described as an "atmosphere of creative tension." Rouse already had acquired a deep admiration for Gruen and advised his architects to consult with him on matters about which they were uncertain.[135] No room existed for dual anchors at Harundale; the site had been purchased well before that arrangement was a concern. Less than half of Southdale's size and on more-or-less flat ground Harundale was only one level as well. Yet it was an important demonstration that the enclosed mall as a mecca for human interaction—with kiosks and fountains, orchids and lilies, palm and pineapple trees—and not just as a utilitarian shelter was indeed a viable enterprise for more than the most prestigious of department store companies—that it could succeed in the retail mainstream.[136] Inside and out, the complex benefited from more rigorous architectural detailing than many shopping centers. Yet the design did not seem extravagant, and it worked effectively as a background for the crowds who frequented the premises (fig. 227).

Over the next several years, Rouse's work, writings, and speeches earned him a national reputation as a leader in the development of the enclosed mall. By the early 1960s, Rouse and his lieutenants repeatedly stated that they would not consider undertaking a shopping center unless it was of this new kind. He used Harundale as a model for several projects undertaken between 1957 and 1959.[137] But it was a break from that physical configuration in a scheme in which, for the first time, Gruen was his architect, that vouchsafed both

228. Cherry Hill Shopping Center, New Jersey Route 38 and Haddonfield Road, Cherry Hill, New Jersey (1959–61). Victor Gruen Associates, architects; Lewis J. Clarke, landscape architect; altered. Strawbridge & Clothier department store at lower center and addition of Bamberger's department store under construction at upper right. Photo Skyphotos, 1961.

men's leadership in the creation of enclosed malls. That complex, Cherry Hill Shopping Center (1959–61), lay some five miles east of downtown Camden, New Jersey. Located amid new middle-class residential areas that were booming as part of greater Philadelphia's growth, Cherry Hill functioned much as Albert Greenfield hoped Lit's Camden branch would function—as a magnet for a large part of southern New Jersey. The shopping center had long been the dream of G. Stockton Strawbridge, who aggressively renewed the pursuit of branch development in conjunction with shopping centers that his firm, Strawbridge & Clothier, had helped pioneer. Other Philadelphia department store companies were still cool to the idea, but Strawbridge was certain this approach would not only keep his business competitive, but also elevate its position, especially in relation to the long-dominant Wanamaker's.

Strawbridge was approached by William Zeckendorf in 1952 for building a shopping center on the Camden fringe, probably on the order of that envisioned for Roosevelt Field, but nothing came of the initiative. The following year local developer Eugene Mori proposed a site farther afield. Negotiations proved fruitful. In January 1955, plans were announced to build a regional mall on the Cherry Hill site. Subsequently, Becket was hired to design the project, but after two and a half years Mori was unable to secure adequate financing. Given the large investment of time and money already made, with plans nearly at the stage where construction could start, Strawbridge was livid. In a memorandum to his board he fumed: "Meanwhile our competitors have moved rapidly in expanding their own branch operations. . . . As a result . . . we have lost position in terms of total corporate sales volume and have been unable to retain our fair share of the consumer's dollar. . . . Since the 1952 opening of [the] Wilmington [branch] we have been static in a period of national and local economic expansion."[138] Yet another year passed before Strawbridge took an option to purchase the land. In seeking a new developer, he consulted with Larry Smith, who advised hiring someone capable of conducting all phases of the operation inhouse—research, planning, financing, construction, and management. Smith's choice was Rouse; certainly no developer in the Delaware Valley could begin to match his credentials. Strawbridge and Rouse were of like minds. Once the latter was part of the team, he recommended Gruen as architect. Finally, in March 1960, Strawbridge unveiled plans for his long-nourished dream, a complex that would encompass 1 million square feet and far surpass any other outlying retail facility in the Philadelphia region.[139]

Gruen was unimpressed by Harundale. At Cherry Hill, he broke from that model and also his own at Southdale, while seeking new ways to integrate the features he and Rouse prized the most. The cluster plan was abandoned for a more straightforward one, with relatively narrow, linear pedestrianways. Gruen appears not only to have taken Graham's criticism to heart, but to have turned to Graham's Gulfgate in developing a modified "T" plan (fig. 228). Here, however, Gruen used it as a means to embrace Rouse's concern for future expansion at one end, with a movie theater and a huge Woolworth's unit as the temporary terminus. At the other end, fronting the supermarket, was an International Bazaar, a new twist on the small specialty establishments Rouse believed could make the greatest difference in profits. Where these two axes converged, fronting the Strawbridge's branch, was a spectacular "Garden Court"—larger, more

229. Cherry Hill Shopping Center, Garden Court, ca. 1961.

230. Cherry Hill Shopping Center, Delaware Mall (*Architectural Record,* June 1962, 178).

231. Cherry Hill Shopping Center, mall kiosk (*Architectural Record,* June 1962, 179).

lush, and more extravagant than anything Gruen or Rouse had done before (fig. 229). The space was in fact pure theater of the sort that Morris Lapidus had popularized for resort hotels—a space that for the first time in a retail setting beyond the city center began to possess the same evocative power as the great atria of Wanamaker's and a few other department stores in the urban core—a space far grander than any in Strawbridge's parent store. At over forty feet high, the court suggested a modernist interpretation of an enormous tent, with a curved ceiling hung from inverted steel trusses supported by mosaic-encrusted columns. A skylight filtered through a suspended trellis extended down the center, augmented by clerestory windows at each end. Circulation paths were irregular and casual, defined by beds of tropical plants, fountains, a gazebo, and changing exhibits. Nor was this space an isolated event. In subtle but effective ways, Gruen played with wall and ceiling surfaces, exposed structure, planting beds, and natural light sources to break down the linear expanses of the pedestrianways into a constantly changing sequence (fig. 230). Even the wood and glass folding kiosks were developed in a lively architectural manner to elicit interest and delight among the throngs that passed them (fig. 231). Here, Gruen and Rouse married spectacle and practicality with greater aplomb than either had done before.[140]

No matter how elaborate the plans to build the finest of regional malls and even to seek regional dominance, the field was too competitive for any one complex to remain in the limelight for long. Despite Rouse's urgings, Strawbridge refused to court Wanamaker's as a second anchor at Cherry Hill. His emporium, after all, had always been the "second" store on Market Street in Philadelphia; it would not be reduced to that position here. In December 1960, with his great regional mall well under construction, Strawbridge changed his mind, but it was too late. Wanamaker's leadership had also long entertained a New Jersey location. While Strawbridge demurred, Wanamaker's had arranged to join Gimbel's at Moorestown Mall (1961–63) under the auspices of the Winston-Muss Corporation, premier New York developers. Designed by John Graham, the complex lacked the ebullience of Cherry Hill but was clearly intended to rival its sense of being a major community center. Strawbridge and Rouse were forced not only to scramble for an alternative but also to look outside the region, as all of Phila-

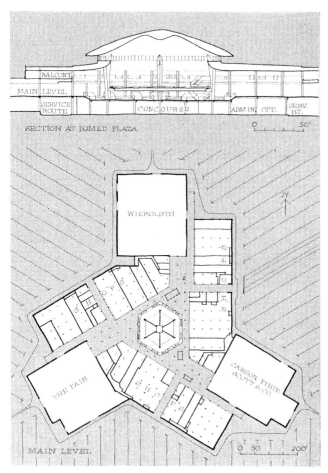

232. Randhurst Center, Rand, Euclid, and Elmhurst roads, Mount Prospect, Illinois (1959–62). Victor Gruen Associates, architects; Franz Lipp, landscape architect; partly demolished 2003–4. Plan of main level and section of central court (*Architectural Forum,* November 1962, 108).

delphia's major stores were committed. Their choice was Bamberger's—respectable enough as an establishment but an unknown to most people in the area. Even then, Strawbridge's dream of hegemony was shattered. Situated along the same highway, just three miles to the east of Cherry Hill, Moorestown Mall attracted a substantial share of the regional market.[141]

Cherry Hill was a suitably grand finale among regional malls initiated in the 1950s, but it was not the only such venture. Department store rivalry also lay behind what was arguably the most ambitious regional mall of the era, Randhurst Center, which opened in 1962. In the wake of Marshall Field's success at Old Orchard, Carson Pirie Scott president Harold Spurway sought to contain its draw by building a complex of equal size nearly ten miles farther to the northwest amid burgeoning new residential tracts attracting higher-medium-income households than those around its predecessor. But Randhurst was not just to be an equivalent to Old Orchard; it would have three major department stores. Spurway convinced not only Wieboldt's, a major area chain, but also The Fair, which had a branch in Old Orchard, to join forces. The three enjoyed parity; there was no "second," let alone "third" department store. Perhaps to ensure this balance throughout the process, the three companies established a subsidiary corporation to develop and manage the center. Randhurst was not only the first regional mall on which three such establishments collaborated from the outset, it was the first to host such a concentration of retail giants. In further distinction to Old Orchard, which celebrated the outdoors, Randhurst was an interior spectacle. Now the acknowledged master of showmanship in shopping centers, Gruen was hired to design the ensemble. To minimize walking distances and maximize exposure of all stores, he developed an ingenious pinwheel plan anchored by a great domed space, 165 feet in diameter, with a "bazaar" of open shops beneath a polygonal "floating" restaurant (fig. 232). In further contrast to Old Orchard— and to Marshall Field's sequel, Oak Brook—plants did not dominate the scene. Instead, spaces were more sculptural in nature, designed to emphasize shelter from the elements but also to highlight through contrast the merchandise in the establishments that lined them.[142]

Coalescence

By the time Randhurst opened in October 1962 the enclosed mall was widely accepted as the preferred—if not yet the ubiquitous—form for new regional shopping centers in an increasing portion of the country. Both the attributes argued by Gruen and Rouse on one hand and by the pragmatists on the other had contributed to the rapid development of the type. David Muss, whose firm had emerged as a major developer of shopping centers, explained in 1963 that his business now focused exclusively on enclosed regional malls, including the much praised Walt Whitman Shopping Center in Huntington, Long Island (1960–62) and Moorestown Mall. The advantages were overwhelming in his opinion. Insurance companies and lending institutions now considered enclosed malls a better investment than any other form of shopping center. Rents were greater and sales about 20 percent higher than in open complexes. Tenants were secured faster, and a higher number of them were top grade. Year-round patronage was greater. The economic benefits of the mall as a focus for promotions and community activities were now indisputable as well. The trend had become a major one. As many enclosed malls were scheduled to open in 1962, he noted, as all those currently operating.[143] Gruen's arguments for Southdale were vindicated.

The regional malls' growth in stature helped generate a shift in popular terminology whereby "mall" or "shopping mall" became virtually synonymous with "shopping center." Increasingly, too, complexes included "mall" in their official name instead of "shopping center" or "plaza."[144] While an ambient newness was paramount in the design of these complexes, they were heralded as having a distinguished pedigree. Since the early 1950s, analogies were made between regional malls and ancient agora, medieval market squares, and similarly venerable precedents.[145] But the enclosed mall carried a more resonant link to the great arcades of Europe, especially the Galleria Vittorio Emanuele II in Milan (1865–67, 1877), one of the few exuberantly eclectic works of that era to enjoy iconic status among modernist designers and the public alike in the postwar years. Gruen first invoked this link, asserting that it was a major source of inspiration for the garden court at Southdale.[146] Thereafter, the image of Old World sophistication, of the casual yet stylish ambience of sidewalk cafes, and of great, soaring, skylit spaces gave the enclosed mall an air of legitimacy that seemed to transcend time and space. On the fringes of the American metropolis would rise huge new centers that defined place as well as served the population.

By the early 1960s, too, the development and operation of regional shopping centers was seen as having reached maturity. When Rouse formed CRD, few firms had much experience in the business, and the most seasoned of developers had only one completed regional mall to their credit. Rouse, Muss, and others had made what once seemed like a rather esoteric pursuit into a major one in the real estate field. The once-feared phenomenon of overbuilding had largely dissipated. Careful planning in all its dimensions would enable for steady growth in the future. The president of the ICSC addressed his colleagues in 1959 by emphasizing that the "Shopping Center industry is not merely a part of this continent's huge industrial strength, it is a manifestation of the new philosophy of 'easy living.' It is the businessman's counterpart to this generation's surge to the suburbs in search of the comfort and joy of suburban leisure." The future looked bright, he intoned. Retail sales were likely to increase by $33 billion over the next half dozen years. More than twice the number of shopping centers that currently existed would be built within that time frame. The development process was fraught with difficulties, and shopping center operation was perhaps the biggest challenge of all. But, he noted, "The shopping center industry which is enacting the tremendous success story of the 20th Century, has come of age. . . . Our industry's dynamic growth will continue to proceed at a startling pace."[147]

Department store executives likewise had cause for self-congratulation. In the course of a decade the regional mall had emerged as a sound and effective means of expansion— of capturing the large new market beyond the established city, of generating new profits, of competing effectively with chain stores—indeed, of controlling the retail environment in a way never before possible. Department stores had made the mall. The great emporia enjoyed privileges there that many developers and some other merchants resented, but without them these complexes would not exist. The generation that created them saw regional malls as bringing a new sense of order and focus in the metropolitan periphery. The many millions invested in expansion were more than justified by the changing nature of the market. "Most of all," declared the real estate director of Allied Stores, summing up conditions in 1960, "America is moving into the very heart of the department store income level—the $6,000 to $12,000 annual income. Discretionary household income is moving into the department store brackets ever faster. . . . These people today want more than the bare necessities. . . . They want quality. They want individuality. They want self-expression, they want service. They want to use their credit. They are not worried about future security. They want to enjoy their discretionary income."[148]

But what of the mall's impact on the established commercial order downtown? During most of the 1950s major retailers with interests in the urban core were convinced, or at least sought to convince themselves, that both worlds could flourish. Toward the decade's end, however, uncertainties about the future of downtown began to escalate among retailers and many other contingents as well. Increasingly, the conviction ran, if the heart of the metropolitan area was to remain viable, large-scale intervention was necessary. As some of the major investors in downtown, it is not surprising that department store companies played a significant role in what was, and what was not, undertaken.

9 Stores in the City

OSCAR WEBBER, president of Detroit's venerable J. L. Hudson Company, may not have been the first prominent retail executive to make the point, but his belief that the regional mall and the downtown emporium complemented, indeed strengthened, each other appears to have had a major impact on the outlook of many colleagues. Large-scale branch building and shopping center development on the metropolitan periphery were not just necessary to best the competition, he argued. Downtown and full-line branch stores were mutually reinforcing. The immense scale of Hudson's operations in both sectors was sufficient in itself to elicit widespread interest within the trade. In 1953, Webber began to make his views known, as construction was progressing on the company's Northland, the largest regional mall yet undertaken. That complex "will attract much new business from people who seldom or never come downtown to shop," he stressed. Furthermore, the "downtown store will continue to be improved and always will be uppermost in our planning." Hudson's treasurer reiterated that Northland "represents no basic change of policy or philosophy. It is simply a new and modern way of meeting an old and accepted principle. If we are to continue to . . . effectively serve the people of Detroit we must grow . . . with Detroit." After Northland opened in 1954, close tabs were kept on its impact by the trade press. Initially, Webber predicted no more than a 5 to 10 percent loss at the main store. Several months later that loss was estimated at over 16 percent, but the following year it had lessened to about 10 percent. Yet even at its peak, Webber emphasized, the loss was no more than a fraction of the gain in business overall. Hudson's was capturing a new market and aggressively improving its great store in the city center. Throughout much of the decade, Hudson's was presented as an exemplar for this dual approach.[1]

A number of other industry leaders were quick to agree. Well before Northland opened, William Crear, Jr., vice president of the Dayton Company in Minneapolis, whose expansion strategy was directly modeled on Hudson's, went so far as to claim that his firm's Southdale "will in no way transfer business from the main store," adding that growth could not be effectively achieved in the core alone. Similarly, a Macy's executive in California emphasized in 1954 that "downtown retail merchandising is not now on the decline, and we need not fear it will be in the future." What was occurring with regional malls, he maintained, was not "decentralization," but simply "expansion." That same year Philip Klutznick, the developer of Old Orchard for Marshall Field's, reiterated that far from undermining the city center, regional malls would "merely take the pressure off" them. That sentiment was likewise stated by Raymond Kramer, board chairman of Interstate Department Stores, adding that while the regional mall appeared to be a "retail revolution," it was simply an "evolution." As part of its publicity for the opening of the 163rd Street Shopping Center in Miami two years later, a feature article proclaimed how such complexes gave cause for downtown stores to expand, citing Allied Stores' allocation of $3 to work on its city center emporia for every $1 channeled to regional mall construction. As late as 1961, Allied's B. Earl Puckett himself declared that downtown and regional malls need not have an adverse effect on each other.[2]

Some retailers were less cheerful, however. Large branch department stores, especially when combined with regional malls, had an increasingly deleterious effect, not just on the parent emporium but on downtown generally. One or two such complexes in a major metropolitan area might not cause a great decline in sales over the long term, many analysts believed. Yet as the number of such retail magnets grew during the second half of the 1950s, the effect became increasingly pronounced. Los Angeles led the nation in this respect thanks to the proliferation of large department store branches—three containing 100,000 square feet or more opened before World War II, six more by the close of 1954, and an additional nine stores five years later.[3] But many in the field regarded Los Angeles as an exception owing to the correspondence between its rise as a major urban area and its diffuse, low-density residential development. New York exceeded Los Angeles with eleven such branches by the end of 1954 and another fifteen between then and 1961, but it, too, was unusual, with an enormous, stable, close-in population with great purchasing power. Philadelphia had more mainstream urban characteristics, but it, too, was subject to the same trend, with five department store branches of 100,000 square feet or more erected prior to 1955, two of them in Wilmington, beyond the city's main trading area. From 1955 through 1960 seven more were completed. By the end of 1960, eight cities had six or more such branches; an additional nine at least three.

Throughout the period *Women's Wear Daily* editors made Philadelphia a poster child for the potential threat that large-scale branch store and shopping center development could pose to the city center. Beginning in 1953, annual accounts correlated the decline in downtown sales with the rise of branches on the periphery and were augmented by numerous other reports. At an early stage, Philadelphia department store executives complained that predictions of doom were greatly exaggerated. Downtown sales would soon stabilize. Echoing the views of Webber, Lit Brothers president Max Robb opined that branches were supplementing, not replacing, downtown stores. Yet by 1956, the picture was consistently one of loss. Two years later, department store executives forecast a rebound that never occurred. By the close of 1961 one account predicted the downward trend was irreversible because of competition not only from branches but also from discount stores and from units established by companies based outside the region.[4]

No other metropolis received comparable scrutiny of its downtown doldrums, but Philadelphia was far from the only place where the phenomenon was chronicled. Washington, Baltimore, Detroit, Minneapolis and St. Paul, Boston, Buffalo, Cleveland, Milwaukee, and San Francisco were among the cities featured in such accounts. Why *should* shoppers from suburban Virginia come to downtown Washington, one journalist queried in 1952, when bus fare could be as much as $1.20. Once in town, local transportation was necessary to get to the city's two best department stores, as well as to some other emporia. Bringing children could easily double fares. The trip might occur at rush hour, when transit facilities were jammed, or at other times when suburban bus schedules were "greatly reduced." Using the car necessitated navigating through heavy traffic en route and searching for off-street parking, the facilities for which were inadequate. The cost of parking was high, and the use of public transit was still required if visiting stores in more than a limited area was on the agenda.[5] Such anecdotes were not as unsettling as either the uncertainty over how big an impact a major new branch or shopping center might have on downtown or the statistics that were disseminated showing the steady erosion of downtown sales.[6] Many prominent retailers tried to allay fears, but some broke ranks. The president of the huge Bond Company apparel chain, who invested heavily in shopping center units, declared in 1959: "We don't open any downtown stores any more. That's what I think of downtown." On the other side of the equation, department store executives in Grand Rapids reportedly agreed among themselves not to enter any shopping centers, a collusion they vehemently denied. The mayor of Akron, however, saw nothing illegal about his banning shopping centers from being constructed in the city, a measure he apparently never implemented.[7]

Another cause for alarm in some circles was the spate of department store closings that began in the mid-1950s and continued into the next decade. A few businesses of this genre had folded during the Depression and in later years, but most such companies were considered especially weak. Others had been purchased and absorbed by prestigious establishments—the Palais Royal by Woodward & Lothrop in Washington (1946), or O'Connor Moffatt in San Francisco (1945) and John Taylor in Kansas City (1947) by Macy's. Now, however, the situation seemed more unsettling. John Wanamaker closed its huge New York complex a week before Christmas in 1954, claiming its location was no longer viable. Hartford's Wise, Smith closed the same year; Alms & Doepke in Cincinnati, Goldenberg's in Washington, Hearn's in New York, and O'Neill's in Baltimore, the next. R. H. White in Boston, Namm-Loeser in Brooklyn, and Frank & Seder in Philadelphia did likewise in 1957, followed by Boggs & Buhl in Pittsburgh (1958), J. N. Adam in Buffalo, and Ernest Kern in Detroit (both 1959). The Hub in Baltimore, Rollamn's in Cincinnati, Rosenbaum's in Pittsburgh, and Mandel Brothers in Chicago all shut their doors in 1960. Eight years after a $5 million remodeling, Snellenberg's closed its downtown store in 1963, its branches taken over by Lit's. The previous year the Bailey Company in Cleveland closed its downtown store but kept its branches operating.[8] Many of these companies catered to the lower-middle market, which was the most susceptible to competition from chains and the rapidly growing number of discount stores. Observers took pains to mention that antiquated physical plants, ineffectual merchandising practices, and/or poor management policies were to blame; the shutdowns were not an omen for the industry as a whole. R. H. White reopened under the aegis of City Stores around 1960. J. N. Adam's building, the largest and newest facility of its kind in Buffalo, was quickly taken over by Adam, Meldrum & Anderson. Rollman's building was replaced by a much larger one for another Allied affiliate, Mabley & Carew. After twice threatening to close its downtown San Francisco store, Broadway-Hale's leadership decided to keep the facility open in December 1962.[9] Still the news, appearing regularly on the pages of *Women's Wear Daily,* was a sobering reminder that retailing downtown was becoming ever more difficult to sustain at traditional levels.

The situation was clear enough that from the mid-1950s on, a substantial number of retailers realized that, however exaggerated they might appear, forecasts of downtown decline were not entirely unfounded.[10] This was also a time when group initiatives to reverse, or at least stem, the decline gained momentum. Increasingly, too, merchants realized that the problems of downtown required a broader scope of measures than they alone could provide. A number of business leaders joined others in calling for sweeping plans that would reinvigorate the city center. Department store executives were extensively involved in the array of undertakings. Traditionally, the department store had fostered urban growth simply by virtue of its existence. Now many industry leaders believed a more aggressive strategy was needed downtown, complementing that undertaken with the development of major branch stores and regional malls. Through such initiatives they believed that they could maintain the equilibrium between downtown and outlying centers that Webber championed. Far from replacing downtown, the regional mall would allow the department store to dominate the new metropolitan periphery *as well as* older parts of the city. Downtown remained central to the equation. But in contrast to the regional mall's relatively swift ascendancy to preeminence as a means of retail expansion, no consensus was reached on an effective means for revitalizing the core shopping district. Opinions indeed were deeply varied. Ultimately no strategy proved effective in reversing the decline to the degree that the core shopping district again became a major center of trade.

Assessment

Part of the problem retailers had in evaluating the condition of downtown was that the problem was new and the bases upon which to determine both symptoms and causes were uncertain. The city center had always faced such challenges as adequate access, street congestion, noise, pollution, infrastructural deficiencies, and spatial constraints on expansion, but these had never threatened the core's hegemony. Public improvements, however slow and inefficient, had headed off any serious, prolonged crisis. Private enterprise, too, had risen to the fore in self-improvement. Whatever its shortcomings, downtown remained the yardstick by which the progress and potential of the city were measured. Even the emergence of chain units and downtown store branches in outlying areas during the interwar decades was seldom seen as an omen of disaster for the core. The volume of sales and the array of goods and services purveyed in the city center were simply too great to be challenged.

Under the circumstances, department store executives and other merchants could not imagine a time when downtown no longer represented the heart and soul of their trade, regardless of how extensive outlying retail operations became. The proliferation of branch stores and regional malls that they themselves created simply could not lead to downtown's demise. More than one department store head insisted that branches would not flourish unless the parent store remained strong. The downtown store, after all, was the flagship; it gave a business the identity, character, and appeal that made the branches viable operations. Similarly, outlying areas could not continue to prosper if the core was rotten. Should blight, which was understood to be the lowering of property values owing to reduced tenant demand, spread unchecked, it would eventually overwhelm the city and its satellite communities alike.[11]

Scenarios of doom were unthinkable to retailers, who reinforced their perspective by incanting the ostensibly immutable advantages offered only in the urban core. Foremost was the combination of variety ("breadth") and quantity ("depth") of merchandise available downtown. No outlying area could boast anything comparable to the assortment of luxury goods, bargains, and everything in between. Downtown enabled comparison shopping to an unparalleled degree as well, exceeding the capacity of the largest regional mall or outlying business district. Large department stores, major specialty stores, and small shops; locally owned and chain establishments; exclusive and popularly priced outlets—all existed in considerable number within a compact area. Even the awkward process of traveling to a number of outlying centers would not yield findings on a par with those contained within a relatively few blocks of the city center. Merchandise alone did not underlie downtown's appeal, proponents insisted. The core also had by far the greatest panoply of restaurants, places of entertainment, and cultural institutions. Downtown might not be as easy to reach as a suburban center, but it was touted as a vastly more rewarding place.[12]

The optimism was reinforced by some of the professionals who also were instrumental in creating the regional mall. Architect Kenneth Welch, who had conceived the regional mall in the mid-1940s, maintained in 1953 that the growth of cities would swell the downtown workforce and with it the demand for goods. As long as offices remained concentrated in the core, the capacity for outlying centers to expand was limited. Larry Smith, dean of real estate consultants for shopping centers, stressed the following year that downtown could take advantage of the demand for higher-priced goods, pampering services, mail and phone orders, and bargains.[13] Even developers and builders specializing in

233. G. Fox & Company, 966 Main Street, Hartford, Connecticut. Main building (upper right), 1917–18, Cass Gilbert, architect; rear additions (center), ca. 1937–39; and extensive side and rear additions (1956–ca. 1958), Abbott, Merkt & Company, architects-engineers; altered. Store parking garage (lower left), ca. 1956–58, Abbott, Merkt & Company. Photo ca. 1958.

shopping centers voiced alarm over accounts of "downtown strangulation," reiterating the need for a strong urban core.[14]

The problem of bolstering downtown was compounded by the fact that prominent retailers held substantially differing views of the situation. In 1957 Fred Lazarus, Jr., president of Federated Department Stores, informed stockholders that all of its downtown operations had experienced "significant record growth and performance" the previous year. Brother Ralph Lazarus, Federated's executive vice president, likewise expressed an "uncompromising faith in 'downtown' as a place to do business" while admitting that "there are almost as many opinions on the business prospects of downtown . . . as there are retailers."[15] For some department store executives, an up-to-date physical plant, aggressive merchandising practices, and top-of-the-line service lay at the heart of revival. As late as 1959, Harold Hecht, president of Buffalo's William Hengerer, reiterated that "downtown merchants can look optimistically to the future if they keep their facilities modern and bring their message to their customers."[16] Huge sums continued to be allocated to store modernization after 1955. New building fronts, improved air conditioning systems, additional escalators, new fixtures and lighting, and reconfigured and sometimes enlarged selling spaces were all undertaken, just as they had been in previous years.[17]

Beyond remodeling, at least twelve companies undertook major additions to their downtown stores between 1956 and 1962, entailing over 1.7 million square feet.[18] The most ambitious among these was the eight-story, 300,000-square-foot addition (1958–60) at the rear of the G. Fox building in Hartford, which allowed for a reconfiguration of the entire facility (fig. 233). F. & R. Lazarus constructed an addition nearly as large (ca. 1959–61) on its recently refaced plant, while Foley's placed a four-story addition of more than 238,000 square feet (1955–57) atop its huge building, which had opened in Houston only a decade earlier. The Jones Store in Kansas City undertook a four-year expansion program (1955–58), completely remaking its existing quarters and erecting a five-story addition that doubled the overall size. In Salt Lake City, ZCMI purchased an adjacent thirteen-story building so as to occupy four of its floors, while Dayton's Rike-Kumler purchased a neighboring hotel for unspecified future expansion (see fig. 64).[19]

Ambitious projects for new store construction were undertaken as well. A year after acquiring Nashville's Cain-Sloan Company, Allied Stores unveiled plans in October 1956 for a six-story, 350,000-square-foot emporium and an adjacent garage containing nearly 370 spaces, a project that allowed for significant expansion of the business. Cain-Sloan was now clearly the principal store in the region and was heralded as a leader in the city's redevelopment.[20] No less enthusiasm greeted Allied's decision to recast Mabley & Carew in Cincinnati. Upon acquiring Mabley's, a major soft goods emporium, in the latter months of 1960, Allied began studies to expand it into a full-fledged department store, using the strategic site of the ailing Rollman's to erect a twelve-story building. Incorporating many of the interior features developed for Cain-Sloan, the facility opened in November 1962 and was hailed as a monument to "splendor and progress." The editors of the *Cincinnati Enquirer* proclaimed it the "kickoff in the modernization and beautification of all downtown," adding that "anyone who inspects the [store] . . . cannot escape a feeling of inspiration in a widespread revitalization of our core." As bland as the hulking, windowless pile might have seemed to some observers, for fashion-conscious consumers and for boosters of a declining retail center, the new premises were nothing short of "exquisite."[21]

Equally aggressive measures to expand its market were taken by the Dayton Company of Minneapolis when in November 1958 it purchased Schuneman's department store, the most prominent emporium in neighboring St. Paul. Soon thereafter Dayton's acquired an entire block across the street, strategically located between high-end specialty shops and other department stores. Work began on the new building three years later. While a subsidiary, the emporium was intended to dominate trade locally, much as the parent store did in Minneapolis, reflecting "Dayton's belief that the hub of an effective merchandising operation in a large city is the operation of a dominant store in the heart of downtown." Containing 380,000 square feet on five stories and an ingeniously integrated garage for over six hundred cars, the building was reportedly the second largest of any kind in downtown St. Paul (fig. 234). More than one-third bigger than the facility it replaced, the structure was designed to support an additional six stories, which would nearly double the size of both store and garage. Once the store opened in August 1963, the 1890 Schuneman building was demolished for Wabasha Court, a complex of specialty stores for which Dayton's was codeveloper. The ensemble formed a compelling anchor for retailing in the city center and was lauded as a catalyst for further renewal.[22]

On the other hand, the construction of large office buildings in the central and eastern ends of downtown Dallas prompted Sanger Brothers to begin searching for a site amid the fast-growing core. The existing store lay in the once booming but now marginal west side. The situation was soon exacerbated after merging with A. Harris, since neither plant could be expanded to meet the amalgamated company's needs. Within a few months Sanger-Harris announced plans for the projected 600,000-square-foot emporium that would exceed its rival, Titche-Goettinger, and indeed all other Texas stores save Foley's in size. Store executives seem to have coordinated their plans with those, by the same architect, for the fifty-two-story First National Building, announced three weeks later, and which lay directly across the street. Accounts emphasized, however, that it was the cumulative effect of over twenty major office buildings and hotels, constructed and planned, plus several large additions, that prompted the move. Store officials proceeded cautiously nevertheless. Not until October 1963 were plans finalized for a somewhat more modest plant of 460,000 square feet. Less than two years later the new Block of Fashion opened, its great mass mitigated by walls covered in mosaic and fronted by a giant arcade sheathed in marble. Looking more like a civic auditorium than a retail facility, the store also drew from its staff's experience with the layout of branches. Sanger-Harris was reversing the trend, its leadership boasted, learning from branch development, then creating a wholly new downtown plant.[23]

As had long been the case, downtown department stores were usually built independent of other facilities. By the late 1950s, however, retailers occasionally took advantage of being part of a mixed-use project. The San Francisco–based White House opted to open a 125,000-square-foot branch in Oakland as part of the Kaiser Center, planned to serve as the international headquarters for the conglomerate of Kaiser companies but also with acreage set aside for stores and parking. Reginald Biggs, head of the comparatively small, fashion-oriented department store, stressed

234. Dayton Company department store, Wabash, Cedar, Sixth, and Seventh streets, St. Paul, Minnesota (1962–63). Victor Gruen Associates, architects. Photo author, 2000.

the importance of a downtown location in the selection of the East Bay's principal city for his company's first branch. The location, several blocks from the retail and office core, boasted vehicular access without congestion and spectacular views. The project also appears to have been planned as a stimulus to extending the business district in a new direction. When it opened in 1960, the Kaiser Center exuded an air of opulence suggestive of a resort hotel. Punctuating the shoreline of Lake Merritt, the gently curving form of the twenty-eight-story tower—touted as the largest office building in the West—was flanked by a vast wing on the other side. The department store was the focal point of this arm, complemented by several high-end specialty outlets. Retail and office functions alike were served by an integral, five-level parking structure with a twelve-hundred-car capacity. Atop garage and stores lay an extraordinary roof garden, designed as an urban oasis, with sensuous, curving forms and a panoply of exotic plants.[24]

A revitalization strategy based on individual projects was bolstered by the opinion among some retail executives that a return to a more centralized urban structure was inevitable. Puckett was bullish on the subject in 1953, when he was paraphrased by a *Women's Wear Daily* columnist: "The downtown store will be 'good but not dynamic' until the 1960s or early 1970s. By then, the trend to the suburbs should reverse itself as cities rebuild their inner cores." In later years, Puckett was somewhat more guarded in his projections, though he remained optimistic. In 1955 he stressed that "downtown metropolitan stores are still the backbone of retailing and will remain so despite mushrooming suburban shopping centers." Others echoed his enthusiasm. That same year David Rike, president of Rike-Kumler, opined: "I am quite sold on the continuing growth of the downtown sections of practically all communities," while Marshall Field's vice president, Lawrence Sizer, dismissed the talk of impending doom as "nonsense." More sweeping were the remarks made by the head of New York's Saks 34th Street in 1959: "The 'population pendulum' will swing back in favor of large . . . cities in the next decade, and downtown retailing will stop losing out." "Suburban areas," he continued, "are becoming fully populated, and the resulting congestion . . . is making it more difficult for the suburbs to expand." Furthermore, as young suburban families "grow older, and children . . . leave home . . . , many of these families will return to the city."[25]

A number of cities indeed experienced little erosion of downtown retailing during at least a good portion of the 1950s. The boom in office building construction in the core of Dallas gave merchants there reason to believe downtown would continue to thrive. The complete dominance of retailing in Hartford by G. Fox, which refused to build branches, kept the city's compact downtown prosperous. Small department store branches were operating in New Orleans by mid-1957, but downtown was unaffected by them. Market analysts reported a similar stronghold enjoyed by downtown Cincinnati stores the following year. More extensive outlying facilities could be found in Milwaukee by 1959, yet the core "remained remarkably healthy in its retail sales," according to that city's Downtown Association.[26] For every account of decline, it seemed, another portrayed a satisfactory or even an improving picture.

Planning

However impressive one or another expansion campaign might appear, by the mid-1950s a number of retailers came to believe that individual action was not enough if downtown was to enjoy a bright future. Besides improving their operations, merchants needed to join forces to advance more sweeping programs. Opinions differed widely in this sphere, too, as to the extent and nature of those programs. Some advocates called for a strong, single-focus agenda; others demanded a multifaceted one; and yet others insisted that only by remaking the central city through comprehensive, long-range planning could the situation improve. None of these options was easily achieved. Retailers were not used to cooperative actions among themselves or with others in the business community. Chambers of commerce generally were advocates of laissez-faire. Many involved were strongly committed to the sanctity of property rights. Most mistrusted local politicians, often for good reason at a time when bosses and party machines remained common. Finally, large-scale planning was still a relatively new phenomenon in many cities; often the municipal mechanisms to implement a coordinated program were fractured by or otherwise riddled with shortcomings. Just what a revitalization plan should be, moreover, was a matter of heated debate.

Not surprisingly, the most widespread cooperative venture among retailers was to establish or reinvigorate a downtown group charged with promoting the district as a whole. While some such organizations had existed during the Depression, when the need to capture scarce dollars was acute, most such efforts had subsided during the prosperous war and immediate postwar years. But now, more than ever, the message of downtown's advantages had to be trumpeted to the public. Newspaper, radio, and even some television advertising were marshaled for the occasion. Catchy slogans were generated to drive home the range and quantity of goods: "Downtown Has Everything"; "It's Smart To Go To Town." Many such campaigns had special events several times a year or even more often to attract crowds. Increasing night hours to stay competitive with shopping centers was implemented in a number of cities. Frequently, too, arrangements were made to provide free or discounted parking and public transportation. Through such inducements retailers believed that they could reacquaint customers who had moved to the periphery and attract newcomers with all that the core shopping district had to offer. Once that experience had taken place, many boosters thought that regular patronage would follow.[27] Just how this strategy equated with that of expanding the market through branch development was never outlined, at least not in print, despite the optimistic scenarios offered by Webber and other leaders in the field.

Department store executives were key figures in orchestrating promotional organizations and their activities. These retailers not only had the managerial experience, they enjoyed prestige within their communities. They also had some of the biggest investments in downtown and stood to lose mightily if the core no longer held its public appeal. Foster Hunter, Hudson's treasurer, was president of Detroit's Central Business Association, which, beginning in 1954, developed highly successful events that were admired nationwide. Alex Lewis, president of Macy's in Kansas City, headed the Downtown Unlimited Committee of the Chamber of Commerce. Likewise, the president of Titche-Goettinger was named chairman of the Downtown Dallas Committee. Operation Downtown Youngstown was launched by a $50,000 pledge from the city's two major department stores in 1955. Similarly, a coalition of leading department and specialty store heads formed a group called Downtown St. Louis to expand promotional activities three years later.[28]

But getting retailers to collaborate, contributing money as well as time and expertise, could prove at least as challenging downtown as it had in the regional mall. While collective efforts yielded substantial results with consumers in such centers as Chicago, Detroit, and Kansas City, they could prove ineffectual elsewhere. Cincinnati, for example, gained some notoriety in this sphere. The Retail Merchants Association, formed by executives of that city's major department stores, achieved very little at first, owing to the pervasive belief that competition from outlying areas would not emerge. Some years later, a *Women's Wear Daily* writer commented that "downtown's competition is from within. Conflicting interests have stymied move after move." By the fall of 1956, Puckett, in town to dedicate Allied's Swifton Center, the city's first regional mall, warned that downtown interests had to unite or risk decline.[29] Cincinnati was not a unique case. An organization also called the Retail Merchants Association in Baltimore refused to participate in Downtown Day, initiated by a large number of stores in 1954, because its membership was citywide and Hutzler's, the city's premier department store, opposed the event because it had a branch in suburban Towson. Following its second annual celebration, the event was postponed indefinitely because of lackluster results. Hutzler's chairman urged extensive building modernization to "save downtown," a program he sought to stimulate through another group, the Association of Commerce.[30] Even when merchants were in agreement on a plan, problems occurred in coordinating efforts. In Providence, for example, a 1958 initiative for downtown stores to adopt a six-day, two-night schedule failed to be synchronized, with the two major department stores among the least responsive to the program.[31]

Early efforts to revitalize downtown were harshly criticized by James Rouse, who was beginning to play an important role in the advancement of the enclosed regional mall but was also involved in, and no doubt frustrated by, the fractured approach to renewal in his adopted city of Baltimore. Addressing department store executives and other retail leaders at the annual convention of the National Retail Dry Goods Association (NRDGA) in January 1957 he minced no words: "I believe that downtown has not yet begun to feel the real impact of the forces working against it. So far the battle for downtown has been waged against the symptoms, not the sources, of its troubles." That campaign had been a "panicky, piecemeal defense consisting largely of tricks, gimmicks and promotional ideas plus a few parking garages and one-way streets." His salvo was reinforced by Victor Gruen: "Sure, many little things are being done. . . . Here a parking garage. . . . There parking meters. . . . Dollar days are being arranged. Sidewalks are being painted green, pink, red and other exciting color schemes. Free bus rides. . . . Advertising campaigns. . . . New lights. . . . Cadillacs are being given away. Parades are being held." But: "All those promotional measures manage for a day or so to bring more people and more cars downtown, increasing traffic jams . . . , and leaving most of the one-time patrons with their minds clearly made up: One time and never again." Both speakers called for comprehensive measures to rectify the situation. Gruen believed that the fully integrated approach to planning employed in developing the regional mall should form the basis for revitalizing downtown. Rouse delineated basic measures to be taken, including making a full assessment of the proper function of a modern city center and giving municipal leaders new powers to implement bold, sweeping plans.[32] None of their proposals was new, yet the frankness of their challenge, the esteem with which both developer and architect were held by retailers, and the increasingly gloomy situation in many city centers helped catalyze some merchants into more concerted action.

Indeed, the shift to a comprehensive approach in the retail sphere was already gaining momentum. Beginning in the Depression, retailers, along with many others with downtown business interests, lobbied for large-scale redevelopment of blighted portions of the central district. The work of Pittsburgh's Allegheny Conference, which was formed in 1945 by an unusual alliance of business and government leaders, had yielded the most tangible manifestation of that approach to date. Renewal efforts focused on the edges of downtown, where blight was deemed the greatest. In addition to a highway system that made the core easily accessible by motor vehicles for the first time, peripheral land was cleared for office and apartment buildings as well as for open space that gave the skyline a distinctly modern profile. By contrast, undertakings in the heart of downtown were of a more individual nature, building on rather than transforming the existing fabric. These included a soaring office tower for Alcoa Aluminum (1951–53) and a 200,000-square-foot addition to Kaufmann's department store (1953–55), as well as a series of parking facilities (see figs. 65, 128). Downtown did not require remaking, in other words, only bolstering at identified weak points.[33] The efforts of Chicago's State Street Council, an alliance of stores and building owners, also attracted widespread attention among retailers. While initiating collective advertisements and other promotions, the organization embraced a range of transportation and housing issues. In 1946, it helped inaugurate a study that eventually led to the city's much-touted municipal parking program. Several years later it played a leading role in advancing legislation to create new tracts of middle-class housing nearby. The organization was also vocal in calling for downtown renewal to be a collective effort, stressing that merchants could not turn the situation around by themselves. Council president Randall Cooper became a national advocate for retailers in the call for cooperative and comprehensive strategies for renewal.[34]

Retailers and other businessmen joined forces to develop a long-term blueprint for revitalization in at least several major cities. Downtown Denver, for example, was formed in 1954 to develop such a plan. Its first project was to secure the services of the Washington-based Urban Land Institute, which had long championed downtown redevelopment, to assess the scope and nature of problems affecting the precinct. Less than three years later a sweeping plan for remaking the core was unveiled as a public-private initiative, produced by the city planning office and local architects.[35] By that time Kansas City's 1943 master plan for downtown was rapidly advancing with vigorous support from the Downtown Committee, an autonomous unit of the Chamber of Commerce and headed by the president of Emery Bird Thayer. While many parties were involved, the committee took a prominent role. In 1952 it established the Redevelopment Corporation with capital stock of $2 million. Working with the municipal government, that entity became the agent for rebuilding the deteriorated area east of downtown into an office and light industrial park.[36]

To facilitate such endeavors, the NRDGA (renamed National Retail Merchants Association [NRMA] in 1957), launched a program of its own in 1955. Incoming president Philip Talbott, senior vice president of Woodward & Lothrop, called for a "frontal attack" on a wide range of contributing urban issues. Through this work he sought to achieve accord on the nature of the problem—no small task in itself—and to develop a basic, comprehensive strategy that would guide individual cities not as advanced in this sphere as Pittsburgh or Chicago. A Downtown Development Committee was established, with Sidney Baer, vice chairman of Stix, Baer & Fuller, as its head. Within four months the group had cosponsored a national conference. Both Talbott and Baer spoke widely on the need for strong, dedicated, private-sector groups to focus on a long-term, full-scale plan for downtown; otherwise decline would only increase. Establishing a set coda for action, however, proved more challenging than anticipated. Two years later, the NRDGA called for a White House conference so that the subject could be explored further at a high level. While the general message continued to be enunciated vigorously, the organization also established an awards program, hoping to influence by example. Equally important, the committee continued to hold panel sessions at annual meetings, where key figures could underscore the issues. If nothing else, the NRDGA sharpened its constituents' consciousness of the complexity of the challenge before them.[37]

The agenda of the Downtown Development Committee and local organizations with similar purposes entailed issues that had been identified for some time in Pittsburgh and elsewhere as key to downtown revitalization.[38] Foremost among these was improving access to the city center with high-speed, limited access highways. Through this system, proponents argued, shoppers could easily drive from outlying residential areas, cutting travel time to a fraction of what it had been. Plans of this kind had been drafted for Los Angeles and Detroit, among other cities, before the federal interstate highway program made millions of dollars available for the purpose nationwide. Kansas City was among the most aggressive in pursuing federal funds early on to construct a loop around the core connected to north-south and east-west highways—a network that retailers saw as ideal for attracting their clientele. The failure of St. Louis to act accordingly, wailed Baer, was causing downtown to stagnate. The fact that these highways were also connecting consumers to regional malls and that they quickly became congested themselves did not enter the discussion. Retailers along with many other interests continued to place these new arterials at the top of their list of needs well into the 1960s.[39]

Equally important was reducing traffic congestion once motorists got off the highway and onto downtown streets. Eliminating curbside parking, converting streetcar lines to bus lines, and changing two-way streets to one-way streets were all widely implemented measures during the 1950s. Providing adequate off-street parking was considered just as important, but it was much more difficult to realize. The failure of the parking industry to meet this need was the primary reason many department store executives undertook building their own facilities, but they also recognized that parking had to be satisfactory for the precinct as a whole if it was to remain strong. Municipal parking authorities were a frequently pursued solution, but such measures were bound to meet fierce opposition from parking facility operators. Initiatives in Pittsburgh, Chicago, and a number of other cities made significant inroads on the parking problem. In many other places, however, the problem was ongoing.[40]

All the focus on accommodating motorists, some parties maintained, was avoiding the issue. Most shoppers still came downtown by public transportation. If transit systems were measurably improved, store patronage would swell. E. Willard Dennis, a director of Rochester's huge Sibley, Lindsay & Curr, remarked in 1958: "Strangely enough, retailers, who stand to gain the most from good public transit, have heretofore shown too little interest." Some colleagues shared his view. A year later George Dayton, executive vice president of the Dayton Company, speaking at the American Transit Association's annual convention, stressed that good mass transit was the lifeblood of a strong downtown. "Transit men and downtown executives," he urged, "should join forces in every city to develop plans for speeding up mass transit." Such improvements, a transit official noted, would cost far less than the "hopeless effort to accommodate the automobile downtown."[41] But by 1960, most such systems were struggling just to maintain the status quo. Municipal authorities had been created to take over numerous failing transit companies, yet cities were strapped for the funds to make the substantial investment while ridership continued to decline as automobile use became ever more intense.

Attracting the middle class back to the city was another priority for retailers—perhaps more so than for any other contingent. Since department stores, especially, depended on large-scale middle-class patronage, the movement of this group ever farther from the core was cause for alarm. Hopes that this trend would not just abate but actually reverse itself lay behind the frequent predictions in the retail press that outlying areas were reaching a saturation point and that the pleasures of urban life would be rediscovered. Eliminating "blight" from precincts close to the core served a double purpose in this regard. Employing a logic that in retrospect seems remarkably naïve, such action was thought to remove a prime cause of urban decay. At the same time, it cleared the ground for large new projects that would attract middle- and upper-middle-class households in sufficient numbers to affect downtown patronage. Lake Meadows, an enormous project and one of the first of this kind, was begun in 1950 on Chicago's South Side, spurred by the State Street Council. Neighboring projects followed, as did others on the Near North Side over the ensuing fifteen years. By the mid-1960s, Baltimore, Boston, Detroit, Minneapolis, Philadelphia, St. Louis, San Francisco, and Washington were among the cities that had created thousands of middle-class dwelling units through new construction or, much less often, the rehabilitation of existing stock under the auspices of federal Urban Renewal monies.[42] The population gains, however, were minuscule compared to the outmigration, increasingly fueled during the late 1950s and the 1960s by racial and class divisions. A large-scale return to the city by these traditional inhabitants never occurred.[43]

Finally, retailers joined others supporting urban revitalization in urging new office building construction in the core. Office workers of all kinds were an important part of the department store's trade; by substantially augmenting that corps some retailers thought they could keep their downtown stores prospering. The long hiatus in downtown construction between the early 1930s and mid-1950s was a source of acute frustration among merchants; never before had the downtown workforce remained static for so extended a period of time. The development of some new office buildings during the second half of the 1950s was applauded. Following Pittsburgh's example, several cities undertook large-scale projects encompassing areas deemed blighted that were tangent to the existing business core. Philadelphia's Penn Center, the construction of which began in 1956, was heralded as a prototype. Numerous office buildings, shops, and a hotel were built close to both the corridor of department stores along Market Street and to high-end specialty stores along the western blocks of Chestnut and Walnut streets. An alliance of business leaders sponsored the plan for one of the most ambitious additions to the office core, Charles Center (begun 1958), which was intended to link the long-separated retail and office districts of Baltimore. The expansion of Hartford's downtown with Constitution Plaza (1959–63) was orchestrated primarily by the city's insurance companies and was to tie into the enlarged G. Fox and a redeveloped retail core.[44]

Malls

Victor Gruen's criticism of piecemeal downtown renewal was based on more than observation and thought.[45] In March 1956, he presented a remarkable plan for Fort Worth on which he had been working for more than a year. The scheme was commissioned by J. B. Thomas, president of the Texas Electric Service Company and a civic leader, in the hopes that it would spur Fort Worth citizens into stemming the erosion of trade from the core. Gruen's approach was far more radical than the Pittsburgh model. Indeed, his plan called for as complete a reconceptualization of the city center as had ever occurred in the United States (fig. 235). The architect emphatically rejected European models, most obviously the grand urban projects that Le Corbusier had advanced since the 1920s, which still retained currency among many colleagues in the United States as well as abroad. His approach also markedly differed from that employed in English and European city centers that were reconstructed following the devastation of World War II. Instead, Gruen drew from his experience in creating regional malls to devise a scheme that, he claimed, was pragmatic and readily achievable without prohibitive cost. Downtown Fort Worth's compact configuration allowed for the elimination of all motor vehicles. Access would be by freeways, connected by a surface-level belt around the core. Directly tied to the inside of the belt, six enormous parking garages, each holding an average of ten thousand cars, would provide ample space for the workforce, shoppers, and everyone else coming downtown. The walking distance from these facilities to any place in the compound would be no more than six hundred feet. Although the character of the precinct would be dramatically altered through embellished pedestrianways

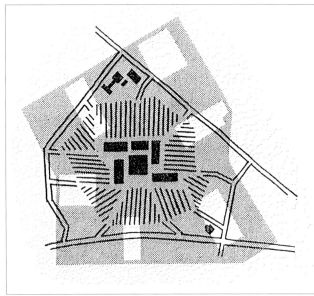

235. Schematic master plan for downtown Fort Worth, Texas (1955–56). Victor Gruen Associates, architects; project.

236. Fort Worth plan, diagram comparing configuration and scale (background, with parking structures in white) with those of Gruen's Northland (line drawing) (*Architectural Forum,* May 1956, 152).

and new construction—greatly increasing retail, office, and hotel space over time—all major existing buildings would be retained. One of the costliest facets of the plan was the system of tunnels servicing the core, but the price tag paled, Gruen maintained, compared to the costs of congestion and efforts to accommodate vehicles in any other way.

Diagrammatically, Gruen's arrangement echoed that designed for Northland; its dimensions were scarcely larger (fig. 236). But the Fort Worth plan was hardly a literal transplantation. Gruen ingeniously adapted lessons learned to be in concert with a wholly urban environment. As the editors of *Architectural Forum* noted in a wildly enthusiastic article, "Perhaps the biggest debt is to the shopping center type of study—the close analysis of the plan's effect on the interests of everyone involved. This is something new for city planning." Praise was also accorded for the plan being essentially a "skeleton"—a framework upon which the details could be developed incrementally by the many private and public parties involved; on the way in which the traffic issue was addressed; on its clarity, logic, and practicality; on its implementation through citizen initiative; on the reintegration of commercial and civic activities; on the freedom of movement accorded to pedestrians, among other attributes. The scheme met with nearly universal acclaim in a wide range of periodicals, becoming perhaps the most extensively publicized city plan in the nation to date. Soon, however, politics and special interests began to undermine the initiative, and although Thomas and some others maintained hope for its realization, the plan was essentially dead three years after its inception.[46] The scope seemed daunting to some observers as well; no other city undertook so extensive a recasting. Yet for some years, Gruen's stillborn plan had a decisive impact on shaping the nature of downtown renewal efforts. Ironically, that influence spurred divisions among retailers and other business interests, planners, and politicians concerning the nature and extent of redevelopment that should occur in the heart of downtown. The proposal to recast the main shopping street as a pedestrian mall became a protagonist in what often was a heated debate.

While Gruen failed to transform Fort Worth, he was at work on a more modest plan that advanced some of the same objectives. Shortly after unveiling the Texas scheme, the architect was commissioned by the Downtown Kalamazoo Planning Committee, an organization of businessmen, to develop a master plan for that Michigan community. Completed in the spring of 1958, the project called for revitalization of a fifty-square-block area over the next twenty-two years. The first component implemented, and the one that received virtually all the public attention, was the pedestrian mall along two blocks of the main (Burdick) street. Opening in August 1959 with a four-day celebration, the Kalamazoo mall was at once hailed as a major step forward in downtown renewal. The project not only heightened awareness of downtown's problems—a $2 million lowering of property value assessments in 1956 among them—but fostered a collaborative spirit among merchants. Property owners bore half the $60,000 cost; shoppers were elated with the product; retailers pleased with the increase in sales.[47] Over the next several years, the mall was extended to additional blocks, but other facets of what Gruen intended to be a comprehensive scheme lagged. The architect soon warned that unto itself a pedestrian mall was not a solution; indeed, without adequate parking facilities, perimeter circulation for motor vehicles, delivery paths, and other coordinated developments to boost the use of the city center, the mall could have a deleterious effect.

Street malls had been proposed for over a decade before Kalamazoo's. The best-known prototype was designed for Rye, New York, in 1946 by Morris Ketchum.[48] The idea remained marginal for some time, however, probably because of the costs entailed, especially those of clearance for new traffic lanes and off-street parking. In European communities, where most residents depended on public transportation, bicycles, and their feet for movement, the mall became a standard feature in the remaking of bombed city centers such as Rotterdam and Coventry and in the creation of centers for new towns such as Vallingby, Tapiola, and Stevenege. Rotterdam's Lijnbaan (1954–56), one of the earliest and most extensive such plans, received considerable coverage in the United States and probably rekindled the interest among planners and architects, including Gruen.[49] As the decline of downtowns continued and the need for projects that affected the whole precinct began to gain acceptance, the mall became a subject of widespread discussion. Such conversions were prominently featured at NRDGA's first conference on downtown renewal in April 1955. The salvation of the downtown shopping district, maintained Brookings Institution transportation authority Wilfred Owen the following year, was to develop the core as a series of malls. Spurred, too, by the Fort Worth scheme, many planners and architects were developing proposals for cities and towns alike nationwide. Schematic designs were prepared for Minneapolis and St. Paul in 1956; Denver, Detroit, Milwaukee, and Philadelphia in 1957.[50] The degree of interest in such projects was reflected by the reception of a four-block temporary mall in Toledo that opened only a week before Kalamazoo's. The scheme attracted delegates from over 230 cities before the fourth week. A month later, a *Women's Wear Daily* writer remarked on the extent of "pilgrimages to the urban redevelopment Mecca which Toledo has become." Erected over a weekend at a cost of $15,000, the mall was intended to last forty-five days. Its popularity led to a three-month extension and a second seasonal trial launched in July 1960. By that year's end, however, the experiment was dead. Retailers had mixed opinions on the matter, but many agreed that challenges such as parking had to be addressed before a permanent mall could be considered.[51]

At a time when most metropolitan areas boasted no more than one or two regional malls, some downtown advocates may have believed that an analogous reconfiguration of the retail core would be an effective instrument of parity. Yet the downtown mall was the subject of broad skepticism as well as of widespread adulation. The editors of *Architectural Forum* reported in February 1958 that nearly one hundred cities and towns were considering such a feature. Numerous communities followed Toledo's lead in erecting a temporary mall to test public reaction and the impact on sales. The interest among retailers was sufficiently strong to prompt Fairchild News Service, publisher of *Women's Wear Daily*, to conduct a survey of the phenomenon in 1959, drawing from its sources in over thirty cities. The resulting report concluded: "For the most part, pilot malls have been short-lived promotional gimmicks. . . . Rarely have they been of sufficient duration to supply valid data on the effectiveness of the mall concept." Furthermore, these endeavors were not integral parts of a broader redevelopment program. The Toledo experiment was singled out as a telling example: How much was the draw due to novelty? How did inadequate parking affect the project? What was the impact of hot weather? Such questions had not been asked and certainly had no authoritative answers.[52] Shortly thereafter the publisher of the New York–based *Downtown Idea Exchange* wrote that although his organization had long championed the mall, he was "opposed to the way in which the mall concept has been footballed. What can be a solid idea is too often being considered a mere gimmick." He had "never seen an idea catch on so quickly. The appeal . . . is so basic that it almost seems to be a heavenly salvation for downtown." Such "sensationalism . . . may ruin any value the mall has as a long-range improvement." Downtown malls were not appropriate for every city, he added. Such a proposal had to be thoroughly researched in each case and always be part of a more comprehensive plan. Gruen contemptuously likened the faddish embrace of malls "to a woman who buys fashion accessories before she has the money to buy a dress."[53]

Major retailers for the most part remained wary of downtown malls as a key agent for revitalization. Those who came to understand the complexities of the renewal process saw the challenges in implementing a mall—financing and close working relationships between property owners, merchants, and public officials among them. Other facets of renewal took priority in the minds of some. Parking stood high as a first step. The only factor that enabled the 1959–60 conversion of Miami Beach's Lincoln Road into a mall, accounts reiterated, was the existence of a 1,000-car municipal parking deck close by. C. Virgil Martin, the outspoken president of Carson Pirie Scott, advocated that an increase in office space downtown and housing nearby were essential to stimulate infrastructural improvements. For some, the time taken to realize a major scheme was too long. Commenting on a plan to redevelop downtown Kansas City with a mall, which would be fully implemented by 1980, Emery, Bird, Thayer president Herbert Wilson dryly noted, "This is not 1980," arguing that there were less expensive and more expe-

237. Howard Street mall, Baltimore, schematic proposal (1959). David Wallace, architect; project. (*Baltimore Post*, 15 May 1959, 1.)

ditious ways to improve the draw of the city center. William Austin, manager of the Kansas City Merchants Association, was blunter. Emulating regional malls was "like the tail wagging the dog." Building a mall downtown was a "huge, expensive problem." The public might like the results, but "closing the streets is not a service to the stores." Similarly, Rouse's repeated calls for wholesale change downtown—the kind of change many mall proponents believed necessary— were openly rebuffed at the 1960 NRMA convention by leaders of downtown business associations who called for more "realistic" strategies, branding large-scale clearance as an experimental measure "that would inflict severe financial damage" to many downtown businesses.[54]

Events in Baltimore around 1960 were a telling indicator of the suspicion and sometimes restrained hostility with which leading retailers came to view large-scale redevelopment plans. That city's Charles Center project, which Rouse touted as exemplary of the kind of transformation the urban core required, was widely heralded by others as well. Spearheaded by the Greater Baltimore Committee, a group of business leaders patterned after Pittsburgh's Allegheny Conference, the scheme skirted the federal urban renewal program, expediting the process and demonstrating the efficacy of projects driven strictly by market demand. For designers and planners the scheme was an exemplar of high standards in both their fields. It was also praised for the extent to which private and public sectors cooperated toward a common goal.[55] But Charles Center triggered a somewhat different reaction from merchants. Once the scheme was under way, *Women's Wear Daily* reported that two hundred businesses would be lost, seventy of them retail establishments, including a number of national chain

units. Space in the main shopping area immediately to the west was limited, and the Charles Center plan would take a decade to realize. Moreover, the scheme would isolate a fading assemblage of elegant specialty shops along Charles Street, effectively ending its viability as a retail node. Indeed, Charles Center could well separate the existing business and retail centers by destroying an admittedly weak link between them rather than taking more decisive steps to bolster that area. One proposal to improve the relationship entailed a moving sidewalk; another limiting Howard Street, the principal retail corridor, to public transit vehicles. Department store executives, the report noted, "do not take kindly to this plan," because they were certain it would erode motorist patronage.[56] The situation came to a head in March 1959 when David Wallace, director of the Greater Baltimore Committee's Planning Council and chief architect of the plan, unveiled a design for a two-level, raised and enclosed mall on Howard Street that would connect to Charles Center via a second mall on Lexington Street, in the process converting the "central shopping core into a regional shopping center" (fig. 237). Included, too, was a 1,500-car garage. The cost would run over $2.5 million. Wallace may have wished to placate the department store heads by retaining vehicular traffic at ground level while connecting the four major emporia by the elevated pedestrianway. It was a realistic scheme, he argued, that could be implemented at once. Retail executives were cool. Martin Kohn, president of Hochschild Kohn, made a point of stating: "We certainly would give such a proposal thorough study though we have not yet been asked to participate in such a venture."[57]

Participate they did thereafter. Hochschild Kohn and the other three major department stores requested outside review of the plan by nationally recognized architects and planners. Presenting its conclusions in July 1960, the group found the mall premature. Before any such scheme was to be implemented, they maintained, four major improvements had to be in place: a highway system allowing easy access to downtown; off-street parking facilities for an additional three thousand cars—half again the current capacity; an updated public transit system serving the area; and provisions for good pedestrian circulation throughout the retail center. This stunning defeat reflected what were likely inner conflicts among those dedicated to revitalizing the core.[58] Hochschild Kohn's chairman, Walter Sondheim, also headed the city's Urban Renewal and Housing Agency, while the Hecht Company's executive vice president, Jay Jefferson Miller, was president of the Committee for Downtown, a group generally in alliance with the Greater Baltimore Committee. Retailers were happy to benefit from the large amount of additional office space Charles Center promised to give but remained cautious about major interventions and were opposed when such endeavors encompassed the shopping district. The divisions were apparently strong enough to prevent any effective tie between the new business area and the retail core from being developed.

The conflicts surrounding the street mall were thus symptomatic of those pertaining to a full-scale remaking of the retail core. Gruen argued against the mall as a panacea, implemented without the other components of a master plan, but many retailers remained leery of any such plan that went beyond the less intrusive approach taken in Pittsburgh. This view appears to have been sufficiently widespread that substantial reconfigurations of downtown retail districts were far more the exception than the rule for some years. Even as part of a less ambitious plan, the downtown mall was seldom adopted for large cities. Not until the late 1960s and 1970s, when downtown retailing experienced a far more precipitous decline than it had during the postwar years, did merchants accept a more radical tack.[59] Department store executives, who tended to be leaders among downtown committees and have the most power to steer organized initiatives and defeat others of which they did not approve, ultimately played a major role in not radically altering the shopping core during the 1950s and early 1960s, even as they continued to reshape outlying areas through the development of regional malls. The embrace of pronounced change on one hand was matched by an innate conservatism on the other. The few large revitalization projects in which these emporia were important participants were not in major cities like Baltimore and Pittsburgh, but in ones of more moderate size. These endeavors suggest that resisting wholesale change downtown was not wholly unwarranted.

Urban Renewal

Initially rivaling Charles Center as a pacesetter for downtown renewal, New Haven's Church Street Redevelopment Area differed in having retail functions as the primary component of the plan. Furthermore, the Church Street project was tied to a comprehensive plan that was for the most part realized by taking full advantage of the then massive federal program for clearance. This ambitious agenda was launched and for many years driven by the city's tireless reform mayor, Richard Lee, who expressed his determination to see New Haven again serve as the dominant regional hub. Church Street was praised for its integral relationship with this broad vision; it was also among the most important facets of Lee's plan to make New Haven a national model of urban regeneration. In the mid-1950s, downtown New Haven had a significantly weaker retail center than did Baltimore and many other cities. During his successful 1953 bid for office, Lee often referred to New Haven as a "dying city." When his lieutenant for redevelopment, Edward Logue, reiterated the phrase two years later, the head of Malley's, the city's largest department store, joined other mer-

238. Church Street Redevelopment Project, business center, Church, Temple, and Chapel streets and North Frontage Road, New Haven, Connecticut, preliminary scheme (1957). John Graham & Company, architects. Existing Malley's department store outlined on left.

chants in vehement protest. Still, New Haven had half the retail sales of Hartford, a city of the same size, where G. Fox enjoyed statewide dominance. Suburban Hamden was also fast emerging as a serious competitor. Sears, Roebuck had recently moved there from Church Street. Two years before, Gamble-Desmond, a small downtown department store, had closed for good.[60]

To make New Haven competitive, Lee orchestrated a bold plan for downtown, which he unveiled in June 1957 (fig. 238). The scheme included three blocks between Church and Temple streets, tying the city core with new limited-access highways—the Connecticut Turnpike (and later I-91) via a spur, the Oak Street Connector. Chapel Street, the northern boundary of the project area, was the principal retail corridor. The proposed $85 million complex comprised an office and hotel block, headquarters for a major bank, parking space for fifteen hundred cars, and an extensive retail area that included a new department store. Occupying the southeast corner of Chapel and Temple streets, Malley's was the sole existing facility not slated for demolition, but the proposed ensemble had no relation to it. Lee had secured Roger L. Stevens as developer; his company had a vast portfolio of real estate holdings nationwide, but he had never realized a new project of this size and complexity.[61]

The plan met with widespread approval among government officials, as well as civic and some business leaders. Lee emphasized that the undertaking would cost the city little. Close to $40 million would come from federal loans and grants. The New Haven Parking Authority and capital improvements would cover more than $10 million. Private investment would run $34 million. The city's share would be slightly over half a million dollars, which would

239. Church Street Redevelopment Project, view showing new Edward Malley Company department store (1959–62), John Graham Associates, architects, demolished; R. H. Macy & Company department store (1962–64), Abbott, Merkt & Company, architects and engineers, demolished. Temple Street parking garage (behind the stores to the left), Paul Rudolph, architect. Undeveloped block (above). Photo 1964.

be recovered through increased taxes once the project was completed. Part of the mayor's strategy was rapid execution. At the announcement ceremony, Lee declared: "This is no dream. This is not just a set of hopes; this is something that has been through the mill—the mill of Federal processing—and is ready to go." By the start of the next decade, he believed, New Haven would be the envy of the nation. The necessary local approvals were quickly secured. Land acquisition began in January 1958.[62]

Early on, however, the process began to unravel. Six weeks after the scheme was presented to the public, concerns began to be voiced by affected merchants. Although the issue was not raised in the press, Lee had orchestrated the Church Street plan to please federal authorities rather than to create a well-structured matrix for business growth. The approach that business leaders, including retailers, had concretized in Pittsburgh was radically altered. Not only was the process here in the hands of the mayor, municipal planners, and outside parties with whom they contracted, the agenda had only a vague programmatic base. A federal agency, not business needs, was the ultimate arbiter of how the project was conceptualized. City authorities could not answer any of the merchants' questions about the specific nature of the proposed retail complex—including whether those displaced could become tenants—because the plan remained largely hypothetical. Sentiment mounted that downtown businesses were being ignored during the months that followed. A lawsuit by one property owner was filed that October and was not settled until a year and a half later, during which time no work could proceed save clearance of most of the site.[63]

Legal opposition was not the only problem. Stevens experienced protracted difficulties in securing financing and in luring a new department store to the project—in all likelihood because the plan was so amorphous. Finally in 1959 he turned to Malley's, hoping to persuade its leadership to relocate in new quarters. Even though Malley executives had been cool to the project and had recently invested about $1 million in their plant, they entered an agreement that September. Within a month a new master plan was developed, making full use of the block Malley's currently occupied.[64] The century-old company's location on the main business street was traded for one three blocks away at the southeast edge of downtown. The appeal of replacing an antiquated assemblage of buildings with a brand-new facility on a site that would be closest to highway connections and parking facilities may have been the decisive factor. Regardless, the complicated land transfers involved took nearly a year to consummate. Stevens still had trouble in securing funding. Only Yale University's pledge to underwrite the project saved it from abandonment.[65] Yet even with this new component in place, the overall plan remained schematic.

Lee, Stevens, and the many others involved hoped that Malley's commitment to build would spur other businesses to do likewise. The department store's decision did induce the Parking Authority to begin work on its mammoth garage. At the May 1960 groundbreaking, the ever-optimistic mayor proclaimed the era as the Golden Age of New Haven. Still, no further progress was made. When Stevens's long-standing overtures to lure Macy's to the project faltered, Lee stepped in and conducted negotiations himself. In September 1962, one month before Malley's and the garage opened, he triumphantly announced that Macy's was in the final stages of striking a deal. This time, work progressed on schedule. Perhaps unbeknownst to the mayor, Macy's leadership saw the New Haven site as a beachhead for an aggressive expansion program into New England. When it opened two years later, the 321,000-square-foot store was the second largest in the state (fig. 239).[66] Over 560,000 square feet of retail space had been added to downtown; Connecticut now had a major New York department store, rising side by side with New Haven's most venerable counterpart. Yet the big emporia stood in isolation. The third and arguably most crucial block, facing Chapel Street, remained empty. Stevens's continued inability to lure investment led the city to secure four additional partners who in effect took charge. Preliminary plans for a complex of hotel, office building, and shops, the latter along a two-tiered, enclosed mall, were released in March 1964. This final component,

232 | STORES IN THE CITY

christened Chapel Square, did not open until March 1967, nearly ten years after initial plan was unveiled with such fanfare (fig. 240).[67]

Even when complete, the complex suffered from shortcomings. Stevens and the others involved appear to have had little experience in retail development or urban planning. John Graham & Company, the architecture firm most responsible for the overall layout, did not possess the urbanistic knowledge or sensitivities of Gruen's office nor did it have a concrete program with which to work.[68] The linear configuration of the project area paralleled that of many regional malls. Here, however, an underlying determinant appears to have been placing the multideck garage close to the highway system while also allowing it to feed directly into the several levels of the projected facilities. As developed, the direct connection between stores and garage at several levels, a relationship perhaps inspired by the Hecht Company's idiosyncratic Parkington a decade earlier, was a source of much favorable attention.[69] Placing Malley's as the southern terminus also made sense in terms of drawing pedestrian shoppers through the complex from Chapel Street at the opposite end. Macy's, however, insisted on comparable garage accessibility, which necessitated placing its store next to Malley's, thus leaving the third block for other shops by default. Without the garage in this latter segment, tenants had the dual disadvantage of not being bracketed by the big emporia and not being as close to parking. The optimal arrangement of retail space never seems to have been the governing factor in the design. As realized, the complex suffered from a piecemeal approach to planning.

To the dismay of some neighboring merchants, the entire complex was inward looking, with few perceptual ties to any of the surrounding blocks. Indeed, its visual effect was to bifurcate the existing retail core. Lee believed, rather naively, that the size of the complex would not only attract a critical mass of shoppers, but that once they had arrived, induce them to freely roam throughout the retail district. Moreover, businesses that had to relocate as a result of the project often were not adequately compensated. "We were all hurt financially," one merchant told a *Wall Street Journal* reporter. "We received the maximum federal allowance for moving, but it didn't nearly cover expenses. It cost me nearly $20,000 to relocate and I received a check for $2,500." Many New Haven retailers felt ignored during the planning and disengaged from, if not set back by, the product.[70] The Church Street Redevelopment Area had been conceived as part of a large, ostensibly holistic program, but its core relationship and arguably its rationale belonged to a broadly defined renewal agenda, not to the specifics of retail functions or to the urban fabric into which they were placed. It was not the regional mall transplanted, as it has often been accused of being, for it lacked the careful planning that went into the

240. Church Street Redevelopment Project, Chapel Square, Chapel, Church, Crown, and Temple streets (1964–67). Lathrop Douglass, architect; William Tabler, architect of hotel (right). Presentation drawing, 1964.

siting, arrangement, and complexion of such projects and had the additional disadvantage of existing in spite of its environs rather than enhancing them. It was the antithesis of Gruen's vision for Fort Worth.

A parallel outcome occurred, albeit for other reasons, with commercial revitalization efforts in downtown Sacramento, California. Sacramento was likewise held as a model for urban renewal at the outset. A redevelopment survey began there in 1948. The following year the City Plan Commission hired the distinguished Los Angeles–based architects Richard Neutra and Robert Alexander to develop a hypothetical plan. That scheme and most of the work that followed over the next two decades focused on a large area that was deemed blighted on the city's west side. Of foremost concern were the blocks lining the boulevard that led from the Sacramento River to the Capitol, which were considered an embarrassing image for the primary route to a major seat of government. Similarly, blocks to the north were felt to undermine the main business district. A substantial portion of this area—fifteen square blocks—was targeted for clearance and redevelopment by the close of January 1954.[71] That measure was probably what attracted the interest of San Francisco developer and real estate magnate Ben Swig, who offered a sweeping proposal for remaking a part of the area six months later. The scheme entailed construction of a "modern retail shopping center" in the six square blocks along K Street, the city's main retail corridor, between Second and Fifth streets, within the targeted precinct. K Street would be transformed into a pedestrian mall, as Neutra and Alexander had envisioned. But Swig was equally concerned with tying this complex to the main shopping district, which lay along K Street several blocks to the east. The Fifth Street boundary of the urban renewal area was determined by "blight," not what would integrate new with existing

241. Schematic proposal for pedestrian mall, K Street between Second and Twelfth streets, Sacramento (1954). Project (*Sacramento Bee*, 1 July 1954, 1).

development on K Street. To achieve the latter end, Swig wished to extend the mall another seven blocks, including those that formed the spine of the retail core between Eighth and Twelfth streets. To mitigate the length of this ten-block path he proposed a pair of moving sidewalks, one for each direction, sheltered by a canopy in the center of the pedestrianway (fig. 241). Swig maintained he had the wherewithal to undertake the $10 million project right away.[72]

City officials greeted Swig's offer enthusiastically, but business interests were less receptive. The manager of the Chamber of Commerce acerbically commented that "local Businessmen can do something like this just as well." Swig bent over backward to placate, emphasizing that his proposals would come at no cost to the municipal government. He also offered to serve as an advisor if local parties wished to seize the initiative. The overriding need, he stressed, was quick, decisive action. Almost no new construction had occurred downtown in years, while businesses were proliferating in outlying areas: "I know of no city the size of Sacramento with as great a decentralization of its business district." F. W. Woolworth announced that it was interested in participating in the scheme. Swig also secured a statement of interest from Sears, Roebuck, which was otherwise planning to build on the urban periphery. Remarkably, the scheme was allowed to die through indecision.[73] Leading merchants apparently were agreeable to redevelopment of K Street's western blocks, but not to change within their own immediate area. A degree of hostility seems to have existed among retailers toward any large-scale project, even one with a sound program.[74] Swig was the first of several prominent developers to commit to revitalizing the commercial core who eventually had nothing to show for their efforts save frustration.

After Swig's rebuff, no concrete initiative for remaking part of K Street surfaced over the next six years. Voters rejected a $1.5 million bond issue for the city's share of the west side's redevelopment in November 1954. To advance their case, city officials decided on a novel alternative procedure: have the redevelopment agency float tax revenue bonds. A master plan for the fifteen-block precinct anchored to the Capitol axis and dubbed Capitol Mall was completed the following August and quickly approved by the necessary authorities. Accord was reached for the federal government's share of implementing the project in April 1956.[75] Despite the ensuing recession, William Zeckendorf, the flamboyant, innovative, and remarkably capable head of Webb & Knapp in New York, expressed interest in undertaking the K Street portion of the area. Zeckendorf had proved himself a master at creating location—to see vast potential in a site that possessed much less current value. As the developer of Roosevelt Field he was also becoming experienced in large-scale retail planning.[76] Like Swig, Zeckendorf understood the need to extend the scope of the work rather than build a large retail facility in isolation. Zeckendorf's bid was conditional on having the urban renewal area extend east to Seventh Street. The City Council approved this measure four months later, but for reasons that remain unclear, his initiative floundered. Calls for a comprehensive study of the retail district were made, but no concrete action was taken until Macy's began to express interest in K Street some two years later.[77]

The California division of Macy's was attracted to Sacramento because of its burgeoning population and its economic stability. Macy's California leadership was impressed with the sweeping urban renewal plans, and the fact that Zeckendorf was still nominally involved may have enhanced the situation. Aspects of the area's two regional shopping centers, for which construction began in 1959, may not have seemed desirable, or Macy's may not have been allowed to participate. Furthermore, most divisions of the company retained a firm commitment to the urban core as the optimal location in relatively small cities such as New Haven; Wichita and Topeka, Kansas; and Augusta and Macon, Georgia. In these places a large, centrally placed store could still enjoy a dominance that no one outlying location afforded.[78] After months of study, Macy's made an offer on a square block in the redevelopment area in May 1960, but the offer came with conditions. Store officials had to be satisfied with the route of, and access from, the freeway (I-70), slated to pass through the western edge of downtown. Two blocks of temporary parking had to be provided by the city until permanent facilities were in operation. Finally, Macy's needed assurance that no department store larger than 100,000 square feet—half the size of its proposed building—would be constructed on K Street in the two adjacent eastern blocks.[79] Complaints from local merchants quickly arose

242. Schematic proposal for "West End Commercial Complex," J, L, Third, and Seventh streets, Sacramento (1961–62). Skidmore, Owing & Merrill, architects; project. View of model, showing Macy's at upper left.

over the last two provisions. The matter of parking was especially volatile, with some store owners complaining that it was unfair to compete with an emporium that offered free parking. In a compromise, which Macy's accepted, the City Council proposed to have the city purchase the lots from the redevelopment agency and open them to the public. Other needed adjustments prolonged negotiations for a year. Federal officials feared that the temporary parking lots might be kept indefinitely and pressed for a master plan of the commercial corridor. Macy's leadership did not stipulate construction of the mall, but clearly it was an important means of linking the site with the shopping core.

In July 1961—seven years after Swig's proposal—the Redevelopment Agency commissioned the San Francisco office of Skidmore, Owings & Merrill to prepare a detailed plan for K Street within the urban renewal area and concurrently gave preliminary approval to Macy's project.[80] Encompassing eight square blocks, the SOM scheme was epic in its scale, rivaling the most ambitious proposals for commercial development of the era. With five large parking garages framing the periphery, an array of retail and other business facilities, including a multistory office building, formed what was tantamount to a new city center (fig. 242). The extent of square footage seemed to reflect the most optimistic projections of a resurgent downtown's capacity to usurp the growth of outlying commercial development. Even if the demand had existed, how such a plan would affect the existing business core to the east was not delineated. Yet the great scope of the proposals appears to have set the tone for what municipal authorities and developers alike would try to create for the site during the better part of the decade that followed.

Once final approval was given to Macy's by the agency eight months later, more opposition was voiced at the City Council hearing over the closing of portions of two side streets to accommodate the store and the adjacent mall. "I do not see," intoned one councilman, "why we have to bend over backwards for Macy's or any other organization to bring them into this town. I cannot see how they can come in here and ask for this." Colleagues fumed that the dispute ignored years of planning, which included approval of the SOM plan a month previous. The campaign to ensure approval that followed met with success. Macy's got the official sanction to build in early May 1962, more than two years after the company's interest in the city was first made public. Construction began soon thereafter. The store opened to much fanfare in November 1963; however, it remained a behemoth in isolation for some time (fig. 243).[81] Even the municipally sponsored pedestrianway along K Street that connected the emporium to the heart of the shopping district several blocks away was delayed by the failure of developers to consummate their proposals.

Reynolds Metals Company was the first concern to embark on the K Street corridor since Zeckendorf, announcing the venture in February 1964. But Reynolds soon bowed out, and over two years elapsed before Tishman Realty & Construction Company committed to the project. The New York–based giant took the scheme much further than any of its predecessors, commissioning Victor Gruen to prepare plans for an elaborate mall, with sunken court and multistory office building spanning its width. The company's spokesman also pledged to realize in two years what he initially calculated would take seven. Yet this developer, too, encountered difficulties, not the least of which entailed plans

243. View of downtown Sacramento, after 1963. At left center: R. H. Macy Company department store, K, L, Fourth, and Fifth streets (1960–63), John S. Bolles, architects. At right center: downtown retail district.

for a second large department store close to Macy's. Failure to secure a tenant for this emporium, along with numerous other problems, caused Tishman to withdraw in September 1967.[82] A local business group, Downtown Plaza Properties, was formed thereafter to continue the effort. After much wrangling with local officials, a scheme for a retail complex to the *west* of Macy's was approved by the Redevelopment Agency in June 1968. Plans were unveiled over a year later, but it, too, failed to materialize.[83]

In the end, no major project was launched. The lack of interest among K Street merchants and other business interests remained an underlying factor. Throughout the process, Sacramento's mayor had experienced difficulty in even scheduling a meeting among these parties, and an initiative to visit the new Fulton Mall in downtown Fresno failed to raise the necessary airfare until an airline donated its services. With prospects for new large-scale construction slim, work finally began on the block of the mall abutting Macy's toward the close of 1967.[84] For a decade, Macy's operated apart from other retail activity, surrounded by cleared land. Eventually, some small-scale retail development was realized, but it fell far short of transforming K Street into a strong, unified retail corridor. Although the particulars differed, Sacramento's redevelopment was like New Haven's in the disconnection between the public-sector agenda and the business sector's inclinations. Under the circumstances, over a quarter century's worth of planning and political maneuvering had not been able to accomplish the equivalent of a regional mall, which routinely took three years or less to realize on the metropolitan periphery.

One reason Zeckendorf may have stepped back once he grasped the extent of the quagmire in Sacramento was the long-standing frustration he had experienced in Denver. His Courthouse Square project in the Mile-High City underscored that even one of the nation's most ingenious, well-financed, and powerful real estate developers working independent of government renewal programs could find the task arduous and costly. In 1945, Zeckendorf purchased the land formerly occupied by the courthouse and situated in the heart of the retail district, believing that Denver would expand greatly during the postwar era. His prediction proved valid, but a lawsuit and other complications forestalled development. Land he acquired one block to the north for an office complex, Mile High Center (1952–56), took precedence under the circumstances.[85] Not until July 1953 did Zeckendorf announce plans for a large department store surmounted by a thirty-story hotel at Courthouse Square. To realize his plan, the developer acquired controlling interest in Daniels & Fisher, the city's premier department store, over the next two months while concurrently negotiating with the Statler organization for the hotel. Zeckendorf hoped to start construction by the close of 1954 but had to resolve a seemingly endless string of complications. Early on, his team discovered that the hotel and department store needed to be configured as separate structures, which required additional land. Zeckendorf pressed ahead with preliminary plans, unveiled in January 1955, but the design of neither building could be resolved until each had a committed tenant.[86]

Zeckendorf thought he had secured the right owners for Daniels & Fisher in May 1954—his own purchase had been to ensure the store would be part of his complex—but the arrangement proved unsatisfactory. Not until the Denver arm of the May Company took over the business more than three years later was the situation rectified. Problems also arose with the hotel. Statler was purchased by Hilton Hotels in August 1954, but Hilton did not agree to lease Zeckendorf's building until September 1958, after the May-D&F store had opened.[87] Delays on realizing both buildings also stemmed from difficulties in assembling land, closing streets, and securing the rights to excavate several levels below grade. As a result, the department store did not open until July 1958, the hotel two years later—fifteen years after Zeckendorf initiated the project. In the meantime, the developer faced accusations of broken promises and had to pay large sums annually to the municipal government as stipulated in the purchase contract.[88]

If realization was agonizing, the result was worthwhile by many accounts, validating Zeckendorf's belief that good design should be an integral part of sound real estate development (fig. 244).[89] Dubbed by *Architectural Forum* as the "greatest design [for a hotel] since the opulence of the twenties," the twenty-one-story Hilton was planned as the premier facility of its kind in the state. It was well equipped with convention facilities in a bid to bolster what client and developer alike saw as a huge untapped trade potential. Enclosing 400,000 square feet, the May-D&F store was probably the largest of its type between the Mississippi and the West Coast. While the mass of the building was windowless, faced in honey-colored aluminum panels, it was fronted by an enormous pavilion of glass with a concrete hyperbolic paraboloid shell—a "gigantic gift box" housing the primary entrance along with jewelry and related merchandise. Here, too, *Forum* editors considered the design well above the industry norm, one that could "breathe new life into urban retailing generally." Adjacent lay a copious plaza, framed by honey locust trees, with a depressed core used as an ice-skating rink in winter (fig. 245). Zeckendorf's architect, I. M. Pei, designed the ensemble as a cool, suave juxtaposition of opposites—the laconic, honeycombed slab of the twenty-one-story hotel facing the plaza and sculptural pavilion, backed by the neutral mass of the emporium. Below lay three levels of parking for over eleven hundred cars. The ensemble was not only seen as a great boost to the area's economy, it was hailed as a linchpin for renewal. Zeckendorf was skeptical, however. After the years he had devoted to strengthening the core with two large projects, he viewed the municipal leadership as ineffectual. His work brought new life to the eastern part of downtown; nothing had happened in the declining western section.[90]

For advocates of having redevelopment initiated and controlled by the private sector, the favorite example was Midtown Plaza in Rochester, New York. Despite its name, Midtown Plaza lay in the heart of the retail district, whose business it was foremost intended to stimulate. The project was initiated in 1956 by Gilbert McCurdy, head of McCurdy's department store, and Maurice Forman, president of B. Forman Company, a major specialty store on the same block. The beginning of a decline in downtown sales was sufficient to prompt their belief that aggressive steps were needed to keep the core vital. They were well aware of competition from outlying areas; each company had a branch store under construction. More important, perhaps, but unstated, was the threat posed by Sibley, Lindsay & Curr, the region's dominant department store, which was constructing two branches close by as well as one in the town of New-

244. Courthouse Square, Sixteenth, Seventeenth, and Tremont streets and Court Place, Denver (1955–60). I. M. Pei & Associates, architects. At right: May–D&F department store (1955–58), front pavilion demolished, remainder altered. At left: Hilton Hotel (1958–60). Photo ca. 1960.

245. May–D&F department store, detail of front plaza. Photo 1958.

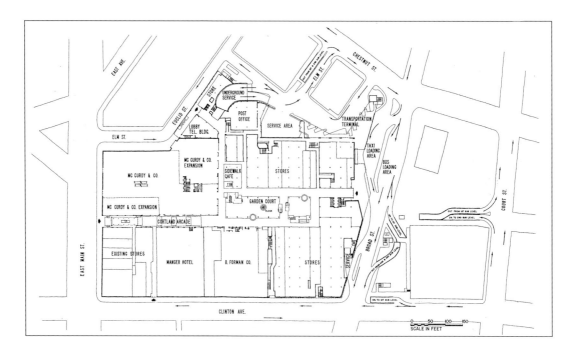

246. Midtown Plaza, Main, Broad, Chestnut, Euclid, and Elm streets and Clinton Avenue, Rochester, New York (1958–62). Victor Gruen Associates, architects; demolished 2008. Ground floor plan.

247. Midtown Plaza, section.

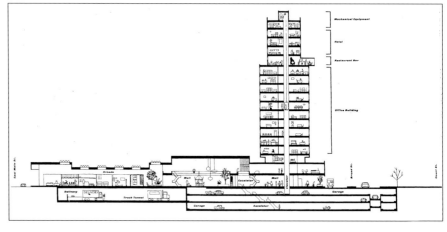

ark, some sixteen miles to the east. Concerned that the city would not furnish adequate off-street parking facilities in a timely manner, McCurdy and Forman hired an architect to design one for them. But this measure, they feared, was not enough, and thus they turned to Victor Gruen on the basis of the plan he had recently done for Fort Worth. Gruen convinced them that a far more ambitious scheme was needed than either had anticipated. His proposal for Midtown Plaza enlarged both stores, tying them to an enclosed mall lined with some fifty shops and services on two levels. At one end lay a bus terminal; on top a hotel and office block—at sixteen stories, the tallest in the city—all served by multilevel underground parking, with a 1,900-car capacity (figs. 246–47). Midtown Plaza, Gruen argued, provided the critical mass to keep downtown in the limelight. The complex also afforded a perceptual sense of equivalency, at least, to Sibley's massive emporium directly across the street.

When the plan was announced in September 1958, it was officially met with enthusiasm. The two retailers had quietly assembled the land for the complex and were willing to foot the bill for its construction under the auspices of the Midtown Holding Corporation. The size of the project—1.3 million square feet on seven-and-a-half acres, costing $16 million, including the land—was ambitious for the period, but the undertaking of such a scheme by retailers was unprecedented. The city would have to contribute, too, by extending Broad Street at the rear of the development—a measure long deemed desirable—and by constructing the underground parking facility. Ultimately the municipal expenditure was high: $9 million. But public officials recognized the value of the endeavor. "To say I am delighted tonight is a gross understatement," gushed the mayor at the unveiling. "This is the first concrete, specific achievement . . . of over 10 years of [hard work by the] City Council, the City Planning Commission and the city administration. . . . We . . . are extremely fortunate in having

248. Midtown Plaza, central court, ca. 1962.

imaginative people willing to invest their savings in a master plan." City officials and the clients alike saw the endeavor as a catalyst. McCurdy proclaimed it the "healthy seed which is destined to germinate and grow into a dynamic new downtown core."[91]

Approval of the scheme was swift given its complexity. When the high cost of the underground parking facility was calculated—far higher than either New Haven or Sacramento were investing in local funds—the city treasurer countered that municipal coffers would receive $17 million back in increased taxes over thirty years. A $12 million appropriation passed the City Council in December 1958. The first contracts were awarded the following March; construction on the first phase of the garage began that July, less than a year after the initial presentation. Well before it received all the necessary approvals, the plan was presented at a meeting in Washington sponsored by the U.S. Chamber of Commerce that addressed what members considered the alarming rise in federal monies for urban redevelopment. Woodward & Lothrop president Philip Talbott warned of the "dragging friction of still higher federal taxation, coupled with constantly diminishing state and local tax revenues to pay for urban programs," and pointed to Rochester as one of the few cities that was taking the right course.[92] But some local merchants were less enthusiastic, complaining that Midtown Plaza would draw business away from them. Others said that the city was playing favorites by "subsidizing" two stores. Well after construction of the garage was under way, the city's involvement became a major issue in the mayoral campaign. Harper Sibley, Jr., head of the realty company affiliated with the family's department store, asserted that insufficient demand existed for the office tower. Many residents also apparently felt that the project was overly ambitious and in the end might hurt downtown through its failure.[93]

When Midtown Plaza opened in April 1962, the skepticism dissipated. The complex not only boasted a full roster of tenants, but many of them were new to the city center. At an early stage of development McCurdy delineated the strategy: "Midtown is dedicated to adding something to Rochester, at bringing new business downtown. We don't want to subtract from—or just redistribute—what's already here." Complementing the new stores was a range of mostly small local and national chain outlets. Early on, too, the management of the adjoining Manger Hotel decided to become an integral part of the project, and two nationally known businesses combined to operate the four-story hostelry and restaurant atop the new office block. Gruen was elated. His regional malls were conceived as substitutes for the urban experience. Here, the project's size and objectives enabled him to create the real thing—a "place where people can meet, can shop, can congregate, where things are happening." The central court "should provide Rochester with a focal point, not only for shopping excursions, but also for entertainment, for meetings, for lectures, for art exhibitions, for musicals" (fig. 248). Here, at last, was a fully realized

249. Midtown Plaza, office tower (center), new and old sections of McCurdy's department store (right), and portion of Sibley, Lindsey & Curr department store (behind McCurdy's). Photo ca. 1962.

embodiment of his vision of a new "town square"—"the first opportunity to show what we have been talking about and writing about and planning about for years." At the opening, consumers raved, state officials praised, local partisanship was put aside. Forman heaved a sigh of relief: "There was so much criticism and apprehension . . . [at the outset] it's a delight to see that the people of Rochester . . . have taken to it and feel it's theirs." The *Rochester Times-Union* went so far as to editorialize that the complex gave the city a "new national image": "It tells young men and women just out of college and looking for places to advance a career that Rochester is a town on the move, a community where spectacular ideas are spectacularly executed."[94]

In concept and execution, Midtown Plaza was "not a shopping center downtown," as Gruen put it, but a business center encompassing a spectrum of civic as well as commercial functions, intended to capitalize on and enhance the traditional strengths of the city center. A local shopping center developer agreed. Midtown Plaza would never compete with his projects; it was a special place, not one for the "routine business of the suburban housewife." Moreover, a writer for *Shopping Center Age* observed, while the regional mall was self-contained, Midtown Plaza was an integral part of its environment. The complex was an unquestioned success in both the business and public realms—including as a symbol of urban regeneration (fig. 249). The real challenge, many commentators agreed, was whether it would spur retail revitalization along the neighboring blocks. Ultimately, Midtown Plaza helped stimulate more office than retail development, but among the major downtown renewal projects it remained the exception in the degree to which it was woven into the existing urban fabric physically and functionally.[95] The acuity for integrating new development into the urban matrix that Gruen revealed in his Fort Worth scheme was well honed in Rochester.

Private-sector initiative was hardly the cure-all in itself, however. Just as many planning agency schemes for downtown renewal remained on paper, so did many others conceived by business interests and reliant strictly on private funds for implementation. One of the grandest of the latter group was proposed for downtown New Rochelle, which had once boasted the major business district serving affluent Westchester County, New York, and neighboring parts of Fairfield County, Connecticut. New Rochelle's draw significantly waned after World War II with the rise of White Plains as a fashion center, where large new branches of B. Altman, Macy's, and Saks Fifth Avenue were erected. The opportunity for New Rochelle to regain some of its former stature occurred almost serendipitously in 1956 when a former New Haven Railroad freight yard adjacent to downtown became available. From the outset, the corporation established to develop the site and the railroad agreed to cooperate closely with municipal officials to ensure speedy realization. Plans for what was called Terminal Plaza, containing a new station, shops, hotel, office building, and parking garage, were drawn the following year. The city's planning board summarily rejected the proposal, however, claiming insufficient time for review.[96] But the problems were more fundamental. In January 1958 the developers announced that an entirely new scheme would be prepared by Victor Gruen and would contain a large branch of Macy's as well as around seventy other stores. The cost was estimated at $42 million. Completed four months later, Gruen's design housed a two-level enclosed mall at the core, anchored by a 225,000-square-foot Macy's at one end. Three levels of parking were set below the shopping center and two above, providing space for fifty-two hundred cars. Surmounting the immense ensemble was a one-hundred-room hotel, rising fifteen stories to afford a dramatic counterpoint (fig. 250). A terminal for trains and buses, containing more stores and parking as well, was planned for the second phase. For the first time, Gruen fully embraced the archetype of the nineteenth-century European arcade, citing the Galleria Vittorio Emanuele II as his primary source of inspiration.[97] Here, too, he took the idea of a single, mixed-use commercial building to a new scale and level of complexity. The scheme was, arguably, a regional mall given a more traditionally urban density, but still a dynamic, freestanding ensemble visually tied more to the adjacent New York Thruway than to the city center it abutted.

Progress snagged due to the death of one of the two

developers. A new party purchased the corporation in September 1959, promising quick action. Impatient, the New Haven Railroad set a completion deadline of two and a half years. Yet dissatisfaction with Gruen's design was apparently sufficient for the developer to commission new plans from John Graham, which were unveiled over a year later (fig. 251). Graham's more staid rendition faced the community's heart, but its scale and massiveness still kept it a thing apart. This reworking was of no help to realization, either. Yet another developer had taken over the project at the close of 1961 only to default in less than twelve months. Extensions were granted until October 1963, when all hope of the project collapsed. New Rochelle's distraught mayor worked directly with Macy's officials to plan a less ambitious complex on urban renewal land closer to the retail core. Macy's agreed to develop its own store in November 1964.[98] A year and a half later, the scheme was finalized with the shopping center developers Winston-Muss, Macy's, and the municipal government each undertaking a portion of the 1.2-million-square-foot complex. When it opened in July 1968, the Mall at New Rochelle was heralded as the city's salvation, but the quest for downtown revival had taken even longer than in New Haven.[99] While not as divorced from the retail core as the stillborn Terminal Plaza, the Mall still was its own, inward-oriented world—a regional shopping center that happened to be at the edge of an existing downtown.

Other proposals had a much briefer lifespan than Terminal Plaza. Capitol Center in Trenton, New Jersey, was one of what perhaps were numerous such endeavors. Shortly before Christmas in 1959 Carl Mark, head of Lit's branch, the largest department store in that city, made an astounding offer. The company would replace its antiquated physical plant with a new 200,000-square-foot emporium, a number of additional stores (for which nearby merchants would receive first priority as tenants), an office building, ample parking for fifteen hundred cars, and a landscaped mall along the Assunpink Creek, which traversed the property. The site lay adjacent to the city's principal shopping corridor on land designated for renewal and owned by the Trenton Housing Authority. Mark's conditions for proceeding with the project were that a long-planned elevated road along the creek not be built and that the state government give concrete assurances that anticipated state office buildings would be constructed on nearby portions of the redevelopment area. So as to preclude any potential conflicts of interest, the retailer concurrently stepped down from his post as chairman of the city's planning board, stating: "I feel I can be of better service to the community by devoting all of my efforts to . . . the project." Local reaction was mixed. The state highway department officials appeared far more concerned with their proposed elevated road, which was still in the middle of engineering assessments. As the months wore on, the "in-

250. Westchester Terminal Plaza, Palmer, North, and Cedar avenues, New Rochelle, New York (1958). Victor Gruen Associates, architects; project. Photomontage.

251. Westchester Terminal Plaza, as redesigned by John Graham & Company, architects, 1960; project. Presentation drawing.

action and indecision" that the press claimed characterized local renewal efforts generally killed hopes for realization. Little was changed in the retail sphere until over a decade later, when hopes for revitalizing downtown were pinned to replacing the main shopping street with a pedestrian mall.[100]

Competition

The divergences of opinion as to how to revitalize the retail core and the multiple frustrations incurred no doubt limited the extent of physical change to a substantial degree. It was much easier for real estate developers and store executives alike to create the advantages of downtown *de novo* by combining a regional mall with dense office building and apartment house construction in a centralized setting. Two projects initiated in the late 1950s—Lloyd Center in Portland, Oregon, and Century City in Los Angeles—set the stage for a number of endeavors that were to follow.

Arguably the most influential retail project of the decade on subsequent urban endeavors, Lloyd Center was born out of paradoxical circumstances. Its site lay just across the Willamette River from downtown—a distance of about two miles and a six-minute drive by car. In the mid-1920s, an unseasoned real estate entrepreneur, Ralph Lloyd, who had amassed a fortune from oil discovered on his family's ranch in southern California, began to acquire property in this near east side location. Like many other speculators of the period, Lloyd harbored dreams of creating an extension of the urban core that would become in effect a "new city." Like most such ventures, Lloyd's failed to materialize, and his efforts to engage the process with projects of his own devising were rendered stillborn by the Depression. He tried twice again, only to be thwarted by World War II and the Korean War. Lloyd died in 1953, but the corporation that bore his name took advantage of the planned confluence of two freeways close by to revive the development objective, now through the unlikely means of proposing a regional shopping center.[101]

Constructing a rival to downtown on nearby land became a realistic goal only because Allied Stores was exploring a way to break into the Portland market. Since 1947, Allied had been aggressively acquiring department stores in Spokane, Walla Walla, Tacoma, and Yakima, Washington, all of which soon became extensions of its Seattle affiliate, Bon Marche. This territorial expansion took a new turn in September 1953, when plans were announced for a Bon Marche branch in Eugene, Oregon, over one hundred miles south of Portland. Nine months later, Allied committed to build an immense (450,000-square-foot) department store on the Lloyd Corporation's property as the centerpiece of a no less ambitious regional mall. Though not stated, Allied's aim was clearly to gain at least parity with Meier & Frank, long the dominant department store in Portland and the surrounding region. Lloyd Center was centrally located as well near the high-speed routes that, when completed, would connect to the great majority of the metropolitan area's population. Though close to downtown, the Lloyd Center site was much more conveniently accessed by motorists, and its projected scope would provide enough amenities that it would rival the city center in many consumers' eyes. It could indeed become a new city.[102]

Perhaps due to strategic error, perhaps because they were cautious about challenging Meier & Frank so close to home, Allied's leadership put its Portland plans on hold, focusing on a major expansion of its Spokane store instead. This neglect prompted Lloyd Corporation officials to court Meier & Frank. Under the circumstances, Meier & Frank executives had few options. If they rejected the offer, they ran the risk of Allied or another department store corporation entering at a later date. If they accepted, on the other hand, they would likely erode some of their own downtown business, but they would achieve hegemony in the shopping center arena for some time to come, precluding a competitor, local or otherwise, from attempting a rival project farther afield. When Meier & Frank's leadership announced their decision in July 1956, they explained that they were simply keeping "pace with the company's growth in the expanding . . . metropolitan area." But shelving plans for a large branch farther afield and erecting a 300,000-square-foot store close to the huge home base would never have been entertained without the threat of outside competition. Once Meier & Frank took the risk, many other downtown stores felt compelled to follow. So large a shopping mall so close to home could not be ignored. By September 1957 most of the retail space was leased. Construction began the following spring, unimpeded by the difficulties of downtown redevelopment. The complex opened slightly more than two years later, in July 1960 (fig. 252).[103]

Throughout the process Lloyd Corporation executives never lost sight of the founder's vision of a new city. By standards of the day, Lloyd Center's size was staggering. The development consumed thirty blocks, eighteen of them unbroken by city streets. While not the nation's biggest shopping center as claimed—Northland, Roosevelt Field, and Garden State Plaza were larger in 1960—Lloyd Center's 1.2 million square feet still made it among the giants, unrivaled in its size west of Chicago. Meier & Frank's emporium enclosed more space than any other store in Oregon save the company's own downtown plant and was balanced by three large junior department stores. Lloyd Center was also by far the densest shopping center development at that time. The cost of land necessitated an interweaving of functions on five levels. Most stores rested on an immense two- and three-level parking structure. The outdoor mall ran at the second level and also differed from others of its kind in having offices above and recreational facilities below (fig. 253). A tunnel and storage basement served major stores, while open vehicular paths allowed smaller businesses to be provisioned at the third level. Touted as the largest fireproof structure in the nation, this vast network encompassed 3.6 million square feet of enclosed and open space. Size was matched by spectacle. From the time it opened, Lloyd Center earned the loyalty of many area residents through a seemingly endless array of special events. At the apex of the T-shaped mall lay an ice-skating rink, operated almost year round, and a unique attraction on the West Coast. Across the street from the department store, a multistory hotel was erected concurrently and an office and medical building

252. Lloyd Center, N.E. Multnomah, Ninth, and Fifteenth streets and N.E. Broadway, Portland, Oregon (1956–60). John Graham & Company, architects. Photo by Delano, 1963.

253. Lloyd Center, plan at mall level (*Architectural Record,* December 1960, 125).

were planned. The whole venture was geared to an upscale market. Lloyd Corporation officials wished to provide all the amenities of downtown with all the conveniences of a regional mall. They did little to disguise their ambition to have the project become the preferred retail center for the metropolis.[104]

Not everyone was optimistic. Considerable nervousness existed among the downtown merchants who had followed Meier & Frank's lead in having branches at the complex. Many who had refused to do so doubted that the new behemoth would succeed. Others were anxious that Lloyd Center would indeed spur downtown decline. After the complex opened, *Women's Wear Daily* kept unusually close tabs on the outcome, issuing monthly reports through the year's end and annual updates for several years thereafter. The initial loss of revenue downtown was in fact pronounced, but soon it partially rebounded due to aggressive group promotional programs. With the passage of time it became clear that downtown would continue to suffer, but not exceedingly so. The biggest losses came from companies with stores in both places, but on average they increased their overall volume by 10 percent. Established outlying business districts nearby, not downtown, took the greatest toll. Lloyd Center was not the commercial folly some skeptics had foreseen. It could hold a sizable, steady clientele, if not quite as large a one as its promoters had predicted.[105]

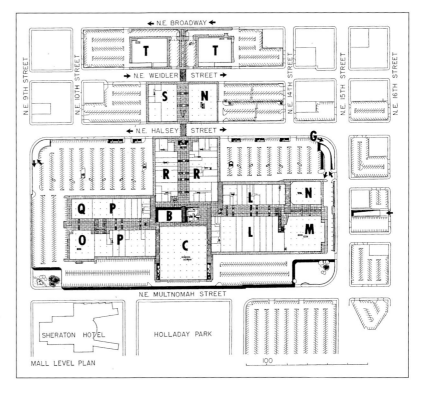

The persistence of this complementarity revealed that the regional mall was not a root cause of downtown's decline as a retail center. A strong shopping core could survive. The density of Lloyd Center, combined with other, complementary functions, became an important precedent for large, mixed-use business facilities in outlying areas, of which Century City was the pioneering example.

Occupying a 263-acre site, Century City eventually

254. Century City, Avenue of the States, between Santa Monica and Pico boulevards, Los Angeles. Welton Becket & Associates, architects; master plan. Aerial view to east. Photomontage of complex as envisioned in 1963, showing Century Square Shopping Center (1960–64, Welton Becket & Associates) at lower left.

255. Century City, aerial view to southeast, with Century Square (3) at lower right. Photo 1967.

became a compound of over a dozen office towers ranging from thirteen to thirty-four stories, five residential towers, two low-rise condominium complexes, two hotels containing nearly eighteen hundred rooms, a hospital, a medical building, and a regional mall. The development took more than thirty years to consummate, but at an early stage was championed as a successful new urban center by business interests of many kinds (figs. 254–55). The site had long served as a back lot of 20th Century–Fox Studios. Situated immediately west of Beverly Hills and in the path of ever more intense high-end development by the late 1950s, the potential value of the property began to escalate. Spyros Skouras, Fox's president, persuaded a member of his board, attorney Edmond Herrscher, to pursue a plan that would make the sale of the tract an attractive one to investors. Herrscher apparently believed that the greatest value lay in creating the blueprint for a business and residential "community" that would attract a broad, high-end clientele. He hired Welton Becket to develop a master plan and attracted the interest of the indomitable William Zeckendorf. Frustrated by urban renewal schemes, Zeckendorf focused attention on advancing a plan that carried few outside restrictions and would be unencumbered by outside interference. In 1960 he found a partner, Alcoa, with sufficient resources to purchase the land and initiate the vast project. The deal was consummated the following year.[106]

For all its size and pretensions of being a distinct community with clearly delineated borders, Century City was developed to function as a business center serving a much larger component of the metropolitan area. This relationship was evident from the start. With his extensive work in the field, Becket realized that a regional mall could be a catalyst for further growth. Even though the western part of Los Angeles was served by numerous neighborhood retail centers, as well as the more stylish Westwood Village and the extravagant stores of Beverly Hills, a number of the amenities offered by a regional mall were found lacking. In addition to ample parking and a pedestrian-oriented atmosphere, such a development could provide a wide spectrum of desirable goods at less than top-end prices. Probably for these reasons the Broadway department store committed to the project over a year before the tract was even purchased.[107] With branches throughout the region, the giant, middle-market emporium was conspicuously lacking a presence on the west side, where, on Wilshire Boulevard, the arch-rival May Company had enjoyed a commanding presence for over three decades. With new, large branches of Bullock's and J. W. Robinson erected nearby after World War II, the Broadway was the only major department store absent in what had become one of the region's strongest markets. The workers and residents who came to Century City over the next twenty years would enhance trade, but it was the half million people living within a five-mile radius that made the real market for the regional mall. Completed in 1964, Century Center, as the retail complex was called, provided a cornerstone for a development still in embryo. As Century City grew over the next two decades, emerging as a true business center far more than those envisioned for Northland, Southdale, and other pioneering examples of the mid-1950s, it became clear that the regional mall could serve a comparatively dense, urban setting well, not by adapting to an ailing core but as part of the city made anew. Through its many transformations the department store not only regenerated its dominant place in retailing, at least for the time being, it regained its role as a catalyst for urban development—now in both inner and outlying parts of the metropolis alike.

Lloyd Center and Century City gave credence to the concept of having a regional mall as a springboard for dense, multipurpose commercial development in more peripheral locations. Among the most ambitious undertakings of that kind was developer Gerald Hines's Galleria in the Post Oak district of Houston (1969–71). Most such concentrations, however, were initiated by multiple parties, owing to the enormous costs—and risks—involved. The physical order of these nodes was looser due to the quest for identity among the individual projects entailed, the absence of a master plan, and the demands of accommodating many thousands of motor vehicles. The regional mall played a catalytic role in the emergence of places such as King of Prussia (Philadelphia), Tyson's Corner (Washington), Buckhead (Atlanta), and Schaumburg (Chicago) and has contributed to their continued expansion into major business centers for their respective regions.[108] The regional mall became the surrogate for the vast downtown department store, but just as those malls and vibrant downtown shopping districts could almost never coexist for long, so the mall has proven an inopportune generator of new, multifunctional centers that offer anything comparable to the downtown environment when it flourished several generations ago.

EPILOGUE

AT THE CLOSE of the 1950s, department store executives were bullish about the future. Growth over the next decade would rival that at the dawn of the twentieth century, according to B. Earl Puckett, chairman of Allied Stores. The middle class was increasing and had ever more disposable income. Federated Stores' Fred Lazarus, Jr., predicted that by 1976, as the baby boomers came of age, a new wave of high-volume spending would occur, and if "we have been able . . . to [continue to] increase the real purchasing power of the average family, the growth in retail sales will be really staggering." Competition would be stiff, Puckett warned, but the department store had the advantage of flexibility to capture an ever expanding and more affluent mass market.[1] Puckett was seasoned in nurturing a corporate strategy conducive to change. He, Lazarus, and other industry leaders had labored hard to transform their businesses in many ways over the previous quarter century. That epic struggle had paid off handsomely. But for the department store to survive, it would have to be reinvented repeatedly in the future.

The physical changes that occurred in department stores after 1960 were not, however, as fundamental or as dramatic as those that had occurred since the 1920s. Instead, change was focused on the regional mall, which remained the preferred instrument of expansion for the great emporia over the next quarter century. The belief held by some leading retailers that the rate of mall development would slow down somewhat proved incorrect. From 1961 to the close of 1970 over 240 such complexes were added to the landscape, more than three times the number constructed in the previous fifteen years. The great majority of the new regional malls were created, owned, and managed by a corpus of developers who made this line of work a specialty, expanding upon the foundation that James Rouse and a few others had laid.[2] In its design the regional mall became larger and more lavish. Almost every example opened after 1960 had dual anchors; at least seventy-two had three; at least eight had four.[3] This expansion rate, in turn, was dwarfed by that of the following decade. Through the 1970s, the growth rate of shopping centers generally, including regional malls, was higher than those of the both the U.S. population and its market potential. Before 1958, regional malls captured 6 percent of shopping goods sales; by 1979 that figure had increased more than sixfold.[4]

Enclosed malls became the industry standard by the mid-1960s. Furthering the increase in scale was the addition of more specialty stores, especially chains; "super-regional" malls, with between one hundred and one hundred fifty stores became increasingly common. The regional mall not only grew laterally but vertically. The Galleria in Houston's Post Oak district conclusively demonstrated what Gruen had sought to advance since the mid-1950s; namely, that through a tiered arrangement more retail space could be organized compactly, attracting ample patronage if the circulation area was made sufficiently appealing and easy to negotiate. Thereafter the largest mall interiors carried more urban overtones, adapting some of the character, and the sensation, of the grandest nineteenth-century arcades.[5] More often, too, mall developers followed the precedent established by Hudson's at Northland and Dayton's at Southdale, purchasing large tracts surrounding the mall site to stave off competition and benefit from other forms of commercial and residential development that the mall's presence could stimulate. The regional mall also became more ubiquitous. Many sizable metropolitan areas boasted ten or more by the early 1970s. Smaller cities also attracted regional malls, because they were positioned to draw from a large hinterland in addition to the population center. By the early 1970s at least some of the major department store corporations, including Allied, generated the majority of their sales volume from units in shopping centers.[6]

The department store, of course, continued to define the

regional mall; any shopping center without these emporia carried far less stature.[7] In its basic size and configuration, however, the department store experienced comparatively minor modifications after 1960. The shifts in design were primarily those affecting image and ambience. A more pronounced change occurred in the scope of goods carried. As regional malls encompassed ever more businesses, as the variety and junior department stores in these complexes continued to expand the range of their merchandise—the latter group becoming full-fledged department stores—and as competition stiffened in the sale of hard goods, especially from the accelerating number of discount stores, major department stores narrowed their offerings, increasingly concentrating on apparel, accessories, and some household goods.[8] By the 1970s the scope of merchandise carried by the mall department store was somewhat akin to that of the large dry goods house of the nineteenth century, while the regional mall emerged as the effective surrogate for the great emporia of the first half of the twentieth century, where most nonessential consumer demands could be addressed under one roof. At the same time, department stores met their competition head on with a fast-increasing reliance on self-service and with a new embrace of goods at lower cost.[9] The department store arguably became a less distinct retail enterprise, but into the 1980s, at least, it remained central among retail destinations.

If leading retailers were skeptical about sweeping plans to remake downtown shopping districts, they were generally confident during the early 1960s that the urban renewal program would effectively eliminate slums, improve automobile access, and bring a large middle-class consumer market back to the commercial core. Such optimism soon proved unfounded. New construction of rental housing fell far below what was necessary to bolster trade. High-speed, limited-access roads allowed city residents to drive outward in search of bargains far more than they drew shoppers inward to the traditional shopping core. The equilibrium that Oscar Webber and many of his colleagues hoped would be maintained between downtown and outlying areas was indeed of very short duration. The finding among St. Louis department store executives that downtown trade had eroded to the point of being a minor component of the region's retail sphere as early as 1963 foretold what became a national pattern by the decade's end.[10]

The exodus of the department store's traditional market was exacerbated by the profound demographic shifts that occurred in U.S. cities during the second half of the 1950s and, especially, the 1960s. Racial issues appear to have been of little concern to prominent downtown-based retailers through the 1950s, since many of them discouraged black patronage until federal laws prohibited them from doing so. The view expressed in 1955 by a Philadelphia real estate broker that downtown stores were missing the "great potential" for business growth by ignoring the nonwhite population was extremely rare. As racial discrimination practices began to erode, African American customer levels began to rise. A 1962 study of eleven major cities showed that such patronage in downtown department stores often exceeded the proportionate size of the black population. As many as 50 percent of customers were black at some Washington emporia; 40 percent at others in Los Angeles, Philadelphia, and Atlanta; overall among more than fifty of the nation's top department stores, black customers accounted for 20 percent. The deep-rooted aversion many whites had toward all but the most formalized, hierarchical interaction with African Americans understandably made retailers nervous about becoming too closely identified with a minority clientele.[11] Ultimately they were hurt as downtown was increasingly perceived as a magnet for minority shoppers during the late 1960s and the 1970s, particularly in the aftermath of race riots that decimated some retail centers serving black neighborhoods in Detroit, Los Angeles, and Washington, among other cities.[12] Given such circumstances, the "economic magnetism of the giant centers," commented a reporter for *Fortune*, "has split asunder the functions of most large cities, as though they were atoms in a cyclotron."[13]

The spiraling decline of downtown led to more radical levels of physical intervention, especially in the 1970s and 1980s. A number of cities converted major shopping streets to malls that were limited to pedestrians and, in some case, public transit vehicles. Baltimore, Boston, Buffalo, Denver, Louisville, Minneapolis, Philadelphia, and Providence were among the metropolises that rapidly executed such plans with little apparent resistance from retailers.[14] A few cities—including Milwaukee, Philadelphia, St. Paul, St. Louis, San Diego, Charleston, West Virginia, and Worcester, Massachusetts—elaborated upon the precedent set by Midtown Plaza in Rochester, undertaking mammoth, mixed-use projects downtown, with the retail components anchored by department stores.[15] Seldom, however, have such ventures met expectations. Pedestrian malls have more often than not discouraged the desired trade—most of them have been dismantled—and, with a few exceptions, the more ambitious projects have failed to attract the huge number of shoppers needed to sustain them profitably.[16]

Since the 1970s external changes affecting department stores have been far more pronounced. The collapse of the downtown market in most cities by the end of that decade or the beginning of the next has left most of the buildings once occupied by the grand emporia adapted to other uses—offices, academic facilities, and housing among them—or in some cases left vacant. Local preservation ordinances have enabled many exteriors to remain intact, but these mammoth buildings are seldom the vibrant centers of human activity they were even in decline. Examples that remain in operation—including Bloomingdale's, Macy's, Lord & Taylor, and Saks Fifth Avenue in New York; Neiman-Marcus in Dallas, Macy's in San Francisco; and the former Marshall Field's in Chicago, Dayton's in Minneapolis, Foley's in Houston, and the Bon Marche in Seattle, all of which became Macy units in the last few years—represent a tiny fraction of the once formidable array. Many freestanding branches have closed as well and, in contrast to their downtown parents, have sustained markedly higher rates of disfiguring alterations or demolition.[17] These tendencies, in turn, pale in comparison to changes in retailing. High-volume discount chains, outlet malls, catalogues, online shopping, and a new, vigorous generation of mid-to-high-end specialty chains have all increased the department store's competition, taking a sizable share of the market in the process.

In an effort to survive, department store companies intensified their acquisition of rivals. Over the past three decades, not only were holdout independent companies such as Strawbridge & Clothier purchased by corporations, those groups, in turn, purchased one another. Among the companies studied, almost as many terminated business during the 1960s as in the previous decade. The rate increased during the 1970s and 1980s. In the 1980s, the number of acquisitions began to soar. Unlike the corporate expansion of the postwar years, which enlarged the trade territory of industry leaders, most purchases of the past three decades have been takeovers by investment companies or by a steadily diminishing number of department store corporations seeking to eliminate competition in an ever smaller market, resulting in the closure not only of dozens of downtown emporia, but major branch units as well.

By the fall of 2006 only Macy's and Bloomingdale's, operating under the aegis of Federated, as well as Lord & Taylor and Saks Fifth Avenue, remain among the national department store companies that enjoyed such prominence over the twentieth century.[18] Allied, Associated Dry Goods, Dayton-Hudson, Gimbel's, and the May Company have all been acquired and, in the process, dissolved. In recent decades, too, all these businesses in reality became chains, not just in their operational practices but in their character. The strong local identity cultivated in the great emporia through the mid-twentieth century has all but vanished. So, too, is the hierarchy that once existed among locally based stores. Today department stores are more alike, catering to a prosperous but generally price-conscious, clientele. They remain strong attractions for shoppers but seldom enjoy the dominance and authority for which they were long known. Edward Filene and Paul Mazur's 1920s prophecies of giant department chains extending coast to coast have in a sense been realized, but the stature of these emporia among retail businesses is hardly what it was two generations ago. Department stores have, in effect, become merely another form of chain retailing.

The changes experienced by department stores have had an impact on the regional mall. Behemoths of this kind more or less saturated their market by the mid-1980s. Since then shopping center development has taken a number of different forms. Many complexes focus on high-volume, low-cost merchandising with immense "big box" or "category killer" stores oriented to a front parking lot and arranged in a straight, L-, or U-shaped pattern—enlarged versions of 1950s patterns for which the regional mall was once seen as a preferable alternative. Outlet centers generally have assumed a configuration of a no-frills kind reminiscent of many of the earliest enclosed malls. Most built over the past decade, however, are building clusters connected by open-air pedestrianways or facing car lots—cost-saving measures predicated on the calculation that poor weather conditions do not significantly inhibit shoppers in search of bargains.[19] The outdoor environment also has acquired positive connotations. An increasing number of high-end shopping centers have assumed a modified Main Street character, with stores fronting sidewalks and vehicular circulation paths in an idealized, nostalgic interpretation of traditional settings that were almost always cast in pejorative terms during the postwar years. Entertainment facilities have played an increasingly important role in the tenant mix. On the other hand, the department store is seldom a part of any of these developments.[20] Some regional malls, on the other hand, have been demolished due to population shifts or to redundancy after the construction of newer, larger rivals nearby, replaced by new, open-air shopping centers or by complexes serving other functions.[21]

The regional mall is hardly a thing of the past, however. Many have been aggrandized since the 1970s. That trend is likely to continue, because the locations of these complexes generally remain strong and the opportunity for shopping center developers to expand through large new ensembles severely diminished over two decades ago. The updating of these complexes is sufficiently frequent that it is difficult to find one from even the 1970s that still possesses anything approximating its original appearance. Like the department store interior of earlier decades, the regional mall is in a more or less continual state of flux.[22] As part of that process, department store buildings vacated by one company are taken over by another of somewhat different stripe—a Penney's or a Sears, perhaps, catering to a less affluent clientele; or a regional chain such as Dillard's that has become a major force in recent decades; or a large, high-end, departmentalized specialty store, among which the Seattle-based Nordstrom's has become especially well known. The regional mall remains a strong destination, not just for retail activity but also for social interaction. Even though many outlying areas have assumed multiple functions once limited to the city, the regional mall remains an important locus of social interaction among groups of all ages—a place for meeting friends, for exchanging pleasantries, for exploring, for exercising, for taking in and being part of the scene.[23] For people who do not frequent the city center, the mall offers an experience that is probably the closest approximation to an urban one. In its traditional form, the downtown department store interior played a key role in defining place, at least for a large contingent of white women with disposable income. The mall interior does likewise for a much broader segment of the population—gender-, age-, income-, and racewise. As an offspring of the department store, the regional mall offers a rich legacy in social no less than in business terms.

Given the attrition and other wrenching changes it has experienced in recent decades, will the department store survive? In all likelihood it will, as few forms of retail distribution disappear completely. Even so archaic a form as the public market has not only remained in a number of communities, it has enjoyed a recent revival in popularity.[24]

But *how* will the department store survive? If history sheds any light on the subject it is that the department store's future has always been impossible to predict. The ways in which it needed to be transformed were never self-evident. Leading retailers and market analysts—those with the most knowledge of the subject—have sometimes forecast trends with a degree of accuracy, but none of them in the 1920s, for example, could have imagined the changes that occurred over the next several decades, and none of their successors around 1960 could begin to fathom what has occurred since. Change is the principal constant. If the department store is to survive, it will need to continue to transform itself. Yet continuity cannot be ruled out of the equation. The department store rose to prominence over a century ago in part because it satisfied some basic human needs beyond the desires of consumption. The department store survived because the regional mall was firmly established in fulfilling that dual role by 1960. Whatever changes occur in the future, they will need to maintain such a balance if the department store is to have any meaning in our lives.

APPENDIX
Department Stores Studied

THE 185 FIRMS listed below provide the basis for this study. They are limited to major, downtown-based department store companies that undertook substantial expansion of their main plants, or the development of branch stores, service buildings, or parking structures, between 1919 and 1960. The rationale for my selection of both cities and companies is outlined in the Introduction.

Company names are cited as they were at the inception of the study period, followed by a later renaming or popular appellation in parentheses. Dates of founding represent the start of a business that was often quite modest in nature and eventually became a full-fledged department store. I have also noted when the company joined, or was acquired by, an ownership group/corporation and, when known, the date of its closing. Many founding, and sometimes closing, dates were drawn from period sources or from a few historical accounts, such as Robert Hendrickson's *The Grand Emporiums* (1979). Jan Whitaker was most gracious in supplying me with a number of dates that I was unable to find. For changes in recent decades I have had to rely primarily on information taken from company websites and the online encyclopedia Wikipedia. The few stores still in operation (as of December 2008) under some variation of the names listed below are marked by an asterisk (*).

AKRON, OHIO

M. O'Neil Company (O'Neil's), founded 1871, acquired by May Department Stores 1912, renamed **May Co.** 1989, renamed **Kaufmann's** 1992, acquired by Federated Department Stores 2005, renamed **Macy's** 2006

A. Polsky Company (Polsky's), founded 1885, closed 1978

ATLANTA

Davison-Paxon Company (Davison's), founded 1890, joined Macy's 1925, renamed **Davison's/Macy** 1985, renamed **Macy's** 1986, closed 2003

M. Rich & Brothers Company (Rich's), founded 1867, acquired by Federated Department Stores early 1980s, renamed **Rich's-Macy's** 2003, renamed **Macy's** 2005

BALTIMORE

Bernheimer-Leader Stores, Bernheimer and Leader companies merged 1923, acquired by May Department Stores and renamed **May Co.** 1927, renamed **Hecht's** 1959; acquired by Federated Department Stores 2005, renamed **Macy's** 2006

Hecht Brothers (Hecht's), founded 1857, acquired by May Department Stores 1959 and consolidated with local May Co. store

Hochschild, Kohn & Company (Hochschild's), founded 1897, closed 1970s

The Hub, established by Hecht Brothers 1897, closed 1960

Hutzler Brothers (Hutzler's), founded 1858, closed 1990

O'Neill's, founded 1882, closed 1955

Stewart & Company, founded 1904, joined Associated Dry Goods Co. 1916, merged with **Caldor** discount stores 1984

BIRMINGHAM, ALABAMA

Loveman, Joseph & Loeb (Loveman's), founded 1887, joined City Stores 1923, closed 1986

Louis Pizitz Dry Goods Company (Pizitz), founded 1899, closed late 1980s

BOSTON

Wm. Filene's Sons (Filene's), founded 1881, joined Federated Department Stores 1929, acquired by May Department Stores 1988, reacquired by Federated 2005, acquired by Macy's and renamed **Macy's** 2006

Gilchrist Company (Gilchrist's), founded 1856, closed ca. 1972

Jordan Marsh Company, founded 1841, joined Allied Stores 1928, consolidated with Federated Department Stores 1988–92, part of Federated merger with Macy's 1994, renamed **Macy's** 1996

R. H. White Company, 1850, acquired by Filene's 1929, acquired by City Stores 1944, closed 1957

BRIDGEPORT, CONNECTICUT

Howland Dry Goods Company, founded 1887, acquired by Genung's 1958

D. M. Read Company (Read's), founded 1857, acquired by Allied Stores 1953, merged with **Jordan Marsh** 1988

BUFFALO

J. N. Adam & Company, founded 1881, joined Associated Dry Goods Co. 1916, closed 1959

Adam, Meldrum & Anderson (AM&A's), founded 1867, acquired by Bon-Ton Stores and renamed **Bon-Ton** 1994

Wm. Hengerer Company (Hengerer's), founded 1874, joined Associated Dry Goods Co. 1916, acquired by Sibley, Lindsay & Curr 1981, acquired by May Department Stores 1986, renamed **Kaufmann's** 1992, acquired by Federated Department Stores 2005, renamed **Macy's** 2006

Hens & Kelly, founded 1892, closed 1980s

CHICAGO

Carson Pirie Scott & Company (Carson's), founded 1854, acquired by P. A. Bergner & Company 1991, acquired by Proffitt's 1998, acquired by Bon-Ton Store 2006

The Fair, founded 1875, acquired by Montgomery Ward 1957

Marshall Field & Company (Marshall Field's), founded 1865, acquired by Batus 1982, acquired by Dayton Hudson 1990, acquired by May Department Stores 2004, acquired by Federated Department Stores 2005, renamed **Macy's** 2006

Mandel Brothers, founded 1855, closed 1960

CINCINNATI

Alms & Doepke, founded 1865, closed 1955

Big Store Company, founded 1896, closed 1947

Mabley & Carew (Mabley's), founded 1877, acquired by Allied Stores 1960

McAlpin Company (McAlpin's), founded 1852, purchased by Mercantile Stores 1914, acquired by and renamed **Dillard's** 1998

H. & S. Pogue Company (Pogue's), founded 1863, acquired by Associated Dry Goods 1961, closed ca. 1980s

Rollman & Son (Rollman's), founded 1867, joined Allied Stores 1928, closed 1960

John Shillito Company (Shillito's), founded 1830, acquired by F. & R. Lazarus 1929 and joined Federated Department Stores 1929, renamed **Lazarus** 1987, part of Federated merger with Macy's 1994, renamed **Lazarus-Macy's** 2003, renamed **Macy's** 2005

CLEVELAND

Bailey Company (Bailey's), founded 1899, joined National Department Stores 1923, closed 1960s

Halle Brothers Company (Halle's), founded 1891, acquired by Marshall Field's 1970, acquired by Associated Investors Corporation 1981, closed 1982

Higbee Company (Higbee's), founded 1860, acquired by Dillard's and Edward DeBartolo 1988, renamed **Dillard's** 1992, closed 2002

May Department Stores Company (May Co.), founded 1877, Cleveland store founded 1898, merged with and renamed May affiliate, **Kaufmann's**, 1992; acquired by Macy's 2005, renamed **Macy's** 2006

COLUMBUS, OHIO

F. & R. Lazarus Company (Lazarus), founded 1851, joined Federated Department Stores 1929, part of Federated merger with Macy's 1994, renamed **Lazarus-Macy's** 2003, renamed **Macy's** 2005

DALLAS

A. Harris & Company (Harris's), founded 1887, acquired by Federated Department Stores, merged with Sanger Bros., and renamed **Sanger-Harris**, 1961, acquired by May Department Stores 1988, reacquired by Federated Department Stores 2005, renamed **Macy's** 2006

*Neiman-Marcus Company, founded 1907, acquired by Broadway-Hale Stores 1969, acquired by General Cinema 1987, acquired by Texas Pacific Group and Warburg Pincus 2005

Sanger Brothers (Sanger's), founded 1868, acquired by Federated Department Stores 1959, merged with A. Harris and renamed **Sanger-Harris**, 1961, acquired by May Department Stores 1988, reacquired by Federated Department Stores 2005, renamed **Macy's** 2006

Titche-Goettinger Company (Titche's), founded 1902, joined Allied Stores 1928, renamed **Joske's** 1979, acquired by and renamed **Dillard's** 1987

DAYTON, OHIO

Rike-Kumler Company (Rike's), founded 1853, acquired by Federated Department Stores 1959, renamed **Lazarus** 1986, renamed **Lazarus-Macy's** 2003, renamed **Macy's** 2005

DENVER

Daniels & Fisher Stores Company, founded 1864, acquired by May Department Stores and renamed **May-D&F** 1957, renamed **Foley's** 1993, acquired by Federated Department Stores 2005, renamed **Macy's** 2006

Denver Dry Goods Company, founded 1882, acquired by Scruggs, Vandervoort & Barney 1924, acquired by Associated Dry Goods Co. 1966, acquired by May Department Stores 1986, most stores closed thereafter

May Department Stores Company (May Co.), founded 1877, relocated to Denver 1888, renamed **May-D&F** 1957, renamed **Foley's** 1993, acquired by Federated Department Stores 2005, renamed **Macy's** 2006

DES MOINES

Younker Brothers (Younker's), founded 1856, Des Moines store founded 1874, acquired by Proffitt's 1996, merged with Saks Fifth Avenue 1998, acquired by Bon-Ton Stores 2006

DETROIT

Crowley, Milner Company (Crowley's), founded 1908, closed ca. 1988

J. L. Hudson Company (Hudson's), founded 1881, merged with Dayton Co. 1969, renamed **Marshall Field's** 2001, acquired by Federated Department Stores 2005, renamed **Macy's** 2006

Ernest Kern Company, founded 1883, closed 1959

FORT WORTH, TEXAS

The Fair of Texas, founded 1891, acquired by Allied Stores and merged with Titche-Goettinger 1962, renamed **Joske's** 1979, acquired by and renamed **Dillard's** 1987

Leonard Brothers (Leonard's), founded 1918, closed 1974

W. C. Stripling Company (Stripling's), founded 1893, closed 2007

GRAND RAPIDS, MICHIGAN
Herpolshiemer Company (Herp's), founded 1870, joined Allied 1928, acquired by Federated Department Stores and renamed **Lazarus** 1987, closed 1992

Wurzburg Company, founded 1872, closed ca. 1960s

HARTFORD
G. Fox & Company, founded 1847, acquired by May Department Stores 1965, renamed **Filene's** 1992, acquired by Federated Department Stores 2005, renamed **Macy's** 2006

Wise, Smith & Company, acquired by City Stores 1949, closed 1954

HOUSTON
Foley Brothers (Foley's), founded 1900, acquired by Federated Department Stores 1945, acquired by May Department Stores 1988, reacquired by Federated Department Stores 2005, renamed **Macy's** 2006

Harris-Hahlo Company, founded 1920

Levy Brothers Dry Goods Company, founded 1887

Sakowitz Brothers, founded 1900, closed 1990

INDIANAPOLIS
L. S. Ayres & Company, founded 1872, acquired by Associated Dry Goods 1972, acquired by May Department Stores 1986, acquired by Federated Department Stores 2005, renamed **Macy's** 2006

Wm. H. Block Company (Block's), founded 1907, acquired by Federated Department Stores and renamed **Lazarus** 1987, renamed **Lazarus-Macy's** 2003, renamed **Macy's** 2005

H. P. Wasson Company (Wasson's), founded 1883, closed 1979

KANSAS CITY
Emery, Bird, Thayer Company, founded 1863, acquired by Scruggs, Vandervoort & Barney, 1951, closed 1968

Jones Store Company, founded 1887, acquired by May Department Stores 1998, purchased by Federated Department Stores 2005, renamed **Macy's** 2006

*R. H. Macy & Company (Macy's), developed as affiliate of New York store 1947 with purchase of **John Taylor Dry Goods Co.** (see New York store for later developments)

LONG BEACH, CALIFORNIA
Buffum's Department Store, founded 1904, closed 1991

Walker's, founded 1906, closed 1979

Wise Company, founded 1902, closed 1950s

LOS ANGELES
The Broadway, founded 1896, merged with Hale Bros. Stores 1950 (renamed Carter Hawley Hale Stores 1974, reorganized as Broadway Stores 1992), acquired by Federated Department Stores 1995, closed 1996

Bullock's, founded 1907, acquired by Federated Department Stores 1964, acquired by Macy's 1988, reacquired by Federated and renamed **Macy's** 1995

B. H. Dyas Company, founded 1914, closed 1933

Fifth Street Store, founded 1905, renamed **Milliron's** 1946, closed 1953

May Department Stores Company, founded 1877, Los Angeles store established with purchase of A. Hamburger & Sons Co. 1922, merged with J. W. Robinson and renamed **Robinsons-May** 1992, acquired by Federated Department Stores 2005, renamed **Macy's** 2006

J. W. Robinson Company (Robinson's), founded 1883, acquired by Associated Dry Goods Co. 1955, merged with May Department Stores and renamed **Robinsons-May** 1992, acquired by Federated Department Stores 2005, renamed **Macy's** 2006

LOUISVILLE, KENTUCKY
J. Bacon & Sons (Bacon's), founded 1845, acquired by Mercantile Stores 1914, acquired by and renamed **Dillard's** 1998

Kaufman-Straus, founded 1879, joined City Stores 1924, closed 1971

Stewart Dry Goods Company, founded 1846, joined Associated Dry Goods Co. 1916, merged with May Department Stores 1986, closed 1987

MEMPHIS
John Gerber Company, founded 1880, purchased by M. M. Cohn, 1975

J. Goldsmith & Sons (Goldsmith's), founded 1870, acquired by Federated Department Stores 1959, renamed **Goldsmith's-Macy's** 2003, renamed **Macy's** 2003

B. Lowenstein & Brother (Lowenstein's), founded 1855, joined City Stores 1923, closed ca. 1982

MIAMI
Burdine's, founded 1898, acquired by Federated Department Stores 1956, renamed **Burdine's-Macy's** 2003, renamed **Macy's** 2005

Cromer & Cassell, founded 1925, closed ca. 1951

Richard's Department Store, founded 1913, joined City Stores 1947

MILWAUKEE
Boston Store, founded 1897, acquired by Federated Department Stores 1948, acquired by Bergner's 1985, acquired by Proffitt's (now Saks) 1998, acquired by Bon-Ton Stores and renamed **Bon-Ton** 2006

T. A. Chapman, founded 1857, closed 1987

Gimbel Brothers (Gimbel's), founded 1842, moved to Milwaukee 1887, acquired by BATTUS 1970s, closed 1986

MINNEAPOLIS
Dayton Company (Dayton's), founded 1902, merged with J. L. Hudson Co. 1969, renamed **Marshall Field's** 2001, acquired by Federated Department Stores 2005, renamed **Macy's** 2006

L. S. Donaldson Company (Donaldson's), founded 1883, joined Allied Stores 1928, purchased by Carson Pirie Scott 1987, purchased by Dayton Hudson and closed 1995

Powers Dry Goods Company, founded ca. 1880s, joined Associated Dry Goods 1916, acquired by Dayton Hudson 1985

NASHVILLE
Cain-Sloan, founded 1903, acquired by Allied Stores 1955, acquired by Dillard's 1987

Castner-Knott Company, founded 1898, acquired by Mercantile Stores 1914, acquired by and renamed **Dillard's** 1998

NEW HAVEN
Edward Malley Company (Malley's), founded 1852, closed 1982

NEW ORLEANS
D. H. Holmes Company, founded 1842, acquired by **Dillard's** 1989
Kraus Company, founded 1903, closed 1997
Maison Blanche, founded 1897, joined City Stores 1923, closed 1992

NEW YORK
Abraham & Straus (A&S), Brooklyn, founded 1865, joined Federated Department Stores 1929, renamed **Macy's** 1995
B. Altman Company (Altman's), founded 1865, closed 1990
Arnold Constable, founded 1825, closed 1975
*Bloomingdale Brothers (Bloomingdale's), founded 1872, joined Federated Department Stores 1929
B. Gertz, Jamaica, founded 1911, acquired by Allied Stores 1941, renamed **Stern's** ca. 1960s, acquired by Campeau Corporation 1986, closed 2001
Gimbel Brothers (Gimbel's), founded 1842, New York store established 1910, acquired by BATTUS 1970s, closed 1986
James A. Hearn & Son (later Hearn Department Stores) (Hearn's), founded 1827, acquired by City Stores 1949, closed 1955
Frederick Loeser & Company (Loeser's), Brooklyn, founded 1869, acquired by A. I. Namm and renamed **Namm-Loeser** 1950s, closed 1957
*Lord & Taylor, founded 1826, joined Associated Dry Goods, 1914, acquired by May Department Stores 1986, acquired by Federated Department Stores 2005, purchase by NDRC Equity Partners 2006
*R. H. Macy & Company (Macy's), founded 1842, purchased by Campeau Corporation 1988, reorganized under bankruptcy as Macy's 1992, purchased by Federated Department Stores 1994
A. I. Namm & Son (Namm's), Brooklyn, founded 1876, renamed **Namm-Loeser** 1950s, closed 1957
*Saks Fifth Avenue (Saks), founded 1924 as affiliate of **Saks 34th Street** (founded 1902 and acquired by Gimbel's 1923), acquired by BATTUS 1973, acquired by Investcorp 1990, acquired by Proffitt's (renamed Saks Incorporated) 1998
Stern Brothers (Stern's), founded 1867, acquired by Allied Stores 1951, acquired by Campeau Corporation 1986, closed 2001

NEWARK
L. Bamberger & Company (Bamberger's), founded 1893, acquired by Macy's 1926, renamed **Macy's** 1986
Goerke Company, founded 1897, closed ca. 1969
Hahne & Company (Hahne's), founded 1862, joined Associated Dry Goods 1916, acquired by May Department Stores 1986, closed 1989
L. H. Plaut & Company, founded 1870, acquired by S. S. Kresge and renamed **Kresge Department Stores** 1923, closed 1964

OAKLAND
H. C. Capwell Company (Capwell's), founded 1889, merged with the Emporium 1927, acquired by Broadway Hale Stores 1969, acquired by Federated Department Stores 1995, renamed **Macy's** 1996
Kahn Brothers (Kahn's), founded 1879, acquired by **R. F. Schlessinger & Son** 1925, reacquired by Kahn family and renamed **Kahn Department Store** 1933, acquired by **Rhodes Department Stores** 1960, acquired by Amfac 1969, closed ca. 1981

OKLAHOMA CITY
John A. Brown Company, founded 1915, closed 1984
Kerr Dry Goods Company, founded 1908, acquired by Boston Store Dry Goods Co. 1953

OMAHA
J. L. Brandeis & Sons, founded 1881, closed 1987
Burgess-Nash Company, closed 1924

PATERSON, NEW JERSEY
Meyer Brothers, founded 1878
Quackenbush & Company, founded 1878, joined Allied Stores 1920s, renamed **Stern's** 1960s, acquired by Campeau Corporation 1986, closed 2001

PHILADELPHIA
Frank & Seder, founded 1918, joined National Department Stores 1923, closed 1957
Gimbel Brothers (Gimbel's), founded 1842, Philadelphia store established 1894, acquired by BATTUS 1970s, closed 1986
Lit Brothers (Lit's), founded 1891, joined City Stores 1928, closed 1978
Snellenbergs, founded 1873, closed 1963
Strawbridge & Clothier (Strawbridge's), founded 1868, purchased by May Department Stores 1996, purchased by Federated Department Stores 2005, renamed **Macy's** 2006
John Wanamaker (Wanamaker's), founded 1861, acquired by Carter Hawley Hale Stores 1978, sold to Woodward & Lothrop 1986, sold to May Department Stores and renamed **Hecht's** 1995, most units renamed **Strawbridge's** 1997, purchased by Federated Department Stores 2005, renamed **Macy's** 2006

PITTSBURGH
Boggs & Buhl, founded 1869, closed 1958
Gimbel Brothers (Gimbel's), founded 1842, Pittsburgh store established with purchase of **Kaufmann, Baer & Company** 1925, acquired by BATTUS 1970s, closed 1986
Joseph Horne Company (Horne's), founded 1849, purchased by Associated Dry Goods 1972, acquired by local investor group 1986, acquired by Federated Department Stores, closed 1998
Kaufmann's, founded 1871, acquired by May Department Stores 1946, acquired by Federated Department Stores 2005, renamed **Macy's** 2006
Kaufmann, Baer & Company, founded 1913, acquired by Gimbel Brothers 1925
Rosenbaum Company, founded 1868, joined National Department Stores 1928, closed 1960

PORTLAND, OREGON

Lipman Wolfe & Company (Lipman's), founded 1850, moved to Portland 1880, acquired by Dayton Hudson 1970s, acquired by Marshall Field's and renamed **Frederick & Nelson** 1980, closed 1986

Meier & Frank, founded 1857, acquired by May Department Stores 1966, acquired by Federated Department Stores 2005, renamed **Macy's** 2006

Olds & King, founded 1878

PROVIDENCE

Outlet Company, founded 1891, closed 1980

RICHMOND, VIRGINIA

Miller & Rhoades, founded 1885, merged with Julius Garfinckel 1967, acquired by Allied Stores 1982, acquired by Kevin Donohue 1987, closed 1990

Thalheimer Brothers (Thalheimer's), founded 1842, acquired by Carter Hawley Hale Stores 1978, acquired by May Department Stores 1990, renamed **Hecht's** 1992, acquired by Federated Department Stores 2005, renamed **Macy's** 2006

ROCHESTER, NEW YORK

McCurdy & Company (McCurdy's), founded 1901, acquired by May Department Stores 1994, closed 1994

Sibley, Lindsay & Curr Company (Sibley's), founded 1868, acquired by Associated Dry Goods Co. 1957, acquired by May Department Stores 1986, renamed **Kaufmann's** 1992, acquired by Federated Department Stores 2005, renamed **Macy's** 2006

ST. LOUIS

Famous-Barr Company, Famous Company and William Barr Company both founded 1849, acquired by May Department Stores 1892 and 1911 (respectively), acquired by Federated Department Stores 2005, renamed **Macy's** 2006

B. Nugent Dry Goods Company (Nugent's), founded 1873, joined National Department Stores 1923, closed 1933

Stix, Baer & Fuller Dry Goods Company (Stix, SBF), founded 1892, acquired by Associated Dry Goods 1966, acquired by and renamed **Dillard's** 1984

Scruggs, Vandervoort & Barney (Vandervoort's), founded 1850, closed 1967

ST. PAUL, MINNESOTA

Emporium, closed 1968

Golden Rule, founded 1868, acquired by Allied Stores 1928, renamed **Donaldson's** ca. 1960s, purchased by Carson Pirie Scott 1987, purchased by Dayton Hudson and closed 1995

SALT LAKE CITY

Auerbach's, founded 1864

Keith O'Brien

Zion's Cooperative Mercantile Institution (ZCMI), founded 1868, acquired by May Department Stores 1999, renamed **Meier & Frank** 2002, acquired by Federated Department Stores 2005, renamed **Macy's** 2006

SAN ANTONIO

Joske Brothers Company (Joske's), founded 1867, joined Allied Stores 1929, acquired by Campeau 1986, acquired by Dillard's and renamed **Dillard's** 1987

Wolf & Marx, joined National Department Stores 1923, acquired by Joske's 1965, renamed **Joske's** 1969

SAN DIEGO

Marston Company, founded 1878, acquired by Broadway-Hale 1960

Walker Scott, founded 1935

Whitney & Company, founded 1905

SAN FRANCISCO

City of Paris, founded 1850, purchased by Liberty House 1972, closed 1974

The Emporium, founded 1896, merged with H. C. Capwell 1927, acquired by Broadway Hale Stores 1969, acquired by Federated Department Stores 1995, renamed **Macy's** 1996

*****R. H. Macy & Company (Macy's),** founded 1842, San Francisco store established with purchase of **O'Connor Moffatt** 1945 (see New York store for later developments)

I. Magnin & Company (Magnin's), founded 1876, purchased by Bullock's 1944, acquired by Federated Department Stores 1964, acquired by Macy's 1988, reacquired and closed by Federated Department Stores

O'Connor Moffatt Company, founded 1866, purchased by Macy's and renamed **Macy's** 1945

The White House, founded 1854, closed 1966

SCRANTON, PENNSYLVANIA

Scranton Dry Goods Company, founded 1912

SEATTLE

Bon Marche, founded 1890, joined Allied Stores 1928, acquired by Campeau 1986, merged with Federated Department Stores 1986, renamed **Bon-Macy's** 2003, renamed **Macy's** 2006

Frederick & Nelson, founded 1890, acquired by Marshall Field's 1929, acquired by BATTUS 1982, acquired by local investors 1986, closed 1992

Rhodes Department Store, founded 1907

SPRINGFIELD, MASSACHUSETTS

Forbes & Wallace, founded 1874, closed 1976

SYRACUSE, NEW YORK

Dey Brothers & Company, founded 1883, joined Allied 1930s, sold 1987

E. W. Edwards & Sons, founded 1889

TAMPA, FLORIDA

Maas Brothers, founded 1886, joined Allied Stores 1929, acquired by Campeau 1986, renamed **Burdine's** 1991, renamed **Burdine's-Macy's** 2003, renamed **Macy's** 2005

TOLEDO

Lamson Brothers, founded 1885

Lasalle & Koch Company, founded ca. 1866, joined Macy's 1924, closed ca. 1976

Lion Store, founded 1857, acquired by Mercantile Stores 1914, acquired by and renamed **Dillard's** 1998

TULSA

Brown-Dunkin Dry Goods Company, founded 1924, closed 1970

Halliburton-Abbott Company (Halliburton's), founded 1882, acquired by Sears, Roebuck, 1931

Vandever Dry Goods Company, founded 1903, closed ca. 1970s

WASHINGTON, D.C.

Julius Garfinckel & Company (Garfinckel's), founded 1905, closed ca. 1985

Goldenberg Company (Goldenberg's), founded 1895, closed 1955

Hecht Company (Hecht's), founded 1857, Washington store established 1896, acquired by May Department Stores 1959, acquired by Federated Department Stores 2005, renamed **Macy's** 2006

S. Kann's Sons (Kann's), founded 1893, acquired by L. S. Good Co. 1971, closed 1975

Lansburgh & Brother (Lansburgh's), founded 1850, closed 1973

Palais Royal, founded 1877, acquired by and renamed **Woodward & Lothrop,** 1946

Woodward & Lothrop (Woodies), founded 1895, purchased by A. Alfred Taubman 1984, closed 1994

YOUNGSTOWN, OHIO

Strouss-Hirshberg Company, founded 1875, acquired by May Department Stores 1947, closed 1987

ABBREVIATIONS

IN THE NOTES, titles of newspapers and trade periodicals in newspaper format are substantially abbreviated and authors' names eliminated. I have also shortened some of the longer article titles and omitted authors' names in other trade periodicals. Abbreviations for frequently cited serials are listed below.

A&B	*Architecture and Building*
A&E	*Architect and Engineer*
ABJ	*Akron Beacon Journal*
AC	*American City*
AF	*Brickbuilder/Architectural Forum*
AJ	*Appraiser Journal*
AR	*Architectural Record*
BE	*Brooklyn Eagle*
BEN	*Buffalo Evening News*
BET	*Beverly Evening Tribune* (Massachusetts)
BG	*Boston Globe*
BH	*Boston Herald*
BHC	*Beverly Hills Citizen/Citizen News* (California)
BW	*Business Week*
CD	*Columbus Post-Dispatch/Columbus Dispatch* (Ohio)
CDN	*Chicago Daily News*
CE	*Cincinnati Enquirer*
CP	*Camden Courier-Post/Camden Post* (New Jersey)
CPD	*Cleveland Plain Dealer*
CSA	*Chain Store Age*
CSA/AE	*Chain Store Age,* Administrative Edition
CSA/GM	*Chain Store Age,* General Merchandise Edition
CSA/VE	*Chain Store Age,* Variety Store Edition
CSE	*Chain Store Age Executive Edition, with Shopping Center Age*
CT	*Chicago Tribune*
CV	*Commercial Vehicle*
DFP	*Detroit Free Press*
DGE	*Dry Goods Economist*
DMN	*Dallas Morning News*
DN	*Detroit News*
DP	*Denver Post*
DSE	*Department Store Economist*
DW	*Display World*
EB	*Evening Bulletin* (Philadelphia)
ENR	*Engineering News-Record*
ES	*Evening Star* (Washington)
FN	*Framingham News* (Massachusetts)
HBR	*Harvard Business Review*
HP	*Houston Post-Dispatch/Houston Post*
HUB	*Bulletin,* Bureau of Business Research, Graduate School of Business Administration, Harvard University
ICSC	International Council of Shopping Centers, Annual Convention Proceedings
IN	*Indianapolis News*
IS	*Indianapolis Star*
ITE	Institute of Traffic Engineers, *Proceedings*
JAPA	*Journal of the American Planning Association*
JEE	*Journal Every Evening* (Wilmington, Delaware)
JR	*Journal of Retailing*
JSAH	*Journal of the Society of Architectural Historians*
LAT	*Los Angeles Times*
MFA	Marshall Field Archives, Target Corporation, Minneapolis
MH	*Miami Herald*
MJ	*Milwaukee Journal*
MLT	*Main Line Times* (Ardmore, Pennsylvania)
MN	*Maryland News* (Silver Spring)
MRSW	*Merchants Record and Show Window*
MS	*Milwaukee Sentinel*
MSJ	*Minneapolis Journal*
MT	*Minneapolis Tribune*
NHJ	*New Haven Journal and Chronicle*
NHR	*New Haven Register*
NRB	*Bulletin,* National Retail Dry Goods Association
NREJ	*National Real Estate Journal*
NSE	*Newark Star-Eagle*
NYT	*New York Times*
OT	*Oakland Tribune* (California)
OWH	*Omaha World Herald*

PA	*Pencil Points/Progressive Architecture*	*SBC*	*Southwest Builder and Contractor*
PI	*Philadelphia Inquirer*	*SCA*	*Shopping Center Age*
PL	*Public Ledger* (Philadelphia)	*SDU*	*San Diego Union*
PP	*Pittsburgh Post*	*SFC*	*San Francisco Chronicle*
PRI	*Printer's Ink*	*SLG*	*St. Louis Globe-Democrat*
PT	*Peabody Times* (Massachusetts)	*SPD*	*St. Louis Post-Dispatch/St. Louis Dispatch*
RC	*Retail Control*	*SPP*	*St. Paul Press*
RDC	*Rochester Democrat and Chronicle* (New York)	*SS*	*Standard Star* (New Rochelle, New York)
RE	*Retail Executive*	*ST*	*Seattle Times*
RL	*Retail Ledger*	*TT*	*Trenton Times*
RM	*Retail Management*	*UL*	*Urban Land*
RMN	*Rocky Mountain News* (Denver)	*ULI*	*Urban Land Institute Technical Bulletin*
RTU	*Rochester Times-Union* (New York)	*WP*	*Washington Post*
SAE	*San Antonio Express*	*WSJ*	*Wall Street Journal*
SB	*Sacramento Bee*	*WWD*	*Women's Wear Daily*

NOTES

Introduction

1. The two principal cultural histories focusing on department stores—William Leach, *Land of Desire: Merchants, Power, and the Rise of a New American Culture* (New York: Random House, 1993) and Susan Porter Benson, *Counter Cultures: Saleswomen, Managers, and Customers in American Department Stores, 1890–1940* (Urbana: University of Illinois Press, 1986)—have been supplemented by a well-researched popular account: Jan Whitaker, *Service and Style: How the American Department Store Fashioned the Middle Class* (New York: St. Martin's, 2006). See also Elaine S. Abelson, *When Ladies Go A-Thieving: Middle-Class Shoplifters in the Victorian Department Store* (New York: Oxford University Press, 1989); Mark Hutter, "The Downtown Department Store as a Social Force," *Social Science Journal* 24, no. 3 (1987): 239–46; and Sarah S. Malino, "Behind the Scenes in the Big Store: Reassessing Women's Employment in American Department Stores, 1870–1920," in Martin Henry Blatt and Martha K. Norkunas, eds., *Work, Recreation, and Culture: Essays in American Labor History* (New York: Garland, 1996), 17–37. The department store has also been featured in broader historical studies such as Gunther Barth, *City People: The Rise of Modern City Culture in Nineteenth-Century America* (New York: Oxford University Press, 1980), chap. 4; and Daniel J. Boorstin, *The Americans: The Democratic Experience* (New York: Random House, 1973), chap. 10. Neil Harris, "Museums, Merchandising, and Popular Taste: The Struggle for Influence," in Ian M. G. Quimby, ed., *Material Culture and the Study of American Life* (New York: W. W. Norton, 1978), 140–74, is a pioneering essay on the underlying cultural importance of these emporia. Studies of consumption have also shed important light on the subject, including Susan Strasser, *Satisfaction Guaranteed: The Making of the American Mass Market* (New York: Pantheon, 1989); Simon D. Bronner, ed., *Consuming Visions: Accumulation and Display of Goods in America* (Winterthur, Del.: Henry Francis du Pont Winterthur Museum, and New York: W. W. Norton, 1989); Rudi Laermans, "Learning to Consume: Early Department Stores and the Shaping of Modern Consumer Culture (1860–1914)," *Theory, Culture, and Society* 10 (Nov. 1993): 79–102; Ann Satterthwaite, *Going Shopping: Consumer Choices and Community Consequences* (New Haven: Yale University Press, 2001); and Lizabeth Cohen, *A Consumers' Republic: The Politics of Mass Consumption in Postwar America* (New York: Alfred A. Knopf, 2004). Hrant Pasadernmadjian, *The Department Store: Its Origins, Evolution, and Economics* (London: Newman, 1954) is a valuable international account from a business perspective. A number of department store companies have commissioned histories, some of which are oriented to a general audience. John William Ferry, *A History of the Department Store* (New York: Macmillan, 1960) and Robert Hendrickson, *The Grand Emporiums: The Illustrated History of America's Great Department Stores* (New York: Stein and Day, 1979) offer copious popular overviews.

2. *Enterprising Emporiums: The Jewish Department Stores of Downtown Baltimore* (Baltimore: Jewish Museum of Maryland, 2001) offers an introductory exploration of the subject. See also Leon Harris, *Merchant Princes: An Intimate History of Jewish Families Who Built Great Department Stores* (New York: Harper & Row, 1979).

3. Exceptions include two brief surveys by Meredith Clausen: "The Department Store—Development of the Type," *Journal of Architectural Education* 39 (fall 1985): 20–29, and "Department Stores," in John A. Wilkes, ed., *Encyclopedia of Architecture, Design, Engineering & Construction,* 4 vols. (New York: Wiley, 1988), 2: 204–22; and case studies, the major example of which is Joseph Siry, *Carson Pirie Scott: Louis Sullivan and the Chicago Department Store* (Chicago: University of Chicago Press, 1988). Louisa M. Iarocci, "Spaces of Desire: The Department Store in America," Ph.D. diss., Boston University, 2003, seeks to integrate material, economic, and cultural aspects, focusing on Wanamaker's in Philadelphia through the early twentieth century. See also Stephanie Dyer, "Markets in the Meadows: Department Stores and Shopping Centers in the Decentralization of Philadelphia, 1920–1980," Ph.D. diss., University of Pennsylvania, 2000. Several aspects of a key prototype have been examined in Mary Ann Smith, "John Snook and the Design for A. T. Stewart's Store," *New-York Historical Society Quarterly* 58 (Jan. 1974): 18–33; Deborah S. Gardner, "'A Paradise of Fashion': A. T. Stewart's Department Store, 1862–1875," in Joan M. Jensen and Sue Davidson, eds., *A Needle, a Bobbin, a Strike: Women Needleworkers in America* (Philadelphia: Temple University Press, 1984), chap. 2; Harry E. Resseguie, "A. T. Stewart's Marble Palace—The Cradle of the Department Store," *New-York Historical Society Quarterly* 48 (Apr. 1964): 131–62; Resseguie, "Alexander Turney Stewart and the Development of the Department Store, 1823–1876," *Business History Review* 39 (autumn 1965): 301–22; and Stephen N. Elias, *Alexander T. Stewart: The Forgotten Merchant Prince* (Westport, Conn.: Praeger, 1992), esp. chap. 4. The department store has also figured prominently in several studies of urban development, including Christine Boyer, *Manhattan*

Manners: Architecture and Style, 1850–1900 (New York: Rizzoli, 1985), 87–120; Jeanne Cather Lawrence, "Geographical Space, Social Space, and the Realm of the Dream Palace," *Urban History* 19 (1992): 64–83; Sharon Zukin, *The Cultures of Cities* (Malden, Mass.: Blackwell, 1995), chap. 6; Mona Domosh, *Invented Cities: The Creation of Landscape in Nineteenth-Century New York and Boston* (New Haven: Yale University Press, 1996), chap. 2; Richard Longstreth, *City Center to Regional Mall: Architecture, the Automobile, and Retailing in Los Angeles, 1920–1950* (Cambridge: MIT Press, 1997); and John Henry Hepp IV, *The Middle-Class City: Transforming Space and Time in Philadelphia, 1876–1926* (Philadelphia: University of Pennsylvania Press, 2003), chaps. 3, 6.

4. Filene's in Boston, Arnold Constable, Lord & Taylor, and Saks Fifth Avenue in New York, Neiman-Marcus in Dallas, Sakowitz in Houston, and I. Magnin in San Francisco.

5. Of the eight other metropolitan areas among the sixty largest in 1960, Sacramento and San Jose, California, had become satellites of San Francisco department stores; San Bernardino–Riverside was likewise tied to Los Angeles, as was Fort Lauderdale–Hollywood to Miami. I could find no developments that lent further insight on the topics discussed in the book among projects done in the Albany-Schenectady, New York, area or in the Norfolk-Portsmouth, Virginia, area. Department store developments in the remaining two cities, Honolulu and Phoenix, likely constitute a richer yield, but only with regional malls created right at the end of the study period.

On the other hand, only three of the sixty largest cities in 1930—Flint, Michigan; Jersey City, New Jersey; and Worcester, Massachusetts—apparently had no department store companies undertaking substantial physical expansion within the study period. I have, however, included Tampa and St. Petersburg as well as Miami and Miami Beach in Florida, as these two pairs in each case formed major metropolitan areas during most of the study period, and in 1930 had combined populations equal to those of a number of the other smaller cities considered. Work undertaken by department store companies based in Miami and Tampa enriches our understanding of the transformations that are the focus of this study.

6. For purposes of this study, a "branch" department store is defined as an outlet of any size and scope that is well removed from the parent store and duplicates some or all of its functions. This range thus encompasses any plant from a small resort shop to a large, full-line facility.

7. Dolores Hayden, *Building Suburbia: Green Fields and Urban Growth, 1820–2000* (New York: Pantheon, 2003) is a recent example from a long line of critiques on retail and other forms of commercial development. The rise of interest among prominent designers in retail architecture is reflected in a project directed by Rem Koolhaas that led to the *Harvard Design School Design Guide to Shopping* (Cologne: Taschen, 2001). A number of pictorial volumes help document the trend; see, e.g., Ian Luna, *Retail Architecture and Shopping* (New York: Rizzoli, 2005) and Stephanie Schupp, *New Architecture of Shopping Complexes* (Singapore: Page One, 2005). That interest, in turn, has fostered a rediscovery of historical precedents such as Jim Heimann, ed., *Shop America: Midcentury Storefront Design, 1938–1950* (Cologne: Taschen, 2007).

CHAPTER 1. Bigger and Bigger Stores

1. "Bamberger Additions," wwd, 12 Dec. 1919, 61; "Work Soon to Begin," wwd, 30 July 1921, 1–2; "To Begin Work," wwd, 2 Aug. 1921, 58; "Novel Features," wwd, 17 June 1922, 40; "Bamberger 'Greater Store,'" wwd, 30 Oct. 1922, 16; nse, 30 Oct. 1922, Bamberger Sect.; "Completion of Bamberger Addition," dge 76 (18 Nov. 1922): 103, 111; "New Addition," a&b 54 (Dec. 1922): 112–13 and pls.

2. "Big Store for Newark," dge 65 (25 Mar. 1911): 81.

3. "New Bamberger," wwd, 18 Dec. 1926, 1, 16; "Bamberger's to Start," rl, 1st Feb. issue, 1927, 10; "Constructing Four Basements," wwd, 26 Apr. 1927, 56; "Bamberger's 16-Story," wwd, 1 May 1928, I-2; "Bamberger's Addition," wwd, 12 Oct. 1928, I-1; "L. Bamberger & Co.'s Department Store," a&b 61 (Oct. 1929): 315–18, 325–26.

4. The extent of department store construction during this period was gleaned from coverage in wwd, dge, and other trade literature of the period. Here I generally define large-scale construction as work entailing at least 100,000 square feet, though I also include the relatively few instances where smaller additions were made to "complete" major work of the previous decade. More research might well yield additional examples, though it is doubtful whether the total would extend much beyond one hundred.

5. "1924 To Be Big Year," wwd, 19 Jan. 1924, 13.

6. Excluding Elizabeth, Jersey City, and Paterson. For the figures and boundaries, I have relied on the *Fifteenth Census of the United States: 1930, Metropolitan Districts, Population and Area*.

7. Department store executives were quite conscious of these factors, as is reflected in period textbooks such as J. Russell Doubman and John R. Whitaker, *The Organization and Operation of Department Stores* (New York: Wiley, 1927), 11–19. See also "What Trends Should Be Watched," rl, 2nd May issue, 1927, 5; and "1918–1928—The Most Important Decade," rl, 1st May issue, 1928, 1. The expanding regional market and women constituting the overwhelming majority of shoppers are addressed in Alison Isenberg, *Downtown America: A History of the Place and the People Who Made It* (Chicago: University of Chicago Press, 2004), chap. 3, although her assertion that the most significant increase in trade came from "small-town and rural women" does not correlate with the great rise in middle-class metropolitan populations of the decade.

8. William Nelson Taft, "1918–1928"; *Twenty-Five Years of Retailing* (New York: National Retail Dry Goods Association, 1936), 22–24. Taft's ranks among the best concise accounts of significant changes in retail practices during the decade. See also "Hahn's Career," wwd, 11 May 1928, I-1, I-16. For a succinct historical account, see Ronald Savitt, "Innovation in American Retailing, 1919–39: Improving Inventory Management," *International Review of Retail, Distribution and Consumer Research* 9 (July 1999): 307–20.

9. Detailed data is found in the "Operating Expenses of Department Stores" issues annually in the hub series. For a summary, see Malcolm P. McNair and Eleanor G. May, "The American Department Store, 1920–1960," hub 166 (1963).

10. A useful overview of the subject is provided in Jan Whitaker, *Service and Style: How the American Department Store Fashioned the Middle Class* (New York: St. Martin's, 2006), chap. 2.

11. For background, see William Leach, *Land of Desire: Merchants, Power, and the Rise of a New American Culture* (New York: Vintage, 1993), 299–302.

12. Charles F. Holt, "Who Benefited from the Prosperity of the Twenties?" *Explorations in Economic History* 14 (July 1977): 277–89; Susan Strasser, *Never Done: A History of American Housework* (New York: Pantheon, 1982), esp. chap. 14; Martha L. Olney, *Buy Now, Pay Later: Advertising, Credit, and Consumer Durables in the 1920s* (Chapel Hill: University of North Carolina Press, 1991), esp. chap. 2.

13. Edward A. Filene, with Werner K. Gabler and Percy S. Brown, *Next Steps Forward in Retailing* (Boston: By the authors, 1937), 10–19; Hrant Pasadermadjian, *The Department Store: Its Origins, Evolution and Economics* (London: Newman, 1954), 51–61;

"Operating Expenses in Department Stores"; McNair and May, "American Department Store."

14. A good sense of the complacency that at least some department store executives had at the decade's beginning is suggested in "Wells Explains History," *WWD*, 7 Oct. 1919, 35.

15. See, e.g., "Circumstances Rather Than Planning Made Present Day Department Store," *DGE* 76 (25 Mar. 1922): 14, 100; "The Department Store and Its Future," *NRB* 10 (Mar. 1928): 100–103. See also "Shops Beat Dept. Stores," *RL*, 2nd Sep. issue, 1927, 6.

16. This pattern is outlined in Richard Longstreth, *City Center to Regional Mall: Architecture, the Automobile, and Retailing in Los Angeles, 1920–1950* (Cambridge: MIT Press, 1997), 36–41. The scope of the current study precludes comparably detailed investigation of other cities; however, the contents of *WWD* and local newspapers suggest similar developments in urban centers nationwide. For a sampling of *WWD* articles, see "Specialty Shop," 6 Oct. 1919, 40; "New Seattle Store," 20 May 1920, 39; "Hailparn's Women's Apparel," 29 Jan. 1921, 40; "Specialty Shop Competes," 5 Oct. 1921, 35; "Rothschild's to Open," 31 July 1923, 58; "Kline's Opens," 5 Nov. 1929, I-10.

17. Carl N. Schumalz, "Operating Results of Department and Specialty Stores in 1929," *HUB* 83 (1930): 3.

18. M. M. Zimmerman, *The Challenge of Chain Store Distribution* (New York: Harper, 1931), 12–13.

19. Mudkins, "Circumstances," 14; William J. Baxter, *Chain Store Distribution and Management,* rev. ed. (New York: Harper, 1931), 113–17; Paul M. Mazur, *American Prosperity: Its Causes and Consequences* (New York: Viking, 1928), 40, 41.

20. Baxter, *Chain Store,* 207, 250–55, 258.

21. *WWD*, 15 Sep. 1922, 34; "Russeks Report," *WWD*, 21 Sep. 1922, 34; "Bedell Co. to Open," *WWD*, 17 June 1920, 1; "Bedell Chain," *WWD*, 14 Sep. 1920, 32; "New Bedell Co. Store," *WWD*, 25 July 1922, 61; *WWD*, 13 Sep. 1923, 42; "Bedell's Open," *WWD*, 1 Oct. 1923, 24; "Complete Plans," 6 Jan. 1925, 55; *WWD*, 30 Apr. 1925, 40.

22. W. D. Darby, "Story of the Chain Store," serialized weekly in *DGE* between 31 Mar. and 4 Aug. 1928. Other important studies of the period include Baxter, *Chain Store;* Zimmerman, *Challenge;* and U.S. Federal Trade Commission, *Chain Stores: Growth and Development of Chain Stores,* 72nd Cong. 1st sess., U.S. Senate Doc. 100, 1932. An authoritative overview is provided in Paul H. Nystrom, *Economics of Retailing,* rev. ed. (New York: Roland, 1930), chap. 8, one of the most widely read and respected texts of the period. An important retrospective account written by a key chronicler of the chain system's rise is Godfrey M. Lebhar, *Chain Stores in America, 1859–1962,* 3rd ed. (New York: Chain Store Publishing, 1963), esp. chaps. 3–5. See also Leach, *Land of Desire,* 272–75.

23. "A Chain Store's Contribution to Retailing," *NRB* 10 (Apr. 1928): 148. See also Darby, "Story of the Chain Store," 12 May 1928, 32–33, 79, and 19 May 1928, 15; John Guernsey, *Retailing Tomorrow* (New York: Dry Goods Economist, 1929), chap. 5; and Mary Elizabeth Curry, *Creating an American Institution: The Merchandising Genius of J. C. Penney* (New York: Garland, 1993), esp. chap. 10.

24. For discussion of Sears and Ward, see Richard Longstreth, "Sears, Roebuck and the Remaking of the Department Store, 1924–1942," *JSAH* 65 (June 2006): 238–79.

25. See, e.g., "Growth of Department Store Chains," *DGE* 78 (4 Oct. 1924): 11–12; "Department Store Consolidation," *JR* 2 (Apr. 1926): 14–15; "Department-Store Consolidations," *HBR* 4 (July 1926): 459–70; "Growth of Department Store Mergers," *WWD*, 17 Mar. 1928, I-1, I-7; "Consolidations and Mergers: Their Potential Advantages and Limitations," *NRB* 11 (June 1929): 324, 362; "Mammoth Stores, Preferred," *Outlook and Independent* 152 (14 Aug. 1929): 606–7; "Merging Seen," *WWD*, 17 Oct. 1929, I-1, I-20; and "Central Buying by Department-Store Mergers," *HBR* 8 (Apr. 1930): 265–73. See also references cited in nn. 26–36, 38–42 below. For a more general discussion of the issue in business, see John Allen Murphy, *Merchandising Through Mergers* (New York: Harper, 1930). A valuable historical account is given in Leach, *Land of Desire,* 24–26, 275–85.

26. "Hamburger Store Sold," *LAT*, 1 Apr. 1923, I-1, I-2; "May to Open," *RMN*, 13 Sep. 1925, 8; "Department-Store Consolidations," 468–69; "May Co. Buys," *WWD*, 9 Sep. 1927, 1; "May Co. Buys," *WWD*, 10 Sep. 1927, II-1, II-16; "Soundness of Organization," *ABJ*, 10 Mar. 1928, O'Neil Sect., 8-B; "May Co. Will Add," *CPD*, 19 Jan. 1931, 11; "May Stores: Watch Them Grow," *Fortune* 38 (Dec. 1948): 152–53. May also purchased a Pittsburgh store, Boggs & Buhl, in 1912, but sold it less than three years later.

27. "Kaufmann-Baer Merge," *WWD*, 3 Dec. 1925, 1, 47; "Kaufmann-Baer Opens," *WWD*, 5 Jan. 1928, I-2. Concerning the company, see "Gimbel's Dedicate," *PL*, 21 Nov. 1926, I-5; and Guernsey, *Retailing Tomorrow,* 121–22.

28. "Organizations Intensively Study," *WWD*, 13 Jan. 1923, 27; "Associated Dry Goods," *WWD*, 2 July 1928, I-1, I-2; "Department-Store Consolidations," 467–68; Theodore J. Carlson, *A Corporate History of Associated Dry Goods Corporation,* rev. ed. (New York: Gould and Wilkie, 1982); "Story of the Chain Store," *WWD*, 21 Apr. 1928, 14.

29. "R. H. Macy," *WWD*, 2 Jan. 1924, 1; "La Salle & Koch," *WWD*, 3 Jan. 1924, 1; "Report Macy's," *WWD*, 6 Mar. 1925, 1, 47; "Davison-Paxon-Stokes," *WWD*, 9 Mar. 1925, 1; "Credit Policy," *WWD*, 1 July 1929, I-1, I-20; "Macy-Bamberger," *DGE* 83 (6 July 1929): 29.

30. "$12,000,000 Dept. Store," *WWD*, 17 Mar. 1927, 1; "F. & R. Lazarus," *WWD*, 11 June 1928, I-1, 19; "Marshall Field & Co.," *WWD*, 14 June 1929, I-1, I-15; "Seattle Store," *WWD*, 5 July 1929, I-1, I-19; "R. H. White Co.," *WWD*, 28 Nov. 1928, I-1, I-2. Filene's purchase proved short-lived.

31. "Lease of Saks," *WWD*, 26 June 1922, 1, 30; "Three Local Gimbel-Saks," *WWD*, 25 Apr. 1923, I-1, I-3; "Stockholders of Gimbels," *WWD*, 11 May 1923, 1, 38; "Gimbels Elect," *WWD*, 12 May 1923, 1; "Gimbel's Now Biggest," *RL*, 1st Oct. issue, 1924, 7; "Saks Is Very . . . ," *Fortune* 18 (Nov. 1938): 64, 126.

32. "S. S. Kresge Buys," *WWD*, 30 July 1923, 1–2; "New Kresge Chain," *WWD*, 1 Aug. 1923, 46; "Plaut Policies," *WWD*, 7 Aug. 1923, 59; "Kresge Start," *WWD*, 14 Aug. 1923, 43; "Palais Royal," *WWD*, 15 Feb. 1924, 1; "The Fair," *WWD*, 24 Feb. 1925, 1, 63.

33. "Lew Hahn Resigns," *WWD*, 11 May 1928, I-1, I-16; "Coordination of Sections," *WWD*, 15 May 1928, I-1, I-20; "Lew Hahn Resigns," *RL*, 2nd May issue, 1928, 2; "Outline Plans," *WWD*, 16 July 1928, I-1, I-2; "Weisenberger Made," *WWD*, 18 July 1928, I-1, I-23; "Report Hahn Chain," *WWD*, 21 Sep. 1928, I-1; "Report Hahn Seeks," *WWD*, 17 Oct. 1928, I-1, I-2; "O'Neill's with Hahn," *WWD*, 5 Dec. 1928, I-1; "Jordan Marsh Denies," *WWD*, 6 Dec. 1928, I-1, I-2; "Aims of Hahn," *WWD*, 11 Dec. 1928, sect. IV; "Billion-Dollar Chain," *RL*, 2nd Dec. issue, 1928, 1, 10; "Joske Brothers Join," *RL*, 2nd Feb. issue, 1929, 1; Guernsey, *Retailing Tomorrow,* 112–13. See also Thomas M. Macioce, *Allied Stores Corporation: 50 Years of Retail Growth* (New York: Newcomen Society, 1979).

34. "Confer on Affiliated," *WWD*, 15 Jan. 1923, 1; "To Give Details," *WWD*, 1 Feb. 1923, 1, 45; "Sincere to Head," *WWD*, 2 Feb. 1923, 1, 53; "Nugent's Tell," *WWD*, 13 Feb. 1923, 57; "Frank & Seder," *WWD*, 20 Aug. 1923, 1; "Frank & Seder," *WWD*, 18 Sep. 1923, 1, 18; Falk, "Central Buying," 266; Darby, "Story of Chain Store," 21 Apr. 1928, 14.

35. "Confirm Purchase," *WWD*, 27 May 1920, 38; "City Stores Co.," *WWD*, 5 Nov. 1923, 1; "City Stores Co.," *WWD*, 8 Nov. 1923, 1, 7; "Fourth Unit," *WWD*, 8 Aug. 1924, 1, 38; "City Stores to Add,"

WWD, 22 Oct. 1925, 1; "Goerke Gains Control," *WWD*, 9 Nov. 1925, 1, 47; "Goerke Gains Control," *RL*, 2nd Nov. issue, 1925, 10; "Will Not Change," *WWD*, 9 Dec. 1925, 5; "City Stores Co.," *RL*, 1st Dec. issue, 1925, 1; "Group Pays," *WWD*, 18 Oct. 1928, I-1, I-2; Guernsey, *Retailing Tomorrow*, 118–19.

36. "Bloomingdale Bros.," *WWD*, 17 Sep. 1929, I-1, I-20; "Name 4 Holding Firms," *WWD*, 17 Oct. 1929, I-1, I-20; "Filene Merger," *WWD*, 26 Nov. 1929, I-1, I-20; "Bloomingdale's Becomes," *WWD*, 19 Dec. 1929, I-1, I-19; "Mr. Fred of the Lazari," *Fortune* 37 (Mar. 1948): 113, 162.

37. Figures are from "Department and Chain-Store Sales in 1927," *JR* 4 (Apr. 1928): 16–17, and *Fairchild's Financial Manual* (New York: Fairchild), issued annually beginning in 1927.

38. "E. A. Filene Advocates," *WWD*, 6 May 1924, 1, 46; "Department Stores Must," *RL*, 7 May 1924, 8; Edward A. Filene, "Just What Does This Chain-Store?" *RL*, 1st Feb. issue, 1929, 1; Filene, "The Present Status and Future Prospects of Chains of Department Stores," address to American Economic Association, Washington, D.C., 27 Dec. 1927; "Filene Predicts," *RL*, 1st Jan. issue, 1928, 1; Edward A. Filene, "What Will the Store," *RL*, 2nd Jan. issue, 1928, 2. Filene opposed the formation of Federated, which his brother Lincoln had orchestrated, due to a deep rift that had developed between them and also because he did not believe it was a true move toward developing a chain operation. For background, see George E. Berkeley, *The Filenes* (Boston: International Pocket Library, 1998), chap. 10.

39. Paul M. Mazur, "The Future of Retailing," *NRB* 7 (Mar. 1925): 19–22, 43 (quote on p. 19); Mazur, "Future Developments in Retailing," *HBR* 2 (July 1924): 434–46; Mazur, "What Developments May," *RL*, 2nd Oct. issue, 1924, 8; "Consolidations Are Inevitable," *RL*, 1st Aug. issue, 1925, 1, 5; "'Consolidation' Is Solution," *RL*, 2nd Feb. issue, 1927, 1. Concerning Mazur himself, see Leach, *Land of Desire*, 285–92.

40. Guernsey, *Retailing Tomorrow*.

41. "Don't Play in the Chain Store's Yard," *DGE* 81 (30 July 1927): 5–6; "Looking Forward," *DGE* 82 (14 Jan. 1928): II-2, II-31; "We Disagree," *DGE* 82 (28 Apr. 1928): 9–10.

42. "Growth of Department Store Mergers," I-1; "Central Buying," 25–26. For an unabashed critique of the whole system, see Edith M. Stern, "Chain Department-Stores," *American Mercury* 30 (Oct. 1933): 152–59.

43. Not everyone subscribed to this view. Mazur was among the first to argue that such expansion was of limited value.

44. *WWD* and other trade periodicals of the period provided the major source on which these numbers are based. For a complete list based on these sources, see Richard Longstreth, comp., "New Buildings and Major Additions for Downtown Department Store Buildings, 1920–1960," at http://www.departmentstorehistory.net and http://www.preservenet.cornell.edu.

45. For a sampling of accounts, see "Gimbel's Buy," *WWD*, 9 Sep. 1921, 1; "Younker Brothers Plan," *WWD*, 28 May 1923, 1; "R. H. White Co.," *WWD*, 2 Jan. 1924, 1; "Burdine's Plan," *WWD*, 20 Nov. 1925, 1; "Issue Stock," *WWD*, 17 Dec. 1925, 1; "Hudson's Offer," *WWD*, 1 Feb. 1927, I-1; and "Strawbridge, Clothier Bonds," *WWD*, 7 June 1928, I-1, I-18.

46. The comparison is based on the number of new buildings, not their collective square footage or the dollar volume of construction. Notes taken during the course of research on stores built prior to the First World War provide the basis for this comparison, but no complete accounting has been made.

47. The few exceptions included new buildings for J. N. Adam of Buffalo (1924–26) and for Hochschild, Kohn of Baltimore (1923–25); enlarged quarters for S. Kann & Sons of Washington (1926–28) and for Hamburger & Sons of Los Angeles (1919–20); and a new building for B. Nugent & Brother of St. Louis (1923), whose existing facility was remodeled instead. Many additional schemes were contemplated during the decade, but never advanced beyond the preliminary discussion stage.

48. For background, see *The Golden Book of the Wanamaker Stores* ([Philadelphia]: John Wanamaker, 1911), 277–88; Robert W. Twyman, *History of Marshall Field & Co., 1852–1906* (Philadelphia: University of Pennsylvania Press, 1954), 155–59; Thomas S. Hines, *Burnham of Chicago: Architect and Planner* (New York: Oxford University Press, 1974), 302–6; Neil Harris, "Shopping—Chicago Style," in John Zukowsky, ed., *Chicago Architecture, 1872–1922: Birth of a Metropolis* (Munich: Prestel, 1987), 142–46; Louisa M. Iarocci, "Spaces of Desire: The Department Store in America," Ph.D. diss., Boston University, 2003, esp. 165–245.

49. "Start Work," *WWD*, 5 Oct. 1922, 31; "Dedicate First Unit," *WWD*, 16 Oct. 1923, 34; "Building Plans," *Birmingham Age-Herald*, 4 May 1924, 1; "To Begin Work," *WWD*, 7 May 1924, 34; "Announce Plans," *WWD*, 18 Nov. 1924, 55; "Kern's Plan," *WWD*, 31 Oct. 1925, 15; "Ernst Kern Co.," *DN*, 24 Feb. 1929, 17; "Convenience to Shoppers Keynote," *DGE* 83 (11 May 1929): 66–67, 82; "Hens & Kelly," *WWD*, 25 May 1922, 29; "Hens & Kelly," *WWD*, 9 June 1922, 43; "Hens & Kelly," *WWD*, 20 Apr. 1923, 28; "Hens & Kelly," *WWD*, 8 Oct. 1923, 22; "Hens & Kelly," *WWD*, 25 Jan. 1924, 32; "Lower Part," *WWD*, 6 Sep. 1924, 49; "Hens & Kelly," *WWD*, 3 Nov. 1924, 25; "Rush Work," *WWD*, 10 Mar. 1925, 57; "4th Unit," *WWD*, 9 June 1925, 56; "Hens & Kelly," *WWD*, 18 Sep. 1925, 41; "Hens & Kelly," *WWD*, 13 Mar. 1926, 16; "Strawbridge, Clothier," *WWD*, 7 June 1928, I-1, I-18; "New Strawbridge Store," *PL*, 17 June 1928, Real Estate Sect., 1, 2; "Work to Start Soon," *DGE* 82 (7 July 1928): 66; "Strawbridge & Clothier to Build," *Building Magazine* 8 (July 1928): 11, 22, 33, 35; "New Department Store," *Commercial America* 25 (Sep. 1928): 22, 44; "Second New Unit," *PI*, 3 Jan. 1929, 4; Strawbridge's Opens," *WWD*, 20 Aug. 1929, I-11, I-12; "Strawbridge & Clothier Open," *Retailing*, 29 Nov. 1930, 5; "Coast Store," *WWD*, 29 Dec. 1920, 37; "Fifth Street Store," *LAT*, 14 Aug. 1921, V-1; "Will Begin Work," *WWD*, 22 Aug. 1921, 27; "Start Work," *WWD*, 26 Oct. 1921, 31.

50. "Big Building Program," *WWD*, 15 Oct. 1919, 48; "L. S. Donaldson Starts," *MJ*, 30 Dec. 1923, 1, 4; "New $6,000,000 Home," *WWD*, 2 Jan. 1924, 1, 3; "Donaldson's Open," *MJ*, 9 Nov. 1924, City Life Sect., 1, 2; "L. S. Donaldson's Open," *WWD*, 17 Nov. 1924, 34; "Greater Namms," *WWD*, 12 Jan. 1924, 12; "A. I. Namm's," *BE*, 3 Feb. 1925, 5; "Formal Opening," *WWD*, 5 Feb. 1925, 56; "Namm's Plans," *WWD*, 18 June 1928, 1; *WWD*, 22 June 1928, I-6.

51. "Move to Erect," *WWD*, 12 Apr. 1927, 1; "Bloomingdale's Develop," *WWD*, 7 June 1928, I-1, I-2; "Bloomingdale Brothers," *NYT*, 17 Feb. 1929, RE2; "A New Bloomingdale's," *DGE* 83 (16 Mar. 1929): 79–80; "Bloomingdale Alterations," *WWD*, 28 Oct. 1929, I-20; "New Bloomingdale," *WWD*, 3 Sep. 1930, I-15; "A & S Plans," *WWD*, 3 Feb. 1927, 1, 63; "New 10-Floor Building," *WWD*, 29 Dec. 1928, 21; "New A & S Building," *WWD*, 23 Aug. 1929, I-2; R. W. Sexton, *The Logic of Modern Architecture* (New York: Architectural Book Publishing, 1929), 56–57.

52. For background and a case study, see Longstreth, *City Center*, 24–34.

53. "$5,000,000 New Store," *ST*, 15 Mar. 1925, 1, 4; "Bon Marche Plans," *WWD*, 16 Mar. 1925, 1, 47; "Bon Marche to Build," *ST*, 7 Aug. 1927, 1, 4; "Bon Marche," *WWD*, 24 Apr. 1928, I-7; "New Bon Marche," *WWD*, 21 May 1929, I-20; "Golden Key," *ST*, 4 Aug. 1929, 161; "Saks,' on Fifth Avenue," *WWD*, 21 Apr. 1920, 47; "Saks Building," *WWD*, 28 June 1921, 46; "Saks Issue," *WWD*, 14 Mar. 1922, 1, 6; "Saks Obtain," *WWD*, 4 May 1923, 1; "Saks-Fifth Avenue," *WWD*, 13 Sep. 1924, 14–15; "Saks-Fifth Avenue," *WWD*, 15 Sep. 1924, 32.

54. "Probable Shift," WWD, 2 Apr. 1926, 6; "O'Neil's Plan," WWD, 7 Dec. 1926, 1; ABJ, 10 Mar. 1928, M. O'Neil Sect.; "O'Neil's New Home," WWD, 13 Mar. 1928, I-1, I-11; "Report Polsky's Preparing," WWD, 4 June 1926, 2; "Akron Gets," ABJ, 9 Apr. 1929, 1; "Polsky's to Open," ABJ, 13 Sep. 1930, 12; "Higbee's Move," CPD, 21 May 1930, 1, 3; "Work Begins," WWD, 23 May 1930, I-2; "Rumor Retail Expansion," WWD, 26 May 1930, I-10; "The Higbee Co. Building," Retailing, 17 Jan. 1931, 9; "Higbee Co. Moves," CPD, 6 Sep. 1931, 4-A; "Higbee's Opens," WWD, 8 Sep. 1931, I-1, I-35; "Here's the Latest Model," RL, Oct. 1931, Magazine Sect., 2; Richard E. Karberg, with Judith Karberg and Jane Hansen, *The Higbee Company and the Silver Grille* (Cleveland: Cleveland Landmarks, 2001).

55. "Will Add," LAT, 9 July 1922, V-1; "Broadway Department Store," WWD, 9 Aug. 1922, 1, 63; "Los Angeles Store," WWD, 23 Dec. 1922, 1; "Work to Start," WWD, 1 May 1923, 42; WWD, 7 May 1923, 27; "Store Unveils," LAT, 9 Nov. 1924, II-2; "F. & R. Lazarus," WWD, 11 June 1925, 1, 2; "Lazarus Co. Makes," CD, 11 June 1925, 1, 6; "J. Horne Co.," WWD, 14 Sep. 1921, 1, 36; "2,300,000 Addition," PP, 14 Sep. 1921, 1, 2; "Big Addition," DGE 75 (1 Oct. 1921): 105; "Joseph Horne's," PP, 23 Apr. 1923, 4; "Neiman-Marcus to Unify," WWD, 8 Jan. 1926, 7; "Floor Plan," WWD, 5 Oct. 1926, 6; "Greater Neiman-Marcus," DMN, 2 Oct. 1927, IX-1 to IX-7 and Rotogravure Sect.; "Expansion Plans," WWD, 4 Feb. 1925, 63; "Woodward & Lothrop," WWD, 22 Apr. 1926, 7; "Enlarged Home," WWD, 4 Nov. 1926, 8, 12; DGE 80 (18 Dec. 1926): 39.

56. "Lasalle & Koch Expansion," WWD, 4 Mar. 1926, 6; "Lasalle & Koch," WWD, 16 Nov. 1927, I-4; "Trade Territory Expanding," DGE 81 (3 Sep. 1927): 60.

57. "Trade Territory Expanding." The company was established three years prior to the expansion ("Brown-Dunkin Opens," *Tulsa Daily World*, 21 Sep. 1924, 1, 2, 7–10; "It's Gala Night," *Tulsa Daily World*, 28 Sep. 1924, 1, 3). Expansion continued in later decades ("Brown-Dunkin Finishes," WWD, 30 Oct. 1931, I-63; "Expansion Planned," WWD, 1 May 1934, 12).

58. "Famous-Barr Co.," WWD, 26 Feb. 1920, 64, 58; "Remodeling of Famous & Barr," WWD, 19 Mar. 1921, 31; "Famous-Barr's Plan," WWD, 10 Feb. 1928, I-6; Famous & Barr Move," WWD, 23 Aug. 1928, I-12; "Famous-Barr's Completing," WWD, 2 Oct. 1928, I-7, 12; "Growing Upward," DGE 82 (22 Dec. 1928): 58, 70–71.

59. "Pogue's to Add," WWD, 26 Aug. 1929, I-15; "Pogue's Plans," WWD, 18 Aug. 1930, I-1, I-20; "Formal Event," WWD, 22 Oct. 1930, I-1, I-16; "Pogue 8-Story Expansion," Retailing, 8 Nov. 1930, 11; "Mabley-Carew Signs," WWD, 9 Dec. 1929, I-1; "Mabley-Carew," WWD, 10 Dec. 1929, I-10, I-15; "Mabley-Carew," WWD, 7 Oct. 1930, 1, 2; "Carew Tower," DW 17 (Nov. 1930): 28–29, 61.

60. "Macy's Buy More," WWD, 2 Apr. 1919, 28; "Macy's Constructing," WWD, 9 Feb. 1922, 1, 5, 49; "A Greater Macy's," DGE 76 (18 Feb. 1922): 32; "Macy's New Building," WWD, 8 Sep. 1924, 33; "R. H. Macy & Co.," A&B 56 (Sep. 1924): 83–88; "Macy's Acquire," WWD, 26 May 1927, 1; "Macy's Start," WWD, 25 Sep. 1928, I-2; Eugene Clute, *The Practical Requirements of Modern Buildings* (New York: Pencil Points, 1928), 169–76; "Macy Building," WWD, 13 Sep. 1929, I-16; "Macy to Erect," RL, 1st Oct. issue, 1929, 5; WWD, 23 Apr. 1930, I-20; "Macy Store Again Enlarged," A&B 63 (June 1931): 114–15.

61. "J. L. Hudson's Ask," WWD, 14 Dec. 1923, 1; "Hudson Store," DN, 11 Jan. 1924, 1, 2; "Hudson Unit," WWD, 17 Jan. 1924, 40; "Entire 15-Story," WWD, 2 Oct. 1924, 25; "Work Starts," WWD, 30 Dec. 1924, 32; "J. L. Hudson Co.," WWD, 9 Dec. 1925, 7; "A Still Greater Hudson Store," MRSW 61 (Oct. 1927): 29; "J. L. Hudson Company," DFP, 4 Nov. 1928, 17; "Hudson's New Unit," WWD, 7 Nov. 1928, I-13, I-20. See also Michael Hauser and Marianne Weldon, *Hudson's: Detroit's Legendary Department Store* (Charleston, S.C.: Arcadia, 2004).

62. "J. L. Hudson Co.," WWD, 25 Aug. 1922, 1; "Hudson's Buy," WWD, 31 Jan. 1927, 1, 63; "Hudson's Buys" and "Progress Mark," DN, 1 Feb. 1927, 1, 2. Later it was reported that Hudson's purchase of Newcomb-Endicott was in part fostered by the May Company's efforts to acquire the latter store; see "Report May Co.," WWD, 8 Feb. 1927, 2.

63. "Bullock's Acquires," LAT, 29 June 1919, V-1; "Bullock's Plans," WWD, 23 July 1919, 56; "Bullock's Plan," WWD, 13 Apr. 1923, 1; "Bullock's Open," WWD, 20 Nov. 1924, 41; "Trio of Major Units," LAT, 2 Oct. 1927, V-1; "Bullock's Will Build," LAT, 26 Feb. 1928, II-1; "Formally Open," WWD, 11 Sep. 1928, I-11.

64. "Crowley-Milner Plan," WWD, 11 Mar. 1919, 1, 12; "Crowley-Milner," WWD, 25 June 1921, 27; "Crowley-Milner Co.," WWD, 23 July 1921, 1; "Crowley-Milner Open," WWD, 5 Oct. 1921, 40; WWD, 7 Jan. 1925, 54; "Crowley-Milner Begin," WWD, 26 Sep. 1925, 31.

65. "Architects Confer," IN, 1 Feb. 1928, 15; "Ayres to Build," IS, 1 Feb. 1928, 1, 2; "L. S. Ayres," WWD, 8 May 1928, I-7; IS, 8 Sep. 1929, 11; IN, 13 Sep. 1929, L. S. Ayres Sect.; "Ayres, Indianapolis," WWD, 18 Sep. 1929, I-10; "Ayres Adds Eleven Stories," DGE 83 (26 Oct. 1929): 65, 67.

66. "Fight Bullock's," WWD, 3 Feb. 1921, 1, 61; "Bullock's Asks," LAT, 4 Feb. 1921, II-1; "J. C. Bullock Expresses," WWD, 7 Feb. 1921, 52; "Hearst's Play," LAT, 8 Feb. 1921, II-1, II-6; "Dry Goods Men," LAT, 9 Feb. 1921, II-1, II-7; "Ask Los Angeles," WWD, 9 Feb. 1921, 56; "Bullock's Bridge," WWD, 14 Feb. 1921, 25; "Hearst Takes Charge," LAT, 26 Feb. 1921, II-1, II-5; "City Not Able," LAT, 2 Mar. 1921, II-1, II-9; "Bullock's Offer," WWD, 5 Mar. 1921, 1, 38; "Los Angeles Still," WWD, 12 Mar. 1921, 30; "Bullock's Wins," LAT, 15 Mar. 1921, II-1.

67. "Halle's Plan," CPD, 28 Feb. 1926, III-6; "Vision Halle Span," CPD, 4 Mar. 1926, 1, 15; CPD, 29 Mar. 1927, Halle Sect.; CPD, 29 May 1929, Halles Bros. Sect.

68. "Our New Music Store," Hudsonian 6 (Apr. 1918): 11; "J. N. Adam's," WWD, 11 Apr. 1930, I-6, I-7; "Adams' Thrift," WWD, 22 Apr. 1930, I-17; "Store Creates Annex," WWD, 21 Jan. 1925, 19.

69. "Carson Pirie Scott," WWD, 15 Nov. 1926, 13; "Carson Pirie's Using," WWD, 18 July 1927, I-12, I-16; "Carson Pirie Scott's," WWD, 12 May 1930, I-13; "Carson Pirie Scott," WWD, 1 Oct. 1930, I-1, I-15. Abraham & Straus opened a men's store the same year; see "A & S Plans," WWD, 3 Feb. 1927, 1. Concerning the Field annex, see Sally A. Kitt Chappell, *Architecture and Planning of Graham, Anderson, Probst and White, 1912–1936: Transforming Tradition* (Chicago: University of Chicago Press, 1992), 66–77. For an overview of the subject, see Whitaker, *Service and Style*, 48–51.

70. "Lincoln-Liberty Building," *Building Magazine* 10 (May 1930): 9, 27; "Skyscraper to Rise," PI, 8 May 1930, 10; "The Lincoln-Liberty Building," *Building Owner and Manager* 11 (Sep. 1931): 5–8; "Symbol of Confidence," PL, 18 Oct. 1931, Editorial Sect., 3; "New Wanamaker Men's Store," *Philadelphia Record*, 16 Aug. 1932, 7; "Wanamaker's, with New Store," Retailing, 22 Aug. 1932, 2; "Business Upturn Speeds," RL, Sep. 1932, 23; "Wanamaker's Store," PI, 14 Sep. 1932, 6; "Open New Store," EB, 12 Oct. 1932, 12; "Wanamaker's New Men's Store," Retailing, 17 Oct. 1932, 1–3, I-7; "Particularly Interested," RL, Nov. 1932, 16; "No. 1 Broad Street, "*Real Estate Magazine* 14 (Nov. 1932): 6–7.

71. The matter is implicit in many period accounts to the point where it seems to have been taken for granted. It is also noted in basic trade studies such as Doubman and Whitaker, *Department Stores*, 153–54, and in articles that appear to be targeted to merchants in relatively small or remote communities. See, e.g., "You Are Judged by Your Store Front," DGE 76 (3 June 1922): 77, 89.

72. "Gimbel's Plan," WWD, 8 May 1922, 1, 7; "Gimbel's Plan," WWD, 17 Sep. 1924, 41.

73. "Lowenstein's Ready," *Commercial Appeal* [Memphis], 7 Sep. 1924, I-13.

74. The new building for Marshall Field (1900–1914) seems to have set the key precedent for this balance at a time when the department store's ascendancy was in full swing. See n. 90 for references.

75. The key precedent for this approach was set by Saks Fifth Avenue store in New York (1922–24).

76. Other examples include Bloomingdale Brothers in New York (1929–31), Thalheimer Brothers in Richmond (1929–30), Wise Company in Long Beach (1929), and Wise, Smith in Hartford (1929).

77. *Twenty-Five Years of Retailing*, 26. A good indication of this pattern is the thirty-page promotional booklet "The Great Department Store of Strawbridge & Clothier," undated but likely printed in the first decade of the twentieth century, Strawbridge & Clothier Collection, series VIII, box 88, Hagley Museum and Library, Wilmington, Del. *The Wanamaker Golden Book* reveals that substantial changes in this approach were under way by 1910. Wanamaker's layout nevertheless represented more the exception than the rule at that time. For a synopsis of planning concerns at the end of the 1920s, see "Today's Department Stores," *American Builder* 48 (Oct. 1929): 95–98.

78. See, e.g., "Department Arrangement and Decoration," MRSW 46 (July 1920): 15–17; "Modern Store Equipment," MRSW 47 (Dec. 1920): 13–15; "Floor Plan," WWD, 11 June 1921, 40; "Eighteen Months Experimenting Brings Splendid Result," DGE 77 (19 May 1923): 89, 93; "Modern Fixtures Show Goods Better," DGE 77 (6 Oct. 1923): 217; "Davis Store Finds Wide Open Display Sells Fabrics," DGE 78 (5 July 1924): 22; "Many Stores Planning New Equipment," DW 7 (Aug. 1925): 44; "Merchandising Methods and Equipment," DW 7 (Sep. 1925): 76–77; "That Sales Asset Called Atmosphere," DW 7 (Nov. 1925): 44–45; "Dreams Fulfilled with Completion of Store," DW 8 (Feb. 1926): 42–43; and "Fixtures—A Wide Selection Has Increased Sales," DGE 80 (31 July 1926): 56–57. Concerning show windows and department store interiors, see Leach, *Land of Desire*, 55–70 and chap. 3.

79. For a sampling of accounts, see "Better Lighting for Better Business," MRSW 45 (Oct. 1919): 15–19; "More Sales Thru Better Lighting," MRSW 45 (Nov. 1919): 13–18; "Light a Selling Help in Merchandising," MRSW 45 (Dec. 1919): 11–15; "Lighting Harmony Pays Well for Investment," DGE 74 (24 Jan. 1920): 99; "These Systems of Lighting Produce Daylight Effect," DGE 74 (10 Apr. 1910): 131; "More Business Thru Better Lighting," MRSW 46 (May 1920): 15–17; "Importance of Proper Store Lighting," DGE 74 (7 May 1920): 108; "Two New Lighting Systems," DGE 74 (5 June 1920): 115; "Surroundings Must Be Reckoned with in Lighting Plans," DGE 74 (31 July 1920): 125; "Lights that Stun the Senses," DGE 74 (25 Sep. 1920): 141; "Turning on Daylight," RL 3 (5 Jan. 1921): 10; "Get 100 Per Cent Efficiency," DGE 76 (11 Feb. 1922): 105; "Principles of Store Lighting," WWD, 11 Feb. 1922, 58; "Customers Demand Good Lighting," DGE 76 (1 July 1922): 73, 84; "Assurance of Customer Satisfaction," DGE 76 (18 Nov. 1922): 107; "You've a Month Before the Fall Opening," DGE 77 (11 Aug. 1923): 65; "The Merchant's First Step Toward Bigger and Easier Sales," DGE 77 (8 Sep. 1923): 83; "Both Customers and Employees Respond to Improved Lighting," DGE 78 (9 Aug. 1924): 65; "Little Extra Work Means Lighting Economy," DGE 79 (14 Mar. 1925): 105; "Planning an Adequate Lighting System," WWD, 4 Apr. 1925, 21; "Good Lighting Brings the Business," DGE 80 (10 Apr. 1926): 127, 149; "Good Lighting," WWD, 10 July 1926, 10; "Lights Need Regular Care," DGE 81 (3 Sep. 1927): 63–64; "Why Merchants Say Good Lighting Pays!" DGE 82 (7 July 1928): 64–65; and "Artificial Daylight," DGE 83 (16 Mar. 1929): 76–77, 96.

80. Notably, the Hecht Company, L. S. Plaut, H. & S. Pogue, and M. Rich & Brothers Company; see "Hecht's Will Open," WP, 12 Nov. 1925, 24; "Building Operations Started," WWD, 20 Oct. 1924, 1; "Pogue's Plans," WWD, 18 Aug. 1930, I-1, I-20; and "M. Rich & Bros.," WWD, 26 May 1922, 1.

81. See, e.g., "Milwaukee Store," WWD, 3 Nov. 1919, 46; "Grand Leader Annex," SLG, 7 Nov. 1920, 14b; "Expansion Plans," WWD, 4 Feb. 1925, 63; "Herpolsheimer's Relocate," WWD, 12 June 1925, 6; "Most Sections Relocated," WWD, 18 Mar. 1926, 7; "Volume Increases Fifty Percent in One Year," DGE 80 (20 Nov. 1926): 78–79, 90; "Gimbel's Add," WWD, 30 Nov. 1926, 1, 63; "Namm's Store," WWD, 2 Sep. 1927, 16; "What's All This About a New Store?" NRB 9 (Oct. 1927): 488–91; "Famous-Barr Move," WWD, 23 Aug. 1928, I-12; "Thousands View," WWD, 10 May 1929, I-8; "Loeser's to Alter," WWD, 17 May 1929, I-1, I-6; "Store Will Build," *Oregonian* (Portland), 13 June 1929, 1, 12; and "Magnin's New," WWD, 19 Aug. 1929, I-14, I-24.

82. For general discussion, see Ruth Leigh, *Elements of Retailing* (New York: D. Appleton, 1923), chap. 2; Doubman and Whitaker, *Organization and Operation*, 157–71; and B. Eugenia Lies and Marie P. Sealy, "Planning a Department-Store Layout," JR 4 (Apr. 1928): 21–28. The arrangement of stores was often described in detail at the time of opening in local papers and also in the trade press.

83. MJ, 9 Nov. 1924, Gen. News Sect., 7; "Donaldson's Open," MJ, 9 Nov. 1924, City Life Sect., 1, 2; "Structure Has Eight Stories," MT, 9 Nov. 1924, 8; "L. S. Donaldson's Open, " WWD, 17 Nov. 1924, 34; "New Store for Gimbel Brothers," MRSW 57 (Aug. 1925): 23; "New Phila. Gimbel," WWD, 13 Nov. 1926, 17; "Gimbel Bros. Open," 58; "New Gimbel Store," RL, 1st Dec. issue, 1926, 9; "New Addition to Gimbel Store Real Engineering Achievement," *Building Magazine* 7 (Feb. 1927): 13–14, 35; "Gimbel Brothers Store," A&B 59 (Apr. 1927): 110, 120; "Interior Windows," RL, 1st Apr. issue, 1927, Graphic Sect.

84. An insightful analysis of the issue was provided by architect Kenneth Welch; see his "Planning Future Expansion for the Department Store," AR 67 (Feb. 1930): 202–4; "How Scientific Store Planning Augments Profits," *Retailing*, 24 May 1930, 3, 14; and "A Profitable Department Doesn't Just Happen," RL, 1st July issue, 1930, Rotogravure Sect., 1.

85. A few of the many accounts of the period are "Macy's to Install," WWD, 29 June 1922, 32; "Stix-Baer-Fuller," WWD, 21 May 1926, 8; "New Escalator System," WWD, 16 Oct. 1926, 9; "Gimbel System," WWD, 12 Nov. 1927, I-7; "Macy's Plans," WWD, 18 Apr. 1928, I-2; and "Escalators Handle Ten Times Elevator Traffic," DGE 84 (15 Feb. 1930): 67, 75. Perhaps the earliest installation in a department store was in 1901 at Gimbel's New York facility; see "Escalators," WWD, 23 July 1947, 58. See also Whitaker, *Style and Service*, 93–95.

86. See, e.g., "Meier & Frank's Convert," WWD, 23 Mar. 1927, 6; "Frederick & Nelson Re-Create Second Floor," DGE 81 (11 June 1927): 50–51, 55; "Miami, Fla., Store Dons New Attire," DGE 81 (3 Sep. 1927): 55; "Individual Shops," WWD, 29 Oct. 1927, I-7; "Kaufmann's Find," WWD, 5 Nov. 1927, I-11; "Marshall Field's New Shoe Salon," DGE 81 (26 Nov. 1927): 45; "Altman's Remodeling," WWD, 7 Sep. 1928, I-1, I-15; "Formally Open," WWD, 11 Sep. 1928, I-11; "Trend Toward Salon Shop Is Apparent," DW 13 (Oct. 1928): 62; "J. L. Hudson Company," DFP, 4 Nov. 1928, I-17; "Apparel Shops," RL, 2nd Nov. issue, 1928, 9; "Specialization by Individual Shops," DGE 82 (24 Nov. 1928): 44–45; "Saks-5th Ave.," WWD, 25 July 1929, I-1; "The Famous-Barr Co. Redecorates," DGE 83 (31 Aug. 1929): 52; and "Beauty Village Springs Up," DGE 83 (5 Oct. 1929): 74–75.

87. Meg Jacobs, *Pocketbook Politics: Economic Citizenship in Twentieth-Century America* (Princeton: Princeton University Press, 2005), chap. 1; Berkeley, *The Filenes*, 123–25, 164–67.

88. See, e.g., "Automatic Bargain Basement," *WWD*, 19 Apr. 1920, 40; "Hamburger's Opens," *WWD*, 8 Mar. 1922, 39; "Strawbridge & Clothier," *WWD*, 20 May 1922, 1; "Bamberger's Basement," *WWD*, 27 July 1922, 1, 39; "New Bargain Basement," *WWD*, 9 Nov. 1922, 1, 5; "Foley Bros.," *WWD*, 5 Dec. 1922, 1; "Abraham & Straus," *WWD*, 23 Feb. 1923, 46; "New Basement," *WWD*, 3 Mar. 1923, 20; "Rollman's First Basement," *WWD*, 2 May 1923, 33; "Abraham & Straus," *WWD*, 6 Oct. 1923, 8; "Edwards' Open," *WWD*, 18 Oct. 1922, 34; "Unusual Features," *WWD*, 20 Oct. 1923, 6; "Kaufman-Straus," *WWD*, 23 Feb. 1924, 3; "Golden Rule," *WWD*, 18 Mar. 1924, 58; "Bargain Basement," 29 Mar. 1924, 21; "Hudson's Open," *WWD*, 7 Aug. 1925, 41; "Gimbel's to Open," *WWD*, 3 Oct. 1925, 20; "Gimbel's Open," *WWD*, 15 Oct. 1925, 40; "Stix-Baer-Fuller," *WWD*, 5 May 1926, 7; "Kaufmann-Baer's," *WWD*, 29 July 1926, 8; "Basement 'Aisle of Thrift,'" *WWD*, 4 June 1927, 17; and "Bamberger's Basement," *RL*, 1st Jan. issue, 1928, 9.

89. All such sources are vague and leave much to inference. I have yet to find a detailed record of exchanges between store executives and designers for the period.

90. Burnham's work for Marshall Field began with an annex to the old store (1892–93) and continued with the new quarters (1900–1914), a major addition for Gimbel Brothers in Milwaukee (1901–2), John Wanamaker in Philadelphia (1902–11) and in New York (1903–6), Selfridge's in London (1906), additions for Alms & Doepke in Cincinnati (1908), Gimbel's in New York (1908–11), and Filene's in Boston (1911–12). See Hines, *Burnham*, 303–7, 378–83.

91. Namely for Donaldson's in Minneapolis (1923–24), major additions to Gimbel's in Philadelphia (1925–27), alterations to Gimbel's in New York (1926–27), M. O'Neil in Akron (1926–28), and Higbee's in Cleveland (1930–31). Earlier, they designed the Marshall Field Annex (1914) and the May Company store in Cleveland (1914–15). See Chappell, *Architecture and Planning,* 63–69, 117, 120–121, 163.

92. Namely for Bamberger's in Newark (1921–22, 1926–28) and the Hecht Company in Washington (1924–25).

93. Namely, additions for Miller & Rhoads in Richmond, Virginia (1921–24); L. S. Plaut in Newark (1924–26); Davison-Paxon in Atlanta (1925–27); additions for F. & R. Lazarus in Columbus, Ohio (1925–26); additions for S. Kann in Washington (1926–27, project); H. C. Capwell in Oakland (1927–29); and Julius Garfinckel in Washington (1928–30). Commissions received from well beyond the New York area in the early 1920s suggests that they had developed a national reputation for store design by that point. Basic biographical information includes obituaries of Starrett (*NYT*, 10 May 1918, 11; *Journal of the American Institute of Architects* 6 [May 1918], 260) and Van Vleck (*NYT*, 9 Aug. 1956, 25), and an entry on the former in the *National Cyclopedia of American Biography,* 24: 42.

94. Advertisements suggest this role in numerous cases, but I have found only three cases where fixture manufacturers are cited in news accounts as being responsible for the interior design: Frederick Loeser and B. Lowenstein (Grand Rapids) and the Fair in Fort Worth (Midwestern Display Equipment Corporation).

95. Known projects include both additions to Bamberger's, Bernheimer-Leader, Capwell's, Gimbel's in New York, L. Pizitz in Birmingham, and Strawbridge & Clothier.

96. "Store Architect Makes Valuable Place for Himself," *DGE* 79 (14 Mar. 1925): 14.

97. "Sales at Peak," *WWD*, 1 Nov. 1932, 1, 34; "New Strawbridge Store," *Philadelphia Record,* 31 Oct. 1932, 5.

98. Mazur, *American Prosperity,* 8; William Trufant Foster and Waddill Catchings, *Business Without a Buyer* (Boston: Houghton Mifflin, 1927). See also Jacobs, *Pocketbook Politics,* 83–85.

CHAPTER 2. Modernizing Stores

1. "Stores Are Translating," *RL*, 1st Dec. issue, 1930, 2; "1932 Will Be," *RL*, Jan. 1932, 1, 8.

2. "Hutzler Bros.," *WWD*, 13 Oct. 1932, 2, 24. For background, see "Hutzler's Buy," *WWD*, 18 June 1923, 1, 2; "Complete Plans," *WWD*, 3 Jan. 1924, 41; "Hutzler Bros.," *WWD*, 18 Jan. 1924, 1; *WWD*, 23 Jan. 1924, 57; "Big Addition," *WWD*, 11 Aug. 1931, I-1, I-28; "Seasonal Expansion," *Retailing,* 27 Feb. 1933, 7; and "Take Advantage," *Retailing,* 28 Jan. 1935, 9.

3. Others included additions to the May Company in Cleveland (1931), Bullock's in Los Angeles (1933–34), J. N. Adam & Company in Buffalo (1935), and Thalheimer Brothers in Richmond (1935–36). The only entirely new facility then, or until after World War II, was Loveman, Joseph & Loeb in Birmingham (1934–35), which replaced an early twentieth-century complex that burned.

4. Malcolm P. McNair and Eleanor G. May, "The American Department Store," *HUB* 166 (1963): 33. These trends are adjusted for inflation. In actual dollars the increases were higher. See also three articles by Walter Alwyn-Schmidt: "Ten Billion Dollar Volume in Sight," *DSE* 10 (Jan. 1947): 20–21, 28, 30; "Sales Will Go Up Again in 1948," *DSE* 11 (Jan. 1948): 14–15, 60–61; and "Your Business in 1949," *DSE* 12 (Jan. 1949): 14–15.

5. McNair and May, "American Department Store," 22–25. More detailed coverage is in the annual issues of *HUB* devoted to the subject, generally titled "Operating Results of Department and Specialty Stores."

6. "Lost or Strayed," *WWD*, 27 Dec. 1954, II-2; Paul H. Nystrom, "The Future of the Department Store," *JR* 8 (Oct. 1932): 68; "Prosperity Returns to the Store," *NRB* 19 (July 1937): 15; B. Earl Puckett, "Post-War Assets and Liabilities!" *DSE* 7 (Dec. 1944): 14–15, 37, 44, 46, 96, 121; "Looking Ahead 5 Years," *DSE* 11 (May 1948): 20, 60; Robert David Entenberg, *The Changing Competitive Position of Department Stores in the United States by Merchandise Lines* (Pittsburgh: University of Pittsburgh Press, 1957), esp. chap. 3.

7. "No Formalities," *WWD*, 28 Oct. 1935, I-1, I-19; Bernice L. Thomas, *America's 5 & 10 Cent Stores: The Kress Legacy* (Washington, D.C.: National Building Museum, and New York: Wiley, 1997), chap. 5; "Luxury Trend," *WWD*, 6 Oct. 1937, II-10; "No Woolworth Policy," *WWD*, 21 Feb. 1938, 4; *WWD*, 24 Feb. 1938, 8; "$1 Goods Tops," *WWD*, 25 Feb. 1938, 1, 39; "Large Crowds," *WWD*, 24 Feb. 1938, 1, 2; "Woolworth Unit," *Retailing,* 7 Mar. 1938, 11.

8. "From Five and Dime to Family Shopping Centers," *CSA/VSE* 26 (June 1950): J6–J9, J72. See, e.g., "Grant Unit Makes News in Display," *NRB* 22 (Jan. 1940): 24–25; *WWD*, 2 Feb. 1942, 21; "Murphy Opens," *CSA/VSE* 24 (Aug. 1948): 62–67, 157; "McCrory Opens," *CSA/VSE* 24 (Oct. 1948): 56–57, 115; "Woolworth's Largest, #28, Opens in Newark, N.J.," *CSA/VSE* 24 (Dec. 1948): 47, 112; "Variety's Biggest," *CSA/VSE* 29 (Aug. 1953): 80; "Woolworth Opens," *CSA/VSE* 30 (Oct. 1954): 12–13; "Grant Opens," *CSA/VSE* 30 (Dec. 1954): 58–59.

9. "Penney's Expands to Bigger Stores," *CSA/GME* 9 (Nov. 1933): 16–17; "J. C. Penney Enters the Large Store Field," *DGE* 88 (July 1934): 12–13, 38–39. Concerning Ward's, see "Montgomery Ward's," *Retailing,* 28 Feb. 1931, 5; "Ward Jamaica," *WWD*, 20 Mar. 1931, I-1, I-2; "New Ward Unit Indicates Trend to Larger Stores," *CSA* 7 (June 1931): 51–54; "Department Store," *WWD*, 24 May 1934, 2; "Ward's to Enter," *WWD*, 24 June 1936, 28; "New Building," *WWD*, 13 Oct. 1936, 7; "Ward's Open," *WWD*, 14 June 1938, 7; "Ward's Big," *WWD*, 12 Oct. 1938, 8; "$1,200,000 New Detroit Unit," *WWD*, 19 July 1939, 1; "2 Stores Open," *WWD*, 16 May 1940, 5; "Ward's Plan," *WWD*, 16 July 1940, 2, 35; and "Ward's Plans," *WWD*, 20 Feb. 1941, 1, 40.

Concerning Sears, see Richard Longstreth, "Sears, Roebuck and the Remaking of the Department Store, 1924–1942," *JSAH* 65 (June 2006): 238–79.

10. In 1935, Penney's profit margin was 6.8 percent, Kresge's 7.4 percent, Woolworth's 11.6 percent. Sears's was only 4.7 percent, but Macy's was 2.5 percent and the May Company's 3.8 percent. By 1940, Macy's and May's had improved (3.7 percent and 5.2 percent, resp.), but so had Penney's (7.1 percent) and Kresge's (8.6 percent). Woolworth's share of business had dropped somewhat, yet its profit margin remained the biggest at 9.2 percent. Among the most detailed sources of data on retail companies is *Fairchild's Financial Manual* (New York: Fairchild), issued annually during these years.

11. "Streamlined vs. Horse," *WWD,* 2 July 1941, 35. For a scathing account of sales force inefficiency of the period, see Frances Taylor, "Who Wants My Money?" *Atlantic Monthly* 147 (May 1931): 607–10.

12. "Flirting with 'Self Service,'" *RE,* 27 Mar. 1940, 2, 6; "'Size Selling' Wins," *RE,* 15 May 1940, 2, 9; "Self-Service," *WWD,* 28 Oct. 1942, 27. See also "Changes in Selling," *RE,* 15 May 1940, 1. An unusual and probably short-lived experiment in self-service was undertaken by John Shillito of Cincinnati in the mid-1920s; see "'Self-Service Squares,'" *WWD,* 28 Aug. 1926, 7.

13. For examples, see "Self-Service," *WWD,* 29 Dec. 1942, II-68; "Pittsburgh Checks," *WWD,* 21 Jan. 1943, 31; "Self-Selection: Present and Future," *DW* 42 (Feb. 1943): 18, 37; L. L. Solomon, "Self-Service: A Revolution," *DW* 42 (Mar. 1943): 6, 39; "Famous-Barr Co. Tries," *WWD,* 23 Mar. 1943, 31; "A Self-Service," *WWD,* 19 Apr. 1943, 19; "'Self-Service' Increasing," *WWD,* 25 May 1943, 33; "Self-Selection Gets," *WWD,* 26 May 1943, 42–43; and "Self-Service," *WWD,* 30 Aug. 1943, 15. See also "Self-Service Experiments in Department Stores," *JR* 18 (Oct. 1942): 74–81.

14. "Self-Service?" *WWD,* 18 Nov. 1942, 27; "Self-Service" *WWD,* 29 Dec. 1942, II-68; Solomon, "Self-Service," 6.

15. "Stiff Post-War Competition Facing Department Stores," *DSE* 6 (Nov. 1943): 10–11; "Fantastic Results Shown by Stores in 1943!" *DSE* 7 (Sep. 1944): 94–95; "Special Services," *WWD,* 1 Jan. 1946, 116. The argument persisted for some time among some merchants; see, e.g., "Reyburn Finds," *WWD,* 12 Mar. 1957, 10.

16. "Department Stores Are Not Mass Media," *DSE* 12 (Aug. 1949): 52–53; "Holds Department Stores," *WWD,* 13 June 1949, 1, 48.

17. Malcolm P. McNair, "The Future of the Department Store," *Stores* 32 (May 1950): 15–19, 81 (quote on p. 18).

18. "The Department Store," *WWD,* 21 Apr. 1952, 28. See also "Helping Customers to Find, See, Touch," *BW,* 30 Sep. 1950, 42–43; Paul M. Mazur, "The Department Store: What Will It Be Like 25 Years from Now?" *Stores* 32 (Nov. 1950): 22–26; Samuel Feinberg, "From Where I Sit," *WWD,* 27 Aug. 1951, 34; 4 Sep. 1951, I-57; and 10 Sep. 1951, 45; "The Trend to Open Selling," *Stores* 34 (Mar. 1952): 16–21; "Conversion to Simplified," *WWD,* 29 Dec. 1952, II-6, II-12; "'Revolutionary' Technics," *WWD,* 15 Jan. 1953, 1, 66; "Planning and Designing for Easy-Selection," *DW* 62 (Apr. 1953): 46–47, 65–67.

19. Albert M. Greenfield, "I Run a Department Store Without Clerks," *Nation's Business* 41 (Oct. 1953): 34–36, 73–75 (quote on p. 36).

20. "More Services," *WWD,* 22 Jan. 1953, 1, 46; "Department Stores Can Stay 'Tops,'" *DSE* 16 (Mar. 1953): 42–43, 78. For examples of store changes, see "Shopping Must," *WWD,* 12 Dec. 1952, 18; "Self-Service," *WWD,* 29 Dec. 1952, II-6, II-13; "Display Role," *WWD,* 15 Jan. 1953, 66; "Self Service," *WWD,* 12 June 1953, 51; "Self-Service Means," *WWD,* 25 Aug. 1953, I-49; "Self-Selection Growth," *WWD,* 15 Oct. 1954, 1, 37. On the shift in chain drug and variety stores, see Richard Longstreth, *The Drive-In, the Supermarket, and the Transformation of Commercial Space in Los Angeles, 1914–1941* (Cambridge: MIT Press, 1999), 163–80.

21. "Conversion . . . Not Simple," *WWD,* 29 Dec. 1952, II-8, II-12.

22. Malcolm P. McNair, "A Perspective on the Department Store Situation," *Stores* 39 (June 1953): 13–15. See also "Department Stores Are Held," *WWD,* 13 Jan. 1955, 16.

23. "Art in Trade Glorified by Macy's," *NRB* 9 (May 1927): 238–41; "Modernistic Apartment," *WWD,* 10 Dec. 1927, I-11, I-29; "Lord & Taylor Exhibit," *WWD,* 17 Mar. 1928, I-1, I-12; "Will Furniture Bow to Modernism?" *DW* 12 (Mar. 1928): 3; "Second Macy," *WWD,* 19 May 1928, I-1, I-13; "With the New York Displaymen," *DW* 12 (June 1928): 14–15, 78; "The Macy Exposition of Art in Industry," *AR* 64 (Aug. 1928): 137–43; "This Modernistic Art," *DGE* 82 (31 Mar. 1928): 58–61, 69. See also "The New Patron of Art—The Department Store," *JR* 4 (July 1928): 3–8. A detailed, lavishly illustrated chronicle of the phenomenon prior to the Depression is contained in Marilyn F. Friedman, *Selling Good Design: Promoting the Early Modern Interior* (New York: Rizzoli, 2003).

24. See, e.g., "Organize to Cooperate," *WWD,* 22 Mar. 1928, I-1, I-2; "Evolution of Modernistic," *WWD,* 31 Mar. 1928, I-1, I-3; "Paul Frankl Plans," *WWD,* 20 Apr. 1928, I-8; Walter Dorwin Teague, "Is a New 'Style,'" *WWD,* 21 Apr. 1928, I-3; Paul T. Frankl, "The Six Fundamentals of Modernism," *DW* 12 (June 1928): 5–7; "'Modernism' to Be Keynote," *WWD,* 21 June 1928, I-1, I-20; "Modernism's Origin and Objectives," *DW* 13 (July 1928): 8–9; "Good Design Is Good Business," *DGE* 82 (4 Aug. 1928): 11–12, 82; and "Lord & Taylor Furniture," *WWD,* 22 Sep. 1928, 1, 13.

25. "'Home Moderne,'" *WWD,* 17 Mar. 1928, I-16; "Some Art Moderne Rooms at Marshall Field's," *DGE* 82 (18 Aug. 1928): 62; "Rike-Kumler Co.," *WWD,* 8 Sep. 1928, 1, 12; "At the Rike-Kumler," *WWD,* 15 Sep. 1928, 15; "Modern Art Takes," *WWD,* 20 Oct. 1928, 15; "Modernism," *WWD,* 27 Oct. 1928, 3; "Permanent Modern Art," *WWD,* 27 Oct. 1928, 18.

26. Quoted in "How the Modernistic Trend," *RL,* 1st Jan. issue, 1929, 8. The major exception to the prevailing pattern nationally among department stores was Bullock's Wilshire in Los Angeles (1928–29).

27. "Edgar J. Kaufmann," *WWD,* 10 Dec. 1929, I-13; "E. J. Kaufmann," *WWD,* 5 June 1929, I-20. The initial, unrealized scheme is illustrated in Randolph Carter and Robert Reed Cole, *Joseph Urban: Architecture, Theatre, Opera, Film* (New York: Abbeville, 1992), 188. Both projects are discussed within the context of the client as patron in Richard L. Cleary, *Merchant Prince and Master Builder: Edgar J. Kaufmann and Frank Lloyd Wright* (Pittsburgh: Heinz Architectural Center, and Seattle: University of Washington Press, 1999), 21–26. Additional material was graciously supplied to me by Albert M. Tannler.

28. "'Art and Industry,'" *WWD,* 28 Apr. 1930, I-1, I-6; "Davis Speaker," *PP,* 28 Apr. 1930, 13; *PP,* 30 Apr. 1930, 16; "Kaufmann Murals," "Modern Construction," and "Kaufmann's Store," *Retailing,* 3 May 1930, 11; "'Radical' Is the Only Name for the New Kaufmann Layout," *DGE* 84 (10 May 1930): 59; *Pittsburgh Sun Telegraph,* 11 May 1930, Kaufmann's Supplement; "Diagonal Aisles," *Retailing,* 14 June 1930, 8; "Distinctively Different: Kaufmann's Main Floor," *DGE* 84 (July 1930): 252–53, 256; "Kaufmann's First Floor" and "Edgar Kaufmann Tells," *Retailing,* 2 May 1931, 2.

29. The scheme did not set an important precedent in its pursuit of fixture arrangement that encouraged freer pedestrian flow, but in later years, this idea was applied in different ways to upper selling floors, not to the main floor.

30. "Saks-5th Ave.," *WWD,* 25 July 1929, I-1; "Modern Architecture," *Retailing,* 21 Sep. 1929, 3; *NYT,* 13 Oct. 1929, II-12; "Saks-Fifth Avenue Goes Modernistic," *DGE* 83 (26 Oct. 1929): 69. By the late

1920s, considerable coverage was given to contemporary Parisian work in a variety of periodicals. Some of the earliest pieces to appear in retail literature was a series in *NRB*: "Ultra Modern Shop Fronts of Paris," 9 (Oct. 1927): 498–500, 505; "The Ultra Modern Notes in Display," 9 (Nov. 1927): 562–64; "Perfumes in Ultra Modern Setting," 9 (Dec. 1927): 604–5; "Paris Modernizes the Average Shop," 10 (Feb. 1928): 82, 84–86; and "Paris Shops Adhere to the Ultra Modern," 10 (May 1928): 206–7. Retailers who bought abroad would probably have been aware of such work firsthand.

31. "Stewart's Plans," *WWD*, 15 June 1928, I-1, I-15; "Stewart & Co.," *WWD*, 16 Oct. 1929, I-1, I-20; "Modern Architecture," 3; "The New Stewart Store," *Retailing*, 26 Oct. 1929, 3, 18; "Stewart & Company's Store," *A&B* 61 (Dec. 1929): 362, 377–84; "The Modernistic Trend," *American Builder* 48 (Feb. 1930): 82–83.

32. "Bonwit Teller Moves," *Retailing*, 20 Sep. 1930, 7. See also "Bonwit Teller," *WWD*, 9 June 1930, I-1; "Quiet Taste," *WWD*, 15 Sep. 1930, I-1, I-20; "Bonwit, Teller & Co., New York, in New Home," *MRSW* 67 (Oct. 1930): 27; and "Simplicity and Elegance Make a Truly Modern Interior," *DGE* 84 (Nov. 1930): 166–67.

33. Much of the ongoing influence stemmed from the rise of New York design firms, including those of Eleanor Le Maire; De Young, Moscowitz & Rosenberg; and, later, Raymond Loewy, all of which enjoyed national prominence. Le Maire did the interiors of Hutzler's; De Young those of the addition to Meier & Frank in Portland, Oregon, both early examples outside New York. Concerning Stern's, see "Accessibility Key," *Retailing*, 2 May 1931, 5; concerning Macy's, see "Macy's New Sixth Floor," *Retailing*, 18 Apr. 1931, 8; "Macy Store Again Enlarged," *A&B* 63 (June 1931): 114–15; and *DGE* 85 (Nov. 1931): 131.

34. "Tomorrow's Stores and Shops Are Being Created Today," *DGE* 86 (May 1932): 116–17, 121.

35. For an exception, see "Big French Exposition," *WWD*, 27 Apr. 1925, 41.

36. Louis Skidmore, "The Architecture of the Century of Progress," *DW* 22 (May 1933): 12–15, 32; "Exhibit Display at the Century of Progress," *DW* 22 (May 1933): 16, 31; "Chicago's World's Fair of Exceptional Interest" (title varies), *MRSW* 72 (June 1933): 3–5; 73 (July 1933): 3–6; (Aug. 1933): 3–5; (Sep. 1933): 11–14; (Oct. 1933): 6–8, 17; "World's Fair a Reservoir," *Retailing*, 10 July 1933, 9. The most detailed historical study of the exposition is Lisa D. Schrenk, *Building a Century of Progress: The Architecture of Chicago's 1933–34 World's Fair* (Minneapolis: University of Minnesota Press, 2007).

37. "Fair in Reality," *WWD*, 28 Apr. 1939, II-4. See also "Whalen Describes," *WWD*, 3 Nov. 1937, 23–24; "Novel Display Will Feature New York World's Fair," *DW* 32 (Mar. 1938): 3; "A New Exposition Offers," *Retailing*, 14 Mar. 1938, 9; "New Selling Themes," *WWD*, 15 June 1938, I-5; "New York Fair to Supply Display Ideas Galore," *DW* 33 (Aug. 1938): 3; "General Motors' 'Futurama,'" *WWD*, 21 Apr. 1939, 6; "Display Inspiration Offered by Fair's Mural Technique," *DW* 34 (Apr. 1939): 3–4; "New York World's Fair," *Retailing*, 22 May 1939, Sect. II; "So You're Going to the Fair!" *DW* 34 (June 1939): 5–7, 52–57, 64–65; "Put Light," *RE*, 25 Oct. 1939, 9; and "Fair of 1940," *WWD*, 10 May 1940, 1, 6.

38. Norman Bel Geddes, "Store of Tomorrow," *WWD*, 27 Dec. 1939, II-16; "Retailing in the World of Tomorrow," *NRB* 21 (June 1939): 12–16.

39. Less coverage was given to the 1937 Exposition of Arts and Technique in Modern Life at Paris and the 1939 Golden Gate Exposition at San Francisco. See "Rising Interest," *Retailing*, 15 Feb. 1937, 3, 13; "Elaborate Ceremony," *WWD*, 24 May 1937, I-1, I-7; "The Paris International Exposition," *Retailing*, 16 Aug. 1937, Sect. II; "Display Will Be Influenced by World Fair's Art," *DW* 33 (Nov. 1938): 6–7, 47; "Boon to Trade," *WWD*, 28 Dec. 1938, II-34, II-70; and "The Golden Gate Exposition," *Retailing*, 13 Mar. 1939, Sect. II.

40. Nystrom, "Future of the Department Store," 67.

41. For an exception, see "Profits When You Modernize," *DSE* 2 (10 Jan. 1940): 30–32. For a sampling of period accounts, see "More Effective Selling," *Retailing*, 6 Feb. 1933, 5, 10; "Modernization a Necessity!" *Retailing*, 17 Sep. 1934, 5; "The Place of Modernization in Store Traffic Control," *DW* 29 (Apr. 1936): 3; "Modernize for Tomorrow's Business," *Retailing*, 30 May 1938, 9; as well as advertisements for the Grand Rapids Store Equipment Company such as in *DSE* 1 (25 Mar. 1938): 13; (25 Apr. 1938): 23; and (25 June 1938): 23. For recent discussion, see Richard Longstreth, *City Center to Regional Mall: Architecture, the Automobile, and Retailing in Los Angeles, 1920–1950* (Cambridge: MIT Press, 1997), 201–3; Alison Isenberg, *Downtown America: A History of the Place and the People Who Made It* (Chicago: University of Chicago Press, 2004), 143–52; and Gabrielle Esperdy, *Modernizing Main Street: Architecture and Consumer Culture in the New Deal* (Chicago: University of Chicago Press, 2008).

42. "Modernizing of Store," *WWD*, 3 May 1935, III-18z; Eleanor Le Maire, "Inviting the Customer Inside," *Retailing*, 24 Apr. 1940, 8; "Blueprint for Modernization," *Retailing*, 29 May 1939, 7. The concept that stores should remain as up-to-date as the goods they carry is analyzed in a larger retail context in Esperdy, *Modernizing Main Street,* chap. 4.

43. "Smarter Homes Call for Smarter Stores," *Retailing*, 11 Jan. 1937, 12. See also "The Store's a Stage," *Retailing*, 2 Aug. 1937, II-6; "Pre-Planning" and "Arranged for Profit," *Retailing*, 29 May 1939, 11, 16; "Modernization's New Materials," *Retailing*, 31 Jan. 1940, 13; and "Store Design as an Active Selling Force," *NRB* 23 (Apr. 1941): 19, 94.

44. For background, see "Do You Bring the Display into the Store?" *DW* 26 (Feb. 1935): 6–7, 32; "Interior Advertising and Display," *DW* 28 (Apr. 1936): 24–25; "Display Has Important Role in Appliance Promotion," *DW* 29 (Dec. 1936): 4–5; "The Part Display Should Play in Internal Store Promotion," *DW* 30 (Feb. 1937): 14–15, 24; "Let's Have More," *Retailing*, 22 Feb. 1937, II-21; "Merchandising Presentation Within the Store," *DW* 30 (June 1937): 6–7; "Showroom Secondary," *WWD*, 6 Oct. 1937, II-7; "Following Through with the Interior," *DW* 32 (Mar. 1938): 9; "Good Interior Settings Are Sales Clinchers," *DW* 33 (July 1938): 26; "Inviting Interiors Help Make Sales," *DW* 33 (Aug. 1933): 18–19; "The Display Industry and Its Accomplishments," *DW* 42 (June 1940): 26, 28, 30, 828–33; and "Interior Display Function," *WWD*, 11 Aug. 1941, 23.

45. Concerning Le Maire, see "She Built Success," *Miami Daily News*, 9 Jan. 1936, 16; "Flair for Interior Decoration," *NYT*, 7 Jan. 1940, II-4; "Women Architects," *NYT*, 11 Apr. 1937, V-92; and "Eleanor Le Maire," *NYT*, 11 Feb. 1970, 47. Concerning Rohde, see *Gilbert Rohde: Modern Design for Modern Living* (New Haven: Yale University Press, 2009). Among interior designers Loewy became the dominant figure during the postwar decade. See Raymond Loewy, *Industrial Design* (Woodstock, N.Y.: Overlook, 1979); and Angela Schoberger, ed., *Raymond Loewy: Pioneer of American Industrial Design* (Munich: Prestel, 1990).

46. The Fox addition was part of a remodeling program, begun in 1931, for the entire store. See "G. Fox & Co.," *Retailing*, 9 Jan. 1933, 5; "Long-Range Modernization," *Retailing*, 14 Oct. 1935, 7–9; "In the Process of Growing," *Retailing*, 5 Dec. 1938, 1–3, 10; and "New Fifth Floor," *WWD*, 20 Feb. 1940, 7.

47. Gilbert Rohde, "The Function of the Designer in Store Remodeling," *NRB* 19 (June 1937): 51–52; "Architect as Merchandiser," *NRB* 19 (July 1937): 41. See also "The Display Man of the Future," *WWD*, 7 Nov. 1941, 39.

48. See, e.g., E. Paul Behles, "Principles of Planning for an

Effective and Economical Retailing Project," *DSE* 1 (25 Jan. 1938): 60–61; Behles, "Dramatized Corners," *DSE* 1 (10 Feb. 1938): 40; Gilbert Rohde, "Better Planning for Better Stores," *WWD*, 28 Dec. 1938, II-64, II-71. An early example was Wm. H. Block Company in Indianapolis; see "'Quiet Corners' Are Now Our Best Sales Spaces," *RL*, June 1931, Magazine Sect., n.p.

49. "Dramatic Fashion Center," *Retailing*, 10 Oct. 1938, 7; "Theatre of Fashion," *DSE* 1 (25 Oct. 1938): 22; "These Firms Make Display a Part of Original Plans," *DW* 33 (Nov. 1938): 12–13.

50. Raymond Loewy, "Today—The Store Is," *Retailing*, 30 May 1938, 11, 18 (quote on p. 11). See also Loewy, "Designing Women's Floors," *Retailing*, 29 May 1939, 9; "Little Shop Idea," *Retailing*, 5 Aug. 1935, 2; "Surrounded Entirely by Shops," *DGE* 90 (26 May 1936): 68; and Meyer Katzman, "Toward a New Floor Design," *Retailing*, 30 May 1938, 15. One of the best examples of the large-scale application of the shops concept prior to the Depression was the 1927–29 addition to I. Magnin & Company in San Francisco; see "I. Magnin's to Add," *WWD*, 11 July 1927, I-1, I-16; "Beauty Marks," *SFC*, 17 Aug. 1929, 4; and "Magnin's New," *WWD*, 19 Aug. 1929, I-14, I-24.

51. "Store Design as an Active Selling Force," *NRB* 23 (Apr. 1941): 19, 94 (quote on p. 94). Concerning Lord & Taylor, see "Remodeling for Lord & Taylor," *AF* 68 (Mar. 1938): 215–22; "Lord & Taylor Presents," *WWD*, 1 Sep. 1938, 28, 27; "Color-Lights Recreate," *Retailing*, 12 Sep. 1938, 16; and "Dramatic New Third Floor for Lord & Taylor," *DW* 33 (Oct. 1938): 18–19. See also "Remodeled Intimate Wear," *WWD*, 24 Feb. 1938, 13. Concerning Bamberger's, see "Specialty Technique," *WWD*, 3 Sep. 1940, 1, 16; "Bamberger's Dress Salon," *WWD*, 4 Sep. 1940, 19; "Three-in-One Shop," *DSE* 3 (25 Sep. 1940): 14; and "Loewy Designs Dress Salon," *DW* 37 (Oct. 1940): 24.

52. "Wanamaker Remodeling," *WWD*, 13 Dec. 1935, I-1, I-24; "Wanamaker's Men's Layout," *DGE* (28 Apr. 1936): 54; "'Presentation' Recognized," *WWD*, 8 May 1936, II-1, II-16; "Entire Men's Store," *RL* 18 (May 1936): 18; "John Wanamaker," *Retailing*, 11 May 1936, 10; "Surrounded Entirely by Shops," *DGE* 90 (26 May 1936): 68; "Wanamaker's New Children's," *WWD*, 25 Aug. 1936, 1, 36; "New Fashion Store," *WWD*, 8 Sep. 1936, I-5. Concurrently, Welch redesigned the ground floor of the newer (1903–6) south building as the Men's Store; see "Wanamaker Shoots," *Retailing*, 6 Apr. 1936, 8; "Entire Men's Store," *RL* 31 (May 1936): 18; and *AR* 80 (Aug. 1936): 117–19.

53. Kenneth C. Welch, "On Men's Departments," *Retailing*, 24 Apr. 1940, 16.

54. "New York Must Shop 'In the Dark,'" *Retailing*, 6 Jan. 1936, 6. See also "Department Stores Notoriously," *WWD*, 29 Sep. 1937, 8. Articles on lighting from the first half of the decade include "Useful Suggestions for Modernizing Your Lighting," *MRSW* 67 (Nov. 1930): 7–9; "Stimulating Sales by Display Lighting," *MRSW* 69 (Aug. 1931): 17–21; "Light, the Big Merchandising Bargain," *RL*, Jan. 1932, 3; "Suit Your Lighting," *Retailing*, 4 Sep. 1933, 11; "Don't Skimp," *Retailing*, 13 Nov. 1933, 12; "Relation of Lighting to Merchandising," *DW* 26 (Mar. 1935): 3–5, 32, and (May 1935): 22–23; "Good Lighting Will Pay Its Own Way in Selling," *DGE* 89 (May 1935): 62–63; and "Store Building Display Lighting as a Business Asset," *DW* 27 (July 1935): 20–21, 29.

55. "'Sunshine' Is Put to Work," *Retailing*, 26 Feb. 1934, 16; "Indirect Light," *Retailing*, 26 Mar. 1934, 13; "Now Stern's," *Retailing*, 2 Apr. 1934, 4; "Relighting Is Rejuvenation," *Retailing*, 25 June 1934, 16; "'Plate' Lighting," *Retailing*, 23 July 1934, 16; "Modernizing with Light," *DW* 28 (Apr. 1936): 4–5.

56. "Fluorescent Illumination—A Lighting Trend," *DW* 33 (Sep. 1938): 3; "New Display and Lighting Possibilities in Fluorescent Lighting," *NRB* 21 (Jan. 1939): 24–25; "Light Conditioning with Fluorescence," *DW* 34 (Mar. 1939): 24, 50; "Numerous Advantages with Fluorescent Installation," *DW* 36 (Feb. 1940): 42–43; "Fluorescent in Display," *RE*, 10 Apr. 1940, 8; "Light Is Not," *WWD*, 25 Nov. 1941, 27. See also "Merchandising with Light," *AR* 96 (Nov. 1944): 104–6.

57. "Cold-Cathode Fluorescent Lighting," *DW* 41 (Oct. 1942): 4–5, 41–42; "Cold Cathode Display Lighting," *DW* 45 (Sep. 1944): 8–9, 40; "Postwar Requirements of Department Store Lighting," *DSE* 7 (Oct. 1944): 72–73; "Your Store Tomorrow," *WWD*, 17 Jan. 1945, 51, and 1 Feb. 1945, 31; "Lighting Store Merchandise," *DSE* 8 (Feb. 1945): 110–11; "The Cold Cathode Way," *DW* 47 (Aug. 1948): 22–23; "Selling with Light," *Stores* 30 (Aug. 1948): 38–39, 42; "Glareless Lighting for Stores," *DSE* 11 (Aug. 1948): 71; "The Silent Salesman," *DW* 53 (Nov. 1948): 72, 102, 104; "Light for Selling in the Department Store," *DSE* 12 (Oct. 1949): 64–65, 102, 104; "Stores Like Spot," *WWD*, 15 Feb. 1950, I-77; "Correlation of Store," *WWD*, 29 Mar. 1950, 53.

58. For a concise synopsis of systems in the late 1920s, see "Store Ventilation," *DGE* 81 (1 Jan. 1927): 17, 53.

59. "Entire Filene's Store," *Retailing*, 24 Sep. 1934, 16; "Cool When You Want It—Warm When You Want It," *DGE* 84 (Sep. 1930): 101, 204–5; "Cool Shopping," *Retailing*, 27 Aug. 1934, 8. Perhaps the first large emporium to be completely air conditioned was Volk Brothers, a departmentalized apparel store that opened in Dallas in 1930. See "Volk Bros. Claim," *Retailing*, 24 Dec. 1934, 6. For an overview of the subject at this early stage, see Godfrey E. Barber, "The Air-Conditioning Equipment Industry," *HBR* 11 (Apr. 1933): 349–58. Important general studies include Darry Donaldson and Bernard Nagengast, *Heat & Cold: Mastering the Great Indoors* (Atlanta: American Society of Heating, Refrigerating and Air-Conditioning Engineers, 1994), 261–301; and Gail Cooper, *Air-Conditioning America: Engineers and the Controlled Environment, 1900–1960* (Baltimore: Johns Hopkins University Press, 1998).

60. "Give Next Summer's," *Retailing*, 28 Nov. 1931, 7. Subsequently the magazine featured a regular column on the subject. See, e.g., 26 Feb. 1934, 10–11; 26 Mar. 1934, 10–11; 25 June 1934, 12; 23 July 1934, 11; 27 Aug. 1934, 8; 24 June 1935, 6; 26 Aug. 1935, 8; 23 Nov. 1936, 6. For later coverage, see "Air Conditioning *Does* Pay Its Way," *DGE* 91 (5 Jan. 1937): 74, 76; "Air Conditioning Seen," *WWD*, 6 Oct. 1937, II-4, II-15; "Air Conditioning for Profit," *DSE* 1 (25 Nov. 1938): 6; "Sales Up," *RE*, 26 July 1939, I-10; and "See All-Year Benefits," *Retailing*, 27 Feb. 1939, 8.

61. "Air Conditioning Now," *WWD*, 25 Feb. 1953, 60; "Air Conditioning Liberates," *WWD*, 25 Feb. 1953, 64. For a sampling of other accounts, see "Post-War Air Conditioning for the Department Store," *DSE* 7 (Mar. 1944): 12–13, 21; "Store Air Conditioning," *DSE* 8 (Jan. 1945): 116–17; "Air Conditioning for Stores," *DSE* 8 (July 1945): 44, 46; "Shoppers Benefit by Conditioned Air Control," *DSE* 10 (Mar. 1947): 144–45; and "How to Create Perfect Selling Weather," *Stores* 31 (Sep. 1949): 40–42.

62. "Modernize the Front," *Retailing*, 30 May 1938, 12–13. See also "Eyes Front!" *Retailing*, 29 May 1939, 8, 10. The great majority of literature on this subject focused on smaller stores.

63. Examples of the former category include additions to Bullock's in Los Angeles (1933–34), Rike-Kumler in Dayton (1936–38), the Dayton Company in Minneapolis (1937–38), Neiman-Marcus in Dallas (1939–41), the May Company in Baltimore (1940–41), A. Polsky in Akron (1941), and Hutzler Brothers in Baltimore (1941–42), the last being a second stage of a scheme prepared a decade earlier. Examples of the latter include G. Fox in Hartford (1937–39), M. Rich & Brothers in Atlanta (1939–40), the Hecht Company in Washington (1940–41), and Miller & Rhoads in Richmond (1940–41). For a listing, see Richard Longstreth, comp., "New Buildings and Major Additions for Downtown Department Stores, 1920–1960," at *http://www.departmentstorehistory.net* and *http://www.preservenet.cornell.edu*.

64. Concerning Robinson's, see "Store Building," *LAT*, 4 Feb. 1934, I-15; "How J. W. Robinson," *WWD*, 9 Feb. 1934, I-22; "Structural Hum," *DGE* 88 (July 1934): 77; *LAT*, 27 May 1934, I-13; "Store Repeats," *LAT*, 3 Sep. 1934, II-8; "New Face," *Retailing*, 10 Sep. 1934, 6; "$300,000 for a Buttered Face," *DGE* 88 (Nov. 1934): 68; and *American Architect* 146 (Apr. 1935): 18–19. For illustration, see Longstreth, *City Center,* figs. 16, 141. The only other prewar instance of such change in a major department store that did not include concurrent additions was Lansburgh & Brother in Washington (1940).

65. See, e.g., "Unique Modern Treatment in New Dutch Store," *NRB* (July 1927): 360–62; "The Most Modern Department Store of the Age," *MRSW* 68 (Mar. 1931): 9–12; and "Should Store Light?" *RL,* Apr. 1932, 3. Coverage in architectural journals was quite extensive but was generally less focused on programmatic aspects.

66. "J. N. Adam & Co.," *BEN,* 11 Apr. 1935, 1, 3; "Elevators in Exact Center," *Retailing,* 4 Nov. 1935, 5 (J. N. Adam); "John Shillito Co.," *WWD*, 15 Sep. 1936, 1, 35; "Grand Opening," *WWD*, 25 Oct. 1937, 1, 2; "Reconstructed Store," *CE*, 26 Oct. 1937, 10; "17 Acres," *Retailing,* 22 Nov. 1937, 7; "The New Shillito's," *DW* 31 (Nov. 1937): 36–37; and "A Department Store Modernization," *AR* 82 (Feb. 1938): 121–25 (Shillito's).

67. "Joske's Store," *SAE*, 4 Dec. 1938, 6A; "Joske's to Dedicate," *SAE,* 19 Nov. 1939, C-1; "Joske's Final," *WWD*, 26 Nov. 1940, 12. Concerning Morgan, Walls & Clements, see "The Spanish Stores of Morgan, Walls & Clements," *AF* 50 (June 1929): 901–16.

68. "H. P. Wasson's," *IS,* 11 May 1936, 1, 10; "H. P. Wasson," *IN,* 11 May 1936, 1; "Windowless Wasson Store Accented by Glass Brick Vertical Panels," *DGE* 91 (5 Jan. 1937): 68; "New Buildings," *IN,* 27 Feb. 1937, II-1. Much more publicity was given to the slightly later "windowless" store built for the Coulter Dry Goods Company on the Miracle Mile in Los Angeles; see Longstreth, *City Center,* 138–39. The prototype for the "windowless" store was developed by Sears, Roebuck two years earlier; see Longstreth, "Sears, Roebuck," 256–58.

69. Despite frequent reference to such criticism in accounts of the period, the critiques themselves are hard to find. Frank Thomson Hypps, "The Department Store—A Problem of Elephantiasis," *Annals of the American Academy of Political and Social Sciences* 193 (Sep. 1937): 70–87, presents one of the most developed analyses of this kind, but in the end argues that the great emporia can survive if they improve merchandising techniques.

70. Not surprisingly, under the circumstances, the postwar period saw a proliferation of material on the design of department stores. See, e.g., "If You Plan to Build or Improve," *Stores* 29 (Jan. 1947): 40–44, 46, 48, 50, 52, 54, 56, 58, 74; Morris Ketchum, *Shops & Stores* (New York: Reinhold, 1948); Louis Parnes, *Planning Stores That Pay* (New York: F. W. Dodge, 1948); and "What Makes a 1940 Store Obsolete?" *AF* 93 (July 1950): 62–79.

71. Allied's major acquisitions included Maas Brothers (Tampa), Dey Brothers (Syracuse), Read's (Bridgeport), and Stern's (New York). Associated's three were J. W. Robinson (Los Angeles), The Diamond (Charleston, West Virginia), and Sibley, Lindsey & Curr (Rochester). Macy's purchase of O'Connor Moffatt (San Francisco) and John Taylor (Kansas City) included substantial transformations of the stores that subsequently bore the Macy's name. May Company acquisitions included Kaufmann's (Pittsburgh), Strous-Hirshberg (Youngstown), and the affiliated Hecht Company stores in Washington and Baltimore. City Stores' purchases included Richard's (Miami), Wise, Smith (Hartford), Lansburgh & Brother (Washington), and Hearn's (the Bronx), as well as two prominent New York specialty stores, Oppenheim Collins and Franklin Simon. Federated's portfolio included the Boston Store (Milwaukee), Foley's (Houston), Halliburton's (Oklahoma City), Burdine's (Miami), Goldsmith's (Memphis), Rike-Kumler (Dayton), and Sanger's (Dallas). Gimbel's did not acquire additional companies during this period. National Department Stores added only small enterprises in the 1930s and almost nothing thereafter, ceasing operations in the 1950s. No new groups of major stores were formed during these three decades. Data was gleaned from editions of *Fairchild's Financial Manual.*

72. "Costs May Cause," *NYT,* 11 July 1949, 28; "Retailing Giants," *WWD,* 21 Oct. 1959, 1, 21; "Path of Independents," *WWD,* 22 Oct. 1959, 1, 42.

73. "Puckett of Allied Stores," *Fortune* 35 (Mar. 1947): 122–25, 162, 164, 166–70 (quote on p. 125); "Dept. Store—Specialty Store," *BW,* 20 Aug. 1949, 64–65; "Stern's Is What Allied's Waited For," *BW,* 31 Mar. 1951, 78, 80–87. See also a ten-part series on Allied by Sam Gottsfeld and Harry Berlfein in *WWD*, 16–27 June 1958.

74. For background, see "May Stores: Watch Them Grow," *Fortune* 38 (Dec. 1948): 108–13, 152–54, 156, 159; "Mr. Fred of the Lazari," *Fortune* 37 (Mar. 1948): 108–15, 162, 165–66, 168, 170, 173–74, 176, 178; "'Intelligent Flexibility,'" *BW,* 17 June 1950, 76–78, 80, 82–83; and Editors of *Nation's Business, Lessons of Leadership: 21 Top Executives Speak Out on Creating, Developing and Managing Success* (Garden City, N.Y.: Doubleday, 1968), chap. 2.

75. Most of this activity was focused on branch store development.

76. "F. & R. Lazarus," *WWD,* 16 Apr. 1945, 19; "Foley Bros.," *WWD,* 22 May 1945, 1, 6; "Federated Policy," *BW,* 10 Aug. 1946, 83–85; "15,000 Jam Foley's," *WWD,* 21 Oct. 1947, 1, 15; "Mr. Fred," 170, 173. Shortly after assuming control of Federated, Lazarus was able to back a major expansion of Abraham & Straus in Brooklyn (1945–47), which had been contemplated in its 1928–29 building program.

77. The Higbee Company store in Cleveland was designed two years later (1930) than Strawbridge's, but completed earlier (1931). Both contained about 1 million square feet, twice that of Foley's. Foley's was designed to carry four additional stories, which were added in 1955–57; see "Foley's to Add," *WWD,* 12 Apr. 1955, 1, 63.

78. See "Escalators and Elevator," *WWD,* 23 Aug. 1945, 30; "Moving Stairways," *WWD,* 23 Apr. 1947, 62; "Stores Install," *WWD,* 3 Dec. 1947, 70; "Relief for Crowded Shopping Floors," *DSE* 11 (Apr. 1948): 124, 128; "As the Traffic Goes So Profits the Store," *DSE* 13 (Sep. 1950): 40–43; and "The Seductive Moving Stairway," *DSE* 16 (Feb. 1953): 56–57.

79. Maurice Lazarus, who was sent to Houston to head the project, emphasized to me that the Loewy firm enjoyed virtually complete charge; Kenneth Franzheim did what they stipulated (interview, Cambridge, Mass., 2 Feb. 2002).

80. "Mr. Fred," 174. For other accounts, see "Break Ground," *WWD,* 18 Feb. 1946, 1, 6; "Foley's New Building," *NRB* 28 (June 1946): 17; "Department Store," *AF* 86 (Apr. 1947): 106–9; "New Departures," *WWD,* 30 July 1947, 51; "New Store, New Methods," *BW,* 18 Oct. 1947, 50, 52, 54; "Foley's Opens New Store," *DSE* 10 (Oct. 1947): 130; "Mechanized Store," *AF* 87 (Nov. 1947): 14; William T. Snaith, "Mechanizing the Store Plant," *Stores* 30 (Feb. 1948): 26–28, 30; "Department Store, Houston Texas," *PA* 29 (July 1948): 49–59; "Mr. Fred's Dream Store," *Saturday Evening Post* 223 (18 Nov. 1950): 42–43, 143–44, 146, 148–50; and "Right Store Layout Can Chart a Retailer's Course," *BW,* 14 May 1955, 102–4, 106, 108, 112, 114.

81. Macy's first acquisition was the large O'Connor Moffatt store in San Francisco (1927–29), which occurred in 1945. Two years later it was renamed Macy's and work was begun on a substantial addition sympathetic to the design of the original building. See "Macy Goes West," *BW,* 14 July 1945, 32, 34; "Look Out Now!" *Time* 46 (16

July 1945): 76, 78; "San Francisco Store," WWD, 17 Oct. 1947, 1, 39; and "It's Macy's," SFC, 17 Oct. 1947, 19.

82. "Macy's Kansas City Store," AF 92 (Feb. 1950): 86–95 (quote on p. 86). See also "Macy's a World Giant," *Kansas City Star,* 30 Mar. 1947, 1A, 7A; *Kansas City Star,* 16 Oct. 1949, Macy's Sect.; "New Store," *Kansas City Star,* 17 Oct. 1949, 1; "Total Flexibility in Macy's, Kansas City," *Stores* 32 (Jan. 1950): 45–46; and "Macy's, Kansas City, Provides Unusual Display Flexibility," DW 56 (Feb. 1950): 32–33.

83. "$3,000,000 GR Store," *Grand Rapids Herald,* 2 Apr. 1947, 1, 13; "Herpolsheimer Acquires," WWD, 3 Apr. 1947, 1; "New Herpolsheimer Store," WWD, 11 June 1948, I-54; "Herpolsheimer," WWD, 10 Feb. 1949, 52; "Flexi-Module Lighting at Herpolsheimer's, Grand Rapids," DSE 12 (Sep. 1949): 108–9; *Grand Rapids Herald,* 13 Nov. 1949, New Herpolsheimer's Store Sect.; "Functionalism," WWD, 14 Dec. 1949, 62; "Distinctive Ceiling," WWD, 21 Dec. 1949, 42.

84. "11,000,000 Store," WWD, 27 Mar. 1947, 1, 10; "Jordan Marsh," BH, 27 Mar. 1947, 1, 4; "New Jordan's," WWD, 14 Oct. 1949, 2; "Jordan Marsh Opens First Unit on Old Site," DSE 12 (Dec. 1949): 80–81; "Boston's Wonder Store," *Stores* 32 (Jan. 1950): 52–53; "Jordan's Will Proceed," WWD, 31 Aug. 1954, 1, 47.

85. Examples include L. S. Ayres in Indianapolis (1945–46), Abraham & Straus in Brooklyn (1945–47), Julius Garfinckel in Washington (1945–46), Halle Brothers in Cleveland (1948–49), J. L. Hudson in Detroit (1945–46), Macy's in San Francisco (1947–48), Neiman-Marcus in Dallas (1951–53), A. Polsky in Akron (1946–47), and Rollman & Son in Cincinnati (1946–47). The same approach was taken to additions made to stores that were products of the 1930s, namely J. N. Adam in Buffalo (1945–48), Burdine's in Miami (1946–48), H. P. Wasson & Company in Indianapolis (1947–48); and, to a lesser degree, Joske Brothers Company in San Antonio (1952–53). Compatible rooftop additions were made to the Bon Marche (1953–54) and Frederick & Nelson (1949–52) in Seattle. Perhaps the last example of this approach used for a major store was at the Marston Company in San Diego (1953–54).

86. "Dayton's Importance," WWD, 13 May 1937, 6; "Rike-Kumler Enlarges 60 Percent," DGE 91 (22 June 1937): 64; "'Greater Rike's,'" WWD, 13 May 1938, 16; "Star in the West," DSE 1 (10 May 1938): 31, 34–35; "Rike-Kumler Co.," *Dayton Daily News,* 27 Dec. 1947, 1; "Rike's Nears Century," WWD, 9 Feb. 1953, 1, 36; "Rike-Kumler," *Dayton Daily News,* 27 June 1954, 1, 8; "Rike-Kumler," WWD, 28 June 1954, 1, 10.

87. WWD, 5 Jan. 1948, 53; WWD, 5 Jan. 1953, 7; WWD, 4 Jan. 1954, 7.

88. "Kaufmann's Sets," WWD, 30 Mar. 1953, 38; "Kaufmann Will Mark," WWD, 8 Nov. 1955, 13; PP, 14 Nov. 1955, 1, 5; "Kaufmann's Opens," WWD, 15 Nov. 1955, 1, 68; "A New Kaufmann's in a New Pittsburgh," *Stores* 38 (Jan. 1956): 16–17.

89. Concerning Lazarus, see "Begin Today," 22 Mar. 1950, 2; "Lazarus to Install," CD, 22 Mar. 1950, 1–4; *Stores* 32 (May 1950): 76; and "Six-Story Facade," WWD, 22 Nov. 1950, 54. Concerning Richard's, see "Richard's Will Build," WWD, 20 June 1950, 9; WWD, 28 June 1950, 58; MH, 4 Nov. 1951, 1-H; and "Richard's New," WWD, 6 Nov. 1951, 13. Concerning the May Company, see "Downtown Denver," WWD, 15 Jan. 1954, 2; and WWD, 1 Feb. 1954, 32.

90. "Thalheimer's Plans," WWD, 16 Mar. 1953, 2; "Thalheimer Sets," WWD, 12 July 1954, 1, 10; "Thalheimer Spends," WWD, 11 Jan. 1955, 10; "World's Largest Curtain," *Richmond Times-Dispatch,* 9 Oct. 1955, B-11; "Aluminum Front," WWD, 11 Oct. 1955, 1, 60.

91. "New Nine-Story," WWD, 27 Oct. 1944, 1; "I. Magnin to Have," SFC, 27 Oct. 1944, 9; "I. Magnin's Puts," WWD, 7 Jan. 1948, 94; "Lavish Fashion Background," DSE 11 (June 1948): 23; AF 88 (May 1948): 106–7; Devin Thomas Frick, *I. Magnin & Co.: A California Legacy* (Orange County, Calif.: Park Place, 2000), chap. 3; Therese Poletti, *Art Deco San Francisco: The Architecture of Timothy Pflueger* (New York: Princeton Architectural Press, 2008), 217–20. The new building made use of the steel frame of the office building erected on the site some forty years previous.

92. "Sackton Realty," WWD, 2 Jan. 1946, 1; "Sakowitz Bros.," HP, 21 Aug. 1949, 1, 18; "New $8 Million," WWD, 23 Aug. 1949, 1, 38; "New Methods," WWD, 5 Apr. 1950, 10; "'Tailored' to Customer," WWD, 24 Jan. 1951, 62; "New Sakowitz Store," WWD, 13 Feb. 1951, I-17; "New Sakowitz Store," HP, 18 Feb. 1951, I-1, I-22, and IV; "Open Sakowitz," 20 Feb. 1951, 1, 51; WWD, 2 Mar. 1951, 14; "New Sakowitz Store," DW 58 (Apr. 1951): 20–23, 60–61.

93. "New Downtown Store," AF 96 (Feb. 1952): 126–33 (quote on p. 127). See also "Rich's to Spend," WWD, 18 Feb. 1946, 2; "Retail Stores, a Critique," PA 28 (May 1947): 53–58; "Rich's Opens," WWD, 18 July 1947, 4; "Rich's Opens," WWD, 30 Sep. 1947, 4; "Complete Store," *Atlanta Constitution,* 28 Mar. 1948, 1-A, 18-A; "Rich's Plans," WWD, 29 Mar. 1948, 12; "Rich's New Store for Homes," *Stores* 30 (May 1948): 20–21; "Rich's Store for Men," DW 58 (Jan. 1951): 78; and "Rich's Opens," *Atlanta Constitution,* 10 Sep. 1951, 19.

94. "Right Store Layout Can Chart a Retailer's Course," BW, 14 May 1955, 102–4, 106, 108, 112, 114.

CHAPTER 3. Service Beyond the Stores

1. "Why the Meier & Frank Delivery," RL, 1st Sep. issue, 1929, 5.

2. Historical accounts of the subject are few. Good case studies can be found in Robert H. Twyman, *History of Marshall Field & Co., 1852–1906* (Philadelphia: University of Pennsylvania Press, 1954), 131–35; and Ralph M. Hower, *History of Macy's of New York, 1858–1919* (Cambridge: Harvard University Press, 1943), 197–98, 279–81, 338–41, 400–401. See also Robert Hendrickson, *The Grand Emporiums: The Illustrated History of America's Great Department Stores* (New York: Stein and Day, 1979), 47–50.

3. For background, see "Motor Car Delivery," MRSW 26 (Feb. 1910): 38–40; "Auto Truck Advantage," DGE 64 (27 May 1911): 69; "Machine Effect Saving in Dry Goods Delivery," CV 6 (June 1911): 300–304; "Growth of Motor Transport in Philadelphia," CV 6 (Nov. 1911): 582–84; "Autos Displace Horses," DGE 64 (25 Nov. 1911): 77; "Traffic Congestion Problems," CV 7 (Jan. 1912): 24–28; "Motor Versus Horse," DGE 65 (24 Feb. 1912): 79; "Motors Save Money," DGE 65 (27 June 1912): 67; "Why Motors Are Used," DGE 66 (25 Jan. 1913): 65; "Motors and Horses," DGE 66 (22 Feb. 1913): 69; "Motors for Delivery Work," DGE 67 (28 Mar. 1914): 15, 31; "Trucks Give Pittsburgh Department Stores Better Service," CV 11 (15 Aug. 1914): 5–8; "Motor Delivery in Department Stores," CV 13 (1 Oct. 1915): 5–9; "Motor Efficiency Proven by Macy & Co. Investigation," CV 13 (15 Dec. 1915): 5–11, 20; "Autos Solve Problems," DGE 70 (24 June 1916): 9; "Development of Retail Delivery," JR 3 (Apr. 1927): 20–22; and "The Evolution of the Retail Delivery Truck," RL, 1st Mar. issue, 1930, 5.

4. So closely was this systemization tied to the acceptance of the truck that the most detailed coverage was given in *Commercial Vehicle,* the organ of the motor truck industry targeted to its purchasers. For examples, see "Internal Systems for Handling Packages in Dry Goods Stores," CV 8 (1 Apr. 1913): 5–11; "Shipping Room Systems in Dry Goods Stores," CV 8 (15 Apr. 1913): 5–13; "Efficient Package Handling Helps Trucks," CV 8 (1 May 1913): 10–11; and "Internal Systems Which Are Responsible for Efficiency of Pittsburgh Trucks," CV 11 (1 Sep. 1914): 20–25. For background on scientific

management, see Samuel Haber, *Efficiency and Uplift: Scientific Management in the Progressive Era, 1890–1920* (Chicago: University of Chicago Press, 1964).

5. For background, see "Loading Methods Retard Delivery Trucks," *CV* 8 (1 Oct. 1915): 22–25.

6. Lord & Taylor was perhaps the pioneer in this arrangement in its store of 1913–14, which used ramps that greatly facilitated traffic flow. See "Truck Efficiency Largely Determined by Speed of Shipping Room Work," *CV* 8 (1 Oct. 1915): 15–20. For other examples, see "100 Per Cent Delivery Performance," *CV* 28 (15 Mar. 1923): 50–53; "Solves Down-Town Congestion," *CV* 28 (15 May 1923): 198–200; "Clear Parking Space by Bringing Store's Truck Inside," *DGE* 78 (14 June 1924): 41; "Off Street Loading of Motor Vehicles," *NRB* 11 (Jan. 1929): 48–54; and "Inside Loading of Vehicles a Great Success," *DGE* 84 (15 Feb. 1930): 69.

7. "Deliveries and Cash," *DGE* 66 (25 Oct. 1913): 79, 95.

8. "Providence a Motor Truck Center," *CV* 10 (1 Mar. 1914): 5–10, 22–24; "Outlet Store Delivery System Meets Every Demand," *DGE* 81 (22 Jan. 1927): 59, 61; "Another Big Department Store Eliminates Sidewalk Loading," *CV* 21 (15 Nov. 1919): 310–12; "Dry Goods Trucks Made More Efficient by Separate Delivery Building," *CV* 13 (1 Sep. 1915): 24–28. Several years before Rosenbaum, the Milwaukee department store E. Schuster & Co. adapted a livery stable for centralized delivery functions, serving the company's two stores, both in outlying areas. See "Time Saving Ideas and Consideration of Details to Quicken Delivery," *CV* 8 (1 May 1913): 5–9.

9. "Wealth of Ideas from Delivery Conference," *DGE* 71 (17 Feb. 1917): 21, 23, 27, 31, 41 (quotes on p. 27). See also "Hudson's Delivery," *WWD*, 20 Nov. 1920, 26, 32.

10. "Wealth of Ideas," 23.

11. "A Model Delivery System," *Dry Goods Reporter* 34 (19 Mar. 1904): 11; E. R. Behnke, "Delivery Service Division," typescript, 1 July 1948, MFA; "Package from Field's," *Field Glass* 19 (4 Sep. 1951): 3–6, MFA; Twyman, *Marshall Field*, 134. The store did not have a fully consolidated remote-site service facility until it purchased an existing plant in 1965.

12. "Wanamaker's Depot," *Yonkers Herald*, 1 May 1931, 1; "Wanamaker's," *Retailing*, 16 May 1931, 10; "Macy's Plan," *WWD*, 7 Apr. 1927, 1, 2; "Macy's Plans," *RL*, 2nd Apr. issue, 1927, 5; "Macy Delivery," *WWD*, 21 Apr. 1928, I-7, I-9; "Macy's Buying," *WWD*, 4 June 1930, I-1; "New Macy," *Retailing*, 9 May 1931, 7; Hower, *History of Macy's*, 338–39. See also "Functions and Advantages," *WWD*, 28 Apr. 1928, I-12, I-14. Several major New York stores, including Lord & Taylor and Bloomingdale's, did build remote-site, consolidated service facilities in the 1920s.

13. I have yet to find detailed accounts of warehousing, comparable to those on delivery systems, in period literature. The requirements of department stores made up a very small portion of the storage trade and thus its principal organ, *Distribution and Warehousing*, gave no coverage of that sphere. Similarly, retail publications accorded scant coverage to this sphere until the 1920s.

14. Letter from George H. Johnson and W. T. Grosscup to Albert M. Greenfield, 6 Mar. 1937, 2, Albert M. Greenfield Papers, box 102, folder 3, Historical Society of Pennsylvania.

15. "A Brief History of the Strawbridge & Clothier Store, Philadelphia Pennsylvania," 15 Apr. 1930, 6–7, Strawbridge & Clothier Papers, series V, box 33, Hagley Museum and Library; "Strawbridge & Clothier Unite," *WWD*, 15 Aug. 1924, 33; "Store Handles," *WWD*, 17 Apr. 1926, 10.

16. "Filene Cambridge," *WWD*, 1 Mar. 1920, 64. See also *Cambridge Tribune*, 8 Jan. 1921, 12; "Filene Service Building," *WWD*, 12 Mar. 1921, 42; "Boston Store Devotes," *DGE* 75 (7 May 1921): 115; and "'Filene's' Symbol," *Cambridge Tribune*, Fiftieth Anniversary Number [21 July 1928], B-1.

17. "Hudson's Delivery." A substantially larger addition was made four years later; see "J. L. Hudson," *WWD*, 15 Aug. 1924, 34; and *DN*, 27 Aug. 1925, 18.

18. These numbers are conservative estimates based on accounts I have been able to find in sources of the period. They do not include buildings used simply for warehousing or for delivery purposes, nor do they include existing buildings adapted for the purpose. For details, see Richard Longstreth, comp., "Purpose-Built Service Buildings for Department Stores, 1913–1960," at http://www.departmentstorehistory.net and http://www.preservenet.cornell.edu. Useful contemporary accounts include a series in *WWD*: "Stores Extend Warehousing," 10 Apr. 1926, 1, 4, 11; "Extend Warehousing," 23 Apr. 1923, 26; "Stores Keep," 17 May 1926, 27; "The Distribution of Costs," 5 June 1926, 12; and "Warehousing Answers," 3 July 1926, 10. See also "The Value of Remote Delivery," *RL*, Sep. 1931, 5; and Hunley Abbott, "Behind the Scenes," *Retailing*, 29 May 1939, 17.

19. In 1927, Lord & Taylor and James McCreery & Company of New York contracted with a third party, the Eleto Company, to construct a warehouse of some 385,000 square feet, probably the only remote-site facility of this kind erected in Manhattan. See "Eleto Plan," *WWD*, 6 Oct. 1927, I-1, I-2; "First Av. Warehouse," *NYT*, 9 Oct. 1927, RE1; "New Lord & Taylor," *WWD*, 26 Apr. 1928, I-16; "New Joint Warehouse," *WWD*, 24 Jan. 1929, I-11, I-18; "Eleto Delivery for Two New York Stores," *DGE* 83 (16 Feb. 1929): 85; and "Lord & Taylor," *WWD*, 18 Apr. 1929, I-13.

20. "Merchant Firm," *ES*, 17 Sep. 1927, 18. See also "Tractor-Trailers Expedite," *RL*, 1st May issue, 1930, 5; and "Our Tractor-Trailer," *RL*, May 1932, 5. The horizontal layout would become the preferred one when the mechanical movement of goods internally became standard after World War II.

21. "Jordan Marsh Acquires," *DGE* 81 (24 Dec. 1927): 50; "Jordan Marsh Company," *Cambridge Tribune*, Fiftieth Anniversary Number [21 July 1928], C-1; "Jordan Marsh Cambridge," *WWD*, 28 July 1928, 10.

22. The building seems to have been converted as part of an expansion campaign for the store; see "Gimbel's Plan," *WWD*, 8 May 1922, 7. While this account does not specify the time of purchase, two photographs in the Gimbel Brothers Papers at the Milwaukee County Historical Society, both of which appear to date from the early 1920s, show the building before and after conversion and reveal minimal changes made to the exterior, at least, in the process.

23. "Hecht's, Washington," *WWD*, 29 June 1933, 23. After less than a decade, both Woodward & Lothrop's and Hecht's service buildings became too small and were replaced by much larger new ones.

24. Concerning Bamberger's, see "Bamberger's Announce," *WWD*, 12 May 1924, 34; "Bamberger's to Build," *WWD*, 20 Dec. 1924, 1, 7; "Bamberger Remote Delivery," *WWD*, 9 Nov. 1925, 41; "Remote Delivery Station," *WWD*, 14 Nov. 1925, 1, 6–7; "Going to the Limit in Delivery Stations," *DGE* 80 (16 Jan. 1926): 64–65; "Bamberger 'Service Building,'" *RL*, 1st Apr. issue, 1926, 5. The large warehouse planned for the site was never built. Rare surviving documents on the development of such facilities exist in the Abbott, Merkt & Company Collection, Avery Architectural and Fine Arts Library, Columbia University. Concerning Famous-Barr, see "New $1,000,000 Warehouse," *WWD*, 16 Jan. 1925, 40; and "Finest Remote Delivery Equipment Seen in New Famous & Barr Station," *DGE* 80 (13 Mar. 1926): 98–99.

25. See, e.g., "Warehouse a Storehouse," *Retailing*, 14 Feb. 1938, 20; and "The Warehouse Manager," *RE*, 13 Dec. 1939, 12–13.

26. "Bloomingdale Warehouse," *WWD,* 7 July 1928, 7. See also "Bullock's System," *RL,* 2nd Mar. issue, 1926, 5; "Scientific Service Plant," *WWD,* 2 Oct. 1926, 10; "This Delivery Depot," *RL,* 2nd July issue, 1927, 3; "Why the Meier & Frank Delivery Depot," *RL,* 1st Sep. issue, 1929, 5; "Meier & Frank's Is a Model Delivery Depot," *DGE* 84 (12 Apr. 1930): 62, 66; "Remote Delivery Station," *WWD,* 3 Dec. 1927, I-8, I-18; "New Horne Warehouse," *WWD,* 17 Nov. 1928, 11–12; "Horne's Sidesweeps Old Traffic Worries," *DGE* 82 (22 Dec. 1928): 60, 69; and "The Palais Royal Warehouse and Delivery Station," *DGE* 86 (Mar. 1932): 116–17, 121.

27. "Long Range Modernization," *Retailing,* 14 Oct. 1935, 7; Dayton Co.'s," *WWD,* 2 Oct. 1928, I-6, I-12.

28. "New Store Plans," *CE,* 8 Mar. 1937, 1, 3; "Shillito Adds," *WWD,* 9 Mar. 1937, 2; "Transportation Speeded," *Retailing,* 11 July 1938, 13.

29. "New Service Building," *WWD,* 13 May 1937, 26; "See Improved Operations," *RE,* 7 June 1939, 15; "Lazarus New," *WWD,* 8 Nov. 1939, 6; "Lazarus Celebration," *CD,* 8 Nov. 1939, A-18; "Horizontal Service," *RE,* 15 Nov. 1939, 3, 14; "Shillito's Buys," *WWD,* 16 July 1941, 34. Accounts do not make clear whether the Lazarus service annex was intended to replace all other service buildings; however, four such facilities, including a six-story warehouse at Third and Chestnut streets, were being used a decade later when they were replaced by a new bulk service facility. See *CD,* 3 Apr. 1949, 14-A, 15-A.

30. One exception is M. O'Neil of Akron, whose original building (1926–28) included a four-hundred-car garage at the rear. In 1941, a three-story service facility was planned atop the garage, but was never realized. See "$500,000 Expansion," *WWD,* 17 June 1941, 1, 2.

31. "Golden Rule to Erect," *WWD,* 18 Aug. 1923, 8; "Vast Expansion," *SPP,* 19 Aug. 1923, I-6; "Golden Rule Occupies," *WWD,* 16 May 1928, I-8, I-20; "Dayton Co.'s," *WWD,* 2 Oct. 1928, I-6.

32. For a sampling of articles on the subject, see Frank E. Wallis, "Is American Architecture a Live Art?" *Architectural Review* [New York], 3 (Oct. 1915): 81–88; "The Modern Manufacturing Building," *AF* 25 (Sep. 1916): 231–38; Albert Kahn, "The Architect in Industrial Building," *A&E* 54 (Sep. 1918): 101–9; "The Modern Industrial Plant of the American Chicle Company," *A&B* 52 (Dec. 1920): 102–4; "Recent Development in the Architectural Treatment of Concrete Industrial Buildings," *Architecture* 43 (Jan. 1921): 18–21; S. Scott Joy, "The Central Manufacturing District, Chicago, Ill.," *AF* 34 (May 1921): 177–82; Moritz Kahn, "The Design of Industrial Buildings," *Western Architect* 34 (Aug. 1925): 80; George Nimmons, "Industrial Buildings," *American Architect* 129 (5 Jan. 1926): 15–27; Moritz Kahn, "The Architect and Industrial Buildings," *Architecture* 59 (Feb. 1929): 67–74; and "The Exterior of Industrial Buildings," *AF* 51 (Sep. 1929): 313–27. The importance this sphere of activity had reached in the profession is suggested by its treatment in G. H. Edgell, *The American Architecture of To-Day* (New York: Charles Scribner's Sons, 1928), 287–94. Valuable historical accounts include C. W. Westfall, "Buildings Serving Commerce," in John Zukowsky, ed., *Chicago Architecture, 1872–1922: Birth of a Metropolis* (Munich: Prestel, 1987), 77–89; and Betsy Hunter Bradley, *The Works: The Industrial Architecture of the United States* (New York: Oxford University Press, 1999), chap. 10.

33. As quoted in "Bloomingdale Warehouse." For other accounts of the building, see "Bloomingdale's to Erect," *WWD,* 2 Nov. 1926, 2; "Bloomingdale's Buy," *WWD,* 26 Jan. 1927, 7; "Bloomingdale's Plans," *RL,* 1st Feb. issue, 1927, 1; *WWD,* 16 Mar. 1928, I-6; "Bloomingdale Opens," *WWD,* 27 June 1928, I-2; and "Remote Delivery Station a New Bloomingdale Project," *DGE* 83 (13 Apr. 1929): 67, 73.

34. Concerning the building, see "May Co. Plans," *WWD,* 2 Mar. 1927, 60; "May Co. Wagers," *CPD,* 27 Mar. 1927, 7B; and "$1,000,000 Warehouse," *WWD,* 25 Feb. 1928, I-14.

35. "Plans Drawn," *WP,* 12 Jan. 1936, R-5; "Speedier Deliveries," *Retailing,* 13 Jan. 1936, 10; "New Hecht Warehouse," *WWD,* 9 July 1936, I-1. Subsequent accounts include "Lay Hecht Co.," *WWD,* 23 Nov. 1936, I-6; "Hecht Officiates," *WP,* 24 Nov. 1936, 12; "Two Glass Buildings," *PA* 17 (Dec. 1936): 679–81; "New Hecht Warehouse," *Retailing,* 8 Mar. 1937, 9; "Hecht Company," *Washington Herald,* 30 June 1937; "A Department Store Builds a New Warehouse," *AR* 86 (July 1937): 78–81; and "Last Word in Warehousing," *Retailing,* 12 July 1937, I-8, I-10. See also Dietrich Neumann et al., "Glass Block," in Thomas C. Jester, ed., *Twentieth-Century Building Materials: History and Conservation* (New York: McGraw-Hill, 1995), 194–98; and Richard Longstreth, *History on the Line: Testimony in the Cause of Preservation* (Washington, D.C.: National Park Service, and Ithaca, N.Y: National Council for Preservation Education, 1998), chap. 2.

36. "Last Word," I-10; interview with Warren O. Simonds, retired senior vice president of Hecht's, Arlington, Virginia, 13 Mar. 1992.

37. This interpretation remains speculative, based on circumstantial evidence. For further discussion, see Longstreth, *History on the Line,* chap. 3.

38. "Lits Buys Site," *WWD,* 8 Aug. 1939, 1, 38; "Plan Warehouse," *PL,* 8 Aug. 1939; "Lit Brothers Warehouse," *Philadelphia* 25 (Sep. 1939): 3, 11; "Warehouse: 1941 Model," *RE,* 4 Sep. 1940, 3, 5; "New Lit Warehouse," *WWD,* 17 Feb. 1941, 25; "Department Store Warehouse," *AR* 90 (Oct. 1941): 60–61. Much additional information is available in the Albert M. Greenfield Papers at the Historical Society of Pennsylvania.

39. "Remote Delivery Stations Urged," *WWD,* 7 May 1924, 1, 3. The account is among the most thorough assessments of the benefits that these facilities could afford. Information on Abbott, Merkt's initial years is meager. For an early advertisement, see *NRB* 7 (June 1925): 39. By 1929, the firm listed itself as "architects and engineers for department stores" and in that year issued a booklet entitled "Department Store Buildings." See *Retailing,* 17 Sep. 1929, 11. The Hecht Brothers store was one of the very few retail buildings known to have been designed by the firm until after World War II, but it began a long and lucrative relationship.

40. Besides the projects noted above, the firm designed consolidated service buildings for S. Kann Sons in Washington (1925–26), H. & S. Pogue in Cincinnati (1926–27), Palais Royal in Washington (1930–31), G. Fox in Hartford (ca. 1929–30), and Hochschild, Kohn in Baltimore (1941–42), as well as an unrealized scheme for James A. Hearn & Son in New York (1928); the extensive remodeling of a loft for service for the Hecht Company (1932); additions to the service building of Stix, Baer & Fuller in St. Louis (1941); and delivery depots for Strawbridge & Clothier (1928) and Gimbel Brothers (1931) in Philadelphia, J. L. Hudson in Detroit (1937–38), and Sibley, Lindsay & Curr in Rochester (1939–40), as well as for the United Parcel Service (1936–37). Other department stores the firm had worked for by 1936 included B. Altman and Arnold Constable in New York, Frederick Loeser in Brooklyn, Halle Brothers in Cleveland, Hess Brothers in Allentown, Pennsylvania, Hutzler Brothers in Baltimore, and Lansburgh & Brother in Washington. The extent of biographical information on the principals, Hunley Abbott and Oswald Merkt, found to date is limited to short obituaries: *NYT,* 26 Oct. 1969, I-82, and *NYT,* 23 June 1943, 21. See also "Hunley Abbott Gets," *NYT,* 29 July 1933, 16. A sense of the esteem in which Abbott was held in the retail sphere is suggested by the National Retail Dry Goods Association's selection of him to write articles on key developments in store buildings and in delivery for an anniversary

volume, *Twenty-Five Years of Retailing* (New York: By the association, 1936), 84–108, 128–34.

41. "Famous-Barr Buys," *SLP*, 29 July 1945, III-1; "Plan 7-Story," *WWD*, 30 July 1945, 1, 4; "Famous-Barr Breaks," *St. Louis Star-Times,* 15 Jan. 1946, 7; "May Co. Starts," *LAT*, 2 Nov. 1945, II-2; "How Service and Delivery Are Expedited at the May Co.," *RM* 43 (Feb. 1948): 16–19.

42. *Branch Stores* (New York: National Retail Dry Goods Association, 1955), 105–6; "Hecht Addition," *WWD*, 22 Jan. 1948, 76. See also "Philadelphia Stores," *WWD*, 5 June 1956, I-25, where the Hecht Company service building is cited as a prototype.

43. For chain company examples, see "Distributing Centers," *LAT*, 11 Mar. 1923, V-1, 9; "Huge Structure," *WP*, 6 May 1923, III-1; "Turnover Is King," *CSA* 1 (Sep. 1925): 9–10, 42; "Sears-Roebuck Need," *WWD*, 3 May 1926, 10; "New Kroger Plant," *CPD*, 8 Jan. 1928, 9-B; "New Penney Warehouse," *WWD*, 3 Feb. 1928, I-16; "When Two Chains Merge," *CSA/GM* 5 (Dec. 1929): 31–33, 50; "Balancing Warehouse Speed with Accuracy," *CSA/GM* 6 (Mar. 1930): 33–35; "New Warehouse," *DMN*, 3 Aug. 1930, 8; "Sears' Chicago," *WWD*, 10 Sep. 1935, 9. Among department stores, Sears was the pioneer in establishing a large, one-story plant. See "Sears to Build," *WWD*, 13 Mar. 1940, 5; and *WWD*, 23 Aug. 1940, II-4.

44. Concerning Abraham & Straus, see "Big Expansion," *WWD*, 14 Sep. 1945, 1, 9; and "A & S 'Housewarming,'" *WWD*, 25 June 1947, I-55. Concerning Foley's, see "Department Store," *AF* 86 (Apr. 1947): 106–9; "New Departures," *WWD*, 30 July 1947, 51; "Foley's Opens New Store," *DSE* 10 (Oct. 1947): 131; and "Department Store, Houston, Texas," *PA* 29 (July 1949): 49–59. The realized service building (1947) was perhaps the first of its type to be organized on a single story, and it no doubt served as a springboard for the more elaborate Lazarus facility begun shortly thereafter. See "Foley, Pogue," *WWD*, 13 Mar. 1947, 62.

45. "Halle's Plan," *WWD*, 24 Nov. 1947, 1, 35; "Halle's Makes Headway," *Halle Bulletin* 14 (3 Apr. 1948): 1, 5–6 [Halle Brothers Papers, Western Reserve Historical Society]; "New West Wing, Service Building," *Halle Bulletin* 15 (30 July 1949): 1; "Complete Halle," *WWD*, 1 Aug. 1949, 2 (Halle's); "Retail Construction," *WWD*, 13 Feb. 1946, 61; "Productivity Stressed," *WWD*, 10 Mar. 1949, 62; and "Service Center," *DSE* 12 (May 1949): 58 (Pogue).

46. "Effortless Delivery," *Retailing,* 9 May 1938, 12; "Hudson's Start," *WWD*, 16 Nov. 1945, 1, 5.

47. "Lazarus Service Building," *WWD*, 20 Apr. 1949, 64; "Following Day Delivery," *WWD*, 7 Apr. 1949, 62. See also "Lazarus to Open," *CD*, 7 Apr. 1949, 2-A; "How Lazarus Cuts Handling Costs," *BW*, 9 Apr. 1949, 39–40, 42, 45–46; "Cutting the Cost of Merchandising," *Stores* 31 (Apr. 1949): 10–13, 52; "Cutting Costs in Handling Bulky Merchandise," *CSA/VS* 25 (May 1949): 171–73, 196; "Lazarus Service Building," *WWD*, 7 Dec. 1950, 57; and "Revolution in the Warehouse," *AF* 93 (Dec. 1950): 108–13.

48. For background, see Martin Greif, *The New Industrial Landscape: The Story of the Austin Company* (Clinton, N.J.: Main Street, 1978). Contemporary coverage was extensive. See, e.g., "Building Types: Factories," *AR* 83 (June 1938): 99–127; "Albert Kahn," *AF* 69 (Aug. 1938): 87–142; Talbot Hamlin, "Factories as Architecture," *PA* 21 (Aug. 1940): 469–80; "Factory Design for Low-Cost Construction," *AR* 98 (Nov. 1945): 118–40; Clarence W. Dunham, *Planning Industrial Structures* (New York: McGraw-Hill, 1948); Randolph W. Mallick and Armand T. Gaudreau, *Plant Layout: Planning and Practice* (New York: Wiley, 1951). Historical accounts, by contrast, are rare and tend to close at the crucial period of transition in the 1930s. See, e.g., Lindy Biggs, *The Rational Factory: Architecture, Technology, and Work in America's Age of Mass Production* (Baltimore: Johns Hopkins University Press, 1996), chap. 7.

49. "'Assembly Line,'" *WWD*, 2 Dec. 1948, 54; "Bamberger Warehouse Will Be Showplace," *Stores* 30 (Dec. 1948): 34, 36. For other accounts of the Bamberger's building, see "Bamberger's Buys," *WWD*, 7 Aug. 1947, 50; "Work on Bamberger," *WWD*, 8 Mar. 1948, 35; "Bamberger's Starts," *WWD*, 9 June 1948, 71; "Superior Warehouse," *DSE* 12 (Jan. 1949): 114; "Bamberger's Opens," *WWD*, 24 May 1949, 23; and R. H. Tatlow III, "Bamberger's One-Story Warehouse," *Stores* 31 (Aug. 1949): 14–17, 36. Concerning Willow Run, see "Willow Run Bomber Plant," *AR* 92 (Sep. 1942): 39–46.

50. See, e.g., "Unimpeded Flow," *WWD*, 21 Apr. 1949, 70; "Carson Warehouse," *WWD*, 14 Feb. 1951, 98; "Thalheimer's Service Building," *Stores* 34 (Nov. 1952): 18–22; "Store Service Center," *DSE* 16 (July 1953): 36–37, 134, 141; "New Denver Warehouse," *WWD*, 30 Apr. 1953, 55; "Filene's Readies," *WWD*, 23 Feb. 1955, I-14; and "The Broadway's New Service Building," *Stores* 37 (Mar. 1955): 22–24, 54.

51. "Heads Engineering Firm," *NYT*, 15 July 1946, 34; R. H. Tatlow III, "Planning a Modern Warehouse," *Stores* 29 (May 1947): 20–26; Tatlow, "Old Service Building," *WWD*, 18 Mar. 1948, 100. See also "More Warehousing," *WWD*, 30 Jan. 1947, 70; and "Warehouse Costs Cut by Mechanization," *DSE* 11 (Nov. 1948): 72–73. Work by Abbott, Merkt was used almost exclusively for examples in addressing the subject in Louis Parnes, *Planning Stores That Pay* (New York: F. W. Dodge, 1948), 132, 147–49, 152–57.

CHAPTER 4. Parking for Stores

1. *LAT*, 14 Sep. 1919, VI-14; "Novel Way," *LAT*, 28 Sep. 1919, V-1, VI-16; "You Motor," *RL*, 15 Oct. 1919, 10. The building was constructed three years earlier for the Ville de Paris, a well-established dry goods store. Dyas shared the building after moving there in 1919, but less than seven months later the two stores merged to form a nascent department store. The name was changed to B. H. Dyas Company in 1926. See "B. H. Dyas," *WWD*, 9 Apr. 1920, 56; and "Ville de Paris," *WWD*, 3 Sep. 1926, 8. The previous year changes were made on the interior that appear to have eliminated the motorists' entrance, converting much of the space to the display of women's sportswear. See "Ville de Paris," *WWD*, 12 Aug. 1925, 56.

2. John A. Miller, "The Chariots That Rage in the Streets," *AC* 39 (July 1928): 111–14.

3. "Parking Space Vital Problem for Retailers with Automobile Trade," *DGE* 76 (4 Mar. 1922): 13. On the situation in Los Angeles, see Scott L. Bottles, *Los Angeles and the Automobile: The Making of the Modern City* (Berkeley: University of California Press, 1987), esp. chaps. 3 and 4; and Richard Longstreth, *City Center to Regional Mall: Architecture, the Automobile, and Retailing in Los Angeles, 1920–1950* (Cambridge: MIT Press, 1997), esp. chap. 1.

4. The data on car registration and use presented in this chapter are from the annual *Facts and Figures of the Automobile Industry* (later *Automobile Facts and Figures*) published by the National Automobile Chamber of Commerce (later Automobile Manufacturers Association).

5. For a sampling of early discussions of the subject, see "The Urban Auto Problem," National Conference on City Planning, *Proceedings,* 1920, 76–106; "Unchoking Our Congested Streets," *AC* 25 (Oct. 1920): 351–54; "Traffic Problems of the Future," *Motor Age* 41 (26 Jan. 1922): 14–18; "Our City Thoroughfares," *AC* 29 (Dec. 1922): 496–500; and "Day and Night Storage and Parking of Motor Vehicles," National Conference on City Planning, *Proceedings* 15 (1923): 176–218. Scholarly studies include Joel A. Tarr, *Transportation Innovation and Changing Spatial Patterns in Pittsburgh, 1850–1934* (Chicago: Public Works Historical Society, 1978), part 2; Howard L. Preston, *Automobile Age Atlanta: The Making of a*

Southern Metropolis, 1900–1935 (Athens: University of Georgia Press, 1979), esp. chap. 5; Bottles, *Los Angeles,* esp. chaps. 3 and 4; R. Stephen Sennott, "'Forever Inadequate to the Rising Stream': Dream Cities, Automobiles, and Urban Street Mobility in Central Chicago," in John Zukowsky, ed., *Chicago Architecture and Design, 1923–1993: Reconfiguration of an American Metropolis* (Munich: Prestel, 1993), 52–73; Robert M. Fogelson, *Downtown: Its Rise and Fall, 1880–1950* (New Haven: Yale University Press, 2001), chap. 6; and Peter D. Norton, *Fighting Traffic: The Dawn of the Motor Age in the American City* (Cambridge: MIT Press, 2008), esp. chap. 5.

6. "What's the Solution?" RL, 6 Feb. 1924, 4; "No Parking," RL, 20 Feb. 1924, 4; "New York Finds," RL, 5 Mar. 1924, 8; "Retail Trade," RL, 19 Mar. 1924, 7; "Columbus Claims," RL, 16 Apr. 1924, 8; "Smaller Cities," RL, 7 May 1924, 8; "Parking Automobiles," NREJ 27 (22 Feb. 1926): 53–54; "Traffic Congestion, Parking Facilities, and Retail Business," AC 34 (June 1926): 664–66; "What 37 Cities," RL, 1st May issue, 1928, 8; "What Merchants Think," RL, 2nd May issue, 1928, 6. A useful overview on this and many other aspects of the subject is contained in John A. Jakle and Keith A. Sculle, *Lots of Parking: Land Use in a Car Culture* (Charlottesville: University of Virginia Press, 2004), chap. 1.

7. Longstreth, *City Center,* 3–5; "Mayors Predict," RL, 20 Feb. 1924, 4.

8. "Syracuse's Merry," RL, 16 Apr. 1924, 8; "Syracuse C. of C.," RL, 6 Feb. 1924, 3; "Merchants of Syracuse," RL, 2nd Oct. issue, 1924, 2.

9. See, e.g., "Gather Favors," *Baltimore American,* 22 July 1925, 1; "Merchants Will Seek," WWD, 16 Feb. 1927, 10; and "Downtown Boston," WWD, 5 Mar. 1930, I-11.

10. "Chicago Study," WWD, 5 Mar. 1927, 1, 10; "Say Loop Parking," WWD, 14 Dec. 1927, I-7; "Most Loop Stores," WWD, 2 Feb. 1928, I-8; "'No Parking' Says Chicago," DGE 82 (7 July 1928): 12–13, 90; Fogelson, *Downtown,* 285–88.

11. "Chicago 'No Parking,'" WWD, 11 Aug. 1928, 1, 4; "Problems and Reactions," WWD, 18 Aug. 1928, 4; "No Parking Plan," WWD, 15 Oct. 1928, I-6; "The Parking Question," NRB 12 (Apr. 1930): 199–200.

12. "Busses to Bring," WWD, 4 Sep. 1925, 2, 4; "Shopping Express," DGE 79 (12 Sep. 1923): 40; "A & S Store," WWD, 23 Nov. 1925, 6; "Arnold Constable's," WWD, 18 May 1926, 7; "Bus Lines Facilitate," WWD, 9 Jan. 1926, 4; "Find Bus Service," WWD, 15 June 1926, 22.

13. "Famous-Barr's," WWD, 4 May 1926, 8; "Plan Terminal," SLP, 23 May 1923, IX-1B; "Famous-Barr," SLG, 2 May 1926, 1a; "Have You a Friendly Department Store Like This One in Your Town?" *Bus Transportation* 6 (May 1927): 254–56. See also, "See Bus Lines," WWD, 28 Dec. 1923, 29.

14. The best source for documenting the development of bus depots is *Bus Transportation,* which contains numerous case studies on the subject. Concerning the rise of the industry, see Albert E. Meier and John P. Hoschek, *Over the Road: A History of Intercity Bus Transportation in the United States* (Upper Montclair, N.J.: Motor Bus Society, 1975); and Oscar Schisgall, *The Greyhound Story: From Hibbing to Everywhere* (Chicago: J. G. Ferguson, 1985).

15. "Busses Carry," RL, 1st May issue, 1927, 5; WP, 25 Oct. 1923, 7; WP, 27 Oct. 23, 2; "Do Your Trucks?" RL, 5 Mar. 1924, 4; "Store in Restricted," WWD, 9 May 1925, 20; "26 Boston Stores," RL, 2nd Oct. issue, 1927, 1.

16. The research necessary to develop a reasonably accurate account of off-street parking facilities in any one city over several decades entails a substantial amount of investigation and so doing for enough cities to provide a comparative base for this study would consume an unrealistic amount of time. Earlier, I provided such details for downtown Los Angeles; see Longstreth, *City Center,* 43–55, 210–15. For additional discussion, see Jakle and Sculle, *Lots of Parking,* chap. 2; and Alison Isenberg, *Downtown America: A History of the Place and the People Who Made It* (Chicago: University of Chicago Press, 2004), 135–40.

17. Brief references in accounts of the period indicate that the practice grew to be widespread during the 1920s. A detailed analysis on store parking from the 1920s is *Vehicular Traffic Congestion and Retail Business,* Trade Information Bulletin #394, Bureau of Foreign and Domestic Commerce, U.S. Department of Commerce, April 1926. Culling information received from over fourteen hundred stores nationwide, the report cited nineteen parking lots and twenty-seven garages related to dry goods houses but did not distinguish between ones owned by the stores and those that were independently owned with which a cooperative arrangement had been made.

18. Concerning Simon's, see "Store Parks Cars," NYT, 14 Dec. 1924, 3; "Garage Parking Plan," WWD, 15 Dec. 1924, 47; "New Simon Parking," WWD, 16 Dec. 1924, 45; and "Shall the Store Provide Parking Facilities?" NRB 6 (Jan. 1925): 37. A Los Angeles counterpart, Meyer Siegel & Co., may have instituted a similar service even earlier; see "Parking Service Asset," WWD, 7 Mar. 1925, 17. Concerning Field's, see "Garage Service," WWD, 28 Aug. 1926, 7; "Chicago 'No Parking,'" 4; and "Suburban Branches," RL, 1st Mar. issue, 1929, 1. Famous-Barr was probably the first department store to introduce this service, using it as a means to transport cars to a garage built for that purpose.

19. To date I have found a copy of only one agreement between the owners of a department store and a parking facility. That document, from P. J. Rossman, manager of the Badger Auto Service Company, to Gimbel Brothers, Milwaukee, 7 Nov. 1929 (Gimbel Brothers Papers, Milwaukee County Historical Society), gives no time frame for which the accord is binding. It is likely that the absence of a specified period was common in the 1920s due to the experimental nature of such ventures and the fact that they did not entail the leasing of space.

20. Concerning Wolff & Marx, see SAE, 16 Feb. 1920, 7; 7 Mar. 1920, 10–11; and 4 Dec. 1920, 9; and "'It's Worth the Cost," RL, 16 Apr. 1924, 2. Concerning the Boston Store, see MS, 16 Nov. 1923, 3; and "Some Solutions," WWD, 9 May 1925, 20.

21. "Paterson Store," WWD, 24 Nov. 1925, 4; *Paterson Morning Call,* 5 Apr. 1926, 7; "Comfort for Customers Who Park Their Cars," DGE 84 (Nov. 1930): 171. Concerning Quackenbush's, see "Plan $500,000," WWD, 10 Apr. 1924, 34; and "Quackenbush's Open," WWD, 9 June 1925, 57.

22. My tabulations draw from the same sources as those for downtown stores and service buildings cited in previous chapters. Of the thirteen I have documented, eleven were newly constructed, one a conversion of a service building, another the conversion of a service garage. For a list of examples, see Richard Longstreth, comp., "Parking Garages Built for Department Stores, 1920–1960," at *http://www.departmentstorehistory.net* and *http://www.preservenet.cornell.edu*. Historical studies of commercial parking garages include Susan West Montgomery, "Making Room for the Automobile: The Parking Garage in the City Center 1920 to 1970," M.A. thesis, George Washington University, 1999; Jakle and Sculle, *Lots of Parking,* chap. 5; and Shannon Sanders McDonald, *The Parking Garage: Design and Evolution of a Modern Urban Form* (Washington, D.C.: Urban Land Institute, 2007).

23. "Store to Build," SLG, 1 Jan. 1922, 14a, 8c; SLP, 1 Jan. 1922, V-14B; SLG, 13 Aug. 1922, 4b; "Providing Place for Customers' Cars," DGE 77 (24 Mar. 1923): 19–20; "Store's Garage Solves," WWD, 8 Mar. 1924, 14; "A Special Garage," RL, 1st June issue, 1924, 4; "Scruggs Garage Parked 26,000 Cars Free in First Year of Operation," DGE 79 (17 Jan. 1925): 67; "Shall the Store Provide?" 37; "Should Stores Give Customers Free Parking Space?" DGE 83 (19 Jan. 1929): 60–61.

Concerning the configuration employed, see "Ramp Design in Public Garages," AF 35 (21 Nov. 1921): 169–75; and "An Analysis of Garage Design," AF 46 (Mar. 1927): 215–16.

24. Concerning Famous-Barr, see "Garage Site," SLP, 5 Feb. 1922, V-1B; "Six-Floor Spiral," SLP, 19 Feb. 1922, 1B; "Three Stores"; and "Stores Find Customer Garage a Service Luxury," NRB 7 (June 1925): 28, which also discusses the rivalry between the three emporia.

25. "4 Seattle Stores," WWD, 11 Nov. 1924, 41; "Four Stores Solve," WWD, 14 Mar. 1925, 15; "Four Stores Building," ST, 5 Apr. 1925, 18–19; "Four Stores Garage," Seattle Post-Intelligencer, 6 Apr. 1925, 3.

26. In at least a few cases during the 1920s, numerous retailers worked together to establish a garage catering to shoppers, but such ventures were not operated by those businesses and major department stores were seldom involved. Among the best known examples of the decade was the Merchants Garage in Columbus, Ohio (1927–28).

27. "Plans 8-Story," BH, 14 June 1924, 1, 13; "Jordan Marsh," WWD, 16 June 1924, 34; "Jordan Marsh's Garage," WWD, 25 Nov. 1925, 47; "Garage Parking," BH, 15 Sep. 1926, 21; "Customer Car Parking a Big Success in Eight-Story Shoppers' Garage," DGE 81 (19 Feb. 1927): 72–73, 77.

28. "Hub Contractors Complete," BH, 2 Jan. 1927, B1–B4; "Now the 'Skyscraper' Garage," Popular Science Monthly 110 (May 1927): 62. On the other hand, the slightly earlier Bowdoin Square Garage had attendant parking; see "New Garage," BH, 9 May 1926, A4.

29. For background, see "The City Parking Garage," AF 46 (Mar. 1927): 234–40; "Multi-Story Garages for Mid-City Plots," NREJ 30 (18 Feb. 1929): 23–25; and "Downtown Parking Garages," Building Owner and Manager 10 (Sep. 1930): 5–7.

30. "May's, Cleveland," WWD, 4 Feb. 1925, 4; "May Co. to Erect," CPD, 1 May 1925, 1-C; "May Co. Patrons," CPD, 21 June 1925, 2-C. Male customers and chauffeurs were asked to drive to the premises. Some two years later, parking demands had increased to the point where the May Company was also using two floors of its remote service building, which lay considerably farther afield, for overflow. See "Free Parking Garage," DGE 81 (1 Oct. 1927): 69.

31. "May's to Build," WWD, 8 Dec. 1926, 1, 2; "Grand Opening," LAT, 4 Sep. 1927, II-10; "Garage Aids," LAT, 6 Nov. 1927, VI-2; "On Trial for Eighteen Months," DGE 84 (3 Aug. 1929): 67, 78; Longstreth, City Center, 49–50.

32. "Dayton Co. Opens," WWD, 28 Sep. 1928, I-8, I-14; "Daniels-Fisher Plan," WWD, 18 Sep. 1929, I-8; "D. & F. Patrons," RMN, 24 Aug. 1930, 12; "Daniels & Fisher's 'Wonder Garage,'" RL, 1st Oct. issue, 1930, 4.

33. Much earlier, J. W. Robinson of Los Angeles had incorporated a small basement garage for customers in its new store of 1914–15, but this feature appears to have been short-lived. See Longstreth, City Center, 31–32. O'Neil's arrangement likely influenced plans for the expansion of the John Shillito store in Cincinnati, new stores for Foley Brothers in Houston, and perhaps other examples discussed in the text below.

34. "Stores Find Customer"; "Garaging Is Too Expensive," RL, 2nd May issue, 1928, 6; "Should Stores Give," 60–61; "Retailing in 1930," WWD, 27 June 1925, 16; "Bigger and Better Parking," DGE 82 (18 Feb. 1928): 61.

35. Increases were substantial in the largest cities as well. Between 1930 and 1940, the total car registrations grew by some 182,000 in Chicago, 62,000 in Philadelphia, 57,000 in Detroit, and 22,000 in Baltimore. Elsewhere increases were smaller, as in, e.g., Dallas (13,000), Washington (11,000), and Kansas City (6,000). These figures are misleading, however, in that they do not include cars owned by the swelling number of inhabitants of surrounding jurisdictions.

36. For background, see "The King's Highway Is not a Stable Yard," Transit Journal 79 (Mar. 1935): 74–77; "They're All Afraid to Mention It," Review of Reviews 9 (Aug. 1936): 54–56; "Traffic Dilemma Returns," Retailing, 12 July 1937, I-19; "Strangled Cities," Toledo Business 17 (May 1939): 11–12; "Solving the Automobile Parking Problem," Public Management 23 (Jan. 1941): 10–14; and "The Parking Problem," AJ 9 (Apr. 1941): 151. First introduced in Oklahoma City in 1935, the parking meter gained rapid acceptance as a means of regulating time spent at the curb, but analysts soon concluded that it had no impact on the causes of traffic or parking problems. For background, see "Nickel in the Slot," Retailing, 12 Apr. 1935, 15; "Regulating Parking by Meters," Public Management 18 (Feb. 1936): 43–44; and "A Promising Solution to the Parking Problem," AC 51 (Aug. 1936): 59–60.

37. For background, see "Parking Lots Offer New Use for Downtown Property," NREJ 30 (23 Dec. 1929): 31–33; "Auto Parks," Los Angeles Realtor 11 (Apr. 1932): 11, 21; "Central Business District Paradox," Journal of the American Institute of Real Estate Appraisers 3 (Jan. 1935): 138–43; "Parking Lots: A New City Activity," AC 53 (Dec. 1938): 59; and "Parking Lots and Garages in Central Business Districts," AJ 8 (Jan. 1940): 62–67.

38. "Traffic Dilemma"; "Should We Get Excited About Retail Decentralization?" NREJ 39 (Dec. 1938): 22–24, 54–55; "Checking Decentralization," RE, 20 Sep. 1939, 2, 15; "'Down Town' Is Losing Out," RE, 15 Nov. 1939, 1; Homer Hoyt, "Urban Decentralization," Journal of Land and Public Utility Economics 16 (Aug. 1940): 270–76; "Diagnosing the Dread," WWD, 26 Dec. 1940, II-20, II-52; "What Is Happening to Our Central Business Districts?" American Planning and Civic Annual, 1940, 231–35; "Decentralization," Buildings and Building Management 41 (July 1941): 21–27; "Effect of Urban Decentralization upon Traffic Problems," ITE, 1941, 64–69. Fogelson, Downtown, chap. 5, provides a valuable historical account.

39. "St. Louis Is Aroused," RE, 24 July 1940, 12; "Kansas City Acts," RE, 25 Sep. 1940, 16.

40. "Parking Facilities for the Detroit Central Business District," ITE, 1939, 73–76; "Traffic Troubles," DN, 8 Oct. 1939, I-17, I-18; "Traffic Jams Business Out," AF 72 (Jan. 1940): 64–65; "Where Is Detroit's Downtown Area Going?" RE, 6 May 1941, 26. The local press was more upbeat. E. A. Baumgarth, real estate editor of DN, covered the issue in a series: 12 Nov. 1939, I-18; 11 Feb. 1940, I-14, I-15; 7 Apr. 1940, I-16, I-17; 21 July 1940, I-14, I-15; and 1 Sep. 1940, I-12, I-13.

41. "Oakland Keeps Shoppers," RE, 21 Feb. 1940, 2–3; "Tonic for Decentralizing Cities," AF 74 (Mar. 1941): 207–11, 42, 44; "26-Year-Old Parking Plan," WWD, 25 July 1956, 3; Division of Research, Bureau of Public Roads, Department of Commerce, Parking Guide for Cities (Washington, D.C.: U.S. Government Printing Office, 1956), 51–54.

42. Among the most detailed studies of the period is Orin F. Nolting and Paul Oppermann, The Parking Problem in Central Business Districts (Chicago: Public Administration Service, 1938). See also "Chicago Succeeds," Retailing, 11 Oct. 1937, 12–13. "Are Business Streets for Parking—or Motoring?" AC 63 (Aug. 1940): 35, 7, 9; "Solving the . . . Problem"; "Financing Off-Street Parking Facilities," Public Management 23 (Apr. 1941): 107–11; "Manager of Revenue," DP, 1 Oct. 1941, 1; "Decentralization and Parking," ITE, 1941, 59–63; "The Parking Problem in the Business District," Civil Engineering 12 (Jan. 1942): 21–23; The Parking Problem: A Library Research (Saugatuck, Conn.: Eno Foundation, 1942); "Providing Off-Street Parking and Terminal Facilities," National Safety

Congress, *Transactions,* 1943, 60–64; "Local Parking Problem Solutions," *Proceedings of the Thirteenth Annual Highway Conference,* University of Michigan Official Publication 46, no. 19, 12 Aug. 1944, 93–117.

43. "An Industry on the Threshold," *Parking,* winter 1954, 19; "Garages Grow Up," *AF* 98 (Feb. 1953): 122; "Unique Structure," *Pittsburgh Press,* 5 Aug. 1936, 9; "A Three-Tier Parking Garage for Kaufmann," *AR* 86 (June 1937): 76–77; Hunley Abbott, "Low Cost Off-Street Parking," *Architectural Concrete* 4:1 [1938]: 6–8; *Parking Manual* (Washington, D.C.: American Automobile Association, 1946), 117–21. An important esthetic model was the PSF Garage in Philadelphia, designed by Howe & Lescaze in conjunction with its landmark Philadelphia Saving Fund Society building (1929–32) a block away; see "Parking Garages," *AR* 90 (July 1941): 94.

44. "Hecht Plans," *WP,* 10 Aug. 1937, 12; "Hecht's Parking," *ES,* 30 Sep. 1937, B-20; Abbott, "Low Cost"; "Stix, Baer & Fuller," *SLP,* 10 Dec. 1939, 14A; "$100,000 Is Paid," *SLP,* 17 Dec. 1939, III-1C; *SLP,* 2 Aug. 1940, 5A; "Four-Way Coupon System," *DSE* 3 (10 Nov. 1940): 29; "Making It Easier," *WWD,* 6 Feb. 1941, 39. Abbott, Merkt designed a number of other parking garages in later years, but never acquired the national reputation for them comparable to the one they had for service buildings.

45. "Parking Deck to Aid Customer Service," *DSE* 3 (25 Sep. 1940): 16; *PI,* 27 Jan. 1941, 14; "Parking Deck Opens," *WWD,* 29 Jan. 1941, 34; "Making It Easier"; "How Stores in Seven Cities Help Customers Park Their Cars," *RM* 36 (15 Mar. 1941): 8, 44; Hunley Abbott, "Metropolitan Store Parking—Philadelphia," *Architectural Concrete* 7:3 [1941]: 32–34.

46. "New Buffum's," *WWD,* 18 Feb. 1941, 5; "New Store, Autoport," *Long Beach Press-Telegram,* 18 Feb. 1941, B-1, B-12; "Buffum's Add Departments and Solve Parking Problem," *RM* 36 (July 1941): 22–23; "Off-Street Parking Garages," *Architectural Concrete* 10:2 [1944]: 34–35.

47. "Architectural Concrete Enhances Beauty of Parking Garages," *Architectural Concrete,* no. 49 [1949]: n.p.; *Off-Street Parking* (Washington, D.C.: Chamber of Commerce of the United States, 1949), 12.

48. "Piano Row to Be Razed," *Real Estate Magazine* [Philadelphia], 20 (Aug. 1939): 2–3; "Board of City Trustees," *Philadelphia* 25 (Aug. 1939): 3; "New Lane Bryant," *WWD,* 22 Mar. 1940, 38; "Store and Garage," *RE,* 10 July 1940, 12; "Stephen Girard Changed His Mind," *Real Estate Magazine* 22 (Feb. 1941): 2–3; "Open New Garage," *WWD,* 12 Mar. 1941, 33.

49. "Auto Parking Problem," *WWD,* 1 Aug. 1946, 38; "Parking Jam," *AF* 85 (Sep. 1946): 8–10 (quote on p. 8).

50. "Gloomy About Downtown," *WWD,* 14 July 1946, 76. Accounts of parking conditions during the second half of the 1940s are numerous. For a sampling, see "Parking and Terminal Problems," *Traffic Engineering* 15 (Feb. 1945): 158–63; "Parking in the Shopping District," *NRB* 27 (Sep. 1945): 44, 78; "The Parking Problem Returns," *Public Safety* 28 (Sep. 1945): 6–7, 36; "Traffic and Parking Snarl Faced by American Cities," *Traffic Engineering* 16 (Feb. 1946): 162–68, 170; "The Parking Problem," *Traffic Engineering* 16 (Sep. 1946): 488–92, 494; "City Highways and City Parking—An American Crisis," *AC* 61 (Nov. 1946): 116–17, 123, 139; "Downtown Must Have," *WWD,* 26 Dec. 1946, II-98, II-106; "Sorry, You Can't Park There," *Nation's Business* 35 (Nov. 1947): 60–64, 86–87; "Parking Problems of American Cities," *American Planning and Civic Annual,* 1950, 132–44; and "Where Can We Park the Car?" *BW,* 28 Oct. 1950, 50, 52, 54–55.

51. *Parking Guide for Cities,* 116–20.

52. "Parking Problem," *WWD,* 11 Apr. 1946, 47. See also "Downtown Merchant Looks at the Future of Downtown Shopping Areas," *Stores* 29 (Nov. 1947): 13, 68, 70; and "The Businessman's Take in the Parking Problem," *ITE,* 1947, 18–21. Good historical coverage is given in Fogelson, *Downtown,* 304–8; and Jakle and Sculle, *Lots of Parking,* chap. 3.

53. "Let's Keep Government Out of the Parking Business," *Stores* 38 (May 1956): 28–29 (quote on p. 28). For a sampling of other accounts, see "Parking Clinic in Kansas City," *UL* 5 (Oct. 1946): 1, 3–4; "Privately Owned Parking Lots," *Traffic Quarterly* 1 (July 1947): 221–27; "A Businessman's View on Off-Street Parking Facilities," *Traffic Quarterly* 2 (July 1948): 267–72; "Private Enterprise in the Parking Field," *UL* 9 (Nov. 1950): 3–7; "Two Approaches to Solution to the Parking Problem," *Parking,* Oct. 1952, 12–13, 54–55; and "Location Factors for Off-Street Parking Facilities," *UL* 13 (Mar. 1954): 3–8.

54. See, e.g., *Parking Manual,* 113, 115; "Garages Grow Up," 125; and "The Merchant Must Be Accessible," *Parking,* spring 1954, 24.

55. "Getting to the Downtown Store," *DSE* 13 (Nov. 1950): 58, 68; "Rx for Parking Ills," *Nation's Business* 41 (Feb. 1953): 35–37, 82–83, 86–88 (quote on p. 82); "Merchant Must Be Accessible," 26.

56. "Adequate Parking," *WWD,* 18 Feb. 1953, 56; "Customer Parking," *Parking,* spring 1954, 36.

57. "Miller & Rhoads," *WWD,* 22 May 1946, 71.

58. "Newark Underground," *WWD,* 12 Dec. 1946, 57; *Off-Street Parking,* 18; "2000 Cars Daily," *WWD,* 16 July 1951, 30.

59. "Fringe Parking Center," *WWD,* 18 June 1947, I-57; "Fringe Parking Center," *RM* 42 (July 1947): 36; "'Fringe' Parking Center," *WWD,* 8 Apr. 1948, 62; *Off-Street Parking,* 32.

60. The council was led by executives from the Fair and Marshall Field's. For background, see "Move to Ease," *WWD,* 12 Sep. 1946, 1, 2; and "Chicago Parking Plan," *DSE* 9 (Oct. 1946): 33. Similar plans were established by merchants' groups in Houston (1951), Kansas City (1953), and Baltimore (1954).

61. "Perimeter Parking," *WWD,* 19 Oct. 1953, 29. In Denver, the May Company took over an existing fringe lot and ran a station wagon shuttle to its store; see "May Co. Provides," *CSA/AE* 23 (Nov. 1947): 38. In Birmingham, Alabama, Loveman, Joseph & Loeb rented a bus to circulate through various residential sections on an eighteen-hour-a-day schedule. Painted like one of the store's gift boxes, the bus may have been a better advertising ploy than conveyance. See "Love that Lovely," *WWD,* 16 Sep. 1953, 79.

62. *WWD,* 16 Apr. 1946, 63; "Lazarus' New," *CD,* 7 Nov. 1947, B-9; "Lazarus Parking," *WWD,* 20 Nov. 1947, 79; "Parking: The Lazarus Solution," *WWD,* 30 June 1948, 54; "Architectural Concrete"; "Lazarus & Co.," *WWD,* 4 Nov. 1953, 70; "Merchant Must Be Accessible," 50; "Work on Third," *CD,* 1 Jan. 1956, 4B; *CD,* 11 Nov. 1956, 32A.

63. "The Zoning Ordinance—A Frontal Attack on the City Parking and Terminal Problem," *ITE,* 1946, 49–58; "Parking Areas for Traffic Generators," *AC* 61 (Sep. 1946): 147; "Tracking Parking Through Zoning," *AC* 62 (Feb. 1947): 109; "Off-Street Parking," *WWD,* 14 Aug. 1947, 62; Longstreth, *City Center,* 214.

64. See "'Ramp' Garage," *WWD,* 19 Dec. 1946, 58; *Off-Street Parking,* 10; and Geoffrey Baker and Paul Funaro, *Parking* (New York: Reinhold, 1958), 78–79.

65. "New Garage," *WWD,* 21 Jan. 1953, 77; "Goldsmith's Looks," *WWD,* 30 Apr. 1953, 53; "Goldsmith's Will Open," *WWD,* 6 Oct. 1953, 12; "Goldsmith's New Garage," *WWD,* 9 Nov. 1953, 38 (Goldsmith's); "Golden Rule to Build," *SPP,* 7 Aug. 1955, I-1, I-8; "Golden Rule Plans," *WWD,* 11 Aug. 1955, I-40; "Bigger Stores," *ABJ,* 20 Apr. 1947, 1-B; *ABJ,* 31 Aug. 1947, 8-A; *ABJ,* 3 Sep. 1947, 21; "New Parking Setup," *WWD,* 18 Nov. 1954, 2 (O'Neil's); "730-Car Parking," *MT,* 28 Aug. 1959, 12; *MT,* 30 Aug. 1959, 7B; "Dayton's Completes," *WWD,* 30 Aug. 1959, 24.

66. "A & S Sets," *WWD,* 19 May 1958, 11; "Confirm A & S Garage,"

WWD, 25 July 1958, 1, 16; "600-Car A & S," *WWD*, 5 Aug. 1959, 17; "600-Car Garage," *Stores* 40 (Oct. 1959): 69–70.

67. Concerning the former, see "Two Close Competitors," *WWD*, 10 Nov. 1949, 50; "Garage Owned," *WWD*, 30 Aug. 1950, 46; *Parking—How It Is Financed* (New York: National Retail Dry Goods Association, 1952), 7–8; and Baker and Funaro, *Parking*, 138. Concerning Hudson's, see *WWD*, 9 Aug. 1950, 55; "Step in Solving," *WWD*, 27 Dec. 1950, 41; "Shoppers Parking Now Ready," *Detroiter* 42 (11 Dec. 1950): 9; and *Parking—How It Is Financed*, 14. Joseph L. Hudson, Jr., recalled that rents from these stores did not significantly offset the garage's operating costs and expressed frustration over the expense of such facilities generally (interview, Detroit, 6 Apr. 2000).

68. "ZCMI Opens," *Salt Lake Tribune*, 1 Nov. 1954, 8–9; "Wall-less Garage Built from Top Down," *ENR* 153 (9 Dec. 1954): 44–47; "Dramatic New Facility Now Open in Salt Lake," *Parking*, winter 1955, 26–27; "Building Engineering," *AF* 102 (May 1955): 164–65; "Parking Plan Big," *WWD*, 15 Nov. 1955, 67; Baker and Funaro, *Parking*, 68–71. A key prototype for the structural approach taken here was a much-praised design by Robert Law Weed for a Miami garage built in 1949. See "Garages Grow Up," *AF* 98 (Feb. 1953): 131; and Baker and Funaro, *Parking*, 148–49. The latter affords a useful overview of some of the many innovations occurring in garage design, but it lacks basic technical analysis. A more insightful perspective in this sphere can be gleaned from Dietrich Klose, *Metropolitan Parking Structures: A Survey of Architectural Problems and Solutions* (New York: Frederick A. Praeger, 1965). Jakle and Sculle, *Lots of Parking*, chap. 6, provides a historical overview.

69. For background, see "Garages Grow Up," 130; "Self-Parking Operations," *Parking*, summer 1954, 38–39; "Industry on the Threshold," 47–48; *Parking Guide for Cities*, 141–44; Edmund R. Rocker, *Traffic Design of Parking Garages*, rev. ed. (Saugatuck, Conn.: Eno Foundation, 1957), 10–11; and "The Parking Picture," *Buildings* 58 (Oct. 1958): 28–31.

70. The self-parking garages for Vandervoort's and Jordan Marsh were anomalies in the 1920s and appear to have had no impact on general practices.

71. *WP*, 2 Nov. 1951, 12C. For analysis of the complex, see Richard Longstreth, "The Mixed Blessings of Success: The Hecht Company and Department Store Branch Development After World War II," in Carter L. Hudgins and Elizabeth Collins Cromley, eds., *Shaping Communities: Perspectives in Vernacular Architecture, VI* (Knoxville: University of Tennessee Press, 1997), 244–62, and references cited in nn. 29 and 30 therein. See also "A 2,000-Car Parking Garage," *AC* 66 (Nov. 1951): 143; "Nation's Largest Parking Building Completed," *ENR* 149 (10 July 1952): 334–39; *Parking: How It Is Financed*, 9; and Baker and Funaro, *Parking*, 140–41.

72. Another important scheme of this genre was built for the May Company's Wilshire Boulevard store in Los Angeles (1952–53). Structurally the design attracted widespread attention as it placed three decks on a nearly flat site without the use of connecting ramps. See "Triple Decker Enables," *WWD*, 30 Oct. 1953, 50; "Designs for Store Parking Areas," *Stores* 38 (Jan. 1956): 18–19; Baker and Funaro, *Parking*, 130–31; and Klose, *Metropolitan Parking*, 192–94. Garages built to serve department stores in outlying areas remained rare before the 1960s. The earliest example I have found of a department store garage built for self-parking in a downtown location was that of G. Fox in Hartford (1952–53); see "Hartford Gets," *WWD*, 15 Oct. 1952, 4; *WWD*, 20 July 1953, 26; and *Parking in the City Center* (New Haven: Wilbur Smith and Associates, 1965), 102–5.

73. "Capital Retailers," *WWD*, 13 Apr. 1955, 6; "Free Parking Plan," *WWD*, 11 May 1955, 6; "Retailer-Subsidized Parking," *WWD*, 17 Aug. 1955, 1, 63; "Baltimore Starts," *WWD*, 1 Aug. 1956, 6; "Baltimore Offered," *WWD*, 5 Mar. 1959, 40; "Downtown Stores," *WWD*, 6 July 1959, 2.

74. "Plan Parking," *WWD*, 14 Feb. 1950, I-1, I-56 [Chicago]; "Privately Financed," *WWD*, 20 Dec. 1950, 58; "Accent on Enterprise in Minneapolis," *Parking*, Oct. 1952, 11, 44; *Parking—How It Is Financed*, 19–20 [Minneapolis]; "Philadelphia Stores," *WWD*, 10 Aug. 1951, 44 [Philadelphia]; "Merchants Offer," *WWD*, 28 Jan. 1953, 16; "Parking Plan," *WWD*, 15 Oct. 1953, I-1, I-39 [Boston]; "Providence Parking," *WWD*, 16 May 1959, 24 [Providence]; "Parking Facility," *WWD*, 23 Oct. 1959, 6 [San Diego]. See also "What's New in Park & Shop," *Parking*, fall 1958, 29–39.

75. "Customer Parking Downtown," *DSE* 9 (Oct. 1946): 126; "Lakefront Parking," *WWD*, 3, 53; "Milwaukee Furthers," *WWD*, 8 Apr. 1953, 75; "Parking Plan," *WWD*, 26 June 1953, 6; "Merchants Take Over Milwaukee's Parking Problem," *DSE* 16 (Aug. 1953): 40–41, 142; "The Solution to Parking Problems in Milwaukee," *DSE* 16 (Sep. 1953): 164, 166; "Milwaukee Group," *WWD*, 8 Mar. 1954, 34; "Milwaukee Group," *WWD*, 8 Feb. 1955, 18; "Downtown Group," *WWD*, 7 June 1955, I-64; "Municipal Aid," *WWD*, 14 Oct. 1955, 1, 16.

76. For an authoritative account of the city's postwar renewal efforts, see Roy Lubove, *Twentieth-Century Pittsburgh: Government, Business, and Environmental Change* (New York: Wiley, 1969), chap. 6. For background on the authority, see "Pittsburgh's Downtown Parking Problem," *ITE*, 1946, 28–40; "Pittsburgh's Approach," *WWD*, 1 July 1948, 42; "Off-Street Parking That Pays for Itself," *AF* 91 (Nov. 1949): 70–71, 112; *Parking: How It Is Financed*, 41–42; Edward G. Morgen, *Parking Authorities* (Saugatuck, Conn.: Eno Foundation, 1953, 74–80; *Parking Programs* (Washington, D.C.: American Automobile Association, 1954), 153–67. Concerning the garages, see "Pittsburgh to Buy," *WWD*, 30 Dec. 1955, 2; *Pittsburgh and Allegheny County: An Era of Accomplishment* (Pittsburgh: Allegheny Conference on Community Development, 1956), 10–11; Baker and Funaro, *Parking*, 64–65; "Parking Garage," *WWD*, 8 Aug. 1957, 6; *PP*, 27 July 1959, 6; and "New Pittsburgh," *WWD*, 30 July 1959, 39.

77. Chicago was an exception; see "Parking: The Crisis is Downtown," *AF* 118 (Feb. 1963): 100–103.

78. See, e.g., "Central Business Districts" and "Downtown Will Always Be There," *Parking*, spring 1954, 18–19, 20–21; and "Parking and Its Relation to Business," *UL* 15 (May 1956): 3–6.

79. "San Francisco Retail," *WWD*, 22 Sep. 1954, 18; "Self Parking Downtown Center Garage," *A&E* 201 (Apr. 1955): 8–15, 22; "Prestressed I-Shaped Wall," *ENR* 154 (31 Mar. 1955): 39–40; Klose, *Metropolitan Parking*, 36; "Self-Service Parking"; "Design and Operation of World's Largest Self-Service Parking Facility," *Parking*, summer 1957, 32–36, 37–39.

80. *ST*, 6 Mar. 1960, 29; *ST*, 7 July 1960, 13. See also *WWD*, 27 Oct. 1958, 1; *ST*, 6 Mar. 1960, 37; "Governor at Garage," *ST*, 7 Mar. 1960, 11; "Store-Connected Parking," *WWD*, 3 Aug. 1960, 55; and *Parking*, fall 1960, 4.

81. "Boost Given," *OWH*, 22 Mar. 1959, 1-B; *WWD*, 12 Nov. 1959, 1; "Air Space Used," *Parking*, fall 1961, 10.

82. "Famous-Barr Plans," *SLP*, 1 Nov. 1960, 1, 6 (quote on p. 6). See also "Famous-Barr Will," *WWD*, 1 Nov. 1960, 12; and "Department Store Garage," *Parking*, winter 1961, 44–45; "The New Face," *SLG*, 30 May 1962, 36; "Famous-Barr," *SLP*, 9 Oct. 1962, 7B; "Paris Store," *SLG*, 21 Nov. 1962, 6A; "New Downtown," *SLP*, 20 Oct. 1963, 2B.

83. This shift occurred more slowly in smaller cities, where immense garages supporting department stores and the shopping district generally continued to be built through the 1960s and into the next decade.

CHAPTER 5. Branch Stores

1. "Department Store of Future," WWD, 13 Feb. 1926, 7. Most of Ilhder's career was devoted to housing reform, directing housing associations in Philadelphia and Pittsburgh and later heading the public housing agency in Washington. I am grateful to Bell Clement for supplying me with details of this important but largely forgotten figure.

2. "Outlying Shops Cited," WWD, 2 July 1927, 6.

3. "Suburban Branch Plan," WWD, 15 Jan. 1927, 1, 15 (quote on p. 15).

4. Concerning Sears's pioneering role in this sphere, see Richard Longstreth, *City Center to Regional Mall: Architecture, the Automobile, and Retailing in Los Angeles, 1920–1950* (Cambridge: MIT Press, 1997), 119–21; and Longstreth, "Sears, Roebuck and the Remaking of the Department Store, 1924–1942," JSAH 65 (June 2006): 238–47.

5. In this chapter I include those large, departmentalized specialty stores that figured in the second as well as the first phase of branch development. They include Wm. Filene's Sons (Boston); Arnold Constable, Lord & Taylor, and Saks Fifth Avenue (New York); Julius Garfinckel & Co. (Washington); and I. Magnin & Co. (San Francisco).

6. The distance from the parent store could vary from a few to several hundred or even thousand miles. The key factor is that for strategic reasons it lay outside the city center and thus not be run simply as an annex, as frequently occurred with the development of men's stores and other operations that were an integral pat of the parent operation.

7. Information on the resort branches operated by these companies is meager at best. For a listing of branch stores, see Richard Longstreth, comp., "Department Store Branches, 1910–1960," at http://www.departmentsstorehistory.net and http://preservenet.cornell.edu.

8. Concerning I. Magnin, see Devin Thomas Frick, *I. Magnin & Co.: A California Legacy* (Orange County, Calif.: Park Place, 2000), 21–25. Concerning Saks, see "Saks-Fifth Ave.," WWD, 13 Nov. 1925, 1, 12; "Saks-Fifth Ave.," WWD, 9 Dec. 1926, 1, 4; "Saks Atlantic City," WWD, 31 Jan. 1927, 9; "Saks May Open," WWD, 19 Feb. 1929, I-24; and "Saks to Open, WWD, 16 May 1929, I-1, I-20. Concerning Filene's, see *The Enterprise* [Falmouth], 25 June 1927, 10; and Stacy Holmes, "A Brief History of Filene's," typescript, 1958, rev. 1972, Filene's Collection, Boston Public Library.

9. "Burdine's Opens," MH, 15 Jan. 1929, 12; "Burdine Branch," 22 Jan. 1929, I-7; "Burdine's to Expand," WWD, 18 Apr. 1929, I-9; "Burdine's Miami Beach," WWD, 29 Nov. 1929, I-6; "Macy's to Open," WWD, 16 Dec. 1929, I-2; "Macy's Palm Beach," *Palm Beach Post*, 31 Dec. 1929, 7; and "Macy's Palm Beach," WWD, 7 May 1930, I-2.

10. *Townsman* [Wellesley], 3 Oct. 1924, 2; *Daily Hampshire Gazette* [Northampton], 16 Dec. 1924, 9; *Mount Holyoke News*, 1 Oct. 1926, 3.

11. MSJ, 17 Sep. 1927, 3; "College Merchandise Is Carried," WWD, 24 July 1936, 6 (Dayton's); "Younkers Proves," WWD, 6 Sep. 1950, 78.

12. "Filene's Opening," *Townsman*, 25 Sep. 1925, 1; "Filene's Starts," WWD, 2 Sep. 1932, I-18; "Opening of Filene's," *Townsman*, 9 Dec. 1932, 1; "Filene's Wellesley Shop," WWD, 21 June 1938, 8; "Record Growth," *Townsman*, 5 Aug. 1938, 1, 8; "Filene's Again Expanding," WWD, 12 Aug. 1938, 20; "Filene's Builds," *Retailing*, 29 Aug. 1938, 8; "3,000 Attend," *Townsman*, 18 Nov. 1938, 1, 7 (Wellesley); "Filene's Has Leased," *Daily Hampshire Gazette*, 29 Mar. 1930, 1; *Daily Hampshire Gazette*, 27 May 1930, 6 (Northampton); "Magnin's Pasadena," WWD, 14 Oct. 1932, I-9; "New I. Magnin," *Pasadena Star-News*, 4 Jan. 1933, 5.

13. A good sense of the branches found in resorts can be gleaned from "Smart Shops"; and "The Magnolia Shops," *North Shore Breeze*, 1 May 1925, 62–63.

14. "Interior Architecture," *American Architect* 129 (5 Feb. 1926): 229–32 (quote on p. 229). See also "Magnins Buy Site," LAT, 19 Nov. 1922, V-1, V-5; "I. Magnin & Co.," WWD, 28 Nov. 1922, 1; "Typical of What Is Best," *Hollywood Daily Citizen*, 3 Aug. 1926, 3; Frick, *I. Magnin & Co.,* 40–44. Concerning Hollywood Boulevard's rise as a regional business center, see Longstreth, *City Center*, chap. 4.

15. "Old World Settings," ST, 29 Aug. 1926, 4. See also "I. Magnin to Add," WWD, 13 May 1925, 1; "I. Magnin & Co.," ST, 16 Oct. 1925, 3; "Magnin Store Wins," ST, 29 Aug. 1926, 1, 4; and "Magnin's Open Million Dollar Seattle Store," DGE 80 (25 Sep. 1926): 140–41.

16. "Magnin Chain," WWD, 23 Aug. 1929, I-1; "Proposed New Magnin," WWD, 7 July 1930, 12; OT, 1 Mar. 1931, I. Magnin Sect.; Frick, *I. Magnin & Co.,* 27–29.

17. Concerning Saks, see "Saks & Co. to Open," WWD, 5 Dec. 1928, I-1, I-20; WWD, 7 Dec. 1928, I-2; "Saks-5th Ave.," WWD, 5 Mar. 1929, I-120; and "Crowds Inspect," WWD, 12 Mar. 1929, I-24. The store was soon expanded; see "Remodeling New Space," WWD, 23 Oct. 1930, I-2. The development of North Michigan Avenue is covered in detail in John W. Stamper, *Chicago's North Michigan Avenue: Planning and Design, 1900–1930* (Chicago: University of Chicago Press, 1991). Concerning Seattle, see Neal O. Hines, *Denny's Knoll: A History of the Metropolitan Tract of the University of Washington* (Seattle: University of Washington Press, 1980), chaps. 5–7.

18. See, e.g., "Is the Down-Town Shopping District?" RL, 1st May issue, 1926, 7; and "Suburban Branch Plan."

19. "Detroit Stores," WWD, 20 Feb. 1926, 5; "Big Detroit Stores," WWD, 2 May 1929, I-10; "Outlying Branch Stores," RL, 2nd Jan. issue, 1930, 3.

20. For discussion, see "Retail Trade Is Moving," RL, 1st Apr. issue, 1926, 7; "The Spread of Branch Retailing," DGE 83 (15 June 1929): 33; "Mrs. Jones Changes Her Shopping Habits," BW, 5 Oct. 1929, 28–30; "Department Store Branches," BW, 1 Oct. 1930, 10–11; "The Growth of Branch Stores," NRB 12 (Oct. 1930): 546–47; "Branch Stores Profitable," *Retailing*, 13 Sep. 1930, 12–14, 23.

21. "Field's Open Store," *Lake Forester*, 7 Sep. 1928, 1; "Marshall Field and Company," *Evanston News-Index*, 13 Sep. 1928, 1; "Marshall Field Unit," WWD, 22 Jan. 1929, I-13; "Field's Solves Loop Shopping Problems with this New Shop," DGE 83 (11 May 1929): 77. Accounts of the Evanston branch make clear that a much larger one would be built if the shop was successful.

22. "Fields Open," *Oak Leaves* [Oak Park], 19 Oct. 1929, 1, 28, 30 (quote on p. 28). For other accounts, see "Marshall Field Store," *Oak Leaves*, 24 Nov. 1928, 1, 30; "Field's Will Have Oak Park Branch," DGE 83 (22 Dec. 1928): 67; "Field's Cornerstone," *Oak Leaves*, 18 May 1929, 1, 10; "Field Store Plan," *Oak Leaves*, 7 Sep. 1929, 4, 24; "Loop Store Features," WWD, 17 Sep. 1929, I-10, I-18; "Field's First Permanent," WWD, 21 Oct. 1929, I-1; "Fields Adapt French Renaissance to West Suburban Store," DGE 84 (23 Nov. 1929): 50, 54 (Oak Park); "Marshall Field to Build," WWD, 1 Mar. 1929, I-1,-15; "Field's Store to be Built," *Evanston News-Index*, 1 Mar. 1929, 1, 3; "Marshall Field & Co.," *Economist* 81 (2 Mar. 1929): 508; *Evanston News-Index*, 22 Nov. 1929, Marshall Field Sect.; "Similarity of Design Identifies Marshall Field Branches," CSA/AE 6 (May 1930): 60, 63.

23. *Hemingway Organizer* 3 (Oct. 1929).

24. For background, see "Evanston Leads," CT, 18 Oct. 1925,

III-8; "Evanston the North Shore Shopping Center," *Economist* 80 (3 Nov. 1928): 1053; "Important Stores," *Evanston News-Index,* 24 Oct. 1929, 16.

25. For other examples, see *Lake Forester,* 7 May 1926, 10; 14 May 1926, 9; 11 June 1926, 10; and *Howard News* [Chicago], 21 Oct. 1926, 10.

26. "Marshall Field & Co.," *Economist* 81 (2 Mar. 1929): 508.

27. "Hub Leases," *Oak Leaves,* 26 Feb. 1927, 1, 8; *Oak Leaves,* 15 Oct. 1927, 7; "Fields' Oak Park," *Economist* 80 (1 Dec. 1928): 1292; "Forsyth Building," *Oak Leaves,* 6 Apr. 1929, 34; *Oak Leaves,* 4 May 1929, 15; *Oak Leaves,* 25 May 1929, 43; "S. H. Goldberg," *Economist* 81 (18 May 1929): 1179; "Forsyth Exposition," *Oak Leaves,* 1 June 1929, 10; *Oak Leaves,* 14 Sep. 1929, 83; *Oak Leaves,* 21 Sep. 1929, 5; "Lerner Stores," *Economist* 83 (14 June 1930): 1371.

28. "New Location," *Lake Forester,* 3 Oct. 1930, 1; "Enlarged Field Unit," wwd, 31 Mar. 1931, I-28; "New Field's Store," *Lake Forester,* 29 May 1931, 1, 13; "To Expand Field's," *Lake Forester,* 14 Aug. 1931, 2; "Marshall Field & Co.," *Lake Forester,* 29 May 1941, 1. Concerning Market Square, see Longstreth, *City Center,* 150–52.

29. Filene's had three suburban branch stores by 1941, but they were all markedly smaller. In Los Angeles, Bullock's and the Broadway each had two big units in outlying areas by 1940, but their thirds would not come until the postwar era.

30. The project was widely noted in the national trade press. For detailed accounts, see "New Store Planned," wwd, 20 Apr. 1927, 5; "Two Chestnut Street Specialty Shops Erect New Buildings," *Building Magazine* 7 (May 1927): 15, 39; "Lay Cornerstone," wwd, 25 Aug. 1927, I-6; "Allen's Open," wwd, 15 Nov. 1927, 11, 22; "30,000 Attend," wwd, 16 Nov. 1927, I-2; "George Allen, Inc., Opens New Million-Dollar Store," *Building Magazine* 7 (Dec. 1927): 19; "Modernness in Every Detail," wwd, 7 Jan. 1928, I-7; and *Architecture* 58 (Aug. 1928): 117–18.

31. "Strawbridge Plans Branch," wwd, 23 Sep. 1929, I-1, I-2 (quote on p. I-2). See also "To Build $1,000,000 Store," rl, 1st Oct. issue, 1929, 2; "2,000 Attend," wwd, 13 May 1930, I-13; "Store Building of Modern Design," *Building Magazine* 10 (May 1930): 25–26; "Perfect in Detail," dge 84 (July 1930): 254–55, 259; ar 68 (Dec. 1930): 464–65; Alfred Lief, *Family Business: A Century in the Life and Times of Strawbridge & Clothier* (New York: McGraw-Hill, 1968), 183–86. Concerning Ardmore, see "Philadelphia Has Gone 'Suburban,'" rl, 2nd Aug. issue, 1930, 10; and "Ardmore Is Fast Becoming," *Ardmore Chronicle,* 15 Sep. 1939, 49.

32. "Branch Stores Profitable," 12–13, 23; "The Problems of Opening a Branch Store," *Retailing,* 28 Dec. 1929, 3.

33. For background, see Richard Longstreth, "The Diffusion of the Community Shopping Center Concept During the Interwar Decades," *jsah* 56 (Sep. 1997): 279–83.

34. Ibid., 281, 284. Concerning Jenkintown, see "Business Center," pl, 13 Nov. 1927, Real Estate Sect., 1; "Figures Which Tell," *Times-Chronicle* [Jenkintown], 12 Feb. 1931, 1, 4; and "Jenkintown in 1942," *Times-Chronicle,* 20 Mar. 1931, 12.

35. *Main Line Times,* 4 Dec. 1930, 2; "Big Store to Serve," pl, 4 Dec. 1930, 10; "Strawbridge Takes," wwd, 9 Sep. 1931, I-5; "Strawbridge Firm," pl, 10 Sep. 1931, 4; "Strawbridge & Clothier," *Retailing,* 12 Sep. 1931, 7–8; "Plenty of Parking Space," rl, Oct. 1931, 10.

36. Longstreth, "Sears, Roebuck," 246–47.

37. "Best's Opens," wwd, 14 Nov. 1929, I-1, I-2 (Garden City); "Best's Opens," wwd, 15 Jan. 1930, I-1; "Best & Co.," nyt, 23 Feb. 1930, 2re (Mamaroneck); "Best Store Plans," *East Orange Record,* 21 Mar. 1930, 14; "Plans for Big Store," *East Orange Record,* 9 May 1930, 1; "Best's East Orange," wwd, 1 Oct. 1930, I-1, I-16; "Throngs at Opening," *East Orange Record,* 3 Oct. 1930, 1. For illustrations, see "The Suburban Branch Department Store," ar 72 (July 1932): 3–6. Concerning LeBoutillier, see "Parking Question," wwd, 14 Mar. 1930, I-7; and "LeBoutillier *Is* Best & Co.," wwd, 26 Dec. 1946, II-40.

38. "Altman Unit," wwd, 10 Feb. 1930, 1, 24; "Altman to Locate," *Daily Press* [White Plains], 10 Feb. 1930, 1, 3; "Altman May Lease," *Daily Press,* 21 Feb. 1930, 1; "B. Altman Unit," wwd, 22 Apr. 1930, I-2; *Daily Press,* 5 May 1930, 1-A, 8-A, 2-B, 13-B, 14-B, 1-C; "Two Views," wwd, 6 May 1930, I-16; "Many Branch Stores," wwd, 30 Oct. 1930, IV-3. The shop was expanded to 5,500 square feet two years later, but was not replaced by a sizable facility until 1951. See "Altman Branch," wwd, 21 Mar. 1932, I-18.

39. "Third Big Store," *East Orange Record,* 4 Apr. 1930, 1; "Altman Store Here," *East Orange Record,* 19 Sep. 1930, 1, 5; "Altman to Open," wwd, 27 Mar. 1931, I-9; "Altman East Orange," wwd, 31 Mar. 1931, I-4, I-5; "Altman Crosses," *Retailing,* 4 Apr. 1931, 5; "Suburban Branch Department Store," 11.

40. "Simon's Opens," wwd, 27 Feb. 1940, 1; "Branch Store Operation," re, 14 Aug. 1940, 3; "East Orange Unit," wwd, 8 Sep. 1949, 2; "Peck & Peck to Expand," wwd, 10 Apr. 1950, 4; "East Orange Is No Lemon," wwd, 16 Mar. 1950, 86.

41. "Former Home," *Stamford Advocate,* 16 May 1930, 1; "Hearn's to Open," wwd, 19 May 1930, I-10; "Hearn's Stamford," *Stamford Advocate,* 3 Sep. 1930, 10; "Hearn Opening," wwd, 2 Sep. 1930, I-1, I-24; "Hearn-Stamford," *Retailing,* 13 Sep. 1930, 12, 23; "Hearn-Stamford," re, 25 Oct. 1930, 11.

42. For background, see Longstreth, *City Center,* 112–13, 136.

43. "Report Dyas' Plans," wwd, 6 July 1927, I-1, I-23; "New Hollywood Store," *Hollywood Daily Citizen,* 9 July 1927, 1, 10; "How New Dyas Branch," wwd, 13 July 1927, I-6; *Hollywood Daily Citizen,* 2 Mar. 1928, B. H. Dyas Co. Sect.; "Shop Idea Carried Out," wwd, 7 Apr. 1928, I-15; "New Dyas Unit Bespeaks Builders Art," dw 12 (May 1928): 32, 68, 72; Longstreth, *City Center,* 86–88.

44. "The Broadway Buys," wwd, 2 Mar. 1931, I-1, I-36; "Broadway Buys," lat, 3 Mar. 1931, II-1, II-2; "Broadway-Hollywood," *Hollywood Daily Citizen,* Sect. II; "Report May Store," wwd, 24 Feb. 1931, 1; "Hollywood Unit," wwd, 25 Feb. 1931, I-1.

45. For further discussion, see Longstreth, *City Center,* 112–27. Additional accounts of the store include "Bullock's-Wilshire," re, 2 Nov. 1929, 18; sbc 74 (22 Nov. 1929): 36; "Bullocks' Wilshire Boulevard Store," a&e 99 (Dec. 1929): 45–49; "Bullock's 'Wilshire,'" dw 15 (Dec. 1929): 38–39, 47; ar 70 (July 1931): 20–26; and Margaret Davis, *Bullock's Wilshire* (Los Angeles: Balcony, 1996).

46. "Art and Business Meet," *Los Angeles Evening Express,* 26 Sep. 1929, 16; Pauline G. Schindler, "A Significant Contribution to Culture," *California Arts & Architecture* 37 (Jan. 1930): 23–28, 74 (quotes on p. 23); "So. Cal. Spirit," *Los Angeles Herald,* 26 Sep. 1929, B1, B4 (quote on B1).

47. Schindler, "Significant Contribution," 23.

48. Peters, working in association with the firm of Feil & Paradise, was in charge of the interior design of the first three floors; the fourth floor was by Webber & Collins, the fifth by Josephine Scheuren. Le Maire's role is discussed in "Bullock's in Debut," lat, 26 Sep. 1929, II-1, II-5; and "Art and Business."

49. "Bullock's in Debut," II-5.

50. "Halle Bros. Co. Opens," wwd, 31 Dec. 1928, I-1, I-20; "Halle's to Expand," wwd, 2 Feb. 1931, I-11 (Erie); *New Castle News,* 3 Sep. 1929, 12; "Halle Bros. Co. Opens," wwd, 5 Sep. 1929, I-12 (New Castle); *Warren Tribune Chronicle,* 9 Dec. 1929, 7; 12 Dec. 1929, 5; 16 Dec. 1929, 9 (Warren); "Halle's, Cleveland," wwd, 11 June 1929, I-1; "Halles Bros. Store," *Canton Repository,* 1 Aug. 1930, 1, 5

(Canton); "Halle Bros. to Open," WWD, 4 Mar. 1929, I-7; "Halle's Mansfield," WWD, 1 Apr. 1929, I-12; James M. Wood, Halle's: Memoirs of a Family Department Store, 1891–1982 (Cleveland: Geranium, 1987), 137, 146. The company also appears to have considered opening a store in Akron; see "Halle's May Open," WWD, 30 Aug. 1929, I-9.

51. The only other major department store that appears to have followed Halle's lead before 1941 was the Youngstown-based Strouss-Hirshberg Company, which opened stores in New Castle and Warren in 1929 and 1940, respectively; see "Strouss-Hirshberg," *Warren Tribune Chronicle*, 6 Sep. 1940, 1, 14. Both communities were much closer to the parent store than in the case of Halle's. On the other hand Strouss also acquired stores in Flint and Pontiac, Michigan, in 1929—communities well removed from its own region. See "New Store for Women," *Pontiac Daily Press*, 1 Mar. 1929, 1; and "New Strouss-Hirshberg," WWD, 13 Sep. 1929, I-5.

52. "Report Fair," WWD, 18 Jan. 1929, I-2; "Fair-Iverson Deal," WWD, 21 Jan. 1929, I-7, I-20 (Milwaukee Avenue); "The Fair to Enter," WWD, 7 Dec. 1928, I-1; "Fair Buys Nicholas," *Oak Leaves*, 20 Apr. 1929, 66; "Fair-Nicholas Story," *Oak Leaves*, 27 Apr. 1929, 1, 14–15; WWD, 28 Aug. 1936, II-6F; "Three Chicago Branch Stores," *Retailing*, 1 Mar. 1937, 6.

53. Victor W. Sincere, "Why We're Opening Branch Department Stores," CSA/GME 6 (Feb. 1930): 5, 6, 81 (quote on p. 6). Concerning the formation of National, see "Confer on Affiliated," WWD, 15 Jan. 1923, 1; "To Give Details," WWD, 1 Feb. 1923, 1, 45; "Sincere to Head," WWD, 2 Feb. 1923, 1, 43; "Frank & Seder May Join," WWD, 20 Aug. 1923, 1; and "Frank & Seder Join," WWD, 18 Sep. 1923, 1, 18.

54. "Nugent's Opens Store," SGD, 13 Apr. 1913, 12; "Nugent's Complete," WWD, 20 Nov. 1923, 49; and SGD, 23 Nov. 1929, 7.

55. "Department Layout," WWD, 8 Nov. 1929, I-12; "Crowds at New Nugent," WWD, 25 Nov. 1929, I-12, I-22 (Nugent's); "Bailey Co. to Open," WWD, 15 Apr. 1929, I-1, I-2; "Bailey Co. Branch," CPD, 19 Apr. 1929, 1-D; CPD, 15 June 1929, 7; "Bailey Co. Opens," WWD, 18 June 1929, I-14 (Bailey Co., Euclid Avenue); "2nd Outlying Unit," WWD, 20 Aug. 1929, I-11, I-12; *Lakewood Post*, 10 Apr. 1930, 7–10; "Bailey Co. Opens," CPD, 11 Apr. 1930, 11 (Bailey Company, Lakewood); "Frank & Seder to Open," WWD, 20 May 1929, I-7; "Frank & Seder Plans," WWD, 19 July 1929, I-16; "5 New Stores Open," PI, 2 Oct. 1929, 6; "New Shopping Center," WWD, 3 Oct. 1929, I-1, I-2; "Frank & Seder Adding," WWD, 6 Nov. 1929, I-8 (Frank & Seder). The Frank & Seder building was constructed for the purpose, but also contained four small chain units.

56. A good historical analysis of Lakewood as a type of outlying community developed during the early twentieth century is found in James Borchert, "Residential Suburbs: The Emergence of a New Suburban Type, 1880–1930," *Journal of Urban History* 22 (Mar. 1996): 283–307. The 69th Street business district in Upper Darby, Pennsylvania, where the Frank & Seder branch was located, was largely developed under the auspices of builder John H. McClatchy and was among the most discussed developments of its kind during the late 1920s. See "Huge Structures," PL, 6 Feb. 1927, Real Estate Sect. (hereinafter RE), 1; "69th St. Growing," PI, 19 Feb. 1928, B16; "Big Developments," PL, 26 Feb. 1928, RE, 1; "Woolworth Plans," PL, 15 July 1928, RE, 1; "Ample Roadways," PL, 30 Sep. 1928, RE, 1; "Stores Spring Up," PL, 2 Dec. 1928, RE, 1; "Rapid Development," PL, 26 May 1929, RE, 1; "Creating a Chain Community by Color, Light and Selling," *Chain Store Review* 2 (Sep. 1929): 9–11, 62, 64; and "Centralized Development," *Retailing*, 21 Dec. 1929, 3.

57. "Growth of Branch Stores," 547. See also "Branch Stores Best," NYT, 19 Oct. 1930, II-18; and "How Are Department Store Branches Operated?" *Advertising & Selling* 16 (7 Jan. 1931): 26, 68–69.

58. Concerning the bankruptcy, see "National Dept. Stores," WWD, 7 Feb. 1933, 1, 2; "Fight Under Way," WWD, 17 Feb. 1933, I-24; "Continue Frank & Seder," WWD, 21 Feb. 1933, 1, 40; "Files Answer," WWD, 8 Mar. 1933, 6; "Nugent Sale," WWD, 31 Mar. 1933, I-9; and "Ask to Keep," WWD, 26 Oct. 1933, 2. Concerning Nugent's, see "Nugent's Vandeventer," WWD, 16 Mar. 1933, 1; and "Big Store," WWD, 23 July 1934, 1, 6.

59. "Plans for Expansion," NYT, 2 Aug. 1936, III-8; "State St. Stores Hesitant," WWD, 4 Sep. 1936, III-52, III-62.

60. "Branch Store Operation," RE, 2 Oct. 1940, 6. The most detailed analysis of situation is "Battle over Suburbia," *Retailing*, 20 Feb. 1939, 4, 9. See also "Operating Problems," HBR 2 (Oct. 1933): 74–83.

61. "Macy's Will Open," *Post-Standard* [Syracuse], 25 Aug. 1940, II-15, II-20; "Macy's Plans," WWD, 26 Aug. 1940, 1; "'No Frills' for Macy's," WWD, 27 Aug. 1940, 1; "Macy's Branches Out," BW, 31 Aug. 1940, 37–38; "Macy Move," *Tide* 14 (1 Sep. 1940): 16; "Low Cost Operation," RE, 4 Sep. 1940, 7; "Syracuse Retailers Show," WWD, 10 Sep. 1940, 7; "Macy Syracuse," WWD, 28 Oct. 1940, 6; "Macy's Seen," WWD, 29 Oct. 1940, 8; "Macy's of Syracuse," RE, 6 Nov. 1940, 3, 5; "Macy's," *Tide* 14 (15 Nov. 1940): 54; "Macy's Chain," BW, 16 Nov. 1940, 54–55; "Macy's of Syracuse," DSE 3 (10 Dec. 1940): 3; "Macy's, Syracuse, Ad," WWD, 31 Dec. 1940, 4. Concerning the supermarket, see Richard Longstreth, *The Drive-In, the Supermarket, and the Transformation of Commercial Space in Los Angeles, 1914–1941* (Cambridge: MIT Press, 1999), chaps. 3, 4.

62. Bill Hart, "Public Being Educated," WWD, 3 Jan. 1941, 49, 52; "Macy's of Syracuse," WWD, 4 Aug. 1941, 20; "Macy's to Close Store," WWD, 26 Dec. 1941, 1; "Experiment Fails," BW, 10 Jan. 1942, 52–53.

63. "Preference for Downtown," WWD, 27 Mar. 1939, 5; "Battle Over Suburbia," *Retailing*, 6 Mar. 1939, 8. For a sampling of accounts of the subject, see "Holds Future of Stores," WWD, 30 Sep. 1936, 2; "Specialty Shops Do It Again," *Retailing*, 21 Feb. 1938, 2, 15; "Battle Over Suburbia," *Retailing*, 27 Feb. 1939, 10; "'Down Town' Is Losing Out," RE, 15 Nov. 1939, 1; "St. Louis Is Aroused," RE, 24 July 1940, 12; "Kansas City Acts," RE, 25 Sep. 1940, 16; Homer Hoyt, "Urban Decentralization," *Journal of Land & Public Utility Economics* 16 (Aug. 1940): 270–76; "Business Districts in Motion," AJ 9 (Jan. 1941): 34–40; and "Unit Expansion," WWD, 29 Dec. 1941, 19.

64. "Saks 5th Ave.," *Greenwich News-Gazette*, 17 Aug. 1937, 1; "Saks Opening," WWD, 19 Aug. 1937, 32 (Greenwich); "To Begin Work," WWD, 15 Nov. 1937, 1, 28; "Saks-Fifth Ave.," WWD, 10 Mar. 1938, 28; "Saks' Beverly Hills," WWD, 23 Apr. 1938, 1, 39; "New Saks-Fifth Ave.," WWD, 29 Apr. 1938, I-12; "Beverly Hills Saks," *Retailing*, 9 May 1938, 6; "Shop Made Like Home," DSE 1 (25 May 1938): 25; "Saks Expansion," WWD, 22 Dec. 1938, 1, 28; "Saks, Beverly Hills," WWD, 17 Aug. 1939, 28; "New York Comes," BHC, 1 Sep. 1939, II-1 (Beverly Hills); "Saks Detroit," WWD, 30 Aug. 1940, 1, 24; "Saks Fifth Avenue," DFP, 4 Sep. 1940, 10; "Saks, Detroit," WWD, 5 Sep. 1940, 40 (Detroit). The firm also opened a new, more elaborate store on Chicago's North Michigan Avenue (1935–36) and a sizable new store in Miami Beach (1939) as well as smaller resort shops in Newport, Westbury (Long Island), and Sun Valley (Idaho).

65. "Magnin Plans," WWD, 14 Feb. 1938, 1; "New I. Magnin Store," WWD, 10 Feb. 1939, 1, 8–9; "Store Holds Gay," LAT, 11 Feb. 1938, I-7; "Thousands Greet," WWD, 13 Feb. 1939, 1, 23; "Beverly-Wilshire Area," BHC, 17 Feb. 1939, 5; "Magnin's in Resplendent," *Retailing*, 20 Feb. 1939, 6; "Old and New Join Hands in New Magnin Store," DSE 2 (25 Apr. 1939): 26; Frick, *I. Magnin & Co.*, 44–67; Therese Poletti, *Art Deco San Francisco: The Architecture of Timothy Pflueger* (New York: Princeton Architectural Press, 2008), 202–8.

66. "New Garfinckel's Store," ES, 14 Aug. 1942, A-2; "Garfinckel's

New Shop," *WWD*, 14 Aug. 1942, 32; "Opening of Garfinckel's," *ES*, 15 Aug. 1942, B-2; "Garfinckel's Opens," *WWD*, 11 June 1947, 2.

67. "Little 'Rockefeller Center' Built in New England Town," *Real Estate Record* 42 (1 Oct. 1938): 30–34; "Filene to Open," *WWD*, 24 Jan. 1940, 44; "Filene's Suburban Store," *DSE* 9 (May 1946): 3 (Winchester); "Modern Block to Rise," *Belmont Citizen*, 16 June 1939, 1; "New Addition," *Belmont Citizen*, 27 Dec. 1940, 1, 8; "Filene to Open," *WWD*, 21 Apr. 1941, 21; "Filene's Belmont," *Belmont Citizen*, 25 Apr. 1941, 1, 10; "Commercial Building Follows Population Trends," *AR* 90 (Dec. 1941): 82–85 (Belmont).

68. "Loeser Building," *WWD*, 27 Jan. 1937, 1; "Loeser's New Garden City," *WWD*, 12 May 1937, 4; "Loeser's Ready," *Garden City News*, 13 May 1937, 1; "Branch Store Idea," *Retailing*, 24 May 1937, 9; "Loeser's New Suburban Branch," *NRB* 19 (May 1937): 52; "Loeser's Garden City," *RL*, Oct. 1937, 15–16; *AR* 83 (Feb. 1938): 126–27 (Loeser's); "Hahne to Open," *Montclair Times*, 11 May 1937, 1; "Parking Meters," *WWD*, 24 Aug. 1937 (Hahne's); "Constable Buys," *WWD*, 24 May 1937, I-1, I-2; "Arnold Constable Files," *NYT*, 8 July 1937, 42; "Arnold Constable Store," *SS*, 28 Oct. 1937, 1, 23; "Open Constable," *WWD*, 1 Dec. 1937, 1, 2; *SS*, 1 Dec. 1937, 5; "Mayor Praises," *SS*, 4 Dec. 1937, 1, 8; "A Community Store," *Retailing*, 20 Dec. 1937, 7 (Arnold Constable New Rochelle); "Constable's to Open," *WWD*, 22 Sep. 1939, 32; "Will Build New Store," *Hempstead Sentinel*, 2 Nov. 1939, 1; "New $750,000 Constable," *WWD*, 12 Mar. 1940, 10; "Branch Store Operation," *RE*, 28 Aug. 1940, 3 (Arnold Constable Hempstead).

69. For background, see Richard Longstreth, "Bringing 'Downtown' to the Neighborhoods: "Wieboldt's, Goldblatt's, and the Creation of Department Store Chains in Chicago," *Buildings & Landscapes* 14 (2007): 13–49.

70. "Hearn Deal," *WWD*, 26 Jan. 1937, 2; "Hearns-Bronx to Open," *Home News* [Bronx], 7 Mar. 1937, 3; "3,000 in Line," *WWD*, 11 Mar. 1937, I-1, I-3; "Hearn's, Bronx," *WWD*, 12 Mar. 1937, I-6; "Rejuvenated in 28 Days!" *Retailing*, 22 Mar. 1937, 3, 9 (Bronx); "Hearn Deal," *WWD*, 17 May 1937, I-1; "Hearns-Newark," *WWD*, 28 Aug. 1939, 1, 19; "Hearns Store Ready," *NSE*, 31 Aug. 1937, 1, 6; "Hearns-Newark Opens," *WWD*, 2 Sep. 1937, 1, 2; "Cash and Carry," *RE*, 30 Oct. 1940, 2 (Newark). According to Hearn's president, the company's expansion program was inspired by the writings of Edward Filene; see "Hearn's Heart," *Tide* 11 (1 June 1937): 26–27.

71. "Macy Branch," *WWD*, 17 July 1940, 1, 6; "Macy to Open," *WWD*, 31 Oct. 1940, 1, 36; "Macy's Chain," *BW*, 16 Nov. 1940, 54–55; "Throngs View," *WWD*, 13 Oct. 1941, 1, 21; "Macy's Branch Unit Opened in New York," *NRB* 23 (Nov. 1941): 15; *AF* 76 (Feb. 1942): 126–28.

72. "A & S Opens," *Retailing*, 10 Dec. 1934, 19; "A & S Opens," *Long Island Daily Press*, 4 Dec. 1934, 9, 14; "Store Is Opened," *Elizabeth Daily Journal*, 15 Mar. 1935, 18; "Department Stores Open," *RL*, Mar. 1937, 8–9.

73. Quoted in "Gerber Branch Store," *Commercial Appeal* [Memphis], 7 Nov. 1941, 12. See also *Commercial Appeal*, 8 Nov. 1941, 4; and "John Gerber Branch," *WWD*, 12 Nov. 1941, 33. Concerning Kerr's, see *Daily Oklahoman*, 30 Nov. 1937, 24; "1,500 Inspect," *Daily Oklahoman*, 1 Dec. 1937, 4; and "Modern Selling," *WWD*, 10 Dec. 1937, 16. Concerning Burdine's, see "Hatch's, Inc., Opens," *Palm Beach Post-Times*, 22 Nov. 1936, 1-A, 10-A; *American Architect* 150 (June 1937): 41–44; "Hatch's Bought," *Palm Beach Post*, 19 Apr. 1941, 1, 3; and "Burdine's Buys," *WWD*, 21 Apr. 1941, 1, 16.

74. *Miami Daily News*, 9 Jan. 1936, 15–16; *MH*, 10 Jan. 1936, 12-A, 13-A; "Burdine's Prestige," *Retailing*, 20 Jan. 1936, 6; "Curves—No Straight Lines in Miami Beach Burdine Shop," *DGE* 90 (17 Mar. 1936): 57–58; *AR* 79 (May 1936): 381–87 (Burdine's); "Saks to Have," *MH*, 18 June 199, 1-C; "Saks to Have," *WWD*, 21 June 1939, 2; "Florida Store Has 4 Shops in 1," *AR* 88 (Aug. 1940): 37–41 (Saks).

75. "Bullock's to Erect," *Westwood Hills News*, 8 Jan. 1932, 1; "Branch Store Welcomed," *LAT*, 10 Jan. 1932, V-2; "Bullock's New Collegienne Branch at Westwood," *DGE* 86 (Aug. 1932): 104; "Expansion for Store," *LAT*, 22 Oct. 1933, I-20; "Bullock's—Westwood," *Westwood Hills News*, 24 May 1935, 1; "Bullock's Enlarged," *Westwood Hills News*, 4 Oct. 1935, 1; "Bullock's Westwood," *LAT*, 22 Jan. 1939, V-2; "New Bullock's," *Westwood Hills News*, 1 Mar. 1940, 1, 2 (Bullock's). "The Broadway to Open," *WWD*, 14 May 1940, 1, 28; "New Broadway-Pasadena," *WWD*, 2 Aug. 1940, 27; "Store to Open," *LAT*, 14 Nov. 1940, II-2; "$1,000,000 Baby," *DSE* 3 (25 Dec. 1940): 28; "Access by Autos," *WWD*, 9 Jan. 1941, 55; "Store's Simplicity of Design Puts Attention on Display," *DW* 38 (Feb. 1941): 36–37; "Broadway Store for Pasadena," *Architectural Concrete* 7:3 (1941): 12–14 (Broadway).

76. For background, see Longstreth, *City Center*, 127–41.

77. "May Co. to Establish," *LAT*, 20 Oct. 1938, II-1; "Work to Start," *LAT*, 13 Nov. 1938, V-1; "May Co. Granted," *LAT*, 1 Dec. 1938, I-8; "May Co. to Open," *LAT*, 3 Sep. 1939, II-2; "May's New Coast Unit," *WWD*, 7 Sep. 1939, 1, 32; *BHC*, 8 Sep. 1939, I-1, I-9, II-2, II-3, II-5 to II-9; "New Steps in Design," *RE*, 20 Sep. 1939, 3, 15; "New Two-Million Dollar Store Building on Wilshire Blvd.," *SBC* 95 (20 Oct. 1939): 12–13; "May Co. Opens," *DSE* 2 (10 Jan. 1940): 34; "Simplicity Marks New Wilshire Store of May's," *RM*, 15 May 1940, 17, 40; "Department Store," *AF* 72 (May 1940): 353–57; Emrich Nicholson, *Contemporary Shops in the United States* (New York: Architectural Book Publishing, 1945), 142–47. Interviews with Albert C. Martin, Jr. (Los Angeles, 11 Feb. 1999), who worked on the project with his father, and Robert Getz (Newport Beach, Calif., 19 Mar. 2000), who directed shopping center development for the May Company in the 1950s and 1960s, provided many additional details.

78. According to Albert C. Martin Jr. (interview), the principal designer in Marx's office was Noel Flint. Martin's father was a good friend of May's, but he focused more on supervision than design. Concerning Marx, see Liz O'Brien, *Ultramodern: Samuel Marx* (New York: Pointed Leaf, 2007).

79. "Manhasset on Display," *Manhasset Press*, 25 Aug. 1950, supplement. Among the stores Atlas lured to the Miracle Mile were B. Altman & Company (opened 1947); Best & Company (1949); Lane Bryant; W. & J. Sloane; McCutcheon (1950); Black, Starr & Frost; Gorham; David's of Fifth Avenue (by 1950); Louis Sherry (1951); and Emily Fifth Avenue (1952).

80. "Lord and Taylor Buys," *Manhasset Press*, 21 Mar. 1940, 1; "Lord & Taylor's Store," *Manhasset Mail*, 1, 7; "Lord & Taylor's Last Word," *WWD*, 27 May 1941, 35; "Crowds Throng," *Manhasset Press*, 30 May 1941, 1, 2; "Lord & Taylor's Manhasset Branch a Brilliant Designing Job," *NRB* 23 (May 1941): 19; "Lord & Taylor Suburban Apparel Shop," *AR* 89 (June 1941): 41–47; "'Country Modern,'" *DSE* 4 (10 June 1941): 33; "Lord & Taylor in Manhasset," *NRB* 23 (June 1941): 14–15; "Lord & Taylor Suburban Store," *Manhasset Press*, 25 Aug. 1950, supplement, 17, 24.

CHAPTER 6. Station Wagon Stores

1. "Start Building," *WWD*, 24 Mar. 1950, 5; "Keyed to the Wide," *WWD*, 13 Feb. 1952, 96. See also "Neiman-Marcus to Establish," *DMN*, 9 Jan. 1949, V-1; "Neiman-Marcus Deal," *WWD*, 10 Jan. 1949, 1, 67; *DMN*, 18 Oct. 1951, I-13; and John Peter, *Aluminum in Modern Architecture*, 2 vols. (New York: Reinhold, 1956), 1: 102–3. See also Stanley Marcus, *Minding the Store, a Memoir* (New York: Signet, 1974), 105–6.

2. "Station Wagon Store," *AF* 96 (Jan. 1952): 136–43, quote on p. 137.

3. Interview with H. Stanley Marcus, Jr., Dallas, 18 Feb. 1997. See also "Branches May Slow," *WWD*, 29 Jan. 1952, 63. Saks's expansion

plans were well known in the trade. See, e.g., "Saks 5th Ave.," WWD, 23 May 1945, 1; and "Saks 5th Plans," WWD, 9 May 1946, 1.

4. Marcus interview. Concerning the initial branch plans, see "Neiman-Marcus Plans," WWD, 22 Mar. 1946, 1, 27; DMN, 24 Mar. 1946, IV-10; and WWD, 10 Apr. 1946, 63. Concerning Highland Park Village, see Richard Longstreth, "The Diffusion of the Community Shopping Center Concept During the Interwar Decades," JSAH 56 (Sep. 1997): 276–79.

5. Marcus interview.

6. E. B. Weiss, "'Aristocratic' Branches for 'Democratic' Department Stores," DSE 12 (May 1949): 90–91, 95.

7. "Retail Rush," AF 85 (Oct. 1946): 10–11. See also "Stores to Expand," BW, 6 Jan. 1945, 86; and 23 Mar. 1946, 80–81; "Department Stores Hurrying for the Suburbs," BW, 4 Oct. 1947, 24–26; "Stores Expected," WWD, 6 Dec. 1950, 5.

8. The figures cited above are derived from the data presented in Richard Longstreth, "Department Store Branches, 1910–1960," at http://www.departmentstorehistory.net and http://www.preservenet.cornell.edu. I selected the years of project announcement rather than completion dates for stores to give a clearer sense of time for the planning agendas of the companies involved. When a new branch was constructed, the process generally took one to two years. When existing stores were purchased, reopening usually occurred within a matter of months, weeks, or days.

9. These figures, derived from the list cited in n. 8 and from Richard Longstreth, "New Buildings and Major Additions for Downtown Department Stores, 1920–1960," at http://www.departmentstorehistory.net and http://www.preservenet.cornell.edu, are quite rough. Throughout I have used gross square footage for buildings, not just selling space. Comparison of dollars expended is more complicated, since even general figures are often missing from period sources, and the figures that are given often do not specify whether they refer to overall project cost, the cost of building and fixtures, or construction cost alone.

10. "Big Stores Follow," NYT, 20 Dec. 1953, III-1, III-6; Richard L. Florida and Marshall M. A. Feldman, "Housing in U.S. Fordism," *International Journal of Urban and Regional Research* 12 (June 1988): 196–97; Barry Checkoway, "Large Builders, Federal Housing Programmes, and Postwar Suburbanization," *International Journal of Urban and Regional Research* 4 (Mar. 1980): 22–23; "Suburbs Gain," WWD, 21 June 1960, 1, 50; Charles F. Holt, "Who Benefited from the Prosperity of the Twenties?" *Explorations in Economic History* 14 (July 1977): 277–89; "'Spending Is Good,'" WWD, 21 Oct. 1957, 1, 16. See also "The Lush Suburban Market," *Fortune* 48 (Nov. 1953): 128–31, 230–32, 234, 237. Lizabeth Cohen, *A Consumers' Republic: The Politics of Mass Consumption in Postwar America* (New York: Alfred A. Knopf, 2003) offers excellent analysis of the new mass market.

11. This is not to imply that department store executives abandoned their concern for their downtown plants. To the contrary, those emporia continued to be objects of considerable attention for some years to come.

12. "Branch Operation," WWD, 2 May 1951, 62; "Parent Store Sales," WWD, 10 Oct. 1951, 49; "Caution Advised," WWD, 10 Jan. 1952, I-62; "Branches Give," WWD, 6 Feb. 1952, I-76; "Bigger Profit Margins," WWD, 2 May 1952, 43; "Branch Returns," WWD, 1 Apr. 1952, 62.

13. "Better Study," WWD, 10 Sep. 1952, I-1, I-77.

14. "Kresge-Newark to Open," *Summit Herald*, 21 Nov. 1946, 1, 7; "L. Bamberger Opens," *Millburn & Short Hills Item*, 4 Dec. 1947, II-2, II-5; "Appliance Center," DSE 11 (Feb. 1948): 112; "Maas Bros. Will Open," WWD, 5 Feb. 1947, 2; *Tampa Tribune*, 23 Feb. 1947, 2-A; "Hearn's First," WWD, 3 Dec. 1947, 61.

15. Woodward & Lothrop acquired the branch as part of its purchase of the Palais Royal department store in 1946; see "Woodward & Lothrop's," *Record of Montgomery County*, 28 Aug. 1953, 1; "Parley Tomorrow," WWD, 20 Dec. 1954, 7; "New, Larger Building," *Bethesda-Chevy Chase Tribune*, 20 Dec. 1954, 1, 4; "Woodward's Store," WWD, 17 Jan. 1955, 6; and "Bethesda Budget Store," ES, 7 Sep. 1955. Concerning Block's, see "Formal Opening," WWD, 9 Sep. 1954, 2; IS, 15 Sep. 1954, 15; and "Over 3,000 Attend," WWD, 17 Sep. 1954, 2. Concerning Saks, see *Princeton Packet*, 2 Nov. 1944, 3; and "Saks Opens," NYT, 9 Oct. 1948, 22. Wm. H. Block opened a store for students at Indiana University in 1942 and enlarged it twice.

16. "S. S. Kresge Purchases," *Asbury Park Evening Press*, 4 Dec. 1934, 1, 2, 16; *Asbury Park Evening Press*, 24 June 1946, 3; "Resort Fashions," *Asbury Park Evening Press*, 25 June 1946, 7; "Kresge, Newark," WWD, 25 June 1946, 46.

17. "M. E. Blatt's," WWD, 12 Aug. 1958, 1, 9; "Snellenbergs Buys," *Atlantic City Press*, 12 Aug. 1958, 1, 9; "Snellenbergs Plans," WWD, 4 Nov. 1959, I-26; "Snellenbergs—Blatt's," WWD, 8 June 1960, 99; "Burdine's to Open," *Miami Daily News*, 15 Nov. 1953, 15-A; "Million Dollar Burdine's," WWD, 8 Jan. 1954, 2; "Burdine's New Store Stresses Display," DW 63 (Dec. 1953): 18–19, 50.

18. "Bullocks Plans," *Desert Sun* [Palm Springs], 14–21 Dec. 1945, 1, 5 (quote on p. 1). See also "Bullock's Buys," WWD, 14 Dec. 1945, 1, 18; "New Bullock's," LAT, 19 Oct. 1947, I-9; "Bullock's Palm Springs Store," AR 103 (Apr. 1948): 123–27 (Bullock's); "Work Starts Soon," WWD, 2 Aug. 1957, 32; *Desert Sun*, 9 Jan. 1958, Robinson's Sect.; "Bazaar in an Oasis," AF 110 (Mar. 1959): 116 (Robinson's); "Saks Fifth Avenue," *Desert Sun*, 22 Dec. 1958, 2; "Saks Will Open," *Desert Sun*, 15 Oct. 1959, 3; "Palm Springs Unit," WWD, 19 Oct. 1959, I-28 (Saks).

19. Weiss, "'Aristocratic' Branches," 90; "Branch Stores," *Stores* 33 (Feb. 1951): 44; "Department Stores: Race for the Suburbs," *Fortune* 44 (Dec. 1951): 101; "Managerial Approach to Branch Stores," RC 20 (Mar. 1952): 3. See also "Six Vital Problems," WWD, 5 Sep. 1951, 75; "Appetite for More," WWD, 26 Dec. 1951, I-26.

20. Concerning Horne's, see "Horne's Will Open," WWD, 14 Mar. 1945, 2; *Practical Builder* 11 (Oct. 1946): 5; *Mt. Lebanon News*, 24 Sep. 1953, 4–5; "Fourth Addition," WWD, 7 Oct. 1953, 18. One of the initial store units was previously occupied by Boggs & Buhl, another Pittsburgh department store, albeit one of decidedly lower standing. Concerning Hens & Kelly, see "Hens & Kelly," WWD, 18 July 1950, 2; "Hens & Kelly," WWD, 17 Oct. 1950, 6; and "Hens & Kelly," WWD, 5 Dec. 1950, 51.

21. "Clear Picture Emerging," WWD, 19 Sep. 1956, I-10; "Suburbs Enjoy," WWD, 16 Feb. 1953, 36.

22. "Branches Held Eventual," WWD, 11 Jan. 1952, 57; "Branches Broaden Department Store Scope," *Barron's* 30 (17 Apr. 1950): 19; "Branch Stores," *Stores* 34 (Feb. 1952): 24; "Creating the Character," RC 20 (Mar. 1952): 24–25; "Good Practice in the Operation of Branch Stores," DSE 15 (July 1952): 38; "Wide Variety," WWD, 16 Feb. 1953, 1, 7; "Solutions to Branch," WWD, 14 Jan. 1954, 72; "Complete Selections," WWD, 5 Mar. 1954, I-1, I-54; "Success of Branches," WWD, 9 Dec. 1954, 9; "Branches Advised," WWD, 14 Sep. 1955, 1, 71; "The Operation of the Branch Store," DSE 38 (Feb. 1956): 19; "Stocks Urged," WWD, 22 Oct. 1959, 1, 12.

23. "B. Altman Will Construct," *Manhasset Press*, 8 Mar. 1946, 1, 4; "Altman Sets," *Manhasset Press*, 12 Sep. 1947, 1, 6; "Suburban Stores Pay," RM 42 (Nov. 1947): 17; "Three Stores," PA 29 (Feb. 1948): 55–60; "East Wing," *Manhasset Mail*, 25 Nov. 1954, 1, 4; "L. Bamberger & Co. Starts," *Morristown Daily Record*, 16 Aug. 1946, 1, 6; "Designed to Fit," WWD, 16 Sep. 1947, 11; "Formal Ceremony Opens," *Morristown Daily Record*, 1 Apr. 1949, 1, 8; "Bamberger's Morristown," WWD, 4 Apr. 1949, 4; "Report Bamberger," WWD, 26 Aug. 1958, I-11; "Lit's Acquires," WWD, 28 May 1948, I-1, I-40; "Lit

Bros. Sees," *Upper Darby News,* 20 Jan. 1949, 1; "Steady Selling," wwd, 20 Oct. 1949, 2; "Lits Opens," *Upper Darby News,* 20 Oct. 1949, 1, 26; "Lit's to Build," wwd, 31 Mar. 1950, 9; "Lit Branch at Upper Darby," dse 14 (Sep. 1951): 142. A small extension was added two years later; see "Lit Bros. Upper Darby," wwd, 25 Aug. 1953, I-44.

24. "Loeser Branch," wwd, 20 Sep. 1950, 1, 40; "No Formality," wwd, 3 Oct. 1950, 1, 59; "A & S to Build," wwd, 13 Oct. 1950, 2; "Mapping a Retailer's Growth," bw, 4 Nov. 1950, 50, 52, 54–55, 58, 60; "New $4,500,000 A & S," wwd, 4 Feb. 1952, 35; "Sets $12 Million" and "Large Selection," wwd, 27 Feb. 1952, 1, 65 (Abraham & Straus); "Scruggs Branch," *St. Louis Star-Times,* 1 Oct. 1945, 8; "Proposed Branch," pa 27 (Aug. 1946): 44–47; "Vandervoort's Suburban," wwd, 23 Mar. 1950, 1, 53; "Scruggs Branch Stresses Easy Selection," *Stores* 33 (Nov. 1951): 56, 58; Morris Ketchum, Jr., *Shops & Stores* (New York: Reinhold, 1948): 257–60 (Vandervoort's).

25. By mid-decade, size requirements were expanding considerably. See "125,000 Sq. Ft. Held Minimum," wwd, 6 Apr. 1956, 1, 29.

26. Richard Longstreth, "The Mixed Blessings of Success: The Hecht Company and Department Store Branch Development after World War II," in Carter L. Hudgins and Elizabeth Collins Cromley, eds., *Shaping Communities: Perspectives in Vernacular Architecture, VI* (Knoxville: University of Tennessee Press, 1997), 244–62 and references therein. Concerning Famous-Barr, see n. 105 below. Concerning Abraham & Straus, see n. 24 above and "A & S Building," wwd, 28 Dec. 1950, 1, 11; "Suburban Department Store," af 96 (May 1952): 127–31; "Display Is the Key-Note of the New A & S Unit," dw 60 (May 1952): 28–29, 70; "Suburban Branch Unit Offers Large-Store Services," csa/vse 28 (Apr. 1952): 200; "A & S Branch Expanded," wwd, 10 Nov. 1954, I-6; and "A & S Will Add," wwd, 23 Jan. 1959, 1, 28.

27. "Branch Store Trend," wwd, 7 Dec. 1951, 1, 34; "Good Practice in Operation of Branch Store," dse 15 (July 1952): 39, 44, 53; "Branches Get Little," wwd, 12 June 1953, 4; "Branch Liaison Problem," wwd, 26 June 1953, 4; "Better Planning," wwd, 31 July 1953, 4; "Imitation of Parent," wwd, 5 Aug. 1953, I-4; "Different Space," wwd, 4 Jan. 1956, 3; "Stores Not Getting," wwd, 2 May 1956, I-1, I-79; "Executive Staff Setup," wwd, 5 Nov. 1956, I-1, I-8; "Buyers Seeking Formula," wwd, 7 Nov. 1956, I-1, I-16; "Branches Problem," wwd, 27 Sep. 1957, 3; "Big Stores Advised," wwd, 9 Oct. 1958, 1, 44; "Wide Interest Indicated," wwd, 13 Jan. 1960, 1, 17; Louis P. Bucklin, "Problems of Organizational Change in Department Store Chains," in William S. Decker, ed., *Emerging Concepts of Marketing* (Chicago: American Marketing Association, 1963), 187–211.

28. "Operational Efficiency," wwd, 15 July 1953, 4; "Complete Selections"; "Shipping Direct," wwd, 17 Dec. 1956, 1, 15; "Communication Difficulty," wwd, 19 Feb. 1959, 14.

29. Within the retail field, "branch" is generally used to denote an operation wholly subservient to the parent one. Here, however, I use the term more broadly to encompass all units of a company that were not annexes to the parent store, irrespective of the degree of autonomy they enjoyed.

30. "Plan Individual," wwd, 30 Mar. 1949, 1, 16; "Buying for the Branch Store," *Stores* 37 (Nov. 1955): 20–23. Concerning branch autonomy, see E. B. Weiss, "Free the Branch from Her Headquarter Apron Strings," dse 12 (July 1949): 40–43; "Branch Stores," *Stores* 34 (Feb. 1952): 21–25; "Good Practice," 38–39, 44, 53–54, 116, 126, 129 and (Sep. 1952): 154–56, 158, 165, 169; "Responsibility for Inventory," wwd, 16 July 1956, 1; "Macy's Testing," wwd, 31 Aug. 1956, 1, 18; "Six Vital Problems"; "Branch Autonomy Gains," wwd, 7 Mar. 1957, I-1, I-36; "Stores Still Sift," wwd, 29 July 1957, 1, 19; and "Report Asks," wwd, 14 Jan. 1960, 1, 44.

31. "New Systems," wwd, 6 Aug. 1957, 1, 33. E. B. Weiss ranked among the most outspoken advocates of department stores learning from chain companies. See his "How to Sell To and Through the *New* Department Store," *Printers' Ink* 221 (28 Nov. 1947): 31–34, 72, 76, 78, and (5 Dec. 1947): 39–40, 62, 66, 68; "The Branch Unit—Hope or Headache?" dse 12 (Mar. 1949): 18, 50–52; "Recentralization vs. Decentralization of Branch Units," dse 12 (Apr. 1949): 24, 32–34; "'Aristocratic' Branches," 90–91, 95; "Make the Branch Unit 'Double in Brass,'" dse 12 (June 1949): 65–67; and "Free the Branch." See also Malcolm P. McNair, "The Future of the Department Store," *Stores* 32 (May 1950): 15–19, 81; Milton P. Brown, "The Trend in Branch Stores," Retail Trade Board, Boston Chamber of Commerce, *Twenty-Fifth Annual Boston Conference on Distribution,* 1952, 77–81; "Stores Not Getting"; "Demand of Suburban," wwd, 30 Nov. 1953, 30; "Liaison Snag," wwd, 12 June 1957, 1, 99; and "Bam Method to Meet," wwd, 11 July 1957, I-1, I-32.

32. "New Surge to Suburbs," wwd, 10 July 1957, 1, 24; "Filene's Branch Setup," wwd, 12 July 1957, 1, 25; "Macy's Intensifies Bid," wwd, 13 Nov. 1958, 1, 11; "Branches Seen Sole," wwd, 3 May 1956, 1, 14; "Los Angeles Area," wwd, 8 May 1956, 1, 14; "Carson's Suburban Units," wwd, 23 Feb. 1960, 1, 22; "May Co. Branch," wwd, 2 May 1960, 1, 28. See also "Branch Volume Contribution," wwd, 5 June 1952, I-1, I-47; "Branches Pace," wwd, 28 June 1954, 1, 25; "Allied Credits Branches," wwd, 13 Apr. 1956, 1, 39; "Branches Did Fourth," wwd, 26 July 1956, 1, 36; and "Branches Keep Boosting," wwd, 6 May 1959, 1, 13.

33. "Branches Held Eventual," wwd, 11 Jan. 1952, 57; "Branches Won't Replace," wwd, 25 May 1953, 36; "Main Tents," wwd, 7 Sep. 1956, 32.

34. Weiss, "The Branch Unit," 18; "Branch Stores," *Stores* 34 (Feb. 1952): 21–25; "Managerial Approach," 3–47. See also "Branch Stores," rm 43 (Feb. 1948): 21–22, 45.

35. "Branch Store Policies," ul 13 (Sep. 1954): 1–6; "Where to Build Your New Store," *Stores* 38 (Aug. 1956): 12–16. Surviving examples of such studies appear to be extremely rare. One I have found is "Department Store Location Study: Study and Recommendations Prepared for Scruggs-Vandervoort-Barney" (St. Louis: Roy Wenzlick & Co., ca. 1945), Missouri Historical Society, St. Louis.

36. For discussion, see Richard Longstreth, *City Center to Regional Mall: Architecture, the Automobile, and Retailing in Los Angeles, 1920–1950* (Cambridge: MIT Press, 1997), 251–54; and Longstreth, "Sears, Roebuck and the Remaking of the Department Store, 1924–1942," jsah 65 (June 2006): 261–64.

37. For background, see "William Snaith, Designer," nyt, 20 Feb. 1974, 40; and Angela Schonberger, "Inside, Outside: Loewy's Interiors and Architecture," in Schonberger, ed., *Raymond Loewy: Pioneer of American Industrial Design* (Munich: Prestel, 1990), 99–106.

38. Interview with Maurice Lazarus, Cambridge, Mass., 2 Feb. 2002. Lazarus worked closely with Snaith in the design of Foley's department store (1945–47) in downtown Houston. Lazarus, who headed the new enterprise, recalled that the final design was really Snaith's; the architect of record contributed little to the scheme. This account corresponds with numerous contemporary ones of branches that describe the Loewy Corporation as the principal designers of the work in question.

39. William T. Snaith, "Planning Branch Store Operation," nrb 27 (Mar. 1945): 18, 48; "On Planning," wwd, 16 May 1951, I-54; "Branches Should," wwd, 21 May 1952, 79; William T. Snaith, "Know Your Total," wwd, 3 Sep. 1952, 74; "Beyond the Suburbs," wwd, 10 Sep. 1952, I-82; William T. Snaith, "Architecture and the Community of Retailing," ar 125 (Apr. 1959): 192–200.

40. Background material on Copeland was gleaned from the

American Institute of Architects (AIA) Archives, Washington, D.C.; "Consulting Architect," NYT, 29 Mar. 1936, III-9; and his obituary, NYT, 31 Jan. 1975, 38. See also "Merchant Prince," NYT, 27 Nov. 1960, VIII-1, VIII-6. For Novak, see George S. Koyl, ed., *American Architects Directory,* 2nd ed. (New York: R. R. Bowker, 1962), 519. For Katzman, see AIA Archives; "'Get off Floor,'" NYT, 29 July 1956, VIII-6; John F. Gane, ed., *American Architects Directory,* 3rd ed. (New York: R. R. Bowker, 1970), 475; and his obituary, NYT, 10 Apr. 1973, 46. Concerning Parrish, see "Mergers Not Doom," NYT, 24 Feb. 1929, II-8; and "Honored by Retailers," NYT, 2 Nov. 1946, 26; and "Stores Welcome," NYT, 13 Sep. 1959, III-6. Quote from "Function Key," WWD, 16 Jan. 1952, 76.

41. For background, see "Perspectives—The Modernist from Wainscott: Morris Ketchum, Jr.," PA 25 (Aug. 1944): 65–66; Koyl, *American Architects Directory,* 376; and Morris Ketchum, Jr., *Blazing a Trail* (New York: Vantage, 1982).

42. "The New Rich's Knoxville," DW 67 (Dec. 1955): 73. See also "Branch Department Layout," WWD, 17 Aug. 1953, 4; and "Suburban Branch Department Stores," AR 115 (May 1954): 178–97. The two major texts on store design of the period were Ketchum, *Shops & Stores* and Louis Parnes, *Planning Stores That Pay* (New York: F. W. Dodge, 1948).

43. See, e.g., Morris Ketchum, Jr., "Suburban 'Store on Stilts,'" WWD, 16 Feb. 1950, I-72; and "One Story Branches," WWD, 6 Aug. 1952, 61, and 13 Aug. 1952, 66.

44. "Functionalism Distinguishes New Bamberger Branch Unit," DW 65 (July–Aug. 1954): 26.

45. E.g., see "Need for More Planning," WWD, 17 June 1954, 6.

46. See, e.g., "Interior Display Role," WWD, 13 Nov. 1958, 6.

47. Concerning Rich's Knoxville, see "The New Rich's"; and "Rich's in Knoxville," *Stores* 37 (Sep. 1955): 7–8, 66. Concerning Burdine's, see n. 17 above.

48. Including B. Altman at Manhasset and White Plains, New York; Lord & Taylor at Eastchester, New York; John Wanamaker at Wilmington, Delaware, and Baederwood, Pennsylvania; Hutzler's at Towson, Maryland; Woodward & Lothrop at Chevy Chase, Maryland, and Alexandria, Virginia; Rich's at Knoxville, Tennessee; and Bullock's at Pasadena.

49. Several exceptions were built in Virginia, ostensibly catering to a strong regional sense of tradition. They included Woodward & Lothrop's unexecuted branch at Arlington, as well as that built at Alexandria, and Miller & Rhoads's at Charlottesville and Roanoke. Hahne's larger branch at Westfield, New Jersey (1960–63), was embellished with a classical portico, probably to assuage fears of incompatibility among the community's well-heeled residents. Similarly, Woodward & Lothrop's Chevy Chase branch had a few historicizing motifs appended to an otherwise conspicuously new building.

50. Two exceptions were Arnold Constable's branch in Hackensack, New Jersey (1945–46), the design of which was patterned after that of its prewar branches in Hempstead and New Rochelle, and the initial design (1945) for Woodward & Lothrop in Chevy Chase, which was discarded for an entirely new one four years later.

51. "Parking Area Determines Store Location," DSE 11 (May 1948): 74–75 (quote on p. 75). See also "Lord & Taylor Planning," WWD, 1 Mar. 1945, 2; "Lord & Taylor to Erect," WWD, 7 Mar. 1946, 1, 44; "Lord & Taylor Opening," WWD, 26 Feb. 1948, 1, 62; "Lord and Taylor's Westchester Store," AR 103 (Apr. 1948): 111–22; "Introducing Lord & Taylor's, Westchester," DW 95 (Apr. 1948): 52–53, 95; and "Fashion Center," *Interiors* 107 (June 1948): 91–93.

52. "Bullock's-Pasadena to Bloom," WWD, 22 Aug. 1947, 7; "Bullock's Opens Here," *Pasadena Star-News,* 9 Sep. 1947, 15, 17 (quotes on p. 15). See also "Bullock's Plans," WWD, 10 July 1944, 1; "Bullock's Pasadena a Postwar Innovation," SBC 105 (5 Jan. 1945): 33–34; "Bullock's Pasadena a Fairyland for Shoppers," SBC 110 (26 Sep. 1947): 9–11, 22; "A Store for the Carriage Trade," AF 88 (May 1948): 102–5; "Bullock's Pasadena," *Architectural Digest* 12:1 [1948]: 103–12; Ketchum, *Shops & Stores,* 260–63; Geoffrey Baker and Bruno Funaro, *Shopping Centers: Design and Operation* (New York: Reinhold, 1951), 164–66.

53. A valuable analysis of the resort hotel from this standpoint is Alice T. Friedman, "Merchandising Miami Beach: Morris Lapidus and the Architecture of Abundance," *Journal of Decorative and Propaganda Arts* 25 (2005): 216–53.

54. See n. 55 below.

55. "Sketch of Hahne," *Montclair Times,* 8 Sep. 1949, 2; "Proposed Hahne's," WWD, 9 Sep. 1949, 9; "Hahne & Co. to Open," *Montclair Times,* 15 Feb. 1951, 1, 12; "Hahne's Opens," *Montclair Times,* 22 Feb. 1951, 1, 11.

56. "Hutzler's Site," WWD, 14 Apr. 1947, I-5, I-37; "Ground Broken," WWD, 23 June 1950, 1, 51; "Hutzler's First," WWD, 21 Nov. 1952, 1, 51; *Sun* [Baltimore], 21 Nov. 1952, 24; "New Lighting, New Parking, Deeper Stock," AF 99 (July 1953): 84–93 (quote on p. 87).

57. Concerning Breuer, see Isabelle Hyman, *Marcel Breuer, Architect: The Career and the Buildings* (New York: Harry N. Abrams, 2001).

58. E.g., see "What's What in New Buildings, No. 87," *Distribution and Warehousing* 24 (Sep. 1925): 30–31, 38; "Household Goods Warehousing," *Distribution and Warehousing* 25 (Jan. 1926): 39–44; and "What's What in New Buildings, No. 130," *Distribution and Warehousing* 29 (Apr. 1930): 35, 58.

59. "Macy Jamaica Store," WWD, 3 Nov. 1944, 1; "Macy's Branch," WWD, 12 Aug. 1947, 2; "Cornerstone Laid," NYT, 30 Aug. 1947, 28; "Jamaica Branch," WWD, 2 Sep. 1947, 12; "Macy's-Jamaica," WWD, 3 Sep. 1947, I-1, I-41; "Macy's-Jamaica a Miracle on 164th Street," RM 42 (Oct. 1947): 13; "Macy's-Jamaica Is Designed Around Merchandising Methods," AF 88 (Feb. 1948): 100–104; "Novel Display Features," DW 51 (Oct. 1948): 46–47, 120–21.

60. See Longstreth, "Sears, Roebuck," 259–61.

61. "Macy Plans," WWD, 29 Jan. 1946, 6; "5-Year Macy's," WWD, 23 Oct. 1947, 1, 56; "Tested Features," WWD, 2 July 1948, I-26; "Macy's-Flatbush," NYT, 4 July 1948, RE 4; "Expect Sales," WWD, 29 Oct. 1948, 1, 48; "Elevator Device," WWD, 3 Nov. 1948, 87 (Flatbush); "$1,000,000 White Plains," WWD, 8 Aug. 1945, 1, 27; "Macy's Start," WWD, 17 Sep. 1945, 15; "New Macy's Branch," WWD, 24 May 1948, 41; "Macy's New Branch," NYT, 22 Mar. 1949, 29 (White Plains); and "Retail Panel Members," WWD, 19 Dec. 1950, 44.

62. Interview with Albert C. Martin, Jr., Los Angeles, 7 Nov. 1989. See also Longstreth, *City Center,* 233–55. For background on the show window, see Leonard S. Marcus, *The American Store Window* (New York: Whitney Library of Design, 1978); Barry James Wood, *Show Windows: Seventy-Five Years of the Art of Display* (New York: Congdon and Weed, 1982); and William Leach, *Land of Desire: Merchants, Power, and the Rise of a New American Culture* (New York: Random House, 1993), chap. 2.

63. Longstreth, *City Center,* 241–46, and references therein; Jeffrey Hardwick, *Mall Maker: Victor Gruen, Architect of an American Dream* (Philadelphia: University of Pennsylvania Press, 2004); and Alex Wall, *From Urban Shop to New City* (Barcelona: Actar, 2005), 42–49. Other accounts include "Milliron's Branch," WWD, 27 Jan. 1949, 62; "Suburban Unit," WWD, 24 Feb. 1949, 2; and "Designed to Attract," WWD, 5 Apr. 1949, 50. "Suburban Store Solves the Parking Problem," *National Real Estate Journal* 50 (Aug. 1949): 51. Milliron's unconventional attributes were not entirely successful.

64. See n.18 above.

65. Some exceptions can be found in new stores erected in the

core small cities or towns beyond the parent company's traditional trading areas. In a few cases, too, municipal parking facilities in suburban communities took the place of store lots.

66. Ketchum, *Shops & Stores,* 248–65; Parnes, *Planning Stores,* 71–76; and Geoffrey Baker and Bruno Funaro, *Parking* (New York: Reinhold, 1958), 29–40, 76–77, 97–113, 128–29, 192–97.

67. Such was the case for many retail outlets of the period. See Richard Longstreth, *The Drive-In, the Supermarket, and the Transformation of Commercial Space in Los Angeles, 1914–1941* (Cambridge: MIT Press, 1999), 110.

68. Concerning Sears, see Longstreth, "Sears, Roebuck," 244–46.

69. "Lord & Taylor Planning," *NYT,* 1 Mar. 1945, 2. Concerning the Eastchester store, see n. 51 above. Concerning the West Hartford store, see "Store Signs Lease," *West Hartford News* (hereafter *News*), 4 Jan. 1951, 1; "Model Shopping Area," *News,* 10 Jan. 1952, 1; "Lord & Taylor," *WWD,* 30 Jan. 1952, 16; "New Lord & Taylor," *WWD,* 23 Feb. 1953, 1, 66; and *News,* 26 Feb. 1953, Lord & Taylor Sect.

70. "Path Seen Clear," *JEE,* 11 Nov. 1947, 1, 4; "Wanamaker Wilmington Site," *WWD,* 17 Nov. 1947, 48; "Wanamaker's New," *WWD,* 10 Feb. 1948, 12; "Wanamaker Plans," *JEE,* 23 May 1949, 1, 18; "Wanamaker's, Wilmington," *WWD,* 24 May 1949, 17; "Wanamaker Store," *JEE,* 15 Nov. 1950, 1, 25; "Wanamaker, Wilmington," *WWD,* 15 Nov. 1950, 61; *AR* 109 (Mar. 1951): 142–43.

71. "Work to Be Started," *SLP,* 1 Jan. 1950, 10G; "Famous-Barr Branch," *WWD,* 3 Jan. 1950, 1, 15; "Famous-Barr Breaks," *WWD,* 13 Apr. 1950, 8; "Famous-Barr Suburban," *WWD,* 21 Aug. 1951, 2; "Famous-Barr Co. to Open," *Observer* [St. Louis], 22 Aug. 1951, 6-A; "Famous-Barr Unit," *WWD,* 23 Aug. 1951, 1, 44; "A Modern Merchandising," *WWD,* 29 Aug. 1951, 58.

72. "Bloomingdale's Buys," *WWD,* 12 Nov. 1947, 1, 7; "Bloomingdale's Buys," *SS,* 11 Dec. 1947, 1, 10; "Ware's Transformed as New Bloomingdale Unit," *DSE* 12 (Feb. 1949): 62–63; "Jordan Marsh Opens," *Malden Evening News,* 29 Mar. 1954, 1, 3; "Jordan's in Malden," *Malden Evening News,* 30 Mar. 1954, 7; "Jordan Marsh Store," *Malden Evening News,* 2 Apr. 1954, 1, 3; "Ceremony Marks," *Independent Journal* [San Rafael], 23 Feb. 1953, 1, 4–5; "It's Macy's Now," *Richmond Independent,* 23 Feb. 1953, 6; "Macy's Plans," *WWD,* 18 May 1953, 2.

73. Namely, Arnold Constable Co. (New York), Bon Marche (Seattle), Boston Store (Milwaukee), Burdine's (Miami), Carson Pirie Scott (Chicago), Castor-Knott (Nashville), Davison-Paxon (Atlanta), Dayton Company (Minneapolis), L. S. Donaldson (Minneapolis), Herpolsheimer's (Grand Rapids), Joske Brothers (San Antonio), Lasalle & Koch (Toledo), Lion Store (Toledo), Lit Brothers (Philadelphia), Maas Brothers (Tampa), R. H. Macy (Kansas City), Meier & Frank (Portland, Ore.), Miller & Rhoads (Richmond), M. O'Neil (Akron), Stewart Dry Goods Co. (Louisville), Thalheimer Brothers (Richmond), and Younker Brothers (Des Moines). The list does not include resort stores or stores such as I. Magnin and Saks Fifth Avenue that were establishing themselves in a number of metropolitan centers.

74. Concerning the purchased stores, see "Say Macy Buys," *WWD,* 3 Aug. 1944, 1; "Saxon-Callum," *WWD,* 17 Aug. 1944, 1, 6; "Saxon-Callum," *Augusta Chronicle,* 17 Aug. 1944, 1, 2 (Augusta); "Davison's Is New," *Macon Telegraph,* 20 May 1945, 2A; "Macon Store," *Macon Telegraph,* 22 May 1945, 6; "Davison's Business," *Macon Telegraph,* 7 Oct. 1945, 20; "Davison-Paxon," *Macon Telegraph,* 22 Oct. 1945, 6; "Davison's Store," *Macon Telegraph,* 20 Nov. 1945, 14 (Macon); "Davison's of Athens," *Banner-Herald* [Athens], 24 May 1953, 1, 8 and sect. A; "Athenians Gather," *Banner-Herald,* 25 May 1953, 1, 2 (Athens); "Davison Paxon," *WWD,* 1 July 1946, 4; and "Davison Opens," *WWD,* 2 Oct. 1950, 43 (Columbia). Concerning the new stores, see "Davison-Paxon," *WWD,* 14 Oct. 1947, 10; "Davison's New," *WWD,* 17 Mar. 1949, 4; "Growth of Augusta" and "Stylish Simplicity," *Augusta Chronicle,* 20 Mar. 1949, A-1, A-5, resp.; *Stores* 32 (Dec. 1950): 26 (Augusta); "Davison's Plans," *Ledger-Enquirer* [Columbus], 4 Aug. 1946, 1-A, 6-A; "Davison Unit," *WWD,* 7 July 1947, 1, 49; "Davison's Fifth," *WWD,* 15 Feb. 1949, 1, 71; and "New Davison's," *WWD,* 16 Feb. 1949, 5 (Columbus).

75. "Froney & Co. Sold," *Sentinel-Tribune,* 22 Dec. 1944, 1, 2 (Bowling Green); "Lasalle's Opens," *Advertiser-Tribune,* 19 Aug. 1947, 1 (Tiffin); "Lasalle & Koch," *WWD,* 30 Oct. 1947, 1; "Lasalle's Projected," *WWD,* 10 Mar. 1948, 71; "Public Is Invited," *Register Star-News,* 27 Oct. 1949, 1, 26 (Sandusky); "Lasalle's to Erect," *Republican-Courier,* 11 Nov. 1954, 1, 15; "Work Starts," *WWD,* 18 Jan. 1955, 2; "Lasalle's New Store," *Republican-Courier,* 15 Aug. 1955, 26 (Findlay).

76. "Macy's Buys," *Joplin Globe,* 10 Sep. 1954, 1A, 2A; "City's Thriving Economy," *Wichita Beacon,* 31 Dec. 1955, 1, 14; "Macy Acquires," *WWD,* 3 Jan. 1956, 1, 67.

77. Concerning the store, see "Innes to Build," *Wichita Beacon,* 14 Nov. 1926, 1A, 3A; *Wichita Beacon,* 7 Nov. 1927, 15–20; *DGE* 82 (14 Apr. 1928): 55; "Innes Will Erect," *Wichita Eagle,* 15 June 1947, 1, 8; "New Innes Building," *Wichita Beacon,* 3 Oct. 1948, A7; and "Geo. Innes Co.," *WWD,* 2 Jan. 1952, 15.

78. "Macy's Mentioned," *WWD,* 17 June 1960, 9; "Macy's Sets," *WWD,* 8 Sep. 1960, 1, 59; "Businessmen Hail," *Topeka Capital,* 8 Sep. 1960, 1, 4; "Macy's Proposal," *Topeka Capital,* 13 Nov. 1964, 1, 2; "Here Are Pros," *Topeka Capital,* 17 Nov. 1963, 29A; "City to Vote," *Topeka Capital,* 20 Nov. 1963, 1, 3; "City Votes Yes," *Topeka Capital,* 20 Nov. 1963, 1, 2; "City Gets," *Topeka Capital,* 2 Oct. 1966, 1, 2.

79. "Crowds Throng," *Spokesman Review* [Spokane], 6 Sep. 1947, 6; Robert B. Hyslop, *Spokane Building Blocks* (Spokane: By the author, 1983), 25–26, 74–75 (Spokane); "Rumbaugh-MacLain's," *Everett Daily Herald,* 29 July 1949, 1 (Everett); "Store Name," *Tacoma News Tribune,* 29 Feb. 1952, 1, 6; "The Bon Marche," *Tacoma Ledger,* 9 Nov. 1952, B-2 (Tacoma); "Remodeled Store," *Walla Walla Union-Bulletin,* 3 Oct. 1951, 1; "Bon Marche Opens," *WWD,* 16 Oct. 1951, 29 (Walla Walla); *Yakima Herald,* 29 Mar. 1953, 9; "Bon Marche Plans," *Yakima Herald,* 1 Jan. 1964, 1, 2 (Yakima); "Doors to Open," *Bellingham Herald,* 8 May 1957, 1, 7, and Bon Marche Sect. (Bellingham); "A Century of Success for the Inland Empire and the Bon Marche," undated (ca. 1989) brochure, Yakima Public Library.

80. "Bon Leases," *Spokesman Review,* 6 Nov. 1954, 1; "A Century of Success."

81. "Bon Marche Plans," *WWD,* 8 Sep. 1953, 1, 11; *Eugene Register-Guard,* 29 Sep. 1954, sect. C (Bon Marche); "M&F Plans," *Oregonian* [Portland], 8 Mar. 1953, 1; "Meier and Frank's," *Oregon Statesman* [Salem], 8 Mar. 1953, 1, 16; "Meier & Frank," *WWD,* 9 Mar. 1953, 1, 34; "Last Minute Flurry," *Oregon Statesman,* 25 Oct. 1955, II-3; "Near 75,000," *Oregon Statesman,* 28 Oct. 1955, I-1, 8; "Speculation Rises," *WWD,* 5 Feb. 1957, 8 (Meier & Frank); *Oregon Statesman,* 3 Sep. 1954, Lipman's Sect.

82. "Dayton Company Buys," *Rochester Post-Bulletin* (hereafter *Bulletin*), 9 Aug. 1952, 1, 3; "Dayton's Plans," *WWD,* 25 Feb. 1954, 1, 58; "Dayton's Store Opens," *Bulletin,* 4 Mar. 1954, 1, 11; "Victor Gruen's Design," *Stores* 36 (Sep. 1954): 20–21; "Flexible Fixturing," *DW* 65 (Sep. 1954): 22–23, 76–77; "Department Store," *PA* 35 (Nov. 1954): 89–96 (Dayton's); "Second Branch," *WWD,* 8 Oct. 1952, I-1, I-28; "Donaldson's Store," *Bulletin,* 15 Oct. 1953, 7 (Donaldson's).

83. Concerning Thalheimer's, see "L. Herman Department Store," *Danville Register,* 26 Apr. 1955, 1, 2; "Thalheimer's Buys," *WWD,* 27 Apr. 1955, 1, 66 (Danville); "Thalheimer's in Expansion," *WWD,* 23 May 1949, I-1, I-37; "Sosnik's, Thalheimer's," *Winston-Salem Journal,* 23 May 1949, 1, 5; "Sosnik's to Get," *Winston-Salem Journal,* 28 Oct. 1949, 10; "Final Stage," *WWD,* 21 May 1959, 9;

"Major Project," *WWD,* 9 Sep. 1959, 22 (Winston-Salem); "Thalheimer's Confirms," *WWD,* 2 Nov. 1957, 11; and "Ellis Stone Store," *Greensboro Daily News,* 12 Nov. 1957, 1, 2 (Greensboro). Concerning Miller & Rhoads, see "Miller & Rhoads in Deal," *WWD,* 2 Apr. 1954, 6; "Miller & Rhoads Announces," *Daily Progress,* 26 Feb. 1955, 1, 9; "First Branches," *WWD,* 28 Feb. 1955, 1, 18; *Daily Progress,* 15 Aug. 1956, sect. II; "Miller & Rhoads Unit," *WWD,* 22 Aug. 1956, 10 (Charlottesville); "Miller & Rhoads Lets," *WWD,* 12 Mar. 1956, 11; "Miller & Rhoads to Open," *Roanoke Times,* 27 Feb. 1955, A-1, A-4; *Roanoke Times,* 4 Sep. 1957, sect. B; "Miller & Rhoads Greets," *Roanoke Times,* 5 Sep. 1957, 4 (Roanoke); "Miller, Rhoads to Acquire," *WWD,* 1 Mar. 1957, 1, 29; "Millner's Merges," *News,* 28 Feb. 1957, 1, 10; and "Miller & Rhoads," *News,* 4 Sep. 1959, C-4 (Lynchburg).

84. "Hear O'Neil Co.," *WWD,* 5 May 1945, 1, 18; "New Store Opened," *Evening Independent,* 30 Nov. 1945, 1, 8 (Massilon); "O'Neil's Store," *Coshocton Tribune,* 15 July 1946, 1; "Ceremonies Mark," *Coshocton Tribune,* 17 July 1946, 1, 7 (Cosochton); "O'Neil's Store," *Mansfield News Journal,* 1 Dec. 1946, 1 (Mansfield); "O'Neil Opens," *WWD,* 6 Oct. 1946, I-14 (Cuyahoga Falls); "Spring-Holzworth Merged," *Alliance Review,* 28 Apr. 1952, 1, 11; "Stark Dry Goods," *Alliance Review,* 18 Dec. 1956, 1, 2 (Alliance); "Stark's 4 Stores," *Canton Repository,* 18 Dec. 1956, 1, 16; "O'Neil Co. Buys," *WWD,* 19 Dec. 1956, 1, 18; *The Place Where 300,000 People Live* ([Akron]: M. O'Neil Co., 1952).

85. "Younkers Plans Post-War Expansion Now," *DSE* 7 (Mar. 1944): 16; "How to Operate," *WWD,* 28 Jan. 1948, 62, and 4 Feb. 1948, 70; "Younkers Proves," *WWD,* 6 Sep. 1950, 78, and 7 Sep. 1950, I-57. Concerning the branches, see "Younker Opens," *WWD,* 28 Nov. 1941, 39; "Younker's Enlarged," *WWD,* 3 Sep. 1942, I-26 (Ames); "Younker's to Open," *WWD,* 3 May 1944, 1; "New Younkers," *Des Moines Register,* 10 Sep. 1944, 8-x; "Accent on Branch," *WWD,* 16 Jan. 1945, 20 (Mason City); "Ft. Dodge Younkers," *Des Moines Register,* 18 Sep. 1947, 7 (Fort Dodge); "Younker's Deal," *WWD,* 24 Dec. 1947, 1, 11 (Sioux City); "Younkers Buy," *Des Moines Tribune,* 26 Dec. 1947, 1; "Younker's Buy," *WWD,* 29 Dec. 1947, I-36 (Marshalltown); "Opens Today," *WWD,* 2 Aug. 1949, I-4; "How Younkers Newest," *WWD,* 28 Sep. 1949, 46; "Younkers Store," *Iowa City Press-Citizen,* 6 Feb. 1951, 12 (Iowa City); "Younkers Store," *Ottumwa Courier,* 5 Nov. 1949, 13; "Younkers to Open," *Ottumwa Courier,* 31 Jan. 1950, 15, (Ottumwa); "Younker's Buy," *WWD,* 14 June 1955, 1, 36; "Younker's Store," *Oskaloosa Herald,* 19 Aug. 1957, 3; "Younkers Store," *Oskaloosa Herald,* 31 Jan. 1958, 2 (Oskaloosa); "Rock Island Gets," *Rock Island Argus,* 22 June 1955, 1, 2; "Ribbon-Cutting," *Rock Island Argus,* 31 Mar. 1956, 12–13 (Rock Island).

86. "Purchases Innes," *Wichita Eagle,* 30 Dec. 1951, 1, 2; "Geo. Innes Co.," *WWD,* 31 Dec. 1951, 1, 2.

87. Concerning the Sioux Falls store, see "Dayton Purchases," *Daily Argus-Leader,* 12 Nov. 1954, 1, 6; and "Dayton's Buys," *WWD,* 12 Nov. 1954, 1, 13.

88. "Carson's Buys," *WWD,* 29 May 1959, 1, 4; "Chicago Firm Buys," *Chicago Heights Star,* 29 May 1959, 1, 2; "The Rau Store," *WWD,* 18 Aug. 1959, I-6 (Chicago Heights); "Carson-Block & Kuhl," *Aurora Beacon-News,* 1 Oct. 1959, 1, 2; "Carson's to Absorb," *WWD,* 24 June 1960, 9; "Carson Name," *Aurora Beacon-News,* 31 July 1960, 1, 3 (Aurora); "Carson's Buys," *WWD,* 27 July 1960, 1, 16; "Fair Store Sold," *Kankakee Daily Journal,* 26 July 1960, 1, 5 (Kankakee). See also "Chicago Stores," *WWD,* 27 Dec. 1956, 1, 33.

89. "George's-Rich's," *WWD,* 5 Aug. 1954, 36; "Finally—Rich's Regionalizes," *BW,* 23 July 1955, 90–94, 97–98, 100; "The New Rich's," 26; "Brief But Significant," *Knoxville Journal,* 28 Aug. 1955, 1-A, 7-A. See also "'Suburban' Unit Downtown," *WWD,* 7 Dec. 1954, 18; "Rich's Opens," *WWD,* 25 Aug. 1955, 2, 41; *Knoxville Journal,* 28 Aug. 1995, 1-B, 2-B; "Rich's, Knoxville, Open," *WWD,* 29 Aug. 1955, 1, 10; "Rich's in Knoxville," *Stores* 37 (Sep. 1955): 7–8; and "Rich Stresses," *WWD,* 26 Oct. 1955, 1, 75. Concerning Eckbo, see Marc Treib and Dorothea Imbert, *Garret Eckbo: Modern Landscape for Living* (Berkeley: University of California Press, 1997).

90. Concerning Greenfield, see "Rules Vast Retail Empire," *WWD,* 13 June 1949, 50; and "A Profile of Mr. Albert M. Greenfield," *Philadelphia* 38 (Mar. 1951): 5–6.

91. "Cites Potential," *WWD,* 9 May 1950, 4; "The Miracle of Upper Darby, Pa.," *WWD,* 19 Sep. 1950, 55; "Favors Developed," *WWD,* 6 Oct. 1950, 2. For background on the Upper Darby commercial center, see "69th Street Business District," *PI,* 15 Dec. 1940, W18; and "Philadelphia's 69th St.," *WWD,* 14 Mar. 1952, 50.

92. "Hear Penney Plans," *WWD,* 10 June 1948, 1, 69; "Set Work," *WWD,* 5 July 1950, 16; "Stern's Opens," *WWD,* 22 Oct. 1951, 4; "Volume Good," *WWD,* 25 Oct. 1951, 8; "Penney Opens," *WWD,* 26 Feb. 1952, I-11; "Hear Blauner Seeks," *WWD,* 15 Sep. 1953, 1; "First Blauner Branch," *WWD,* 10 Dec. 1953, I-1, I-11; "Blauner's Branch," *WWD,* 3 Aug. 1954, 12.

93. "Lit Brothers Sets," *NYT,* 11 Apr. 1949, 35. For reasons that are unclear, no coverage of the purchase is given in local papers. Newspaper advertisement first notes that Swern's was affiliated with Lit's on 5 March 1950. The Lit's name was not used for the store, however, until 1 September 1953 and was not used exclusively until five months later. Such a gradual transition often occurred when an out-of-town company acquired a well-known local store in order not to make customers feel the establishment to which they were loyal had been eradicated.

94. "Freeholders Vote," *CP,* 21 Mar. 1951, 1, 2; "Department Store," *CP,* 22 Mar. 1951, 1; "Lit's to Erect," *CP,* 29 Mar. 1951, 1, 3; "Lit's Acquires," *WWD,* 30 Mar. 1951, 1, 47; "Lits Will Erect," *CP,* 23 Apr. 1953, 1, 3; "Lits Asks Delay," *CP,* 25 Aug. 1953, 1; "Lit Bros. Takes," *CP,* 24 Sep. 1953, 1, 2; "4-Story, $3,445,000 Parkade," *CP,* 8 Jan. 1954, 1, 18; "Lit Bros. May Drop," *WWD,* 11 Jan. 1954, I-4; "Lit Pact Signed," *CP,* 4 Mar. 1954, 1, 5; "Fee for $10,000," *CP,* 11 Aug. 1955, 1, 16; "'Shopping City,'" *CP,* 11 Oct. 1955, 13–14, 16, 24, 48.

95. "Camden Lits," *PI,* 12 Apr. 1954, 19; "Greenfield Predicts," *CP,* 11 Oct. 1955, 13. See also "Concept Differ," *WWD,* 12 Sep. 1951, 85. As early as 1938, the president of Lit's was exploring the development of a branch on the Camden outskirts patterned after the precedent Strawbridge & Clothier was instrumental in fostering in Ardmore (letter from Jack E. Lit to Albert M. Greenfield, 28 Nov. 1938, Albert M. Greenfield Papers, box 102, folder 5, Historical Society of Pennsylvania). Greenfield's focus on bolstering the city center was expressed early on, see "American Merchandisers Told of Danger Which Threatens Business Districts," *UL* 3 (Jan.–Feb. 1944): 4–6.

96. "Camden Area Held," *WWD,* 6 Jan. 1960, I-27.

97. "Lord & Taylor Plans," *WWD,* 10 May 1945, 1, 50; "Lord & Taylor," *WWD,* 15 May 1945, 1, 23; "New Rochelle," *WWD,* 9 Aug. 1945, 1, 4; "Lord & Taylor," *WWD,* 21 Aug. 1945, 1; and numerous accounts in *SS* between 11 May and 21 Aug. 1945.

98. "Opposition," *Millburn and Short Hills Item,* 31 Oct. 1946, 1. See also "Lord & Taylor Plans," *WWD,* 4 Sep. 1946, 2; "Lord & Taylor," *WWD,* 1 Nov. 1946, 1, 4; "Lord & Taylor," *WWD,* 4 Dec. 1946, 5; and numerous accounts in the *Item* between 5 Sep. and 26 Dec. 1946.

99. "Sues to Stop," *WWD,* 24 Dec. 1946, 1, 27; "Move to Block," *WWD,* 26 June 1947, 2. See also "Woodward's Buy," *WWD,* 25 Nov. 1946, 1, 6; "Woodward's Plans," *WWD,* 9 Dec. 1946, 1; "Arlington Rezoning," *WP,* 13 Dec. 1946, 43; "Court Upholds," *WWD,* 14 Mar. 1947, 1, 10; "Woodward's Files," *WWD,* 3 July 1947, 8; "Court Upholds," *WWD,* 16 Nov. 1947, 7; "Renew Efforts," *WWD,* 13 Dec. 1948, 4; "No Deals Made," *WWD,* 22 Dec. 1949, 38; "Arlington Residents," *WWD,*

17 Jan. 1950, 8; "Woodward Unit," WWD, 14 Feb. 1950, I-4; "Woodward's Wins," WWD, 27 Feb. 1950, 5; and "Decision Favoring," WWD, 4 Dec. 1951, 55.

100. "Wanamaker's Plans," WWD, 21 Aug. 1947, 1, 52; "Wanamaker's Appeals," JEE, 22 Aug. 1947, 11; "Council Hears," JEE, 5 Sep. 1947, 6; "Child Safety," JEE, 11 Sep. 1947, 1, 4; "Proponents of Wanamakers," JEE, 12 Sep. 1947, 2; "Wanamaker's Reveals," JEE, 18 Sep. 1947, 1; "Wanamaker's Gets," WWD, 22 Sep. 1947, 1, 4; "Council Takes," JEE, 26 Sep. 1947, 6; "Hecht Company's Bid," *Bethesda Record*, 7 Feb. 1957, 1; "Somerset Grids," *Bethesda Record*, 14 Feb. 1957, 1; "Somerset Citizens Committee," *Bethesda Record*, 21 Feb. 1957, 1; "Somerset Meeting," *Bethesda Record*, 28 Feb. 1957, 1; "Chamber Reaffirms," *Bethesda Record*, 4 Apr. 1957, 1; "Hecht Co. Withdraws," *Bethesda Record*, 11 Apr. 1957, 1.

101. "South Lake Showing," WWD, 19 Dec. 1957, 10; "New Concept of Shopping," LAT, 16 Sep. 1958, III-1, III-28. The success of this precinct was such that it ranked among the very few that was not an integrated business developed to be listed in early editions of the *Directory of Shopping Centers in the United States and Canada* (Chicago: National Research Bureau, 1957, et seq.).

102. The Sears Wisconsin Avenue store is discussed in Longstreth, "Sears, Roebuck," 264–67. On Garfinckel's Spring Valley branch, see chap. 5, n. 66.

103. "Two District Stores," ES, 31 Aug. 1945, B-1; "Chamber OKs," *Bethesda Journal*, 2 Nov. 1945, 1; "Woodward Store," MN, 7 Dec. 1945, 1, 5; "Montgomery Refuses," ES, 29 Dec. 1945, B-1; "Land Rezoned," MN, 4 Jan. 1946, 1, 2.

104. "Woodward's Branch," WWD, 18 Oct. 1949, 16; "Inaugurate New Woodward," WWD, 31 Oct. 1950, 55.

105. "Bethesda Busy," WP, 11 Oct. 1953, 1R; "Throngs See Opening," ES, 16 Sep. 1954, A-12; "First Suburban Unit," WWD, 3 Dec. 1954, 1, 9; "Associated D. G. Files," WWD, 3 June 1958, I-8; "Lord & Taylor," WP, 29 June 1958, B1; "Day-Long Party," WP, 30 Sep. 1959, D3; "Chevy Chase—and How It Grew," WWD, 19 Jan. 1960, 13; "Chevy Chase Store," WP, 30 Nov. 1960, B6; "Saks Store Zoning," WP, 5 Mar. 1961, D21; "Hearing Divided," WWD, 22 Apr. 1961, 51; "Rezoning Hurdles," WWD, 24 May 1961, 26; "Saks Store Wins," WP, 23 Nov. 1961, D1; "Saks 5th Avenue," WP, 15 July 1964, C8.

106. "$7,500,000 Postwar Program," SLP, 15 Oct. 1944, 1, 3; "Famous-Barr Plans," WWD, 16 Oct. 1944, 1, 23; "Post-War Expansion," DSE 7 (Dec. 1944): 129, 135; "Famous-Barr's Clayton," WWD, 4 Oct. 1948, 1, 42; *St. Louis Star-Times*, 7 Oct. 1948, Famous-Barr Sect.

107. Concerning the Vandervoort store, see n. 24 above. Concerning the community, see "The Story of Clayton, Mo.," *Freehold* 4 (1 Mar. 1939): 161–66; and Earl W. Kersten, Jr., and D. Reid Ross, "Clayton: A New Metropolitan Focus in the St. Louis Area," *Annals of the Association of American Geographers* 58 (Dec. 1968): 637–49.

108. "Maryland's '2nd' City," WP, 4 Aug. 1946, 4R; "Silver Spring," *Washington Daily News*, 14 Nov. 1946, 28; "Free Parking Lots Help Create 'Fastest Growing City in U.S.,'" *Automobile Facts* 8 (Dec. 1949): 6; "Park Your Car," WP, 4 Apr. 1948, 1R; "Silver Spring Solves," ES, 24 Sep. 1950, Pictorial Magazine, 3; "Silver Spring," ES, 6 Nov. 1950, B-1. Historical accounts include Mark Wallston, "The Commercial Rise and Fall of Silver Spring: A Study of the 20th Century Development of the Suburban Shopping Center of Montgomery County," *Maryland Historical Magazine* 81 (winter 1986): 330–39; and Richard Longstreth, "Silver Spring: Georgia Avenue, Colesville Road, and the Creation of an Alternative 'Downtown' for Metropolitan Washington," in Zeynep Celik et al., eds., *Streets: Critical Perspectives on Public Space* (Berkeley: University of California Press, 1994), 247–58.

109. "Top Retailers Join," WWD, 15 Sep. 1948, 71; "Murphy's New Modern," *Silver Spring Post*, 22 Nov. 1946, 1, 8; "Sears Roebuck Plans," MN, 22 Oct. 1948, 1; "Open Jelleff's," WWD, 23 Jan. 1949, 13; "Jelleff's Opens," WWD, 16 Feb. 1949, 5; "Sherer Will Hold," MN, 20 May 1949, B-1; "Mangums to Open," MN, 24 June 1949, B-1; "9 More Stores," WWD, 1 Aug. 1949, 6; "Hahn Shoe Co.," WP, 14 Aug. 1949, 4R; "New P. J. Nee," MN, 6 Jan. 1950, B-1; "New J. C. Penney," MN, 11 Aug. 1950, A-1, A-3; "Eig Starts," MN, 22 Sep. 1950, 1; "New Morton's Store," WP, 24 June 1951, 3R; "Silver Spring Hangs," WP, 4 Nov. 1951, 1R; "New Chandler's," MN, 20 Mar. 1953, 1.

110. "Move by Hecht's," WWD, 29 Nov. 1951, 45; "Hecht's Deal," WWD, 5 Dec. 1951, 2. Concerning the additions, see n. 26 above.

111. "Suburban Branches," 43; "Department Stores," 102.

CHAPTER 7. Stores in Shopping Centers

1. Samuel Feinberg, "From Where I Sit," WWD, 23 Mar. 1960, 14, and 25 Mar. 1960, 8. In his opening article (19 Oct. 1959, 1), Feinberg wryly admitted that Steffens had uttered those words to describe his trip to Russia not long after the Revolution.

2. Homer Hoyt, "The Current Trend in New Shopping Centers: Four Different Types," UL 12 (Apr. 1953): 1; "Shopping Centers: A Way to More Sales if You Know How to Use Them," *Tide* 28 (24 Apr. 1954): 21. "The Rise of Shopping Centers," JR 31 (spring 1955): 25. Hoyt repeated his analogy two years later in "The Status of New Suburban Shopping Centers," UL 14 (June 1955): 1.

3. Victor Gruen, "Twelve Check Points," WWD, 28 Dec. 1953, II-35.

4. Concerning Nichols, see Richard Longstreth, "J. C. Nichols, the Country Club Plaza, and Notions of Modernity," *Harvard Architecture Review* 5 (1986): 121–35; William S. Worley, *J. C. Nicholas and the Shaping of Kansas City* (Columbia: University of Missouri Press, 1990), chap. 8; and Robert Pearson and Brad Pearson, *The J. C. Nichols Chronicle* (Kansas City: Country Club Plaza Press, and Lawrence: University Press of Kansas, 1994), esp. 91–106, 123–33. Nichols's own writings are key documents on the subject; see "Planning Shopping Centers," NREJ 8 (22 Mar. 1926): 48–49; "Developing Outlying Shopping Centers," AC 41 (July 1929): 98–101; "A Few Suggestions on Developing Outlying Business Property," NREJ 38 (Apr. 1937): 38–39; and "Mistakes We Have Made in Developing Shopping Centers," ULI 4 (Aug. 1945): whole issue. The importance of Nichols for the next generation of shopping center developers is noted in "Instant Main Street: The Shopping Center Saga," UL 45 (June 1986): 18–19.

5. Richard Longstreth, "The Diffusion of the Community Shopping Center Concept During the Interwar Decades," JSAH 56 (Sep. 1997): 268–93; Longstreth, *City Center to Regional Mall: Architecture, the Automobile and Retailing in Los Angeles, 1920–1950* (Cambridge: MIT Press, 1997), chap. 6 and pp. 185–97; Longstreth, "The Planned Neighborhood Shopping Center in Washington, D.C., 1930–1941," JSAH 51 (Mar. 1992): 268–93; Longstreth, *The Drive-In, the Supermarket, and the Transformation of Commercial Space in Los Angeles, 1914–1941* (Cambridge: MIT Press, 1999), 148–61.

6. "What and Where to Build," RC 20 (Mar. 1952): 7–16; "Warns Traffic," WWD, 8 May 1952, 1, 55; William Snaith, "Beyond the Suburbs," WWD, 10 Sep. 1951, I-82; "Parent Trees," WWD, 5 Feb. 1954, 40; Richard Longstreth, "Silver Spring: Georgia Avenue, Colesville Road, and the Creation of an Alternative 'Downtown' for Metropolitan Washington," in Zeynep Celik et al., eds., *Streets: Critical Perspective on Public Space* (Berkeley: University of California Press, 1994), 251–52; Longstreth, "The Mixed Blessings of Success: The Hecht Company and Department Store Branch Development after World War II," in Carter L. Hudgins and Elizabeth Collins Cromley, eds., *Shaping Communities: Perspectives in Vernacular Architecture*, VI (Knoxville: University of Tennessee Press, 1997), 249.

7. "Parent Trees," WWD, 5 Feb. 1954, 40; "Shopping Centers: A Way to More Sales," 21; "Distribution—The Role of the Department Store," ICSC, 1960, 34–35.

8. The shift is evident in myriad new items contained in major trade periodicals of these years: *Super Market Merchandising, Variety Store Merchandiser,* and *Chain Store Age*. For further discussion, see Longstreth, *Drive-In*, 176–80. "Junior department store" is now an archaic term. Leading companies in this sphere have either gone out of business (W. T. Grant) or expanded into what is now deemed a full-fledged department store (J. C. Penney).

9. "Plan 2 Major," WWD, 6 Sep. 1949, 1, 12; "Emery, Bird to Open," WWD, 15 Feb. 1950, I-2; "Novel Fixtures," WWD, 2 Mar. 1950, 49; "Emery, Bird, Thayer Branch," *Stores* 32 (Apr. 1950): 26–27 (Emery, Bird, Thayer); "Hear Sanger's Negotiating," WWD, 16 Nov. 1949, 2; "Deal Completed," WWD, 22 Dec. 1949, 1, 36 (Sanger's); "Shaker Square Store," WWD, 2 Jan. 1947, 1, 12; "First Unit," WWD, 16 Sep. 1948, 51; "A Branch Store at Shaker Square," *Clevelander* 23 (Sep. 1948): 11; "Branch Store," AF 92 (Feb. 1950): 96–101; Geoffrey Baker and Bruno Funaro, *Shopping Centers: Design and Operation* (New York: Reinhold, 1951), 186–87 (Halle's Shaker Square); "Halle's Opens," *Halle Bulletin* 16 (24 July 1950): 1, 3; "Halle's Open," WWD, 4 Aug. 1950, I-2; "Halle's Cedar-Center," *Halle Bulletin* 16 (14 Aug. 1950), 1 (Halle's Cedar Center). See also Edwin W. Crooks, Jr., "The History of the Halle Bros. Co.," Ph.D. diss., Indiana University, 1959, 284–88. Concerning Highland Park Village and Shaker Square, see Longstreth, "Diffusion," 274–79. A list of branches in shopping centers of all the department store companies studied is contained in Richard Longstreth, comp., "Branch Department Stores, 1910–1960," http://www.departmentstorehistory.net and http://www.preservenet.cornell.edu.

10. "Frederick & Nelson," *Bellevue American,* 27 Sep. 1945, 1; *Bellevue American,* 15 Aug. 1946; "Frederick & Nelson, Seattle," RM 41 (Aug. 1946): 28; "First Suburban Store," DSE 9 (Oct. 1946): 28–29, "Bellevue Shopping Square," *American Builder* 68 (Nov. 1946): 74–77; "Shopping Center," AF 86 (Apr. 1947): 76–78; Baker and Funaro, *Shopping Centers,* 222–31 (Frederick & Nelson); "Edmondson Village," WWD, 28 May 1947, 61; "Hochschild's Suburban Unit," WWD, 4 June 1947, I-14; "Off to the Suburbs!" RM 42 (Aug. 1947): 41; "Edmondson Village," *American Builder* 70 (Feb. 1948): 114–19; Baker and Funaro, *Shopping Centers,* 138–39; W. Edward Orser, *Blockbusting in Baltimore: The Edmondson Village Story* (Lexington: University Press of Kentucky, 1994), 49–57 (Edmondson Village); "Wanamaker's Plans," WWD, 8 June 1950, I-1, I-53; "Wanamaker's Branch," WWD, 12 June 1950, 8; "North Shore Mart," WWD, 7 Aug. 1950, 42; "Selling on a Curve," CSA/AE 26 (Oct. 1950): 49; "Wanamaker's, Great Neck," WWD, 16 May 1951, I-1, I-55; "Hens & Kelly," WWD, 16 June 1950, 2; "New Edwards Store," WWD, 2 Oct. 1951, 7; "Hens & Kelly," WWD, 19 Oct. 1951, 2 (L. B. Smith Plaza).

11. These figures, like many others that I have developed for this chapter, are approximations. I have documented sixteen shopping centers that contained a department store branch or had one constructed on adjacent land between 1946 and 1950; sixty-five between 1951 and 1955. Among these there is a small percentage of stores for which I have been unable to obtain square footage counts. On the other hand, a few shopping centers contained more than one department store branch during the latter period. I have included shopping centers to which a department store was built adjacent, but not as an integral part, since those complexes provided the raison d'etre for that emporium. On the other hand, I have not included departmentalized specialty stores such as Saks Fifth Avenue or I. Magnin when they did not serve as anchor stores in a shopping center. See also "125,000 Sq. Ft. Held," WWD, 4 Apr. 1956, 1, 29.

12. No two definitions of the period for shopping center types are precisely the same. The synopsis presented in the text is derived from what appears to have been the most commonly agreed upon characteristics. See Baker and Funaro, *Shopping Centers,* 10; Hoyt, "Current Trend," 3–4; J. Ross McKeever, "Shopping Centers: Principles and Policies," ULI 20 (July 1953): 6; "Rise of the Shopping Center," 14–15; "Shopping Center Here to Stay," WWD, 27 Dec. 1955, II-6; Paul Smith, *Shopping Center Planning and Management* (New York: National Retail Merchants Association, 1956), 12; Eugene Kelly, *Shopping Centers: Locating Controlled Regional Centers* (Saugautuck, Conn.: Eno Foundation, 1956), 5–7; and J. Ross McKeever, "Shopping Centers Re-Studied: Emerging Patterns and Practical Experiences," ULI 30 (Feb. 1957): I-9–10.

13. Dating is based on the year in which the department store branch (the initial one in the case of dual anchors) opened. Sometimes this was concurrent with the opening of the center, but often at least a portion of the center already existed. On a number of occasions, too, the department store was the first unit to open; many, sometimes all, of the remaining businesses opened weeks, months, or even years later. The number of shopping centers cited is based on those with department stores from the sixty cities studied. Additional examples could be found incorporating department stores based in cities such as Harrisburg, Pennsylvania, and Phoenix, Arizona.

14. For discussion, see Longstreth, *City Center,* 227–38.

15. "A Center's Financial Case History," CSA 30 (May 1954): 27, 87.

16. "Branches for Bloomingdale's," RM 42 (Dec. 1947): 15; "Bloomingdale's Unit," WWD, 24 May 1949, 1, 20; "Fresh Meadows," AR 106 (Dec. 1949): 85–97; Baker and Funaro, *Shopping Centers,* 248–57; and "Suburban Retail Center," WWD, 10 Apr. 1952, 49.

17. "A Case in Contrast in Suburban Stores," UL 11 (Feb. 1952): 3–4 (quote on p. 4); Homer Hoyt, "Impact of Suburban Shopping Centers in September, 1956," UL 15 (Sep. 1956): 3. For background, see Longstreth, "Mixed Blessings," 252–57 and references cited therein.

18. "Kann's Building," *Arlington Sun,* 1 Dec. 1950, 3; "Kann's Branch," WWD, 31 Oct. 1951, 71; "Kann's Opens," ES, 15 Nov. 1951, A-29; McKeever, "Shopping Centers," 50–53, 55.

19. Hoyt, "Impact of Suburban Shopping Centers," 3.

20. "Hear Lansburgh's," WWD, 23 July 1953, 4; "Lansburgh's First," WWD, 8 Sep. 1953, 1, 11; "Lansburgh's New Store," WP, 23 Oct. 1955, L4; *Stores* 37 (Nov. 1955): 48.

21. "Lits, Food Fair," EB, 21 Aug. 1952, 1, 3; "Lit's Branch," WWD, 22 Aug. 1952, 1, 51; "$5 Million Shopping Center," WWD, 1 Sep. 1950, 9; "Lits-Northeast," WWD, 1 Oct. 1952, I-58; "Outward Bound," *Greater Philadelphia Magazine* 41 (Feb. 1954): 36–37, 54–55, 58; "New Lit's Unit," WWD, 17 Feb. 1954, 1, 56 (Lit's); "Branch Sites," WWD, 5 May 1960, 1, 19; "Gimbel's Plans," PI, 6 May 1960, 1, 8; "Castor Avenue," WWD, 13 June 1961, 1, 38; "Gimbel's, Phila.," WWD, 10 Oct. 1961, 18; and "Gimbel's Store Opens," PI, 15 Oct. 1961, B-1 (Gimbel's).

22. "Construction Begun," MLT, 3 Aug. 1950, 1; "Two Retailers," WWD, 2 Dec. 1952, 2; "New Major Branch," WWD, 18 Dec. 1952, 1, 42; "John Wanamaker Will Build," MLT, 27 Aug. 1953, 1, 2; "Bonwit Teller to Establish," MLT, 1 July 1954, 1, 3; "New Big Store," WWD, 17 Dec. 1954, 9; "Contemporary and Tradition Unite in New Wanamaker Store," DW 66 (June 1955): 46–47, 108–9; "Elegance in Suburbia," *Stores* 37 (Dec. 1955): 11–13; "Bonwit's Wynnewood," DW 68 (Mar. 1956): 16–17, 49. The Philadelphia-based Bonwit Teller was an outgrowth of, but continued no affiliation with, its famous New York namesake.

23. In some cases a master plan called for the implementation of

a scheme in phases, but a department store branch was almost always part of the initial phase. In those cases noted in the text, some developers may have hoped eventually to attract a department store, but I have found no evidence in contemporary accounts that such a unit provided a basis for the layout of the complex from the start.

24. "Shirlington Center," *WWD*, 11 Mar. 1957, 12; "$3 Million Unit," *WWD*, 21 Aug. 1957, 1, 47; "Lansburgh Branch," *WWD*, 18 Aug. 1958, I-14 (Shirlington); "Hear Jordan's Plans," *WWD*, 21 Jan. 1957, 1, 36; "New $7 Million," *WWD*, 25 Feb. 1957, 1, 44; "Jordan Starts," *WWD*, 9 Nov. 1959, 1, 37; "Jordan Marsh Opens," *Fort Lauderdale News and Sun Sentinel*, 30 Oct. 1960, 9-D; McKeever, "Shopping Centers Re-Studied," 87–88 (Sunrise); "Emporium Sets," *WWD*, 9 Aug. 1960, 1, 44; "Emporium Opens," *SPP*, 7 Sep. 1961, 1 (Signal Hills); "300,000 Sq. Ft.," *WWD*, 3 June 1959, I-6; "Parmatown's Five-Unit," "Council to Hear," and "An Editorial," *Brooklyn-Parma News*, 17 May 1956, 1; "Parmatown Center," *WWD*, 9 Aug. 1960, 1, 14 (Parmatown); "May Co. Planning," *DP*, 29 Nov. 1953, 1A, 2A; "May Co. Plans," *WWD*, 30 Nov. 1953, 1, 10; "New May Co. Store," *DP*, 27 Sep. 1955, 1, 2; "New May Co. Unit," *WWD*, 28 Sep. 1955, I-1, I-21 (University Hills).

25. Longstreth, *City Center*, 246–48, and references cited therein.

26. Namely at Eastway Plaza (1955–57), Irondequoit Shopping Plaza (1955–57), and South Town Plaza (1957–58). See "Sibley's Will Open," *RDC*, 10 Sep. 1955, 13; "Multi-Million Expansion," *WWD*, 12 Sep. 1955, 1, 36; "Sibley Branch Caters," *RDC*, 28 Aug. 1956, 23 (Eastway); "Sibley's Planning," *WWD*, 12 Dec. 1955, 11; "Sibley's Intends," *WWD*, 28 Mar. 1956, 3; "Sibley's Signs," *RDC*, 12 Oct. 1956, 25; "New Sibley's," *RDC*, 30 Sep. 1957, 16 (Irondequoit); "Sibley's to Add," *RDC*, 4 July 1957, 28; "Sibley's Opens," *RDC*, 4 Mar. 1958, 21 (South Town Plaza).

27. Larry Smith, "Department Store Trends in the Development of Shopping Centers," *UL* 11 (Mar. 1952): 5; "The Chains Want to Know," *CSA/AE* 29 (May 1953): 29. Other examples include L. S. Donaldson Co. (1952–53) at the Miracle Mile Shopping Center (1951–52), Rochester, Minn.; H. C. Capwell Co. (1952–54) at the Broadway Shopping Center in Walnut Creek, Calif.; Gimbel Bros. (1953–54) at Southgate Shopping Center (1950–51), Milwaukee; Snellenbergs (1954–55) at Oregon Avenue Shopping Center (1953–54), Philadelphia; Olds & King (1955–56) at Gateway Shopping Center (1953–54), Portland, Ore.; Halle Bros. (1955–57) at Southland Shopping Center (1954–55), Maple Heights, Ohio; Sanger Bros. (1956–57) at Preston Center Plaza (early 1950s), Dallas; Hens & Kelly (1958–59) at Transittown Plaza (1956–57), Clarence, N.Y.; Kaufman-Straus Co. (1958–59) at Dixie Manor Shopping Center (1954–55), Louisville; Snellenbergs (1959–60) at Lawrence Park Shopping Center (1956–57), Broomall, Pa.; Richards Department Stores (1959–60) at Cutler Ridge Regional Shopping Center (1958–59), Miami; The Fair of Texas (1958–60) at Wynnewood Village Shopping Center (1948–49) and Lochwood Village Shopping Center (1956–57), Dallas; Gilchrist Co. (1960–61) at Redstone Shopping Center (1956–57), Stoneham, Mass.; and Hens & Kelly (1960–61) at Northtown Plaza (1952–53), Amherst, N.Y.

28. "Hecht Branch," *WWD*, 16 Apr. 1953, 1, 52; "Hecht Branch Opens," *WWD*, 14 Sep. 1954, 1, 51; "Initial Expectations," *WWD*, 29 Sep. 1954, 1, 42; McKeever, "Shopping Centers Restudied," 112–13; "The Hecht Store in Northwood," *Stores* 36 (Dec. 1954): 46–49 (Northwood); "Newest Hecht Branch," *WWD*, 25 May 1953, 13; "Hecht Co. Opens," *WWD*, 15 Oct. 1956, I-10 (Edmondson Village); "May Co. Plans," *WWD*, 12 May 1955, 1, 15; "May's Store," *CPD*, 12 May 1955, 1, 10; "May Co. Branch," *CPD*, 3 Feb. 1957, 23-A; "May's on the Heights," *CPD*, 1 Nov. 1957, 33, 38; "A Department Store on Two Levels," *AR* 125 (Apr. 1959): 201–4 (May Co.); "Kaufmann's Buys," *WWD*, 10 Feb. 1959, 1, 52; "Kaufmann's Will Build," *WWD*, 27 Apr. 1959, 33; "Kaufmann's Branch," *Pittsburgh Press*, 5 May 1961, I-7 (Kaufmann's).

29. May Company officials sought to have their San Fernando Valley store (1954–55), which at 452,000 square feet was one of the largest branches ever built, an integral part of Valley Plaza shopping center, whose owner was stymied in assembling sufficient land. A parcel close by was eventually secured by the department store. Thereafter, both parties were eager to cooperate, and Valley Plaza was marketed as if the May Company store was an integral part of the complex. See Longstreth, *City Center*, 263–64.

30. "Plans Progress," *WWD*, 25 Apr. 1951, 10; "Design for Shopping," *NRB* 53 (Mar. 1952): 26–28; "Carson's Plan," *WWD*, 29 July 1952, 1, 31; "Late Mondays," *WWD*, 26 Aug. 1952, 4; "New Fair Unit," *WWD*, 17 Sep. 1952, 62; "First Branch," *WWD*, 4 Dec. 1952, I-1, I-55; "Branch Uses," *WWD*, 30 Jan. 1953, 56; Baker and Funaro, *Shopping Centers*, 118–21; McKeever, "Shopping Centers Restudied," 85–86. Concerning Rubloff, see Miles L. Berger, *They Built Chicago: Entrepreneurs Who Shaped a Great City's Architecture* (Chicago: Bonus, 1992), 271–82.

31. "Parking Shortage," *WWD*, 3 Dec. 1952, 58; Smith, *Shopping Centers*, 68.

32. "Permit Building," *WWD*, 8 Feb. 1951, 1, 10; "Strawbridge & Clothier," *JEE*, 22 Feb. 1951, 1, 4; "Strawbridge's Branch," *WWD*, 21 Aug. 1952, 12; *JEE*, 30 Sep. 1952, Merchandise Mart Sect.; *JEE*, 19 Nov. 1952, Merchandise Mart Sect.

33. "Gimbel Branch," *WWD*, 22 Apr. 1955, 6; "Gimbels Plans," *PP*, 22 Apr. 1955, 6; "North Hills," *PP*, 17 Feb. 1957, I-10; "Gimbels Officially Opens," *PP*, 20 Feb. 1957, 26–29 (North Park); "Famous-Barr to Build," *SLG*, 24 Sep. 1952, 1A; "Famous-Barr Opens," *SLG*, 19 Aug. 1955, 1A, 4A; "Famous-Barr, Northland," *DW* 68 (Feb. 1956): 24–25, 54 (Northland). Concerning DeBartolo, see "Portrait of a Pro," *SCA* 1 (Mar. 1962): 28–30, 50; and "No. 1 Builder of Shopping Malls," *NYT*, 29 Apr. 1973, 167.

34. "Shopping Center," *NYT*, 3 Jan. 1954, VIII-1, VIII-2; "Babylon to Have," *NYT*, 26 Sep. 1954, VIII-1; "Shopping Center Rises," *NYT*, 19 Dec. 1954, VIII-1; "A & S Plans," *WWD*, 16 Nov. 1955, 1, 67; "Babylon Area," *WWD*, 17 Feb. 1956, 1, 40; "A & S to Launch," *WWD*, 25 Sep. 1957, 3; "A & S Babylon," *WWD*, 9 Oct. 1957, 1, 20 (South Bay); "Hutzler's Buys," *WWD*, 16 Oct. 1947, 1; "Major Branch," *WWD*, 19 June 1957, 10; "Oasis in the Suburbs," *AF* 110 (Mar. 1959): 117 (Westview); "Million Crowley Center," *Dearborn Press*, 9 May 1957, 1; "$5 Million Westborn," *Dearborn Press*, 25 Feb. 1959, 1, 17; "Westborn Built," *Dearborn Press*, 25 Feb. 1959, 13–14 (Westborn).

35. Feinberg, "Where I Sit," 21 Dec. 1959, 6. See also "Expansion in Branches," *WWD*, 20 Sep. 1957, 1, 23. Concerning University Plaza, see "Buffalo Store," *WWD*, 23 July 1947, 51; "Adam, Meldrum," *WWD*, 1 Sep. 1949, 8; and "Branch Expansion," *WWD*, 7 Jan. 1959, 1. Subsequent branches were at Airport Plaza in Cheektowaga (1949, adds. 1950s), Sheridan Plaza in Buffalo (1950, adds. 1955 and later), and L. B. Smith Plaza in Lackawanna (1952).

36. "Edwards to Open," *RTU*, 15 Jan. 1960, 1, 21; "Big Grand Opening," *Greece Press*, 6 Oct. 1960, 1; "Edwards Expands," *WWD*, 7 Oct. 1960, 2 (Ridgemont Plaza, Greece); "Edwards Is First," *Brighton-Pittsford Post*, 5 Oct. 1961, 1, 5 (Pittsford Shopping Plaza, Pittsford); "McCurdy's to Build," *RDC*, 14 Apr. 1953, 19; "McCurdy Plans," *WWD*, 15 Apr. 1953, 1, 26; "Plans Completed," *Greece Press*, 15 Oct. 1953, 1, 2; *RDC*, 25 Oct. 1953: 10B–22B (Northgate Plaza, Greece); "McCurdy & Co.," *RTU*, 27 Sep. 1955; "McCurdy's of Geneva," *Geneva Times*, 27 Feb. 1957, 7; McCurdy Opens," *WWD*, 5 Mar. 1957, 11 (Town & Country Plaza, Geneva).

37. "$400,000 Fair Oaks," *Fort Worth Star-Telegram*, 17 Jan.

1951, 1; "First Suburban Branch," WWD, 2 July 1952, 50 (Fair Oaks); "Second Branch," WWD, 16 Sep. 1953, 1, 79; "Says Department Stores," WWD, 19 Oct. 1953, 29 (Fair East Shopping Center, 1952–53); "New Business Center," *Fort Worth Star-Telegram,* 11 Oct. 1953, 15; "Fair, Fort Worth," WWD, 25 Oct. 1954, I-3 (Fair Ridgelea Shopping Center, 1953–54); "Dallas to Get," DMN, 23 Nov. 1958, II-7; "Fair of Texas," *Dallas Times-Herald,* 9 Aug. 1960 (Wynnewood Village and Lochwood Village, Dallas).

38. Namely, branches for J. Bacon at the Youngstown Shopping Center in Jeffersonville, Ind., and Bacon's Shively Shopping Center in Shively, Ky. (both 1955–56); for Kaufman-Straus at the Dixie Manor Shopping Center, Louisville (1959–60); for Castor-Knot at Green Hills Village, Nashville (1954–55), and at Donelson Village, Donelson, Tenn. (1959–61); for B. Lowenstein at Poplar-Highland Plaza, Memphis (1947–49), and at Whitehaven Plaza, Whitehaven, Tenn. (1955–56); for Maison Blanche at the Crescent Airline Shopping Center, New Orleans (1956); for Miller & Rhoads at the Willow Lawn Shopping Center, Richmond (1959–61), and for Macy's at the Mission Shopping Center in Mission, Kansas (1954–56), and The Landing, Kansas City (1959–61).

39. Namely, Joseph Horne branches at the Brentwood-Whitehall Shopping Center, Brentwood, Pa. (1950–51), and at Natrona Heights Plaza, Natrona Heights, Pa. (1954–56); and McAlpin branches at Western Hills Plaza, Bridgetown, Ohio (1954); at Kenwood Plaza, Cincinnati (1955–56); and at Cherry Grove Plaza, Cherry Grove, Ohio (1958–59).

40. See, e.g., "Caution Is Advised," NYT, 1 June 1952, VIII-1, VIII-3; "Will Today's Shopping Centers Succeed?" NRB 54 (Feb. 1953): 22–23; "Too Many Shopping Centers?" WWD, 21 May 1953, 58; "Stores Warned," WWD, 14 Oct. 1953, 1, 71; "Keen Competition," WWD, 15 Jan. 1954, 1, 46; "Emporium Capwell President," WWD, 9 June 1954, I-31; "Shopping Center 'Craze,'" WWD, 28 June 1954, 1, 25; "Shopping Centers: The Boom Raises Problems," ENR 153 (29 July 1954): 21–23; "Shopping Centers: How Many Are Enough?" AF 101 (Aug. 1954): 41–42; "Motorized Customers," WWD, 3 Mar. 1955, 1; "Rise of Shopping Centers," 24–26; "Long Island Told," NYT, 19 July 1956, 37; "Store Over-Expansion," WWD, 10 Oct. 1956, 17; "Shop Center Developers," WWD, 16 Oct. 1956, I-6; "Shopping Center Here," NYT, 21 Oct. 1956, III-1, III-11; "Too Many Shopping Centers?" BW, 17 Nov. 1956, 136–38, 140, 142, 144; "Shopping Centers Still," NYT, 2 Jan. 1957, 54; "Shopping Centers Urged," NYT, 25 Aug. 1957, VIII-1, VIII-5.

41. Quoted in "Shopping Center Boom Poses Problems," *Journal of Commerce,* 1 Oct. 1954, 1, 14; and "Watch Out for Pitfalls," WWD, 15 Feb. 1955, 27.

42. For a brief account of the organization, see "Historical Timeline," http://www.icsc.org/srch/about/icschist.php.

43. Thomas W. Hanchett, "U.S. Tax Policy and the Shopping-Center Boom of the 1950s and 1960s," *American Historical Review* 101 (Oct. 1996): 1082–110. Hanchett's exceptional research makes a conclusive argument, but the impact of shopping center development was varied, as discussed in Chapter 8.

44. "Shopping Centers," NYT, 29 June 1958, VIII-1, VIII-10; quote on p. 1. Concerning DeBartolo, see "Portrait of a Pro," 28, 50. His company's holdings as of 1961 were gleaned from the *Directory of Shopping Centers in the United States and Canada* (Chicago: National Research Bureau, 1961).

45. Rubloff was among the early advocates to write about the regional mall as a corrective agent to the overbuilding of shopping centers; see Arthur Rubloff, "Regional Shopping Centers and Their Effect on the Future of Our Cities," *American Planning and Civic Annual,* 1953, 45–49. See also "Financing Seen," WWD, 18 Sep. 1957, I-1, I-71; and "Developer Sees," WWD, 30 Apr. 1959, 9.

CHAPTER 8. Stores Make the Mall

1. Sidney Nichols Shurcliff, *The Day It Rained Fish and Other Encounters of a Landscape Architect* (By the author, 1978), 161–62. Shurcliff's views are evident in this and the previous chapter of his memoir, both of which are devoted to Shoppers' World. At the time of its completion, however, he was eager to capitalize professionally on the national publicity the project received; see Sidney N. Shurcliff, "Shoppers' World: The Design and Construction of a Retail Shopping Center," *Landscape Architecture* 42 (July 1952): 144–51.

2. "Department Stores: Race for the Suburbs," *Fortune* 44 (Dec. 1951): 164; obituary, NYT, 20 Oct. 1962, 25.

3. "Await Information," BET, 28 Oct. 1946, 1, 8; "$2,500,000 Trading Center," BET, 29 Oct. 1946, 1, 3; "$2,500,000 Business," WWD, 30 Oct. 1946, 4; "For Easy Shopping," BW, 9 Nov. 1946, 24, 26; "'Recentralization,'" WWD, 20 Nov. 1946, 71.

4. "Department Stores," 164. For background on Welch, see "Shoppers' World," AF 95 (Dec. 1951): 184; "Aerial Study," OWH, 23 Oct. 1955, 2-J; and material in Baldwin Memorial Files, American Institute of Architects Archives, Washington, D.C.

5. Right after the North Shore Center was announced, Welch began to publish his ideas in a spectrum of retail, architectural, planning, and other periodicals, to the point where he emerged as the leading advocate of the regional shopping center during the immediate postwar years. See, e.g., "Suggests Planned," WWD, 14 Nov. 1946, I-6; "Convenience vs. Shopping Goods," WWD, 26 Dec. 1946, II-82, II-96; "Regional Shopping Centers," JAPA 14 (fall 1948): 4–9; "The Relocation of Commercial Areas," *Planning,* 1948, 101–10; AJ 17 (Jan. 1949): 45–52; "More Modern," WWD, 6 Apr. 1949, 52; "Regional Shopping Centers," AR 109 (Mar. 1951): 121–31; and "Location and Design of Shopping Centers," *American Planning and Civic Annual,* 1951, 131–39.

6. For background, see "The Modernist from Wainscott: Morris Ketchum, Jr.," AF 81 (Aug. 1944): 63–64; "Shopping Center Districts," *Planning* (Chicago: American Society of Planning Officials, 1953), 111–14; and material in Baldwin Memorial Files, American Institute of Architects Archives, Washington, D.C. Ketchum wrote one of the standard texts on retail design of the period, *Shops & Stores* (New York: Reinhold, 1948; rev. 1957), and his firm designed several prominent department store branches, including ones for Hutzler's and Davison-Paxon.

7. "Architectural Staffs," BET, 23 Nov. 1946, 1, 5; "$6-Million," BET, 9 June 1947, 1, 3; "Shopping Center," AF 86 (June 1947): 84–93; "The North Shore Shopping Center," AC 62 (July 1947): 124–25; Morris Ketchum, Jr., "Regaining Advantages," CSA/AE 23 (July 1947): 16–17; "Ultimate Success," BET, 10 Mar. 1948, 1, 5; "Recentralization Is Growing!" RM 43 (Apr.–May 1948): 32–37; "Beverly Shopping Center," WWD, 27 Dec. 1948, I-4; "N. Beverly, Mass.," WWD, 20 Mar. 1953, 51; WWD, 1 Apr. 1953, 62; "Plans Abandoned," BET, 19 Nov. 1954, 1, 6.

8. To create a multistate network of regional malls, Rawls formed a new company, National Suburban Centers, in addition to forming the Middlesex Trust to build Shoppers' World. In 1948 and 1949 National Suburban Centers announced plans for similar complexes in Paramus and Livingston, New Jersey; Harrison and later White Plains, New York; and Cleveland, none of which was realized. See "Mammoth New Shopping Center," AC 64 (Feb. 1949): 78–79; "Back Huge Store Center," CPD, 30 July 1949, 2; "Trust Rides Shopping Center Boom," BW, 22 July 1950, 80–81, 84; and "Shopping Center," NYT, 9 May 1951, 35.

9. "Plan New Mass.," WWD, 7 Jan. 1948, 8; "Work on Shopping Center," FN, 17 Feb. 1948, 1, 2; "Middlesex Trust Plans," FN, 20 Feb. 1948, 7.

10. "Filene's Plans," *BG*, 23 Jan. 1949, 24; "New Unit," *WWD*, 24 Jan. 1949, 4.

11. "Jordan's Deal," *WWD*, 10 Mar. 1948, 1, 60; "Jordan Marsh Co.," *FN*, 10 Mar. 1948, 1, 12; "Shoppers' World," *FN*, 4 Oct. 1951, 1; "$8 Million Store," *WWD*, 4 Oct. 1951, 2; "What's New About the New Shopping Centers?" *PRI* 237 (Nov. 1951): 37–39, 72, 74, 76, 79; "Shoppers' World at Framingham Applies New Ideas," *AR* 110 (Nov. 1951): 12–13; "Shoppers' World," *AF* 95 (Dec. 1951): 180–85; "Retailing Booms in the Outskirts," *Steel Construction Digest* 9 (Jan. 1952): 8–9; Shurcliff, "Shoppers' World"; "Sports-Field-Type Floodlighting," *AC* 67 (Aug. 1952): 163; "Shoppers' World," *WWD*, 29 Dec. 1952, II-32; "Can You Top This?" *Steelways* 9 (Apr. 1953): 31; "Shopping for Tomorrow," *Coronet* 34 (Oct. 1953): 30–33; Eugene J. Kelley, *Shopping Centers: Locating Controlled Regional Centers* (Saugatuck, Conn.: Eno Foundation, 1956), chap. 10; Samuel Feinberg, "From Where I Sit," *WWD*, 9 Dec. 1959, 8. (The last citation is one in a 110-part series on shopping centers, to which the author devoted his column from 19 October 1959 to 23 March 1960. Subsequent references abbreviate author and title but give the date of the cited installment.) For a recent account, see Kathleen Kelly Broomer, "Shoppers' World and the Regional Shopping Center in Greater Boston," *Society for Commercial Archeology Journal* 13 (fall–winter 1994–95): 2–9.

12. "Gilchrist's of Boston," *FN*, 10 Mar. 1948, 1; "New Suburban Unit," *WWD*, 5 Feb. 1951, 2.

13. "New Plan," *WWD*, 13 July 1953, 14; "Hearing Today," *WWD*, 14 Jan. 1954, 4; "Center in a Fix," *BW*, 23 Jan. 1954, 51–52; "Other Centers Can Learn," *WWD*, 10 Feb. 1954, 71; "Shoppers' World, National Pioneer," *AF* 100 (Feb. 1954): 37; "Court Confirms," *WWD*, 24 Jan. 1956, 6; "Dilemma at Framingham," *Tide* 28 (24 Apr. 1954): 22; "Allied Stores Negotiating," *WWD*, 12 July 1956, 1; "Shop Center Trend," *WWD*, 16 July 1956, 1, 21; "Shoppers' World Tenants," *WWD*, 24 July 1956, 1, 47; "Filene's Seen Sure," *WWD*, 26 July 1956, 6; "Framingham Center Bought," *WWD*, 28 June 1957, 1, 7; Feinberg, "Where I Sit," 5 Nov. 1959, 51; "Shoppers' World," *WWD*, 24 July 1962, 36.

14. "Peabody May Have," *PT*, 2 Dec. 1954, 1; "Jordan Marsh Sets," *WWD*, 15 Dec. 1954, 1, 67; "Times Prediction," *PT*, 16 Dec. 1954, 1, 6; "Latest Rumors," *PT*, 20 Jan. 1955, 1; "Peabody OK's," *WWD*, 7 Mar. 1955, 11; "Filene-Jordan Rivalry," *WWD*, 12 Aug. 1955, 1, 28. Concerning Filene's aborted project at the Townlyne Shopping Center, see n. 46 below.

15. "Largest Filene Branch," *WWD*, 17 Sep. 1957, 1, 30; "Filene's in Peabody," *PT*, 19 Sep. 1957, 1, 8; "Allied Center's Sales," *WWD*, 2 May 1958, 6; "Specially Designed," *WWD*, 25 July 1958, 2; "Jordan Marsh Opens," *PT*, 31 July 1958, 2; Feinberg, "Where I Sit," 14 Dec. 1959, I-10, I-27.

16. See, e.g., "Shopping Centers—The Pattern of the Future," *PRI* 230 (23 June 1950): 34–36, 40–41, 44; "The Marketing Revolution III: One-Stop Shopping Is Making Some Radical Changes in Old Patterns," *Tide* 26 (26 Sep. 1952): 36–39; "Planned Postwar Shopping Centers Come Big," *BW*, 11 Oct. 1952, 124–25; "Boomtown on the Byways," *Time* 62 (20 July 1953): 72–73; "Shopping Centers: A Way to More Sales if You Know How to Use Them," *Tide* 28 (24 Apr. 1954): 21–23; and "Regional Shopping Grows Fast," *PRI* 247 (14 May 1954): 37–39, 74–75. For a list that includes branches in regional malls of all the department stores studied, see Richard Longstreth, comp., "Department Store Branches, 1910–1960," at http://www.departmentstorehistory.net and http://www.preservenet.cornell.edu.

17. "Shopping Centers . . . Story of 3 New Giants," *DSE* 17 (July 1954): 41; Welton Becket, "Parking Poses Perennial Problem," *CSA/VS* 27 (July 1951): 186.

18. See also Richard Longstreth, *City Center to Regional Mall: Architecture, the Automobile, and Retailing in Los Angeles, 1920–1950* (Cambridge: MIT Press, 1997), 286–304.

19. Welch took pride in this early venture, as he used it in accounts of his career given to the press in the 1950s; see, e.g., "Aerial Study." For background on Strawbridge's and Suburban Square see Richard Longstreth, "Diffusion of the Community Shopping Center Concept During the Interwar Decades," *JSAH* 56 (Sep. 1997): 279–83.

20. Homer Hoyt, "Impact of Suburban Shopping Centers," *UL* 15 (Sep. 1956): 6; "The Future of Regional Shopping Centers," *Stores* 40 (Jan. 1958): 14.

21. Quoted in "Shopping Centers: A Way to More Sales," 22. The most detailed account of the complex's development is Meredith L. Clausen, "Northgate Regional Shopping Center—Paradigm from the Provinces," *JSAH* 43 (May 1984): 144–61. Contemporary writings include "Bon Marche," *WWD*, 24 Feb. 1948, I-1, I-63; "Shopping Center for Suburban Seattle," *Stores* 30 (Sep. 1948): 42; "Bon Marche," *WWD*, 24 Dec. 1948, 1, 24; "Expect Seattle," *WWD*, 18 Jan. 1950, 5; "Suburb Unlimited," *Time*, 8 May 1950, 83–84; "Display Is Different at the Bon Marche-Northgate," *DW* 57 (July 1950): 26–27, 84; "New Bon Marche," *WWD*, 9 Aug. 1950, 54; "Northgate—Suburban Shopping Center," *A&E* 182 (Sep. 1950): 14–19, 21; and "Northgate," *WWD*, 23 Jan. 1953, 52. See also Feinberg, "Where I Sit," 22 Oct. 1959, 8, 22. Kelley, *Shopping Centers*, 129.

23. Quoted in "Shopping Centers and a Way to More Sales," 22. See also "The Marketing Revolution," 36–39; B. Earl Puckett, "Planned Growth for Retailing," *Stores* 38 (Jan. 1956): 9–12, 51–52. Concerning the shopping centers, see "Allied Plans," *WWD*, 21 Jan. 1953, 1, 71; "Allied Planning," *WWD*, 20 July 1953, 1, 7; "Allied to Build," *WWD*, 6 Aug. 1953, 1, 42; "Allied Units," *WWD*, 13 Jan. 1955, 1, 74; "10 Shopping Centers," *NYT*, 13 Jan. 1955, 37, 39; and "The Super Centers," *Time*, 24 Jan. 1955, 82.

24. "Coast May Co.," *WWD*, 29 June 1950, 1, 48; "Work Started," *SBC* 116 (27 Oct. 1950): 30–31 (Lakewood); "Sign Emporium Lease," *WWD*, 12 Jan. 1950, I-1, I-67; "Plan Full-Scale," *WWD*, 13 Apr. 1950, 4 (Stonestown); "Field's Plans," *WWD*, 7 Aug. 1950, 1, 43 (Old Orchard); "J. L. Hudson to Build," *DFP*, 4 June 1950, 1, 10; "Hudson's First Branch," *WWD*, 5 June 1950, 1, 50 (Eastland); "Hudson's Plans Confirmed," *WWD*, 9 Oct. 1950, 1, 42 (Northland). Wanamaker's announced plans to build a shopping center in Yonkers in 1947 ("Councilmen Told," *Herald Statesman* [Yonkers], 10 Dec. 1947, 1, 2). A design for the mall was developed ca. 1950 (Geoffrey Baker and Bruno Funaro, *Shopping Centers: Design and Construction* [New York: Reinhold, 1951], 172–73), but the scheme does not seem to have been finalized until some three years later ("Wanamaker Branch," *NYT*, 24 May 1953, VIII-12; "$30,000,000 Yonkers," *NYT*, 2 July 1953, 1, 14). The complex did not open until 1957. Similarly long periods of gestation occurred at Eastland, which opened that same year, and Old Orchard, which opened the year previous.

25. "Shopping Centers . . . Story of 3 New Giants," 41.

26. For background, see Larry Smith, "Department Store Trends in the Development of Shopping Centers," *UL* 11 (Mar. 1952): 1, 3–6; "Shopping Center Trends," *CSA/VE* 34 (May 1958): 144; and Feinberg, "Where I Sit," 3 Dec. 1959, 14.

27. "Shop Center Construction," *WWD*, 15 Oct. 1956, 1, 14; "May Co. Likes," *SDU*, 19 Nov. 1959, a8. See also "Shopping Center Trends," 144.

28. "Field's Plans Set," *WWD*, 7 Mar. 1952, 7; "Report Field's," *WWD*, 11 Dec. 1953, 8; "Field's Plans," *WWD*, 16 Dec. 1953, 4.

29. "Shop Center Construction," 14; "Stores Eye," *WWD*, 5 Dec. 1956, 1, 8.

30. "Emporium Capwell President," *WWD*, 9 June 1954, I-32;

"Shopping Centers Enjoy," *WSJ*, 8 Apr. 1959, 26; Feinberg, "Where I Sit," 2 Dec. 1959, 8.

31. Concerning Cherry Creek and Buell, see "Sketch of Proposed," *DP*, 9 Nov. 1950, 47; "Denver Dry Goods," *WWD*, 26 Dec. 1950, 1, 43; and Diane Wilk Shirvani, "A Century of Exploration in Civic Architecture: Temple Hoyne Buell," *Avant Garde,* Journal of the School of Architecture and Planning, University of Colorado at Denver, 1 (winter 1989): 10–31. Buell's later claim that Cherry Creek was the first regional mall in the country was unfounded. Counting the opening of the department store as the completion date, it was the sixth, but some time had elapsed before the complex approached completion. It does not seem to have had a detailed master plan at the outset, and it received relatively little coverage in trade literature of the period. Concerning Lakeside and von Frellick, see "Denver Dry Sets," *DP,* 6 Mar. 1955, 1A, 22A; and "Plans Underway," *DP,* 29 Aug. 1956, 46. Concerning Roosevelt Field and Webb & Knapp, see "New History for Old," *Time* 63 (16 July 1956): 80–81; "Plan Stores," *WWD,* 8 Aug. 1950, 8; "Macy's Roosevelt Field," *WWD,* 10 Nov. 1953, 1, 60. Concerning 7 Corners and Kass, see "Woodward's Third Branch," *WWD,* 18 Oct. 1954, 8; and "7 Corners Builder," *WP,* 3 Oct. 1956, 42. Early plans for 7 Corners called for a mall configuration (*WP,* 24 May 1953, 7B); however, the design was subsequently modified because of the irregular topography. Concerning Hillsdale and Bohannon, see "Bohannon Building Team," *AF* 82 (June 1945): 133–36, 138, 142, 146; David D. Bohannon, "Look Out for Those Shopping Centers!" *AC* 65 (Dec. 1950): 114–15; "Macy's to Have," *San Mateo Times,* 28 May 1952, 1, 4; "New Macy Store," and "One of Nation's," *San Mateo Times,* 18 Nov. 1954, 1A, 2A.

32. Concerning Mid-Island Plaza, see "Builders Enlarge," *NYT,* 4 Oct. 1953, VIII-8; "Gertz to Build," *WWD,* 17 Mar. 1955, 1, 40; and "Shopping Marts Get," *NYT,* 30 Sep. 1956, VIII-1, VIII-14. Concerning Swifton Center, see "Rollman Leases," *CE,* 21 July 1953, 1; and "Retail 'City Within City,'" *CE,* 24 Oct. 1956, Swifton Center Sect., 7. Concerning Plaza de Las Palmas, see "Pletz Developed," *SAE,* 17 Mar. 1957, 4-B.

33. Concerning Westgate, see "Halle's Plans," *WWD,* 30 July 1951, 1; and "5,000 Expected," *Lakewood Post* [Ohio], 26 Mar. 1954, 11. Concerning Cross County and Atlas, see "$30,000,000 Yonkers"; "Shopping Center Set," *NYT,* 29 July 1956, VIII-8; and "British Purchase," *NYT,* 14 Jan. 1960, 55. Concerning Gulfgate, Northline, and Berenson, see "Gulfgate Gets," *HP,* 21 Mar. 1954, I-1, I-15; "Texas Size," *NYT,* 21 Sep. 1956, 33; "Northline Shopping City," *HP,* 8 Aug. 1960, I-1, I-5; and "Three Businessmen," *HP,* 14 Mar. 1963, IX-2. Concerning Ayres, see "130,000 Sq. Ft.," *WWD,* 25 Mar. 1954, 1, 44; and "Ayres Plans," *IS,* 25 Mar. 1954, 12. Concerning Oakbrook, see "Suburb Shop Center," *CT,* 7 June 1960, D5; "Oakbrook Bows," *WWD,* 2 Mar. 1962, 1, 6; "Big Oakbrook," *CT,* 4 Mar. 1962, 28; and Miles L. Berger, *They Built Chicago: Entrepreneurs Who Shaped a Great City's Architecture* (Chicago: Bonus, 1992), 219–32. Concerning Mayfair, see "Field, Gimbel," *WWD,* 7 Apr. 1953, 1, 51; and "Mayfair Dream," *MS,* 1 Aug. 1960, MX-4. Earlier Froedtert developed Southgate Shopping Center (1950–51), to which Gimbel's added a large branch in 1953–54. Concerning the Tri-County Center, see "$24 Million Tag," *CE,* 18 Dec. 1955, I-1; "Shillito's and Pogue's," *CE,* 1 Feb. 1959, 1A, 8A; and "Tri-County Developer," *CE,* 25 Sep. 1960, III-2.

34. "Emporium Unit," *WWD,* 25 Mar. 1954, 2; "Stanford Builds," *NYT,* 28 Nov. 1954, 43 (Stanford Shopping Center); "32 Million Center," *AJ,* 12 May 1957, 1-A, 6-A; "Rich's Joining," *WWD,* 13 May 1957, 1, 37; "Charity Funds," *WWD,* 10 Aug. 1959, 1, 24 (Lenox Square); "Woodward & Lothrop Plans," *WP,* 27 Mar. 1958, B8; *ES,* 30 Nov. 1958, A-22; "Wheaton Plaza," *ES,* 30 Mar. 1960, H-2; "Business Team," *Washington Daily News,* 6 Apr. 1960, 56 (Wheaton Plaza).

35. Concerning Hoyt, see "Homer Hoyt," *NYT,* 1 Dec. 1984, 28. Concerning Smith, see "Editor's Note," *UL* 11 (Mar. 1952): 1. In 1970, the former issued a compendium of his writings, comprising over 850 pages: *According to Hoyt: 53 Years of Homer Hoyt, Articles on Law, Real Estate Cycle, Economic Base, Sector Theory, Shopping Centers, Urban Growth, 1916–1969.*

36. A good sense of the growth in the complexity of this process can be gleaned from sequential publications by the Urban Land Institute. See Homer Hoyt, "Market Analysis of Shopping Centers," *ULI* 12 (Oct. 1949): whole issue; J. Ross McKeever, "Shopping Centers: Principles and Policies," *ULI* 20 (July 1953): 11–16; J. Ross McKeever, "Shopping Centers Re-Studies," *ULI* 30 (Feb. 1957): 19–34, 43–51; and *The Community Builders Handbook* (Washington, D.C.: Urban Land Institute, 1954 and 1960), sect. 2. See also "Pitfalls Stressed," *NYT,* 26 Aug. 1951, R4; Victor Gruen and Lawrence P. Smith, "Shopping Centers: The New Building Type," *PA* 33 (June 1952): 79–90; "Shopping Center Requires," *WWD,* 20 Nov. 1953, 42; "The Planned Shopping Center," *CSA/AE* 30 (May 1954): 13–19; "The Rise of the Shopping Center," *JR* 31 (spring 1955): 17–24; Larry Smith, "Analyzing the Shopping Center Market," *UL* 16 (Jan. 1957): 1, 3–8; "Public Policy and the Outlying Shopping Center," *JAPA* 24:4 (1958): 215–22; Paul E. Smith, *Shopping Centers: Planning and Management* (New York: National Retail Merchants Association, 1958), 24–33; and Victor Gruen and Larry Smith, *Shopping Towns USA: The Planning of Shopping Centers* (New York: Reinhold, 1960).

37. See, e.g., "Where Do Customers?" *WWD,* 13 Sep. 1957, 1, 45. Insightful social analysis of the regional mall during the period is afforded by Lizebeth Cohen, "From Town Center to Shopping Center: The Reconfiguration of Commercial Marketplaces in Postwar America," *American Historical Review* 101 (Oct. 1996): 1050–81; and by Cohen, *A Consumers' Republic: The Politics of Mass Consumption in Postwar America* (New York: Alfred A. Knopf, 2003), chap. 6. Contemporary accounts stress past and future growth of areas chosen for regional mall development. Field trips to most of those areas taken over the past decade confirm the nature of housing stock from the period.

38. "Work Started on Large Shopping Center," *SWBC* 116 (27 Oct. 1950): 30–31; "Shopping Center," *NYT,* 9 Jan. 1955, VIII-1.

39. "Stores Do $88 Million," *WWD,* 19 Mar. 1956, 1; "Three Successful Shopping Centers," *AF* 167 (Oct. 1957): 112 (Northland); "Shopping Centers," *WWD,* 12 Nov. 1952, 118; "Winter or Summer," *AF* 98 (Mar. 1953): 132–33; *MT,* 7 Oct. 1956, Southdale Sect., 19; "Southdale Shopping Center: An Investment in Good Planning," *Building* 58 (Oct. 1958): 37; M. Jeffrey Hardwick, *Mall Maker: Victor Gruen, Architect of an American Dream* (Philadelphia: University of Pennsylvania Press, 2004), 154–56 (Southdale). See also "Shopping Centers Need," *WWD,* 12 Nov. 1952, 113; "From Joe's Hot Dog Stand to a Regional Shopping Center," *AC* 68 (Apr. 1953): 98–99; "Shop Centers Held," *WWD,* 18 Apr. 1957, I-8. Though the acreage around Northland and Southdale developed in ways that were somewhat different from those envisioned in the master plans, the basic objective of having complementary functions was consummated. At the same time, these precincts were a far cry from the traditional town center, since all components were laid out to accommodate motorists.

40. "Shopping Centers: An Analysis," *ULI* 11 (July 1949): 42–43; "Community Builders' Council," *UL* 9 (Dec. 1950): 3; Becket, "Parking Poses Perennial Problem," 186, 210; "Will Today's Shopping Centers Succeed?" *NRB* 54 (Feb. 1953): 27–29; J. Ross McKeever,

"Shopping Centers: Principles and Tested Policies," ULI 20 (July 1953): 20–23. See also "Parking Needs in the Development of Shopping Centers," *Traffic Quarterly* 5 (Jan. 1951): 32–37; "Planning Suburban Shopping Centers," *Appraisal Bulletin* 20 (28 Feb. 1951): 90–105; "Retail Shopping Centers," WWD, 8 Aug. 1951, 54; "Three to One," WWD, 14 Aug. 1953, 44; "Shopping Centers," AR 114 (Oct. 1953): 192–97; "Parking Points That Make the Difference," CSA 30 (May 1954): 20–25; "Both Quality and Quantity Are Vital to Good Parking," CSA/VE 33 (May 1957): 188–90; Feinberg, "Where I Sit," 16 Nov. 1959, 10. The matter was continually restudied; see, e.g., "Parking Requirements for Shopping Centers," ULI 53 (1965): whole issue.

41. "Marshall Field's New Shopping Center," AF 95 (Dec. 1951): 186.
42. "Three Successful," 112.
43. "Traffic Planning Opportunities in Shopping-Center Design," *Traffic Quarterly* 5 (Oct. 1951): 383–92.
44. Kelley, *Shopping Centers*, 106–7; "Roosevelt Field Gets," *Garden City Times*, 21 Apr. 1955, 1; "Three Shopping Areas," NYT, 5 July 1956, 27; HP, 20 Sep. 1956, VII-1; HP, 21 Sep. 1956, 1; "Tri-County Center," CE, 25 Sep. 1960, J-5. See also "Shopping Center Trends," 144; and Feinberg, "Where I Sit," 16 Dec. 1959, 10.
45. "Shopping Center," NYT, 21 Oct. 1956, III-11. "Shopping Center Trends," 144; "Shopping Centers Fed," WWD, 8 Apr. 1959, 22.
46. The Townlyne debate was covered in PT between 26 Mar. 1948 and 8 July 1949; the Lexington controversy in the *Lexington Minuteman* from 18 Apr. to 5 Dec. 1957.
47. As covered in the *Garden City News* between 20 May 1954 and 17 Mar. 1955.
48. "May Co. Wins," WWD, 11 June 1958, 1, 90; "May Co. Meeting," WWD, 15 July 1958, 42; "Steering Group Named," WWD, 18 July 1958, 1, 22; "San Diego D.A.," WWD, 24 July 1958, 6; and in SDU from 26 Mar. to 10 Oct. 1958.
49. Hoyt, "Impact of Suburban Shopping Centers," 6; "What Next in Shopping Centers?" AF 112 (Apr. 1960): 129.
50. "Initial Profit," WWD, 19 May 1960, 1, 61. Concerning options for financing, see "A New Look at Shopping Centers," UL 13 (May 1954): 4–5.
51. Thomas W. Hanchett, "Financing Suburbia: Prudential Insurance and the Post–World War II Transformation of the American City," *Journal of Urban History* 26 (Mar. 2000): esp. 314–15, 319–20; "Suburban Developments—Capital Investment Opportunities," RC 23 (Dec. 1954): 10–11. See also "Shop Center," WWD, 13 Nov. 1957, 6; Feinberg, "Where I Sit," 24 Nov. 1959, 12; 27 Nov. 1959, 32; 30 Nov. 1959, 6, 28; and Carlson, "What Next?" 129–31, 236.
52. "A Center's Financial Case History," CSA 30 (May 1954): 27.
53. The list of companies I have compiled from contemporary accounts of shopping centers is by no means complete but it is revealing. It includes Connecticut General, Connecticut Mutual, Equitable, John Hancock, Massachusetts Mutual, Metropolitan Life, Nationwide, New England Mutual, New York Life, Northwestern Mutual, Pacific Mutual, and Prudential. Contemporary accounts include Hoyt, "Impact of Suburban Shopping Centers," 6; and "Shop Center Developers," WWD, 16 Oct. 1956, 6. For case studies, see "Faith in Future," *Montgomery [Ala.] Advertiser*, 9 Sep. 1954, 13-F; "Financing Completed," NYT, 7 Sep. 1956, 31; and "Wheaton Plaza Loan," ES, 20 May 1960, B-6. At least one regional mall, Monmouth Shopping Center (1958–60), was developed by an insurance company, Massachusetts Mutual. See "One of Country's Oldest," *Long Branch Daily Record*, 29 Feb. 1960, 18.
54. "Shopping Centers Move Ahead," ICSC, 1961, 3. See also "Small Store Advantages," WWD, 15 Oct. 1956, I-29; "Centers Seen," WWD, 5 June 1957, 1, 83; "Future of Regional Shopping Centers," 15; Feinberg, "Where I Sit," 25 Nov. 1959, 14. The same held true for community shopping centers as well; see "Columbus Discovers," WWD, 18 Feb. 1953, 58.
55. "Independents Lost," WWD, 19 Oct. 1956, 1, 29; "Centers Hurt," WWD, 1 Oct. 1957, 1, 54; "Shop Center Bias," WWD, 10 Mar. 1959, 1, 47; "Keynote Address," ICSC, 1959, 11; "Shop Center Bar," WWD, 28 Apr. 1959, 1, 49; "Centers in High Gear," CSA/VE 35 (May 1959): E34; "U.S. Small Store," WWD, 28 Sep. 1959, I-1, 8; "SBA Plan," WWD, 22 Aug. 1960, 1, 17; "SBA Clarifies," WWD, 25 Aug. 1960, 1, 39; "SBA Plan," WWD, 29 Aug. 1960, 7; "SBA Hopes," WWD, 6 Apr. 1961, 11; "New SBA Aid," WWD, 22 June 1961, 1, 10; "Small Concern," WSJ, 19 Dec. 1961, 30.
56. "Expansion Is Termed," WWD, 1 Sep. 1957, 1, 40; "A Variety Chain's Experience in Shopping Centers," ICSC, 1959, 74–77; Feinberg, "Where I Sit," 25 Nov. 1959, 14; Homer Hoyt, "The Status of Shopping Centers in the United States," UL 19 (Oct. 1960): 4–5.
57. "Shopping Centers in the '60s," ICSC, 1960, 6. See also "Independents Lost," 1, 29.
58. Feinberg, "Where I Sit," 18 Nov. 1959, 20; "Shopping Center Tenants," WWD, 7 July 1952, 51.
59. "Shopping Centers," NYT, 18 July 1956, 35; "Promotion Duties," WWD, 14 Oct. 1957, 1, 31; "Promotion Stressed," WWD, 16 Oct. 1957, 1, 59; "New Competition," NYT, 13 Nov. 1958, 57; Smith, *Shopping Centers*, 83–89; "Merchants Associations," ICSC, 1959, 119–32; Feinberg, "Where I Sit," 19 Nov. 1959, 8; 20 Nov. 1959, 6; 15 Dec. 1959, 15; "Merchants Associations in Shopping Centers," ICSC, 1962, 129–30.
60. "The Chain Faces Special Problems," CSA/AE, 34–37; "Centers Seen," 83; "In-Center Liaison," WWD, 10 July 1957, 1, 82; "Shopping Centers . . . Still Going Strong," CSA/VE 33 (May 1957): 171; "Promotions Pay Profits in Shopping Centers," *Journal of Property Management* 23 (Dec. 1957): 98–100; "Centers in High Gear," E36; "Shopping Centers Hotter Than Ever," CSA/VE 36 (May 1960): E27; "Lack of Big Chain Aid," WWD, 18 Oct. 1960, 1, 51.
61. "The Chain Wants to Know," CSA/AE 29 (May 1953): 29; "Shopping Centers Revisited," WWD, 28 Dec. 1953, 30–31; "Shopping Centers: The Boom Raises Problems," ENR 153 (29 July 1954): 22; "Some Big Stores," WWD, 15 May 1957, 1, 83; "Dangers in Shopping Center Leasing Today," *Journal of Property Management* 23 (Dec. 1957): 103–5; "Split Rate Plan," WWD, 26 Feb. 1958, I-1, I-15; "Atlas Assails," WWD, 28 Feb. 1958, 1, 29; "Big Stores Advised," WWD, 23 Apr. 1959, 8; "Shortcomings of Big Stores," WWD, 9 Apr. 1959, 1, 62. For a differing view, see Larry Smith, "Analyzing the Shopping Center Market," UL 16 (Jan. 1957): 7.
62. Smith, *Shopping Centers*, 34–35; Hoyt, "Impact of Surburban Shopping Centers," 1.
63. "$30,000,000 Yonkers"; "Gimbel-Wanamaker Project," WWD, 3 July 1953, 1, 26; "Gimbel Branch," WWD, 8 July 1953, 1, 13; "New Branch," NYT, 10 Jan. 1954, VIII-1 (Cross County). "The Fair to Have," WWD, 12 Jan. 1955, 30 (Old Orchard).
64. Interviews with Eaton Ballard, former senior vice president of Carter Hawley Hale, Pasadena, Calif., 14 Nov. 1989; and R. Dean Wolfe, then executive vice president, May Department Stores Company, St. Louis, 17 Mar. 1999.
65. The intention to have a second major department store at Garden State Plaza is noted in "Bamberger Plans," NYT, 25 May 1957, VIII-1, 7. Concerning the negotiations, see "Macy's to Develop," NYT, 7 Aug. 1953, 23; "R. H. Macy to Build," WWD, 5 Feb. 1954, 1, 39; and "The Suburb That Macy's Built," *Fortune* 61 (Feb. 1960): 196. See also "Macy-Allied," WWD, 21 Sep. 1954, 1, 56; "North Jersey," WWD, 16 Nov. 1955, 1, 67; "Ample Trade" NYT, 29 July 1956, III-1, III-7; Smith, "Analyzing the Shopping Center," 4; and Fein-

berg, "Where I Sit," 19 Feb. 1960, 8; 23 Feb. 1960, 10; 24 Feb. 1960, 12.

66. Interview with George G. Rinder, former executive vice president, Marshall Field & Co., Burr Ridge, Ill., 4 Nov. 1999; Hoyt, "Impact of Suburban Shopping Centers," 3. Concerning Edens Plaza, see "Hear Carson's," WWD, 13 Oct. 1950, 1, 47; "Details Given," WWD, 6 May 1953, I-1, I-20; and "Carson's New," WWD, 21 May 1956, 8. See also "Will Today's Shopping Centers," 23.

67. "Why Aren't There More Good Shopping Centers?" AF 105 (Dec. 1956): 170, 174.

68. "3 Shopping Areas," NYT, 5 July 1956, 27. "Long Island Told," NYT, 19 July 1956, 37; "L. I. Retailers," WWD, 4 Oct. 1956, 2; "Store Over-Expansion," WWD, 10 Oct. 1956, 17; Feinberg, "Where I Sit," 10 Mar. 1960, 8; 11 Mar. 1960, 9; 14 Mar. 1960, 9; 15 Mar. 1960, 8; 16 Mar. 1960, 12.

69. "Major Project," WWD, 18 June 1952, 1, 68; "Dayton Plan," Edina-Morningside Courier, 19 June 1952, 1, 21; "$20 Million," WWD, 1 Oct. 1952, I-1, I-52; "$10 Million," Richfield [Minn.] News, 2 Oct. 1952, 1; "Donaldson's and Dayton's," MT, 25 Oct. 1953, 1, 7; "L. S. Donaldson Joins," WWD, 26 Oct. 1953, 1, 30; "Donaldson's Had Planned," MT, 7 Oct. 1956, Southdale Sect., 5. Slightly earlier, Marshall Field and Gimbel's had agreed to do the same thing at the Mayfair Shopping Center in Milwaukee; see "Field, Gimbel Planning," WWD, 7 Apr. 1953, 1, 51; and "Field, Gimbel Plan," MS, 7 Apr. 1953, 1, 2. However, the project did not begin construction until 1957, opening in 1959.

70. Concerning Eastpoint, see "Hochschild, Kohn to Build," WWD, 25 Jan. 1954, 2, 35; and "Hutzler Unit," WWD, 18 Apr. 1955, I-2. Concerning Glendale, see n. 33 above and "Block's Sets," WWD, 9 Mar. 1955, 1, 59.

71. Followed by Macy's (1960–61) at Stanford Shopping Center, Palo Alto, Calif.; Higbee's (1960–61) at Westgate Shopping Center outside Cleveland; the Emporium (1960–62) at Hillsdale Shopping Center, San Mateo, Calif. (1960–62); and Bamberger's (1961–62) at Cherry Hill Shopping Center.

72. Beginning with Crestwood Plaza near St. Louis—Sears (opened 1957) and Scruggs, Vandervoort & Barney (opened 1958). Of twenty-six regional malls with dual anchors secured prior to construction and opened by 1961, ten had either Sears or Montgomery Ward as the second anchor. See Richard Longstreth, comp., "Dual Anchor Shopping Centers, 1950–1960," at http://www.preservenet.cornell.edu.

73. Including Northway Mall (1960–62) with Joseph Horne, near Pittsburgh; Cottonwood Mall (1960–62), with ZCMI in Salt Lake City; Dadeland (1960–62), with Burdine's, near Miami; Eastland (1960–63), with Gimbel's, near Pittsburgh; and South Shore Mall (1960–63), with Macy's, in Bay Shore, Long Island.

74. "Shopping Habits," WP, 3 Oct. 1956, 54.

75. "Problems Beset," NYT, 3 July 1955, VIII-1; "Shopping Centers—Retailing in Transition," ICSC, 1959, 72. See also "Night Hours," WWD, 13 June 1957, 1, 40; "Los Angeles Centers," WWD, 12 July 1957, 1, 8; "Opinion Split," WWD, 11 Nov. 1957, 1, 28; and "Study Shows," WWD, 2 Dec. 1957, 1, 16.

76. "Suburb Shop Centers," NYT, 13 June 1953, 25.

77. Joseph Reiss, "Shopping Centers—Retail Result of the Auto Age," Printers' Ink 230 (9 June 1950): 47; "Branch Business Is Different," Stores 36 (June 1954): 24, 66; "Shopping Centers: A Way to More Sales," 21; "Shopping Centers—Retailing in Transition," ICSC, 1959, 70–73. See also "Shift in Retailing," NYT, 3 May 1957, 29.

78. "Buying Patterns Changed," ES, 30 Mar. 1960, H-8; "Evening Shopping," NYT, 16 Jan. 1961, 29. See also Reiss, "Shopping Centers," 25, 44; "Shopping after Dark," Fortune 46 (Nov. 1952): 120–23, 198, 200, 204; "Convenience Is King in the New Shopping Centers," PRI 24 (12 Dec. 1952): 50–51; "Regional Shopping Grows Fast," PRI 247 (14 May 1954): 74; "163rd St. Will Revive," Miami Daily News, 31 Oct. 1954, 10E; "Public Asks," WWD, 17 May 1956, 14; "Swing to Evening," NYT, 15 July 1956, VIII-4; Smith, Shopping Centers, 94, 98; Slocum, "Shopping Centers Enjoy," 26; "Detroit Store Growth," WWD, 11 Nov. 1957, 1, 28; and Feinberg, "Where I Sit," 17 Nov. 1959, 10. Cohen, Consumers' Republic, 278–86, emphasizes the importance of the regional mall as space that empowered female leadership of family outings, but also discusses the limitations these complexes had for women.

79. "Paramus Booms," NYT, 5 Feb. 1962, 33; "Center Developers Stress," WWD, 1 Jan. 1956, 1.

80. "Art Show Gets," WWD, 8 Oct. 1957, 1, 36 (quote on p. 36).

81. "Christmas Fetes," NYT, 22 Dec. 1960, 16. See also "John Wanamaker Opens," NYT, 24 Apr. 1955, III-1, III-9; "'Christmas City' Opens," NYT, 24 Nov. 1955, 31; "Public Relations Drive," WWD, 25 Apr. 1956, 9; "Promoting Traffic," WWD, 4 Oct. 1957, 1, 6; Feinberg, "Where I Sit," 23 Nov. 1959, 8; 25 Feb. 1960, 10; "Shop, Culture, Centers—and More," NYT Magazine, 18 Nov. 1962, 24–25, 109–10, 112, 114; "Community Promotions: Big Bang—Small Cost," SCA 2 (Nov. 1963): 10–13. See also "How to Open a Shopping Center," Journal of Property Management 23 (Dec. 1957): 87–97.

82. "Film House," WWD, 8 June 1960, 24; "Victorian Village," Bergen Evening Record, 13 Nov. 1957, 66; "Bergen Mall Pioneering," WWD, 17 Sep. 1962, 21; "Roosevelt Field," WWD, 30 Sep. 1957, 1, 4. For other examples, see "Hall Will Be Used," Lorain [Ohio] Journal, 30 Apr. 1952, 25; "A Welcome Sign," SFC, 16 July 1952, 4ES; "Concourse Planned," NYT, 15 Apr. 1956, VIII-8; "Story of Modern," Daily Breeze [Redondo Beach, Calif.], 21 Aug. 1957, 10c; "Big Community Hall," Pittsburgh Press, 31 July 1962, 58; and "Community Groups," Arlington Heights [Ill.] Herald, 16 Aug. 1962, 71.

83. "Shopping Centers: A Way to More Sales," 22.

84. "The Emporium-Stonestown Is Geared to Self-Selection," DW 63 (July 1953): 35; "Emporium Stonestown," WWD, 27 Apr. 1953, 2. See also "The Big 'E' Flies over Stonestown," Stores 32 (Apr. 1952): 55, 79; "Emporium Opens," WWD, 16 July 1952, 1, 30; SFC, 16 July 1952, Emporium Sect.; "Emporium's Stonestown Unit Engineered for Selling," DW 61 (Sep. 1952): 34–35, 86; and "New Shopper Magnets," AF 98 (Mar. 1953): 143–45. Concerning Sears stores, see Richard Longstreth, "Sears, Roebuck and the Remaking of the Department Store, 1924–1942," JSAH 65 (June 2005): 256–66.

85. Longstreth, City Center, 335–41.

86. Including Hillsdale, 163rd Street, Bergen Mall, Prince Georges Plaza, and Mid-Island Plaza.

87. "New Dome Design," NYT, 20 Sep. 1948, 33; "Formal Opening," FN, 3 Oct. 1951, 10.

88. Ketchum employed the wide landscape court on a smaller scale for the one-level Princeton Shopping Center in Princeton, New Jersey (1950–54), but this complex, too, went bankrupt a year after opening. The two-tier configuration around a wide court was used by developer James Rouse in his first shopping center, Mondawmin, in Baltimore (1954–56), where Sears was the anchor store. Other examples that employed a broad central green include Cheery Creek and O'Neil-Sheffield Shopping Center.

89. Gruen is the subject of two recent biographies—Hardwick, Mall Maker; and Alex Wall, Victor Gruen: From Urban Shop to New City (Barcelona: Actar, 2005)—focusing on his work in the retail field. See also Howard Gillette, Jr., "The Evolution of the Planned Shopping Center in Suburb and City," JAPA 51 (autumn 1985): 449–60; and Longstreth, City Center, 302–4, 323–31. Gruen wrote an array of articles, some of which are cited in these notes, but his ideas on the subject are well covered in Gruen and Smith, Shopping

Towns. He was also the subject of an insightful journalistic profile: "An Architect of Environments," *Fortune* 65 (Jan. 1962): 76–80, 134, 136, 138.

90. Interviews with the late William McAdam, former senior vice president of Coldwell Banker, Newport Beach, Calif., 8 Apr. 1988, and Eaton Ballard. For further discussion of Milliron's and Gruen's unrealized regional shopping center designs in Los Angeles, see Longstreth, *City Center,* 242–46, 323–31; Hardwick, *Mall Maker,* 94–105; and Wall, *Victor Gruen,* 42–49, 70–73. Hardwick and Wall also discuss the architect's work for Grayson's (chap. 2 and pp. 36–40, resp.).

91. Interview with Joseph L. Hudson, Jr., former president of J. L. Hudson Company, Detroit, 6 Apr. 2000. Hudson joined the firm, replacing James B. Webber, Jr., as heir apparent after the latter's unexpected death in August 1954. Oscar Webber's great-nephew and namesake of the store's founder, Hudson was propelled to the senior ranks of management. Gruen's claim that it was all his idea, on the other hand, makes little sense. It is highly unlikely that an architect, unsolicited and with no experience in large-scale retail planning, could persuade one of the nation's leading department store executives to adopt a policy of building branch stores, of developing shopping centers as part of that strategy, and indeed of building the biggest such facilities in the nation. Gruen's account has nevertheless been accepted, including in Hardwick, *Mall Maker,* 105–11. See also Feinberg, "Where I Sit," 12 Dec. 1959, 8, 40. A more skeptical view is expressed in "Architect of Environments," 80.

92. Concerning the scheme, see "J. L. Hudson," *DFP,* 4 June 1950, 1, 10; "Hudson's First Branch," *WWD,* 5 June 1950, 1, 50; "Hudson's Finally Goes Suburban," *BW,* 10 June 1950, 80–81; "Suburban Retail Districts," *AF* 93 (Aug. 1950): 111–15; Victor Gruen, "Circular Store for Traffic Flow," *CSA/VE* 27 (July 1951): 180–81, 213–14; Baker and Funaro, *Shopping Centers,* 200–207; and Wall, *Victor Gruen,* 74–77. Concerning the plan's wartime delay, see "Hudson's Store," *WWD,* 25 Apr. 1951, 1, 71.

93. "Hudson Shifts," *WWD,* 26 Dec. 1951, 1; "Hudson to Settle," *Community News* [Detroit], 17 Jan. 1952, 1, 2; "Hudson Land Swap," *Harper Woods Herald,* 6 Feb. 1952, 1, 5. Hudson's intention eventually to build Northland was disclosed not long after Eastland's original plans were unveiled; see "Hudson's Plans," *WWD,* 9 Oct. 1950, 1, 42.

94. "Construction Starts," *WWD,* 12 May 1952, 1, 45; "Huge New Shopping Center Sets Detroiters Buzzing," *Automobile Facts* 12 (Dec. 1953): 4–5; "Hudson's Northland," *WWD,* 5 Feb. 1954, 1, 39; "Hudson's Sets," *WWD,* 16 Mar. 1954, 1, 59; "Shopping Convenience," *WWD,* 22 Mar. 1954, 31; "Northland: A New Yardstick for Shopping Center Planning," *AF* 100 (June 1954): 103–17; Kelley, *Shopping Centers,* chap. 15; Feinberg, "Where I Sit," 28 Dec. 1959, 7; 29 Dec. 1959, 8; 30 Dec. 1959, 10; Hardwick, *Mall Maker,* 124–38; Wall, *Victor Gruen,* 81–91.

95. "Northland: A New Yardstick," 104; "Northland," *Stores* 36 (Apr. 1954): 20; "Commercialism Takes—and Wears—a New Look," *Ladies' Homes Journal* 71 (June 1954): 11, 14 (quote on p. 11).

96. Concerning sales, see "Hudson Northland Branch," *WWD,* 15 Sep. 1954, I-3; "Hudson Doing," *WWD,* 28 Dec. 1954, 1, 33; "Sales of Center," *NYT,* 22 Feb. 1955, 26; "Hudson Northland," *WWD,* 17 Mar. 1954, 1, 63; "Stores Do $88 Million," *WWD,* 19 Mar. 1956, 1, 23; and "Three Successful Shopping Centers," 112–13.

97. "New Hudson's," *WWD,* 18 July 1955, 1, 10; "Art and Sculpture," *WWD,* 10 July 1957, 20; "Curtains Going Up," *DN,* 22 July 1957, 34; "Hudson's Eastland," *WWD,* 23 July 1957, 1, 44; "Three Successful Shopping Centers," 114–17; Feinberg, "Where I Sit," 31 Dec. 1959, I-4, I-32, and 4 Jan. 1960, 8.

98. Which regional malls may have been planned so that a second anchor department store could be added is difficult to ascertain since these intentions were not always noted in period accounts. Such an expansion plan was definitely a part of the Broadway-Anaheim Shopping Center; see Longstreth, *City Center,* 343–44. Other examples of the linear end configuration include Westgate Shopping Center, near Cleveland (1952–54); Los Altos Shopping Center, Los Altos, Calif. (1954–55); Swifton Center, Cincinnati (1954–56); University Village Shopping Center, Seattle (1954–56); Eastgate Shopping Center, Indianapolis (1955–57); Eastland Shopping Center, West Covina, Calif. (1955–57); East Hills Shopping Center, Pittsburgh (1959–60); Lakeside Shopping Center, New Orleans (1958–60); and Westland Shopping Center, near Denver (1958–60).

99. "Marshall Field's New Shopping Center," *AF* 95 (Dec. 1951): 185–99.

100. "Wanted Something 'Human,'" *Evanston Review,* 5 Dec. 1968. See also "Elegance, Luxury Mark," *WWD,* 17 Oct. 1956, 1, 59; "Random Observations on Shopping Centers" and "Garden Setting Lends Charm to Suburban Center," *AR* 122 (Sep. 1957): 217–19, 220–28, resp.; "Let's Build a Center That Sells," *SCA* 2 (June 1963): 30–32, 34.

101. "It's Fun to Visit America's Largest Shopping Center," *AR* 122 (Sep. 1957): 206–15; Robert L. Zion, "The Landscape Architect and the Shopping Center," *Landscape Architecture* 43 (Oct. 1957): 6–12.

102. "Flowers and Shrubs," *MH,* 1 Nov. 1956, 3-C; "Landscaping Planned," *CE,* 25 Sep. 1960, J-5; "Landscaping Beauty," *MS,* 4 Apr. 1960, III-2.

103. "Famed Artist," *DP,* 31 July 1960, Westland Sect., 8; "Variety of Plants," *SDU,* 28 July 1960, x-3; "Landscaper Uses," *MH,* 30 Sep. 1962, 16-J.

104. "Report Dayton Co.," *WWD,* 17 June 1952, 1; "Major Project," *WWD,* 18 June 1952, 1, 68; "Dayton Plan Stuns," *Edina-Morningside Courier,* 19 June 1952, 1, 17, 20–22.

105. Concerning the unrealized Montclair Shopping Center, see "First Part of $12 Million," *HP,* 17 Dec. 1950, 10; "109-Store Houston," *WWD,* 3 Jan. 1951, 85; Hardwick, *Mall Maker,* 112–15; and Wall, *Victor Gruen,* 91–92.

106. "Winter or Summer," *AF* 98 (Mar. 1953): 127; "June in January," *Minnesota Engineer,* May 1956, 4–6; "Southdale Will 'Save,'" *MT,* 7 Oct. 1956, Southdale Sect., 2; "Natural Gas Operates World's Largest Heat Pump," Minneapolis Gas Company, Suburban Division, Nov. 1956, brochure, Southdale file, Target Company archives, Minneapolis; "600 Ton Heat Pump System," *Heating, Piping & Air Conditioning* 29 (Jan. 1957): 143–45; "Cut Shopping Center Costs," *Heating, Piping & Air Conditioning* 31 (Dec. 1959): 103–4; "Southdale up to Date," *MT,* 19 Aug. 1979, 1D, 3D. Other technical innovations are noted in "Architect of Environments," 134.

107. During the 1950s, regional shopping centers were seldom divided on two levels. In most such cases, the configuration was in response to topography—Evergreen Plaza, Famous-Barr's Northland, and 7 Corners, for example—and they did not employ the mall arrangement. On the other hand, a number of regional malls existed when the pedestrianway was set at one level, but the department store at one end also had a major entrance at a lower level, including Jordan Marsh at the North Shore Center, Hutzler's at Westview Shopping Center, Marshall Field's at Mayfair Shopping Center, Rollman's at Swifton Center, and Gimbel's at Cheltenham Shopping Center.

108. "Winter or Summer," 126–33; "A Break-Through for Two-Level Shopping Centers," and "Two-Level Southdale," *AF* 105 (Dec. 1956): 114–15 and 116–23, resp.; *MT,* 7 Oct. 1956, Southdale Sect.; *Edina Morningside Courier,* 11 Oct. 1956, 13–20; "Southdale

Shopping Center," *Buildings* 58 (Oct. 1958): 34–37; Hardwick, *Mall Maker,* 142–55; Wall, *Victor Gruen,* 92–102.

109. "He Brought Charm," MT, 7 Oct. 1956, Southdale Sect., 26. See also "3-Story Garden," in the same sect., p. 19.

110. The relationship between shopping centers and redeveloped commercial centers in the United States during the 1950s and the concurrent rebuilding of city and town centers in Europe has yet to be carefully examined, but some preliminary observations are offered in Chapter 9.

111. "Center Breaks Art Barrier," MT, 7 Oct. 1956, Southdale Sect., 32; "Convenience, Beauty," WWD, 13 Mar. 1957, 1, 78 (quote on p. 78); "Brisk Business for a Bright Shopping Center," *Fortune* 55 (Feb. 1957): 14; "Southdale Shopping Center," 34.

112. "Enclosed Malls," WSJ, 11 Oct. 1961, 1. As the "second" store, Donaldson's was perhaps less enthusiastic about Southdale's broader role. The company insisted on owning its own land, designing and building its own store, and even having it use separate systems, as seems to have occurred in a number of instances when two department store companies did not collaborate on planning a regional mall at the outset. John Graham, working here as he did for other Allied stores, also apparently argued against Gruen's design for the court; see Hardwick, *Mall Maker,* 150.

113. Concerning The Center, see "Omaha Store Plan," *Des Moines Register,* 20 Dec. 1953, 1-L; "Center on 42nd," OWH, 27 Sep. 1953, 1-B; "Shopping Center," OWH, 7 Feb. 1954, 4-B; and OWH, 23 Oct. 1955, Center Shopping Center Sect. Kenneth Welch was hired to conduct the market survey and select the site; he also seems to have had a hand in developing the unorthodox configuration of the complex; see "Integrated Shop Center," WWD, 14 Feb. 1956, 30. Concerning Lakeside, see "Denver Dry Sets," DP, 6 Mar. 1955, 1A, 22A; "Denver Store," WWD, 7 Mar. 1955, 1, 10; and DP, 29 Aug. 1956, 45–74.

114. Joshua Olsen, *Better Places, Better Lives: A Biography of James Rouse* (Washington, D.C.: Urban Land Institute, 2003), 80. Olsen's claim was perhaps based on comments from former Rouse employees, although he cites no source for it. Much the same argument was made concerning Hudson's and Northland; see Smith, *Shopping Centers,* 50–51.

115. The *Directory of Shopping Centers in the United States and Canada,* 5th ed. (Chicago: National Research Bureau, 1961) notes many enclosed malls among its listings, based on data submitted by owners and/or managers, but a substantial portion of these seem to refer to canopies or some other form of shelter without full enclosure. The notation "air conditioned" with other listings is probably a better indicator. Among those so noted with less than 150,000 square feet, thirteen were opened between 1958 and 1962.

116. "2 More Branches," WWD, 26 Apr. 1947, 3; "Million-Dollar Shopping Center," *Newton Daily News,* 16 Apr. 1957, 1; "Younkers First," *Newton Daily News,* 22 Apr. 1957, 1; *Newton Daily News,* 30 Nov. 1960, 3-B, 4-B. See also "Small Towns 'a Shopping Center Vacuum,'" SCA 3 (Jan. 1964): 16–17.

117. Those with branches of the department stores studied included Harundale, near Baltimore, 1956–58 (Hochschild-Kohn); Big Town Shopping Center, Dallas, 1957–58 (Sanger's); North Star Mall, San Antonio, 1958–60 (Wolff & Marx); Crossroads Shopping Center, Omaha, 1959–60 (Brandeis, Sears); River Roads Shopping Center, near St. Louis, 1959–61 (Stix, Baer & Fuller); Sharpstown Center, near Houston, ca. 1958–61 (Foley's, Montgomery Ward); Cherry Hill Shopping Center, near Philadelphia, 1959–61 (Strawbridge & Clothier, later Bamberger's); The Mall, Louisville, 1959–62 (Kaufman-Straus); Cottonwood Mall, Salt Lake City, 1960–62 (ZCMI); Walt Whitman Shopping Center, Huntington, Long Island, ca. 1959–62 (Abraham & Straus, Macy's); Northway Mall, near Pittsburgh, 1960–62 (Joseph Horne); and Randhurst Center, near Chicago, 1959–62 (Carson Pirie Scott, Wieboldt's, The Fair). Others greater than 300,000 square feet include West Park Plaza, Billings, Mont. (Sears); Eastwood Mall, Birmingham, Ala. (J. C. Penney); Sunset Shopping Center, Amarillo, Tex. (Sears, J. C. Penney) (opened in 1960); Rogers Plaza, Grand Rapids, Mich. (Montgomery Ward); Winrock Shopping Center, Albuquerque (Fedway); Lake Air Center, Waco, Tex. (Goldstein-Miguel); Chris-Town Shopping City, Phoenix (Montgomery Ward, J. C. Penney); and Apache Plaza, St. Anthony, Minn. (Montgomery Ward, J. C. Penney) (opened in 1961).

118. "Construction and Costs," ICSC, 1961, 111; "Malls Call for Exciting Use of Materials," CSA/VE 37 (July 1961): E35–36.

119. "Sanger's to Build," DMN, 11 Mar. 1956, 1, 10; DMN, 26 Feb. 1959, sect. 6; "Throngs Crowd," DMN, 27 Feb. 1959, I-1.

120. "New Designs," NYT, 9 Mar. 1958, VIII-1; "More Enclosed Malls?" CSA/VE 35 (Nov. 1959): E23; "Malls Call," E34–E35; "Many Developers Can't 'See' Enclosed Malls," SCA 1 (Apr. 1962): 26–27.

121. "Enclosed Mall Centers Are Costing Less to Build," CSA/VE 36 (May 1960): E34–E35 (quote on p. E34). See also "Closed Mall," WWD, 3 May 1961, I-6; "Closed Mall Centers," ICSC, 1961, 109–18; "Enclosed Malls May Be the Next Big Development," CSA/VE 37 (May 1961): E22–E25; "Malls Call," E34–E36, E39, E41; "47 Individual Heat Pumps Cut Costs at Eastwood Mall," CSA/VE 37 (Oct. 1961): E30–E31, E35; "Many Developers Can't," 26–27, 43, 46; and "Enclosed Malls: What Do They Really Cost?" SCA 2 (July 1963): 16–19.

122. "The Future of Regional Shopping Centers," *Stores* 40 (Jan. 1958): 15; "Malls Call," E39.

123. John Graham, "Air Conditioned and Enclosed Malls," ICSC, 1962, 20–22. See also Graham, "The Enclosed Mall Is Here to Stay," SCA 1 (May 1962): 27; and "Economics, Planning, and Prospects," AR 127 (Mar. 1960): 211.

124. "Tug of War: How Centers Can Get Harmony of Design," SCA 1 (Jan. 1962): 26–29, 55–57 (quotes on pp. 27–28).

125. Besides Northland, Eastland, and Southdale, Gruen's regional malls that had department stores studied include Valley Fair Shopping Center in Santa Clara, Calif., ca. 1955–57 (Macy's); Bay Fair Shopping Center, San Leandro, Calif., 1955–57 (Macy's); South Bay Shopping Center, Redondo Beach, Calif., 1955–57 (collaboration; built in conjunction with a May Company branch); Glendale Shopping Center, Indianapolis, 1955–58 (Ayres, Wm. H. Block); South Shore Plaza, Braintree, Mass., 1959–61 (Filene's); Cherry Hill Shopping Center, Cherry Hill, N.J., 1960–61 (Strawbridge & Clothier, later Bamberger's); Northway Mall, near Pittsburgh, 1960–62 (Joseph Horne); and Randhurst Center, Mount Prospect, Ill., 1959–62 (Carson Pirie Scott, Wieboldt's, and The Fair)—the latter three enclosed. Besides Stonestown, Becket's regional malls included Hillsdale, San Mateo, Calif., 1952–54 (Macy's, later Emporium); Oak Cliff Shopping Center, Dallas, 1953–56 (collaboration; A. Harris); Los Altos Shopping Center, Los Altos, Calif., 1954–56 (Walker's); Stanford Shopping Center, Palo Alto, Calif., 1954–56 (Emporium, later Macy's); Hillside Shopping Center, Hillside, Ill., 1954–56 (Carson Pirie Scott, Goldblatt's); Broadway-Anaheim Shopping Center, Anaheim, Calif., 1954–57 (Broadway, later J. W. Robinson); Del Amo Center, Torrance, Calif., 1957–60 (Broadway, Sears); Westland Shopping Center, Lakewood, Colo., 1957–60 (collaboration; May Co.); Grossmont Shopping Center, La Mesa, Calif., 1958–61 (Marston's); and Walt Whitman Shopping Center, Huntington, Long Island, 1960–62 (Abraham & Straus, Macy's)—the last enclosed. In addition to Northgate, Graham's regional malls include Capitol Court, Milwaukee, opened 1956 (T. A. Chapman, Shuster's); Gulfgate Shopping City, Houston, 1954–56 (Joske's, Sakowitz);

North Shore Shopping Center, Peabody, Mass., 1955–58 (Filene's, Jordan Marsh); Bergen Mall, Paramus, N.J., 1955–57 (Stern's); College Grove Shopping Center, San Diego, 1957–60 (Walker Scott); Lloyd Center, Portland, 1956–60 (Meier & Frank); Parmatown Shopping Center, Parma, Ohio, 1958–60, major addition (collaboration; May Co. store by Gruen); River Roads Shopping Center, Jennings, Mo., 1959–61 (Stix Baer & Fuller); and Cottonwood Mall, Salt Lake City, 1960–62 (ZCMI)—the latter two enclosed. No other architectural firm came close to these three in receiving commissions for regional malls.

126. Olson, *Rouse,* 52–63, 77–78; "Mid-City Shopping Center," *AF* 98 (Mar. 1953): 134–39; "Two-Level Mondawmin," *AF* 105 (Dec. 1956): 124–26.

127. Concerning Atlas, see "Shopping Center Set," *NYT,* 16 May 1956, 55; "Shopping Center Set," *NYT,* 29 July 1956, VIII-8; "Connecticut Site," *NYT,* 24 Jan. 1957, 48; Feinberg, "Where I Sit," 8 Mar. 1960, 10; obituary, *NYT,* 31 July 1973, 40.

128. "Public Firms Seen," *WWD,* 3 July 1957, 1, 10; "Corporate Shop Center," *WWD,* 15 Aug. 1957, 1, 36; "Shopping Centers Urged," *NYT,* 25 Aug. 1957, VIII-1, VIII-5.

129. James W. Rouse, "Planning for America's Future," *ICSC,* 1960, 143–49 (quote on p. 146); Willard G. Rouse, "Construction and Operation," *ICSC,* 1961, 114; James W. Rouse, "Must Shopping Centers Be Inhuman?" *AF* 116 (June 1962): 105–7 (quote on p. 105); James W. Rouse, "The Regional Shopping Center: Its Role in the Community It Serves," *Ekistics* 16 (Aug. 1963): 96–100 (quote on p. 99).

130. Rouse, "Planning for America," 145.

131. "Why Aren't There More?" 178, 184. This important article, placed immediately after a feature on Southdale and Mondawmin, is unsigned. The depth of its argument, based strictly on business considerations, make it unlikely that a member of *Forum*'s staff developed it fully. Much more plausible is that the content was given by Rouse.

132. Kelley, *Shopping Centers,* chap. 13; "Garden State Plaza," *WWD,* 28 Feb. 1956, 13; *Bergen Evening Record,* 30 Apr. 1957, Garden State Plaza Sect.; "Here Paramus Center," *WWD,* 13 June 1958, 1, 35; "Gimbel Now Macy," *WWD,* 5 Sep. 1958, 1, 38; "Paramus Center," *NYT,* 7 Sep. 1958, 61.

133. "Why Aren't There More?" 184. Based on interviews with former associates, Olsen, *Rouse,* 77–78, argues convincingly that Rouse was more concerned with societal goals than business ones—that he assumed that one would lead to the other. Early on, however, he seems to have developed a way in which that connection could be specifically realized, not just assumed. Rouse's acumen in the practical arena of regional mall planning is evidenced by his building upon Welch's approach to assessing the market of a potential site; see James W. Rouse, "Estimating Productivity for Planned Regional Shopping Centers," *UL* 12 (Nov. 1953): 1, 3–5.

134. "Hochschild, Kohn Silent," *WWD,* 5 Oct. 1954, 8; "Hochschild's Confirms," *WWD,* 22 Dec. 1954, 1, 36; "Two Multi-Million," *Sun* [Baltimore], 28 Sep. 1958, 1C; "Harundale Shopping Center," *Baltimore News-Post,* 30 Sep. 1958, Harundale Mall Sect.; "Harundale Center," *Baltimore News-Post,* 1 Oct. 1958, 3-C; Olsen, *Rouse,* 77–81.

135. Interview with Charles Lamb and Francis Taliaferro, Annapolis, Md., 28 Oct. 2003. According to them, Rouse first hired the senior partner, Archibald Rogers, to assist him in securing a zoning variance for the land since Rogers had been the first zoning commissioner for Ann Arundel County and knew the system well. Soon thereafter he gave the newly established firm the commission to design the complex.

136. Olsen, *Rouse,* 80, maintains that Harundale became a more important model for the enclosed mall than Southdale. If this is true, the influence would have been through informal transmissions, for Harundale received scant coverage in retail journals and none that I have found in popular or technical ones, in striking contrast to Southdale.

137. See, e.g., "Enclosed Malls Help," *WSJ,* 11 Oct. 1961, 1; and "Cherry Hill," *SCA* 1 (Jan. 1962): 46. Realized work using the Harundale model included Charlottetown Mall, Charlotte, N.C. (1957–59); North Star Mall, San Antonio (1957–60); and The Mall, Louisville (1959–62).

138. "New Suburb Rises," *NYT,* 7 Oct. 1956, 296; memorandum, 24 July 1957, Strawbridge & Clothier papers, series V, box 33, Hagley Museum and Library, Wilmington, Del.

139. The best background account on the development is "Cherry Hill," *SCA* 1 (Jan. 1962): 50–51. See also "Strawbridge & Clothier Plans," *CP,* 11 Jan. 1955, 1; "S. & C. Plans," *PI,* 27 Apr. 1956, 33; "New Suburb Rises," *NYT,* 7 Oct. 1956, VIII-10; "Option Taken," *WWD,* 15 Aug. 1958, 7; Feinberg, "Where I Sit," 18 Feb. 1960, 8; "Store Plans," *PI,* 13 Mar. 1960, 1B; "Big Store Set," *WWD,* 14 Mar. 1960, 1, 28; Stephanie Dyer, "Designing 'Community' in the Cherry Hill Mall: Social Production of a Consumer Space," in Alison K. Hoagland and Kenneth A. Breisch, eds., *Constructing Image, Identity, and Place: Perspectives in Vernacular Architecture, IX* (Knoxville: University of Tennessee Press, 2003), 267–68; and Wall, *Victor Gruen,* 103–5.

140. For background, see "New Cherry Hill," *CP,* 15 Sep. 1961, 1; "Neither Snow, Nor Rain," *EB* 8 Oct. 1961, IV-6; "Dignitaries Will Attend," *CP,* 11 Oct. 1961, 1a–38a; "Largest All-Weather," *EB,* 11 Oct. 1961, 1, 3; "Enclosed Mall with an Outdoor Feeling," *AR* 131 (June 1962): 174–79; "Cherry Hill," 41–55; "Shops, Culture, Centers— and More," *NYT Magazine,* 18 Nov. 1962, 34–35, 109–10, 112, 114; Dyer, "Designing 'Community,'" 263–75; and Olsen, *Rouse,* chap. 5. Concerning Lapidus, see Alice T. Friedman, "Merchandising Miami Beach: Morris Lapidus and the Architecture of Abundance," *Journal of Decorative and Propaganda Arts* 25 (2005): 216–53.

141. Olsen, *Rouse,* 105; Dyer, "Designing 'Community,'" 271. Concerning Bamberger's, see "Bamberger's Chain," *CP,* 17 Mar. 1961, 1, 2; "12-Million Bamberger Store," *PI,* 17 Mar. 1961, 1, 21; "Bamberger's Mall Store," *CP,* 26 Sep. 1962, 1, 2; and "Bamberger Store," *NYT,* 27 Sep. 1962, 61.

142. "Carson's Slates," *WWD,* 18 Aug. 1958, 20; "Ward's, Carson's," *WWD,* 26 Feb. 1959; "3 Chains Develop Closed-Mall Center," *CSA/VE* 35 (May 1959): E35; "3 Big Chicago Retailers," *WWD,* 2 July 1959, 1, 32; Feinberg "Where I Sit," 29 Jan. 1960, 10; "At Randhurst a Floating Restaurant," *SCA* 1 (Feb. 1962): 20–21; "Randhurst Bows," *WWD,* 15 Aug. 1962, I-8; *Arlington Heights [Ill.] Herald,* 16 Aug. 1962, 32, 69, 71, 77–78, 85; "Grand Opening," *Des Plaines [Ill.] Journal,* 16 Aug. 1962, 3A; "Randhurst Center: Big Pinwheel on the Prairie," *AF* 117 (Nov. 1962); 106–11; "Pace Setters in Mall Design," *SCA* 1 (Nov. 1962): 18–19; and Wall, *Victor Gruen,* 106–7.

143. David Muss, "Why Winston-Muss Went 100% Enclosed Mall," *SCA* 2 (July 1963): 17, 48–49. Concerning Walt Whitman Shopping Center, see "Big Garden-Like Mall," *NYT,* 24 Nov. 1962, 26; and "Variety Without Clutter," *SCA* 2 (July 1963): 12–15. See also "The Enclosed Mall and Other Development Trends in the Shopping Center Business," *UL* 21 (Sep. 1962): 3–5.

144. The earliest case I have found is Allied's Bergen Mall (1955–57), which was not enclosed. That complex, however, does not seem to have had much of an impact on nomenclature. The next project was Harundale, followed by (between 1959 and 1962) Charlottetown Mall in Charlotte, Eastwood Mall in Birmingham, North Star Mall in San Antonio, The Mall in Louisville, Green Springs Mall in Birmingham, Cottonwood Mall in Salt Lake City,

and Northway Mall near Pittsburgh—all enclosed malls and four of them developed by Rouse. Olsen, *Rouse*, 81, states he was a key figure in popularizing the term.

145. See, e.g., Victor Gruen and Lawrence P. Smith, "Shopping Centers: The New Building Type," *PA* 33 (June 1952): 68–70; "Ancient Shopping Center," *WP*, 3 Oct. 1956, 38 (7 Corners); "Roman Forum," *MH*, 1 Nov. 1956, 3-C; and "Northland: A New Yardstick," 104.

146. The analogy was in fact initially made in print by the editors of *AF*; see "The Big New Ideas in the Big New Shopping Centers," *AF* 98 (Mar. 1953). Whether or not Gruen was the source, he soon embraced it as his own and continued to use it for his work over a period of a number of years. However, it was not until the Galleria at Post Oak in Houston (1969–71)—by Hellmuth, Obata & Kassabaum—that a formal correspondence occurred, with multiple shopping levels around a space covered by a glazed, arched roof.

147. "Keynote Address," *ICSC*, 1959, 8–9.

148. "Distribution—The Role of the Department Store," *ICSC*, 1960, 33.

CHAPTER 9. Stores in the City

1. "Cites Hudson's," *WWD*, 5 Jan. 1953, 4; "Expanded Market," *WWD*, 2 Feb. 1953, 35; "Hudson's Northland," *WWD*, 17 Mar. 1954, 1, 63; "Hudson's Northland," *WWD*, 21 July 1954, 3; "Hudson's Northland," *WWD*, 21 July 1955, 1, 47; "Downtown and Suburban," *Buildings* 58 (Feb. 1958): 36–38; "The Downtown Recovery," *Stores* 40 (Oct. 1959): 13.

2. "Dayton Branch," *WWD*, 21 Jan. 1953, 78; "No Downtown," *WWD*, 30 Sep. 1954, I-6; "Shopping Centers Help," *NYT*, 30 Sep. 1954, 53; "Ills of Downtown," *WWD*, 10 May 1956, 2, 44; "Suburban Centers Help," *MH*, 1 Nov. 1956, 25-c; "Plea to Revitalize," *WWD*, 12 Dec. 1961, 14. See also "Big Retailers," *WWD*, 23 Nov. 1957, 7.

3. Richard Longstreth, *City Center to Regional Mall: Architecture, the Automobile, and Retailing in Los Angeles, 1920–1950* (Cambridge: MIT Press, 1997), 86–89, 112–27, 139–41, 168–69, 182–83, 223–48, 254–55, 262–64, 334–47. For period discussion, see, e.g., "Branches Seen," *WWD*, 3 May 1956, 1, 14; "Los Angeles Area," *WWD*, 8 May 1956, 1, 14; "Downtown LA," *WWD*, 15 Mar. 1962, 1, 8; and "Los Angeles Branches," *WWD*, 24 Aug. 1962, 1, 20. Even in southern California hope remained strong that downtown Los Angeles would regain some of its former strength; see, e.g., Samuel Feinberg, "From Where I Sit," *WWD*, 8 June 1953, I-42; and "Downtown Halting in Los Angeles," *CSA/VE* 33 (Feb. 1957): 209–10.

4. "Downtown Philadelphia," *WWD*, 2 Feb. 1953, 1, 31; "Is Urban Hurt?" *WWD*, 8 Oct. 1953, 42; "Philadelphia Sees," *WWD*, 27 Dec. 1954, II-29; "Philadelphia Suburbs," *WWD*, 14 Jan. 1955, 7; "Downtown Philadelphia," *WWD*, 13 Dec. 1961, 50. See also "Central City," *WWD*, 10 Nov. 1953, 8; "Branches Key," *WWD*, 15 Feb. 1954, 1, 23; "Healthy Future," *WWD*, 12 Nov. 1954, 26; "Philadelphia Store Executives," *WWD*, 6 Dec. 1954, 14; "Suburban Retail," *WWD*, 9 Feb. 1955, 1, 75; "Find Suburbanites," *WWD*, 13 Oct. 1955, I-1, I-14; "Suburban Sales," *WWD*, 6 Feb. 1956, 1, 42; "Philadelphia Store Results," *WWD*, 6 July 1956, 21; "$10 Million Suburban," *WWD*, 11 Feb. 1957, 1, 29; "See New $10 Million," *WWD*, 10 July 1957, 24; "Philadelphia Stores," *WWD*, 2 Oct. 1957, 1, 58; "Philadelphia Downtown," *WWD*, 13 Feb. 1958, 1, 47; "Downtown Off," *WWD*, 23 Sep. 1958, 15; "Downtown Still," *WWD*, 20 Nov. 1958, 13; "Philadelphia Big Stores," *WWD*, 3 Jan. 1959, 1, 60; "Downtown Lag," *WWD*, 17 Mar. 1959, 1, 40; "Philadelphia Stores," *WWD*, 7 Oct. 1959, 11; and "Philadelphia Still Lags," *WWD*, 1 Mar. 1962, 1, 8.

5. "Branches Boom," *WWD*, 30 Apr. 1952, 70.

6. See, e.g., "Detroit Suburbs," *WWD*, 5 Nov. 1954, 13; "Suburbia's Gain," *WWD*, 27 Dec. 1954, II-28; "Suburban Center," *WWD*, 10 Mar. 1955, 1, 44; "First Half Sales," *WWD*, 14 July 1955, I-1, I-37; "Shop Center Encirclement," *WWD*, 16 Feb. 1956, 25, 35; "Thruway Plaza Luring," *WWD*, 4 Sep. 1956, 1, 46; "Buffalo Stores," *WWD*, 16 July 1957, 1, 50; "Downtown Cleveland," *WWD*, 31 Oct. 1957, 1, 43; "Downtown Area Decline," *WWD*, 12 Dec. 1957, 1, 12; "Shop Centers Drain," *WWD*, 7 Apr. 1959, 1, 48; "Washington Sales," *WWD*, 5 May 1959, I-25; "Capital Stores," *WWD*, 13 May 1959, 113; "Shop Centers," *WWD*, 19 May 1959, 16; and "Branches Halt," *WWD*, 20 May 1959, 8.

7. "Bond Stores Head," *WWD*, 1 May 1959, 1, 14; "Grand Rapids Stores," *WWD*, 8 Mar. 1956, 2; "Akron Mayor," *WWD*, 27 Apr. 1959, 16. See also "Retailers Step Up," *NYT*, 3 Jan. 1955, 99.

8. For a sampling of accounts, see "Wanamaker's Will Close," *WWD*, 26 Oct. 1954, 1, 72; "Wanamaker's Main Store," *WWD*, 7 Dec. 1954, 1, 56; "Wanamaker's Will End," *WWD*, 13 Dec. 1954, 1, 43; "Wanamaker's, N.Y.," *WWD*, 17 Dec. 1954, 1, 17; "Alms & Doepke," *WWD*, 13 Apr. 1955, 17; "O'Neill & Co.," *WWD*, 27 Sep. 1954, 1, 14; "White Closing," *WWD*, 18 June 1957, 1, 60; "Namm-Loeser's," *NYT*, 13 Feb. 1957, 1, 51; "Goldenberg's Will Liquidate," *WWD*, 6 June 1955, 1, 20; "Goldenberg's Sets," *WWD*, 7 June 1955, I-82; "Downtown Store," *WWD*, 22 July 1955, 35; "Crowds Jam," *WWD*, 6 Sep. 1956, 1, 37; "Hear Snellenbergs," *WWD*, 25 Jan. 1962, 1, 24; "Report Lit's," *WWD*, 31 Jan. 1962, 1, 51; "Snellenberg, Lit Tied," *WWD*, 1 Feb. 1962, 1, 15; "Snellenbergs Fades," *WWD*, 18 Feb. 1963, 1, 10; "Hear . . . Bailey's," *WWD*, 25 Jan. 1962, 1, 24; "Bailey Shuts," *WWD*, 15 Feb. 1962, 2. See also "Old Stores Die," *NYT*, 17 Feb. 1957, III-1, III-8.

9. "City Stores Denies," *WWD*, 27 July 1960, 6; "AM&A Renovates," *BEN*, 26 July 1960, 20; "AM&A Begins," *BEN*, 28 July 1960, 31; "Traffic Is Heavy," *WWD*, 2 Aug. 1960, 40; "Set to Build," *WWD*, 4 Dec. 1961, 1, 4; "Broadway-Hale's," *WWD*, 18 May 1960, 36; "Broadway-Hale," *WWD*, 31 May 1962, I-13; "Confirm Closing," *WWD*, 25 May 1962, 6; "Hale's to Stay," *WWD*, 6 Dec. 1962, 2. "List of Independent Stores," *WWD*, 21 Oct. 1959, 18, 67, affords a useful though not completely accurate compendium of store closings.

10. Historical studies of downtown decay in the mid-twentieth century include Mark I. Gelfand, *A Nation of Cities: The Federal Government and Urban America, 1933–1965* (New York: Oxford University Press, 1975), esp. chap. 4; Marc A. Weiss, "The Origins and Legacy of Urban Renewal," in Pierre Clavel et al., eds., *Urban and Regional Planning in the Age of Austerity* (New York: Pergamon, 1980), 53–80; Jon C. Teaford, *The Rough Road to Renaissance: Urban Revitalization in America, 1940–85* (Baltimore: Johns Hopkins University Press, 1990), esp. chap. 4; Robert M. Fogelson, *Downtown: Its Rise and Fall, 1880–1950* (New Haven: Yale University Press, 2001), 357–94; and Alison Isenberg, *Downtown America: A History of the Place and the People Who Make It* (Chicago: University of Chicago Press, 2004), chap. 5. For a concise period synopsis, see George Sternlieb, "The Future of Retailing in the Downtown Core," *Journal of the American Institute of Planners* 29 (May 1963): 102–12.

11. "Advises Stores," *WWD*, 17 Nov. 1950, 1, 41; "Downtown Vital," *WWD*, 17 Dec. 1952, 54; Samuel Feinberg, "From Where I Sit," *WWD*, 12 June 1953, 51; "Albert Greenfield," *WWD*, 16 Oct. 1953, 1, 46; "Vast Potential," *WWD*, 11 Jan. 1956, 1, 17; "Downtown Aid," *WWD*, 27 Feb. 1958, 1, 12; "Sears Head Urges," *WWD*, 16 Jan. 1959, 1, 7; "Wanamaker's Stress," *WWD*, 4 Mar. 1960, 7, 32.

12. "Field's Official," *WWD*, 13 Mar. 1953, 8; "Downtown Isn't Dead by a Long Shot," *BW*, 24 Oct. 1953, 41–42, 44; "Future of Downtown," *WWD*, 16 Dec. 1953, 4; "Survey Reveals," *WWD*, 3 May 1954, 31; "Store Centers," *WWD*, 10 Oct. 1954, I-21; "Improved Shopping," *WWD*, 12 Oct. 1954, 1, 48; "Chairman of Allied," *NYT*, 10 Apr. 1955, III-1, III-12; "Talbott Sees Downtown," *WWD*, 12 July 1955, 1,

60; "Suburban Shopping," WWD, 14 Feb. 1956, 28; "Merchandising the Downtown Shopping Center," *Stores* 39 (Jan. 1957): 47–49; "Downtown Is Held," WWD, 5 Mar. 1957, 3. The strengths of the downtown shopping district at that time are argued in Michael Johns, *Moment of Grace: The American City in the 1950s* (Berkeley: University of California Press, 2003), chap. 2.

13. "Hold Downtown," WWD, 19 Jan. 1953, 2; "Big Potential," WWD, 16 Sep. 1954, I-2. See also Larry Smith, "Commercial Real Estate Relationships—Downtown and Suburban," UL 15 (Mar. 1956): 3–5; and "Architect Sees," WWD, 22 Oct. 1956, 1, 7.

14. "Center Heads," WWD, 19 Feb. 1957, I-1, I-56.

15. "Lazarus Cites," WWD, 29 Apr. 1957, 1, 15 (quote on p. 1); "Ralph Lazarus," WWD, 27 May 1955, 6. See also "Detroit Merchants," WWD, 8 May 1956, 6.

16. "Special Customer," WWD, 14 Oct. 1953, 70; "Efficiency Rise," WWD, 19 Nov. 1956, 1, 10; "Downtown Buffalo," WWD, 11 Sep. 1959, 12; "Normand Offers," WWD, 15 Jan. 1957, I-59; "Grand Court," WWD, 7 Mar. 1960, 9; "May Co. Head," WWD, 18 Oct. 1960, 1, 43; "High Priority," WWD, 12 Apr. 1961, 8.

17. See, e.g., "Downtown Unit," WWD, 1 May 1956, I-8; "Branch Lesson," WWD, 11 June 1956, 1, 14; "Downtown Chicago," WWD, 19 Feb. 1957, I-23; "Big Downtown Plans," WWD, 15 Jan. 1958, 6; "Modernization: Key to Downtown Renewal," CSA/VE 34 (Feb. 1958): 174–83; "Downtown Refurbishing," WWD, 6 Aug. 1959, 7; and "Downtown Recovery," 13–59.

18. For a listing, see Richard Longstreth, comp., "New Buildings and Major Additions for Downtown Department Stores, 1920–1960," at http://www.departmentstorehistory.net and http://www.preservenet.cornell.edu. This compilation does not include a number of downtown stores that were extensively remodeled during the same period.

19. "G. Fox Plans," WWD, 11 July 1956, 1, 58; "G. Fox Wants," *Hartford Courant,* 20 June 1958, 1; "Fox Preparing," *Hartford Times,* 17 Nov. 1958, 25; "G. Fox & Co.," *Hartford Courant,* 8 Feb. 1959, 1A, 10A; "G. Fox Stresses," WWD, 11 Feb. 1959, 1, 66; "G. Fox & Co. Will More Than Double Its Downtown Space," *Stores* 40 (Mar. 1959): 25; "New $8 Million," *Hartford Courant,* 24 Nov. 1960, 1; "F. & R. Lazarus," WWD, 12 Nov. 1956, 1; "Foley's to Add," WWD, 12 Apr. 1955, 1, 63; "Work Stride," *Kansas City Star,* 6 Jan. 1957, 4A; "New Jones Penthouse," *Kansas City Star,* 30 June 1957, 17G; "Work on Store," *Kansas City Star,* 5 Oct. 1958, 3A; "Downtown Recovery," 52–53; "ZCMI to Add," WWD, 1 June 1959, 1, 14; "ZCMI Downtown," WWD, 20 Apr. 1961, 8; "Rike-Kumler Buys," WWD, 14 Jan. 1959, 16; "Rike-Kumler Plans," WWD, 7 Mar. 1961, I-44; "Rike's Remodeling," WWD, 26 July 1962, 7.

20. "Allied Stretches Its Arms," BW, 6 Aug. 1955, 60; "Store to Cost," WWD, 30 Oct. 1956, 18; "New Cain-Sloan," *Nashville Tennessean,* 20 Oct. 1957, 6-A; "New Downtown," WWD, 28 Oct. 1957, 1, 20.

21. "Work to Start," CE, 3 Dec. 1961, 1; "Set to Build," WWD, 4 Dec. 1961, 1; "Full Details," WWD, 15 Nov. 1962, 6; "Splendor and Progress," CE, 18 Nov. 1962, 2-H (quotes); "Nearly All," CE, 19 Nov. 1962, 1.

22. "Fact Sheet, Dayton's St. Paul," undated press release [ca. Aug. 1963], Target Corporation archives, Minneapolis, quote on p. 3. See also "Dayton-Schuneman," SPP, 29 Nov. 1958, 1, 2; "Dayton's Plan Set," SPD, 9 Feb. 1962, 1, 3; "Cost Put Over," WWD, 12 Feb. 1962, 2; "Dayton, Sears Set," WWD, 25 July 1963, 2; "Initial Response" and "New Structure First," SPP, 4 Aug. 1963, 1, 2, and 14, resp.; Jeffrey A. Hess and Paul Clifford Larson, *St. Paul's Architecture: A History* (Minneapolis: University of Minnesota Press, 2006), 201–4.

23. "Hear Sanger's," WWD, 19 May 1960, 1, 13; "Sanger-Harris Due," WWD, 20 Sep. 1961, 2; "Downtown Store," DMN, 24 Sep. 1961, 14; "Sanger-Harris," WWD, 16 Oct. 1961, 2; "Sanger-Harris Confirms," WWD, 16 Oct. 1961, 2; "Sanger-Harris Discloses," DMN, 27 Oct. 1963, 1; "New Store Plans," DMN, 11 Feb. 1965, 1; "Sanger-Harris Sets," DMN, 25 June 1965, 1; "Sanger-Harris Ready," DMN, 1 Aug. 1965, C1. See also "Dallas Develops Its Downtown," AC 79 (Oct. 1964): 145, 147.

24. "Oakland Gets," OT, 31 May 1959, 1, 12; "Rites Open," OT, 13 July 1960, 1, 19. Concerning the Kaiser Center, see "Kaiser Buys," OT, 28 June 1955, 1, 8; "'Raft' Foundation," OT, 11 May 1956, 3; "Contract Awarded," OT, 11 Mar. 1958, 1, 3; "The Kaiser Vistas," *San Francisco Examiner,* 9 Oct. 1960, *Highlight* magazine, 11; "Kaiser Center," AR 128 (Dec. 1960): 117–22; "Lakeside Colossus," A&E 220 (Dec. 1960): 17–21; "New Rooftop Garden in Downtown Oakland," *Sunset* 126 (May 1961): 220–22; "Kaiser Center Roof Garden," *Landscape Architecture* 53 (Oct. 1962): 14–17; and "J. Magnin Using," WWD, 6 Nov. 1961, 6. Falling on financial hard times, the White House ceased all operations only five years later.

25. Feinberg, "Where I Sit," 51; "Chairman of Allied," WWD, 10 Apr. 1955, III-1; "Enhancing Entire," WWD, 12 Jan. 1955, 30; "Careful Planning," WWD, 4 May 1955, I-3; "Population Swing," WWD, 17 Sep. 1959, I-6. See also "Downtown Stores," NYT, 12 Jan. 1955, 37; and "Wagner Derides," NYT, 11 Jan. 1956, 41, 48.

26. "Dallas Develops," WWD, 27 Dec. 1954, II-33; "Hartford Stores," WWD, 16 July 1956, 7; "Downtown Is Stressed," WWD, 31 July 1957, 1, 42; "Downtown Cincinnati," WWD, 19 Aug. 1958, 1, 40; "Progress Seen," WWD, 10 Feb. 1959, 2.

27. See, e.g., "Downtown Stores," WWD, 17 Apr. 1952, 52; "San Diego Promotions," WWD, 13 Jan. 1953, I-76; "Downtown Merchants," WWD, 22 Apr. 1953, 86; "'Downtown Has Everything,'" WWD, 28 May 1953, 50; "Volume Ahead," WWD, 21 May 1954, 1, 42; "Baltimore Group," WWD, 1 Dec. 1954, 8; "$60,000 Ad Drive," WWD, 19 Jan. 1955; "Year-Round Program," WWD, 21 Jan. 1955, 1, 39; "Pittsburgh Stores," WWD, 28 Jan. 1955, 6; "'Downtown Louisville Days,'" WWD, 2 Mar. 1955, I-19; "Paterson Initiates," WWD, 7 June 1955, I-68; "Many Areas Step," WWD, 7 July 1955, 36; "Promotional Plan," WWD, 16 Aug. 1955, 20; "Campaign Set," WWD, 22 Aug. 1955, 8; "Drives Found," WWD, 18 Oct. 1955, 10; "Main Street . . . Bulwark of Retailing," CSA/VE 33 (Feb. 1957): 199; "Downtown Kansas City," WWD, 5 Sep. 1957, 2; "Downtown Providence," WWD, 6 Aug. 1958, 1, 55; "Shoppers Jam," WWD, 21 May 1959, 3; "Downtown Providence," WWD, 16 Sep. 1959, I-23; "Miami Merchants," WWD, 16 June 1960, 13; "Group Formed," WWD, 1 Sep. 1960, 8; "Downtown St. Louis," WWD, 20 Oct. 1960, 6. For a good illustration of an elaborate promotional feature in the press, see MJ, 2 Sep. 1951, Up and Down the Magnificent Mile Sect., which inaugurated the first Downtown Days event sponsored by the Milwaukee Downtown Association. For a case study, see Longstreth, *City Center,* 207–14.

28. "Year-Round"; "Campaign Set"; "Group Formed"; "All-Out Promotion," WWD, 6 July 1955, 12; "St. Louis Retailers," WWD, 17 Nov. 1958, 3.

29. "Downtown Program," WWD, 24 Nov. 1950, I-53; "Cincinnati Stores," WWD, 27 Dec. 1954, II-24; "United Effort," WWD, Oct. 1956, 14.

30. "First 'Downtown Day,'" WWD, 18 Feb. 1954, 2; "Baltimore Downtown," WWD, 3 Nov. 1955, 1, 50; "Action Pressed," WWD, 10 Oct. 1954, I-14.

31. "Downtown Providence," WWD, 6 Aug. 1958, 1, 56; "Downtown Stores," WWD, 29 Aug. 1958, 7.

32. "Retail Impact," WWD, 9 Jan. 1957, 1, 11. See also "Reversing the Down Trend in Downtown Volume," *Stores* 39 (Feb. 1957): 22–26. Rouse's talk was published as "Will Downtown Face Up to Its Future?" *Buildings* 57 (Oct. 1957): 54–57.

33. Coverage of the endeavor in retail publications includes

"A Downtown Area Refuses to Die," *Stores* 35 (May 1953): 13–15, 50; "Combined Downtown Effort," WWD, 27 Feb. 1953, 6; "Pittsburgh Proves," WWD, 24 Feb. 1954, 61; "Downtown Unites," WWD, 27 Dec. 1955, II-28; "Pittsburgh Was the First to Rebuild Downtown," CSA/VE 34 (Feb. 1958): 209; and "Result Cited," WWD, 1 Oct. 1958, 10. "Pittsburgh in Progress," PA 28 (June 1947): 67–72, covers an early and more radical scheme sponsored by Kaufmann's. For a good overview of the program, see Jeanne R. Lowe, *Cities in a Race with Time* (New York: Random House, 1967), chap. 2; Roy Lubove, *Twentieth Century Pittsburgh* (New York: Wiley, 1969), 87–141; and Teaford, *Rough Road*, 46–48. See also "Pittsburgh Renascent," AF 91 (Nov. 1949): 59–73, 110.

34. "Retailers Make," WWD, 15 May 1952, 53; "Says Population," WWD, 12 Oct. 1953, I-18; "Support by Other," WWD, 1 Feb. 1955, 17; "Wagner Derides," NYT, 11 Jan. 1956, 41, 48; "Downtown Unit," WWD, 28 Apr. 1958, 1, 10; "Downtown Chicago," WWD, 6 June 1958, 10; "$500,000 Project," WWD, 26 Aug. 1958, I-1, I-13.

35. "Downtown Denver," WWD, 27 Dec. 1954, II-32; "Downtown vs. Suburbia," WWD, 15 Aug. 1955, 1, 16; "Master Plan," DP, 25 Jan. 1957, 25; "Master Plan Unveiled," WWD, 29 Jan. 1957, 1, 40.

36. "Kansas City Creates a New Downtown," *Stores* 39 (Nov. 1957): 14–15, 18–19; "The Planned City: Main Street Is One Part of the Problem," CSA/VE 34 (Feb. 1958): 198–202, 213–14.

37. "Techniques Detailed," WWD, 13 Jan. 1955, 22; "Retailers' Problems: Reviving Sick Old 'Downtown,'" BW, 15 Jan. 1955: 42–44, 46, 50; "How to Rebuild Cities Downtown," AF 102 (June 1955): 122–31, 164, 170, 176, 182, 188, 192, 200, 206, 212, 216, 220, 224, 228, 232, 236; "Rebuilding the Downtown Centers," *Stores* 37 (June 1955): 16–17, 40, 48–49; "Talbott Sees"; "Unified Drives," WWD, 24 Oct. 1955, 1, 13; "Retailers Preparing," WWD, 11 Jan. 1956, 1, 14; "NRDGA Acts," WWD, 11 June 1957, I-1, I-48; "Comeback of the Central City," *Stores* 39 (Aug. 1957): 5–7; "Key Steps," WWD, 10 Jan. 1958, 1, 44; "Retail Lead," WWD, 2 Oct. 1958, 3.

38. See, e.g., Josep Luís Sert, *Can Our Cities Survive?* (Cambridge: Harvard University Press, 1942); Louis Justement, *New Cities for Old: City Building in Terms of Space, Time, and Money* (New York: McGraw-Hill, 1946); Arthur B. Gallion and Simon Eisner, *The Urban Pattern: City Planning and Design* (Princeton, N.J.: D. Van Nostrand, 1950); Miles E. Colean, *Renewing Our Cities* (New York: Twentieth Century Fund, 1953); and Hal Burton, *The City Fights Back: A Nationwide Survey of What Cities Are Doing to Keep Pace with Traffic, Zoning, Shifting Population, Smoke, Smog, and Other Problems* (New York: Citadel, 1954); as well as such specialized articles as "What Can Be Done to Conserve and Revitalize Our Downtown Business Areas?" UL 4 (Oct. 1945): 1, 3–4; "A Downtown Merchant Looks at the Future," *Stores* 29 (Nov. 1947): 13, 68, 70; and "Our Cities Are Worth Saving," *Stores* 30 (Mar. 1948): 19, 54, 56.

39. "Downtown Vital"; Better Roads Will Help," CSA/VE 33 (Feb. 1957): 211.

40. See, e.g., "Act Now," WWD, 21 May 1953, 58; "Traffic Biggest Problem," WWD, 19 Oct. 1953, 28, 31; "Kansas City Taking," WWD, 21 Oct. 1953, 70; "Downtown Isn't Dead," 42; "Center City Recovery: A Nationwide Report," *Stores* 37 (Jan. 1955): 8–11, 51–52; "Parking . . . a Fighting Word in San Diego," CSA/VE 33 (Feb. 1957): 207–8; "How Cities Are Trying to Relieve the Traffic Squeeze," and "How Main Streets Get More Parking," CSA/VE 34 (Feb. 1958): 184–87, 188–93, resp.; "Parking Lots Aid," NYT, 6 Apr. 1958, III-1, III-10.

41. "Public Transit," WWD, 24 June 1958, 1, 49 (quote on p. 1). See also "Downtown Isn't Dead," 29–30; "Public Transit," WWD, 31 July 1958, 6; "Mass Transportation," WWD, 24 Sep. 1959, 45; and "Downtown Held," WWD, 20 Oct. 1960, 1, 45.

42. "City Stores Asked," NYT, 16 Oct. 1960, VIII-1, VIII-8. See also "Shouldn't Department Stores Invest in 'Human Parking' Downtown?" *Journal of Property Management* 25 (Dec. 1959): 85–89.

43. In a few cities such as Boston, New Orleans, San Francisco, and Seattle a large middle- and upper-middle-class contingent remained close to downtown, but these were exceptions. Among the largest return of these groups has occurred in Chicago and Washington during the past several decades.

44. Concerning Charles Center, see n. 55 below. Concerning Constitution Plaza, see "Financing Set," WWD, 2 Feb. 1960, 6; "Hartford: Renewal in the Round," AF 113 (Dec. 1960): 72–76; and "Planning the Downtown Center," AR 135 (Mar. 1964): 177–85. See also Bernard J. Frieden and Lynn B. Sagalyn, *Downtown, Inc.: How America Rebuilds Cities* (Cambridge: MIT Press, 1989), chap. 13; and Alexander Garvin, *The American City: What Works, What Doesn't* (New York: McGraw-Hill, 1996), chap. 6. In reality, none of these undertakings proved effective in bolstering nearby retail activity for a sustained period.

45. See, e.g., Victor Gruen, "Dynamic Planning for Retail Areas," HBR 32 (Nov.–Dec. 1954): 53–62; and Gruen, "Urban Renewal," AJ 24 (Jan. 1956): 23–29.

46. "Typical Downtown Transformed," AF 104 (May 1956): 146–54 (quote on p. 150). For a sampling of other accounts, see "Traffic-Less Streets," WWD, 13 Mar. 1956, 1, 40; "Greater Fort Worth Plan," *Buildings* 56 (June 1956): 46–48; and "Fort Worth Aims to Remake Downtown," CSA/VE 33 (Feb. 1957): 202–3. For discussion of the plan's failure to be implemented, see "What's Happened in Fort Worth?" AF 110 (May 1959): 136–39; and "Upgrading Downtown," AR 137 (June 1965): 176–78. See also Victor Gruen, *The Heart of Our Cities, the Urban Crisis: Diagnosis and Cure* (New York: Simon and Schuster, 1964), 214–20. The plan's history is covered in detail in M. Jeffrey Hardwick, *Mall Maker: Victor Gruen, Architect of an American Dream* (Philadelphia: University of Pennsylvania Press, 2004), chap. 7; and in Alex Wall, *Victor Gruen: From Urban Shop to New City* (Barcelona: Actar, 2006), 126–38.

47. "1st Permanent Mall," WWD, 13 Aug. 1959, 1, 40; "Kalamazoo Mall," NYT, 4 Oct. 1959, I-78; "Will Downtown Malls Work?" CSA/VE 35 (Oct. 1959): E19–E22, E31, E34, E38, E41; "Mall Is First Step in Long-Range Kalamazoo Plan," *Stores* 40 (Oct. 1959): 56–57; "Kalamazoo Mall," WWD, 14 Jan. 1960, 10; "Kalamazoo's Permanent Mall," CSA/VE 36 (Oct. 1960): E30–E33; Hardwick, *Mall Maker*, 193–97; Wall, *Victor Gruen*, 178–81.

48. For discussion, see Longstreth, *City Center*, 269–71, 324–25.

49. For background, see "Shopping Precincts," *Architectural Review* [London] 118 (Aug. 1955): 106–10; "Europe's Reborn Cities," ULI 28 (Mar. 1956): whole issue; "Hubs Without Wheels," *Architectural Review* 123 (June 1958): 373–92; "Shopping," *Architectural Design* 29 (July 1959): 258–65; Frederick Gibberd, *Town Design*, 1953; 5th rev. ed. (New York: Frederick A. Praeger, 1967), esp. chap. 5; and Percy Johnson-Marshall, *Rebuilding Cities* (Chicago: Aldine, 1966). For a recent overview, see Kathryn A. Morrison, *English Shops and Shopping* (New Haven: Yale University Press, 2003), chap. 11. Concerning the Lijnbaan, see "Holland's Fifth Avenue," DW 64 (Mar. 1954): 54–55; "Europe's Fifth Avenue," UL 13 (Oct. 1954): 3–6; and "The Shopping Center: Back Where It Started," BW 17 (July 1954): 106–8.

50. "Rebuilding the Downtown," 48–49; "Turn Main Streets," WWD, 10 Dec. 1956, 1, 13. Concerning the proposals, see "Elevated Shopping Plaza," MSS, 14 June 1956, 22A; "Plan for Plaza," WWD, 18 June 1956, 7 (Minneapolis); "Air-Conditioned Mall," WWD, 18 July 1956, 1, 51 (St. Paul); "Master Plan," WWD, 29 Jan. 1957, 1, 40 (Denver); "The Planned City," 203–4 (Detroit); "Downtown Plan," MJ, 1 May 1957, 1, 2; "Big Plan Ready," WWD, 6 May 1957, 8 (Milwaukee);

"A Mall for Philadelphia," CSA/VE 33 (Feb. 1957): 227. See also "Mall Plans," NYT, 22 Mar. 1959, VIII-1, VIII-6.

51. "Downtown Mall Fever," WWD, 23 Sep. 1959, 1, 99; "A Mall in Toledo," NYT, 4 Aug. 1959, 19; "Downtown Pedestrian Malls," WWD, 4 Aug. 1959, 32; "Parklike Malls," NYT, 23 Aug. 1959, 46; "Downtown Stores," WWD, 31 Aug. 1959, 1, 7; "Decide Today," WWD, 21 Sep. 1959, 1, 29; "Toledo Ending," WWD, 19 Nov. 1959, 1, 49; "Toledo Razes," NYT, 22 Nov. 1959, 60; "Malls in Toledo," WWD, 20 May 1960, 7; "New Toledo Malls," NYT, 12 July 1960, 72; "Toledo Malls," WWD, 17 Nov. 1960, 10; "Toledo Backers," NYT, 4 Dec. 1960, 35.

52. "Closed to Traffic," AF 110 (Feb. 1958): 88–93; "Valid Data," WWD, 24 Sep. 1959, 1, 43.

53. "Some Second Thoughts on Downtown Malls," Stores 40 (Oct. 1959): 55–56; "Malls Held," WWD, 25 Sep. 1959, 1, 6; "The Downtown Mall Experiment," Journal of the American Institute of Planners 30 (Feb. 1964): 66–74. For a recent assessment, see Garvin, American City, chap. 7.

54. "How Leading Chains View Downtown Malls," CSA/VE 35 (Dec. 1959): E20–E22; "What Makes a Mall Plan Practical?" CSA/VE 35 (Mar. 1959): E28–E30; "Lincoln Road," NYT, 24 Jan. 1960, XI-3; "'Fifth Avenue,'" NYT, 27 Nov. 1960, II-2, II-3; "Miami Beach Mall," MH, 27 Nov. 1960, 1H, 8H; "City Stores Asked"; "Malls Held," 6; "Mall not Figured," WWD, 8 Sep. 1959, 6; "Demolition and Rebuilding," WWD, 15 Jan. 1960, 10. See also "Clash Marks Session," WWD, 14 Jan. 1959, 23.

55. "City to Join," WWD, 23 Sep. 1957, 9; Jane Jacobs, "New Heart for Baltimore," AF 108 (June 1958): 88–92; Archibald C. Rogers, "Charles Center, Baltimore," AIA Journal 31 (Mar. 1959): 30–40; "Baltimore's Charles Center: A Case Study in Downtown Renewal," ULI 51 (Nov. 1964): whole issue; "Charles Center in Baltimore: How the Plan Didn't Get Compromised," Landscape Architecture 59 (Jan. 1969): 122–27; Katharine Lyall, "A Bicycle Built-for-Two: Public-Private Partnership in Baltimore," National Civic Review 72 (Nov. 1983): esp. 546–51; Marion E. Warren and Michael P. McCarthy, The Living City: Baltimore's Charles Center & Inner Harbor Development (Baltimore: Maryland Historical Society, 2002); David A. Wallace, Urban Planning My Way (Chicago: Planners Press, American Planning Association, 2004), chaps. 1–3.

56. "Baltimore Plan," WWD, 18 Mar. 1959, 1, 49; Wallace, Urban Planning, 39–43. Concerning Rouse's involvement, see Joshua Olsen, Better Places, Better Lives: A Biography of James Rouse (Washington, D.C.: Urban Land Institute, 2003), 93–95, 169–70.

57. "$470 Million Downtown," Baltimore Post, 15 May 1959, 1, 2, 10; "Covered Mall," WWD, 18 May 1959, I-6.

58. "Study Group," WWD, 1 July 1960, 22.

59. Only twenty-one permanent malls were developed in communities of any size during the 1960s. For background, see Roberto Brambilla et al., American Urban Malls: A Compendium (Washington, D.C.: U.S. Government Printing Office, 1977); and Harvey M. Rubenstein, Center City Malls (New York: Wiley, 1978). A particularly influential book on later work was Bernard Rudofsky, Streets for People: A Primer for Americans (Garden City: N.Y.: Doubleday, 1969).

60. "'Dying City' Label," NYT, 22 May 1955, 123.

61. "City Reveals," NHR, 12 June 1957, 1, 2; "Project Is Record," NHR, 12 June 1957, 1, 5; "Big Redevelopment," NHR, 12 June 1957, 80; "Stevens Picks," NHR, 13 June 1957, 1, 2; "Church Street Redevelopment Project, New Haven, Connecticut," brochure [1957], New Haven Free Public Library. For background, see "Planning with You," AF 82 (Jan. 1945): 113–18; Maurice E. H. Rotival, "An Experiment in Organic Planning for New Haven," U.S.A. Tomorrow 1 (Jan. 1955): 16–23; "Forward Look in Connecticut," Time 69 (24 June 1957): 28–29; "He Is Saving a 'Dead' City," Saturday Evening Post 230 (19 Apr. 1958): 31, 115–16, 118; "New Haven: Test for Downtown Renewal," AF 109 (July 1958): 78–81, 152; and "New Haven and Its Mayor," Holiday 39 (May 1966): 62–63, 117–18, 120–22, 126. Rotival's 1941 master plan formed the framework for the city's postwar redevelopment program. For recent critical analyses of the project, see Jeff Hardwick, "A Downtown Utopia? Suburbanization, Urban Renewal and Consumption in New Haven," Planning History Studies 10 (1996): 41–54; and of the city's urban renewal program, see Douglas W. Rae, City: Urbanism and Its End (New Haven: Yale University Press, 2003), chaps. 9–10. For a more balanced overview, see Lowe, Cities in a Race, chap. 9; and G. William Domhoff, Who Really Rules? New Haven and Community Power (New Brunswick, N.J.: Transaction, 1978). Useful pictorial coverage is offered by New Haven Colony Historical Society, New Haven: Reshaping the City 1900–1980 (Charleston, S.C.: Arcadia, 2002), esp. chaps. 2 and 3.

62. "Chamber of Commerce" and "Realty Heads," NHR, 13 June 1957, 19; "City Plan Group," NHR, 20 June 1957, 54; "Development . . . Gets," NHJ, 11 July 1957, 1; "Church Street Project," NHJ, 4 Sep. 1957, 1, 6; "Church Street Acquisitions," NHR, 13 Jan. 1958, 14; "The Real Story," NHR, 2 Oct. 1959, 1.

63. "Project Hearing," NHJ, 23 July 1957, 1, 5; Merchants Now Oppose," NHJ, 16 Nov. 1957, 1, 15; "Sawitt Asks," NHJ, 15 Oct. 1957, 1, 5; "Redevelopment Agency," NHJ, 9 Nov. 1958, 4; "City Reaches," NHR, 20 Apr. 1959, 1, 2.

64. "The Real Story," 1, 8; "Malley Vote," NHJ, 14 Oct. 1959, 1; "Church Street Redevelopment," NHR, 1 May 1960, 27. Concerning improvements to the existing store, see "Edw. Malley Co.," NHR, 16 May 1955, 1; "Malley Store," NHR, 5 Oct. 1955, 1, 2; "Malley Store," NHR, 15 Mar. 1956, 1, 4; and "Malley Opens," NHR, 20 Aug. 1956, 1, 2.

65. "Stockholders Favor," NHJ, 28 Nov. 1959; 1, 5; "Building Requirements," NHR, 11 May 1960, 1; "Aldermen Deny," NHJ, 3 May 1960, 4; "Malley Pact," NHJ, 20 Aug. 1960, 16; "Hearing Set," NHJ, 2 July 1960, 1, 10; "Malley-Stevens Deal," NHR, 20 Aug. 1960, 7; "Delay of Year," NHR, 13 Dec. 1961, 1, 8; "Final Church Street," NHJ, 24 May 1962, 1, 6; "Demolition of Old," NHR, 26 Mar. 1963, 38.

66. "$7,000,000 Construction," NHR, 16 May 1960, 1, 2. Concerning Malley's opening, see "Oct. 1 Opening," NHR, 24 May 1962, 1, 2; "Opening of Malley's," NHR, 25 Oct. 1962, 1, 2; and "Eager Crowds," NHJ, 26 Oct. 1962, 1, 15. Concerning the garage, see "Rudolph's Roman Road," AF 118 (Feb. 1963): 104–9; and "Paul Rudolph Designs a Place to Park," AR 133 (Feb. 1963): 145–50. Concerning Macy's, see "Macy's Shows Interest," NHR, 17 Sep. 1962, 1, 32; "Macy Deals," WWD, 18 Sep. 1962, 1, 21; "Businessmen Cheer," NHJ, 18 Sep. 1962, 1; "Stevens Says," NHR, 25 Sep. 1962, 1, 7; "Macy's Nears," NHR, 9 Nov. 1962, 4; "Church Street Plans," NHR, 29 Nov. 1962, 1, 11; "Macy's Plan," NHR, 19 Dec. 1962, 1, 72; "New Macy's," WWD, 20 Dec. 1962, 6; "City Forwards," NHJ, 3 Jan. 1963, 1; "Negotiations Completed," NHR, 25 Mar. 1963, 1, 2; "Contract Approved," NHR, 29 Mar. 1963, 1, 15; "Dwight Firm," NHR, 19 Apr. 1963, 1, 4; "Lee Describes," NHR, 5 Dec. 1963, 64; "Macy New Haven," WWD, 24 Sep. 1964, 13.

67. "'Front Block' Development," NHR, 6 Jan. 1963, 2; "Central Boom," NHR, 24 Jan. 1963, 48; "Church St. . . . Unveiled," NHR, 15 Mar. 1964, 1, 2; NHR, 1 Mar. 1967, Chapel Square Sect.; "At Long Last," NHR, 13 Mar. 1967, 1, 2; "Chapel Square," AR 146 (July 1969): 139; Louis G. Redstone, The New Downtowns: Rebuilding Business Districts (New York: McGraw-Hill, 1976), 84–85.

68. Graham was responsible for the 1957 and 1959 schemes and designed the Malley store. Macy's was designed by Abbott, Merkt. Chapel Square was the work of Lathrop Douglass, except for the hotel, which was designed by a leading specialist in that sphere, William Tabler. The soon infamous Temple Street Garage was the work of Paul Rudolph, then dean of Yale's School of Art and Architecture.

69. "Temple Garage," NHR, 25 Oct. 1962, 64.

70. "Future of Chapel Street," NHJ, 11 Mar. 1963, 1, 6; "Rx for Downtown?" WSJ, 28 Sep. 1960, 1, 23 (quote on p. 23).

71. "Sacramento . . . a Model for Small City Redevelopment," AF 102 (June 1954): 152–59; "Council Adds," SB, 20 Jan. 1954, 21.

72. "Redevelopment of Whole," SB, 1 July 1954, 1, 19.

73. Ibid., 19; "Capital Leaders," SB, 2 July 1954, 1; "Swig Pledges," SB, 9 July 1954, 1, 8; "Woolworth Is Interested," SB, 9 July 1954, 1; "Swig Tells," SB, 14 July 1954, 1.

74. Later, the city's redevelopment agency divided the fifteen-block urban renewal area into several sections, primarily to "encourage local investors to develop one or more of the parcels"—an objective not realized until the late 1960s. See "Slum Agency," SB, 7 Aug. 1957, A-1.

75. "Backers of Mall," SB, 17 Sep. 1954, 1, 4; "Downtown Improvement," SB, 17 Sep. 1954, 23; "Big Drive Set," WWD, 20 Sep. 1954, 1, 36; "Redevelopment Plan's," SB, 25 Oct. 1954, 21; "City Council Orders," SB, 25 Nov. 1954, 1, 8; "US Agrees," SB, 2 Dec. 1954, 1, 8; "Officials See," SB, 27 Aug. 1955, 1, 7; "Agency Okehs," SB, 1 Sep. 1955, 1; "City Plans Board," SB, 7 Sep. 1955, 1; "Officials Sign," SB, 26 Apr. 1956, 1, 8.

76. Zeckendorf's role in shaping the post–World War II landscape begs detailed analysis. For a sampling of contemporary accounts, see "The Newsworthy Webb & Knapp: Real Estate Plus Imagination," BW, 31 Oct. 1953, 130–33; "Webb & Knapp—and Zeckendorf," Fortune 49 (Mar. 1954): 113–15, 131–32, 136, 138, 141–42, 144; "He Dreams Colossal—Some Come True," BW, 14 Jan. 1956: 54–56, 60; "Zeckendorf: He's the Biggest Real Estate Tycoon in America," House & Home 12 (Oct. 1957): 82–94; "The Wheeling and Dealing of William Zeckendorf," AF 112 (June 1960): 130–31, 195, 198, 202, 210; "Man in a $100-Million Jam," Fortune 62 (July 1960): 104–9, 244, 246, 249–50; and Eugene Rachlis and John E. Marquesee, *The Land Lords* (New York: Random House, 1963), chap. 9. The developer made no mention of Sacramento in his autobiography, *Zeckendorf* (New York: Holt, Rinehart & Winston, 1970).

77. "Mall Project," SB, 24 Jan. 1957, E1; "Bill Says," SB, 13 Mar. 1957, 1; "NY Builder," SB, 21 Mar. 1957, A1; "NY Firm Plans," SB, 10 Dec. 1957, A1, A8; "NY Firm Will," SB, 10 Feb. 1958, C1; "Business Center," SB, 11 Feb. 1958, D1; "$10,000,000 West End," SB, 24 Mar. 1958, C1; "City Plan Chief," SB, 7 Apr. 1958, B1; "City Councilmen Okeh," SB, 5 June 1958, F1; "Coordinated Planning," SB, 16 Apr. 1957, A1; "'Core Area' Plans," SB, 23 June 1958, D1.

78. "Bright Future," WWD, 24 Sep. 1963, 11; "Many Favorable," SB, 3 Nov. 1963, M2. The Topeka store was announced in 1960 but not completed until six years later due in part to problems in securing adequate municipal support for locating in a physically constrained and economically fragile central business district.

79. "Macy's Negotiates," SB, 12 Apr. 1960, A1, A4; "Traffic Plan," SB, 13 May 1960, C1; "Macy's Acts," SB, 31 May 1960, A1, A6; "200,000 Sq. Ft. Branch," WWD, 1 June 1960, I-1, I-54.

80. "Slum Unit," SB, 1 July 1960, B2; "Council Okeh's," SB, 22 July 1960, C1; "Macy Is Due," SB, 30 Jan. 1960, C1; "Redevelopment Agency," SB, 31 Jan. 1961, B1; "Density Control," SB, 21 Mar. 1961, C2; "City Planners," SB, 29 Mar. 1961, C1; "SRA Sets," SB, 26 June, 1961, C1; "Macy Plan," SB, 8 July 1961, A1. Concerning the SOM plan, see "SF Firm Will," SB, 8 July 1961, A1; "Redevelopment Unit," SB, 20 Mar. 1962, A1, A4; "C of C Board," SB, 13 Apr. 1962, C1; and "West End Commercial Complex, Sacramento, Skidmore, Owings & Merrill, Architects," May 1962, copy in Sacramento Room, Sacramento Public Library.

81. "Macy's Slates," SB, 6 Mar. 1962, C2; "Redevelopers Study," SB, 10 Mar. 1962, A1, A5; "SRA Acts," SB, 6 Apr. 1962, C1; "Council Argues," SB, 7 Apr. 1962, A1, A4 (quote on A4); "Public Has," SB, 10 Apr. 1962, C1; "Ex Mayor Backs," SB, 11 Apr. 1962, C1; "Council Sets," SB, 13 Apr. 1962, A1, A4; "Macy's Starts," SB, 27 June 1962, C1; "New Department Store Opened," *Journal of Housing* 20 (Oct. 1963): 577; SB, 3 Nov. 1963, Macy's Sect.

82. "$35 Million Reynolds," SB, 12 Feb. 1964, A4; "Special Tishman Report," SB, 13 Dec. 1966, C1; "Future of Capital City," SB, 14 Dec. 1966, A1, D1; "Tishman Pledges," SB, 16 Dec. 1966, A1; "Mall Planning," SB, 17 Dec. 1966, C1; "Tishman Site," SB, 10 Jan. 1967, A1, D1; "Delay Looms," SB, 15 Feb. 1967, H1, H2; "Some Progress," SB, 28 Mar. 1967, B2; "Tishman Action," SB, 5 June 1967, B1; "Tishman Co.," *Sacramento Union*, 19 Sep. 1967, 1, 2; "Request Is Expected," SB, 9 Oct. 1967, B1.

83. "Plant Marks," *Sacramento Union*, 9 Apr. 1968, Dedication ed., 19; "City Council Speeds," *Sacramento Union*, 26 Apr. 1968, 3; "Parking, Office Sites," *Sacramento Union*, 4 June 1968, 3; "Redevelopment Unit," *Sacramento Union*, 18 June 1968, 1, 3; "West End Plaza," *Sacramento Union*, 26 Aug. 1969, B3; "Mall Shops," SB, 26 Aug. 1969, A1.

84. "Mayor Opens Drive," SB, 9 Dec. 1966, A1; "Mayor Asks," SB, 15 Dec. 1966, C1; "Mall Plan," SB, 17 Dec. 1966, C1; "K Street Mall," SB, 5 Feb. 1967, B7; "Start on Mall," SB, 14 Mar. 1967, C1; "Fresno Center," SB, 28 Mar. 1967, B1; "Building of Mall," SB, 16 May 1967, A1; "K Street Pedestrian," SB, 1 Aug. 1967, 3; "K Street Mall," SB, 17 Oct. 1967, B1; *Sacramento Union*, 28 Nov. 1967, C1.

85. "Lease Signing," DP, 18 Sep. 1958, 42. The project is discussed at some length in *Zeckendorf*, chap. 10.

86. "15 to 18 Story Hotel," DP, 8 July 1953, 1, 3; "It's 30-Story," DP, 9 July 1953, 1; "Zeckendorf Buys," RMN, 19 July 1953, 1, 5, 6; "Zeckendorf, Statler," DP, 20 Sep. 1953, 3-A; "Start Seen," DP, 23 Jan. 1954, 1; "1,000 Room Hotel," DP, 5 Apr. 1954, 1; "Hotel 'Reversal,'" DP, 10 Nov. 1954, 3; "Original Plan Enlarged," DP, 23 Jan. 1955, 1-A.

87. "2 Department Chains" and "Webb & Knapp Sifted," DP, 23 May 1954, 1-A, 3-A, resp.; "Statler Sale," DP, 20 June 1954, 2-A; "Start on Hotel," DP, 24 June 1954, 3; "Hilton Hotel," DP, 3 Aug. 1954, 1; "Zeckendorf Capitulates," RMN, 5 Aug. 1954, 10; "Work to Start," RMN, 8 Aug. 1954, 5; "Zeckendorf Hails," DP, 3 Nov. 1954, 3; "Hotel to Start," DP, 9 Nov. 1954, 1; "D&F Store," DP, 16 Aug. 1957, 1; "May Clears," DP, 20 Aug. 1957, 1; "May Co. Seeks," WWD, 21 Aug. 1957, 1, 13; "D&F Board," DP, 6 Sep. 1957, 1; "Daniels, Fisher Holders," WWD, 9 Sep. 1957, 1, 18; "May Co. Deal," WWD, 14 Nov. 1957, 1, 52; "Zeck Arrives," RMN, 18 Nov. 1957, 5; "May Co.–D&F Merger," WWD, 19 Nov. 1957, 1, 19; "Zeck, Hilton," RMN, 23 May 1958, 8; "Hilton Leases," DP, 18 Sep. 1958, 1.

88. "Zekendorf's 'Diggings,'" DP, 19 Nov. 1954, 20; "Do Cowtown Denverites," RMN, 19 Feb. 1956, 16; "Hotel in Doubt," DP, 26 June 1956, 1, 19; "Zeckendorf Will," RMN, 10 July 1956, 12; "Zeckendorf Arrives," RMN, 30 July 1956, 40; "Councilman Claims," RMN, 19 Nov. 1957, 5.

89. "Newsworthy Webb & Knapp," 133; "Mr. Zeckendorf and Architecture: A Communication," *Horizon* 5 (Jan. 1963): 115.

90. "D&F Predicts," DP, 23 Jan. 1955, 15-A; "Gold-Covered Aluminum," DP, 14 Feb. 1957, 2; "New May-D&F," WWD, 30 June 1958, 1, 33; "Interior of May-D&F," DP, 14 July 1958, 27; "Special Décor," WWD, 17 July 1958, 3; "Huge Crowds," WWD, 5 Aug. 1958, 1, 36; "Architect I. M. Pei," RMN, 2 Aug. 1958, 19; "Mid-City 'Shopping Center,'" AF 109 (Nov. 1958): 142–45 (quotes on p. 144); RMN, 3 Apr. 1960, Denver Hotel sect.; "Hilton Sees," DP, 7 Apr. 1960, 3; "Grand Hotel—1960 Style," AF 113 (Aug. 1960): 94–99 (quote on p. 95); "Zeckendorf Assails," DP, 14 Feb. 1961, 1, 31; "Denverites Challenge," DP, 15 Feb. 1961, 2.

91. "Here's What," RDC, 26 Sep. 1958, 7. See also "Bold 15 Million," RDC, 26 Sep. 1959, 1, 6; "Plaza Plan Heralds," RTU, 26 Sep. 1958, 1, 4; "A Downtown Garden Spot," RTU, 26 Sep. 1958, 48; "A

Chance Meeting," *RTU*, 26 Sep. 1958, 27; "Big Enclosed Plaza," *WWD*, 29 Sep. 1958, 1, 24; "Renaissance on the Genesee," *AF* 111 (July 1959): 104–9; "Center for Rochester," *AF* 116 (June 1962): 108–13; "Rochester's Midtown Plaza," *Journal of Housing* 19 (June 1962): 261; Gruen, *Heart of Our Cities*, 300–321; Wall, *Victor Gruen*, 142–48. Hardwick, *Mall Maker*, 197–204, provides a useful historical perspective, although McCurdy's and Forman's were not the city's two largest department stores (p. 198) and the mall did not exclude small local stores (p. 203). See also Karen McCally, "The Life and Times of Midtown Plaza," *Rochester History* 69 (spring 2007): whole issue.

92. "City Council Gives," *RDC*, 30 Sep. 1958, 1; "Estimates, Plans," *RDC*, 8 Nov. 1958, 17; "City's Share," *RDC*, 8 Dec. 1958, 21; "Planning Commissioners," *RDC*, 18 Dec. 1958, 1, 11; "City Council Gives," *RTU*, 24 Dec. 1958, 1, 10; "Midtown Pact," *RTU*, 11 Mar. 1959, 33; "Award of Contract," *RDC*, 25 Mar. 1959, 19; "Council Authorizes," *RDC*, 24 June 1959, 19; "Midtown Plaza Garage," *RDC*, 3 July 1959, 18; "City's Plaza Plan," *RTU*, 24 Nov. 1958, 29. See also "Midtown Plaza Receives," *RTU*, 5 Feb. 1959, 23.

93. "Group Maps," *RTU*, 22 Dec. 1958, 21; "There'll Be Debate," *RTU*, 23 Dec. 1958, 11; "Center Developer," *RDC*, 23 Dec. 1958, 58, 15, 16; "Stone St. Merchants," *RDC*, 26 Dec. 1958, 23; "Midtown Reassurance," *RTU*, 7 Feb. 1959, 3; "Merchant Hits," *RTU*, 11 Aug. 1960, 26; "Midtown Plaza," *RTU*, 24 June 1961; Hardwick, *Mall Maker*, 203–4.

94. "Adding Something," *RTU*, 12 Nov. 1959, 22; *RDC*, 10 Apr. 1962, Midtown sect.; "87 Per Cent," *RTU*, 17 Apr. 1963, 30; "Midtown Leases," *RTU*, 15 Feb. 1962, 25; "Midtown Plaza," *WWD*, 20 Mar. 1962, 2; "Designer Hails," *RDC*, 4 Apr. 1962; "Bipartisan Spirit" and "Mall's 'Fabulous,'" *RDC*, 11 Apr. 1962, 23, 24; "Midtown: 1958 and Today," *RTU*, 17 Apr. 1963, 29; "Midtown Gives," *RTU*, 26 Apr. 1962, 14.

95. Gruen, *Heart of Our Cities*, 300–321 (quote on p. 312); "What Happens to Shopping Centers When the Downtown Core Is Revitalized?" *SCA* 1 (Aug. 1962): 18–19, 29–31 (quote on p. 18); "Midtown Plaza," *UL* 21 (June 1962): 3–5; "New Rochester Plaza," *WWD*, 10 July 1962, 15; "Midtown Plaza," *WWD*, 20 Sep. 1962, 16; "Rochester Plaza," *WWD*, 11 Apr. 1963, 12; "The Vision that Saved the City" and "Mr. Midtown," *RDC*, 12 Apr. 1970, *Upstate* magazine, 4, 6–7, 25, 27, resp.; Robert E. Witherspoon et al., *Mixed-Use Developments: New Ways of Land Use* (Washington, D.C.: Urban Land Institute, 1976), 91; interview with Angelo J. Chiraella, former manager of Midtown Plaza, Rochester, 18 June 2002.

96. "$41 Million Plaza," *SS*, 24 May 1957, 1, 2; "City Council Juggles," *SS*, 19 Sep. 1957, 1, 5; "Plaza Job Begins," *NYT*, 6 Oct. 1957, VIII-6; "Plaza City Hall," *SS*, 15 Oct. 1957, 1.

97. "Macy's to Lease," *SS*, 18 Jan. 1958, 1; "Shop Center Design," *SS*, 13 May 1958, 1, 3; "Skyscraper Shopping Center," *WWD*, 14 May 1958, 1, 17; "Milan Center Gave," *NYT*, 25 May 1958, VIII-1, VIII-13.

98. "New Buyer," *SS*, 30 Sep. 1959, 1; "Plaza Promoter," *SS*, 1 Oct. 1959, 1; "Plaza Deadline," *SS*, 2 Oct. 1959, 1; "Urban Renewal Job," *SS*, 17 Nov. 1960, 1, 2; editorial, *SS*, 18 Nov. 1960, 4; "Work Now Getting," *WWD*, 15 Dec. 1961, 2; "Bake a 7-Layer Cake," *SCA* 2 (July 1963): 28–30; "Macy to Build," *SS*, 5 Nov. 1964, 1, 2.

99. "Agreement Seen," *SS*, 17 Mar. 1966, 1, 2; "Shop Center," *SS*, 18 Jan. 1967, 1, 37; "Macy's Opens," *SS*, 13 Sep. 1967, 1, 3; "The Mall to Open," *SS*, 31 July 1968, 1 and A sect.

100. "Lits Proposes," *TT*, 14 Dec. 1959, 1, 2; "Mark Resigns," *TT*, 14 Dec. 1959, 1; "Disturbing Indecision," *TT*, 14 Dec. 1959, 12; "9-Acre Shop Tract," *NYT*, 15 Dec. 1959, 41; "Road Plan Factor," *TT*, 15 Dec. 1959, 1, 2; "Capitol Center," *TT*, 15 Dec. 1959, 14.

101. E. Kimbark MacColl, *The Growth of a City: Power and Politics in Portland, Oregon, 1915 to 1950* (Portland: Georgian, 1979), chap. 12. See also "Ben Holladay First," *Oregonian* (Portland), 31 July 1960, C-4.

102. "8 Million Allied," *WWD*, 24 May 1954, 8.

103. "M&F Gets," *Oregonian*, 29 July 1956, 1; "Eastside Shopping Center," *Oregonian*, 18 Nov. 1956, 44; "Meier & Frank," *Oregonian*, 24 July 1957, 24; "100 Million," *Oregonian*, 1 Dec. 1957, 1; "Record $21,300,000 Permit," *Oregonian*, 11 Apr. 1958, 1; "Building Giant Lloyd," *Oregonian*, 28 Dec. 1958, 32; "Large Downtown," *WWD*, 20 Aug. 1959, 9.

104. As is evident in the lavish section devoted to the center's opening; see esp. "Lloyd's Bring New Era," *Oregonian*, 31 July 1960, M-1. Useful material also can be found in "Portland's Lloyd Center," *WWD*, 20 Jan. 1960, 18; "Economics, Planning, and Prospects," *AR* 127 (Mar. 1960): 211–12; "New *Downtown* Portland Center," *CSA/VE* 36 (Sep. 1960): 85; "Design for Merchandising," *AR* 128 (Dec. 1960): 123–28; and "Trends from Regional Center to 'Complete City,'" *UL* 21 (Sep. 1962): 9–10.

105. "Threat of Lloyd Center," *WWD*, 20 Oct. 1959, 1, 42; "Portland Retail Scene," *WWD*, 8 July 1960, 3; "Convenient Parking," *WWD*, 3 Aug. 1960, 6; "Lloyd Center Has Lead," *WWD*, 6 Sep. 1960, 51; "Downtown Portland," *WWD*, 6 Oct. 1960, 1, 37; "Lloyd Center Lag," *WWD*, 1 Nov. 1960, 1, 16; "Business Trails," *WWD*, 6 Dec. 1960, I-6; "Lloyd Center Inroads," *WWD*, 14 Mar. 1961, 1, 41; "Lloyd Center," *WWD*, 4 Aug. 1961, 1, 20; "Lloyd Center Well," *WWD*, 19 July 1962, 6.

106. For background, see "LA Planners," *BHC*, 17 Feb. 1961, 1, 2; "Real Estate Values," *BHC*, 24 Mar. 1961, 1, 2; "C-City Plans," *BHC*, 9 July 1962, 1; "ALCOA . . . and Redevelopment," *AR* 34 (Sep. 1964): Western Sect., 36–37; "Century City's 2nd Milestone," *LAT*, 11 Oct. 1964, J-1, J-20; *Zeckendorf*, 244–54; Witherspoon et al., *Mixed-Use Developments*, 27–33; Cheryl G. Cummins et al., "*ULI* 1987 Fall Meeting Project Brochure, Los Angeles Metropolitan Area . . . Today" (Washington, D.C.: Urban Land Institute, 1987), 110–24; and Garvin, *American City*, 291–94.

107. "Century City," *WWD*, 4 Apr. 1960, I-6; "Broadway Department Store," *BHC*, 5 Apr. 1960, 1, 2; "200,000 Sq. Ft." *WWD*, 27 Dec. 1960, 1, 28; "Century City Action," *BHC*, 28 Dec. 1960, 1, 2; "Century City Men," *BHC*, 24 Feb. 1961, 1; "Plans Are Rounded," *WWD*, 11 June 1962, 2; "Century Square's Parking," *SCA* 1 (Aug. 1962): 8; "Work Starts on Century Square," *SCA* 2 (Jan. 1963): 9; "Century Square Will Park 2,700 Cars *under* the Center," *SCA* 2 (Feb. 1963): 25–27; "Century City Broadway," *BHC*, 6 Oct. 1964, B-1.

108. For discussion, see, e.g., Peter O. Muller, *The Outer City: Geographical Consequences of the Urbanization of the United States* (Washington, D.C.: Association of American Geographers, 1976); Thomas Baerwald, "The Emergence of a New 'Downtown,'" *Geographic Review* 68 (June 1978): 308–18; and Truman Hartshorn and Peter O. Muller, "Suburban Downtowns and the Transformation of Metropolitan Atlanta's Business Landscape," *Urban Geography* 10 (July–Aug. 1989): 375–95.

EPILOGUE

1. "Allied Looking," *WWD*, 13 Feb. 1959, 1, 32; "Big Retail Gains," *WWD*, 26 Dec. 1956, II-2; "Big Stores Told," *WWD*, 21 Oct. 1959, 1, 20.

2. A useful compendium of prominent regional mall developers can be found in *CSE* 65 (May 1989): 43–93. See also A. Alfred Taubman, *Threshold Resistance: The Extraordinary Career of a Luxury Retailing Pioneer* (New York: HarperCollins, 2007).

3. The figures cited in the text were compiled from a page-by-page culling of information from the *Directory of Shopping Centers in the United States and Canada*, 13th ed. (Burlington, Iowa: National Research Bureau, 1972). The rate of construction picked up early on in the decade so that by 1967 and thereafter the number of regional malls opening annually was generally more than double

what it had been. Over half of these malls had at least one national chain department store—Sears, Montgomery Ward, J. C. Penney, etc.—as an anchor, along with a downtown-based department store.

4. Grady Tucker, "The New Economics of Shopping Center Location and Scale," and Thomas Muller, "Regional Malls and Central City Retail Sales: An Overview," in *Shopping Centers: U.S.A.*, ed. George Sternlieb and James W. Hughes (Piscataway, N.J.: Center for Urban Policy Research, Rutgers University, 1981), 46, 180–81, resp.

5. Handbooks of the period that afford a useful indicator of trends include Louis G. Redstone, *New Dimensions in Shopping Centers and Stores* (New York: McGraw-Hill, 1973); William Applebaum and S. O. Kaylin, *Case Studies in Shopping Center Development and Operation* (New York: International Council of Shopping Centers, 1974), esp. chap. 3; David Gosling and Barry Maitland, *Design and Planning of Retail Systems* (New York: Whitney Library of Design, 1976), 28–47; J. Ross McKeever et al., *Shopping Center Development Handbook* (Washington, D.C.: Urban Land Institute, 1977); John Casazza et al., *Shopping Center Development Handbook,* 2nd ed. (Washington, D.C.: Urban Land Institute, 1985); Barry Maitland, *Shopping Malls: Planning and Design* (London: Construction Press, 1985), chaps. 2, 3; Robert Davis Rathburn, *Shopping Centers & Malls 1* (New York: Retail Reporting Corporation, 1986), and Rathburn, *Shopping Centers & Malls 3* (New York: Retail Reporting Corporation, 1990). See also "Shopping Centers and Stores," *AR* 139 (Apr. 1966): 149–70; "Shopping Malls in Suburbia," *AR* 151 (Mar. 1972): 113–28; and "Retail Malls," *AR* 165 (Feb. 1979): 117–52. An insightful analysis of the situation in the early 1970s is afforded by "'Downtown' Has Fled to the Suburbs," *Fortune* 86 (Oct. 1972): 80–87, 156, 158, 162. Concerning the Galleria, see "The Galleria," "Galleria Mall," and "Galleria Patterned," *HP*, 15 Nov. 1970, BB1, BB8, CC6, and 10–16, resp.; "Supermall," *AF* 136 (Apr. 1972): 30–33; Redstone, *New Dimensions,* 174–75; and Robert E. Witherspoon et al., *Mixed-Use Developments: New Ways of Land Use* (Washington, D.C.: Urban Land Institute, 1976), 148–53.

6. "'Downtown' Has Fled," 87.

7. After 1960, however, a substantial number of regional centers with forty or more units were anchored by a national chain department store, not one traditionally based downtown. Around sixty-five such complexes were opened by the close of 1970, indicating that at least in some market areas a downtown-based department store was not necessary. The dynamics of mall tenancy continued to change in the decades that followed. See, e.g., "Opinions Differ on Anchorless Centers," *CSE* 64 (May 1988): 59–60, 62.

8. Ronald W. Stampfl and Elizabeth Hirschman, eds., *Competitive Structure in Retail Markets: The Department Store Perspective* (Chicago: American Marketing Association, 1980), 33–42, 119–23; Barry Bluestone et al., *The Retail Revolution: Market Transformation, Investment, and Labor in the Modern Department Store* (Boston: Auburn House, 1981); Eleanor G. May and Malcolm P. McNair, "Department Stores Face Stiff Challenges in Next Decade," *JR* 53 (fall 1977): 47–58. For a sampling of early accounts, see the eight-part series by Fred Eichenbaum in *WWD* from 22 June to 7 July 1959; "Discounters Feel," *WWD*, 16 Jan. 1961, 1, 12; "May, Allied Plan," *WWD*, 13 Mar. 1961, 1, 28; "Competitors Ready," *WWD*, 5 Apr. 1961, 1, 51; "Sharp Competitive Battle," *WWD*, 22 May 1961, 1, 28; "J. C. Penney Chain," *WWD*, 29 Sep. 1961, 1, 47; and "Discounter Called Hypo," *WWD*, 7 May 1962, 10. The nomenclature itself varied over the period. In January 1981, for example, *Standard & Poor's Industry Surveys* classified the traditionally downtown-based emporia as "department stores," while the diverse group of Sears, Penney's, Woolworth's, Murphy's, and K Mart were classified as "general merchandise chains." Caldor, Wal-Mart, and Zayre, on the other hand, were categorized as "discount department stores" (vol. 2, R99, R100). By 2004, in contrast, Sears, Penney's, Federated, May Company, Dillard's, Nordstrom, Saks, and Neiman-Marcus were all classified as "department stores"; Wal-Mart, K Mart, and Target as "discount stores" (3 [17 Nov. 2005]: Retail General, 30). Penney's was first listed as a department store in July 1973 (vol. 2, R103).

9. For a sampling of early accounts, see "Allied Will Establish," *WWD*, 13 Apr. 1961, 1, 35; "Branches Neglect," *WWD*, 24 May 1961, 1, 91; "*Big* Store Self-Help," *WWD*, 21 Aug. 1961, 1, 12; "Dayton Co. Discount," *WWD*, 2 Oct. 1961, 17; "Big Store Strength," *WWD*, 19 Oct. 1961, 1, 20; "Macy's Stepping Up," *WWD*, 15 Nov. 1961, 1, 16; "Federated, May Co.," *WWD*, 27 Apr. 1962, 1, 28; "Macy's Kansas City," *WWD*, 17 July 1962, 12; "Branch Treasure," *WWD*, 24 Sep. 1962, 1, 8; and "Basement Sections Held," *WWD*, 27 Dec. 1962, I-1, I-48.

10. "Downtown Status Minor," *WWD*, 16 Jan. 1963, 6. Useful, concise retrospective accounts include Muller, "Regional Malls," 177–99; Kent A. Robertson, "Downtown Retail Activity in Large American Cities, 1954–1977," *Geographical Review* 73 (June 1983): 314–23; and George Sternlieb and James W. Hughes, "The Demise of the Department Store," *American Demographics* 9 (Aug. 1987): 30–33, 59.

11. "Large-Non-White Market," *WWD*, 12 Oct. 1955, I-14; "Negro Population Move," *WWD*, 17 Aug. 1959, 1, 28; "Job Level Rise," *WWD*, 18 Aug. 1959, I-1, I-52; "Negro Said to Constitute," *WWD*, 24 Apr. 1962, 24; "Face of Chicagoland," *WWD*, 24 Oct. 1962, 16; George Sternlieb, "The Future of Retailing in the Downtown Core," *Journal of the American Institute of Planners* 29 (May 1963): 102–12; "Negro Market Potential," *WWD*, 15 Oct. 1963, 14. A good case study of postwar segregation policies is found in Patricia Cooper, "The Limits of Persuasion: Race Reformers and the Department Store Campaign in Philadelphia, 1945–1948," *Pennsylvania Magazine of History and Biography* 126 (Jan. 2002): 97–126. An insightful historical account is afforded in Allison Isenberg, *Downtown America: A History of the Place and the People Who Made It* (Chicago: University of Chicago Press, 2004), chap. 6. See also Robert E. Weems, Jr., *Desegregating the Dollar: African American Consumerism in the Twentieth Century* (New York: New York University Press, 1998).

12. For a recent, concise overview, see Jon C. Teaford, *The Metropolitan Revolution: The Rise of Post-Urban America* (New York: Columbia University Press, 2006), 126–56. See also "Inner-City Decay," *NYT*, 19 July 1971, 1, 29.

13. Breckenfeld, "'Downtown' Has Fled," 82.

14. E.g., see Harvey M. Rubenstein, *Center City Malls* (New York: Wiley, 1978); and Rubenstein, *Pedestrian Malls, Streetscapes, and Urban Spaces* (New York: Wiley, 1992).

15. Namely, in order of completion: The Center in Worcester (1972); The Gallery in Philadelphia (1977, 1982–83), Town Square in St. Paul (1980), Grand Avenue in Milwaukee (1982), Charleston Town Center in Charleston, West Virginia (1983), St. Louis Centre in St. Louis (1985), and Horton Plaza in San Diego (1985). Besides Midtown Plaza, Boston's Prudential Center (1959–68, et seq.) provided an important precedent. In that case, however, the department stores were among the last components developed.

16. Less sweeping projects, especially ones intended to bolster retail areas that remained strong, such as Water Tower Place on North Michigan Avenue in Chicago, fared markedly better.

17. See Richard Longstreth, comp. "New Buildings and Major Additions for Downtown Department Stores, 1920–1960"; and Longstreth, comp., "Department Stores Branches, 1910–1960," at http://www.departmentstorehistory.net and http://www.preservenet.cornell.edu.

18. For a sampling of period accounts, see "The Merger Spree,"

NYT, 20 May 1984, F1, F26; "B.A.T. Will Sell," WSJ, 14 Jan. 1986, 2; "Associated Dry Goods Accepts," WSJ, 17 July 1986, 2; "Allied Stores," WSJ, 3 Nov. 1986, 3; "Campau's Victory," WSJ, 4 Nov. 1986, 2; "Canadian Offering $4 Billion," NYT, 25 Jan. 1988, D1, D9; "Campau-Federated Is Off," WSJ, 13 May 1988, 22; "Squeezed Stores," WSJ, 14 Dec. 1988, A8; "B.A.T.-Man Caper," WSJ, 12 July 1989, A4; "Saks and Marshall Field," NYT, 8 Feb. 1990, D20; "Arab Group to Buy," WSJ, 26 Apr. 1990, B1, B10; "Macy's Board Backs," NYT, 15 July 1994, A1, D4; "Federated to Buy Broadway," NYT, 15 Aug. 1995, D1, D2; "Federated Unveils," WSJ, 20 Nov. 1995, C13; "Federated Shows," NYT, 21 Jan. 2005, C1, C4; "Federated Agrees," WSJ, 28 Feb. 2005, A1, A6; "Federated Unveils," WSJ, 1 Mar. 2005, A3; "Anchors Away!" WSJ, 1 Mar. 2005, B1, B7; "What's in a Store's Name?" NYT, 29 July 2005, C1, C2; "Federated to Hang," WSJ, 29 July 2005, B3; "Saks Urged to Offer," WSJ, 29 July 2005, C4; "Marshall Field's Becomes," WSJ, 21 Sep. 2005, A15; "Federated to Sell," WSJ, 13 Jan. 2006, A11; "Loss of Marshall Field," NYT, 17 Jan. 2007, 13. See also John Rothchild, *Going for Broke: How Robert Campeau Bankrupted the Retail Industry, Jolted the Junk Bond Market, and Brought the Booming Eighties to a Crashing Halt* (New York: Simon & Schuster, 1991); and Jeffrey A. Trachtenberg, *The Rain on Macy's Parade: How Greed, Ambition, and Folly Ruined America's Greatest Store* (New York: Random House, 1996).

19. Concerning the former group, see "Power Centers: Everybody Wins," CSE 62 (Sep. 1986): 35–36, 38; "Power Centers Flex Their Muscles," CSE 65 (Feb. 1989): 3A–4A; "At Issue: Over'power'ing the Strip," CSE 65 (Oct. 1989): 29–31; and Robert Spector, *Category Killers: The Retail Revolution and Its Impact on Consumer Culture* (Boston: Harvard Business School Press, 2005). Concerning the latter group, see "Outlets' Balancing Act: Low Prices vs. Quality," CSE 58 (May 1982): 110, 113; "Off-Price Shopping Centers: Developers' High-Caliber Weapon," CSE 59 (Oct. 1983): 46–48; "Off-Price Centers: Offbeat or Off-Stride?" CSE 62 (May 1986): 94, 96, 100, 102; "Factory Outlet Centers Keep Their Distance," CSE 66 (Apr. 1990): 39, 40, 42; and David A. Weiss and David M. Lummis, *Value Retailing in the 1990s: Off-Pricers, Factory Outlets, & Closeout Stores* (New York: Wiley, 1995), chap. 4.

20. Howard L. Green and David L. Huntoon, "Regional Shopping Center Issues in the 1980s," in Sternlieb and Hughes, *Shopping Centers*, 55–61; "Now That the Nation Is 'Malled,'" WSJ, 31 July 1985, 21; "Regional Mall Developers," WSJ, 2 Sep. 1987, 21; "Development of Big Shopping Malls," WSJ, 24 Apr. 1991, B1; "Retailing: When Decking the Halls," WSJ, 10 Dec. 1992, B1, B6; "Reinventing the Regional Mall," UL 53 (Feb. 1994): 24–27; "Retail Entertainment," UL 58 (Feb. 1999): 34–37, 94–95; "The De-Malling of America," UL 66 (Feb. 2001): 72–77; "Town Watch," UL 60 (May 2001): 36–45; "Lifestyle Centers," UL 61 (Feb. 2002): 59–64; "The Community Mall," UL 61 (Nov.–Dec. 2002): 100–105; "Back to the Basics," UL 62 (Feb. 2003): 44–48; "Lifestyle Retail," UL 63 (Feb. 2004): 48–56; "A Breath of Fresh Air," WSJ, 4 Aug. 2004, B4; "Entertaining Development," UL 64 (Jan. 2005): 54–58; "Centering Towns," UL 64 (Apr. 2005): 90–93; "A Choice of Lifestyles," UL 64 (Oct. 2005): 88–93; "Alternative Anchors," UL 64 (Oct. 2005): 96–102. For examples, see Barry Maitland, *The New Architecture*; International Council of Shopping Centers, *Winning Shopping Center Designs*, nos. 6–9 (New York: Visual Reference Publications, 1999–2002); and Michael D. Bayard et al., *Developing Retail Entertainment Destinations* (Washington, D.C.: Urban Land Institute, 2001). The proliferation of new types rendered the long-used distinctions of neighborhood, community, and regional shopping center somewhat obsolete. New categories such as "town center" and "lifestyle center" have generated as much confusion as clarification; see "Lost in Translation," UL 64 (Jan. 2005): 74–79.

21. "The Dead Mall," *Metropolis* 13 (Nov. 1993): 44–47, 61, 63; "The Aging Shopping Mall," WSJ, 16 Apr. 1996, B1, B16. See also Francesca Yurchiano, "The (Un)Malling of America," *American Demographics* 12 (Apr. 1990): 36–39. A long list of moribund centers is posted on http://www.deadmalls.com. Among the regional shopping centers initiated by 1960 that were visited as part of this study, the great majority remain in operation, albeit in substantially altered condition.

22. See, e.g., "Competition Strong for Prime Centers," CSE 61 (Apr. 1985): 41–42, 44, 47; Dean Schwanke et al., *Remaking the Shopping Center* (Washington, D.C.: Urban Land Institute, 1994); and "Mall Turnarounds," UL 63 (June 2004): 22–23.

23. Jerry Jacobs, *The Mall: An Attempted Escape from Everyday Life* (Prospect Heights, Ill.: Waveland, 1984), chap. 5; William Severini Kowinski, *The Malling of America: An Inside Look at the Great Consumer Paradise* (New York: William Morrow, 1985); Ira G. Zepp, Jr., *The New Religious Image of Urban America: The Shopping Mall as Ceremonial Center* (1986; Niwot: University Press of Colorado, 1997); Richard A. Feinberg et al., "There's Something Social Happening at the Mall," *Journal of Business and Psychology* 4 (fall 1989): 49–63; Peter H. Bloch et al., "Leisure and the Shopping Mall," in Rebecca H. Holman and Michael R. Solomon, eds., *Advances in Consumer Research, Vol. XVIII* (Provo, Utah: Association for Consumer Research, 1991), 445–52; Feinberg et al., "The Shopping Mall as Consumer Habitat," *Journal of Retailing* 70 (spring 1994): 23–42; Ozlem Sandikci and Douglas B. Holt, "Malling Society: Mall Consumption Practices and the Future of Public Space," in John F. Sherry, Jr., ed., *Servicescapes: The Concept of Place in Contemporary Markets* (Chicago: NTC Business, 1998), 305–36; James J. Farrell, *One Nation Under Goods: Malls and the Seduction of American Shopping* (Washington, D.C.: Smithsonian, 2003); "Our Malls, Ourselves," *Fortune* 150 (18 Oct. 2004): 243–45; Paco Underhill, *Call of the Mall* (New York: Simon & Schuster, 2004); Mark Moss, *Shopping as an Entertainment Experience* (Lanham, Md.: Rowman & Littlefield, 2007), chap. 4.

24. Theodore Morrow Spitzer and Hilary Baum, *Public Markets and Community Revitalization* (Washington, D.C.: Urban Land Institute, and New York: Project for Public Spaces, 1995).

A NOTE ON THE SOURCES

READILY AVAILABLE archival information concerning the business and the building of department stores is slim. Material of this kind consulted during the course of this project is noted in the Acknowledgments. I have relied most heavily on two types of period sources: trade publications and newspapers. Books and periodicals pertaining to advertising, architecture, business in general, engineering, landscape architecture, planning, motor vehicles and related transportation issues, and retailing were all of great value. Among them, the most important was *Women's Wear Daily,* which, for the period examined, was a rich source of information pertaining to virtually all the topics addressed in this book.

Besides myriad insights on retailers' interests in a wide spectrum of areas, *WWD* provided invaluable data, including literally hundreds of key dates when new stores and additions to existing ones, as well as service and parking facilities, were announced and when those projects were completed. This information allowed me to search efficiently through myriad newspapers for additional material. Newspaper clipping files or card indices in many urban libraries further facilitated the process. In many other instances, the search for information about a branch store in a suburban or other outlying location required scanning multiple issues. The great majority of this research was conducted before Proquest Historical Newspapers provided a digital search tool for the *Chicago Tribune, Los Angeles Times, New York Times, Washington Post,* and a few other major dailies. This database has nonetheless proved very helpful in augmenting information for the manuscript in recent years.

Site visits were made to the great majority of the projects examined in this study. Even when the facilities in question have been demolished or altered, visitation often yielded important information about the environs—both commercial and residential—in which they operated.

All the above sources assisted in developing detailed lists of the new downtown department stores, major additions to existing ones, department store branches of every kind, purpose-built service buildings, and garages built for department store companies nationwide for the decades that are the focus of the study. This material provided an essential basis upon which I could delineate expansion, innovation, and other trends in the industry, as well as placing major examples in a broader context. While those lists are far too extensive to include in the book, they are included on two websites: http://www.departmentstorehistory.net and http://www.preservenet.cornell.edu.

Interviews with a number of retailers and architects who contributed to the department store's progress in the post–World War II era yielded an array of insights that would otherwise have been difficult or impossible to glean. These individuals are cited in the Acknowledgments. Regrettably, time precluded searching for many others who could have enriched the picture in any number of ways.

Historical sources on department stores and related retail facilities, as well as on pertinent retailing practices and patterns of consumption, have helped frame a number of topics that I have sought to address. While many of them are cited in the notes, the rather varied nature, but relatively limited number, of such studies that include twentieth-century developments invites their listing, by subject, below.

Department Stores

Baker, Henry Givens. *Rich's of Atlanta: The Story of a Store Since 1867.* Atlanta: Division of Research, School of Business Administration, Atlanta Division, University of Georgia, 1953.

Beaumont, Matthew. "Shopping in Utopia: *Looking Backward,* the Department Store, and the Dreamscape of Consumption." *Nineteenth-Century Contexts* 28 (Sep. 2006): 191–209.

Benson, Susan Porter. *Counter Cultures: Saleswomen, Managers, and Customers in American Department Stores, 1890–1940.* Urbana: University of Illinois Press, 1986.

———. "Palace of Consumption and Machine for Selling: The American Department Store, 1880–1940." *Radical History Review* 21 (fall 1979): 199–221.

Bigson, George T., and Earle Dunford. *Under the Clock: The Story of Miller & Rhoads.* Charleston, S.C: History Press, 2008 (Richmond, Va.).

Birmingham, Nan Tillson. *Store.* New York: G. P. Putnam's, 1978.

Bradley, Martha Sonntag. *ZCMI: America's First Department Store.* Salt Lake City: ZCMI, 1991.

Brady, Maxine. *Bloomingdale's.* New York: Harcourt Brace Jovanovich, 1980.

Buenger, Victoria, and Walter L. Buenger. *Texas Merchant: Marvin Leonard and Fort Worth.* College Station: Texas A&M University Press, 1998.

Clausen, Meredith. "The Department Store—Development of the Type." *Journal of Architectural Education* 39 (fall 1985): 20–29.

———. "Department Stores." In Joseph A. Wilkes, ed., *Encyclopedia of Architecture, Design, Engineering and Construction,* 2: 204–22. New York: Wiley, 1988.

Cohen, Nancy Elizabeth. *Doing a Good Business: 100 Years at the Bon Ton.* Lyme, Conn.: Greenwich, 1998.

Cooper, Patricia. "The Limits of Persuasion: Race Reformers and the Department Store Campaign in Philadelphia, 1945–1948." *Pennsylvania Magazine of History and Biography* 126 (Jan. 2002): 97–126.

Costello, Brian J. *Canal Street and Beyond: Louisiana's 20th-Century Department Stores.* New Orleans: By the author, 2003.

Covington, Howard E., Jr. *Belk: A Century of Retail Leadership.* Chapel Hill: University of North Carolina Press, 1988.

Davis, Margaret. *Bullock's Wilshire.* Los Angeles: Balcony, 1996.

Emmet, Boris, and John E. Jeuck. *Catalogues and Counters: A History of Sears, Roebuck and Company.* Chicago: University of Chicago Press, 1950.

Enterprising Emporiums: The Jewish Department Stores of Downtown Baltimore. Baltimore: Jewish Museum of Maryland, 2001.

Faircloth, Christopher. *Cleveland's Department Stores.* Charleston, S.C.: Arcadia, 2009.

Ferry, John William. *A History of the Department Store.* New York: Macmillan, 1960.

Firestone, Mary. *Dayton's Department Store.* Charleston, S.C: Arcadia, 2007.

Frick, Devin Thomas. *I. Magnin & Co.: A California Legacy.* Garden Grove, Calif.: Park Place, 2000.

Grippo, Robert M. *Macy's: The Store, the Star, the Story.* Garden City Park, N.Y.: Square One, 2009.

Guilford, Martha C. *From Founders to Grandsons: The Story of Woodward & Lothrop.* Washington, D.C.: By the store, 1955.

Harris, Leon. *Merchant Princes: An Intimate History of Jewish Families Who Built Great Department Stores.* New York: Harper and Row, 1979.

Hauser, Michael, and Marianne Weldon. *Hudson's in the Early 1940s.* Charleston, S.C.: Arcadia, 2004.

Hendrickson, Robert. *The Grand Emporiums: The Illustrated History of America's Great Department Stores.* New York: Stein and Day, 1979.

The History of Lord & Taylor 1826–2001. [New York]: by the company, 2001.

Hower, Ralph M. *History of Macy's of New York, 1858–1919.* Cambridge: Harvard University Press, 1943.

Hungerford, Edward. *The Romance of a Great Store.* New York: Robert M. McBride, 1922. [Macy's]

Hutter, Mark. "The Downtown Department Store as a Social Force." *Social Science Journal* 24, no. 3 (1987): 241–46.

Karberg, Richard E., with Judith Karberg and Jane Hazen. *The Higbee Company and the Silver Grille.* Cleveland: Cleveland Landmarks, 2001.

La Pointe, Patricia M. "The Goldsmiths: A Memphis Department Store Family." *West Tennessee Historical Society Papers* 47 (December 1993): 1–9.

Lawrence, Jeanne Catherine. "Geographical Space, Social Space, and the Realm of the Department Store." *Urban History* 19 (1992): 64–83.

Leach, William R. *Land of Desire: Merchants, Power, and the Rise of a New American Culture.* New York: Random House, 1993.

———. "Transformations in a Culture of Consumption: Women and Department Stores, 1890–1925." *Journal of American History* 71 (Sep. 1984): 319–42.

Lewis, Russell. "Everything Under One Roof: World's Fairs and Department Stores in Paris and Chicago." *Chicago History* 12 (fall 1983): 28–47.

Lief, Alfred. *Family Business: A Century in the Life and Times of Strawbridge & Clothier.* New York: McGraw-Hill, 1968.

Lindstroom, Richard. "'It Would Break My Heart to See You Behind a Counter!': Business and Reform at L. S. Ayres & Company in the Early Twentieth Century." *Indiana Magazine of History* 93, no. 4 (1997): 345–76.

Longstreth, Richard. "Bringing 'Downtown' to the Neighborhoods: Wieboldt's, Goldblatt's, and the Creation of Department Store Chains in Chicago." *Buildings and Landscapes* 14 (fall 2007): 13–49.

———. "The Mixed Blessings of Success: The Hecht Company and Department Store Branch Development After World War II." In Carter L. Hudgins and Elizabeth Collins Cromley, eds., *Shaping Communities: Perspectives in Vernacular Architecture, VI,* 244–62. Knoxville: University of Tennessee Press, 1997.

———. "Sears, Roebuck and the Remaking of the Department Store, 1924–42." *Journal of the Society of Architectural Historians* 65 (June 2006): 238–79.

Lyons, Bettina O'Neil. *Zeckendorfs and Steinfelds: Merchant Princes of the American Southwest.* Tucson: Arizona Historical Society, 2008.

McNair, Malcolm, and Eleanor May. *The American Department Store, 1920–1960: A Performance Analysis Based on the Harvard Reports.* Boston: Harvard University, Graduate School of Business and Administration, 1963.

Mahoney, Tom. *The Great Merchants: The Stories of Twenty Famous Retail Operations and the People Who Made Them Great.* New York: Harper and Row, 1955.

Malino, Sarah S. "Behind the Scenes in the Big Store: Reassessing Women's Employment in American Department Stores, 1870–1920." In Martin Henry Blatt and Martha K. Norkunas, eds., *Work, Recreation, and Culture: Essays in American Labor History,* 17–37. New York: Garland, 1996.

Marcus, Stanley. *Minding the Store.* Boston: Little, Brown, 1974.

Mayfield, Frank M. *The Department Store Story.* New York: Fairchild, 1949.

Morgan, Robert. *It's Better at Burdine's: How the Famous Store Grew Hand in Hand with Florida.* Miami: Pickering, 1991.

O'Connor, John E., and Charles F. Cummings. "Bamberger's Department Store, *Charm* Magazine, and the Culture of Consumption in New Jersey, 1924–1932." *New Jersey History* 102 (fall–winter 1984): 1–33.

Pasdernmadijan, H. *The Department Store: Its Origins, Evolution and Economics.* London: Newman, 1954.

Perry, Charles R. *The Negro in the Department Store Industry.* Report 22, Industrial Research Unit, Department of Industry, Wharton School of Finance and Commerce, University of Pennsylvania, 1971.

Pitrone, Jean Maddern. *Hudson's: Hub of America's Heartland.* West Bloomfield, Mich.: Altwerger and Mandel, 1991.

Reilly, Philip J. *Old Masters of Retailing.* New York: Fairchild, 1966.

Rodriguez, Aimmee L. *The Harris Company.* Charleston, S.C.: Arcadia, 2008 (San Bernardino, Calif.).

Rosenberg, Leon Joseph. *Dillard's: The First Fifty Years.* Fayetteville: University of Arkansas Press, 1988.

———. *Sangers': Pioneer Texas Merchants.* Austin: Texas State Historical Association, 1978.

Sibley, Celestine. *Dear Store: An Affectionate Portrait of Rich's.* Garden City, N.Y.: Doubleday, 1967.

Siry, Joseph. *Carson Pirie Scott: Louis Sullivan and the Chicago Department Store.* Chicago: University of Chicago Press, 1988.

———. "Louis Sullivan's Building for John D. Van Allen and Son." *Journal of the Society of Architectural Historians* 49 (Mar. 1990): 67–89.

Smart, Samuel Chapman. *The Outlet Story, 1894–1984.* Providence: By the store, 1984.

Spector, Robert. *More Than a Store: Frederick & Nelson, 1890 to 1990.* Bellevue, Wash.: Documentary, 1990.

Sternberg, Hans J. *We Were Merchants: The Sternberg Family and the Story of Goudchaux's and Maison Blanche Department Stores.* Baton Rouge: Louisiana State University Press, 2009 (Baton Rouge and New Orleans).

Strom, Steven R. "Modernism for the Masses." *Cite* 62 (fall 2004): 30–33, 161–72.

Thrower, Kristin Terbush. *Miller & Rhoads Legendary Santa Claus.* Richmond, Va.: Dietz, 2002.

Traub, Marvin, and Tom Teicholz. *Like No Other Store: The Bloomingdale's Legend and the Revolution in American Marketing.* New York: Times Books, 1993.

Twyman, Robert W. *History of Marshall Field & Co., 1852–1906.* Philadelphia: University of Pennsylvania Press, 1954.

Tyler, Linda L. "'Commerce and Poetry Hand in Hand': Music in American Department Stores, 1880–1930." *Journal of the American Musicological Society* 45 (spring 1992): 75–120.

Veale, Frank R. *Family Business: Strawbridge & Clothier, the Momentous Seventies.* Philadelphia: Strawbridge & Clothier, 1981.

Webb, Bruce C. "The Incredible Shrinking Store: Foley's Department Store, Downtown Houston." *Cite* 23 (fall 1989): 10–11.

Weil, Gordon L. *Sears, Roebuck, U.S.A.: The Great American Catalog Store and How It Grew.* New York: Stein & Day, 1977.

Wendell, Ann. *Frederick & Nelson.* Charleston, S.C: Arcadia, 2008 (Seattle).

Wendt, Lloyd, and Herman Kogan. *"Give the Lady What She Wants": The Story of Marshall Field & Company.* Chicago: Rand McNally, 1952.

Whelan, Frank A., and Kurt D. Zwikl. *Hess's Department Store.* Charleston, S.C.: Arcadia, 2008 (Allentown, Pa.).

Whitaker, Jan. *Service and Style: How the American Department Store Fashioned the Middle Class.* New York: St. Martin's, 2006.

Wood, James M. *Halle's: Memoirs of a Family Department Store, 1891–1982.* Cleveland: Geranium, 1987.

Related Writings on Retail Architecture

Borking, Seline. *The Fascinating History of Shopping Malls.* The Hague: MAB, 1998.

Broomer, Kathleen Kelly. "Shoppers World and the Regional Shopping Center in Greater Boston." *SCA Journal* 13 (fall–winter 1994–1995): 2–9.

Clausen, Meredith. "Northgate Regional Shopping Center—Paradigm from the Provinces." *Journal of the Society of Architectural Historians* 43 (May 1984): 144–61.

Cohen, Lizabeth. "From Town Center to Shopping Center: The Reconfiguration of Community Marketplaces in Postwar America." *American Historical Review* 101 (Oct. 1996): 1050–81.

Cohen, Nancy E. *America's Marketplace: A History of Shopping Centers.* Lyme, Conn.: Greenwich, 2002.

Crawford, Margaret. "The World in a Shopping Mall." In Michael Sorkin, ed., *Variations on a Theme Park: The New American City and the End of Public Space,* 3–30. New York: Hill and Wang, 1992.

Dart, Susan. *Market Square, Lake Forest, Illinois.* Lake Forest, Ill.: Lake Forest–Lake Bluff Historical Society, 1985.

Dyer, Stephanie. "Designing 'Community' in the Cherry Hill Mall." In Alison K. Hoagland and Kenneth A. Breisch, eds., *Constructing Image, Identity, and Place: Perspectives in Vernacular Architecture IX,* 263–75. Knoxville: University of Tennessee Press, 2003.

Esperdy, Gabrielle. *Modernizing Main Street: Architecture and Consumer Culture in the New Deal.* Chicago: University of Chicago Press, 2008.

Friedman, Marilyn F. *Selling Good Design: Promoting the Early Modern Interior.* New York: Rizzoli, 2001.

Geist, Johann Friedrich. *Arcades: The History of a Building Type.* Cambridge: MIT Press, 1985.

Gillette, Howard, Jr. "The Evolution of the Planned Shopping Center in Suburb and City." *Journal of the American Planning Association* 51 (autumn 1985): 449–60.

Hanchett, Thomas. "U.S. Tax Policy and the Shopping-Center Boom of the 1950s and 1960s." *American Historical Review* 101 (Oct. 1996): 1082–1110.

Jacobs, Jerry. *The Mall: An Attempted Escape from Everyday Life.* Prospect Heights, Ill.: Waveland, 1984.

Liebs, Chester. *Main Street to Miracle Mile: American Roadside Architecture* (1985). Reprint, Baltimore: Johns Hopkins University Press, 1995.

Longstreth, Richard. *The Buildings of Main Street: A Guide to American Commercial Architecture* (1987). Reprint, Woodland Hills, Cal.: Alta Mira, 2000.

———. *City Center to Regional Mall: Architecture, the Automobile, and Retailing in Los Angeles, 1920–1950.* Cambridge: MIT Press, 1997.

McCally, Karen. "The Life and Times of Midtown Plaza." *Rochester History* 69 (spring 2007).

Marcus, Leonard S. *The American Store Window.* New York: Whitney Library of Design, 1978.

Prosser, Daniel. "The New Downtowns: Commercial Architecture in Suburban New Jersey, 1920–1970." In Joel Schwartz and Daniel Prosser, eds., *Cities in the Garden State: Essays in the Urban and Suburban History of New Jersey.* Dubuque, Iowa: Kendall/Hunt, 1977.

Satterthwaite, Ann. *Going Shopping: Consumer Choices and Community Consequences.* New Haven: Yale University Press, 2001.

Sewell, Jessica. "Sidewalks and Store Windows as Political Landscapes." In Alison K. Hoagland and Kenneth A. Breisch, eds., *Constructing Image, Identity, and Place: Perspectives in Vernacular Architecture IX,* 85–98. Knoxville: University of Tennessee Press.

Sternlieb, George, and James W. Hughes. *Shopping Centers: U.S.A.* Piscataway, N.J.: Center for Urban Policy Research, Rutgers University, 1981.

Webb, Bruce C. "City Under Glass." *Cite* 65 (winter 2005): 20–23 [Galleria, Houston].

Wood, Barry James. *Show Windows: 75 Years of the Art of Display.* New York: Gordon and Weed, 1982.

Retailing and Consumerism

Barger, Harold. *Distribution's Place in the American Economy Since 1869.* Princeton: Princeton University Press, 1955.

Beniger, James R. *The Control Revolution: Technological and Economic Origins of the Information Society.* Cambridge: Harvard University Press, 1986.

Bird, William L., Jr. *Holidays on Display.* Washington, D.C.: Smithsonian Institution, National Museum of American History, and New York: Princeton Architectural Press, 2007.

Blaszczyk, Regina Lee. *Imagining Consumers: Design and Innovation from Wedgewood to Corning.* Baltimore: Johns Hopkins University Press, 2000.

Bronner, Simon J., ed. *Consuming Visions: Accumulation and Display of Goods in America 1880–1920.* Winterthur, Del.: Henry Francis du Pont Winterthur Museum, and New York: W. W. Norton, 1989.

Bucklin, Louis P. *Competition and Evolution in the Distributive Trades.* Englewood Cliffs, N.J.: Prentice Hall, 1972.

Cameron, Mary Owen. *The Booster and the Snitch: Department Store Shoplifting.* New York: Free Press, 1964.

Chandler, Alfred D., Jr. *The Visible Hand: The Managerial Revolution in American Business.* Cambridge: Belknap Press of Harvard University Press, 1977.

Cohen, Lizabeth. *A Consumers' Republic: The Politics of Mass Consumption in Postwar America.* New York: Alfred A. Knopf, 2003.

Cross, Gary. *An All-Consuming Century: Why Commercialism Won in Modern America.* New York: Columbia University Press, 2000.

Dickinson, Roger. "Innovations in Retailing." In Stanley C. Hollander and Ronald Savitt, eds., *First North American Workshop on Historical Research in Marketing, Proceedings of a Conference Held at Michigan State University, East Lansing, Michigan, June 1983,* 89–101. East Lansing: Department of Marketing and Transportation Administration, Graduate School of Business Administration, Michigan State University, 1983.

Harris, Neil. *Cultural Excursions: Marketing Appetites and Cultural Tastes in Modern America.* Chicago: University of Chicago Press, 1990.

Jacobs, Meg. *Pocketbook Politics: Economic Citizenship in Twentieth-Century America.* Princeton: Princeton University Press, 2005.

Lebhar, Geoffrey M. *Chain Stores in America, 1859–1962* (1952). 3rd ed. New York: Chain Store Publishing, 1963.

McGovern, Charles F. *Sold American: Consumption and Citizenship, 1890–1945.* Chapel Hill: University of North Carolina Press, 2006.

Miller, Roger. "Selling Mrs. Consumer: Advertising and the Creation of Suburban Social-Spatial Relations, 1910–1938." *Antipode* 23 (July 1991): 263–301.

Monod, David. *Store Wars: Shopkeepers and the Culture of Mass Marketing, 1890–1939.* Toronto: University of Toronto Press, 1996.

Moss, Mark. *Shopping as an Entertainment Experience.* Lanham, Md.: Lexington, 2007.

Savitt, Ronald. "Innovation in American Retailing, 1919–39: Improving Inventory Management." *International Review of Retail, Distribution and Consumer Research* 9 (July 1999): 307–20.

———. "Looking Back to See Ahead: Writing the History of American Retailing." *Journal of Retailing* 65 (fall 1989).

———. "Time Paths in the Diffusion of Retail Innovations: E. A. Filene's Model Stock Plan." *Essays in Economic and Business History* 10 (1992): 201–17.

Segrave, Kerry. *Shoplifting: A Social History.* Jefferson, N.C.: McFarland, 2001.

Shapiro, Stanley J., and Alton F. Doody, eds. *Readings in the History of American Marketing, Settlement to Civil War.* Homewood, Ill.: Richard D. Irwin, 1968.

Shields, Rob, ed. *Lifestyle Shopping: The Subject of Consumption.* London: Routledge, 1992.

Strasser, Susan. *Satisfaction Guaranteed: The Making of the American Mass Market.* New York: Pantheon, 1989.

Tedlow, Richard S. *New and Improved: The Story of Mass Marketing in America.* New York: Basic, 1990.

Twitchell, James B. *Lead Us into Temptation: The Triumph of American Materialism.* New York: Columbia University Press, 1999.

Weems, Robert E., Jr. *Desegregating the Dollar: African American Consumerism in the Twentieth Century.* New York: New York University Press, 1998.

Wrigley, Neil, and Michelle Lowe. *Reading Retail: A Geographical Perspective on Retailing and Consumption Spaces.* London: Hodder Headline Group, and New York: Oxford University Press, 2002.

———, eds. *Retailing, Consumption and Capital: Towards the New Retail Geography.* Harlow, U.K.: Longman, 1996.

Zukin, Sharon. *Point of Purchase: How Shopping Changed American Culture.* New York: Routledge, 2004.

Architects, Retailers, and Shopping Center Developers

Appel, Joseph H. *The Business Biography of John Wanamaker, Founder and Builder* (1930). Reprint, New York: AMS, 1970.

Berkeley, George E. *The Filenes.* Boston: Branden, 1998.

Bloom, Nicholas Dagen. *Merchant of Illusion: James Rouse, America's Salesman of the Businessman's Utopia.* Columbus: Ohio State University Press, 2004.

Bruegmann, Robert. *The Architects and the City: Holabird & Roche of Chicago, 1880–1918.* Chicago: University of Chicago Press, 1997.

Chappell, Sally. *Architecture and Planning of Graham, Anderson, Probst and White, 1912–1936: Transforming Tradition.* Chicago: University of Chicago Press, 1992.

Ershkowitz, Herbert. *John Wanamaker, Philadelphia Merchant.* Conshocken, Pa.: Combined, 1999.

Gibbons, Herbert Adams. *John Wanamaker* (1926). Reprint (2 vols.), Port Washington, N.Y.: Kennikat, 1971.

Goldblatt, Louis. *Life Is a Game, Play to Win.* N.p. [U.S.]: by the author, 1994.

Hardwick, M. Jeffrey. *Mall Maker: Victor Gruen, Architect of an American Dream.* Philadelphia: University of Pennsylvania Press, 2003.

Hines, Thomas. *Burnham of Chicago: Architect and Planner.* New York: Oxford University Press, 1974.

Holleman, Thomas, and James Gallagher. *Smith, Hinchman & Grylls: 125 Years of Architecture and Engineering, 1853–1978.* Detroit: Wayne State University Press, 1978.

Johannesen, Eric. *A Cleveland Legacy: The Architecture of Walker and Weeks.* Kent, Ohio: Kent State University Press, 1999.

O'Brien, Liz. *Ultramodern: Samuel Marx, Architect, Designer, Art Collector.* New York: Pointed Leaf, 2007.

Olsen, Joshua. *Better Places, Better Lives: A Biography of James Rouse.* Washington, D.C.: Urban Land Institute, 2003.

Poletti, Therese. *Art Deco San Francisco: The Architecture of Timothy Pfleuger.* New York: Princeton Architectural Press, 2008.

Rhodes, Henry A. *Memoirs of a Merchant.* Seattle: Metropolitan, 1952.

Schaffer, Kristen. *Daniel H. Burnham.* New York: Rizzoli, 2003.

Taubman, A. Alfred. *Threshold Resistance: The Extraordinary Career of a Luxury Retailing Pioneer.* New York: HarperCollins, 2007.

Wall, Alex. *Victor Gruen: From Urban Shop to New City.* Barcelona: Actar, 2005.

Worthy, James C. *Shaping an American Institution: Robert E. Wood and Sears Roebuck.* Urbana: University of Illinois Press, 1964.

Locational Studies

Deegan, Gregory G., and James A. Toman. *The Heart of Cleveland: Public Square in the 20th Century.* Cleveland: Cleveland Landmarks, 1999.

Hauser, Michael, and Marianne Weldon. *20th-Century Retailing in Downtown Detroit.* Charleston, S.C.: Arcadia, 2008.

Hess, Jeffrey A., and Paul Clifford Larson. *St. Paul's Architecture: A History.* Minneapolis: University of Minnesota Press, 2006.

Karberg, Richard E., and James A. Toman. *Euclid Avenue: Cleveland's Sophisticated Lady, 1920–1970.* Cleveland: Cleveland Landmarks, 2002.

Laborde, Peggy Scott, and John Magill. *Canal Street: New Orleans' Great Wide Way.* Gretna, La.: Pelican, 2006.

Longstreth, Richard. "Building for Business: Commercial Architecture in Metropolitan Washington." In C. Ford Peatross, ed., *Capital Drawings: Architectural Designs for Washington, D.C., from the Library of Congress,* 109–50, 208–12, 238–42. Baltimore: Johns Hopkins University Press, and Washington: Library of Congress, 2005.

———. "The Unusual Transformation of Downtown Washington in the Early Twentieth Century." *Washington History* 13 (fall–winter 2001–02): 50–71.

Rizzo, Michael F. *Nine Nine Eight: The Glory Days of Buffalo Shopping.* Morrisville, N.C.: Lulu, and Buffalo: Western New York Wares, 2007.

Roderick, Kevin, with J. Eric Lynxwiler. *Wilshire Boulevard: Grand Concourse of Los Angeles.* Santa Monica, Cal.: Angel City, 2005.

Shand-Tucci, Douglass. *Built in Boston: City and Suburb, 1800–2000* (1978). Rev. ed., Amherst: University of Massachusetts Press, 1999.

Stern, Robert A. M., et al. *New York 1900: Metropolitan Architecture and Urbanism, 1890–1915.* New York: Rizzoli, 1983.

———. *New York 1930: Architecture and Urbanism Between the Two World Wars.* New York: Rizzoli, 1987.

———. *New York 1960: Architecture and Urbanism Between the Second World War and the Bicentennial.* New York: Monacelli, 1995.

Zukowsky, John, ed. *Chicago Architecture, 1872–1922: Birth of a Metropolis.* Munich: Prestel, 1987.

———. *Chicago Architecture and Design, 1923–1993.* Munich: Prestel, 1993.

Urbanism

Baerwald, Thomas. "The Emergence of a New 'Downtown.'" *Geographical Review* 68 (June 1978): 308–18.

Barth, Gunther. *City People: The Rise of Modern City Culture in Nineteenth-Century America.* New York: Oxford University Press, 1980.

Berry, Brian J. *Geography of Market Centers and Retail Distribution.* Englewood Cliffs, N.J.: Prentice Hall, 1967.

———. "Ribbon Developments in the Urban Business Pattern." *Annals of the Association of American Geographers* 49 (Mar. 1959): 145–55.

———, and Yehoshua Cohen. "Decentralization of Commerce and Industry: The Restructuring of Metropolitan America." In Louis Masotti and Jeffrey Hadden, eds., *The Urbanization of Suburbs,* 431–55. Beverly Hills: Sage, 1973.

Cervero, Robert. *America's Suburban Centers.* Boston: Unwin Hyman, 1989.

Cohen, Saul B., and George K. Lewis. "Form and Function in the Geography of Retailing." *Economic Geography* 43 (Jan. 1967): 1–42.

Erickson, Rodney, and Marilyn Gentry. "Suburban Nucleations." *Geographical Review* 75 (Jan. 1985): 19–31.

Fogelson, Robert M. *Downtown: Its Rise and Fall, 1880–1950.* New Haven: Yale University Press, 2001.

Goss, Jon. "The 'Magic of the Mall': An Analysis of Form, Function and Meaning in the Contemporary Real Estate Environment." *Annals of the American Association of Geographers* 83 (Mar. 1993): 18–47.

Hartshorn, Truman A. *Interpreting the City: An Urban Geography.* New York: Wiley, 1992.

———. "Suburban Downtowns and the Transformation of Metropolitan Atlanta's Business Landscape." *Urban Geography* 10 (July–Aug. 1989): 375–95.

———, and Peter O. Muller. "Suburban Business Centers: Employment Implications." Washington, D.C.: U.S. Department of Commerce, Economic Development Administration, Technical Assistance and Research Division, Nov. 1986.

Hepp, John Henry IV. *The Middle-Class City: Transforming Space and Time in Philadelphia, 1876–1926.* Philadelphia: University of Pennsylvania Press, 2003.

Isenberg, Alison. *Downtown America: A History of the Place and the People Who Made It.* Chicago: University of Chicago Press, 2004.

Jakle, John A., and Keith A. Sculle. *Lots of Parking: Land Use in a Car Culture.* Charlottesville: University of Virginia Press, 2004.

———. *Signs in America's Auto Age: Signatures of Landscape and Place.* Iowa City: University of Iowa Press, 2004.

Kersten, Earl W., Jr., and D. Reid Ross. "Clayton: A New Metropolitan Focus in the St. Louis Area." *Annals of the Association of American Geographers* 58 (Dec. 1968): 637–49.

Longstreth, Richard. "Silver Spring: Georgia Avenue, Colesville Road, and the Creation of an Alternative 'Downtown' for Metropolitan Washington." In Zeynep Celik et al., eds., *Streets: Critical Perspectives on Public Space,* 247–58. Berkeley: University of California Press, 1994.

Muller, Peter O. *The Outer City: Geographical Consequences of the Urbanization of the United States.* Washington, D.C.: Association of American Geographers, 1976.

Panetta, Roger, ed. *Westchester: The American Suburb.* New York: Fordham University Press, and Yonkers, N.Y.: Hudson River Museum, 2005.

Robertson, Kent A. "Downtown Retail Activity in Large American Cities, 1954–1977." *Geographical Review* 73 (June 1983): 314–23.

Sewell, Jessica. "Gender, Imagination, and Experience in the Early-Twentieth-Century American Downtown." In Chris Wilson and Paul Groth, eds., *Everyday America: Cultural Landscape Studies after J. B. Jackson,* 237–54, 346–48. Berkeley: University of California Press, 2003.

Stamper, John W. *Chicago's North Michigan Avenue: Planning and Development, 1900–1930.* Chicago: University of Chicago Press, 1991.

Zukin, Sharon. *The Cultures of Cities.* Cambridge: Blackwell, 1995.

INDEX

Store companies and shopping centers are listed under the names used during the period studied. Individuals in several fields pertinent to this study are listed by professional group: architects, interior designers/ architects, landscape architects, real estate developers, and retail executives. "Department store" includes all of the 185 companies examined for this study and "branch" entails the range of outlets presented in Chapters 5–8. Page numbers in **boldface** indicate illustrations.

Abercrombie & Fitch apparel and accessories store, New York, 29
Abraham & Straus department store, Brooklyn, 12, 37, 86, 102, 199, 263n69, 269n76; downtown store, 15, 23, **23**, 29, 78–79, 270n85; Garden City branch, 143, 154; Hempstead branch, 143, 144, 150, 154, 161, 196; other branches, 131, 180, 296nn117 and 125; parking garage, 102; service building, 78–79
Adam, J. N., & Company department store, Buffalo, 11, 20, 48, **48**, 220, 262n47, 265n3, 270n85
Adam, Meldrum & Anderson department store, Buffalo, 180, 220, 289n35
Affiliated Retail Stores, research association, 12
Airport Plaza shopping center, Cheektowaga, New York, 289n35
Akron, Ohio, 13, 220; parking garages in, 93, 275n33; stores in, 11, 15, **16**, 23, 93, 163, 265n91, 268n63, 272n30, 280n50
Albert's department store, Richmond and San Rafael, California, 159
Allegheny Conference, Pittsburgh, 225, 230
Allen, George, Company dry goods store, Philadelphia, 117, 121
Allentown, Pennsylvania, parking facilities in, **89**; stores in, 272n40
Allied Stores, department store ownership group/ corporation) (*see also* Hahn Department Stores), 50–51, 54, 55, 162, 169, 184, 185–86, 188, 189, 190, 191, 196, 197, 217, 219, 220, 222, 225, 242, 247, 249, 269n71, 296n112, 297n144
Alms & Doepke department store, Cincinnati, 220, 265n90
Altman, B., & Company department store, New York, 153, 156, 272n40; East Orange branch, 121, **121**; Miracle Mile branch, 143, 281n79;

284n48; White Plains branch, 120–21, **120**, 161, 240, 279n38, 284n48
American Architect, 112
architects, 29, 76, 146–47
Architectural Forum, 53, 138, 191, 202, 228, 229, 237, 297n131
architects, 29, 76, 146–47
  Abbott, Hunley, 74, 77, 272n40; Abbott, Merkt & Company (New York) (*see also* Merkt, Oswald), **71, 72, 74–76**, 76–77, 80, 81, **81**, 97, **98, 104**, 146, 147, **151, 155–56, 176, 177**, 212, **212, 222, 232**, 272n39, 273n51, 276n44, 301n68
  Adams, Frederick (Boston), 184
  Ahlschlager, Walter W. (Chicago), **17**
  Alexander, Robert (Los Angeles), 233
  Anderson & Beckwith (Boston), 184, **184**
  Applegarth, George (San Francisco), **106**
  Armstrong, Harris (St. Louis), **144**
  Ashford, L. K. (Washington), **16**, 30
  Austin Company (Cleveland), **78, 79, 80**, 81
  Ballinger Company (Philadelphia), **99**
  Barber & McMurry (Knoxville), **149**, 164
  Becket, Welton (Los Angeles) (*see also* Wurdeman & Becket), 152, 186, 191, 199, 210, 211, 214, 244, 296; Welton Becket & Associates (Los Angeles), 147, 199, **244**
  Behles, E. Paul (New York), 42, 43
  Behrens, Peter (Berlin), 37
  Belluschi, Pietro (Portland, Oregon), 211
  Bennett, Richard (Chicago) (*see also* Loebl, Schlossman & Bennett), 204–5
  Boehler & Brugman, **203, 206**
  Bohn, Arthur (Indianapolis), **44**
  Bolles, John M. (San Francisco), **236**
  Breuer, Marcel (New York), 154
  Buell, Temple (Denver), 190, 292n31
  Bulfinch, Charles (Boston), 54
  Burnham, D. H., & Company (Chicago), **22**, 29, 265n90
  Carneal & Johnson (Richmond), **57**
  Cobb, Henry Ives (Chicago), **16**
  Cocke, Bartlett (San Antonio), **49**
  Conrad, Hays, Simpson & Ruth (Cleveland), **172**
  Copeland, Peter (New York), 146–47; Copeland, Novak & Associates / Copeland, Novak & Israel (New York) (*see also* Novak, Adolph), **57**, 146, **165**

Crisp, H. C. (Baltimore), **32**
Daverman, J. & G., Company (Omaha), **209**
Delano & Aldrich (New York), **17**
De Lemos & Cordes (New York), **18**
De Witt & Swank (Dallas), **137**
Douglass, Lathrop (New York), **193, 233, 301n68**
Dreher & Churchman (Philadelphia), **118, 119**
Dudok, W. M. (Hilversum, the Netherlands), 48
Eberson, John (New York), 147
Edmunds, James R. (Baltimore), **32, 155**
Ely, George (New York), 54, **55**
Esser, Herman J. (Milwaukee), **22**
Fellheimer & Wagner (New York), 154
Finn, Alfred C. (Houston), **58**
Fisher, Howard T. (Chicago), **179**
Flint, Noel (Chicago) (*see also* Marx, Flint & Schonne), 281n78
Franzheim, Kenneth (Houston), **51, 102,** 269n77
Frost Frederick G. (New York), **121**
Gardner, Albert B. (Los Angeles), **175**
Gilbert, Cass (New York), **222**
Good & Wagner (Akron), **16**
Graham, John (Seattle), 187, 188, 203, 210–11, 215, 241, 296nn112 and 125, 301n68; John Graham & Company, 147, **162, 188, 199, 203**, 214, **231–32**, 233, **241, 243**
Graham, Anderson, Probst & White (Chicago), **15, 16, 27,** 29, 114
Greene, Herbert M. (Dallas), **23**
Gruen, Victor (Los Angeles), 146, 156, 170, 180, 194, 195, 200, 201–2, 206–08, 210, 211–12, 213–15, 216, 225, 227–29, 231, 235, 238, 240, 241, 295n91, 296n112, 295n125, 297n125, 298n146; Victor Gruen Associates, 17, **192, 201–2, 207–9, 214–16, 223, 228,** 233, **238–40, 241;** Gruen & Krummeck, 53, **157,** 180, 201
Hanke, Harry and Harry, Jr., 78
Harding, Clarence (Washington), **16**
Hawker & Cairns (Memphis), 27
Heatley, Harold M., **161**
Hellmuth, Obata & Kassabaum (St. Louis), 298n146
Hentz, Reid & Adler (Atlanta), **8, 26**
Hobart, Lewis (San Francisco), 29
Hoener, P. John (St. Louis), **160**

| 313

architects (continued)
    Hoffmann, Josef (Vienna), 37
    Hoffmann & Crumpton (Pittsburgh), **57, 105**
    Holabird & Roche (Chicago), **63**; Holabird, Root & Burgee, **179**
    Holmes, J. E., **112**
    Hunt, Jarvis (Chicago), 5, **6**, 29
    Hunt, Myron (Los Angeles), 112, **112**; Hunt & Chambers, **130**
    Janssen & Cocken (Pittsburgh), **38**
    Kahn, Ely Jacques (New York), 39; Kahn & Jacobs, **104, 156, 176**
    Katzman, Meyer (New York), 146, 147
    Kellum, John (New York), **46**
    Ketchum, Gina & Sharp, 146, **155, 161, 184–85, 200**
    Ketchum, Morris (New York), 147, 184, 186, 200, 203, 229, 290n6, 294n88
    Kivett & Myers (Kansas City), 53, **53**
    Klein, Irving R. (Houston), **203**
    Knight, John J. (New York), **156**
    Kohn, Robert D. (New York), **18, 156**
    La Roche & Dahl (Dallas), **23**
    Lapidus, Morris (New York), 215
    Larson & McLaren (Minneapolis), **192, 207–9**
    Le Corbusier (Paris), 227
    Lehman & Schmidt (Cleveland), **94**
    Leland, Schmidt & Company (Cleveland), **74**
    Lescaze, William (New York), 37
    Levy, Will (St. Louis), **71**
    Little, Robert A. (Cleveland), **172**
    Loebl, Schlossman & Bennett (Chicago) (*see also* Bennett, Richard), **204–5**
    Lorenz & Williams (Dayton), **56**
    Marham, Charles O. (Los Angeles), **150**
    Martin, Albert C. (Los Angeles), **133**
    Martin, Albert C., Jr. (Los Angeles), 200, 281n78
    Marx, Samuel (Chicago), 132, **133**, 281n78; Marx, Flint & Schonne, **179**
    Massena & du Pont (Wilmington), **160**
    Mauran, Russell & Crowell (St. Louis), **21, 64**; Russell, Mullgardt, Schwarz & Van Hofen, **179**; Schwarz & Van Hoefen, **107**
    McLaughlin, James (Cincinnati), **48**
    Mendelsohn, Eric (Berlin), 48
    Merkt, Oswald (New York) (*see also* Abbott, Merkt & Company), 272n40
    Miller, Kenneth Cameron (Baltimore), **173**
    Moore, Joseph (San Francisco), **43**
    Moore & Massar (Seattle), **173**
    Morgan, Walls & Clements (Los Angeles), 49
    Morris & Weinberg (Cleveland), **128**
    Neutra, Richard (Los Angeles), 233
    Novak, Adolph (New York) (*see also* Copeland, Novak & Associares), 147
    Parkinson & Bergstrom (Los Angeles), **19**; John and Donald B. Parkinson, 29, **123**, 124, **125–27**
    Parsons, Brinckerhoff, Hall & Macdonald (New York), **149**
    Paul, Bruno (Berlin), 37
    Pei, I. M., & Associates (New York), **203**, 205, **206, 237**, **237**
    Pereira & Luckman (Los Angeles), **44, 150, 157, 158**

    Perry, Shaw & Hepburn (Boston), 54, **55**
    Pfleuger, Timothy & Milton (San Francisco), **58, 130**
    Pissis, Albert (San Francisco), **43**
    Potter, Tyler & Martin (Cincinnati), **48, 66, 123**
    Price & McLanahan (Philadelphia), **141**
    Pyle, Frederick (Washington), **16**
    Rambush & Hunter (Indianapolis), **49**
    Richards, McCarthy & Bulford (Columbus), **72**
    Rogers, Archibald (Baltimore), 297n135
    Rogers, Taliferro & Lamb (Baltimore) (*see also* Taliferro, Frank), 213, **213**
    Rudolph, Paul (New Haven), **232**, 301n68
    Schein, Sumner (Rochester), **177**
    Schenck & Williams (Dayton), **56**
    Schwarzmann, David (New York), 53, **156**
    Silverman & Levy (Philadelphia), **97**
    Simon & Simon (Philadelphia), **14, 77**
    Skidmore, Owings & Merrill (New York), 205, (San Francisco), 235, **235**
    Smith & May (Baltimore), 29
    Smith, Hinchman & Grylls (Detroit), **15, 18, 19, 20**, 29, **66, 78**
    Snaith, William (New York) (*see also* interior designers, Loewy, Raymond), 47, 53, 54, 146, 152, 181, 200, 283n38
    Snyder & Babbitt (Columbus), **57**
    Starr, Arthur P. (Washington), **141**
    Starrett, Goldwin, 29
    Starrett and Van Vleck (New York) (*see also* Van Vleck, Ernest), **14, 23, 26**, 29, **40**, 48, **48, 57, 63**, 134, **134, 152**
    Stevens & Wilkinson (Atlanta), **59, 149, 164**
    Tabler, William (New York), **233**, 301n68
    Taliferro, Frank (Baltimore) (*see also* Rogers, Taliferro & Lamb), 213
    Tatlow, Richard, III (New York) (*see also* Abbott, Merkt & Company), 81
    Thalheimer & Weitz (Philadelphia), **165**
    Thomas & Grainger (Seattle), **92**
    Tombs & Creighton (Atlanta), **59**
    Van Vleck, Ernest Alan (New York) (*see also* Starrett & Van Vleck), 29, 38
    Vonnegut, Bohn & Mueller, **22, 44**
    Voorhees, Walker, Foley & Smith (New York), **176**
    Walker, William E., (Chicago), **66**
    Walker & Weeks (Cleveland), **20**, 29
    Wallace, David (Baltimore), 230, **230**
    Walter, Frank C. (Tulsa), **28**
    Warren & Whetmore (New York), **40**
    Weed, Robert Law (Miami), **131**, 277n68
    Welch, Kenneth (Grand Rapids), 42, **44**, 45, **46**, 98, **156**, 184, 187, 188, 191, 200, 211, **211**, 212, 221, 268n52, 290n5, 291n19, 296n113, 297n133
    Weile, Emile (Memphis), **27**
    Whitten & Sons, **111**
    Windrim, John T. (Philadelphia), **21**
    Wurdeman & Becket (Los Angeles) (*see also* Becket, Welton), **142, 153**
Ardmore, Pennsylvania, 118
Arlington/Arlington County, Virginia, 103–4, 175–76, 177, 187
Arnold Constable department store, New York,

39, 86, 272n40, 278n5; branches, 130, 134, 284n50, 285n73
Associated Dry Goods Corporation, department store ownership group/corporation, 11, 50, 249
Atlanta, Georgia, 13, 59; stores in, **8**, 11, **26**, 37, 43, **44**, 58–59, **59**, 161, 163, 190, 248, 265n93, 268n63
automobiles, widespread us of, 3, 83, 84–85, 95, 98, 113, 140, 275n35
Ayres, L. S., & Company department store, Indianapolis, 199, 211; downtown store, 19-20, **22**, 47, 270n85; Glendale branch, 190, 196, 296n125

Bacon, J., & Sons department store, Louisville, 180, 290n38
Bacon's Shively Shopping Center, Shively, Kentucky, 290n38
Bailey Company department stores, Cleveland, 12, 127–28, **128**
Baltimore, Maryland, 104, 190, 206, 211, 220, 225, 276n60; department store service building in, 76; downtown revitalization in, 225, 227, 230–31, **230**, 248; stores in, 11, 29, **32**, 33, 59, 144, 153–54, 156, 173, **173**, 177–78, 180, 196, 211, 213, **213**, 225, 231, 262n47, 268n63, 269n71, 272n40, 294n88
Bamberger, L., & Company department store, Newark, 5, 6, 11, 14; Cherry Hill branch, **214**, 216, 294n71, 296nn116 and 125; downtown store, 5, **6**, 16, 17, **25**, 45, **45**, 164, 265nn92 and 95; other branches 140–41, 143, 148, 159, 189; parking lots, 100; service buildings, 70, 73, 77, 80–81, **81**, 271n24
Barr, William, Dry Goods Company, St. Louis (*see also* Famous-Barr), 11
Bay Fair Shopping Center, San Leandro, California, 189, 296n125
Bedell Company, women's apparel store chain, 9
Bellevue Square shopping center, Bellevue, Washington, 172–73, **173**
Bergen Mall, Paramus, New Jersey, 188, 196, 198, 297nn125 and 144
Bernheimer-Leader department store, Baltimore (*see also* May Company, Baltimore store), 11, 29, 265n95
Bertoia, Henry, sculptor, 208
Best & Company women's and children's apparel store, New York, 119–20, 134, 281n79
Beverly Hills, California, 129, 131, 132, 149, **150**, 159, 244
Big Town shopping center, Dallas, 210, 296n117
Birmingham, Alabama, stores in 12, 14, 265 nn 95 and 3, 276n61, 297n144
Block, William H., Company department store, Indianapolis; branch stores, 141, 146, 196, 282n15, 296n125; downtown store, **44**, 196, 268n48
Bloomingdale Brothers department store, New York, 51, 146, 249; branch stores, **149**, 159, 175, **176**; New York store, 15, 29, 264n76; service buildings, **71**, 74, **74**, 271n12
Boggs & Buhl department store, Pittsburgh, 220, 261n26, 282n20
Bon Marche department store, Seattle, 12, 144, 162, 163, 187, 285n73; downtown store, 15, 47, 249, 270n85; Northgate branch, 147, 187–88,

188, 199, **199;** other branch stores, 162, **162,** 242; parking facilities, 91–92, **92,** 106, **106**
Bond Company, men's clothing store chain, 9, 220
Bonwit Teller apparel store, New York, 39, 288n22
Bonwit Teller apparel store, Philadelphia, 177, 288n22
Boston, Massachusetts, 68, 92, 183, 190, 220, 227, 248, 300n43, 304n15; department store service building in, 68, **68,** 69–70; parking garages in, 92–93, **93,** 97, 275n28; stores in, 11, 12, 54, **55–56,** 59, 69, 86, 109, 110, 111, 146, 220, 265n90, 278n5
Boston Store, department store, Milwaukee, 68, 104, 269n71; branch stores, 146, 285n73; downtown store, **43;** parking lot, 89
Bowdoin Square Garage, Boston, 275n28
Brandeis, J. L., & Sons department store, Omaha, 163, 189, 296n117; parking garage, 106, **106**
Brentwood-Whitehall Shopping Center, Brentwood, Pennsylvania, 290n39
Bridgeport, Connecticut, 86; stores in, 269n71
Broadway department store, Los Angeles (see also Broadway-Hale), 29, 121, 279n29; Anaheim branch, 189, 296n125; Century City branch, 244, **244;** Crenshaw branch, 174–75, **175,** 189, 195, 196; Del Amo branch, 189, 296n125; downtown store, 16; other branch stores 122, 131, 132, 177
Broadway-Anaheim Shopping Center, Anaheim, California, 189, 295n98, 296n125
Broadway-Crenshaw Center, Los Angeles, 174–75, **175,** 176, 194, 203
Broadway Shopping Center, Walnut Creek, California, 289n27
Broadway-Hale department stores, 220
Bronx, New York, 131
Brookings Institution, Washington, D.C., 229
Brooklyn, New York, 86; department store service buildings in, **71, 74,** 78–79; Flatbush district, 156, 159; Fulton Street, 102; stores in, 15, 23, **23,** 78–79, 102, 220, 269n76, 270n85, 272n40
Brown-Dunkin Dry Goods Company, Tulsa, 13, **16,** 17
Buffalo, New York, 220, 248; stores in, 11, 14, 20, 48, **48,** 144, 146, 180, 220, 222, 262n47, 265n3, 270n85
Buffum's Department Store, Long Beach, California, parking garage of, 97
Bullock's department store, Los Angeles, 8, 29, 68, 121, 129, 155, 157, 158, 244, 279n29; downtown store, 19, **19,** 20, 265n3, 268n63; Palm Springs branch, 142, **142;** Pasadena branch, 147, 152–53, **153,** 159, 166, 199, 284n48; other branch stores, 131, 189; Wilshire Boulevard branch, 122–24, **123, 125–27,** 130, 132, 134, 145, 159, 166, 171, 266n10, 279n48
Burdine's department store, Miami, 111, 146, 147, 154, 269n71; branch stores, 111, 131, 133, **133,** 141–42, **148,** 150, 285n73, 294n73; downtown store, 270n85
busses, as feeders to department stores, 86–87, 93, 96, 100
Bus Transportation, 274n14

Cage Garage, Boston, 97
Cain-Sloan department store, Nashville, 222

Calder, Alexander, sculptor, 137
Cambridge, Massachusetts, 68, 70
Camden, New Jersey, 164–65, 214
Capitol Court shopping center, Milwaukee, 296n125
Capwell, H. C., Company department store, Oakland (see also Emporium-Capwell), 11, 265nn93 and 95, 289n27
Carson Pirie Scott & Company department store, Chicago, 50, 86, 117, 196, 211, 216, 229; branch stores, 163, 178, 189, 216, **216,** 285n73, 296nn117 and 125; men's store, 21
Castor-Cottman Shopping Center, Philadelphia, 176–77
Castor-Knott department store, Nashville, 180, 285n73, 290n38
Catchings, Waddill, banker, 31
Cedar-Warrensville Center, shopping center, University Heights, Ohio, 172, 178
Center, The, mixed-use development, Worcester, Massachusetts, 304n15
Center, The, shopping center, Omaha, 207
Century City, mixed-use development, Los Angeles, 242, 243–45, **244**
Chain Store Age, 195, 210
chain stores, 78, 145, 230, 239; as competitors to department stores, 31, 34–35, 36, 140, 187, 220, 249; development of in outlying areas, 96, 113, 115, 116, 128, 129, 140, 168, 176, 195, 221; influence on department stores, 77, 109, 110, 112, 129, 139, 145, 146, 158; rise of, 2, 6, 9–10; in shopping centers, 172, 173, 194–95, 203, 209, 247, 304
Chapman, T. A., department store, Milwaukee, 296n125
Charleston, West Virginia, 248, 269n71, 304n15
Charleston Town Center, mixed-used development, Charleston, West Virginia, 304n15
Charlottetown Mall, Charlotte, North Carolina, 297nn137 and 144
Cheltenham Shopping Center, Cheltenham, Pennsylvania, 179, 295n107
Cherry Creek Shopping Center, Denver, 190, 294n88
Cherry Grove Plaza shopping center, Cherry Grove, Ohio, 290n39
Cherry Hill Shopping Center, Cherry Hill, New Jersey, 190, 214–16, **214–15,** 294n71, 296nn117 and 125
Chevy Chase, Maryland, 166–67, 168, 284nn48–50
Chicago, 5, 29, 41, 54, 86, 109, 114–17, 118, 163, 225, 276n60, 300n43; Century of Progress Exposition of 1933, 40–41, 43; department store service buildings in, 66, **66,** 68, 109; North Michigan Avenue, 86, 113, 114, 278n17, 280n64, 304n16; parking issues in, 85–86, 96, 100; revitalization in, 225, 226, 227; State Street, 86, 114, 126, 196; stores in 8, 12, 21, 37, 59, **63, 64,** 86, 109, 113, 114, 115, 117, 118, 124, 126, 128, 130, 178–79, **179,** 196, 220, 249, 304n16
Chicago Tribune, 197
Chula Vista Shopping Center, Chula Vista, California, 189
Cincinnati, 225; Carew Tower, 17, **17;** department store service buildings in, 72, 76, **78,** 79, 272n40; parking garages in, 97, 101, 275n33; stores in, 11, 12, 17, 48, **48,** 180, 188, 190, 205–6,

219, 220, 222, 224, 265n90, 266n10, 270n85, 295n98
Cincinnati Enquirer, 222
City Stores Company, department store ownership group/corporation, 12, 36, 50, 56, 67, 164, 176, 220, 269n71
Claflin, H. B., Company, retail ownership group, 11
Claflin, John, wholesaler, 11
Clayton, Missouri, 107, 143, 144, 161, 167, 168, 171
Cleveland, 15, 79, 109, 126, 163, 177, 220; department store service building in, 74, **74;** parking facilities in, 93, **94, 95;** stores in, 8, 11, 12, 15, 20, **20, 24,** 29, 59, **63,** 68, 124, 127–28, 172, **172,** 178, 190, 265nn91 and 3, 269n77, 270n85, 272n40
Coldwell-Banker, real estate brokers, 166
College Grove Shopping Center, San Diego, 206, 297n125
Columbus, Ohio, 59, 94; department store service buildings in, 72, **72,** 73, 76, 78, **78,** 79–80, **80;** parking garages in, 101, **101,** 275n26; stores in, 11, 16, 35, 56, **57,** 72–73, 265n93
Commercial Vehicle, 270n4
Cottman-Bustleton Shopping Center, Philadelphia, 177
Cottonwood Mall, Salt Lake City, 294n73, 296n117, 297n125 and 144
Coulter Dry Goods Company, Los Angeles, 132, 269n68
Country Club Plaza shopping center, Kansas City, 170, 172, 194, 198, 212
Crescent Airline Shopping Center, New Orleans, 290n38
Crestwood Plaza shopping center, Crestwood, Missouri, 294n72
Cross County Center, shopping center, Yonkers, New York, 189, 190, 192, **193,** 196, 198, 211, 291n24
Crossroads Shopping Center, Omaha, 189, 296n117
Crowley-Milner & Company department store, Detroit, 113; branch store, 180; downtown store, 19, **19,** 29
Culbertson's Department Store, Spokane, **162**
Cutler Ridge Regional Shopping Center, Miami, 289n27

Dadeland Shopping Center, Dade County, Florida, 206, 294n73
Dallas, Texas, 13, 224, 225; department store parking lot in, 100–101, **101;** stores in, 12, 16, **23,** 47, 55, 57, 99, 137, 137–38, 172, 180, 189, 210, 223, 268n59, 268n63, 269n71, 270n85, 296n117, 296n125
Daniels & Fisher Stores Company (see also May Co.) Denver, **95,** 163, 236; parking garage, 93, **95**
Davison-Paxon Company department store, Atlanta, 11, 37, 147, 161, 163; branch stores, 161, **161,** 285n73, 290n6; downtown store, **26,** 43, **44,** 265n93
Dayton, Ohio, 59, 192; stores in, 37, 55, **56,** 222, 268n63, 269n71
Dayton Company department store, Minneapolis, 147, 191, 198, 209, 211, 219, 222, 227, 247, 268n63; branch stores, 111, 163, 189, 285n73; Minneapolis store, 208–209, 249; parking garage of, 72, 93, 102; St. Paul store, 222–23, **223;** service facilities, 72, **73,** 93

| 315

de Forest, Robert, museum director, 37
decentralization of business, 96, 105, 113, 129, 139, 184, 219, 234
Del Amo Center, shopping center, Torrance, California, 189, 295n125
Denver, Colorado, 190, 226; department store parking facilities in, 93, **95**, 276n61; downtown revitalization in, 226, 229, 236–37, 248; stores in, 11, 59, 93, **94**, 163, 177, 189, 190, 209
Denver Dry Goods Company, Denver, 190, 209
Department Store Economist, 100, 186, 189
department stores, advertising of, 9, 62, 73; air conditioning in, 1, 47, 49, 148, 222, 268n59; bargain departments (basements) in, 20, 28–29, **28**, 47; bus services of, 85–86, 93, 100, 276n61; closings of, 220–21, 231, 249; customers of, 1, 7, 8, 36; delivery of goods from, 7, 61–66, 78; design of (downtown buildings), 1, 21–26, 28–30, 34, 38–40, 41–49, 51–59; display of goods in, 1, 23, 24–25, 34, 41, 42, 52, 148, 156–57; as emblems of modernity, 1, 34, 37–41, 47–49; elevators in, 5, 26, 28, 43, 149; escalators in, 26, **27**, 28, 38, 49, 52–53, 149, 222, 264n85; expansion of, 3, 5, 13–31, 33, 34, 48–49, 51–59, 61, 222, 224; financing of, 11, 13, 194; impact of Depression on, 15, 30–31, 33–35, 40, 42, 47, 95, 110, 119, 128, 220; impact of World War II on, 35, 81; layout of, 1, 24–26, 28–29, 38–39, 43, 45–47, 49, 52, 53, 114–15, 124, 131, 132, 134, 148–50, 152; lighting, use of in, 1, 23, 25–26, 38, 45, 46–47, 48, 49, 148; management and operation of (downtown buildings), 1, 7; men's stores in, 20–21, 124; mergers and acquisitions, *see* ownership groups/corporations of; operating costs of, 6, 8, 34; ownership groups/corporations of, 6, 10–13, 50–51, 160–63, 187–89; parking services of (downtown), 87–94, 96–107, 272n30, 274n19, 275nn30 and 33, 276n61, 277nn67, 70, 72; profits of, 34–35, 36, 41, 266n10; as purveyors of elegance and fashion, 8, 41, 41; remodeling of, 3, 34, 41–43, 45–49, 222; sales force of, 9, 35; sales volume of, 8, 34, 36; self-selection/self-service of goods in, 2, 35–36, 53, 129, 148, 248, 266n10; services provided by, 7, 8, 35, 36, 42; shoplifting in, 35; size of (downtown buildings), 5, 17, 21, 30, 34, 48, 56, 222; telephone orders to, 5, 7, 61, 62; trade radius of, 7, 10; use of shops concept in, 28, **28**, 39, **40**, 43, **44**, 45, **52**, 53, 112, 114–15, 121, 124, 130, 132, 149; "windowless" exteriors of, 49, 51, 58, 155, 222
department store branches, 1, 2, 3, 4, 59, 61, 109–35, 221, 279nn29 and 38, 280nn50–51, 55–56, 64, 281n79, 282nn15 and 20, 284nn48–50, 285n73, 286nn93 and 95; advantages of, 113; appliance outlets, 131, 140–41; in college communities, 111, 124, 141; definition of, 110, 260n6, 278 n.6, 283n29; design of, 112–13, 114–15, 118, 123–24, 132, 134–35, 146–58; furniture outlets, 140–41; grassroots opposition to construction of, 165–66; operation of, 121, 128–29, 142–43, 144–45; parking accommodations at, 118, 124, 126, 127, 130, 132, 150, 152, 154, 164–65, 166, 167–68, 174–76, 178, 179, 185, 187, 201, 209, 223; percentage of sales made in, 145; planning for, 146–47; in resorts, 110–11, 131; location of, 109, 113, 114–16, 118, 121, 123, 124, 126, 128, 129, 132, 134, 146,
156, 158–68; size of, 110, 111, 112–13, 114, 116, 117, 118, 120, 121, 123, 126, 127, 129, 130, 131, 132, 139, 142, 143–44, 146, 152, 155–56, 159, 161, 163, 164, 166, 167, 172, 173, 174, 175, 176, 177, 178, 179, 180, 186, 196, 201, 204, 219, 220, 223, 234, 240, 242
department store service buildings, 2, 3, 53, 62–81, 93, 271nn6, 8, 11–12, 19, 23–24, 272nn29–30, 39–40; delivery facilities of, 62–66; integrated service buildings of, 68–81; use of motor trucks with, 3, 7, 61, 62, 64, 65–66, 69, 113; warehousing facilities of, 64–65, 66–68, 70, 72, 113, 172, 271nn19 and 24, 272n29
Des Moines, Iowa, 59, 163
Detroit, Michigan, 13, 76, 80, 94, 96, 113, 129, 145, 147, 219, 220, 224, 225, 226, 227, 229; department store service buildings in, 65–66, **66**, **78**, **79**, 272n40; parking facilities in 96, 102; stores in, 9, 12, 14, **15, 18**, 19, **19, 20, 24, 25**, 29, 59, 65, 113, 129–30, 180, 189, 200–202, **201–2**, 220, 270n85
Dey Brothers department store, Syracuse, 269n71
Diamond, The, department store, Charleston, West Virginia, 269n71
Dillard's department store chain, 249, 304n8
discount stores, 171, 219, 220, 248, 249
Dixie Manor Shopping Center, Louisville, 289n27, 290n38
Donaldson, L. S., Company department store, Minneapolis, 12, 196, 210, 212, 296n112; branch stores, 163, 196, 207, 289n27; downtown store, 15, **15,** 26, **30, 88,** 265n91; use of parking facilities, **88**
Donaldson Village shopping center, Donaldson, Tennessee, 290n38
downtown commercial districts, 105, 217, 219; advantages of, 221–22; decline of/threats to vitality of, 96, 107, 140, 219–21, 248; impact of department stores on, 15, 34, 48, 52; impact of motor vehicles on/traffic congestion in, 2, 3, 61, 65, 66, 69, 84–86, 95, 96, 109, 113, 126–27, 220, 225; land values in, 2, 3, 9, 69, 87, 96, 101; parking in, 83–107, 109, 113, 200–201, 220, 225, 226, 227, 229, 230, 231, 232, 233, 234–35, 237, 238–39, 240; pedestrian malls in, 227–31, 233–36, **234–35,** 248, 301n59; revitalization / renewal of, 4, 56, 105, 106–7, 221–41, 248, 300n43
Downtown Parking Garage, San Francisco, 105–6
Dry Goods Economist, 10, 13, 37, 38, 83
Dyas, B. H., Company sporting goods (later department) store, Los Angeles, downtown store, 83, **84,** 121, **122,** 273n1; Hollywood branch, 121–22, **122**

East Hills Shopping Center, Pittsburgh, 295n98
East Orange, New Jersey, 119, 121
Eastgate Shopping center, Indianapolis, 295n98
Eastland Center, shopping center, Harper Woods, Michigan, 189, 201, **201,** 202, 203, 210, 295n93, 296n117
Eastland Shopping Center, West Covina, California, 295n98
Eastland Shopping Plaza, North Versailles Township, Pennsylvania, 294n73
Eastpoint Shopping Center, Baltimore, 196, 211
Eastwood Mall, Birmingham, 297n144
Edens Plaza Shopping Center, Wilmette, Illinois, 189, 196

Edmondson Village shopping center, Baltimore, 173, **173,** 178, 211
Edwards, E. W., & Sons department store, Syracuse, 173, 180
Emery, Bird, Thayer Company department store, Kansas City, 172, 226, 229
Emporium, The, department store, Detroit, 19, **19**
Emporium, The, department store, San Francisco (*see also* Emporium-Capwell), 11, **94**; branch stores, 188, 199, **199,** 294n71, 296n125; downtown store, **43**
Emporium, The, department store, St. Paul, 177
Emporium-Capwell department stores, San Francisco (*see also* Capwell, H. C.), 190
Evanston, Illinois, **114,** 115–16, **116,** 120, 121, 171
Evergreen Park Shopping Plaza, Chicago, 178–79, **179,** 196, 295n107

Fair, The, department store, Chicago, 12, 126, 128; Evergreen branch, 178, 196; Milwaukee Avenue branch, 126; Oak Park branch, 126; Old Orchard branch, 204; Randhurst branch, 216, **216,** 296n117
Fair, The, of Texas department store, Forth Worth, 180, 265n94; branch stores of, 180, **180,** 289n27
Fair Oaks Shopping Center, Forth Worth, 180, **180**
Fairchild News Service, 229
Famous-Barr Company department store, St. Louis, 68, 86, 144, 274n18; branch stores plans, 77; Clayton branch, 107, 161, 167; downtown store, 17, 64–65, **64**; Northland branch, 179, **179,** 295n107; parking garages, 91, 106–7, **107;** service buildings, 64–65, **65,** 70–71, **71,** 72, 73, 77; Southtown branch store, 107, 159, **160**
Famous Company department store, St. Louis (*see also* Famous-Barr), 11
Federal Department Stores, chain company, 200
Federal Housing Administration, 171
Federated Stores/Federated Department Stores, ownership group/corporation, 12, 50, 51, 53, 78, 80, 101, 163, 222, 247, 249, 262n38, 269nn71 and 76, 303n8
Feinberg, Samuel, journalist, 169, 181, 287n1
Field, Marshall, & Company department store, Chicago, 6, 8, 11, 29, 37, 62, 88, 113, 117, 119, 128, 129, 132, 153, 166, 189, 196, 203, 211, 216, 219, 276n60; downtown store, 14, 63, **64,** 115, 118, 249, 264n74, 265n90; Evanston branch, 114, **114,** 115, 118; Lake Forest branches, 114, 116; men's store, 21; Milwaukee branch, 294n69, 295n107; Oak Park branch, 114, **114,** 115, **117,** 118, 126; Old Orchard branch, 189, 204, **204;** other branch stores, 189, 190; parking services, 88, **88;** service buildings, 66, **66,** 271n11
Fifth Street Store, department store, Los Angeles (*see also* Milliron's), 13, 14
Filene's Sons, William, department store, Boston, 8, 11, 12, 51, 111, 145, 183, 184, 185, 193, 211, 278n5; branch stores, 111, **111**–12, 130, **130,** 189, 159, 279n29, 296n125, 297n125; downtown store, 28–29, 47, 93, 286n90; service building, 68, **68,** 70, 73
Foley Brothers department store, Houston, 51, 269n71; branch store, 296n117; downtown store, 51–53, **51–52,** 54, 57, 59, 80, 101, 163, 222,

316 | INDEX

223, 249, 269n77; parking garage, 101–2, **102,** 275n33; service facilities of, 79, 102, 273n43

food stores/supermarkets, 2, 35, 36, 103, 109, 129, 138, 173, 174, 176, 177, 178, 180, 203, 209, 214

Forman, B., Company, apparel store, Rochester, 237, **238,** 303n91

Fort Worth, Texas, downtown revitalization plan for, 227–28, **228,** 229, 233, 238, 240; stores in, 180, **180**

Fortune, 50, 248

Foster, William Trufant, educator, 31

Fox, G., & Company department store, Hartford, 141, 224, 231; downtown store, 42, 222, **222,** 227, 267n46, 268n63; parking garage, **222,** 277n72; service facilities of, 72, 272n40

Framingham, Massachusetts, 147, 161, 185

Frank & Seder apparel (later department) store, Detroit, Philadelphia, and Pittsburgh, 12, 127, 143, 159, 220, 280nn55–56

Frederick & Nelson department store, Seattle, 11; branch store, 172–73, **173;** downtown store, 270n85

Fresh Meadows Shopping Center, Queens, New York, 175, **175,** 194

Fresno, California, Fulton Mall, 236

furniture stores, 37, 171

Galleria, mixed-use development, Post Oak district, Houston, 245, 247, 298n146

Gallery, The, mixed-use development, Philadelphia, 304n15

Gamble-Desmond department store, New Haven, 231

Garden City, New York, 119, 120, 134, 143, 154, 193

Garden State Plaza shopping center, Paramus, New Jersey, 189, 192, 196, 198, 212, **212,** 242

Garfinckel, Julius, & Company department store, Washington, D.C., 13, 278n5; branch stores, 166, 196; downtown store, 130, 265n93, 270n85

Gateway Shopping Center, Portland, Oregon, 289n27

Gerber, Joseph, Company department store, Memphis, 131

Gertz, B., department store, Queens, New York, 190, 196

Gilchrist Company department store, Boston, 161, 185, 289n27

Gimbel Brothers department store ownership group/corporation, 11, 249

Gimbel Brothers department store, Milwaukee, 11, 104, 146; branch stores, 289n27, 294n69; downtown store, 11, 22, **22,** 265n90; service building, 70, **70**

Gimbel Brothers department store, New York, 264n85, 265nn90, 91, and 95; branch stores, 196, 198, 212; New York store, 11; service building, 65

Gimbel Brothers department store, Philadelphia, 11; branch stores, 177, 295n107; downtown store, 11, 26, **27,** 265n71; parking garage, 97, **98;** service building, 272n40

Gimbel Brothers department store, Pittsburgh, 11, **63;** branch stores, 179, 294n73

Glendale Center, shopping center, Indianapolis, 190, 196, 296n125

Goerke Company department stores, Elizabeth and Newark, New Jersey, 12

Goldblatt's department store chain, Chicago, 296n125

Golden Rule department store, St. Paul, 12; parking garage, 102; service building, 72, **73**

Goldenberg Company (Goldenberg's) department store, Washington, D.C., 220

Goldsmith, J., & Sons department store, Memphis, 269n71; parking garage, 102

Grad, F. W., Company variety store chain, 9

Grand Avenue, mixed-use development, Milwaukee, 304n15

Grand Rapids, Michigan, 220; stores in 54, **55,** 141

Grant, W. T., Company, junior department store chain, 10, 288n8

Grayson-Robinson, apparel store chain, Los Angeles, 200

Green Acres Shopping Center, Valley Stream, New York, 196

Green Hills Village, shopping center, Nashville, 290n38

Green Springs Mall, Birmingham, 297n144

Grossmont Shopping Center, La Mesa, California, 296n125

Guernsey, John, retail analyst, 13

Gulfgate Shopping City, Houston, 188, 192, 203, **203,** 210, 214, 296n125

Hahn Department Stores (*see also* Allied Stores), ownership group, 12, 50

Hahne & Company department store, Newark, 11, 29, 144; branch stores, 130, 154, **154,** 159, 161

Halle Brothers Company department store, Cleveland, 8, 29, 95, 124, 146, 190, 272n40, 280nn50 and 51; branch stores, 79, 124, 126, 172, **172,** 178, 289n27; downtown store, 20, **20, 24, 63,** 270n85; service building, 79

Halliburton-Abbott Company department store, Tulsa, 23, **28,** 269n71

Hamburger & Sons department store, Los Angeles, 11, 262n47

Hartford, Connecticut, 13, 76, 224; department store service building in, 72; stores in, 42, 220, 222, 231, 264n76, 268n63, 269n71, 272n40, 277n72

Harris, A., & Company department store, Dallas (*see also* Sanger-Harris), 189, 223, 296n125; parking lot, 100–101, **101**

Harundale Mall, Glen Burnie, Maryland, 213, **213,** 214, 296n117, 297nn136–37 and 144

Harvard University, Bureau of Business Research, 7; Graduate School of Business Administration, 36

Hearn, James A., & Son (later Hearn Department Stores), New York, 110, 141, 220, 269n71, 272n40; branch stores, 120, 121, 130

Hearst, William Randolph, 20

Hecht Brothers department store, Baltimore, 76, 178, 269n71, 272n39

Hecht Company department store, Washington, D.C., 13–14, 20, 77, 103, 144, 154, 168, 264n80, 265n92, 268n63, 269n71; parking garage, 97, 103–4; Parkington branch, 103–4, **104,** 175–76, 187, 233; service buildings, 70, 74–75, **75,** 76, 271n23, 272n40, 273n42; Somerset branch project, 166; Silver Spring branch, 144, 150, **151,** 154, **155,** 161, 167–68, **167,** 175

Hempstead, New York, 130, 134, 143, 154, 161, 171, 190, 196

Hengerer, Wm., Company department store, Buffalo, 11, 144, 222

Hens & Kelly department store, Buffalo, 14, 142, 173, 289n27

Herpolsheimer Company department store, Grand Rapids, 54, **55;** branch stores, 141, 285n73

Hess Brothers department store, Allentown, Pennsylvania, 272n40

Hicksville, New York, 188

Higbee Company department store, Cleveland, 15, 265n91, 269n77, 294n71

Highland Park Village shopping center, Highland Park, Texas, 138, 172

highways, limited-access, as a factor in siting regional shopping centers, 184, 185, 192, 240; impact on downtown, 107, 226, 227, 230, 231, 234

Hillsdale Shopping Center, San Mateo, California, 190, 191, 294n71, 296n125

Hillside Shopping Center, Hillside, Illinois, 198, 296n125

Hochschild, Kohn & Company department store, Baltimore, 213, 230, 262n47, 272n40; branch stores, 156, 173, **173,** 178, 196, 213, 296n117

Horne, Joseph, Company department store, Pittsburgh, 199, 211; branch stores, 142, **143,** 180, 282n20, 290n39, 294n73, 296n117; downtown store, 16; parking garage, 105; service building, 73

Horton Plaza, mixed-use development, San Diego, 304n15

Houston, Texas, 192, 269n77, 276n60; parking garage in, 101–2, **102;** stores in, 51, **51,** 53, 57, **58,** 59, 101, 163, 188, 203, **203,** 206, 210, 245, 247, 249, 269n71, 275n33, 283n38, 296nn117 and 125, 298n146

Hovey, C. H., department store, Boston, 54

Hoyt, Homer, planner, real estate analyst (Chicago), 169, 191, 195

Hub, The, department store, Baltimore, 220

Hudson, J. L., Company department store, Detroit, 29, 50, 65, 113, 147, 191, 200–201, 206, 211, 219, 263n62, 295n91; downtown store, 17, **18,** 23, **24, 25,** 46, 47, 208, 270n85; Eastland Center, 189, 201, **201,** 202, 295n93; music store, 20, **20;** Northland Center, 189, 201–2, **201–2,** 203, 204, 206, 247, 295n93, 296n114; parking garage, 102, 277n67; service buildings, 65–66, **66,** 68, **78,** 79, 272n40

Hull & Dutton department store, Cleveland, 11

Hutzler Brother Company department store, Baltimore, 153–54, 225, 272n40, 290n6; branch stores, 147, 154, **154,** 161, 180, 196, 225, 284n48, 295n107; downtown store, **32,** 33, 40, 267n33, 268n63

Ihlder, John, housing reformer, 109, 278n1

Indianapolis, Indiana, 94; stores in, 19–20, **22, 44, 49, 49,** 59, 141, 146, 190, 268n48, 270n85, 295n78, 295n125

Innes, George, Company department store, Wichita, 161, 163

| 317

interior designers/interior architects
    Brochstein, I. S. & S. J., **58**
    Carlu & Boyle (New York), **40**
    De Young, Moskowitz & Rosenberg (New York), 267n33
    de Wolfe, Elsie (New York), 146
    Feil & Paradise (Los Angeles), **123**, 279n48
    Frankl, Paul (New York), 37
    Grand Rapids Show Case (later Store Equipment) Company (Grand Rapids), 29, **42**, 184
    Heller, Robert (New York), 42
    Le Maire, Eleanor (Los Angeles, New York), 41, 42, **43**, **59**, 124, 131, **131**, 137, **137**, 147, 267n33, 279n48
    Loewy, Raymond (New York), 42, 45, 267n33 (*see also* architects, Snaith, William); Raymond Loewy Associates, **45**, **51**, 53, 56, **57**, 129, 134–35, **134**; Raymond Loewy Corporation, 47, 146, 147, **148–50**, **152**, 158, 269n77, 283n38
    Parker, Neal, **58**
    Parrish, Amos, & Company (New York), **144**, 146, 147
    Peters, Jock (Los Angeles), **123**, 124, **125–27**, 279n48
    Platt, Joseph B., **160**
    Rohde, Gilbert (New York), 42–43
    Scheuren, Josephine (Los Angeles), 279n48
    Schoen, Eugene (New York), **40**
    Stetson, David, **44**
    Swanson Associates, **160**
    Taussig & Flesch (Chicago), 29–30, 43, **160**
    Urban, Joseph (New York), 38
    Weber, Kem (Los Angeles), 37
    Webber & Collins (Los Angeles), 279n49
    Welch-Wilmarth Corporation (Grand Rapids), 29, **30**
    Whitman & Goldman (New York), **40**
    Williams, Sue (New York), **151**
International Council of Shopping Centers (ICSC), 181, 194, 198, 210, 217
Interstate Department Stores, chain company, 219
Irondequoit Shopping Center, Irondequoit, New York, **177**
Iverson, E., department store, Chicago, 126

Jenkintown, Pennsylvania, 118
Jones Store, department store, Kansas City, 221
Jordan Marsh Company department store, Boston, 12, 92, 184, 185, 186, 188; downtown store, 54, **55–56**; Fort Lauderdale branch, 177; Malden branch, 159; North Shore branch, 185, 186, 295n107, 297n125; parking garage, 92–93, **93**, 277n70; service building, 69–70; Shoppers' World branch, 185, **185**, 200
Joske Brothers Company department store, San Antonio, branch stores, 190, 203, **203**, 285n73, 296n125; downtown store 49, **49**, 270n85
Joslin Company department store, Malden, Massachusetts, 159

Kalamazoo, Michigan, Burdick Street Mall, 228–29
Kann, S., Sons (Kann's) department store, Washington, D.C., 68, 176, 187, 262n47, 265n93, 272n40

Kansas City, Missouri, 59, 96, 170, 225, 226, 229–30, 276n60; stores in, 50, 53, **53**, **54**, 180, 221, 224, 229, 269n71
Kaufman-Straus department store, Louisville, 12, 180, 289n27, 290n38, 296n117
Kaufmann, Baer & Company department store, Pittsburgh (*see also* Gimbel Brothers, Pittsburgh), 11, **63**
Kaufmann's department store, Pittsburgh, 59, 269n71; branch store, 178; downtown store, 38, **38**, **39**, 40, 55–56, **57**, 225; parking garages, 97, **97**, 101, 102, 105, **105**
Kenwood Plaza shopping center, Cincinnati, 290n39
Kern, Ernest, Company department store, Detroit, 14, **15**, 29, 113, 220
Kerr Dry Goods Company, Oklahoma City, 111, 131
King of Prussia, Pennsylvania, 245
Knoxville, Tennessee, 148, 163, 284n48
Kresge, .S. S., Company, variety store chain, 9
Kresge Department Stores, Newark (*see also* L. S. Plaut & Company), 131, 140–41
Kress, S. H., Company, variety store chain, 9, 34

L. B. Smith Plaza shopping center, Lackawanna, New York, 173, 289n35
Ladies' Home Journal, 202
Lake Forest, Illinois, 116
Lakeside Center, shopping center, Denver, 190, 209, 210
Lakeside Shopping Center, New Orleans, 295n98
Lakewood Center, shopping center, Lakewood, California, 188, 191, 199–200
Landing, The, shopping center, Kansas City, 290n38
landscape architects
    Church, Thomas (San Francisco), 184
    Clark, Lewis J., **214**
    Eckbo, Garrett (San Francisco), **149**, 163, **164**
    Funnell, Martin (Baltimore), 206
    Halprin, Lawrence (San Francisco), **204**, **204–5**
    Lipp, Franz, **216**
    Moore, William Lee, **152**, **160**
    National Landscaping Organization, **206**
    Ratekin, John (Beverly Hills), 206
    Seymour, Jonathan (Coral Gables, Florida), 206
    Shurcliff, Arthur (Boston), **184**, **185**, **200**
    Shurcliff, Sidney (Boston), 183, **184**, **184**, 186, **200**
    Zion Robert L. (New York), **203**, 205, **206**
Langley Park Shopping Center, Langley Park, Maryland, 176, **176**
Lansburgh & Brother department store, Washington, D.C., 269n71, 272n40; branch stores, 176, **176**, 177
Lasalle & Koch Company department store, Toledo, 11, 161; branch stores, 161, 285n73; downtown store, 16, 29
Lawrence Park Shopping Center, Broomall, Pennsylvania, 289n27
Lazarus, F. & R., Company department store, Columbus, Ohio, 11, 12, 35, 50; downtown store, 16, 56, **57**, 222, 265n93; parking garages,

101, **101**; service buildings, 72, **72**, 73, 76, 78, **78**, 79–80, **80**, 81, 272n29, 273n44
Lee, Richard, mayor, New Haven, 231–33
Lenox Square shopping center, Atlanta, 190
Lerner Shops, women's apparel store chain, 9
Lion Store, department store, Toledo, 285n73
Lipman Wolfe & Company department store, Portland, Oregon, 162
Lit Brothers department store, Philadelphia, 12, 67, 70, 164, 219, 220, 285n73, 286n95; branch stores, 143, 159, 164–65, **165**, 176–77, 286n93; service buildings, 67, 76, **77**
Lloyd Center, shopping center, Portland, Oregon, 242–43, 297n125
Lochwood Village Shopping Center, Dallas, 289n27
Loeser, Frederick, & Company department store, Brooklyn (*see also* Namm-Loeser), 29, 265n94, 272n40; Garden City branch, 130, 134, 143
Logue, Edward, planner (New Haven), 231
Long Beach, California, 199, 264n76; parking garage in, 97
Long Island, New York, 130, 131, 134, 143, 173, 175, 180, 190, 196
Lord & Taylor department store, New York, 11, 37, 134, 143, 146, 153, 155, 156, 158, 159, 165, 185, 204, 278n5; Eastchester branch, 152, **152**, 159, 165, 284n48; Manhasset branch, 134–35, **134**, 146, 151, 152, 158, 159; Millburn, New Jersey, branch, 159, 165; New Rochelle branch project, 158–59, 165; New York store, 29, **37**, 45, 249, 271n6; service buildings, 271nn12 and 19; Washington, D.C., branch, 167; West Hartford branch, 159
Los Altos Shopping Center, Los Altos, California, 295n98
Los Angeles, 49, 113, 177, 199, 200, 226, 244; department store service buildings in, 77, 79; downtown, 132, 298n3; Hollywood district, 112, 121–22, 123, 132, 147; outlying commercial centers, 96, 113, 132; parking issues in, 85, 101, 104–5; stores in, 8, 13, 14, 16, 19, **19**, 29, 47, 59, 68, 83, **84**, 112, 112,121–24, **122–23**, **125–27**, **130**, 131–32, **133**, 144, 145, 146, 147, 156, **157**, 161, 174–75, **175**, 177, 219–20, 248, 265n3, 266n10, 268n63, 269nn68 and 71, 274n18, 275n33, 277n72, 279n29; Westwood, 132, 244; Wilshire Boulevard, 121, 130, 132, 134, 159, 167, 244
Los Angeles Evening Express, 123
Los Angeles Examiner, 20
Los Angeles Times, 124
Louisville, Kentucky, 248; stores in, 11, 12, 180, 296n117, 297nn137 and 144
Loveman, Joseph & Loeb department store, Birmingham, 12, 265n3, 276n61
Lowenstein, B., & Brothers department store, Memphis, 12, 22, **27**, 265n94; branch stores, 180, 290n38
Lytton's apparel store, Chicago, 178

Maas Brothers department store, Tampa, 154, 269n71, 285n73
Mabley & Carew apparel (later department) store, Cincinnati, 17, 220, 222
Macy, R. H., & Company department store ownership group/corporation, 11, 35, 37, 43, 50, 62, 80, 129, 145, 147, 161, 196, 266n10, 269nn71 and 81

318 | INDEX

Macy, R. H., & Company department store, Kansas City, 220, 269n71; branch stores, 161–62, 163, 180, 234, 285n73, 290n38, 302n78; downtown store, 50, 53, **53,** 54, 161–62

Macy, R. H. & Company department store, New York, 144, 156, 190, 196; Manhattan store, 17, **18, 37,** 39, 40, 47, 86, 249; Jamaica branch, 154–55, 156, **156,** 159; New Haven branch, 232, **232,** 233, 234, 301n68; other branch stores, 111, 129, 131, 144, 155, 156, 159, 160, **212,** 294n73, 296nn117 and 125; Roosevelt Field branch, 196, 203, **203, 205;** service buildings, 66; Syracuse branch, 129, 130, 146

Macy, R. H. & Company department store, San Francisco (*see also* O'Connor Moffatt), 50, 190, 211, 219, 220, 249, 269n71; downtown store, 270n85; other branch stores, 159, 189, 294n71, 296n125; Sacramento branch, 234–35, 236, **236**

Magnin, I., & Company department store, San Francisco, 110, 124, 143, 147, 278n5; downtown store, 56–57, 58, **58,** 112, 268n50; Los Angeles branches, 111, 112, **112,** 130, **130;** other branches, 111–14

mail-order companies, 6

Main Line Shopping Center, Wynnewood, Pennsylvania, 177

Maison Blanche department store, New Orleans, 180, 290n38

Mall, The, Louisville, 296n117, 297nn137 and 144

Malley, Edward, Company department store, New Haven, 231, **231,** 232, **232,** 301n68

Mandel Brother department store, Chicago, 220

Manhasset, New York, 131, 134

Market Square shopping center, Lake Forest, 116

Marston Company department store, San Diego, 270n85, 296n125

May Company department store, Baltimore (*see also* Bernheimer-Leader), 268n63

May Company department store, Cleveland, 11, 68, 265nn91 and 3; branch stores, 117, 297n125; parking garage, 93, **94;** service building, 74, **74,** 275n30

May Company department store (May D&F), Denver, 11, 276n61; branch stores, 177, 206, 296n125; downtown store, 236–37, **237**

May Company department store, Los Angeles, 11, 77, 121, 122, 131–32, 193–94; Crenshaw branch, 174, **175,** 176, 187, 195; other branch stores, 122, 132, 188, 200, 289n29, 296n125; parking garages, 93, 277n72; service building, 77, 79; Wilshire Boulevard branch, 132, **133,** 135, 167, 277n72

May Department Stores Company (May Company) ownership group/corporation, 11, 12, 13, 17, 50, 55, 64, 77, 93, 106, 157, 167, 179, 188, 189, 236, 249, 261n26, 263 n. 62, 266n10, 269n71, 304n8

May Shopping Centers, Los Angeles, 189

Mayfair Shopping Center, Wauwatosa, Wisconsin, 190, 192, 194, 206, 294n69, 295n107

Mazur, Paul, retail analyst, 9, 13, 31, 36, 50, 110, 249, 262n43

McAlpin Company department store, Cincinnati, 180, 290n39

McClintock, Miller, traffic analyst, 85, 86

McCreery, James, & Company department store, New York, 11; service building, 271n19

McCurdy & Company department store, Rochester, 180, 237, **238, 240,** 303n91

McNair, Malcolm, retail analyst, 36

Mears, Charles, marketing consultant, 109

Meier & Frank department store, Portland, Oregon, 62, 162, 242, 243, 267n33, 285n73; Lloyd Center, 242–43, **243,** 297n125; service building, 61

Memphis, parking garage in, 102; stores in 12, 22, **27,** 269n71

merchants, property-owner, and other, related business associations, 94, 96, 98, 100, 195, 198, 224–25, 276n60

Merchants Garage, Columbus, Ohio, 275n26

Metropolitan Merchandise Mart shopping center, Wilmington, Delaware, 179

Metropolitan Museum of Art, New York, 37

Meyer Brothers department store, Paterson, New Jersey, parking facilities, 89, **90**

Meyer Siegel apparel store, Los Angeles, 274n18

Miami, 111, 146, 154, 277n68; stores in, 269n71, 294n73

Miami Beach, 111, 131, 141–42, 229, 280n64

Miami Herald, 205

Mid-Island Shopping Plaza, Hicksville, New York, 188, 192, 196

Midtown Plaza, mixed-use development, Rochester, 237–40, **238-40,** 248, 303n91, 304n15

Milan, Italy, Galllleria Vittorio Emanuele II, 207, 217, 240

Miller & Rhoads department store, Richmond, Virginia, 265n93, 268n63; branch stores, 163, 180, 284n49, 285n73, 290n38; parking garage, 100, 102

Millburn, New Jersey, 159, 165

Milliron's department store, Los Angeles, Westchester branch, 147, 156, **157**

Milwaukee, 220, 224, 229, 248; department store service building in, 70, **70;** parking facilities in, 104; stores in, 11, 22, **22, 42,** 59, 68, 89, 104, 146, 190, 206, 265n90, 269n71, 274 n.19, 294n69, 296n125, 304n15

Minneapolis, 209, 227, 229, 248; department store parking garage in, 93; department store service buildings in, 72, **73;** stores in, 12, 15, **15,** 26, **30,** 72, 88, 163, 189, 219, 249, 265n91

Miracle Mile, Los Angeles, 132, 269n68

Miracle Mile, Manhasset, New York, 132, 134, 190, 281n79

Miracle Mile Shopping Center, Monroeville, Pennsylvania, 178

Mission Shopping Center, Mission, Kansas, 290n38

Mission Valley Shopping Center, San Diego, 189, 193–94

Mondawmin Shopping Center, Baltimore, 211, 212, 213, 294n88, 297n131

Monmouth Shopping Center, Eatontown, New Jersey, 293n53

Montgomery Ward department store chain, 10, 35, 189, 197, 294n72, 296nn117 and 125

Moorestown Mall, Moorestown, New Jersey, 215–16

Motor Mart Garage, Boston, 93

Murphy, G. C., Company, variety store chain, 9

Namm, A. I., & Sons department store, Brooklyn (*see also* Namm-Loeser), 15

Namm-Loeser department store, Brooklyn, 102, 220

Nashville, 59, 180, 222

Nassau County, Long Island, 175, 196

National Department Stores, ownership group, 12, 126–28, 269n71

National Parking Association, 99

National Retail Dry Goods Association (NRDGA), 7, 12, 13, 76, 109, 128, 202, 210, 225, 226, 229, 272n40

National Retail Merchants Association (NRMA), 226, 230

Natrona Heights Plaza, shopping center, Natrona Heights, Pennsylvania, 290n39

Neiman-Marcus Company department store, Dallas, 57, 99, 138, 139, 155, 172, 249, 304n8; downtown store, 16, 268n63, 270n85; University Park branch, 138–39, **138,** 142, 147

New Haven, Connecticut, 86, 141; downtown revitalization in, 231–33, **231-32,** 239, 241, 301n68

New Orleans, 180, 224, 295n98, 300n43

New Rochelle, New York, 136, 158–59, 165, 240–41

New York, New York (*see also* Bronx, Brooklyn, and Queens), 13, 15, 29, 33, 37, 39–40, 52, 54, 75, 76, 88, 119, 163, 189, 215; architects and designers in, 29, 41, 53, 146–47, 184, 267n33; department store service buildings in, 66, 68, 271n19, 272n40; Fifth Avenue, 15, 88, 120, 120, 202; Rockefeller Center, 205; stores in, 5, 9, 11, 15, **18,** 29, 34, 37, **37,** 39–40, **40,** 45, **46,** 59, 86, 89, 109, 110, 111, 112, 113, 119–21, 123, 124, 130–31, 134, 138, 144, 146, 156, **156,** 175, **176,** 220, 224, 232, 249, 264n76 and 85, 265n90, 269n71, 272n40, 278n5; World's Fair of 1939, 40–41, 46, 198

New York Life Insurance Company, 175, 194

New York Times, 128, 197, 198

Newark, New Jersey, parking lots in, 100; stores in, 5, **6,** 11, 14, **14, 25,** 29, **45,** 89, 130, 140, 144, 164, 265nn92 and 93

Newberry, J. J., Company, variety store chain, 9, 191

Newcomb-Endicott Company department store, Detroit, 17, **18,** 263n62

Newton Shopping Center, Newton, Iowa, **209**

Nordstrom's apparel and accessories store, 249, 304n8

North Hills Village shopping center, Ross Township, Pennsylvania, 179

North Shore Center, shopping center project, Beverly, Massachusetts, 183–84, **184,** 188, 191, 200, 290n5

North Shore Center, shopping center, Peabody, Massachusetts, 186, 188, 189, 192, 193, 194, 201, 203, 205n107, 297n125

North Shore Mart shopping center, Great Neck, New York, 173

North Star Mall, San Antonio, 296n117, 297nn137 and 144

Northgate Shopping City, Seattle, 147, 163, 187–88, **188,** 189, 191, 192, 195, 199, **199,** 201, 202, 203, 204, 210, 296n125

Northland Center, shopping center, Southfield, Michigan, 189, 191, 192, 201–2, **201-2,** 203, 204, 206, 208, 210, 212, 219, 228, **228,** 242, 245, 247, 292n39, 295n93, 296nn114 and 117

| 319

Northland Shopping Center, Jennings, Missouri, 179, **179,** 189, 295n107
Northline Shopping Center, Houston, 190
Northtown Plaza shopping center, Amherst, New York, 289n27
Northway Mall, Ross Township, Pennsylvania, 294n73, 296nn117 and 125, 298n144
Northwestern Mutual Life Insurance Company, 194
Northwood Shopping Center, Baltimore, 177–78
Nugent, B., Dry Goods Company, St. Louis, 12, 127, 128, 262n47
Nystrom, Paul, retail analyst, 41

O'Connor Moffatt Company department store (San Francisco) (*see also* Macy, R. H. & Company, San Francisco), 29, 220, 269nn71 and 81
O'Neil, M., Company, department store, Akron, 11, 15, 93; branch stores, 163, 285n73; downtown store, 15, **16,** 265n91, 272n30; parking garage, 93, 102, 272n30, 275n33
O'Neil-Sheffield Shopping Center, near Lorain, Ohio, 188, 189, 294n88
O'Neill's department store, Baltimore, 87, 101, 220
Oak Brook shopping center, Oak Brook, Illinois, 190, 216
Oak Cliff Shopping Center, Dallas, 189, 296n125
Oak Park, Illinois, 115–16, **115–17,** 120, 121, 126
Oakland, California, 96; Kaiser Center, 223; parking facilities in 96, 105; stores in, 11, 112–13, 189, 223, 265n93
Oklahoma City, Oklahoma, 275
Old Orchard shopping center, Skokie, Illinois, 189, 191, 192, 203–5, **204–5,** 211, 216, 219
Olds & King department store, Portland, Oregon, 289n27
Omaha, Nebraska, 59; department store parking garage in, 106, **106;** stores in, 163, 189, 209, 296n117
Oppenheim Collins, apparel store, New York, 269n71
Oregon Avenue Shopping Center, Philadelphia, 289n27
Outlet Company department store, Providence, service building, 65, 72
outlying commercial districts, 1, 4, 96, 105, 112, 113–24, 128, 129–30, 132–35, 159, 161, 163–64, 171, 172, 184, 195, 245

Palais Royal department store, Washington, D.C., 12, 220, 282n15; service building of, 272n40
Palm Springs, California, stores in, 142, **142,** 157, **158**
Panorama City Shopping Center, Los Angeles, 177
Paramus, New Jersey, 188, 196, 290n8
Paris, France, Rue de la Paix, 38, 112; 1925 decorative arts exposition in, 37, 40
Park Forest Plaza shopping center, Park Forest, Illinois, 198, 211
parking, 2, 3, 4, 171, 187–88, 200–201, 225, 226, 229, 234–35, 274n19; curbside, 83, 85–86, 95–96, 118, 226; meters, 275n36; municipal programs for, 98–99, 134, 164–65, 167–68, 226, 231, 232, 233; parking garages, 72, 87, 88, 89–95, **91–95,** 96–98, **97–99,** 99, 100–107, **101–7,** 118, 164–65, 175–76, 209, 222, **222,** 223, 225, 229, 232, **232,** 233, 235, 237, 238, **238,** 239, 242, 272n30, 275nn26, 28, 30, 33; 276n44; 277nn67–68, 70, 72; 301n68; parking lots, 86, 88–89, **89–90,** 96, 99, 100–01, **101,** 107, 124, 126, 127, 130, 134, 138, 150, 152, **153,** 154, **155,** 157–58, 159, **160,** 166, 167–68, **167,** 170, **173,** 174–7, 175, **175–77,** 178, **179–80,** 183, 185, **185,** 186, 187, **188,** 199, 201, **201, 204, 207,** 210, **214,** 234, **241,** 276n61; restrictions on, 83, 85–86, 96
Parkington shopping center, Arlington, Virginia, 103–4, **104,** 106, 233
Parmatown Shopping Center, Parma, Ohio, 297n125
Pasadena, California, 111, 131, 147, 159, 166, 287n101
Paterson, New Jersey, parking facilities in, 89, **90;** stores in, **23,** 89
pedestrian malls. *See* downtown commercial districts, pedestrian malls in
Penney, J. C., Company, junior department (later department) store chain, 10, 35, 50, 191, 249, 266n10, 288n8, 303n8
Philadelphia, 40, 59, 76, 118, 129, 147, 159, 164, 176, 179, 184, 190, 214, 215, 227, 229, 248; department store parking garage in, 97, 98, **98–99;** department store service buildings in, 67–68, **67, 72,** 76, **76,** 272n40; Germantown district in, 117; Liberty-Lincoln Building, 21, **21;** stores in, 8, 11, 12, 14, **14,** 17, 21, **21,** 26, **27,** 30, 47, 59, 67, 98, 117, 121, 122, 144, 176–77, 215, 220, 248, 265nn90 and 91, 304n15
Pittsburgh, 94, 179; department store service buildings in, 65, **65,** 73, 94; downtown revitalization in, 225, 226, 227, 231, 232; parking facilities in, 94, 97, **97,** 100, 102, 105, **105,** 225; stores in, 11, 12, 16, 38, **38, 39,** 55–56, **57,** 59, **63, 64,** 65, 73, 142, 180, 220, 231, 269n71, 294n73, 295n98
Pizitz, Louis, Dry Goods Company, Birmingham, 14, 265n95
Plaut, L. S., & Company department store, Newark (*see also* Kresge department Stores), 11; downtown store of, 14, **14,** 264n80, 265n93
Plaza de las Palmas shopping center, San Antonio, 190
Pogue, H. & S. Company department store, Cincinnati, 17, **17;** service building, **78,** 79, 272n40
Polsky, A., Company department store, Akron, 15, **16,** 23, 93, 268n63; parking garage, 93
Poplar-Highland Plaza shopping center, Memphis, 290n38
Portland, Oregon, 59, 162, 242; department store service buildings in, 61; Lloyd Center, 242–43, **243,** 245, 297n125; stores in, 61, 112, 162
Powers Dry Goods Company, Minneapolis, 11, 68
Preston Center Plaza shopping center, Dallas, 289n27
Princes Georges Plaza shopping center, Hyattsville, Maryland, 190, 194, 198
Princeton Shopping Center, Princeton, New Jersey, 294n88
Providence, Rhode Island, 225, 248; department store service building in, 65
Prudential Center, mixed-use development, Boston, 304n15
Prudential Life Insurance Company, 194
public transportation systems, use of, 7, 62, 83, 85, 100, 140, 171, 226–27, 230

Quackenbush Company department store, Paterson, New Jersey, **24;** parking lot, 89
Queens, New York, 86; stores in, 131, 154–55, 156, **156,** 159, 175, **176**

Randhurst Center, shopping center, Mount Prospect, Illinois, 189, 216, **216,** 296n117
Read, D. M., Company, Bridgeport, Connecticut, 269n71
real estate developers
  Atlas, Sol (New York), 132, 190, 196, 211, 281n79
  Berenson, Theodore W. (Boston), 190
  Bohannon, David (San Francisco), 169, 190
  Chevy Chase Land Company (Washington), 167
  Community Research & Development (CRD) (Baltimore), 190, 211, 213, 217
  De Bartolo, Edward J. (Youngstown), 179
  Eastern Shopping Centers (Yonkers), 190
  Eichenbaum, Joseph (Los Angeles), 200
  Eig, Sam (Washington), 168
  Food Fair Properties (Philadelphia), 181
  Froedtert Enterprises (Milwaukee), 190, 292n33
  Hines, Gerald (Houston), 245
  Kass, Garfield (Washington), 190
  Klutznick, Philip (Chicago), 189, 211, 219
  Landau & Pearlman (Chicago), 190
  Lloyd, Ralph (Portland, Oregon), 242
  Lofus, Don (Wilmington, Delaware), 179
  McClatchy, John H. (Philadelphia), 280n56
  Meyerhoff, Joseph (Baltimore), 190, 211
  Mori, Eugene (Camden County, New Jersey), 190, 214
  Muss, David (New York) (*see also* Winston-Muss), 216
  Nichols, J. C. (Kansas City), 170, 187, 194, 198, 211, 212
  Pletz, Roy (San Antonio), 190
  Rawls, Huston (Boston), 183, 184–86, 187, 188, 191, 195, 203, 290n8
  Ross, A. W. (Los Angeles), 132
  Rouse, James (Baltimore) (*see also* Community Research & Development), 190, 191, 211–15, **212,** 217, 225, 230, 247, 294n88, 296n114, 297nn131, 133, 135; 298n144
  Rouse, Willard, 211
  Rubloff, Arthur (Chicago), 178, 181, 290n45
  Stackler & Frank (New York), 190
  Stevens, Roger L. (New York), 231, 232, 233
  Suburban Company (Ardmore, Pennsylvania), 118
  Swig, Ben (San Francisco), 233–34
  Tishman Realty & Construction Company (New York), 235–36
  Visconti, Anthony (Cleveland), 190
  von Frellich, Gerri (Denver), 190
  Webb & Knapp (New York) (*see also* Zeckendorf, William), 234
  Winston-Muss Corporation (New York) (*see also* Muss, David), 215, 241
  Woodner, Jonathan, Company, 190
  Zeckendorf, William (New York) (*see also* Webb & Knapp), 190, 214, 234, 235, 236–37, 244
Redstone Shopping Center, Stoneham, Massachusetts, 289n27

retail executives
  Adam, Robert B. (Adam, Meldrum & Anderson), 180
  Allison, Rex (Bon Marche), 187, 188, 189
  Baer, Sidney (Stix, Baer & Fuller), 226
  Biggs, Reginald (White House), 223
  Bullock, John (Bullock's), 122–23
  Clark, Frank, Jr. (May Company), 189
  Clothier, Isaac (Strawbridge & Clothier), 30
  Cohen, George (Foley's), 51
  Crear, William (Dayton's), 219
  Dayton, Donald (Dayton's), 206, 209
  Dayton, George (Dayton's), 227
  Dennis, E. Willard (Sibley, Lindsay & Curr), 226
  Dyas, Bernal (B. H. Dyas), 121, 122, 123, 124
  Filene, Edward A. (Filene's), 12–13, 110, 249, 262n38, 281n70
  Filene, Lincoln (Filene's), 262n38
  Forman, Martin (B. Forman), 237, 238, 240
  Gimbel, Adam (Gimbel's), 11
  Goerke, Rudolph J. (Goerke's), 12
  Greenfield, Albert M. (City Stores), 36, 67, 164, 165, 176, 214
  Greenhut, Eugene, 12
  Hahn, Lew (Hahn Department Stores), 7, 12, 13
  Hecht, Harold (Hengerer's), 221
  Hodgkins, Harold (Filene's), 183, 184
  Hoving, Walter (Lord & Taylor), 134, 158, 165
  Hudson, Joseph L., Jr. (Hudson's), 277
  Hunter, Forest (Hudson's), 224
  Kaufmann, Edgar (Kaufmann's), 38–39, 56, 105
  Kohn, Martin (Hochschild, Kohn), 230
  Kramer, Raymond (Interstate Department Stores), 219
  Kresge, Sebastian S. (Kresge's, Kresge Department Stores), 11, 12, 14
  Lazarus, Fred (Lazarus, Federated), 50, 51, 53, 56, 59, 72, 73, 78, 79, 222, 247, 269n76
  Lazarus, Maurice (Federated), 269n79, 283n38
  Lazarus, Ralph (Lazarus, Federated), 222
  LeBoutiller, Philip (Best & Company), 119, 120, 121
  Lewis, Alex (Macy's, Kansas City), 224
  Martin, C. Virgil (Carson Pirie Scott), 229
  Marcus, H. Stanley (Neiman-Marcus), 99, 138, 140
  Marcus, Herbert (Neiman-Marcus), 138, 140
  Mark, Carl (Lit's, Trenton), 241
  May, Morton J. (May Company, St. Louis), 167
  May, Tom (May Company, Los Angeles), 132, 167, 196
  McBain, Hughston (Marshall Field's), 189
  McCurdy, Gilbert (McCurdy's), 237, 238, 239
  Mitton, Edward (Jordan Marsh), 54
  Moss, John (Marshall Field's), 205
  Myers, Perry (Allied Stores), 197
  Puckett, B. Earl (Allied Stores), 50, 169, 184, 186, 188, 189, 219, 224, 225, 247
  Rich, Richard (Rich's), 59, 163
  Rike, David (Rike-Kumler), 224
  Robb, Max (Lit's), 220
  Sams, E. C. (J. C. Penney), 10
  Sincere, Victor (National department Stores), 126, 127
  Sizer, Lawrence (Marshall Field's), 224
  Spurway, Harold (Carson Pirie Scott), 216

  Stewart, A. T. (A. T. Stewart), 45
  Strawbridge, G. Stockton (Strawbridge & Clothier), 214, 215
  Strawbridge, Justus (Strawbridge & Clothier) 30
  Talbott, Philip (Woodward & Lothrop), 226, 239
  Tily, Herbert J. (Strawbridge & Clothier), 30–31, 33, 117–18
  Webber James B., Jr. (Hudson's), 295n91
  Webber, Oscar (Hudson's), 200–201, 206, 219, 220, 221, 224, 248, 295n91
  Weisenberger, Arthur, 12
  Whelan, Groves (Wanamaker's New York), 40–41
  Wilson, Herbert (Emery, Bird, Thayer), 229–30
Retail Ledger, 7, 33
Retail Research Association (RRA), 11, 13
Reynolds Metals Company, Richmond, Virginia, 56, 235
Rhodes Department Store, Seattle, parking facilities, 91–92, **92**
Rich, M., & Brothers Company department store (Rich's), Atlanta, 163, 190; downtown store, **8**, 58–59, **59**, 264n80, 268n63; Knoxville branch, 148, **149**, 150, 163, 284n48
Richard's Department Store, Miami, 56, 269n71, 289n27
Richmond, Virginia, 59; parking garage in, 100, 102; stores in, 56, **57**, 163, 180, 264n76, 265nn93 and 3, 268n33
Rike-Kumler Company department store, Dayton, 37, 224, 269n71; store of, 55, **56**, 222, 268n63
River Roads Shopping Center, Jennings, Missouri, 296n117, 297n125
Robinson, Boardman, muralist, 38–39
Robinson, J. W., Company department store, Los Angeles, 8, 121, 122, 146, 269n71; branch stores, 142, 149, **150**, 159, 244, 296n125; downtown store, 47, 275n33
Rochester, New York, 76, 226, 239; department store service building in, 272n40; Midtown Plaza, 237–40, **238-40**, 248; parking facilities in 100, 238–39; stores in, 269n71
Rochester Times-Union, 240
Rollman & Son department store, Cincinnati, 12, 190, 220, 222, 270n85, 295n107
Roosevelt Field shopping Center, Hempstead, New York, 190, 191, 192, 193, 194, 196, 198, 203, **203**, 205, **206**, 214, 234, 242
Rosenbaum Company department store, Pittsburgh, 12, **64**, 220; parking garage, 94; service building, 65, **65**, 94, 271n8
Rothschild & Company department store, Chicago, **63**
Rotival, Maurice, planner, 301n61
Rotterdam, the Netherlands, Lijnbaan, 227
Russek's, women's apparel store chain, 9
Rye, New York, revitalization plan for, 229

Sacramento, downtown revitalization of, 233–36, **234-36**, 239
Sakowitz Brothers department store, Houston, 57–58, **58**; branch stores, 159, 203, **203**, 296n125
Saks Fifth Avenue department store, New York, 11, 113, 124, 128, 138, 143, 145, 156, 185, 278n5, 281–82n3, 304n8; Chicago branch, 113, 114, 280n63; Detroit branch, 129–30; Miami Beach branch, 111, 131, 280n63; New York store, 15, 29, 39, 40, **40**, 249, 264n75; other branches, 111, 129, 141, 142, **156**, 181, 167, 240
Sales Management, 129
Salt Lake City, Utah, parking garage in 102–3, **103**; stores in, 222, 294n73, 296n117, 297nn125 and 144
San Antonio, Texas, stores in, 49, **49**, 88, **89,** 190, 270n85, 296n117, 297nn137 and 144
San Diego, California, 193–94, 248; stores in, 189, 194, 206, 270n85, 297n125, 304n15
San Francisco, California, 13, 163, 190, 204, 220, 227, 233, 235, 300n43; parking garage in, 105–6; stores in, 11, 29, **43,** 50, 56–57, **58,** 59, 94, 109, 110, 111, 112, 161, 188, 199, **199,** **207,** 211, 268n50, 269nn71 and 81, 270n85, 278n5
San Mateo, California, 171, 190, 296n125
Sanger Brothers department store, Dallas) (*see also* Sanger-Harris), 172, 223, 269n71, 289n27, 296n117
Sanger-Harris department store, Dallas, 223
Schaumburg, Illinois, 245
Schindler, Pauline, journalist, 124
Schuneman's department store, St. Paul, 222
Schuster, Ed., & Company department store, Milwuakee, 271n8, 296n11
Scruggs, Vandervoort & Barney department store, St. Louis, 91; branch stores, 143, 144, **144,** 167, 294n72; parking garage, 91, **91,** 277n70
Sears, Roebuck & Company department store chain, 10, 35, 109, 119, 121, 139, 145, 155, 156, 158, 159, 166, 191, 197, 199, 231, 234, 249, 266n10, 269n68, 273n43, 294n72, 294n88, 296nn117 and 125, 304n8; Pico Boulevard store, Los Angeles, 146
Seattle, Washington, 13, 98, 172, 188, 211, 300n41; parking garages in, 91–92, **92,** 106, **106;** stores in, 11, 12, 15, 47, 59, 112, 163, 187–88, **188,** 199, **199,** 249, 270n85, 295n98
Seattle Times, 12
Seventeen, 197
Shaker Square shopping center, Cleveland, 172, **172**
Sharpstown Center, Sharpstown, Texas, 296n117
Sheridan Plaza shopping center, Buffalo, 289n35
Shillito, John, Company department store, Cincinnati, 11, 266n10; branch store, 190; downtown store, 48, **48,** 50; parking garages, 72, 97–98, 100, 275n33; service facilities, 72, 76
Shirlington shopping center, Arlington, Virginia, 177
Shoppers' World shopping center, Framingham, Massachusetts, 147, 183, 185–86, **185,** 196, 200, **200,** 207–9, 211, 212, 290n8
Shopping Center Age, 240
shopping centers, 4, 116, 118, 138, 167, 168, 169–81, 183–217, 249, 289nn27, 29, 35; 290nn38–39, 45, 5; 292n31; arrangement/layout of, 178, 179, 186–87, 201–3, 209–10, 212, 214, 216, 289n23, 292n31, 294n88, 295n107, 296n112; characteristics/definitions of, 170, 173–74, 216–17, 249, 288n12, 304n8; cost of, 187; design of, 199–216; department stores added to, 172, 177–78; department store as anchor of, 155, 157, 172–73, 174–76, 178–80, 183–86;

| 321

shopping centers *(continued)*
  developers of, 172, 179, 181, 189–90, 217, 240, 290nn45 and 8; enclosed malls, 163, 195, 204, 206–16, 225, 247, 295n117, 296nn115 and 125, 297n136, 298n144; financing of, 194, 214, 293n53; grassroots to development of, 193–94; location of, 184, 191; origins of, 170–71; planning of, 171, 190, 191–94, 292n39, 296n113; parking accommodations of, 170, 171, 174–76, 178, 179, 183, 185, 186, 187, 191–92, 201, 209, 241, 242; regional shopping centers/ regional malls, 1, 2, 4, 101, 105, 138, 147, 163, 166, 174, 178, 179, 180, 181, 183–217, 219, 221, 225, 229, 231, 233, 234, 239, 240–43, 244, 245, 247–48, 249, 290n8, 291n24, 292nn31 and 39, 293n53, 294nn69, 71–73, 88; 295nn90, 93, 98, 107; 296nn112, 115, 117, 125; 297nn131, 133, 137, 144; 298n146, 304n7; relation to city center, 187, 219–21, 243, 248; role of chain store in, 172, 173, 194, 195, 209, 217; size of, 174, 185, 186, 188, 196, 201, 203, 209, 210, 214, 242; as a social center, 197–98, 203, 207, 211–12, 216; tenant mix of, 173–74, 178, 190, 194–97, 203, 205, 212, 214; with dual anchors, 173, 184, 195–97, 202–3, 206, 207, 211, 212, 213, 247, 294nn69 and 71–73, 295n98; with three or four anchors, 203, 247
Sibley, Lindsay & Curr Company, Rochester, 226, 237; branch stores, 177, **177**, 237; service building, 272n40
Signal Hills Shopping Center, St. Paul, 177
Silver Spring, Maryland, 144, 150, 154, 161, 167–68, **167**, 171
Simon, Franklin, apparel store, New York, 88, 269n71
Small Business Administration, 195
Smith, Larry, planner, real estate analyst (Seattle), 191, 200, 206, 214, 221
Snellenbergs department store, Philadelphia, 220; branch stores, 141, **141**, 289n27, 289n27; parking facilities, 98, **99**
South Bay Shopping Center, Redondo Beach, California, 296n125
South Bay Shopping Center, West Babylon, New York, 180
South Shore Mall, Bay Shore, New York, 294n73
South Shore Plaza shopping center, Braintree, Massachusetts, 189, 296n125
Southdale shopping center, Edina, Minnesota, 163, 189, 191, **192**, 194, 196, 206–9, **207–9**, 210, 212, **212**, 213, 214, 216, 217, 219, 245, 247, 292n39, 296nn112 and 117, 297nn131 and 136
Southgate Shopping Center, Milwaukee, 289n27, 292n33
specialty stores, 2, 6, 9, 39, 78, 115, 129, 223
Spokane, Washington, 59, 162
Sports Illustrated, 198
St. Louis, 76, 91, 96, 163, 225, 226, 227, 248; department store service buildings in, 70–71, **71**, 272n40; parking facilities in, 91, **91**, 92, 106–7, **107**; Railway Exchange Building, 17, **64**; stores in, 11, 12, 17, **21**, 59, 64–65, 68, 86, 96, 97, 107, 127, 143, 144, **144**, 159, **160**, 161, 179, **179**, 262n47, 294n72, 304n15
St. Louis Centre, mixed-use development, St. Louis, Missouri, 304n15
St. Paul, 220, 229, 248; parking garage in, 102; department store service building in, 72, **73**; stores in, 12, 72, 222–23, **223**, 304n15
Stamford, Connecticut, 86, 121, 171
Stanford Shopping Center, Palo Alto, California, 190, 294n71, 296n125
Stanford University, 190
Stern Brothers department store, New York, 39, 269n71; branch store, 297n125
Stewart & Company apparel store, New York, 39, **40**
Stewart & Company department store, Baltimore, 11
Stewart Dry Goods Company, Louisville, 11, 285n73
Stiffel, Geo., Company department store, Wheeling, 12
Stix, Baer & Fuller Dry Goods Company, St. Louis, 167, 226; branch store, 296n117, 297n125; downtown store, **21**; parking facilities, 91, 97; service building, 272
Stonestown shopping center, San Francisco, 188, 191, 199, **199**, 201, 202, 203, 210, 296n125
Stores, 202
Strawbridge & Clothier department store, Philadelphia, 8, 33, 116–17, 121, 122, 129, 132, 153, 157, 166, 184, 190, 211, 214, 249; Ardmore branch, 118, **118**, 121, 172, 184, 187, 286n95; Cherry Hill branch, 179, 214–15, **214**, 296nn117 and 125; downtown store, 14, **14**, 30, 47, 51, 63, 215, 265n95, 269n77; Jenkintown branch, 118–19, **119**; service buildings, 67–68, **67**, **72**, 272n40; Wilmington branch, 179, 214
Strouss-Hirshberg Company, Youngstown, Ohio, 269n71, 280n51
Suburban Square shopping Center, Ardmore, Pennsylvania, 118, 172, 179, 184, 187
Sun [Baltimore], 33
Sunrise Shopping Center, Fort Lauderdale, 177
supermarkets. *See* food stores
Swern's department store, Trenton, New Jersey, 164, 286n93
Swifton Center, shopping center, Cincinnati, 188, 190, **206**, 225, 295n98, 295n107
Syracuse, New York, 129; parking issues in, 85; stores in, 129, 130, 146, 269n71

Taft, William Nelson, editor, 7
Tampa, Florida, stores in, 141, 154, 269n71
Taylor, Frederick Winslow, 63
Taylor, Geo., Company department store, Wheeling, 12
Taylor, John, Dry Goods Company, Kansas City, 53, 220, 269n71
Thalheimer Brothers department store, Richmond, Virginia, branch stores, **149**, 163, 285n73; downtown store, 56, **57**, 264n76, 265n3; parking garage, 102
Thurway Plaza shopping center, Cheektowaga, New York, 180
Tide, 169
Titche-Goettinger Company (Titche's) department store, Dallas, 12, **23**, 47, 55, 223
Toledo, Ohio, 229; stores in, 11, 16, 29
Town Square, mixed-use development, St. Paul, 304n15
Townlyne Shopping Center, Peabody, Massachusetts, 195

Towson, Maryland, 147, 154, 161, 225, 284n48
Transittown Plaza shopping center, Clarence, New York, 289n27
Trenton, New Jersey, 164, 165, 241
Tri-County Shopping Center, Glendale, Ohio, 190, 192, 205–6
Tulsa, Oklahoma, stores in, 13, **16**, 17, 23, **28**
Turner Construction Company, New York, 33
Tyson's Corner, Virginia, 245

U.S. Chamber of Commerce, 109, 239
U.S. Department of the Treasury, 7
University Plaza shopping center, Amherst, New York, 180
University Village Shopping Center, Seattle, 295n98
Upper Darby, Pennsylvania, 143, 159, 164, 165, 280n56
Urban Land Institute, Washington, D.C., 98, 170, 176, 191, 226
urban renewal. *See* downtown commercial districts, revitalization of

Valley Fair Shopping Center, Santa Clara, California, 189, 296n125
Valley Plaza shopping center, Los Angeles, 289n29
variety stores, 9, 11, 34–35, 36, 109, 129, 172, 173, 174, 178, 209
Venice, Italy, Piazza San Marco, 207
Vincennes, Indiana, 11
Volk Brothers apparel store, Dallas, 268n59

Walker's department store, Long Beach, California, 296n125
Walker Scott department store, San Diego, 297n125
Wall Street Journal, 233
Walt Whitman Shopping Center, Huntington, New York, 216, 296nn117 and 125
Wanamaker, John, department store, Philadelphia and New York, 6, 8, 29, 37, 40, 50, 62, 117, 144, 147, 153, 158, 190, 196, 214, 215; downtown stores: New York, 45, **46**, 220, 265n90, 268n52; men's store, Philadelphia, 21, **21**; other branch stores, 173, 177, 215, 284n48; service buildings, 66; Philadelphia, 14, 17, 215, 264n77, 265n90; Wilmington, Delaware, branch, 156, 159, **160**, 166, 179, 284n48; Yonkers branch, 189, 291n24
Ware department store, New Rochelle, New York, 159
Washington, D.C., 13, 76, 109, 147, 154, 163, 166, 167, 168, 170, 176, 190, 196, 220, 226, 227, 239, 300n43; department store service buildings in, 69, **69**, 70, 74–76, **75–76**, 272n40; parking facilities in, 97, 104; stores in, 12, 13–14, 16, **16**, 20, **28**, 30, 59, 68–69, 70, 74, 86, 103, 130, 141, 146, 154, 166, 176, 196, 220, 248, 262n47, 265nn92 and 93, 268n63, 269n71, 270n85, 278n5
Wasson, H. P., & Company department store, Indianapolis, 49, **49**, 270n85
Water Tower Place, mixed-use development, Chicago, 304n16
Weiss, E. B., retail analyst, 138–39, 145, 152, 155, 283n31
Wess, Harold, educator, retail analyst, 36

Westborn Shopping Center, Dearborn, Michigan, 180
Westchester County, New York, 119, 120, 121, 130, 156, 240
Westchester Terminal Plaza, mixed-use development, 240–41, **241**
Western Hills Plaza shopping center, Bridgetown, Ohio, 290n39
Westgate Shopping Center, Fairview Park, Ohio, 190, 294n71, 295n98
Westland Shopping Center, Lakewood, Colorado, 189, 206, 295n98, 296n125
Westview Shopping Center, Catonsville, Maryland, 180, 295n107
Westwood Village, quasi-planned shopping enclaves, Los Angeles, 131
Wheaton Plaza shopping center, Wheaton, Maryland, 190
Whitaker, Amy, journalist, 124
White, R. H., Company, department store, Boston, 11, 185, 220
White House department store, San Francisco, 223, 299n24
White Plains, New York, 120, **120**, 121, 152, 156, 161, 165, 240, 284n48, 290n8

Whitehaven Plaza shopping center, Whitehaven, Tennessee, 290n38
Wichita, Kansas, 161, 163
Wieboldt's department store chain, Chicago, 189, 216, **216,** 296nn117 and 125
Williamsburg, Virginia, 173, 184
Willow Lawn Shopping Center, Richmond, 290n28
Wilmington, Delaware, 156, 159, 166, 179, 284n48
Wise Company department store, Long Beach, California, 264n76
Wise, Smith & Company department store, Hartford, 220, 264n76, 269n71
Wolf & Marx department store, San Antonio, **89;** branch store, 296n117; parking facilities, 88, **89**
Woodward & Lothrop department store, Washington, D.C., 30, 68, 86, 99, 144, 146, 154, 190, 220, 226, 239; branch stores, 159, 166–67, 196, 284nn48–50; budget store, 141, **141,** 282n15; bus service of, 86, **87;** downtown store of, 16, **16, 28;** parking garage, 97; service buildings, 69, **69,** 74, 75–76, **76,** 271n23
Woolworth, F. W., & Company variety store chain, 9, 34, 214, 234, 266n10, 304n8

Women's Wear Daily, 35, 36, 71, 109, 110, 137, 152, 166, 169, 208, 220, 221, 224, 225, 229, 230, 243
Worcester, Massachusetts, 185, 248, 304n15
Wynnewood Village Shopping Center, Dallas, 289n27

Yale University, 233, 301n68
Yonkers, New York, 189, 291n24
Youngstown, Ohio, 163, 225, 269n71
Youngstown Shopping Center, Jeffersonville, Indiana, 290n38
Younker Brothers department store, Des Moines, 163; branch stores, 111, 163, 209, **209,** 285n73

ZCMI department store, Salt Lake City, 222, 294n73, 296n117, 297n125; parking garage, 102–03, **103,** 1057 Corners Shopping Center, Falls Church, Virginia, 190, 196, 292n31, 295n107; 163rd Street Shopping Center, Miami, 205, 219

ILLUSTRATION CREDITS

The photographers and the sources of visual material other than the owners indicated in the captions are as follows. Every effort has been made to supply complete and correct credits; if there are errors or omissions, please contact Yale University Press so that corrections can be made in any subsequent edition.

Architectural Archives, University of Pennsylvania, Philadelphia, by the gift of Lawrence Halprin, fig. 216; Avery Architectural and Fine Arts Library, Columbia University, New York (Abbott, Merkt Collection), figs. 87–89, 127, 181, 197, 233; Author's collection, figs. 54–57, 65, 75, 80, 108, 124, 128, 136, 179, 185, 190, 196, 199, 210, 251; Trustees of the Boston Public Library, Rare Books, fig. 83; California State Library, Sacramento, California History Room, figs. 147, 149–52; Chicago History Museum, figs. 135, 140 (Marshall Field Collection), 198 (HB 14148A), 214, 215 (HB-20652D), 217 (HB-20652I); Meredith L. Clausen, fig. 206; Cleveland Public Library, figs. 16, 25; Columbia Archives, Columbia, Maryland, fig. 228; Dallas Public Library, Texas/Dallas History and Archives Division, figs. 161, 162; Detroit Public Library, Burton Historical Collection, figs. 5, 12, 13, 15, 17, 26–28, 79, 99; ESTO Photographics, figs. 178, 218; Grand Rapids Public Library, Local History Department, fig. 61; Hagley Museum and Library, Wilmington, Delaware, Strawbridge & Clothier Collection, figs. 81, 82, 141–43, 229; Michael Hauser, figs. 22, 24; Historical Society of Pennsylvania, Philadelphia (Albert M. Greenfield Collection) fig. 97, (Wanamaker Collection) figs. 18, 184; Historical Society of Washington, D.C., figs. 8, 34, 84, 106, 163; Houston Public Library, Houston Metropolitan Research Center, fig. 69; Indiana Historical Society, Indianapolis, figs. 21, 52, 53; © J. Paul Getty Trust. Used by permission. Research Library, Getty Research Institute, Los Angeles, Julius Shulman Photography Archive, figs. 167, 175, 176, 182, 183; Kansas City Public Library, Special Collections, fig. 58; Lehigh County Historical Society, Allentown, Pennsylvania, fig. 110; Library of Congress, Geography & Maps Division, fig. 205, (Nierenstein National Realty Company Collection) figs. 7, 227; Library of Congress, Prints & Photographs Division, figs. 168 (LC- G613-T-64734), 169 (LC-G613-T-68079), 170 (LC-G613-T-56490), 171 (LC-G613-74751), 174 (LC-G613-77470), 177 (LC-G613-T-58733), 188 (LC-G613-T-68112), (Gruen Collection) figs. 246–49, (HABS Collection) fig. 71 (GA-2290–21), (Loewy Collection) fig. 47; Robert A. Little, fig. 191; Los Angeles Public Library (Herald-Examiner Collection) figs. 254 (HE-002–686), 255 (HE-002–687), (Security Pacific Collection) fig. 194 (A-003–052); Maryland Historical Society, Baltimore, fig. 37; Milwaukee County Historical Society, figs. 20, 85; Museum of the City of New York, Irving Underhill Collection, fig. 11 (C20508); New Haven Museum & Historical Society, figs. 238–40; Ohio Historical Society, Columbus, figs. 66, 90, 102, 123; Oregon Historical Society, Portland, fig. 252 (OrHi 106182); Pei Cobb Freed & Partners, New York, figs. 212, 244, 245; Perry Dean Rogers & Partners, Architects, Boston, figs. 60, 62, 63; Queens Borough Public Library, Long Island Division, fig. 180; Sacramento Public Library, figs. 242, 243; San Francisco Public Library, San Francisco History Center, fig. 207 (AAC-6780); Target Corporation, Minneapolis (courtesy Anthony K. Jahn), figs. 220, 222; Temple University Libraries, Urban Archives, Philadelphia, fig. 189; Alex Wall, figs. 204, 223, 235, 250